CHRISTOPHER LEE

The Authorised Screen History

CHRISTOPHER LEE

THE AUTHORISED SCREEN HISTORY

JONATHAN RIGBY

REYNOLDS & HEARN LTD
LONDON

BACK COVER
Dracula (Hammer Film Productions/Rank Film Distributors, 1957)
The Man With the Golden Gun (Eon Productions/United Artists, 1974)
The Wicker Man (British Lion, 1972)
Sherlock Holmes und das Halsband des Todes (CCC Filmkunst/Critérion Film/INCEI Film, 1962)
The Man With the Golden Gun (Eon Productions/United Artists, 1974)
Rasputin the Mad Monk (Hammer Film Productions/Associated British Pathé, 1965)

FRONTISPIECE
Portrait by Gered Mankowitz, 2000

CONTENTS
A Tale of Two Cities (1957)
The Mummy (1959)
El Conde Drácula (1969)
The Young Indiana Jones Chronicles: Austria March 1917 (1991)

First published in 2001 by
Reynolds & Hearn Ltd
61a Priory Road
Kew Gardens
Richmond
Surrey TW9 3DH

© Jonathan Rigby 2001
Reprinted 2001

Second edition © Jonathan Rigby 2003

All rights reserved. No part of this publication may be reproduced,
in any form or by any means, without permission from the publisher.

A CIP catalogue record for this book is available from the British Library.

ISBN 1 903111 64 1

Designed by Peri Godbold.

Printed and bound in Great Britain by Biddles Ltd, Guildford, Surrey.

Contents

Author's Note & Acknowledgments	6
Foreword by George Lucas	7
Introduction	8
Part One: Rank Charmer 1922-1952	12
Part Two: TV and Other Trials 1952-1956	32
Part Three: Malignant Heroes 1956-1959	50
Part Four: Euro-Actor 1960-1964	78
Part Five: Homecoming 1964-1968	104
Part Six: Beyond the Graveyard 1969-1971	128
Part Seven: From Scaremonger to Scaramanga 1972-1975	148
Part Eight: From Belgravia to Bel-Air 1976-1981	170
Part Nine: Another Homecoming 1982-1989	192
Part Ten: New Horizons 1990-1999	214
Part Eleven: Indian Summer: 2000 and beyond	232
Film and Television Chronology	246
Source Notes	260
Index	264

Author's Note and Acknowledgments

On May 2002, Christopher Lee was asked about this book and its author by David Edelstein of the *New York Times*. His reply was characteristically droll: 'I felt badly for the poor fellow. Can you imagine having to watch all my movies? I haven't seen most of them; I can think of few prospects more horrifying.' With any luck, the reader will be inspired to test the validity of this statement and find, like me, that the prospect wasn't really so horrifying after all.

In order to set the record straight about a career that seems to have attracted misinformation like a magnet, the dates attached to films in this book are, wherever possible, those of production rather than release. Films are referred to under the titles by which they're known in their native countries, or, in the complicated area of co-productions, the nationality of the credited producer has generally been taken as the nationality of the film. English titles of foreign language films are given in italics; when the English title doesn't directly correspond to the original, a literal translation is given in parentheses but not in italics. Quotations from Lee and others are numbered in order that their source can be found in the relevant appendix; where a Lee quote is not numbered, it is drawn from one of three sources – his autobiography, letters printed in his fan club bulletins (in which he often looked back on his old films as well as dealing with the current ones) or interviews conducted by the author. The latter quotes are identifiable by the use of the present tense rather than the past in ascribing them to him; ie, the use of 'he says' rather than 'he said'.

The publication of a second edition has provided the opportunity, not merely to update the book's final section, but also to incorporate the results of new research elsewhere. In particular, the section detailing Lee's stint as a 'Euro-actor' has benefited from information unavailable to the author three years ago.

Research associate on *Christopher Lee: The Authorised Screen History* was Julian Grainger, whose zeal for fact-finding – and provision of rare films on video – was of enormous help in making sense of the many complexities thrown up in the writing of the book. My thanks also to Claudia Andrei, Charlie Baker, Chris Bentley, the BFI reference library and its staff, Simon Flynn, Renée Glynne, Richard Golen, Bruce G Hallenbeck, David Hanks, John Herron, Tony Mechele, David Miller, Gareth Owen, Andrew Pixley, Philip Spedding, Pam Stockbarger, Tise Vahimagi and John Willmer, archivist of the Connaught Theatre Worthing.

Further thanks go to David McGillivray for his collection of faded *Picturegoer*s; Peri Godbold for designing this and my previous book, *English Gothic*, so splendidly; Lynne Hale, Chris Holm, Jonathan Rinzler and Lucy Autrey Wilson at Lucasfilm; Tom Johnson and Mark A Miller for graciously comparing notes; my mother and father for their continued support; Peter Nicholson for his astonishing photo archive; Marcus Hearn and Richard Reynolds for commissioning the book in the first place, and to George Lucas for pausing amid *Star Wars: Episode II* to provide an illuminating foreword. And a special thank you to Josephine Botting, my British Film Institute mole and all-round muse.

Sincere thanks are also due to the many production and distribution companies responsible for the films discussed, all of whom are acknowledged in the chronology.

A final thank you goes to Christopher Lee himself and to his unfailingly hospitable wife, Gitte. Reports of Lee's unapproachability go hand in hand with reports of his loquaciousness. The latter quality is true enough, and is an invaluable boon to any interviewer and even more so to anyone writing a book about him. Reports of his presumed aloofness, however, have been greatly exaggerated. His enthusiasm regarding this book never flagged and his sense of humour while dealing with nit-picking questions about his distant past was just as unquenchable. Fact-finding missions to his London home were never dry-as-dust research assignments; on the contrary, they were more often than not an absolute hoot.

Jonathan Rigby
London
July 2003

Foreword

When I was asked to write the foreword for this book I was incredibly pleased for a number of reasons. For one, I have the utmost respect for Christopher Lee as an actor and a person, and have thoroughly enjoyed working with him. Additionally, I feel an amazing body of work such as his deserves to be captured in a book to be studied by generations to come.

Writing this tribute prompted me to recall how I came to know and work with such a talented and distinguished man.

I first became aware of Christopher Lee when I studied film at the University of Southern California. Like everyone in film school, I was captured by the Dracula films and absolutely mesmerised by Christopher's chilling portrayal of the vampire Count. Little did I know that what was then a fascinating study would decades later become a mutually enriching work experience.

I next came 'face-to-face' (so to speak) with Christopher Lee when I was working on *Star Wars: A New Hope* in London. My office was situated in the same building as the Hammer Films headquarters. The walls of the studio were lined with photos of Britain's most distinguished actors – amongst them, Peter Cushing and Christopher Lee. Looking up at those photos every day inspired me to cast Peter Cushing as Grand Moff Tarkin, the dreaded servant to Emperor Palpatine. Working with Peter was such a joy, I vowed to continue using British actors who were seasoned in the art of playing larger-than-life characters and villains.

Twenty-five years later, I still hold these actors in the same esteem. When it was time to cast the role of Count Dooku in *Star Wars: Episode II* my casting director suggested Christopher Lee and I jumped at the opportunity to work with him.

I knew that I needed someone who could convey evil. But in addition, I needed someone to bring stature, strength, and wisdom to the role. There was no doubt in my mind that Christopher Lee was the right person. His villainous resumé speaks for itself – he has defined macabre for generations of horror enthusiasts. But his talent reaches far beyond that genre. With 54 years in the film business, the breadth of his experience is tough to beat. He has a regal physical appearance and an elegant style. But most importantly he genuinely loves acting and breathes life into every character he plays, no matter how large or small the role.

Christopher Lee is a giant of a man in all respects. His intelligence is matched only by his elegance and style. He is a classic.

George Lucas
Skywalker Ranch
January 2001

INTRODUCTION

Writing a 'screen history' of Christopher Lee is tantamount to writing a history of post-war popular cinema. He has been an actor for over half a century, and in that time the techniques available to filmmakers have changed almost beyond recognition. One of his earliest films, the aptly titled *Prelude to Fame*, was made late in 1949 and utilised the ill-fated Independent Frame process, a Rank-sponsored scheme involving multiple back-projection plates, trundled around Pinewood Studios on wheeled rostra. One of his latest, *Star Wars: Episode II*, was made in the year 2000 and makes use of new technology likely to have a more long-lasting impact than Independent Frame; not only has back-projection given way to computer generated imagery, it was also the first feature film to be shot and edited with digital cameras.

Between these technological extremes, Lee's career has taken in almost all the phases of popular filmmaking: breezy British farce and stiff-upper-lip derring-do in the 1950s, the dazzling efflorescence of Hammer Horror at the end of that decade, so-called 'krimis' in West Germany, lurid Gothics in Italy, a James Bond picture, a Walt Disney picture, all-star 1970s blockbusters, straight-to-video fodder in the 1980s, glossy TV movies and mini-series in the 1990s and, at the turn of the century, a few projects that are unquestionably the most successful films he's ever been involved in. His dizzying number of credits bears witness not only to a man in demand, but also to a man easily bored by inactivity, a workaholic. The films that have resulted vary sharply in quality but constitute a body of work unrivalled by any other living actor.

In many of his films, Lee has been cast as the villain, more often than not bringing to his performances a baleful charisma beside which the average hero pales into insignificance. Indeed, these characters were dubbed by a French admirer 'héros maléfiques' (a phrase Lee treasures). Embodying these malignant heroes, Lee also embodies a contradiction common to most of the other gentlemanly actors who have become indelibly associated with horror films (a phrase Lee dislikes). 'No one less like the roles he plays with such ferocity can be imagined,' commented an American journalist in 1960. 'Off screen Lee is a pleasant, good-humored, well-mannered young man. He is extremely good-looking, a fact the make-up men work hard to cancel out. His appearance is intellectual (which he is) and somewhat ascetic. Besides these more obvious qualities, he possesses that most saleable quality – sex appeal. This latter factor came through his characterisation of the vampire in *Horror of Dracula* with such force that it made the picture one of the top box-office successes of 1958. It also provoked a landslide of fan mail from a multitude of women who apparently regarded Lee as anything but horrible.'[1]

'The dead, when frightening, are apt to be very erotic,' Raymond Durgnat confirmed in 1961. 'I have it on the authority of one intelligent teenager that Christopher Lee in *Dracula* was the sexiest male in English pictures since James Mason in *The Seventh Veil*.'[2] Lee nevertheless pronounced himself baffled by the response of his female fans. 'I certainly don't want to be a romantic actor,' he insisted, apparently unaware of his expertise in engendering romantic longing mixed with mortal dread. 'I've always considered they're the dullest parts you can possibly play, and the most unrewarding ... Apart from that, I haven't got the face for it, or the figure, or the approach.'[3]

Several other ironies are embodied in Lee's marathon career. An actor hamstrung early on by the assumption among casting directors that he looked too Continental, he now seems the epitome of patrician Englishness. (He remains, nevertheless, the least parochial of English film stars, his numerous Continental credits owing much to his command of several languages: fluent French, more than adequate Spanish, Italian and German, a smattering of Russian, Swedish, Greek and Finnish.) Possessing one of the most distinctive voices in British cinema – together with a singing voice that he still regrets not having made more use of – he was nevertheless called upon to be mute in some of his most important performances. He compensated for this with a really impressive flair and fluidity in

Faust metamorphoses into Mephistopheles in the extraordinary Katarsis *(1963)*

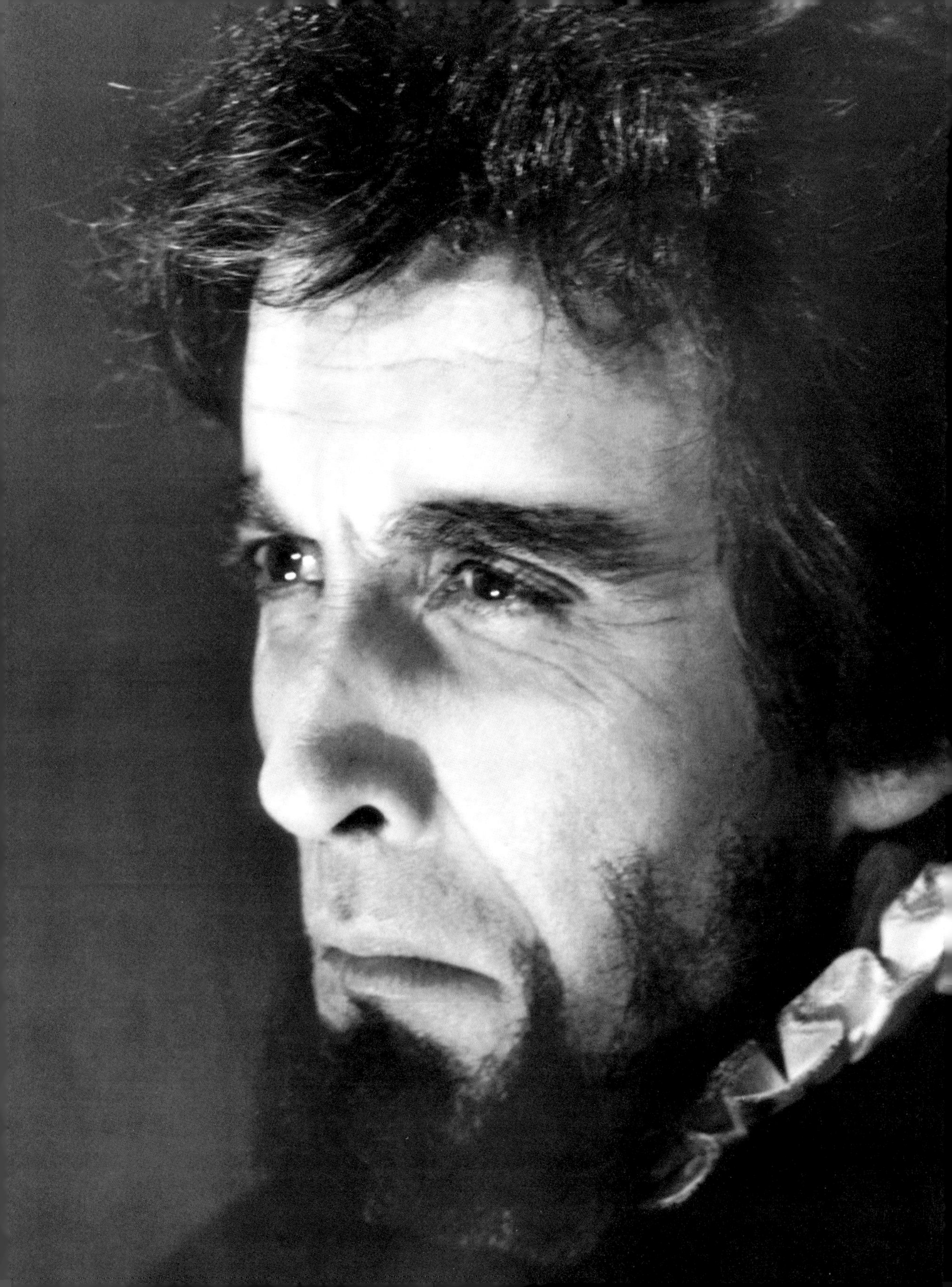

movement and mime, a fluidity in sharp contrast to the stiffness he displayed in some of his fledgling appearances. Lee explained in his autobiography that 'the cameras in those days were enormous boxes painted greenish blue and rather alarming to see dancing down on you ... Somebody said to me, "You must tone everything down for a close-up. You mustn't move too much, either, or you'll go out of focus. And if you go sideways you go out of frame." Because of these inhibiting warnings ... I was so scared of moving any part that it looked as if I had locked into position.'

In a final irony, hard-won stardom brought with it a procession of boringly similar roles in boringly similar films, with the result that Lee's early inflexibility resurfaced from time to time in the 1960s. This inflexibility was an asset where Fu Manchu was concerned – a characterisation in which stiffness was translated, in mesmerising fashion, into stillness – but, by and large, the versatility and vulnerability Lee had been able to show in the 1950s was temporarily stifled. Fortunately, more imaginative casting from the 1970s onwards has seen both qualities roaring back in recent years with a vengeance.

Vulnerable or invulnerable, Lee brings to all his roles a dominating physical presence, his preference for 'larger than life' characters being a matter of temperament as well as physique. The 'kitchen sink' explosion in 1950s theatre began to take root in British cinema during the 1960s and Lee was dismayed by it. 'Why do they have to make so many films about little people?' he demanded of *Titbits* columnist David Hunn in 1965. 'If they're not small in stature, they're small in personality. Insignificant. They say it's more real, more lifelike. Maybe – but who the hell cares?' And by 1967 he appears to have lost all patience. 'For God's sake,' he stormed, 'let's get back to the people who can act. People with an impact – who set the screen alight when they walk on. There's a Niagara of mediocrity among our 'stars' today.'[4]

Lee himself is quite clear about the actors who influenced him, who 'set the screen alight'. 'The finest actor I've ever seen on screen was Walter Huston, the father of the film director John Huston,' he claimed in 1991. 'He was a character man rather than a glamorous actor, but he appeared to be able to play anything. I've seen most of his films and, no matter what he did, he had real gunpowder ... an essential, immensely important quality to an actor.'[5] Lee identified the same 'gunpowder' in his friend George C Scott and also sees it in Gene Hackman. But the greatest influence on him was an actor who was character man and sex symbol combined – Conrad Veidt. Over 50 years after first seeing Veidt in the 1939 film *The Spy in Black*, Lee explained that 'Claude Rains, George Sanders and Basil Rathbone were my models; Veidt was my idol. And he still is, really, because he had an unearthly quality about him ... It was a combination of the voice and his face; it was mesmerising for me. I couldn't take my eyes off him – his power, his presence – the two most important qualities for an actor to have. You must be born with them.'[6]

The Spy in Black was the first feature film from Michael Powell and Emeric Pressburger, and in 1956 Lee would appear in the last, *Ill Met By Moonlight*. This is only one of numerous parallels between the two actors. Veidt had risen to prominence in the many morbid classics produced in Germany during the silent era and a 1940 description of him by journalist Theodore Strauss could easily be transposed, with only a few cosmetic adjustments, onto his postwar successor. 'Six foot three, spare of frame and severely featured, his right eye immobilised by a monocle, he might be an urbane Mephistopheles,' Strauss explained. 'One searches the lean features, the cold blue eyes, for a resemblance to those other faces that have peopled midnight with a macabre procession – somnambulant murderers, misshapen clowns, sinister magicians, intriguing statesmen, maniacal Hindus.'[7] Strauss also admitted,

An urbane Mephistopheles: Conrad Veidt (1893-1943) in a 1933 publicity photo, complete with characteristic monocle

almost grudgingly, that 'There has been a saint or two in his repertoire.'

Veidt's repertoire anticipated Lee's almost step-for-step. Both actors acquired fame as mute, murderous, white-faced puppets controlled by an evil genius (Veidt in *Das Cabinet des Dr Caligari*, Lee in *The Curse of Frankenstein*) and, in 1928, Veidt was strongly tipped to play Count Dracula, the role Lee would make his own nearly 30 years later. Lee would inherit many other Veidt roles – Jekyll and Hyde, Rasputin, a wicked Caliph, duelling Teutonic students, assorted Nazi officers, even the saint or two referred to by Strauss – and he nursed an unrealised desire to star in a remake of Veidt's Hollywood vehicle, *The Man Who Laughs*. He would also share with Veidt a peculiar heart-throb status founded on monsters and hypnotic demons. Lee's tireless globe-trotting from film to film echoes Veidt's facility for filming in France, Sweden, Italy, the UK and America as well as Germany. When casting directors permitted, Lee would also reproduce Veidt's faintly manic sense of fun. He would even inherit Veidt's extra-curricular passion for golf.

Most importantly, however, Lee would strive to humanise his malevolent characters with what he calls 'the loneliness of evil'. At work on *The Two Faces of Dr Jekyll* in 1960, he claimed that 'In all [my roles] I have searched for the human being trapped within the outer shell, as in [*The Curse of*] *Frankenstein* and *The Mummy*, or in an inescapable web of evil, as in *Dracula*.'[8] Veidt had much the same idea while making *A Woman's Face* in 1941, expressing a wish to 'make people feel that this man, this spirit of evil, is an unhappy human being. Sick with unhappiness, the unhappiness of Lucifer, the angel cast out of Heaven.'[9]

Lee's attempts to humanise his monsters did not go unnoticed by critics who were otherwise ill-disposed towards Hammer's horror product. One called his Creature in *The Curse of Frankenstein* 'a sad, bewildered thing, infinitely pathetic.'[10] Another, faced with *The Mummy*, described Lee's Kharis as 'a figure of imperishable sadness whose expressive, sorrowful eyes his reanimated mummy retains.'[11] Gratified by plaudits such as these, Lee was content for a time to continue in Grand Guignol vein. 'I can honestly say that, from every angle, horror films have been a considerable asset in my screen career to date,' he wrote in 1959. 'Working on horror films has been a fascinating and absorbing experience, since they call for complete sincerity in one's acting. I have always felt the dividing line between conviction and absurdity to be very slight. I think that all of us who have been connected with these films at Bray Studios have managed to achieve that conviction.'[12]

As Franz, a scar-faced student at old Heidelberg, in Douglas Fairbanks Presents: American Duel (1952)

Lee's zeal for his macabre characterisations became increasingly difficult to maintain, however, as the 1960s proceeded, an era he describes ruefully as his 'Graveyard Period'. Being arguably the most viscerally frightening actor ever to grace the screen would have been enough of an achievement for most actors, but not for Lee. Unwilling to rest on his laurels, he determined to break the mould in which he had been unexpectedly 'typed', and in 1969 Billy Wilder provided a timely springboard with *The Private Life of Sherlock Holmes*. Moving to America, Lee was finally able to exploit a hidden talent for droll comedy, starting with a wildly successful collaboration on *Saturday Night Live* with a daunting collection of cutting-edge comedians. 'There are few actors,' he pointed out, 'who would not benefit from having to take off their trousers in front of 30 million people. Most of all, he who (as a rule) plays the King.'

Christopher Lee will remain forever linked with the horror genre, and rightly so; his achievements in it, after all, stamp him as a worthy successor to Lon Chaney and Boris Karloff as well as Conrad Veidt. But this 'screen history' may remind people familiar only with the 'King of Horror' that he has plenty of other achievements under his belt, and that his Graveyard Period is just one feature of a long and many-faceted career.

PART ONE

RANK CHARMER
1922–1952

On his mother's side, Christopher Lee can trace his antecedents to the first century, with any number of Italian Counts and Cardinals adorning the family tree but precious few actors. When Lee decided on an acting career in 1946, his only precedent was an Antipodean one dating back 100 years. The tumult of the Risorgimento had forced Lee's great-grandfather Girolamo to decamp from Italy to Australia, where he married another European exile, Marie Burgess, daughter of a Brixton coachman. Together they sang opera in an itinerant theatre company before setting up a dancing school in Sydney. Their five singing daughters followed suit, bringing high culture to some of Australia's wildest and least hospitable areas. The girls' elder brother, Francesco Giacomo, became a cavalry officer instead and in due course consented to the union of his daughter, Contessa Estelle Marie Carandini, with Captain (later Lieutenant Colonel) Geoffrey Trollope Lee of the 60th King's Royal Rifle Corps.

They were married in 1910 and produced a daughter, Xandra, in 1917. Five years later, on Saturday 27 May 1922, a son, Christopher Frank Carandini Lee, was born at 51 Lower Belgrave Street, London. Lee's first memory is related to his father. 'I was four when I was grasped by my ankles by my father and shaken upside down because I was choking on a lollipop,' he recalls. 'The lollipop clattered out onto a dish on a beige carpet.' Lee was also four when his father suddenly left the family home, prior to a divorce being granted in 1928. 'He was a very good-looking man and a professional soldier – a dear, sweet man, brave as a lion, served in the Boer War and the First World War, and a wonderful sportsman – but he was a gambler,' Lee pointed out. 'Well, nobody's perfect.'[1]

A spell in Switzerland brought forth Lee's stage début in the title role of *Rumpelstiltskin* at Miss Fisher's Academy, from which he tended to run away about once a week. 'I learnt at the outset,' he wrote later, 'that the best lines are given to the baddies and that these make the most impact on the audience – especially if there is some pathos in their situation.' Back in London, he was educated at a Queen's Gate establishment called Wagner's before being sent away to Summer Fields prep school in Oxford. There, he played the Dauphin in *Henry V* – Patrick Macnee stole the show in the title role – and Mowbray in *Richard II*, with Macnee as Bolingbroke. In the meantime, his mother had remarried. Harcourt George St Croix Rose, popularly known as Ingle, was a small whirlwind of a man and uncle to the writers Peter and Ian Fleming. A prosperous banker, he returned Lee's mother to the glamorous existence she had formerly enjoyed; as Lee put it, 'It began to rain silver-fox furs and diamond pendants.'

Subject to these upheavals, Lee became a loner – even his tolerant grandmother described him as 'a tiresome boy' – and all the more so at school, where his Italian ancestry cut no ice with snobbish under-tens in the same way that it would prove a stumbling-block when he first became an actor. 'I once made a girl stand up against a door and threw knives around her,' he confessed. 'She's still alive, I'm glad to say. I was a rebel all the time at school. I was beaten, too; it didn't do me any harm, I can assure you.'[2] It may not have done him any harm, but he still felt, on being transplanted to Wellington College in January 1936, that 'I had fallen among barbarians, with nothing to be done about that but grit it out for the next four years.'

His resentment was increased by the fact that he had sat an examination for the much more congenial Eton, gaining an Oppidan scholarship but just missing out on the more generous Kings scholarship. With his stepfather's fortunes beginning to wane, it was decided that Wellington was the more affordable option. The Eton scholarship nevertheless threw up an interesting encounter – with M R James, Provost

Too tall and too foreign-looking: one of J Arthur Rank's newest recruits, 1947

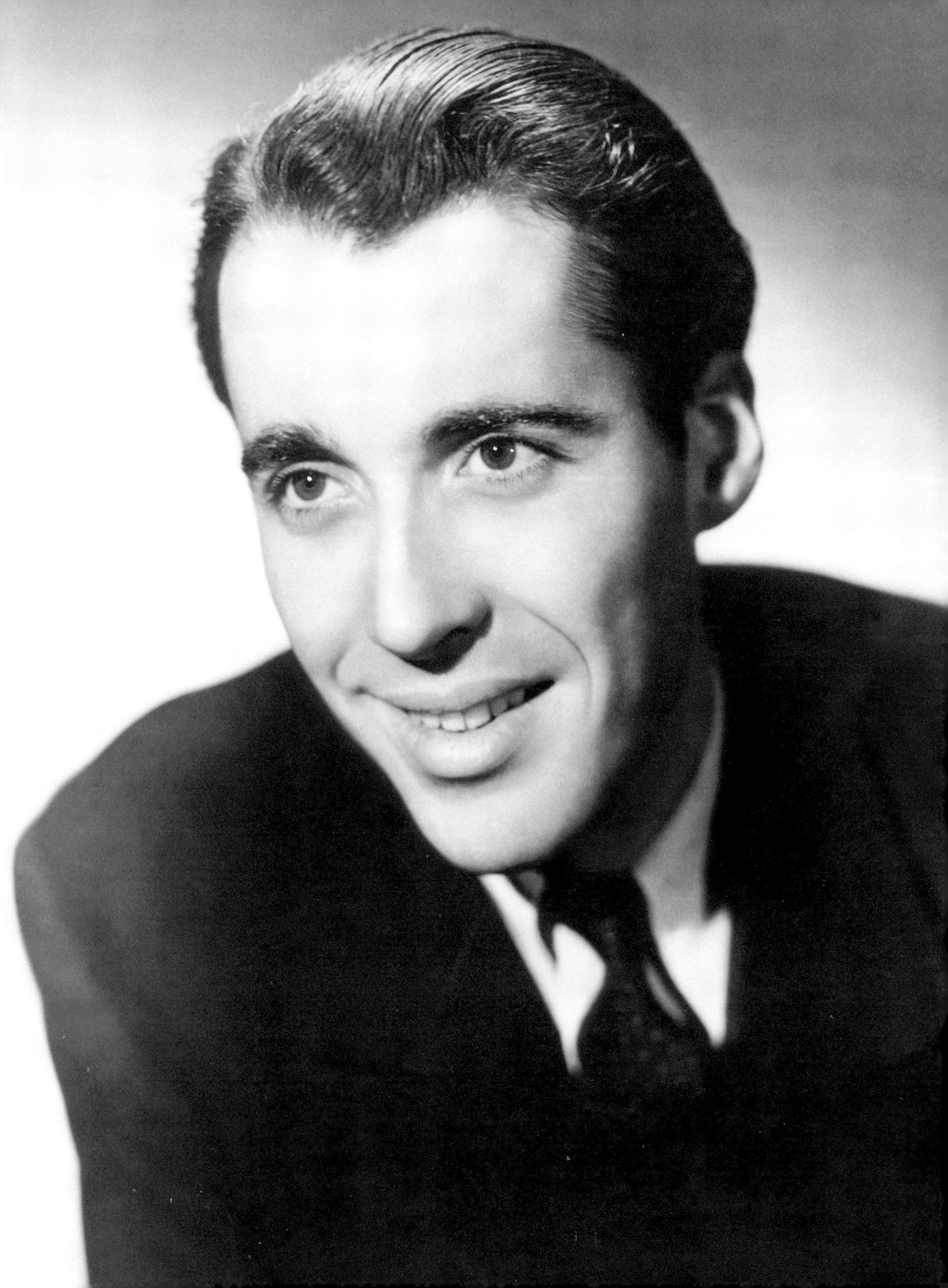

of the College and the master of scholarly but extremely gruesome horror stories. To the 13-year-old Lee, he was 'a little old man in glasses with a skin like parchment.'

Despite its Spartan unpleasantness, Wellington managed to provide Lee with a further crack at acting, this time in a pirate entertainment concocted by an American colleague and starring the future film composer John Addison. But in July 1939 he was suddenly withdrawn from the school. Ingle had gone bankrupt, resulting in a second separation for his mother. There had been several warning signs. 'He was drunk every night and lost every penny,' Lee recalled. 'I didn't know that he drank at the time but I do remember him once with a revolver, waving it around in my general direction. I suppose a psychiatrist or a psychologist would say, "Ah, well, yes, a broken home after a so-called privileged background" – although it wasn't, believe me. Both times the money went totally. My mother was left at the age of 50 with two teenage children and nothing.'[3]

DESTINY ON THE LINKS

Aged 17, Lee was already a lanky 6'4" and was put to work for a City shipping firm as an all-purpose mail/tea/errand boy at £1 a week, later transferring, for the same wage, to Beecham's in Pall Mall, a company which itself transferred to Watford as the Blitz took hold in 1940. As an alternative to the dreary round of licking stamps and making tea, Lee developed an interest in the more exotic and fantastic branches of literature. Schooled, almost literally, in M R James, he also absorbed Edgar Allan Poe, Algernon Blackwood, E F Benson, Conan Doyle, Bram Stoker and others, as well as finding further outlets for this tendency in both theatre and cinema.

At the New (now Albery) Theatre in 1939, he saw the great Leslie Banks playing 'homo immortalis' John Thackeray in Barré Lyndon's *The Man in Half Moon Street*, little dreaming that in due course he would be cast in a lurid film version of Lyndon's play, or that his first role in Hollywood would be scripted by Lyndon. And, as well as enjoying the cinematic exploits of Tod Slaughter, the so-called 'Horror Man of Europe', Lee was scared witless by Wilfrid Walter in *The Dark Eyes of London*, a Bela Lugosi vehicle that was Britain's first film to be granted an 'H' (for 'Horrific') certificate. He had also fallen under the spell of Conrad Veidt, perhaps the most mesmeric of all film stars between the wars. In September 1939, only two days after seeing Veidt in *The Spy in Black* at the King's Road Gaumont, Lee was astonished to bump into the man himself while strolling on Wentworth golf course. Veidt graciously interrupted his game for half an hour to chat with his awestruck admirer. Given the number of parallels between Veidt's career and Lee's, it could be said in hindsight that Destiny – a powerful force in many of Veidt's macabre motion pictures – was at work in this chance meeting.

Early in 1941, Lee's father succumbed to double pneumonia and pleurisy, aged 62. 'There were very few people at the funeral,' Lee remembers. 'He was cremated on a cold day. Just before that I had joined up, and subsequently I saw many funerals, but they were slightly different: holes in the ground with a cross put over them and a name if possible.' Having enlisted in the RAF, Lee soon found himself at the Hillside training grounds near Bulawayo in Rhodesia, looking forward excitedly to the day when he should start flying. A faulty optic nerve put paid to this ambition – 'It was the end of my world,' Lee reported – and he was passed on to the Rhodesian police as a warder at Salisbury Prison. This was followed by a spell in Egypt and several bouts of malaria, after which, to Lee's astonishment, he was attached to 260 Squadron as Intelligence Officer. As 'Spy', Lee co-ordinated the Squadron's strafing missions and bomb strikes, acutely conscious of the fact that his airmen 'were obliged for their lives to depend on me.' The Squadron made some five missions per day and moved inexorably west, originating at El Alamein and ending up in Tunisia.

Lee was mentioned in despatches at the end of 1944 but remains circumspect about his experiences outside North Africa, and not merely because of the Official Secrets Act. 'That is a part of my life I never

Christopher Frank Carandini Lee, circa 1932

talk about, except to those who were around at the time,' he maintained in 1995. 'Look at what is happening in the world today: Bosnia, Rwanda. Who wants to talk about something that happened 50 years ago? Nobody but a lot of old men and a lot of old women.'[4] In the second edition of his autobiography, however, he chose to insert an extra paragraph to the effect that 'before catching my boat from Naples for demobilisation in Britain, I served with the Central Registry of War Crimes and Security Suspects, or Field Securities Sections (the Americans called these mixed groups of British, Russian, French, American and Palestinian investigators 'Counter Intelligence Corps'). Starting in Austria, we had dossiers on men and women wanted for interrogation and orders to arrest them on suspicion, and this took me to a number of concentration camps which had only just been cleaned up, and some that hadn't.'

Kicking his heels on demob and unsure of his direction, Lee found himself having lunch one day with his cousin Niccolò Carandini. The scene was the Italian Embassy in Grosvenor Square, Niccolò having become Italy's first post-war envoy to the Court of St James. Listening to a colourful account of Lee's recent vicissitudes, complete with much spot-on mimicry of the equally colourful characters involved, Niccolò sat back and said simply, 'Have you ever thought of becoming an actor, Christopher?'

Intrigued, Lee took up Niccolò's suggestion that he should meet another Italian, Filippo del Giudice of Two Cities Films. 'So off I went to Hanover Square,' Lee recalls, 'and Del, as he was known, said, "You are just what we are looking for!" He then sent me along the corridor to see his associate, Josef Somlo.' Somlo was less enthusiastic, telling Lee that he was much too tall and foreign-looking to be an actor. 'We make *British* pictures,' Somlo emphasised in his thick Hungarian accent. Even so, Lee came away clutching a seven-year contract with the Rank Organisation, Two Cities being one of several companies under the paternalistic control of the North Country flour tycoon J Arthur Rank. With very little ado, Lee had become an actor with a starting salary of £10 a week. His mother was scandalised, coming out with the classic – and, as it turned out, prophetic – remark, 'Just think of all the appalling people you'll meet!'

Industry mismanagement, exacerbated by the unhelpful attitude of Clement Attlee's government, would bring about a severe crisis in film production by the end of the 1940s, but the immediate post-war period nevertheless marked an artistic high watermark for British cinema. This was the era of *Odd Man Out*, *Dead of Night*, *Green for Danger*, *Black Narcissus*, *Great Expectations*, *Hue and Cry* and scores of others, a period dominated by Carol Reed, David Lean, Launder and Gilliat, Powell and Pressburger, the burgeoning Ealing comedies and the bodice-ripping Gainsborough melodramas. For the time being, however, Lee was to remain on the industry's lowest rung. Armed with his seven-year contract, he had his first 'Spotlight' photos taken by Alexander Bender and acquired his first agent, Vivienne Black. He was then enlisted in the J Arthur Rank Company of Youth, which operated from Highbury Studios in Islington.

Contemptuously dubbed the Rank Charm School, this was one of four Rank initiatives in the late 1940s that proved to be expensive failures; the others were the establishment of an animation unit to rival Disney, a newsreel magazine to rival *The March of Time* and a heavy investment in the so-called Independent Frame process, which aspired to reduce production costs via the wonders of back-projection. The Charm School was run by David Henley and Olive Dodds, with fencing and 'rough-house' looked after by Patrick Crehan and Rex Rickman, singing and dialect by Helen Goss (later to appear with Lee in *The Hound of the Baskervilles*), diction by Miss Hartley-Milburne and acting itself by the fearsome Molly Terraine. Also involved was Rank's charming PR chief, Theo Cowan.

'No special standard of education is expected from prospective members – students can and do come from all standards of British living,' declared a Rank press release. 'The subjects include fencing, breathing exercises, play reading and play rehearsals, movement and gesture, diction, muscular exercises, accent correction, microphone technique and lessons in film technique ... Members of the Company of Youth are allowed to live at their own homes and receive a salary considered sufficient for principle [sic] needs ... It is intended, by this training, to build many of these promising young people into fully fledged British and later, it is hoped, international stars.'

Of the Charm School's pupils, only Lee would fulfil the latter hope on a long-term basis. One other graduate, however, would have a brief taste of international notoriety during the 1950s. Diana Mary Fluck was being groomed as 'Britain's baby Lana Turner' under the name Diana Dors, and her account of the Highbury training is as vivid as any. 'For myself, I'll tell you outright that I loathed the Charm School and practically left show business because of the depressing effect it had on me,' she wrote in 1960. 'We met in a disused church hall in North London under the supervision of a crowd of rather frustrated old actresses ... Still, it was a good thing for many of the youngsters, some of whom had been found in beauty contests and who had been given film contracts without even being able to read properly.

'Looking back, I can remember many who came through those rather grubby portals,' she continued. 'I wonder now where many of them are. Of the ones who remained steadily successful over the years, I can recall Susan Shaw, Christopher Lee (now making a bit of a splash in horror films), Pete Murray (who abandoned acting for the disc jockey business), Dennis Vance (who became a television producer) and likewise Philip Saville, Patricia Owens (who went to Hollywood and starred in *The Fly* among others), Barbara Murray, Pat Goddard, Anthony Steel, Dana Wynter, Constance Smith, Rosemary Treston (who left the business and married into the peerage), Zena Marshall, Sandra Dorne, Dermot Walsh, Hazel Court, Bill Travers, Conrad Phillips (now *William Tell* on TV) and so on.'[5]

Fresh from his life-or-death experiences in the war – and, at 24, somewhat older than the majority of his fellow students – Lee was more conscious than most of the Charm School's in-built absurdities, but conceded that it 'was a brave idea, even a good idea ... The Method Acting was amazing. Each in turn we'd hurl ourselves through a doorway and register horror, rage, love or resignation at the sight of a pair of spectacles in an otherwise bare room, simultaneously declaiming "That is a *red* cash register" or "*That* is a red cash register." The permutations were infinite. Molly took no impertinence, nor idleness, and she was a great elocution coach.'

MEANINGLESS SPECKS

The Rank contractees were further bedevilled by a programme of public appearances in the shadow of real movie stars, presumably in the hope that they would pick up some glamour-by-association. Lee's first encounter with Merton Park Studios, for instance, took place at a Rank-sponsored fête in which he had to cower bashfully in the back of a Jeep alongside Jack Benny and Ingrid Bergman. Even more horrific, through a link-up with BBC Television it was arranged that selected members of the Company of Youth should form part of an occasional magazine programme, broadcast from Alexandra Palace, called *Kaleidoscope*. The Charm School's slot was called 'Word Play' and involved performing a charade in which viewers were encouraged to guess a concealed word. The first show was a success, a BBC spokesman noting that 'many viewers have written saying they were so engrossed in the plot of the first charade that they forgot to guess the word.'[6] It was therefore decided to press on with the 'Word Play' concept. As a result, Lee's first ever screen appearance took place, live, soon after 8.30 pm on Friday 20 December 1946.

Presented by John Irwin, the programme was the third in the *Kaleidoscope* series and featured seven items; the Company of Youth went on second, directly after an appearance by 'Memory Man' Leslie Welch. Lee's companions on this occasion were John Stone, Robert Parker and June Melvin. 'The above cast of four,' noted the BBC archivist, 'enacted a charade written by Rodney Hobson ... Outside rehearsals for the Company were directed by Miss Molly Terraine for the Rank Organisation.' Other items included Iris Brooke's Collector's Corner ('Miss Brooke showed viewers antiques she had bought, antiques she would like to buy and some that none of us could buy') and a 'How To...' feature ('Miss Sonstagen showed viewers how to decorate a Christmas Tree'). There was also an item called 'The Tight Spot', in which 'Captain Easton's Stunt Team of three' gave tips on self-defence. Jock Easton had met Lee as a fellow member of the SAS during the war and, exactly ten years after *Kaleidoscope*, he would be consumed in flames on Lee's behalf at the end of *The Curse of Frankenstein*.

Lee was presumably considered a promising student, because on Friday 17 January 1947 he was back at Alexandra Palace for a further 'Word Play' in *Kaleidoscope*'s fifth instalment, accompanied this time by Norma Simpson, Pete Murray and Jane Hylton. All the *Kaleidoscope* regulars were back in place, although the 'How To...' spot was filled not by Miss Sonstagen but by W O Goss, who 'demonstrated the best and easiest way to clean shoes.' Of Lee's fellow actors that evening, Jane Hylton had already done two years at RADA and would prove the most immediately successful Charm School graduate, giving sensitive performances in films like *My Brother's Keeper* and *Dance Hall*.

Having finished *Kaleidoscope*, Lee went straight into his first film appearance. *Corridor of Mirrors* was the first picture directed by 32-year-old Terence Young, who had begun his career as a screenwriter at Elstree. The film was the brainchild of the South African actress Edana Romney; having tried to set it up for several years, she eventually got together with the future TV director Rudolph Cartier to present it as 'A Cartier-Romney Production for Apollo Films'. For Lee, *Corridor of Mirrors* was prophetic in several ways. It tells a faintly macabre story and spends a lot of time in Mme Tussaud's Chamber of Horrors. Prefiguring Lee's penchant for filming on the Continent, it was shot at the Studios Radio-Cinéma, Buttes-Chaumont, Paris. And Lee's first on-camera line namechecks a historical personage who fancied himself as a vampire.

'Mr Rex Rickman is an important visitor to Mr J Arthur Rank's Company of Youth, now located at Highbury Studios. Rickman, fencing and 'rough-house' instructor, is seen here in the midst of a thrust and parry session with a promising bunch of lithe lads and lasses. On your right, coming down from the doorway: Christopher Lee, Shaun Noble, Maura Kelly and Zena Marshall. On your left: Peter Murray, Pat Goddard, Sheila Martin and Carol Marsh.' (1946)

Romney is Mifanwy Conway, a haughty beauty who falls under the spell of obsessive artist Paul Mangin, played by Eric Portman, the British cinema's psychopath of choice in the late 1940s. (He had come straight to *Corridor of Mirrors* from making *Dear Murderer* at Islington.) Mangin and Mifanwy first meet at a nightclub, where she is surrounded by her feckless friends Babs (Mavis Villiers), Lois (Lois Maxwell), Bing (Hugh Latimer), Brandy (John Penrose) and Charles (Lee). 'The young people she runs around with are all like her,' we have been told, 'just marking time waiting for something to happen to them.' A chanteuse croons 'These Foolish Things' as Mangin appears in the doorway. 'Look who's dropped in,' says Brandy. 'Dropped in is hardly the phrase I should have chosen,' Charles drawls off-camera. 'And who are we all pulling to pieces this time?' asks Mifanwy. The camera then settles on Mifanwy and Charles as he replies, with a nonchalant wave of his cigarette, 'Take a look, standing in the entrance: Lord Byron.'

Charles is relegated to the background for the remainder of the scene, looking surprised when Mangin approaches the group's table and then posing with his fellow drones for a group photo. Young minimised Lee's height problem by confining him to a chair throughout. He also lent him his own dinner jacket for the scene, though it was hardly sufficient to protect Lee from the extreme January cold that pervaded the studio. The film itself, a glamorous but rather gloomy confection, was met with mixed reviews on its release the following year. Richard Winnington observed in the *News Chronicle* that Edana Romney 'has ... a glimmer of that disgracefully un-British quality – sex mystery,' while the *Observer*'s C A Lejeune claimed that 'I came away feeling rather as if I had been watching the long, slow smear of a slug.'

Back at Highbury, Molly Terraine had further horrors in store for her young charges. Journalist Norman Hudis – later the scriptwriter for the first six

Carry On films – reported that 'The "children" as Miss Terraine calls them (freely interspersing this affectionate label with the good old theatre standbys of "darling" and "ducky") ... get a period of solid stage work with the rep company at Worthing, one of the best shop windows in the country for potential talent. Molly decides when they go.'[7] For Lee, the time came in the second week of July. The Connaught Theatre was run by Melville Gillam and its acting company was known as the Overture Repertory Players. As was common practice at the time – a practice most actors today would find unthinkable – the Connaught's bill changed weekly, meaning that the company would be rehearsing the following week's show during the day while playing the current one during the evening. As a result, Lee had barely arrived in the Sussex coastal town when he found himself pressed onto the stage in *The Constant Nymph*, a 1920s West End hit by Margaret Kennedy and Basil Dean. Opening night was Monday 14 July 1947.

The director, who also acted in the play, was Guy Verney and the stars were Robin Bailey and Patricia Dainton, daughter of Lee's agent. The cast also included Sheila Keith, Charles Morgan and Michael Bates, with Lee as Roberto the butler. 'I went on believing that to be an actor you had to act,' Lee reported. 'All the time. Non-stop. I buttled unrelentingly.' Dismayed by Lee's unwitting tendency to upstage his fellows by silently echoing all their emotions, Verney came round in the interval and suggested that he should finish the play on his own. ('I was very hurt. It was like a cold shower. I'd had no idea I'd offended.') By Friday, however, Verney found himself bracketed with Lee in the local newspaper's review. With a mere 150 words at his disposal and a cast of 22 to choose from, the reviewer singled out only Lee, Verney and the two leads. 'Guy Verney, with a delightful little sketch of the too intense pseudo-enthusiast for music, Leyland, enlivens and steals scenes in which he appears and Christopher Lee provides similar welcome light relief as Roberto.'[8] The following week Lee moved from butler to waiter. As Joseph in Harry Graham's *By Candlelight*, another 1920s West End warhorse, 'I was given more bits of business carrying dishes about than any servant before or since.'

The week after that, Terence Young's second picture began at Denham after five weeks on location around Italy's Lake Maggiore. Lee gratefully exchanged the stage of the Connaught for Denham's Stage 7, where a shimmering 'production suite' set had been built for Two Cities' *Fugue for Two Voices*. The film was rapidly retitled *One Night With You* and in it, Lee recalled, 'I played the director's assistant. I don't think I even said anything. I just sat around looking idiotic.' Though wordless, Lee received billing as 'Pirelli's assistant' and was able to observe the hyperactive comic actor Charles Goldner at work as Fogliati, a combustible film producer cudgelling the brains of his director, Pirelli (Willy Fueter), and lowly script doctors Brian Worth, Judith Furse and Stuart Latham. Lee collects a telegram from a fat young man directly after the credits, hands it to Goldner and then lapses into virtual invisibility. The main business of the film takes the form of the fantastic story dreamt up by Fogliati's writers – 'So artistic, and so box-office!' he enthuses – and lumbers the gorgeous Patricia Roc with a charisma-free co-star in Nino Martini, a celebrated tenor from New York's Metropolitan Opera. The film was a mis-step for Young after the atmospheric *Corridor of Mirrors*; even seasoned comic actors like Stanley Holloway and Richard Hearne are made to seem unfunny.

Living in a basement flat in Chelsea, Lee rapidly developed a routine for fulfilling his minuscule movie commitments. Rising at 4.30 am, he would take the tube from Sloane Square followed by a train for the studio, arriving there at seven. 'We, the meaningless specks,' he explained, 'had to be got rid of to frowst in the canteen before the stars arrived at 7.45.' The stars were often of considerable radiance, however. *One Night With You*'s first week at Denham corresponded with *Hamlet*'s sixteenth and, urged on by a fellow 'speck', Lee sneaked across to watch Laurence Olivier, just knighted in the King's Birthday Honours List, at work on his neo-Expressionist masterpiece. Unknown to Olivier, Lee struggled into a spear carrier's costume and joined in a general chorus of 'Lights!' when Basil Sidney's King, his conscience caught by Hamlet's accusatory play-within-a-play, made his anguished plea for illumination. Also at Denham that day were Olivier's right-hand man Anthony Bushell (later to act with Lee in *Bitter Victory* and direct him in *The Terror of the Tongs*), together with Lee's future co-star Peter Cushing, cast as the courtly 'waterfly' Osric.

CURTAIN RAISERS AND THE CUTTING-ROOM FLOOR

Continuing to trumpet the Rank Company of Youth, Norman Hudis observed that 'Just as the RAF pupil-pilots used to champ through their initial training, gasping for the sight of real live aircraft, so do the stars-in-embryo sigh for close contact with the studio.'[9] Hudis' analogy was a particularly apt one for Lee, but he would have preferred a continuing diet of small parts in big pictures rather than the next quixotic scheme hatched at Highbury, which basically

'People are not always what they seem.' As young cartoonist Jonathan Blair in the Highbury 'curtain raiser', Penny and the Pownall Case (1947)

involved giving the new recruits big parts in small pictures. Supervised by John Croydon, Highbury's so-called 'curtain raisers' were inaugurated on 7 July when production began on Terence Fisher's début film, a ghost comedy called *Colonel Bogey*, and the programme continued with Fisher's drunk-driving shocker, *To the Public Danger*.

The third film, a comedy-thriller called *Penny and the Pownall Case*, began on 6 October under the direction of an Ealing production manager called H E 'Slim' Hand. It turned out to be the first of the Highbury featurettes to reach the public and in it, says Lee, 'I played a part I was quite incapable of playing; it was quite beyond my professional competence ... I suppose it's the same for most actors, when they're just starting out and have no experience and don't get any guidance. I gave some ghastly performances at the beginning of my career.'

The curtain raisers were made for around £20,000 each and took five weeks to shoot, though *Penny* took rather longer, thanks to being closed down for a while when Lee's co-star, Peggy Evans, was involved in a road accident. The films also had several established actors in them to give the proceedings a stiffening of 'professional competence'. In *Penny*, the personable Ralph Michael is Scotland Yard's Detective Inspector Carson, investigating the murder of secret service agent Pownall and discovering that cartoonist Jonathan Blair is part of a plot to liberate German war criminals. Looking callow but glamorous, Lee gives a well-practised beaming smile on his first entrance and, looming over his transparent easel, is photographed from below as he instructs his young model, Penny Justin, to 'Lean forward and lift up your skirt, will you? That's it. Hold it there.'

As the winsome Penny, Peggy Evans is required to model numerous up-to-the-minute outfits ('Dresses executed by Horrockses Fashions Ltd,' the credits inform us), as well as a couple of fetching swimsuits and some utterly ridiculous hats. Despite being called 'a very indifferent model' by Jonathan, she nevertheless agrees to accompany him to Spain. There, he lets slip that 'People are not always what they seem' and ticks off a scar-faced associate called Von Leicher (Olaf Pooley). Smooth and relaxed in the opening scenes set in Blair's London studio, Lee becomes stiff and unconvincing in the scenes set in Madrid; it's a fair bet, in fact, that the Spanish sequences were shot first. The denouement is equally limp. Previously quite stylish, Blair is now, as Lee put it, clothed in 'an ancient brown leather raincoat which might have been worn by Tree playing Fagin.'

As Auguste, MC of Cirano's nightclub, with James Hayter, Evelyn McCabe and Ralph Michael in Terence Fisher's Song for Tomorrow (1948)

Eyes fixed uncertainly on some point in the middle distance, Blair is shown in close-up as he tells Penny that 'I'm no murderer: I kill as a soldier kills in a war: for a belief!' 'You're mad!' she quavers. 'Possibly to you,' he replies in clipped tones before bundling her into a car with Carson and his men in hot pursuit.

Blair is finally cornered in a Home Counties village, the footage alternating weirdly between genuine location work and studio shots in which even the parked cars are painted on the backdrop. Blair tries to use the squirming Penny as a shield but is summarily shot down by Carson. Lee merely stares fixedly, bites his lip and raises a hand to his ribs, the scene fading tactfully before he can sink to the ground. Abducting the heroine, issuing Fascist manifestos, being killed in the final reel – Lee would do all these things on a regular basis in future films, but with a great deal more conviction. Blair's death scene, in particular, was met with thinly veiled derision from Slim Hand and his crew. 'Having seen people shot,' Lee explained, 'I knew that they don't always go hurtling into the air; they're inclined just to jerk slightly and then quietly fold up and hit the floor.

Well, they all thought this was *appalling*...' Lee learnt from *Penny and the Pownall Case* that the 'truth' is not always dramatically expedient and realised 'a need to polish up my dying.'

Jonathan Blair's controversial death sequence was filmed on Highbury's Stage 1 on the last day of production, 9 December. Lee's other commitments at this time were more discreet, and sometimes completely invisible. He was in demand as a stand-in for lofty male stars – the few that there were – in camera tests for their prospective female co-stars. He doubled for the Australian star Chips Rafferty in tests for Harry Watt's *Eureka Stockade* (part of Ealing's brief flirtation with Antipodean 'Westerns') and for Stewart Granger on Basil Dearden's *Saraband for Dead Lovers*, a lavishly budgeted Hanoverian epic with which Ealing hoped to lend some historical seriousness to the bodice-ripping subjects popularised by Gainsborough. Granger disconcerted Lee by watching his efforts from the sidelines, but then 'showed me an unforgettable courtesy by driving me back from the studio in his own car.' In the *Saraband* test footage, Lee was required to act opposite Moira Lister,

Coral Browne and Flora Robson; the coveted role of Countess Platen went to Robson.

Lee, too, was given a role in the picture for his pains. 'I played Duke Anthony von Wolfenbuttel, who was supposed to be either the brother or the lover or something (I could never find out which) of Joan Greenwood,' he recalled. 'I sat on a horse on Christmas Eve in Ealing Studios, with Basil Dearden looking at me with something approaching despair on his face. I was wearing a fixed grin, which was supposed to be a very winning smile, and a blond wig, because Stewart Granger had insisted that I couldn't appear looking like myself, as I slightly resembled him in those days ... I rode a horse across the set with this manic grin on my face, looking over my shoulder and bidding my love "Goodbye", and I believe I'm right in saying that it was removed from the picture in its entirety.' It was.

Another film from which Lee's footage was dropped was *Double Pursuit*, a gripping Gainsborough thriller directed by the prolific editor Alfred Roome. The film started at Shepherd's Bush late in November, was completed in January 1948 and went on release that summer as *My Brother's Keeper*. In it, Jack Warner and the young George Cole are escaped convicts joined at the wrist by handcuffs and pursued by the massed police forces of several counties. 'I played a tall policeman standing in the dark by a wall,' Lee remembered. 'I wasn't allowed to come near anybody because I was too tall ... Certainly, my contribution was virtually nil and very possibly it was cut out of the picture.' Long thought lost, the film was recently rediscovered by the National Film Archive, confirming Lee's suspicions.

Mae West was in town at the end of 1947, preparing to remount her notorious 20-year-old hit *Diamond Lil* in the West End before taking it on a marathon tour that stretched to 1951. Lee auditioned for the role of Lil's Latin lover at the Prince of Wales Theatre and then went for a 'call-back' in the star's suite at the Savoy. Everything was 'perfectly detached and proper,' Lee reported, and the part went to Bruno Barnabe. After these disappointments, Lee returned to Highbury to appear in a film for Terence Fisher, the director who would eventually take charge of Hammer's Gothic horrors in the late 1950s. The fourth Rank curtain raiser, *Song for Tomorrow* had started back on 17 December with the Irish singer Evelyn Dale making her film début. Adjusting her name to Evelyn McCabe, she was cast as Helen Maxwell, who is recruited by Colonel Roger Stanton (Ralph Michael again) to use her voice in restoring the memory of a wounded pilot, Derek Wardell (Shaun Noblye).

The crucial scene in which Stanton realises the therapeutic potential of Helen's voice takes place at Cirano's nightclub, where Wardell has taken a job as a pianist. Lee appears here as the club's MC, Auguste, looking uncomfortable with his hair plastered in silver paint and cajoling Helen into treating his patrons to a song. The film is marginally more lavish than *Penny and the Pownall Case* and also longer, its 61 minutes just qualifying it as a feature film. But it overstretches its resources in a climax purporting to be set at Covent Garden Opera House, where Helen performs Saint-Saens' *Samson and Delilah* with the Charm School's fight instructor, Rex 'Ricky' Rickman, pressed unwillingly into a leopard skin as Samson.

The film's nightclub scenes were shot in mid-January 1948, and in the same week Lee returned to Ealing to start work on Charles Frend's *Scott of the Antarctic*. The film had been in preparation for two years and had already spent some six months on snowbound locations in Norway. Lee was cast as expedition member Bernard Day, a rather smaller role than those given to other up-and-coming youngsters like Kenneth More, John Gregson and Derek Bond. Looking extremely aquiline and glossy-haired, Day first turns up puffing on a pipe as Scott (John Mills) briefs his men. He subsequently joins the team's 1911 Christmas party and finally appears bearded in the Ealing Antarctic astride one of his large motor-sleighs.

Realism had been the keynote in Norway and the same was true in London; the actors were given a week off in mid-February to perfect real beards. The

As Australian motor-sleigh supervisor Bernard Day in Basil Dearden's Scott of the Antarctic (1948)

Dancing attendance on Jean Kent, accompanied by Roger Moore (left), in Trottie True *(1948)*

snow, however, was bogus and caused Lee to 'dry' quite literally. 'In the middle of a particularly long scene where everybody had a great deal of dialogue,' he remembered, 'I had to come hurtling out of a hut in the snow and say one line. Of course, true to theatrical and film tradition, I blew it. As it was the end of a long scene, with a lot of snow and a lot of people – and everybody was getting very tired and it was very, very hot on the set – the director, Charles Frend, gave me a look the like of which I have never seen since. I don't blame him a bit.' Graced by a stirring Vaughan Williams score, the film wound up as a suitably patriotic choice for the Royal Command Film Performance on 29 November.

PINEWOOD GARDENS AND POST-WAR RUINS

Lee's next commitments were theatrical ones. Though he had long since shaken off his commitment to the Charm School, he was still required to earn his keep at Worthing from time to time. Peter Streuli's production of Noël Coward's *Design for Living* started on 17 May. The company was led by Sheila Keith and Lee was cast in the third act as Henry Carver. 'Mona Berridge, Jennifer Maddox and Christopher Lee provide the right touch in the American scene, in which John Elliott gets a great reception as Matthew, the Negro servant,'[10] commented a local critic. A courtroom drama called *Libel* was produced the next week – Lee played the Junior Counsel – and Guy Verney's gala production of *As You Like It* followed on 7 June, marking the Overture Players' fourth anniversary at the Connaught.

Patricia Burke was imported from the Old Vic to play Rosalind, Hugh Cross from Alliance Film Studios to play Orlando and Lee was on hand to play both 'First Lord attending the banished Duke' and Orlando's younger brother Jacques de Boys, who pops up at the very end to resolve the plot. 'Until an actor has performed Shakespeare before schoolchildren, all of whom turn the pages of the book in their laps, and has heard the gasps of indrawn breath when he gets a word wrong, he has never acted,' Lee observed. Sharing this disconcerting experience with him were three other striplings: Paul Eddington (Silvius), Tony Britton (Dennis) and, as Celia, Carol Marsh, who had recently appeared in *Brighton Rock*. She would later become Count Dracula's first female victim while

Eddington would turn up in *The Devil Rides Out*. 'We have no doubt that our present company contains stars of the future,' predicted the souvenir programme. 'Meanwhile they are Worthing's players, your own stars.'

In the first week of September, Lee resumed his stop-start cinema career with an uncredited role in *Trottie True*. Another Two Cities production, this was the first film in Technicolor from the Irish director Brian Desmond Hurst and Lee's first encounter with Pinewood Studios. A cloying music hall confection, it charts the progress of Gaiety girl Trottie True from Camden Town to Edwardian high society. 1940s favourite Jean Kent puts Trottie over with enormous vim and is surrounded by a pack of silly-ass Stage Door Johnnies straight out of P G Wodehouse.

Lee is the Hon Bongo Icklesham, looking lanky in a pearl-grey frock coat and forming an unlikely double act with Trottie's portly Gaiety co-star, Daisy Delaware (Hattie Jacques). Bongo is first seen with a rather more lissom Gaiety girl on his arm (Tamara Lees), but the provocative Daisy has only to snap her teeth at him for his monocle to pop out in mingled alarm and excitement, a gag repeated several times later in the picture by Michael Medwin's Monty, Marquis of Maidenhead. The scenes at the Gaiety stage door were filmed at Denham in October, but the gaily coloured communal picnic that ensues had been captured in the Pinewood gardens back in September. There, Bongo is shown in hot pursuit of Daisy, who pauses to say 'Oh, Bongo, you *are* dreadful: I thought I could trust you.' 'Oh, you certainly can, old girl,' he replies, whereupon she looks crestfallen and the chase continues.

Lee was by no means the only actor whose contribution to *Trottie True* went unacknowledged; other nameless ones included Patrick Cargill, Ian Carmichael, Anthony Steel and Roger Moore, with whom Lee shared a dressing room. There were also numerous uncredited starlets, notably the Irish beauty Constance Smith 'and a marvellous and enchanting person called Natasha Parry, who's now married to the director Peter Brook. I was so overcome by her, I once gazed into her eyes, saying "Would you like some tea?" – and all I succeeded in doing was to flood the entire table top, because I just kept pouring and pouring.'

Having doubled for Stewart Granger again, this time in test footage for Harold French's Two Cities comedy *Adam and Evelyne*, Lee began 1949 with a further month spent in Worthing. Edward Percy's blackmail thriller *The Shop at Sly Corner* had recently been made into a gripping film by George King; the Connaught version began on 24 January and cast Lee as Robert Graham, the doctor hero. A fey bit of Welsh whimsy, E Eynon Evans' *The Wishing Well* followed on the 31st and featured Lee as the wheelchair-bound John Pugh and Gaynor Woods as his sweetheart, Delith Gwyn. According to the local press, 'Gwen Williams as the wealthy visitor and Christopher Lee as the war-wounded grandson gave fine performances.'[11]

On the second night, however, part of the set fell down as Lee was being wheeled on-stage and on the Wednesday he found himself careering towards the orchestra pit in his wayward wheelchair and was forced to fling himself out of it two acts too soon. (The play was filmed five years later, incidentally, as *The Happiness of Three Women*; Donald Houston played John, Petula Clark was Delith and Eynon Evans himself played Amos, the resident postman-poet.) Winding up this Worthing stint, Lee then played Angelo de Medici in Elmer Rice's *See Naples and Die*. 'Christopher Lee and Hazel Penwarden contribute the Italian exotic,' opined a local critic, 'the first with mandolin and song and the latter with brown skin and not much on.'[12] Connaught records show that Lee returned to Worthing for a final appearance as late as 17 October 1955, playing opposite Virginia Maskell in Merton Hodge's medical student saga *The Wind and the Rain* – but Lee recalls nothing of this last theatrical engagement.

Only ten pictures were filming in British studios during March 1949, so Lee was lucky to receive another call from Terence Young. *They Were Not Divided* got well away from British studios in any case, starting at Soltau, near Hamburg, in the last week of April. About 12 weeks of location work also took in Munster Lager on the Lüneburg Heath, followed by a 300-mile trip to Vogelsang and then even further afield to Brussels, before moving to Caterham Barracks and Denham Studios. '*They Were Not Divided* is not an orthodox film,' announced Wardour Street newshound C H B ('Willy') Williamson. 'The story is based on fact, and tells of a wartime comradeship between two Guards officers – an Englishman and an American ... Almost a documentary approach is being used. All the male actors are ex-Servicemen, either professional or amateurs ... The director feels that so many members of the public have had first-hand experience of the incidents in the story that it would be a mistake to emphasise personalities. It is to be an anonymous tribute to every soldier who fought in the war. The actors are not 'stars' and the technicians will not take any screen credit for their contribution.'[13]

They Were Not Divided is a flawed but extremely powerful picture, expertly disguising its handful of

At Gmünd-Eiffel for They Were Not Divided *(1949), with Michael Trubshawe (seated on tank turret), Rupert Gerrard (sprawled on front of tank) and Ralph Clanton (behind Lee)*

studio shots with a documentary verisimilitude that was like no other 'fiction' film before it. Its English and American protagonists (Edward Underdown and Ralph Clanton) are brutally snuffed out at the end, the flags on their snow-covered graves intertwining as the cast list quietly unfolds. Despite this heavy dose of last-minute sentiment, and some out-of-kilter scenes with the heroes' sweethearts back home (Helen Cherry and Stella Andrew), the film is gruellingly realistic and features engaging performances from RSM 'Tibby' Brittain, with his trademark yell of 'Never seen anything like it in all my life!', and the impressively moustachioed Michael Trubshawe, subsequently immortalised by David Niven in *The Moon's a Balloon*. Lee is a young tank commander called Lewis – Trubshawe refers to him amiably as 'Chris' at one point – and is seen playing Snap with the two leads, lolling outdoors with a pipe, giving a suave victory sign from his tank turret as the Guards Division rolls into a French town, munching nonchalantly on an apple as the locals swarm round excitedly, and listening to an American chaplain just before the final push.

'It was the first time I'd been back to Germany since the end of the war and most of the country was still partly in ruins,' Lee recalled. 'Almost every single person one saw seemed to be up at dawn, if not before, working on rebuilding and clearing the rubble away. Great whole sweeps of land were still heavily sown with mines, so one was back in a place that was still far from safe and back among desolation and destruction with a beaten people who didn't exactly welcome you with open arms. And Lüneburg Heath, of course, was where Field Marshal Montgomery received the surrender of the German armed forces, so we were right in the middle of history.' As well as seeing the mass graves at nearby Belsen, Lee took more congenial trips up and down the Rhine, visiting the Court Theatre at Zell and Beethoven's house in Bonn.

Work on the film itself was pretty dangerous, including a scene in which Lee's tank, shaken by an over-generous explosive charge from the local special effects team, crashed into a wall. 'There was an almighty concussion and a cascade of bricks came down on me. The driver bailed out with a wild yell and I only just made it in time.' In another scene, not included in the final cut, Lee had to sprint through a flock of sheep and jump onto the running board of a moving three-ton truck. 'My feet went through the front of the driver's cabin onto the front axle. I really thought, for one terrifying second, that I was going to lose my legs.'

Winter Light, Mediterranean Sun

Lee's next Two Cities engagement started at Pinewood on 14 November. Based on an Aldous Huxley story, Fergus McDonell's *Prelude to Fame* is a charming drama about a bitter, childless woman (Kathleen Byron) who manipulates boy prodigy Guido (Jeremy Spenser) into undertaking a concert tour as a conductor. Unbilled, Lee is one of several Italian music journalists awaiting an audience with Guido, reacting rather wildly – facially, at any rate – when Byron's embarrassed Signora Bondini informs them that the boy will not be forthcoming. Looking slick in natty co-respondent shoes and well-oiled hair, Lee also has a brief moment in the aisle of the concert hall when he consults the crusty old conductor Dr Freihaus (Hugo Schuster). 'Would you give me an opinion, Maestro?' he asks. 'Do you think the boy will be a success?' The real maestro in *Prelude to Fame*, however, was Rank's musical director Muir Mathieson, who whipped up bits of Borodin, Bach, Beethoven and others into a delightful musical mélange.

Lee's duties in *Prelude to Fame* were hardly taxing but still succeeded in destroying his one-and-only appearance on the West End stage. He was given the lead in a three-act drama called *The Flat Next Door* by the Under 30 Group, and the play's one-off Sunday night performance at the Whitehall Theatre was a disaster attended, to Lee's dismay, by the Group's president, Alec Guinness. The director was the brilliant comic actor Colin Gordon, a snooty civil servant in innumerable British films. But Lee had been able to attend no more than half a dozen rehearsals, and the evening accordingly became 'the actor's recurrent nightmare come true: that he is pushed on the stage not knowing what he's doing, what the play is about or what his lines are ... When the curtain went up I was so badly under-rehearsed that I shook with fright.' Lee dried repeatedly, a contagious problem soon picked up by his co-star, Edwin Richfield. Radio engagements were less nerve-wracking, including a broadcast of Somerset Maugham's *The Noble Spaniard* during which Lee and Roger Delgado engaged in a fully fledged sword fight in the studio.

The 1950s began for Lee with *Captain Horatio Hornblower R.N.*, which started at Denham on 23 January, later transferring to Elstree. Based on C S Forester's famous sea stories, the film was directed by the one-eyed Raoul Walsh, an associate of D W Griffith during the silent era and later the director of hard-edged classics like *They Died With Their Boots On*, *High Sierra* and *White Heat*. An epic Technicolor endeavour, the film's action set-pieces required Captain Jock Easton and 65 of his stuntmen chums to be in more-or-less constant attendance, while Denham's Stage 4 was given over to a 70-ton

The captain of the Natividad and Lady Barbara Wellesley (Virginia Mayo) stand by while Captain Entenza (John Witty) confers with Gregory Peck's Captain Horatio Hornblower R.N. (1950)

representation of HMS Lydia which was later converted into the even bigger Spanish galleon, the Natividad.

Lee's audition for the Natividad's swarthy captain was conducted in a Denham corridor, Walsh asking him only two questions, 'Speak Spanish?' and 'Can you use a sword?' As well as marking Lee's first encounter with a big Hollywood director, the film also marked his first encounter with big Hollywood stars and his first of many on-screen sword fights. Gregory Peck had come over from the US to play Hornblower but his choice of a leading lady, the British stage star Margaret Leighton, was rejected by Walsh with the simple phrase, 'No tits.' Virginia Mayo better suited Walsh's requirements but was the subject of an official complaint from Equity. 'To put American stars in the lead in such films,' said a spokesman, 'will, we believe, destroy such character as our industry still possesses, and in addition will reduce the status of British artistes by condemning them to play only supporting roles.'[14]

'I had a sword fight with Gregory Peck,' Lee recalled, 'and not a very good one. We got far too close to each other, which is always a mistake in sword fights. There's no jumping forward, and your arms are moving instead of your legs, which never looks good. Gregory Peck had never used a sword in his life; I think he found it difficult and he said so.' To cover Peck's inexperience, Hornblower was given lines indicating that his clash with the Spanish captain of the Natividad was his first sword fight since flunking fencing classes as a midshipman. The encounter is a convincingly savage one, nevertheless, and after it Lee's captain argues hotly with the Spanish envoy, their argument providing a Hispanic backdrop to the first meeting between Hornblower and the Duke of Wellington's sister, Lady Barbara Wellesley. Lee finally gets a line in English when, faced with Hornblower's magnanimity, the captain blusters, 'But we have surrendered; there are rules of war.'

After *Hornblower* finished in April there was a pause, by Lee's standards quite a lengthy one. His Rank contract had not been renewed after *Prelude to Fame* – he had survived for three out of a possible seven years – and life as a freelance during some of the British film industry's darkest days was not easy. As a result, he spent the remainder of 1950 earning £8 a week as an interpreter in the export department of Simpson's, the famous department store in Piccadilly. Having doubled as a floorwalker during the January sales, Lee was bailed out once more by the faithful Terence Young. While most of Equity's membership was occupied with John Boulting's Festival of Britain production, *The Magic Box*, Young's *Valley of Eagles* started in Stockholm on 22 January 1951 and Lee went with it in the uncredited role of Holt, right-hand man to Jack Warner's Inspector Petersen. 'It was the middle of winter and incredibly cold,' Lee recalls. 'I remember wearing rubber shoes and having to hurtle across a frozen lake. I had to come to a mark, stop dead and then give my lines to Jack Warner, who was standing behind the camera. Well, I just went sailing straight past.' The scene was restaged on the bank.

Valley of Eagles is a tale of industrial espionage that starts from a vaguely science fiction standpoint – the theft of a device that converts sound into electricity – and ends with a protracted pursuit through the snow-covered wilderness. For the first section, scenes were shot inside Stockholm's Nobel Institute, for the last the unit went to Nystuen in the mountains of central Norway, where it was even colder than in Sweden. As in *Scott of the Antarctic*, Lee was not required on the Norwegian trip. Instead, he shot a few scenes in Sweden's winter light – as in *They Were Not Divided*, Harry Waxman's photography artfully obscures most of the actors' heads in these outdoor sequences – and, back at Pinewood's C Stage, held a gun on John McCallum's youthful boffin, Nils Ahlen. 'This flat belongs to Sven Nystrom,' he says quietly. 'What are you doing here?' Accompanied by fellow cop Ewen Solon, Lee is present only for the film's first act; the remainder is devoted, as one trade critic put it, to 'spectacular thrills [that] have not been matched in any previous motion picture, presenting as they do an amazing stampede of reindeer over a precipice and the killing-off of marauding wolves by trained eagles.'[15] In fact, much of this thrilling footage came courtesy of the National Geographic Society.

Valley of Eagles finished at Pinewood in the first week of April, but Lee felt himself irresistibly drawn back to the scenes of its location shooting. 'Sweden

As Holt, lieutenant to Inspector Petersen (Jack Warner) in Valley of Eagles (1951)

Restraining Eva Bartok in Robert Siodmak's The Crimson Pirate *(1951)*

I loved: the comfort and the luxury were almost unheard of so soon after the war. Over here there was still rationing,' he observed. 'I remember everybody on that picture; the beauty of Stockholm; the marvellous food that we had and the friends that we made.' Among these friends was the famous tenor Jussi Björling, who picked Lee out of the crowd at Stockholm's Tivoli Gardens for a schnapps-fuelled sing-song and invited him to the Opera House next day to meet the great baritone Joel Berglund. There, Lee was told he could well be enrolled in the Swedish Opera if he were to stay behind in Stockholm, but he elected to return to the UK and an uncertain acting career.

Lee kept his singing voice in trim, however. In the early 1950s he would assuage his operatic leanings – and indulge his new-found love for Northern Europe – with cycling trips round Sweden, Norway and Finland, during which he adopted fanciful pseudonyms and performed operatic excerpts with various backwoods opera companies. In the same way, he would descend unannounced on obscure theatre troupes in Germany and France, mucking in with backstage duties as well as playing roles like the malevolent Iago in a potted version of *Othello*.

Having continued at Simpson's both during and after the *Valley of Eagles* schedule, Lee's next port of call was Teddington Studios. *The Crimson Pirate* was a lavish buccaneering romp conceived as a follow-up to *The Flame and the Arrow*, in which Burt Lancaster and his diminutive partner from vaudeville, Nick Cravat, had scored a major hit. Directing the new film was Robert Siodmak, master of paranoid 1940s thrillers like *The Spiral Staircase* and the Lancaster vehicles, *Criss Cross* and *The Killers*. At Teddington, Lee stood in for Lancaster, back-to-camera, in test shots and Siodmak accordingly offered him a part in the film itself.

Accompanied by George Woodbridge and other British character actors, Lee left for Ischia aboard a specially chartered Sabena aircraft on 1 July 1951. Shooting began immediately, all of it some 20 miles out to sea, utilising a three-masted Spanish frigate and a two-masted brig, plus a sophisticated ship-to-shore radio service to communicate with the mainland production office. According to Lee, Siodmak took a hard look at the script of *The Crimson Pirate* and within 48 hours had cannily decided to play it for laughs. 'We had a great time,' Lee reported. The unit took up residence at Teddington in mid-October and the film's athletic star finally managed to fly back to Hollywood on 8 December. He had in the meantime taught Lee much about the art of screen fighting, notably the need to keep one's distance – a rule disregarded in *Hornblower*. Siodmak himself found Lancaster less amenable, ascribing the star's numerous temperamental outbursts to mental illness.

The film is one of the most memorable examples of the early 1950s vogue for highly coloured

Christopher Lee – Part One

Talking terms with Caliph Macdonald Parke in Babes in Bagdad *(1951)*

swashbucklers, presenting Lancaster at the peak of his physical prowess and the Hungarian star Eva Bartok at the height of her beauty. Uncredited, Lee is Joseph, assistant to the swarthy Baron Grude (Leslie Bradley), who helps his devious master recapture his hijacked ship, manhandles Bartok a bit and coldly stabs a whiskery insurgent (Noel Purcell) when he cries 'Death to Grude!' He's also involved in the climactic shipboard skirmish, but otherwise doesn't do much more than stand around looking exotic in a bottle-green uniform and tricorn hat, plus a dashing goatee that would stay with him for some 12 months. 'It was Otto Heller's first essay in colour,' Lee commented, 'and, despite the discomfort of wearing green velvet under the Mediterranean sun, I was delighted to come up resplendent as the waves.'

A Desultory Crop

While *The Crimson Pirate* was settling into Teddington, Lee polished off a brief job that would prove to be his last role for BBC Television for 45 years. It was not an auspicious occasion, though it would provide him with invaluable talk-show material in years to come. *I Made News* was what would later become known as a drama-documentary and a large cast was lined up at Alexandra Palace for its third instalment. Directed and presented by Leonard Brett,

The Theft of the Pink Diamond was broadcast, live, at 8.15 pm on Friday 2 November 1951. It featured, among others, Anton Diffring, Richard Molinas, Marne Maitland, Everley Gregg and John Fabian. 'Monsieur Raymond Lacoste, former correspondent of *L'Echo de Paris*, describes the part he played in this case,' explained the *Radio Times*.

Among the sound effects culled from various BBC discs were 'Grandfather clock', 'Paris street noises', 'typewriter', 'printing press' and 'alarm bell'. But Richard Molinas – overcome by the nervous tension inseparable from live television – provided some thunderous sound effects of his own as a Parisian inspector cowed by Lee's Commissaire de Police. 'We played a ten-minute scene without once looking at each other,' Lee reported. 'And he never stopped farting ... People behind the camera were rolling in agony, but there was nothing they could do to help us. The glory and the confusion were all ours. I racked my brains unavailingly for a way to let the viewers know that the credit should all go to Richard. It was hopeless.'

Further embarrassment followed in December. A limp Arabian Nights burlesque, *Babes in Bagdad* was filmed in Spain by Edgar G Ulmer, the now-venerated Austrian director who had been scenic artist on *Der Golem* as well as directing Bela Lugosi and Boris

Karloff in *The Black Cat*. The film's American producers were the Danziger Brothers, who would soon take root in the UK as the country's foremost purveyors of B-pictures. 'I played a slave trader,' Lee reported, 'feeling somewhat uncomfortable in black satin which didn't fit very well.' And he certainly looks it when dragging in a gaggle of comely harem candidates at the end of a chain for the delectation of Macdonald Parke's elderly Caliph.

Jack Cox's 'Exotic Color' photography provides occasional travelogue-style distractions from a ludicrous plot, in which wisecracking Americanisms are allowed to intrude for supposedly comic effect. Rebellious harem girl, Kyra, is plotting the emancipation of women and the institution of monogamy in old Bagdad, and to this end enlists the aid of the Caliph's erstwhile favourite, Zohara. As the *Monthly Film Bulletin* ungallantly put it, 'The 'babes' are led by Paulette Goddard and Gypsy Rose Lee, scantily clad but clearly in their thirties.' Kyra's master, meanwhile, is played by the ageing matinée idol John Boles in his final screen appearance; one of the earlier ones had been in *Frankenstein* 20 years before. 'It was the first time I'd ever been to Spain,' Lee pointed out. 'Barcelona at Christmas. I remember seeing my first bullfight on Boxing Day.' It was also Lee's first American picture, though not an encouraging one.

Yet another first followed in 1952 – Lee's first 'red herring' role. *Paul Temple Returns* began at Nettlefold Studios in Walton-on-Thames on 7 April, the third of three small-scale pictures starring John Bentley as the amateur sleuth created by Francis Durbridge. This one was based on Durbridge's BBC radio play *Paul Temple Intervenes* and only secured Bentley's services at the last minute; he had been occupied with *Men Against the Sun* in Kenya and rumours of his unavailability had caused one industry observer to complain that 'A Paul Temple film without John Bentley playing the title role is ... almost as unthinkable as Quo without Vadis.'[16] Advertised as 'His Toughest Assignment Yet,' the film pits Temple against a narcotics baron and triple murderer known only as the Marquis. Dark doings in Docklands, two further murders, a road accident, an attempt to kill Temple's plucky wife Steve (Patricia Dainton) and a climactic warehouse conflagration are all squeezed into a breathless 70 minutes by the veteran director Maclean Rogers, who was then in his seventies.

According to Lee, 'All I remember about that film is sitting down in a lot of the scenes because I was too tall to stand up.' Sir Felix Raybourne is a famous explorer suspected of being the Marquis and is twice visited in his country retreat by Temple and wife. Strangely prescient, the scene in which the Temples first drop in on Sir Felix is creepily done, with a number of Arab servants, notably Abdullah (George Patterson), ushering them into an inner sanctum done up like an Ancient Egyptian temple. Quizzed

An early interest in Egyptology: as Sir Felix Raybourne opposite Patricia Dainton and John Bentley in Paul Temple Returns *(1952)*

about a recent archaeological find in the desert that may have a bearing on the case, Sir Felix is conspicuously unco-operative, though on the Temples' second visit to his domain all is revealed and the fiery Docklands denouement is precipitated. Bespectacled and still bearded, Lee handles Sir Felix with a lofty hauteur that would be perfected in many similar roles, though somewhat hampered by Rogers' confinement of him, *Corridor of Mirrors* style, to a chair.

Lee then did a very brief 'bit' in Mario Zampi's *Top Secret*, which started at Elstree on 28 April. A follow-up to Zampi's wildly successful comedy *Laughter in Paradise*, this has Sanitary Engineer Potts (George Cole) being appropriated by the Russians in the belief that he is an atomic expert rather than a lavatorial one. The film's title oscillated during production from *Top Secret* to *Laughter Behind the Curtain* and then back again, and this uncertainty is reflected in the tone of the finished product, despite a galaxy of comic talent and a typically charming performance from Oscar Homolka, looking very like Leonid Brezhnev. That persistent goatee still in place, Lee appears fleetingly in a hotel lobby, observing the movements of Comrade Potts from behind a newspaper and then going into a phone booth. Addressing Frederick Valk at the other end, he says simply, 'He is on his way to Comrade Ivanova's room.'

Lee turned 30 on 27 May and soon after gained a small role in a very big movie indeed, *Moulin Rouge*. John Huston, director of *The Maltese Falcon*, *The Treasure of the Sierra Madre*, *Key Largo* and others, had just made *The African Queen* for John and Jimmy Woolf of Romulus Films and felt disinclined to return to America. He agreed to direct *Moulin Rouge* for them if they could secure José Ferrer for the role of Toulouse-Lautrec. This they did and four weeks of Paris location work began, in the midst of a ferocious heatwave, early in July. Fully bearded by now, Lee was cast as the creator of Pointillism, Georges Seurat, seen lolling outside a Parisian café with Toulouse-Lautrec and two other members of the Society of Independents. Toying with a glass of absinthe, Seurat suggests that 'We will go to the Louvre and refresh our souls.' Lautrec dismisses it as a 'graveyard' and stumps off. 'I wonder what has made him so unhappy,' Seurat mutters to himself in close-up as the scene fades.

Considerate and sensitive, Seurat is very different from his skittish fellows, Anquetin and Gauzi, played

'Just be yourself, kid.'
With director John Huston outside Aux Deux Magots for Moulin Rouge (1952)

Innocents in Paris: rib-tickling antics with Ronald Shiner (in drum) and Alf Goddard (1952)

by two French actors, Jean Landier and Robert Le Fort, who have been conspicuously dubbed. 'My small part was played in the actual café, Aux Deux Magots, frequented by Toulouse-Lautrec,' Lee claimed. 'The temperatures were in the nineties. It was Paris at the height of the tourist season and José Ferrer and I could hardly hear what we were saying because of the traffic, the screeching of the gendarmes' whistles and the constant coming and going of the tourists.' Lee was also faintly disconcerted by the supreme nonchalance of Huston himself, who gave him only four words by way of direction ('Just be yourself, kid') and then sat across the street flipping through a copy of *Time* magazine while the scene was being shot. Lee goes unbilled in the film, but his role is more substantial than the one played by Peter Cushing, who *does* receive a credit.

While shooting *Moulin Rouge*, the Woolf brothers cannily began work on Gordon Parry's *Innocents in Paris*, a bitty and unamusing comedy redeemed only by the incomparable Alastair Sim. Lee has a 'blink and you'll miss it' part as Lieutenant Whitlock, an unsmiling (and non-speaking) military bandleader whose instrumentalists – apart from star comic Ronald Shiner and sidekicks Alf Goddard and Philip Stainton – were the real thing, specially imported from Chatham. On the tarmac at the airport, Whitlock's pint-sized French liaison tries to kiss him on both cheeks but is confounded by his great height, a gag Lee would restage much more elaborately over 40 years later in *Police Academy: Mission to Moscow*. 'Those tourists who already had me in their albums as part of the French art scene,' he commented, 'must have been taken aback to see me striding out in front of the band in the Avenue Foch.' They may not have recognised him, however; for *Innocents in Paris*, Lee's tenacious facial hair finally got the chop.

During this period, Lee further occupied himself as a film dubber, most notably providing the voices for the English version of Jacques Tati's *Monsieur Hulot's Holiday*, a task that offered greater challenges than his desultory crop of on-screen appearances. But, unknown to him, help was already at hand. While *Paul Temple Returns* was shooting at Nettlefold in April, Douglas Fairbanks Jr – actor, producer, socialite, diplomat and honorary KBE – was in Britain making three pilot pictures for a proposed series of TV films for NBC. The first was made at Isleworth's Worton Hall Studios, which, despite having recently played host to *The African Queen*, would be gutted at the beginning of June to make way for the Coal Board, a fate emblematic of the British film industry itself as it struggled through another of its periodic crises. The Fairbanks scheme fared better than Worton Hall, however, and in the process it would revolutionise Lee's career.

PART TWO

TV And Other Trials 1952–1956

In the early 1950s, filmmakers were becoming increasingly queasy about the threat posed to them by television. Glamorous innovations cunningly designed to dwarf TV, like 3-D and Scope screen ratios, were all very well for monied American producers but their British counterparts were cautious about splashing out on such luxuries. 'The whole medium gave the impression of being on the skids,' Lee wrote later, noting also the ironic fact that 'in that slack time for the film business, my only way forward was through television.'

More precisely, his way forward was provided by Douglas Fairbanks Jr, who with his fellow producer Peter Marriott and the fledgling casting director Lionel Grose was setting up a series of 39 films for American TV under the umbrella title *Douglas Fairbanks Presents*. Each show cost around £7,500, was shot in five or six days and lasted 26 minutes. The whole 'programme' began at Borehamwood's British National Studios on 22 September 1952, winding up some six months later. 'I became intrigued with the idea of making the highest quality films in the least possible time, turning out Rolls-Royces on Ford assembly line methods,'[1] Fairbanks explained. As the project got into its stride in November, features being shot elsewhere included *Will Any Gentleman?* at Elstree, *Genevieve* at Pinewood, *The Beggar's Opera* at Shepperton and *Meet Mr Lucifer* at Ealing (ironically, this was a rather desperate satire on the threat of television), while Hammer Film Productions, who would later play a decisive role in Lee's career, were making *Spaceways* at Bray. For the time being, however, Lee was much better off under the Fairbanks wing, honing his skills on an extraordinary variety of parts and enjoying 'the kind of experience actors dream about.'

Industry observers were at first sceptical about the validity of TV movies, particularly because the programmes US audiences would see on their television sets were due to be packaged into 'portmanteau' pictures for UK cinemagoers. 'British actors and British technicians find that such productions afford them a means to sustaining a living in our erratic and unreliable industry,' sniffed C H B Williamson in July 1952. 'Yet they have to ask whether the quality of the results can assist their professional reputation.'[2] The following February, however, Williamson was entirely won over to what he called 'the new industry in this country' – and it was a visit to the Fairbanks unit that effected the conversion. 'Harold Huth, who is in charge of production for Fairbanks, took me on a tour of production activity and, very rapidly, I saw that not a moment could be wasted, that there was no time for temperament nor, indeed, for the creation of 'Rembrandts' as one assistant director put it – but the effect on the screen was there and good enough to satisfy cinema patrons ... I decided that here was scope for testing new talent, for developing it until such time as it was ripe for stardom in major product.'[3]

Of the new talent developed by Fairbanks, Lee would appear in 16 programmes across a four-year period and act with Fairbanks himself in five of them. In the course of their work together, the pair became good friends – though, as Fairbanks put it in 1983, 'I could not let sentiment interfere with business if he were not so damned *good*. He just happens to be one of the most thoughtful, sensitive and intelligent actors around, and one of the most versatile. I do not think people realise how versatile he is. He was called upon with me to play every kind of part: serious and comic, romantic and villainous, old and young, fat and thin – everything that you can imagine ... He just stood out. Whenever anyone was stuck, they always knew – whatever the part, almost – that Christopher could do it; or, if he could not, they would change the writing of the part to get him in.'[4]

Fairbanks and Beyond

Charting the progress of *Douglas Fairbanks Presents* can be a bewildering business, thanks not only to

With Boris Karloff, Eileen Moore and (in background) Frances Rowe in At Night All Cats Are Grey, *a 1953 instalment of* Colonel March of Scotland Yard

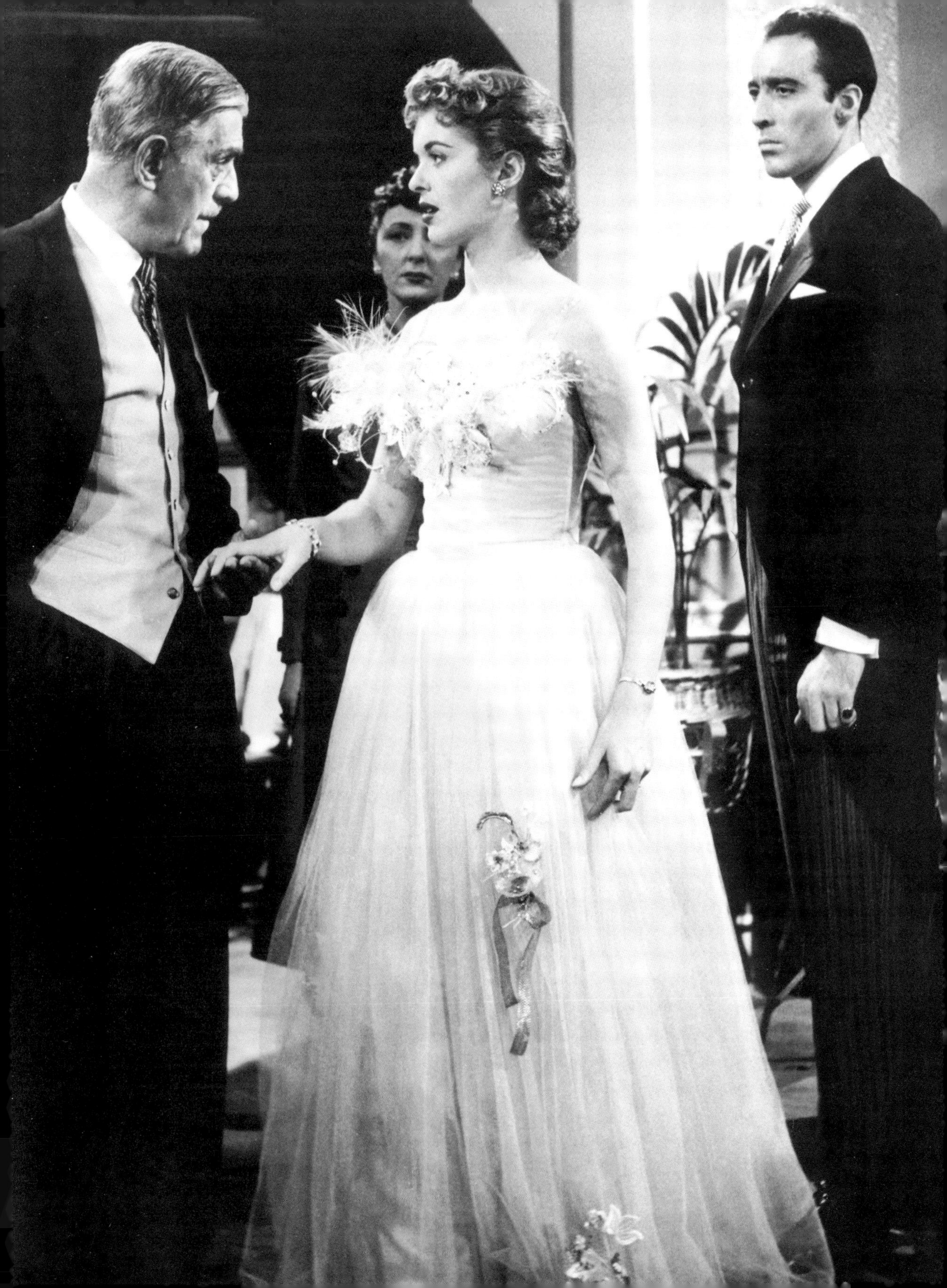

As Radenko, 'a half-witted Yugoslav soldier in a Dalmatian Laurel and Hardy act,' with Martin Benson's Lenkov in Douglas Fairbanks Presents: The Death of Michael Turbin (1953)

Fairbanks' habit of pasting selected episodes together to form theatrical features but also to a further habit, acquired after the arrival of Independent Television in 1955, of allowing instalments to bleed out onto British TV screens under a variety of other 'umbrella' titles, such as *Crown Theatre*, *Summer Theatre* and *Saturday Playhouse*. As one commentator put it in the run-up to ITV's inception, 'These films contribute to satisfying the insatiable demands of American television, and what American television needs today, British television may need tomorrow when it goes commercial.'[5]

Fairbanks himself pointed out that 'It's all a question of packaging. We pick only a certain type of story – one that is universally understandable. Anything too localised is out. We take care to avoid over-English accents ... Americans just don't understand the Mayfair drawl.'[6] Lee would generally be cast as non-English characters, in any case, and in the first season he acted in six stories: Lawrence Huntington's *International Settlement*, *Destination Milan* and *The Parlour Trick*, Bernard Knowles' *The Death of Michael Turbin* and Lance Comfort's *Moment of Truth* and *American Duel*. The last would form part of a 1953 compendium called *The Triangle* while *The Parlour Trick* was one of the three components of *Thought to Kill* later that year. As for *Destination Milan* and *The Death of Michael Turbin*, they provided the collective titles for two further portmanteaux put together at the end of 1954; *International Settlement* was put out by itself as a short and *Moment of Truth* was confined to TV.

These first season assignments offered Lee a typically eclectic range of parts. In *The Death of Michael Turbin*, he was teamed with Martin Benson as East European soldiers Radenko and Lenkov, selling the victims' boots after a stint on a firing squad and discovering that one of them, Turbin (Christopher Rhodes), is still alive. Indulgently allowing him to get away, Radenko then discovers that Turbin has swiped all the valuable boots in the process. *The Parlour Trick* offered Lee a less prominent role, as a Junior Counsel in what Fairbanks' publicity called 'The remarkable story of a grocery clerk who sued his wife for divorce because she would not let him carve the roast.' The cast here is a pretty juicy one, including Bill Owen, Lana Morris and Bartlett Mullins as the pint-sized Judge. Lee made a similarly fleeting appearance alongside Philip Friend and Elizabeth Sellars in the bullfighting drama *Moment of Truth*, as a priggish torero dressed in full 'suit of lights' rig.

In *International Settlement* a US pilot (played by Fairbanks himself) crash-lands on an isolated Pacific island and finds that the polyglot inhabitants – including Lee as the resident Italian, Antonio – are blissfully unaware that the Second World War is in progress. As a Swedish huckster called Svenson in *Destination Milan*, Lee tries to talk a lion-faced man (Tommy Duggan) into signing an exclusive circus contract aboard the Orient Express, and in *American*

Duel he is Franz, a scarred Prussian swordsman who challenges an American student (Ron Randell) to a duel for the affections of Mitzi (June Thorburn). Set in 1912, this segment was written by the young novelist and screenwriter Nelson Gidding and focused on 'the duelling ritual of the Mensur, as practised by the students in old Heidelberg,' Lee reported. 'It was very formal and stately, our bodies padded up like ice-hockey goalkeepers while we chanted in unison, "Ein, zwei, drei – zurück," and repeated it, our swords clashing in time.'

The Fairbanks connection bore further fruit when shooting on the first season drew to a close in March 1953. Fairbanks' casting director, Lionel Grose, returned to acting for a project that took him to Stockholm on 10 April; the handful of other English performers included Lee and the child actor William Simons, plus the half-Swedish ingenue Doreen Denning. *Tales of Hans Andersen* was produced by the Norwegian shipping magnate Karl Moseby for American TV and was no doubt designed to tap into the huge success enjoyed by Danny Kaye in the film *Hans Christian Andersen*. Tom Connochie, Fairbanks' production supervisor, alternated as director with Åke Ohberg and Lee appeared in four of the stories: *The Nightingale*, *Wee Willie Winkit*, *The Cripple Boy* and *The Old House*. Production values were high and much enhanced by extensive use of Stockholm's Skansen Park, with its multiple show-houses rendered in different styles and periods.

Lee's roles were as testing as any Fairbanks could have thrown at him, ranging from a romantic student and a chess-playing old man to a swarthy peasant, husband to Hollywood star Signe Hasso in *The Cripple Boy*. His role as the Emperor of China in *The Nightingale* marked his first of eight appearances in Oriental make-up, with a bald cap thrown in to increase his discomfort. The Emperor's dream sequence as he hovers near death was augmented by Elsa-Marianne von Rosen and other members of the Swedish Ballet, with Death himself personified by the diminutive Julius Mengarelli and the choreography handled by Mengarelli and his brother Mario. The Skansen Park, meanwhile, was temporarily abandoned in favour of the Chinese Pavilion in the grounds of the royal castle of Drottningholm, and the 'set' was duly visited by King Gustav VI Adolf. The series started being shown in the UK as a teatime attraction on 24 September 1955 – the very first Saturday of commercial television – though for some reason *The Nightingale* and *The Old House* weren't included.

While the Hans Andersen stories were in production, Stockholm was in the midst of its seventh centenary celebrations (albeit a year late), and Lee returned home in time for London's own celebrations attendant on the Coronation. Later in the year he was at Southall Studios for *Colonel March of Scotland Yard*, a series based on John Dickson Carr's *The Department of Queer Complaints*. Three pilot episodes had been made back in 1952 only to be composited, Fairbanks-style, into a feature called *Colonel March Investigates*. Also in Fairbanks mould, production on the 23-episode series was stretched from 9 November 1953 to the following April. The first ten instalments were completed by Christmas and Lee appeared as a fey French designer, Jean-Pierre, in the fifth. *At Night All Cats Are Grey* was directed by Phil Brown and dealt with the mystery surrounding a murdered fashion model. Colonel March himself was Hollywood's very own London-born 'Monster', Boris Karloff.

Lee little suspected then how closely his persona would soon be interlinked with Karloff's, but an indication of sorts was provided by a Motley TV film shot at Nettlefold Studios in the week beginning on 14 December. John Lemont's *The Mirror and Markheim* is a 29-minute Robert Louis Stevenson adaptation in which Lee was cast as a ghostly visitant who appears in a mirror to a downtrodden young man (Philip Saville), dissuading him from the murder of pompous antiques dealer Arthur Lowe. The story is set on Christmas Day, and making the film in the run-up to Christmas perhaps helped in creating the appropriate atmosphere. Narrated by Marius Goring, it was produced by Norman Williams (husband of Patricia Dainton, with whom Lee had worked on *Paul Temple Returns*) and was well received by the US TV executives it was aimed at. It was tradeshown in London as a theatrical short in January 1955 before acquiring an ITV afterlife the following year.

In it – blandly smiling throughout the better to prick Saville's conscience – Lee laid down in embryo the method he would bring to similar roles, taking his cue from Stevenson's suggestion that 'this thing was not of the earth and not of God ... and yet the creature had a strange air of the commonplace ... [speaking] in the tones of everyday politeness.' The film also provides an echo of the looking-glass climax of Conrad Veidt's doppelgänger classic, *Der Student von Prag*. By coincidence, at the time that *Markheim* was being made, Laurence Olivier had recorded the original story for BBC Radio under the auspices of Harry Alan Towers, an entrepreneur who would loom large in Lee's career during the 1960s.

Another portent of things to come was provided at Bushey Studios in 1954. In *Crossroads*, a 19-minute Butcher's vignette, Lee was cast as a young man returning from the grave to avenge himself on a callous impresario who caused the death of his sister

Jack Dunscombe (Douglas Fairbanks Jr) threatens gang boss Gravat (Peter Illing), while Gravat's henchman Maurice looks on, in Douglas Fairbanks Presents: Street of Angels *(1954)*

(Mercy Haystead). 'Neat lead performances in miniature from Christopher Lee as the avenger and Ferdy Mayne as the showman,'[7] enthused one critic. Lee received top billing for the first time – as, prophetically, 'the Ghost' – but the film was memorable for him less as a forecast of future roles than as a threat to his professional reputation. Laughing hysterically at a joke told him by Ferdy Mayne, he was sent home and reported to Equity for misconduct. 'The director, John Fitchen, soon afterwards committed suicide,' Lee points out.

Douglas Fairbanks Presents Mark Two had begun, meanwhile, on 16 December 1953 with Lance Comfort in overall charge of a 39-picture programme that stretched to May 1954. In Derek Twist's *Border Incident*, Lee is an 'Official' coping with William Sylvester and a stolen passport in a French border town, while in Arthur Crabtree's *Street of Angels* he plays Maurice, bodyguard to a gangster (Peter Illing) in a North African port who avenges the death of his master at the hands of an American petty crook (Fairbanks).

Lee's four remaining contributions that season were all directed by Michael McCarthy, who also wrote the first two. Set on the border between East and West Germany, *The Refugee* revolves around a beautiful spy (Ingeborg Wells) who gives herself away by trying to kill the German-Jewish Carl (Lee). *The Last Knife* features Lee as Tolsen, a scar-faced Russian lion-tamer vying for the circus limelight with Fairbanks' jaded knife-thrower Karoff, and in *A Line in the Snow* Lee is Brackett, a murderer pursued through a blizzard by a couple of Canadian Mounties, Robert Beatty and Patrick Holt. Also in the cast was Carol Marsh from the Connaught *As You Like It*, whom Lee would meet again in momentous circumstances at Bray Studios late in 1957. Filming of the blizzard sequence saw Lee and Beatty, bombarded by a nasty mixture of salt and minced polystyrene, coming close to asphyxiation.

A Moroccan pimp, a genial Italian, a German Jew, a Russian circus performer and a Canadian convict – Lee's roles were even more wide-ranging than those in Fairbanks' first season. Better still, he was also cast as a factory boss in McCarthy's *The Awakening*, an accomplished adaptation of Gogol's *The Overcoat* which succeeded in luring Buster Keaton to Borehamwood. Arriving for the rushes, Keaton astonished Lee by emerging unexpectedly from behind the screen and somersaulting deftly into his seat. As for McCarthy, he interleaved his directing career with the proprietorship of a hotel in St Leonard's on Sea. He would die there, aged 42, in May 1959, causing Lee to observe that 'had he lived he would have been one of the great directors.'

During the second Fairbanks season, and with feature film opportunities still thin on the ground, Lee auditioned at the Globe Theatre for *After the Ball*, Noël Coward's musical version of *Lady Windermere's Fan*. Robert Helpmann and Michael Benthall joined

Coward in listening to Lee's spirited rendition of the Serenade from *Don Giovanni*, and the part went to Peter Graves. But by the time the show opened on 10 June 1954, Lee had been in Spain for over a fortnight, filming a lavish CinemaScope adventure for the faithful Terence Young. Budgeted at over $1 million, *That Lady* remained in Spain for six weeks before transferring to MGM Borehamwood early in July. Its credentials were impressive. Cinematographer Robert Krasker, veteran art director Alfred Junge, costume designer Mariano Andreu and Lee's Wellington contemporary, composer John Addison, supplemented what producer Sy Bartlett called 'as powerful and impressive a cast as I have ever known in the last 15 years.'[8] The locations were just as impressive, ranging from the huge Escorial monastery, the Escorial-Madrid road and the banks of the Guadalquivir to the ancient university town of Salamanca and the Alcazar in Segovia.

However scenic, the film was by no means a holiday for Lee; Terence Young's old maxim – 'Do anything for me, that boy!' – was never put into practice more remorselessly than here. Unknown to Lee, casting director Maude Spector had cannily included in his contract the phrase 'to play the Captain of the Guard and other parts'. Lee was therefore required to play several other roles, heavily disguised as muffled horsemen and masked assassins. A river duel with the Hollywood star Gilbert Roland yielded a classic whispered warning from Roland – 'Be careful, amigo! I can't see a thing without my glasses!' – and also involved Lee being thrown from his horse in full armour. To add insult to injury, the scene was cut from the film.

A florid 16th century court intrigue, the film was based on a novel and play by Kate O'Brien, which coincidentally had been produced by the BBC a few weeks before Terence Young's unit started work in Spain. A complicated, and ultimately tragic, love triangle develops between King Philip II, his flamboyant minister, Perez, and the one-eyed beauty Ana de Mendoza – so complicated, and ultimately turgid, that a narrator is required to guide the bewildered viewer through it. The deluxe supporting cast provides some compensation, however, including Dennis Price, Robert Harris, Anthony Dawson and the distinguished French actress Françoise Rosay. Roland was cast as Perez and Olivia de Havilland as Ana, while Paul Scofield had been lured away from *A Question of Fact* at the Piccadilly Theatre to essay his first screen role as the King. Professing little enthusiasm for the medium, he returned to it only sporadically thereafter.

Lee learned a useful lesson from *That Lady*. In his big scene with Olivia de Havilland, the captain takes Ana into custody and informs her that 'This is not an

Bringing bad news to Olivia de Havilland and Françoise Rosay in That Lady *(1954)*

CHRISTOPHER LEE – PART TWO

arrest but a measure of protection for her Highness' own safety.' The scene was democratically shot on both messenger and recipient but ended up in the finished film as an uninterrupted de Havilland reaction shot and an extended view of the back of his head. The star was full of surprises all round. Sleepless in Segovia, Lee appealed for a sleeping pill and obediently swallowed the foul-tasting item she offered him, only to be told it was a suppository. Lee was happy, however, to share his single day off with the affable Gilbert Roland, joining him in a pilgrimage to the grave of Roland's bullfighter father.

HOME COUNTIES PSYCHO

After *That Lady*, Lee switched to a small role, uncredited, in another swashbuckler, this time a vehicle for Errol Flynn. Shot in lustrous CinemaScope, Henry Levin's *The Black Prince* started on location at Tring on 26 July, moved into Elstree on 2 August and was finished by mid-October. A week later its title was changed to *The Dark Avenger* – the original may have been considered too close to Tay Garnett's Alan Ladd vehicle *The Black Knight* – and it would be changed again, to *The Warriors*, for its US release. At some point in the picture's lengthy schedule, Lee filmed a couple of brief scenes in a French tavern, where the lovely Yvonne Furneaux trills 'Everybody knows I am the girl for quelque chose' and tells Lee's loutishly attentive soldier that 'You have enough girls already, Captain.'

The princely Flynn and his trusty right hand (Rupert Davies) are at the tavern incognito and Lee, resplendent in dark tunic and stripey tights, addresses them, for no accountable reason, in an American accent. 'You're noo to this village,' he says aggressively. At dead of night, Lee wakes from a drunken stupor to find Flynn and Davies attempting to steal a suit of armour. 'Besides stealing, you dare to impersonate a knight?' Lee storms, US twang still in place. 'D'you know what the punishment for that is, you dog?' A bludgeoning fight with broadswords ensues – Flynn's stunt double was Britain's Olympic sabre champion, Raymond Paul – and, having been thumped in the face with a wooden stool, Lee ends up impaled and sprawling in death across an upended table. Lee ended up, for real, with a permanently crooked little finger on his right hand; in his enthusiasm, Flynn had slipped and almost cut the digit off. The injury would lend a peculiarly spidery quality to many future scenes of Lee's hand groping its way out of coffins.

Nursing his injured finger, Lee went into *Police Dog*, a theatrical second feature with which the Fairbanks team prefaced its third batch of TV half-hours at British National. Produced by Harold Huth, the film was written and directed by Derek Twist, a noted editor for Powell and Pressburger among others, and began on location in Kentish Town on 18 October. Very much a latterday quota quickie, it sets up a ludicrous love triangle between plucky copper Tim Turner, his doting fiancée Joan Rice and

In The Dark Avenger *(1954), Errol Flynn almost succeeded in cutting off the little finger on Lee's right hand*

the heroic Alsatian, Rex III. With the Blitz a relatively recent memory, Rex is found 'nosing around a bomb site' and is rapidly co-opted into the police force.

Lee is an anti-dog PC, first encountered in the canteen as he nurses a bitten hand and challenges Turner 'to let him have a whiff of your pong.' With a pleasantly muted East End accent, Lee is confounded when cop and dog take to each other like old pals. 'I always said he was a son of a – ' Lee exclaims (the final word has been erased by a clumsy blip in the soundtrack), and struts out with the surly observation, 'See you at Crufts!' Later, he cowers from Rex in a police station doorway and has his helmet knocked off by a gang of toughs outside a pub, cravenly running away when Rex bounds to his rescue. The film's resident crook is hugely unconvincing, dropping all his H's with great care and burdened with unfortunate lines like 'I can smell a dick three streets away.' His moll (Sandra Dorne) is rather better, but the film as a whole is a slog to sit through.

Police Dog's three-week schedule was succeeded at British National on 8 November 1954 by the revived Fairbanks TV 'programme'. In Michael McCarthy's *The Immigrant*, Lee plays Makarenko, a Polish ship's officer involved in the efforts of a police spy (André Morell) to thwart two crew members' attempts to jump ship, and in Roy Rich's *The Wedding Dress* Lee is an East European officer, Lieutenant Krainski, watching from the sidelines as his superiors (Mary Morris and André Morell again) clash over a handmade bridal gown.

Douglas Fairbanks Presents wound up with a fourth and final batch of dramas filmed at the end of 1955. McCarthy's *The Man Who Wouldn't Escape* cast Fairbanks himself in two roles, as a South American dictator and his scholarly brother who leads the Resistance movement against him. Lee is Luis, a convict hired to kill the liberal Fairbanks when he's imprisoned. Francis Searle's *Crown of the Andes* has Christopher Rhodes as spy Hugh Diamond, hot on the heels of Lee's rogue agent Felipe Nagy, who has stolen the titular treasure and at one point resorts to disguising himself as a Sikh. During the filming of this final season, Fairbanks' considerable back catalogue began to appear on the fledgling ITV, starting with André Morell in *Atlantic Night* on 7 December. 'Since the formation of the company some $4,000,000 have been brought into this country by our export business,'[9] Fairbanks proudly pointed out.

The Man Who Wouldn't Escape and *Crown of the Andes* brought an end to an invaluable professional relationship that significantly increased Lee's self-confidence and flexibility. 'Douglas Fairbanks, Peter Marriott and Lionel Grose gave me the priceless

Felipe Nagy and Hugh Diamond (Christopher Rhodes) struggling against a painted sky in Douglas Fairbanks Presents: Crown of the Andes *(1955)*

opportunity to learn my craft in front of a camera, and I shall be eternally grateful to all three,' he asserted 20 years later. 'In those half-hour shows, I played everything you can imagine, from one word and one day to the lead in several of the pictures. I was able to get such a solid professional grounding in the technique of acting in front of a camera that the camera ceased to frighten me and never has since.'

But Fairbanks wasn't the only TV producer prepared to take a chance on Lee. Edward J and Harry Lee Danziger were a pair of expatriate American brothers who, as well as owning hotels in Mayfair and Monte Carlo and residing on Park Lane, also turned out hordes of series episodes and threadbare second features throughout the 1950s. The Australian actor Vincent Ball remembered that they 'used to do four-minute takes, which was very demanding on the actors. Half the time you didn't have time to learn the dialogue. Doing a Danziger was really the end of the line ... You would play a lead for ten days and get your money – in cash, which was most unusual. The films were made on a shoestring, with minimum crews.'[10] And according to Francis Matthews, the Danziger philosophy was perfectly summed up in Harry's end-of-picture remark, 'You wanna carry on and do the next one? Because you might as well go straight into the next one; change your suit.'[11]

Lee himself has acknowledged that Danziger assignments 'could only be mentioned in whispers. They were made mainly under the direction of David MacDonald and his henchman Ernest Morris.' After *Babes in Bagdad* in 1951, Harry and Eddie came back into Lee's life in September 1954, around the time that a couple of major opportunities eluded him. He had tested with director William Dieterle for the Rita

Hayworth vehicle *Joseph and His Brethren* – the film was eventually abandoned altogether – and also for the fearsome Count de la Marck, Wild Boar of the Ardennes, in Richard Thorpe's *Quentin Durward*. (The role went to Duncan Lamont.) Taking a leaf out of the Fairbanks book, the Danzigers were producing a dozen small dramas for American TV at MGM Borehamwood, packaging them as portmanteau pictures for release to UK cinemas through Associated British. 'Using a crew of British technicians,' reported *Films and Filming*, 'director David MacDonald has turned out a film every three days and has kept on schedule.' What *Films and Filming* didn't mention was that MacDonald was assisted not only by Ernest Morris but also by the fugitive American director Joseph Losey, working incognito for fear of the House Un-American Activities Committee.

Lee appeared in three of these quickies. *Final Column* was transmitted in the US in January 1955 before lending its name to a doubledecker anthology tradeshown in London in February. The other story, starring Laurence Naismith and Sandra Dorne, was *Dr Damon's Experiment* and the linking commentary was provided by Ron Randell. In *Final Column* itself, Lee is matched against John Longden, star of several early Hitchcock films, as the devious newspaperman Larry Spence and his employer Albert Lake. With designs not only on promotion but also on Lake's daughter (Jeanette Sterke), Spence kills Lake's mistress (Kay Callard) as the prelude to a blackmail plot. Even the normally indulgent *To-Day's Cinema* drew attention to the film's 'somewhat limited production values,' but also took the trouble to praise Lee's 'smoothly villainous' performance.

Strangle Hold was put out by itself as a short in March before being aired in America in July. Playing another blackmailing murderer in a story remarkably similar to *Final Column*, Lee is Brookes, the valet to a young businessman (John 'Paul Temple' Bentley), who kills his employer's wife, whom the businessman had long thought dead anyway, and then tries to do the same to his fiancée. *Man in Demand* was reviewed as a film in May and its component parts screened on US television the same month. Lee wasn't in *Man in Demand* itself but featured in the second segment, *The Price of Vanity*, with Eric Lander, Muriel Young and Lloyd Lamble. As bearded art critic Richard Martell, Lee is deceived by Lander's artful copies of Old Masters – a prelude of sorts to the clean-shaven, but just as easily deluded, art critic he would play ten years later in *Dr Terror's House of Horrors*.

Early in 1955, Lee reported to MGM once more for a fully fledged Danziger second feature, and judging from David MacDonald's *Alias John Preston* it's easy to see how the Danzigers acquired their 'bottom of the barrel' reputation. This was Lee's first leading role in a feature film – he's billed below Betta St John and Alexander Knox but above the title – and garnered him the Danzigers' top-whack fee of £75. Mention of the film, however, causes him to blanch to this day. 'That's the one with me going mad on a grave, clawing at tufts of grass. God! When I think what a terrible actor I was in those days, it's a wonder I've ever lasted.'

A whiff of fleabitten amateur dramatics hangs over great chunks of *Alias John Preston*. It's packed with unspeakable dialogue – there's no screenplay credit but the story is attributed to the Danzigers' regular ideas man Paul Tabori – and in it Lee plays a psychotic businessman who moves to the sleepy backwater of Deanbridge and becomes a conceited pillar of the community in record time. 'We need some new blood in our town!' chuckles Sandford, the local bank manager (John Longden), while enthusiastically endorsing Preston's romance with his daughter Sally (Betta St John). For some reason – no doubt a pathetic attempt to make the film appeal to US audiences – Lee is required to play Preston as a laconic American. Dark of eye and chin, he looks distinctly haggard and has grey-streaked temples to indicate the streak of madness that becomes all too apparent as Preston's affair with Sally continues.

The charming smile he gives her on their first date is very frightening indeed, but the first flash of real mania is reserved for an altercation in a French restaurant, when Preston tells the waiter in no uncertain terms that 'I don't care if the people who reserved this table eat in the kitchen!' He gets even twitchier when attending a hospital council meeting and it's revealed that a psychoanalyst is coming to Deanbridge. 'I don't altogether approve of this Freudian mumbo-jumbo,' he explains weakly. Bob,

Scrutinising a fake Old Master as conceited art critic Richard Martell in The Price of Vanity *(1954), a Danzigers TV half-hour included in the theatrical feature* Man in Demand

TV AND OTHER TRIALS 1952-1956

'Was she in love with a man – or a murderer?' asked the Danzigers pressbook. As David Garrity, Alias John Preston, with Sandra Dorne (1955)

Sally's former beau (played very badly by St John's real-life husband Peter Grant), complains that 'There's something strange about him, something I can't put my finger on' – and the newly arrived Dr Walton (Alexander Knox) determines to get to the bottom of the problem.

Preston toys obsessively with an unlit cigarette as he tells Walton of his troubled sleep. 'In these dreams,' he stammers, 'I'm somebody else ... assuming the identity of John Preston ... a criminal, David Garrity.' The film then completely falls apart under the weight of several stubbornly un-dreamlike dream sequences, in which Preston strangles a blonde floozy (Sandra Dorne) and shares some tense exchanges with a detective, played with a ridiculous French accent by Dorne's real-life husband, Patrick Holt. The ensuing fight is mainly played out by a pair of laughably obvious stuntmen, though Lee recalls that, in the close shots, Holt failed completely to pull his punches. Back in Walton's office, Preston is finally led away by the police and the doctor gives Sally a ponderous account of her fiancé's dual personality that anticipates the ending of *Psycho*. In a typically glib 1950s fade-out, Sally is then re-delivered into the arms of Mr Suburban Stodge, Bob.

'Paul Tabori has rigged up a lively little heebee-jeebee,' commented *To-Day's Cinema*, noting also that 'Christopher Lee foams around town convincingly as a psycho.' Lee's foaming is certainly over-pitched from time to time but the performance contains a handful of intriguing moments modelled, consciously or not, on Conrad Veidt, whose 1920s output had contained several roles as split personalities. A nasty close-up as Preston throttles his blonde victim is supplemented by his windswept breakdown over her shallow grave, Lee cramming his fingers into his mouth in the style perfected by Veidt in *Orlacs Hände*. And Preston's final burst of giggling hysteria in Walton's office as the truth sinks in echoes Veidt's Hollywood classic *The Man Who Laughs*. Whatever his inspiration, Lee wears a strangely hunted look throughout, appropriate to the character but also arising, perhaps, from the sheer horror of having to tackle an extraordinarily demanding role in the crank-'em-out context of the Danzigers.

LEVIATHANS '55

The Danzigers gave rise to a queasy moment for Lee when he was invited to dinner by family friends and discovered, to his astonishment, that the fourth guest was Sir Alexander Korda, the legendary Hungarian entrepreneur behind London Films and Denham Studios. 'And what are you doing now, Lee?' Korda asked politely through a haze of cigar smoke, and an awkward silence fell when Lee blurted out the embarrassing truth that he was working for the Danzigers.

CHRISTOPHER LEE – PART TWO

Among the many classics masterminded by Korda, *The Four Feathers* came up for remake treatment at Shepperton and the Sudan in January 1955. Directed, as before, by Korda's brother Zoltán – but this time in collaboration with Terence Young – the film was announced as *White Feathers* and shot as *None But the Brave*, eventually winding up as *Storm Over the Nile*. It was fitted with a cast of popular 1950s faces and, because the 1939 version had already featured breathtaking Technicolor photography, was in need of further hi-tech bait with which to lure telly-saturated cinemagoers. 'There are many who will remember the original,' commented Zoltán Korda, 'but there are many to whom the story is fresh. What we have done is to remake an excellent tale in the new medium of CinemaScope.'[12]

The excellent tale was a chunk of turn-of-the-century, true-Brit derring-do by A E W Mason, in which young Lieutenant Harry Faversham (Anthony Steel) resigns his commission at the very moment his regiment is ordered to join Kitchener's army in the Sudan. He redeems himself by posing as a member of the outcast Sangali tribe, heroically keeping alive one of his colleagues (blinded by sunstroke) and springing the other two from an Omdurman gaol. Though efficient enough, *Storm Over the Nile* can't help but seem a little unnecessary given the brilliance of its forebear; it even incorporates battle footage from the earlier film, ingeniously 'scoped' to fit the new widescreen requirements. According to Ian Carmichael, 'This resulted in one actor, Jack Lambert, appearing in the picture twice. A shot of him in the previous film, in which he portrayed a drummer boy, was included in the new remake in which he appeared as the colonel of the regiment.'[13] What's worse, the leads are a major come-down. Anthony Steel, Laurence Harvey and James Robertson Justice are mere shadows of John Clements, Ralph Richardson and C Aubrey Smith.

Trapped in a fetid Shepperton dungeon with Ian Carmichael, Anthony Steel and Ronald Lewis in Storm Over the Nile *(1955)*

Cast towards the end of the film's schedule in March, Lee is the deposed Sudanese governor, Karaga Pasha, imprisoned alongside Burroughs (Ronald Lewis) and Willoughby (Carmichael) in a fetid Shepperton dungeon. He appears some 80 minutes in, daubed in filth and further obscured by a straggling, matted beard. Grey and weary, Karaga has been incarcerated for 13 years ('since [General] Gordon was killed') and uses his command of Arabic and Greek to rally the prisoners behind Faversham's proposed uprising. Lee described his squalid scenes as 'another peak in the sado-masochistic graph' and also recalled that Zoltán Korda's broken English frequently gave rise to misunderstandings on set. 'There was one time when he said to Ian Carmichael, "Now, Ian, I want you to do this scene with butter on your head" – which is a German expression, 'butter an dem kopf', meaning 'in an ingratiating, slightly oily way'. I shall never forget the expression on Ian's face when he was asked to play the scene with butter on his head.'

A more up-to-date war subject, *The Cockleshell Heroes* had been touted throughout 1954 and finally began in Lisbon on 7 April 1955 under the auspices of Warwick partners Irving Allen and Albert R 'Cubby' Broccoli. Directed by and starring Lee's *Moulin Rouge* companion José Ferrer, the film abounds with familiar British faces, ranging from Percy Herbert, David Lodge and Anthony Newley to Victor Maddern, Dora Bryan, Gladys Henson and Sydney Tafler. Lee was cast as Submarine Commander Alan Grieves, who crops up nearly an hour in to convey the titular heroes to the scene of their commando mission and says things like 'Shut off the depth charge attack' and 'Stand by to surface.' After shooting exteriors off Cascais, near Estoril, the unit returned to Shepperton and Lee met the original Grieves there – real name R P Raikes, by then a Marconi publicity manager in Chelmsford. Raikes noted without rancour that his film counterpart was 'Tall, dark and handsome, whereas the original is short, bald and chinless.'[14]

Though directed by an American, the film is a monument to the kind of true-Brit pluckiness which its writer, Bryan Forbes, would later lampoon in *The League of Gentlemen*; assembled in front of a firing squad on the Shepperton lawn, the unruffled Trevor Howard tells his companions, Peter Arne and John Van Eyssen, to 'Keep the line straight, boys.' The film premièred at the Empire Leicester Square on 16 November, six days after *Storm Over the Nile* had opened at the Odeon Marble Arch, and both premières were attended by the Duke of Edinburgh.

Having finished *The Cockleshell Heroes* for José Ferrer, Lee next appeared under the aegis of Orson Welles. Welles' play-within-a-play, *Moby Dick Rehearsed*, had opened at the Duke of York's on 16 June, with Welles himself as 'An Actor Manager, afterwards Father Mapple and Ahab.' According to critic Ivor Brown, it was 'an evening for which the word unusual was altogether inadequate. Through our quiet theatre of the cocktail-tinkle came the shivering of timbers and the roar of the hurricane: instead of anchovy sandwiches we had great slabs of whale-meat and the bulk of Leviathan himself, Leviathan Welles in full spout.' Brown also pointed out, however, that the supporting cast, though 'superbly schooled in the kind of mime [Welles] wanted, became more puppets than persons.'[15] The show's limited run ended on 9 July and six days later Welles was shooting it as a TV movie at the Scala Theatre and also at the Hackney Empire, where the schedule was tailored around the evening bill headed by instrumental parodists Sid Millward and his Nitwits.

Of Welles' theatre cast, Patrick McGoohan (A Serious Actor, afterwards Starbuck), Kenneth Williams (A Very Serious Actor, afterwards Elijah and others), Joan Plowright (A Young Actress, afterwards Pip), Gordon Jackson (A Young Actor, afterwards Ishmael) and Wensley Pithey (A Middle-Aged Actor, afterwards Stubb) were still available. Peter Sallis (A Stage Manager, afterwards Flask) was not, however, and made way for the much taller Christopher Lee. The improvisational nature of the play was reproduced during the filming, with much careening about the stage to simulate being at sea. 'Hours and hours are wasted on this kind of nonsense,' complained the 29-year-old Williams in his subsequently notorious diary, adding, 'I wish to God I had never *seen* this rotten play, and Orson Welles and the whole filthy tribe of sycophantic bastards connected with this bogus rubbish.'[16] Whether the show was bogus rubbish or not is hard to judge, because the film seems to have been left unfinished. While it lasted, however, Lee was given the signal honour of driving the mountainous Welles to and from the 'studio', Welles having rented a house in Chester Row near Lee's bedsit in Eaton Terrace.

More conventional TV roles were still to be had, like the executioner Sanson in the Marius Goring vehicle *The Adventures of the Scarlet Pimpernel*, which took Lee back to British National Studios. Lee's episode, *The Elusive Chauvelin*, was directed by Michael McCarthy and the production company was Towers of London. As already indicated, Harry Alan Towers was due to employ Lee on a regular basis in the ensuing decade. There was also a spell at Nettlefold later in the year, playing Inspector Hollis in the *Cut Glass* episode of *The Adventures of Aggie*. Joan Shawlee was the eponymous globe-trotting fashion designer under the fussy direction of John Guillermin.

There followed a brief assignment, uncredited, as a Nazi officer in the Boulting Brothers' *Private's Progress*, which started at Shepperton on 12 August. Its satirical barbs blunted by the passage of nearly 50 years, the film is in most respects a rather pallid forerunner to later Boulting Brothers comedies like the ever-relevant *I'm All Right, Jack*. The sardonic sting of its service-life comedy was vividly present to contemporary audiences, however, and it proved a smash hit across the country. In the first film of a five-picture contract with the Boultings, the incomparable Terry-Thomas as the CO remains the best reason for watching it, whether uttering his generic cry of 'You're an absolute shower' or hissing 'Schnell, you stinker!' Lee's presence is first felt when Dennis Price's Brigadier Tracepurcel, impersonating a Nazi high-up, has to speak in German; Lee's is the voice that issues forth. Confusingly, Lee then turns up in person as Major Schultz and is required to talk to Tracepurcel – that is, to himself. Held at gunpoint by another disguised Brit, Stanley Windrush (Ian Carmichael), Schultz contrives to take a suicide pill, observing that 'Defeat is less bitter at ze hands of a civilised opponent' and expiring as an ornate clock chimes 'Deutschland Deutschland über alles.'

Over at Pinewood in November, Michael Powell and Emeric Pressburger were perfecting a wartime drama, *The Battle of the River Plate*, about the 1939 sinking of the Graf Spee off Uruguay. Deciding to insert some comic scenes set in Montevideo itself, Powell put out a call for Spanish speakers through his associate producer, Sydney Streeter. 'The next day,' Powell recalled, 'Syd brought a very striking-looking actor onto the set to meet me, for Manolo. He was very tall, and had a remarkably large and long skull. His eyes were beautiful, large and expressive. He vibrated with energy. "Do you speak Spanish?" "Si, señor." He burst into a whole speech in Spanish. "But I also speak French." He shifted the clutch again. "And German." He quoted a piece of Heine. The man had the most powerful voice and presence, and all this energy. The way he gave the whole of his attention to me was quite disturbing. "Do you want me to read the part, Mr Powell?" "The part isn't written yet. The scene is a waterfront café in Montevideo. We'll ad-lib most of it." "Good." His assurance was impressive. "Okay, Mr..." "Lee, Christopher Lee."'[17]

Lee soon found himself billeted in the same dressing room as Lionel Murton (cast as Mike Fowler, the US radio reporter who keeps up a breathless commentary on the Graf Spee's progress) and the statuesque ballet dancer April Olrich, playing the Café

'The scene is a waterfront café in Montevideo. We'll ad-lib most of it...' Coping with April Olrich, Lionel Murton and Edward Atienza in Powell and Pressburger's The Battle of the River Plate (1955)

Manolo's resident spitfire songstress, Dolores. The finished film would be selected as the 10th Royal Film Performance the following year, but was dismissed by critics as an uncharacteristically stodgy addition to Powell and Pressburger's distinguished repertoire. It sparks into last-minute life, however, with the rumbustious café scenes; as one latterday critic has put it, 'There's more fun here, in the play of national stereotypes and competing voices, than in the ponderous allegory of *A Matter of Life and Death*.'[18]

Manolo first appears in pointy sideburns, Gilbert Roland moustache and white tuxedo for an explosive row with Dolores, all of it conducted in high-speed Spanish; trying to get through a full-throated Latin number, she eventually kicks him in the shins for silence. The following morning, he reappears in a purple vest and makes vain attempts to turf Fowler out, struggles for control of 'the last bottle' with Edward Atienza's elderly 'Pop', and finally sorts disinterestedly through his receipts as the Graf Spee commits hara-kiri out at sea. In rehearsal, Powell noted, 'Christopher Lee was everywhere at once, curling and uncurling like a hissing cobra. His entrances were stormy, his exits abrupt.'[19] The same is true of the finished product; Manolo is a delightfully combustible comic creation, brilliantly matched by Olrich's truly eye-popping Dolores.

MOROCCO TO MOMBASA

Lee's stint as Manolo came halfway through the schedule of an exotic murder-mystery called *Port Afrique*. This started in Tangiers, in what was then known as Spanish Morocco, on 24 October 1955 before transferring to MGM Borehamwood in late November. By that time Kathryn Grayson, the soprano star of numerous MGM musicals, had bowed out 'due to illness' and the porcelain Italian beauty Pier Angeli had taken her place. Sharing his Moroccan billet with Anthony Newley, Lee was cast as Franz Vermes, a French sculptor who is one of several red herrings involved in the efforts of a crippled ex-army pilot (Phil Carey) to find out who murdered his wife. Based on a novel by Bernard Victor Dryer, the plot is a hackneyed one, with our hero, 'Rip' Reardon, finally discovering that the culprit was his business partner's wife (Rachel Gurney) and settling down with gentle Spanish chanteuse Ynez.

The film's location work was done in the thick of terrorist disturbances and in Ceuta, a sea port opposite Gibraltar, Lee was deputed every morning to fish one of his fellow actors, Eugene Deckers, out of the red light district. At the unit's next port of call, Tetuan, an already volatile situation was made worse by Anita Ekberg, starring nearby in Terence Young's *Zarak*, who offended Muslim sensibilities by sunbathing topless on the roof of her hotel. Unfortunately, the fraught atmosphere did not translate into *Port Afrique* itself; its echoes of *Casablanca* are faint indeed and interest is maintained only by Wilkie Cooper's handsome Technicolor photography of the Moroccan locations. Lee also looks handsome in a Bohemian sort of way – plaid shirt, corduroy trousers, neatly chiselled goatee – and does some nifty verbal fencing with Deckers' Colonel Moussac and his fez-wearing assistant Abdul (Guido Lorraine). The film's atmosphere was reportedly redirected, not by the political situation, but by the torrential rain falling in Morocco at the time – and not for the better.

The director was the Polish-born Rudolph Maté, who claimed to have prepared Method-style dossiers on all the protagonists. 'This way I build myself a Frankenstein-like character,' he observed. 'What he does, therefore, must be logical according to his background and experiences.'[20] The cardboard figures perambulating through *Port Afrique* hardly measure up to Maté's hopes for them, nor to his distinguished pedigree as director of film noir classics like *The Dark Past* and, before that, as the innovative cinematographer on Carl Dreyer's *Le passion de Jeanne d'Arc* and *Vampyr*. Maté had also photographed Laurel and Hardy in *Our Relations* and, at some point during December, a fellow Laurel and Hardy veteran wandered onto *Port Afrique*'s Borehamwood set. George Marshall had worked with many other legendary comics, notably W C Fields and Bob Hope, and had directed the classic comedy Western, *Destry Rides Again*. Now he was preparing a picture called *The Mark of the Leopard*, based on a James Eastwood novel of the same name. He saw Lee working away as Franz Vermes and lost little time in offering him a prominent role – as another Frenchman – in his new film.

On Thursday 5 January 1956, Lee accordingly attended a Savoy press reception for the picture, by then retitled *Beyond Mombasa*, alongside its stars, Cornel Wilde, Donna Reed, Leo Genn and Ron Randell. The following weekend, cast and crew left for locations in Mombasa, Nairobi, Malindi and Zanzibar for what Columbia's publicists called an 'adventure drama which tells of the clash between the Africa of today and the primitive voodoos of yesterday.' For Lee, the film was something of a breakthrough: fifth billing in a major Columbia picture that only boasted five major characters. Smiling, relaxed and still sporting his *Port Afrique* goatee, Lee plays a shady character but a distinctly glamorous one, and the film could have nudged him towards stardom had it been more successful.

Deputising for Aldo Ray, Cornel Wilde is Matt Campbell, a no-nonsense American whose brother has been murdered while searching for

Thursday 5 January 1956: with co-stars Dan Jackson, Donna Reed and Leo Genn at a Savoy pre-production party for Beyond Mombasa

Challenging Errol Flynn to another duel – over Lisa Daniely – in The Fortunes of War, *shot at Bray Studios in summer 1956*

valuable uranium deposits. Randell and Lee are Elliot Hastings and Gil Rossi, former associates of Campbell's brother who are now co-opted by Campbell into resuming the search. Though trying to curry Campbell's favour, Rossi bluntly announces that 'I'm not very interested in being an all-American boy; by passport I'm French, by profession international.' He tries a different tack with Donna Reed's Ann Wilson, oiling up to her with lines like 'You could do worse, you know; I might even give up being a White Hunter.' Though nominally the hero, Campbell is just as boorish, regarding Ann as she takes an alfresco shower and saying, 'You know, for a lady anthropologist you're pretty well stacked,' to which she playfully replies, 'Anthropology had nothing to do with it.'

When a native bearer is mysteriously killed on the trek, Rossi puts it down to 'a dart from a pygmy blowgun,' subsequently succumbing to one himself when the uranium mine is finally discovered. Patrolling above ground with only Leo Genn's white-haired missionary for company, Rossi tries to raise his rifle when hit by the poisoned dart but tumbles instead down a dusty incline. The missionary is revealed as a religious maniac who killed Campbell's brother in order to preserve the locale from Western encroachment – Genn, unfortunately, is seriously miscast – and the film winds up with a most peculiar climax set in the ruins of a 15th century Arab city called Gedi. According to Lee, Gedi 'had survived with a strange and eerie beauty,' but Marshall and his cinematographer Freddie Young don't really capture it.

Beyond Mombasa is a charming entertainment, nevertheless, and comes complete with a memorably funky theme arranged by Norrie Paramor and played by 'the Man with the Golden Trumpet', Eddie Calvert.

Lee enjoyed himself playing golf with Genn and their extremely affable director 'on some of the wildest courses I had ever seen' – he had taken up the game shortly after the war and rapidly developed a fanatical devotion to it – but also suffered a recurrence of his wartime malaria and badly injured his arm when performing his death fall. The unit had returned to MGM Borehamwood by mid-February and Lee was further injured by a (not very convincing) mechanical crocodile in the tank there.

Memories of his old injury on *The Dark Avenger* resurfaced in April when Lee went to Bray Studios for three episodes of *The Errol Flynn Theatre*. 'Now watch it, sport,' Flynn said, resurrecting his long-suppressed Tasmanian twang while preparing for a climactic duel in *The Fortunes of War*. 'Don't forget: it was an accident...' Domiciled throughout the series' schedule in sumptuous twin caravans parked in the studio grounds, Flynn told the press that 'Right now I'm on my best behaviour. Got to be. I've got money in this company ... Don't call them films,' he added. 'Don't call them playlets. Let's call them features in miniature – that's what they really are. I'll be in half-a-dozen of the first 26. But I'll be the host of every one.'[21]

A French Revolutionary tale, *The Fortunes of War* cast Flynn as the aristocratic Comte Henri de Dairval, a powdered wig sorting oddly with his trademark pencil moustache. Lee is the people's representative General Hamelin and Lisa Daniely the woman they fight over, Hélène de Mailly. Lee also appeared as impoverished painter Maurice Gabet in *The Model* – Flynn's third wife, Patrice Wymore, played Gabet's girlfriend, Pat – while in *Love Token* he was cast as a jealous husband, the Comte de Merret, in a story loosely derived from Balzac's *La Grande Breteche*. A more faithful adaptation would be made 17 years later as part of *Orson Welles Great Mysteries*, with Peter Cushing as the Comte. In the Flynn version, the Comte walls up his rival (John Van Eyssen) as per Balzac but then has to fight a duel with him on his brick-busting escape. The prodigiously bosomed Rosanna Rory played the Comtesse and reportedly spent a lot more time in Flynn's mobile home than in the studio.

Lee would do battle with Van Eyssen again the following year, this time in the library of Castle Dracula, but in the meantime the Flynn series began unspooling in the UK in September. Maximising Lee's contribution, Motley Films expediently dusted off their three-year old production of *The Mirror and Markheim* for use as the series' Christmas instalment, retitling it *The Evil Thoughts* and fitting it with a Flynn prologue. The series then entered US syndication from May 1957. 'World-Famous Stars – Intriguing Romantic Stories Featured in a Top Quality Dramatic TV Series,' enthused the sales brochure, illustrating Lee alongside such luminaries as Brian Aherne, Patricia Roc, Jean-Pierre Aumont, Ronald Howard, Mai Zetterling, Glynis Johns, Herbert Lom and Paulette Goddard. The 26 episodes of *The Errol Flynn Theatre* were obviously modelled on the success of *Douglas Fairbanks Presents* and gave Flynn the opportunity to indulge his little-known literary bent, all the films being based on classic short stories. He died, aged 50, in October 1959 and, some 25 years later, Lee was chosen as host-cum-narrator of a syndicated TV documentary, *Errol Flynn: Portrait of a Swashbuckler*.

DOMINATING THE FRAME

Other TV engagements included two episodes apiece of the Merle Oberon vehicle *Assignment Foreign Legion*, shot at Beaconsfield by Lance Comfort, and the Lorne Greene vehicle *Sailor of Fortune*, back with Michael McCarthy at British National. In the former series Lee played a mad Arab called El Abba in *The Anaya* (co-star: Eddie Byrne) and Rodin, a murderous French gardener with a pronounced limp in *As We Forgive* (co-stars: Peter Arne and Andrée Melly). In the latter series he played another foaming Arab, Yusif, in *The Desert Hostages* and Carnot, an upright officer of the Foreign Legion in *Stranger in Danger*. Lee's Carnot earned him high praise from Stanley 'Billy' Moss, whose wartime heroics would be immortalised in one of Lee's upcoming films. In a brief incarnation as a tabloid TV critic, Moss pointed out that 'Lorne Greene was admirably supported by Esmond Knight, whom it was good to see on the screen again, and, in particular, by Christopher Lee, who gave a subdued and convincing performance as a French officer which might be imitated to advantage by the gentlemen of the Foreign Legion.'

The Danzigers, meanwhile, were sufficiently emboldened by their TV successes to build their own studio for large-screen as well as small-screen purposes. New Elstree was positioned on the Watford Road and formally opened for business in May 1956. A Fantur production called *The Traitor* was one of the first features to make use of the facility, which, according to Lee, still came complete with 'water pouring down the cement walls ... duckboards between the stages traversing a sea of mud ... lights that didn't work,' and many other Spartan delights. As a much-needed distraction, Lee lent his copy of J R R Tolkien's *The Hobbit* to one of his fellow sufferers, the legendary actor-manager Donald Wolfit, who adored it.

The Traitor was written and directed by Michael McCarthy, who uses a profusion of interesting camera set-ups and smoothly executed tracking shots in order to squeeze his large ensemble cast into virtually every frame. The country house interior is highly impressive, too, betraying no hint of the primitive conditions Lee remembers. But, for all the artful dodges cooked up by McCarthy and his design department, the film's *Ten Little Indians*-style scenario remains obstinately stagey. Using much the same German accent heard in *Private's Progress*, Lee is Dr Neumann, one of a group of wartime Resistance fighters who rendezvous, one tense post-war evening,

A man strangely ill at ease: Dr Neumann and Major Shane (Robert Bray) in Michael McCarthy's The Traitor (1956)

to work out once and for all which of them betrayed their deceased associate, Keller, to the Nazis. Others include the beetle-browed Wolfit and an extremely fey Oscar Quitak, while John Van Eyssen and Robert Bray (Marilyn Monroe's co-star from *Bus Stop*) are the probing military policemen who turn up when murders start to be committed.

Lee acts conscientiously throughout, in striking contrast to the attitudinising-by-numbers of Anton Diffring, who eventually turns out to be the culprit on both counts. A man strangely ill at ease, Lee's Dr Neumann is often seen standing slightly adrift from his former colleagues. He adjusts his spectacles a great deal; has trouble settling his hand on his hip; stands stiffly while clutching the upper slopes of his waistcoat; comes out with spasmodic and unconvincing smiles, and, as in *Alias John Preston*, is much given to nervous fumblings with his cigarette. All these tiny details build up an intriguing picture, particularly by comparison to Neumann's succinct and matter-of-fact way with words. As Wolfit's Colonel Price waffles inconclusively at the head of the table, Neumann cuts him short with a blunt 'What are you trying to say, Charles?' And he responds to a prolonged interrogation by Bray's Major Shane with an exasperated 'I don't want any part of your game!'

Lee's performance is a discreetly clever one and the film's denouement is startlingly ghoulish; one of the murdered men is propped up in an armchair and armed with a cigarette holder to smoke out the villain quite literally. But, by that stage, the intrigue has become so talky and incomprehensible that audience interest has long since waned.

Another Michael Powell assignment followed at Pinewood. *Ill Met By Moonlight* was based on the wartime exploits in Crete of Patrick Leigh-Fermor and Billy Moss, and started in France on 16 July. Lee's contribution was filmed back in the studio and caused Powell, ruminating over 1950s actors in his memoir *Million Dollar Movie*, to give special mention to 'Christopher Lee, the great Christopher Lee, in his masterful performance of a German soldier in *Ill Met By Moonlight* where he dominates every frame of the scene.' This is true enough – Dirk Bogarde in a dentist's chair with a metal clamp in his mouth doesn't present much competition – but the scene is extraordinarily brief. Lee has barely whipped Bogarde's sheet aside and yelled (in German) 'You are a damned spy!' when he's summarily gunned down and his uniform is appropriated by David Oxley's Moss for the upcoming mission. Indeed, in some versions of the film, Lee's scene is left out altogether. Their last major collaboration, the dreary *Ill Met By Moonlight* was something of a low point for Powell and Pressburger. As one critic has put it, this and *The Battle of the River Plate* were 'rattling good yarns that, alas, were widely perceived as rattling just a bit too much.'[22]

Lee's next performance was not much more substantial, and involved the minor humiliation of having to mime an operatic aria. In *Fortune is a*

With dentist Peter Augustine, patient Dirk Bogarde and onlooker Rowland Bartrop (far left) in Ill Met By Moonlight *(1956)*

Woman, his role as a conceited Welsh pop singer was to be introduced with a section of the largo al factotum from Rossini's *The Barber of Seville*, a passage too high for Lee's voice; the scene didn't make it into the final cut. The film began on location outside Lloyds of London on 10 September prior to settling into Shepperton a week later. The writer/producers were Frank Launder and Sidney Gilliat, legendary architects of the script for *The Lady Vanishes* and the later St Trinian's series. The source here was a 1953 Winston Graham novel and it fell to Gilliat to direct it.

'A masterly thriller of torment and terror!' shrilled the posters, but the picture carries little of the tension Gilliat brought to the splendid *Green for Danger* ten years before. Jack Hawkins is Oliver Branwell, a Lloyds insurance assessor investigating the death of Tracey Moreton (Dennis Price) in a blaze at Lewis Manor and becoming infatuated with the chief suspect, Tracey's glamorous widow Sarah (US import Arlene Dahl). Much was made of the fact that it was Hawkins' first romantic role – after several kissing sessions with Arlene Dahl he confessed to realising what he'd been missing – and to the fact that he indulged in some eyebrow-singeing heroics in the conflagration footage. The film is replete with good-value character actors (Ian Hunter, Michael Goodliffe and particularly Bernard Miles as a slimy blackmailer), but, unlike Lewis Manor, it never quite catches fire.

Lee appears early on, resplendent in a velvet-collared dressing gown, recumbent on a plush sofa and nursing a boot-polish black eye. Branwell has been sent by his father-and-son bosses (played by Malcolm Keen and his real-life son Geoffrey) on 'a tricky assignment' to assess whether 'the singing miner' Charles Highbury needs the month's rest he claims; the underwriters of the film he's starring in stand to lose up to £40,000. 'You can tell them from me,' Highbury scowls, 'that I'm going back when I'm fit and not before.' Lee's Welsh accent is pretty wobbly and his scene lasts all of a minute, but he provides the first link in Branwell's investigation, leading him to Greta Gynt's amusingly vampish Mrs Litchen. She reports that Highbury invited her to look at his scrapbooks with him and, to her dismay, that was precisely what they did – until his wife turned up, misconstrued the situation and punched him in the eye.

The 34-year-old Lee had now been an actor for ten years and, as 1956 drew to a close, still felt hamstrung by his impressive height and faintly Continental appearance. Apart from a notable hiccough in 1950, he had been in pretty consistent employment but felt no nearer to public recognition than he had as a member of the Rank Charm School. In the bloodless, antiseptic environment of 1950s

Charles Highbury argues over an insurance claim with Oliver Branwell (Jack Hawkins) in Fortune is a Woman *(1956)*

British cinema, he was a square peg in a round hole; there was no place for his glamorous yet baleful presence in reassuring popular hits like *Doctor in the House* or *Reach for the Sky*.

But if Lee's career needed a shot in the arm, then so did the British film industry itself, strangling as it was on a diet of Home Counties domesticity. After their blazing achievements of the late 1940s, British studios had lapsed into a corseted blandness reflected in their abandonment of the full-blooded female stars of the 1940s – Margaret Lockwood, Googie Withers, Jean Kent among others – in favour of a new breed of male stars, notably Dirk Bogarde, Kenneth More and the aforementioned Jack Hawkins. And, according to Michael Powell, the new men simply weren't up to it. 'I don't think anybody has ever realised why English films after the war tended to be unexciting,' he wrote. 'After the war was over there was a great scarcity of leading men in all the lively arts: theatre, film, radio, television. Most of the top talent went off to America.' [23] Enumerating actors like Marius Goring, David Farrar, Anthony Steel, Carl Boehm and Lee himself – but excepting Peter Finch, who 'had that little extra that makes an actor a star, like Conrad Veidt' – Powell concluded that they were 'all character actors, you see – no stars, present or potential, except Peter Finch.'

Lee certainly wasn't a potential star in the eyes of an industry crippled by good taste. 'None of us would ever suggest any subject, whatever its box-office potential, if it were socially objectionable or doubtful,' observed Ealing chief Michael Balcon in 1951. 'We want to achieve box-office success, of course, but we consider it our primary task to make pictures worthy of that name.' [24] Over at Bray Studios, however, there was a small but aggressive film company with an exactly opposite outlook. Keen to embrace the dreaded 'X' certificate, Hammer Film Productions provided a decidedly uncorseted context in which Lee could become a star after all – and a star, what's more, just like Conrad Veidt.

PART THREE

MALIGNANT HEROES
1956–1959

In August 1956, C H B Williamson, affable king of Wardour Street tittle-tattle, reported that James Carreras and Anthony Hinds of Hammer Films – their fortunes recently rescued from the brink of disaster by the phenomenal success of *The Quatermass Xperiment* – were planning to move into the long-abandoned field of Gothic horror. Something called *Frankenstein and the Monster* was scheduled to wind up a 1956 production programme that had comprised *X the Unknown*, *Quatermass 2* and *The Steel Bayonet*. 'Wonder who will do the Karloff this time?'[1] Williamson mused.

Hammer were pondering exactly the same question, as well as rapidly changing the film's title to *The Curse of Frankenstein*. The title character had come their way with no trouble at all. When Peter Cushing noticed the trade announcements and expressed an interest in playing Baron Frankenstein, Hammer leapt at the opportunity. An actor who had worked with Olivier but whose fame rested on his achievements in television, Cushing had been pursued by Hammer without success for several years, and now he was volunteering his services. So far, so good.

But what of the Monster, made immortal by Boris Karloff in the 1930s and here rechristened the Creature? Hammer briefly toyed with the notion of casting Bernard Bresslaw, the lofty comic actor who, at 6'5", was an inch taller than Lee. Cushing's agent John Redway was also Lee's, however. 'They obviously wanted a very tall man,' Lee recalled, 'a man who had some knowledge and experience of movement and mime and who was able to act without speaking if necessary. My agent suggested me, I went up to see them and they said "Yes." It was as simple as that.'[2] There had been one potential stumbling block, however: Lee had worked with the film's director, Terence Fisher, on *Song for Tomorrow* in 1948 and 'wondered if he would be influenced by that dread memory. But he'd either repressed it or thought I'd been so grotesque as the MC that I'd be just right for the Creature.'

Filming began at Hammer's Bray Studios on 19 November, with the all-important Creature make-up not yet finalised. The legendary visage devised by Jack Pierce for Karloff was strictly out of bounds for copyright reasons. It was just as well that Lee's contract contained a clause stipulating that 'For any days on which the artiste is called for make-up and/or photographic tests, he shall be paid the full daily rate,' because many hours were spent in Phil Leakey's make-up chair in the search for a satisfactory 'look'. Among half-a-dozen outlandish variations, Lee found himself looking at one point like the Elephant Man and at another like a pig-faced refugee from *The Island of Dr Moreau*. The ordeal was lightened, however, by Lee and Leakey's shared enthusiasm for the Olympic Games coverage on the radio.

In the end, Leakey had to whip up a final make-up a matter of hours before Lee was due to make his first appearance on the set. 'It was all such a mad rush,' Leakey wrote in 1987, 'with no proper preparation, no understanding from the producers of what the job entailed ... and none of the materials to make up the parts to stick to poor old C Lee's face. A bit of a cock-up, in fact, as far as I was concerned.'[3] Barely had the make-up been settled than Lee was required to appear in it at a Brooks Wharf press reception in Lower Thames Street, making a dramatic entrance with Hazel Court in his arms and reportedly causing 'some of the 200 guests [to] reach for their smelling salts.'[4] Happily, Lee was not required to mingle in make-up but was hustled away while the impact of his sudden appearance remained fresh.

That smelling salts were required is hardly surprising, because Lee's Creature has been described on several occasions as looking like a road accident. But, for all its water-logged pallor and grisly accretions

An unusually pensive Count Dracula, photographed by Tom Edwards (1957). 'It is possible to compare his striking first entrance and descent of the staircase as Dracula, in stature and presence,' observed theatre critic Audrey Williamson in the Times, 'with a Wotan of Mr Hans Hotter, a great actor-singer whose work Mr Lee (himself a bass singer) has long studied and admired.'

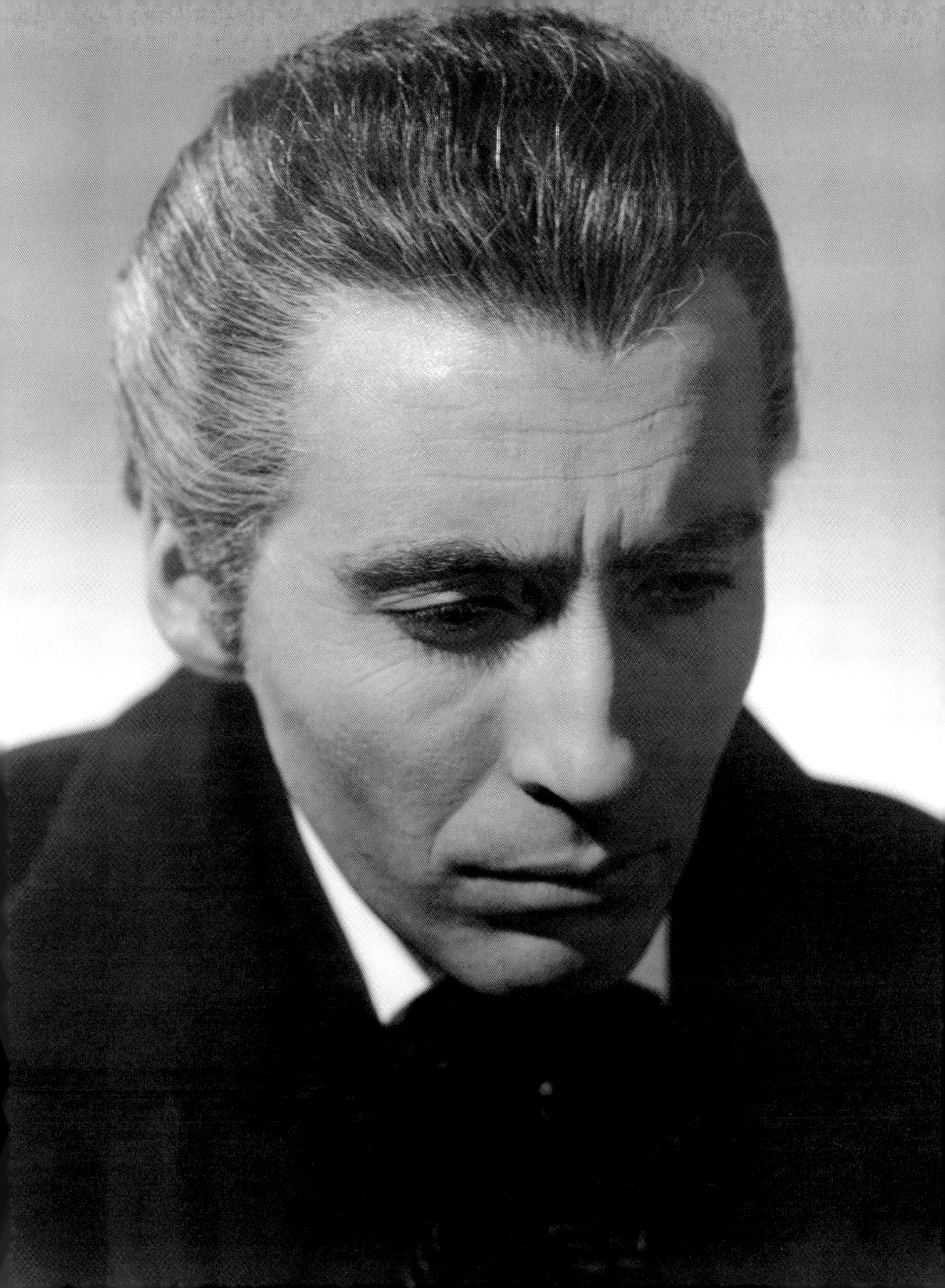

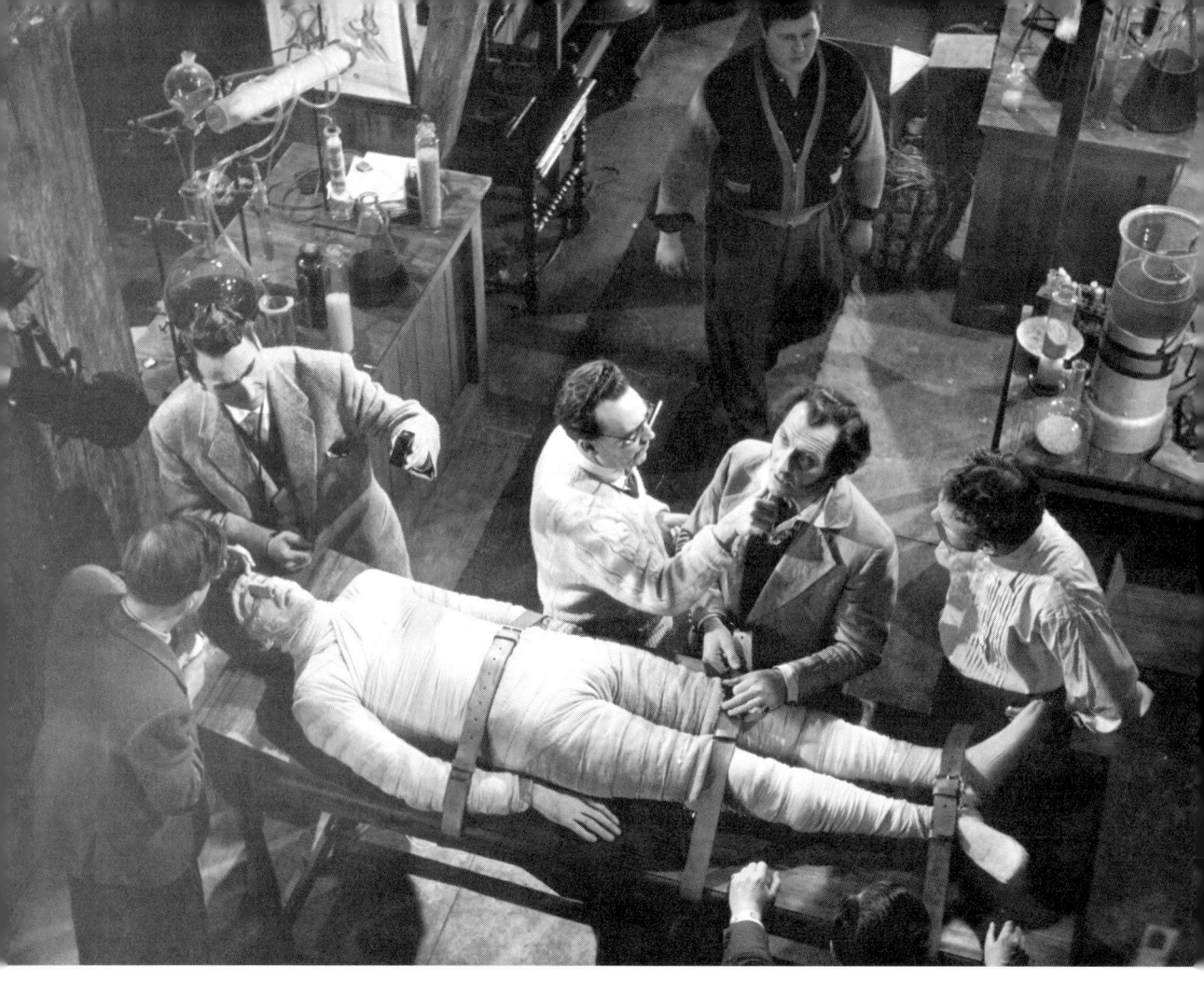

With, left to right, Phil Leakey, Jack Asher, make-up assistant George Turner, Peter Cushing and Robert Urquhart on the set of The Curse of Frankenstein (1956)

of scar tissue, the make-up allowed Lee to remain recognisably human, thus underlining the tragedy of the film – for not only is Lee recognisably human under Leakey's gruesome overlay, he's also a potentially good-looking specimen. Baron Frankenstein had been reconceived by screenwriter Jimmy Sangster as a Promethean overreacher, careless of anything or anyone that stands in his way and interpreted by Cushing as a genuinely frightening monomaniac and murderer. He gives his Creature the capacious brain of a professor, the delicate hands of a sculptor and the face of a once-handsome highwayman. Lee determined, therefore, to present the Creature as a brain-damaged child, the dislocated brain struggling to co-ordinate the component parts of an unfamiliar body, and the Creature's spastic attempts at interaction with other humans are deeply upsetting to watch as a result.

The Creature's first appearance is a classic shock sequence that determined the 'in your face' approach of what would become known as Hammer Horror. Having discovered a bandaged phantom framed menacingly in the laboratory doorway, the camera tracks in rapidly as the Creature's white hand plucks the covering from its face. Before being cowed by Frankenstein's programme of Pavlovian training, this is a Creature that's simply furious about being born, and Lee is careful to put a look of recognition, as well as hatred, into the Creature's eyes as it seizes Frankenstein and starts to throttle him. The damaged brain still retains vestiges of its former owner, Professor Bernstein, who presumably recognises Frankenstein as the man who murdered him. Later, the Creature escapes its confinement and, outfitted in a shabby military greatcoat, encounters an elderly blind man in the forest. Emerging from foliage, the Creature regards the old man with dead-eyed, mouth-lolling incomprehension, recoiling like a frightened animal when he attempts to make contact and finally snapping the staff with which the old man prods him. As the Creature considers its next move – which is to murder the old man – Lee stands for a moment with both hands suspended at chest level as if on strings, making the Creature's resemblance to a marionette, subject to a malign will that is not its own, movingly apparent.

The Creature's next scene provided Lee with the first of several injuries he would sustain in Hammer's service. Shambling across a carpet of autumn leaves, the Creature is shot in the eye by Frankenstein's associate, Paul Krempe (Robert Urquhart). The effect was a startlingly gruesome one in its day but simple enough to execute: Lee had a dollop of Kensington Gore in his palm and slapped it into his face at the appropriate moment. But the stage blood got underneath the contact lens in his right eye and, as well as being in agony, Lee spent an hour fearful that he would lose his sight. The scene remains one of the most powerful in the picture, however, particularly for the way it confounds the viewers' expectations. The audience has waited some 50 minutes for the Creature to arrive, and within ten minutes it's dead again? But no. Frankenstein proceeds to his greatest atrocity yet, digging the Creature up and putting it through a further bout of brain surgery.

The results are truly pitiful. Lee reappears in a modified make-up, a hideously scarred bald patch the most conspicuous refinement. The Creature is now tethered to an iron ring in the laboratory wall and its coat is smeared with mud from its temporary grave. It recoils bashfully at the approach of Krempe – this could be Professor Bernstein again, shrinking in shame from the gaze of his former admirer – and struggles upright in answer to Frankenstein's commands. Reaching the end of its tether (literally), the Creature looks off in the opposite direction in an attempt to locate its master's voice and finally sprawls on the floor when commanded by Frankenstein to sit down. 'Is this your creature of superior intellect?' Krempe sneers. 'Your perfect physical being? This animal?'

As well as being exquisitely observed, Lee's mime work in *The Curse of Frankenstein* was unlike anything seen in British cinema up to that point. The same applied to the film as a whole. Britain's first horror picture in colour (and lusciously rendered Eastmancolor at that), it would revolutionise the horror genre worldwide when unveiled in 1957. Like Cushing, Lee has always graciously attributed Hammer's success to the unassuming but inspirational personnel behind the camera; as well as Terence Fisher, the team included Jack Asher (cinematographer), Bernard Robinson (production designer), James Needs (editor) and James Bernard (composer). But the contributions of Cushing and Lee themselves cannot be overestimated. They struck up an immediate rapport behind the scenes, Lee treating Cushing to bursts of opera in full Creature regalia and the pair of them entertaining the crew with softshoe-shuffle routines while waiting for the rushes to be screened.

Two French Farces

The Curse of Frankenstein finished filming on 3 January 1957, and Lee returned to his customary diet of TV episodes. *Gay Cavalier* was a 13-part adventure produced by Tod Slaughter's old associate, George King, and starred Christian Marquand as Royalist highwayman Captain Claude Duval. Lance Comfort and Terence Fisher alternated as director, and Lee appeared in the sixth instalment, Comfort's *The Lady's Dilemma*. 'Lady Jane (Gene Anderson) discovers that her trust in her Roundhead suitor, Colonel Jeffries (Christopher Lee), is misplaced,' explained the *TV Times*. Lee's duel with the left-handed Marquand was something of an ordeal. 'When the time came to shoot,' Lee explained, 'the routine went out of his head completely and I was faced with a human windmill.' That summer, Lee's next trial of strength took the form of a bludgeoning fight with claymores in a sunny Beaconsfield meadow. Directed by C M Pennington Richards, *German Knight* was the seventh of 39 episodes of the Sydney Box production *Ivanhoe*, and Lee was cast as the titular Sir Otto, bent on the destruction of Ivanhoe himself, Roger Moore.

Back on 11 February, Lee had received bad news from his friend José Ferrer, at work in Culver City on his upcoming dramatisation of the Dreyfus case, *I Accuse!* 'They [MGM] seem to think that a "name" is necessary for the part of Picquart,' he wrote. 'They were, however, properly impressed with your acting talents.' Leaving Picquart to Leo Genn, Lee started work on his next film on the 15th. *Bitter Victory* was an Anglo-French co-production (French title: *Amère victoire*), with a six-week shoot in the Libyan desert supplemented by interiors at the Studios de la Victorine in Nice. The director was Nicholas Ray, a fragile 46-year-old responsible for classics like *In a Lonely Place* and *Rebel Without a Cause*. A posthumous cult has grown up around Ray among cinéastes but *Bitter Victory* is not among his best works. Indeed, Lee remembers it as 'the only film I ever worked on in the whole of my life that I instantly wanted to leave after one day of shooting. A nightmare – there's no other word for it.'[5]

Desert line-up (l to r): Harry Landis, Sean Kelly, Lee, Curt Jürgens (seated), Nigel Green, Raymond Pellegrin (supine), Ronan O'Casey, Fred Matter and Sumner Williams in Nicholas Ray's gruelling Bitter Victory (1957)

The story of a group of World War II commandos undertaking a dangerous mission behind enemy lines, the film stars Curt Jürgens and the young Richard Burton as group leaders Brand and Leith. Their men are seen in procession behind the opening credits (Lee taking the lead), and, as the film wears on, they grow increasingly disenchanted when the antagonism between their leaders becomes embarrassingly apparent. At perpetual loggerheads over the same woman (Ruth Roman), Brand and Leith are also divided over more abstract problems. 'I'm a kind of mirror of your own weakness,' sneers Leith, 'and it's unbearable, isn't it?' Which of the film's several writers – Ray, Gene Hardy, Gavin Lambert or Paul Gallico – was responsible for this philosophical gem is unclear. As if to punish him for such clunky sophistry, Leith is then bitten by a scorpion (the craven Brand stands by and allows it to happen), whereupon the unit's Arab bearer (Raymond Pellegrin) eviscerates a camel for its ammonia. 'Finest medicine chest in the desert, the camel,' observes Lee's lanky Sergeant Barney.

Barney exchanges many dark looks with Nigel Green's equally disenchanted Wilkins, as well as displaying occasional flashes of grim humour. 'Tired, Sergeant?' asks Brand in the thick of the unit's desert trudge. 'I'll be all right for another five days, sir,' replies Barney, 'soon as I get my tablespoonful of water.' The first action set-piece sees the unit disguised as gun-toting Arabs and is poorly staged; when his pal successfully opens a safe, Barney brings the scene to a close with a sardonic cry of 'Wilkie's won the war!' At the opposite end of the film, the entire cast are required to squint against a climactic sandstorm, which the ailing Leith does not survive. Back at base, Brand is given the DSO and his men file out in reproachful silence. Sick at heart and given to symbolism, Brand pins the medal to the heart of a suspended combat dummy and the film ends. It's a powerful conclusion to a strangely boring film, made particularly gruelling by Maurice Le Roux's relentlessly doom-laden score.

The off-screen chaos began on the actors' arrival in Tripoli, when they were transported to the Marcus

Aurelius ruins and Ray, no doubt in search of challenge and spontaneity, doled out the parts more or less piecemeal. Only Jürgens and Burton had joined up knowing in advance what roles they were to play, and the situation inevitably led to a certain amount of simmering discontent between the actors. Ray may have been in search of spontaneity, but authenticity was pretty low on his list of priorities. Saddled with the rough-and-ready Sergeant Barney, Lee was staggered to be told by his director 'not to bring all this British Army nonsense into it.'

In Tripoli, cast and crew were billeted at a former brothel called the Hotel Mahari, while at Nice's Hôtel Negresco Lee was woken up one night to attend to a fellow actor whose bed was awash with blood after he had slashed his wrists and throat. (The actor, who had received a 'Dear John' letter from his boyfriend back home, had previously appeared with Lee in *Trottie True*.) To add to the film's horrors, Ray's drug addiction was plainly visible to all and the distinguished cinematographer Michel Kelber suffered a broken collarbone. Richard Burton, meanwhile, felt that the film was beneath him and arrogantly questioned his fellow actors' professionalism while drinking himself into a stupor.

Back in London, the première of *The Curse of Frankenstein* took place at Leicester Square's Warner Theatre on Thursday 2 May, enjoying a record-breaking first weekend and outstripping that record the following weekend. Soon it was installed in a second Leicester Square cinema, the Ritz. 'You should see the audience,' James Carreras crowed in the *Sunday Express*. 'They squeal, gasp and shriek. Some of them even run out of the cinema in panic. It's wonderful!' As the picture concluded its first blockbusting week, Lee reported to Shepperton on Wednesday 8 May for a 'business as usual' role in *The Truth About Women*. Production had begun on 18 March and Lee was added in the film's final fortnight, completing his scenes as Monsieur le Deputé François Thiers on 10 and 13 May. A glossy turn-of-the-century comedy of manners chronicling the romantic misadventures of Laurence Harvey's Humphrey Tavistock, the film was the brainchild of Muriel Box, England's only female director of mainstream pictures during the 1950s, but the end product was only a moderate success.

'*The Truth About Women* was the most difficult film I ever made,' she recalled in 1989, 'and Laurence Harvey was the most difficult artiste ... The Rank group wasn't behind us as they should have been,' she added. 'The publicity people knew that I was doing a comedy and they expected belly laughs, but it wasn't like that; it was ironical, pure satire really. It was mainly to show up the situation of women that I agreed to make the film at all.'[6] Unfortunately, the picture is too lightweight, and Harvey too listless a lead, to fulfil Box's ambitious brief. Her feminist pill is voluptuously sugared, however – Otto Heller's Eastmancolor photography and Cecil Beaton's exquisite costumes see to that – and it has a truly deluxe roster of international leading ladies for Humphrey to encounter: Diane Cilento, Julie Harris, Mai Zetterling, Eva Gabor. Just as deluxe is the British supporting cast, including Wilfrid Hyde-White, Thorley Walters, Roland Culver and the inimitable Ernest Thesiger. Lee appears in the Paris segment as the conceited husband of Gabor's Louise, returning home unexpectedly and performing some very funny calisthenic exercises on one balcony as the concealed Humphrey cowers on another.

The performance is repeated the following night, only this time an argument erupts from the marital bedroom – conducted by Lee and Gabor in blisteringly effective off-screen French – whereupon Humphrey trips up on his way out and the alerted François bursts in upon him. 'Cet homme est votre amant?' he demands of Louise's maid, afterwards realising his mistake and challenging Humphrey to a duel with a cold 'My carte, monsieur.' Humphrey's embarrassment is increased by the fact that he has been formally introduced to François that very day, a friendly Comtesse (Elina Labourdette) explaining to him that François is 'an honoured member of the French National Assembly.' The proposed duel never takes place, however, for François is killed in another

Farce à la Feydeau: Monsieur le Deputé François Thiers and wife Louise (Eva Gabor) in the glossy Muriel Box satire, The Truth About Women *(1957)*

'Drive him fast to his tomb': showing Marie Versini the Marquis St Evrémonde's fatal wound during the Pinewood filming of A Tale of Two Cities *(1957)*

one only moments before the appointed time. The wily Comtesse explains that, as well as being her own lover 'for ten beautiful years,' François was also indulging in a politically advantageous affair with the horse-faced wife of the Minister of State. Lee's scenes are straight out of a Feydeau farce and his enjoyment of the film was in stark contrast to his miserable experiences on *Bitter Victory*.

The Curse of Frankenstein, meanwhile, began its general release on 20 May and smashed records across the country. Its American progress was equally phenomenal, and in the end the film reportedly grossed over 70 times its cost. By Sunday 7 July, James Carreras was cabling his American associate Eliot Hyman to the effect that 'England is sweltering in a heatwave and NOTHING is taking any money except *The Curse of Frankenstein*' – adding a tantalising postscript that read simply, '*Dracula*???'

DRIVE HIM FAST TO HIS TOMB

On Monday 8 July, a lavish remake of the Charles Dickens classic *A Tale of Two Cities* went into production at Pinewood as the centrepiece of that studio's 21st anniversary celebrations. The film's credentials were impeccable: Ealing veteran T E B ('Tibby') Clarke as screenwriter, producer Betty Box and director Ralph Thomas of the hugely popular *Doctor* films and Dr Simon Sparrow himself, Dirk Bogarde, shifting gears to play the heroically dissipated Sydney Carton. The cast also boasted Dorothy Tutin, Cecil Parker, Stephen Murray, Donald Pleasence, Rosalie Crutchley, Athene Seyler, Freda Jackson, Duncan Lamont, Ian Bannen, Alfie Bass – and, as the pressbook put it, 'Christopher Lee (famous as the Monster in *The Curse of Frankenstein*) is an 18th century monster – an arrogant, dissolute nobleman, the Marquis St Evrémonde.'

Lee's involvement was perhaps facilitated by the fact that he had just played a Frenchman for Betty Box's sister-in-law, Muriel – also, of course, by his sudden notoriety as the cinema's newest fiend. '*A Tale of Two Cities* had the best cast of, I think, any picture I've ever worked on,' Lee remembers. 'It was unbelievable; it was really like a Who's Who of the British theatre and film world. They only made one big mistake on that picture. I remember saying to Betty Box at the time, "Why on earth aren't you making this in colour?"' Similar misgivings were expressed by Dirk Bogarde himself and, by 1990, Box had come round to their point of view. 'Looking back, I realise what an idiot I was,' she admitted. 'At that time Rank would have said OK if I'd told them I wanted to make it in purple.' Nor was the miscalculation regarding colour the film's only problem. 'We shot in Bourges in central France for four or five weeks,' Box added, 'and it poured with rain the whole bloody time. It was fated from beginning to end.'[7]

Lee's scenes were filmed at the Chateau de Valençay on the Loire, home of the Talleyrand family. Playing what he called 'a top-level swank villain,' Lee is first seen in a flashback narrated by Cecil Parker's avuncular Jarvis Lorry. The camera pans up from the chateau's carved eagles to the Marquis glaring from an upper window, the cry of his resident peacocks issuing from the lawns below. Much play is made of the peacocks, strutting in their plumed finery as a metaphor for the gilded uselessness of the French aristocracy. St Evrémonde himself is the film's flesh-and-blood symbol of all the upper class evils that precipitated the French Revolution. He gags a hapless servant girl with a silken sash that bears his family crest and, as Lorry discreetly recounts it, 'She died that same day, from the violence she had suffered in body and mind.'

Decked out in powdered wig, beauty spot and extravagant jabot, St Evrémonde then intervenes in the stables as Dr Manette (Stephen Murray) ministers to another of his abused domestic staff. 'Doctor, you were not summoned here to listen to the babblings of this hind,' he says, simultaneously cuffing aside his majordomo Gabelle (Ian Bannen). Lee brings a genuine whiff of spiritual evil to this stony-faced decadent, in sharp contrast to the way the character was presented in MGM's famous Hollywood version of 1935. There, the Marquis was played as a preening pansy by Basil Rathbone and carried no threat whatsoever. Lee's St Evrémonde really means business – and proves it when the action moves forward 18 years and he reappears looking not much older but appreciably more corrupt.

The weasel-faced Barsad (Donald Pleasence) rolls up at the chateau and interrupts the Marquis as he debauches Gabelle's doe-eyed daughter Marie (Marie Versini). The Marquis explains that his depravity is merely 'one of the benefits of our own good French system,' but retribution is imminent. Relaxing in his baronial coach, he finds that a tiny street urchin has been crushed under its wheels. As a ragged, reproachful crowd starts to gather, St Evrémonde leans from the window and slings a sou in recompense. 'You dogs,' he hisses, 'I would ride over all of you willingly, and exterminate you from the earth.' The coach rumbles on, but the boy's vengeful father (Sacha Pitoeff) is attached to the undercarriage. After a brief dinner scene with his shamefaced cousin Charles Darnay – dripping with contempt for Darnay's notion of getting a proper job, Lee's diction is a model of crystalline clarity here – the Marquis is found dead in bed the following morning, grotesquely contorted, wigless and stabbed to the heart. The peacocks shriek in terror off screen.

Attached to the knife is a note that reads 'Drive him fast to his tomb.' Lee's next major picture would have a noble tomb as virtually its opening image, bearing the name 'Dracula' rather than 'St Evrémonde', and in many ways Lee's performance in *A Tale of Two Cities* represents a dress rehearsal for Count Dracula. Like Dracula, St Evrémonde's domain is decorated with stone eagles. Like Dracula, he takes the notion of droit de seigneur to monstrous extremes. Like Dracula, his screen time is relatively limited but his presence, even in death, permeates the whole film. (Darnay's fateful affiliation to the hated St Evrémonde name propels Dickens' entire plot.) Also like Dracula, Lee plays a melodramatic role straight, disdaining camp asides and stripped of all theatrical flourishes. The result is that the Pinewood *Two Cities* carries a disturbing undertow which the Culver City one never captured.

'There has probably never been a more thoroughly downtrodden French populace, a more scrofulous Madame Defarge (Rosalie Crutchley), or a more detestable Marquis St Evrémonde (Christopher Lee),' claimed *Newsweek*. By and large, the film was politely reviewed on its release in February 1958 but failed to ignite much excitement. Its scenes of the storming of the Bastille are epic by British standards but still seem puny by comparison to the MGM precedent, while the film's youthful imports from the Comédie Française – Paul Guers as Darnay and the 17-year-old Marie Versini as Marie – are transparently dubbed. Dorothy Tutin's Lucie Manette redefines the word 'radiant' and the supporting actors are priceless. But the film somehow lacks grip. 'As a classic adaptation,' suggested Dirk Bogarde, 'it could not be faulted, but it did not transfer to the screen of the late fifties. It was not of the time. And I fear, because of my position in popular cinema then, it just came over as 'another Dirk Bogarde piece'. OK for the fans, but not really suitable for the nobs.'[8]

Preparing for his undead incarnation of St Evrémonde, Lee rapidly polished off what he dismissed as 'a no-account picture ... made near Brighton.' Based on a Bernard Newman bestseller called *They Saved London*, Vernon Sewell's *Battle of the V.1* imported Michael Rennie and Patricia Medina from Hollywood, together with the glamorous Milly Vitale from Rome, and kicked off with a Café Royal press reception at the end of September. The film was based at the tiny Brighton Studios but mainly filmed around Shoreham and Hove. The Sussex countryside stood in for wartime Warsaw and an experimental research station at Peenemünde, target of a British raid that sets back the German war effort by six months. The film's centrepiece was a full-scale replica of a V.1 rocket, the so-called 'robot bomb', weighing more than a ton and measuring over 22 feet in length.

Lee's role as a conventionally hissable Nazi officer called Brunner is pretty negligible, and his insistence that SS officers wore grey in the concentration camps was disregarded in favour of symbolic black. Charged with rounding up Poles for forced labour, he announces that 'I have a special job for two of you, requiring brains and skill,' after which our heroes are discovered cleaning the floor of a public lavatory. As Peenemünde is rocked by the British bomb strike, he shoots various Polish escapees and then, reeling from the proximity of an exploding bomb, is choked with an iron bar by Stefan (Rennie). Rather gratuitously, Stefan proceeds to bash Brunner's head in with a large rock, afterwards appropriating his uniform, as previously occurred in *Ill Met By Moonlight*. Lee's presence in the film is fleeting, but his presence in West Sussex caused an unforeseen stir when he accepted a lift in Vernon Sewell's bubble car, only for Sewell to crash it into a Daimler. For reasons unknown, there was a bottle of ether in Sewell's car, which smashed and sent Lee, still in costume, groping woozily among the citizens of Hove, who fled in panic at the approach of what they presumed to be an SS officer.

Interleaved with original German newsreel footage of the robot bombs under construction, *Battle of the V.1* is awkwardly poised between documentary seriousness and wartime melodramatics and, at 109 minutes, it's also seriously overlong. It was designed to form part of the 1958 release schedule of Eros Films, an independent distributor which thrived on a diet of sub-Hammer horror pictures. Their most exact Hammer pastiche, the Donald Wolfit vehicle *Blood of the Vampire*, started production at Twickenham on 21 October 1957 but was rapidly eclipsed by a much more formidable British vampire. For on 29 October, Lee signed his second Hammer contract, this time to play Count Dracula.

An Odd Sex Manifestation

'Top Horror Stars in *Dracula*,' announced the *Daily Cinema* on Tuesday 12 November. 'Peter Cushing and Christopher Lee, who sent shudders around the world when they appeared in *The Curse of Frankenstein* ... are together again in a new exercise in British screen horror. This time it is Bram Stoker's *Dracula*, which Hammer Films – the world's top horror specialists – have put into production at Bray Studios ... The new *Dracula*, according to Tony Hinds, will have a greater shock-impact than the version in which the late Bela Lugosi starred nearly 30 years ago.'

The film had started shooting the day before, with Cushing on hand to give a youthful make-over to Bram Stoker's elderly vampire hunter Van Helsing and Lee primed to do the same for Stoker's ancient vampire Count. The technical personnel, headed by director Terence Fisher, also reproduced the winning dynamics of *The Curse of Frankenstein*. Jimmy Sangster had prepared a no-nonsense adaptation of Stoker's novel, ditching great chunks of it (the Count's deranged disciple Renfield, even the vampire's all-important transfer to London) but expertly distilling the basic storyline into a headlong, three-act format. At a little over £81,000, the budget exceeded that of the Frankenstein film by some £16,000 and greater opulence was further ensured by Bray's newly built 90' by 80' sound stage. Having passed through the hands of German and American filmmakers, Count Dracula was at last restored to the London showbusiness world of which Stoker himself had been a part 60 years before.

There were no auditions for the title role; Lee was the obvious choice and turned to the novel for inspiration in creating the character anew. Phil Leakey's task was considerably less arduous this time around, though Dracula's make-up was carefully thought out nevertheless. Lee was given a facial caste more swarthy than pallid and a grey wig in sharp contrast to the oily black one worn by Bela Lugosi 27 years before. Lugosi's evening dress and opera cape were also out, in favour of a plain black suit and floor-length cloak. Though in a fantastic context, realism was again the key note, with Dracula denied the power to transmogrify into bats and wolves and

Burying stunt double Daphne Baker against an impressive Bernard Robinson backdrop in Terence Fisher's Dracula *(1957)*

his castle converted from a cobwebbed ruin into a beautifully maintained Gothic showroom. Tellingly, Lee had never seen the Lugosi version and made no efforts to do so.

The Hammer philosophy was later expounded, in its simplest terms, by James Carreras. 'We've found a formula for spine-chillers that never misses,' he boasted. 'You make the villain of your story look just like the good-looking man, or the pretty girl, you might see on the underground any evening. You imagine you could trust him anywhere. Then suddenly, when you find yourself alone with him – wham! He starts to do terrible, awful, ghastly things.' Carreras' interviewer, Leonard Mosley, pronounced the film 'one of the most revolting pictures I have seen for years,' claiming, however, that 'Count Dracula himself ... looks like a model for one of those Men of Distinction advertisements. Then why am I revolted by this picture?' Mosley asked himself. 'Because Mr Carreras does not let [him] stay that way all the time.'[9]

Mosley's answer points to the enduring power of the film and of Lee's performance in it. In America it was retitled *Horror of Dracula*, and Terence Fisher crystallises that horror in the first 15 minutes by carefully juxtaposing two screen-filling views of Lee's face. The silhouetted Count sweeps down his baronial staircase to greet Jonathan Harker in close-up, revealing a crisply good-looking aristocrat, slightly chilly in manner but by no means a monster. In no time at all, however, he reappears in truly explosive fashion as Harker succumbs to the bite of Dracula's faithless vampire bride. This second close-up, luridly lit by Jack Asher, caused petrified baby-boomers around the world to choke on their popcorn. Red eyes ablaze with hellfire, crude daubs of blood smeared on his mouth and chin, and 'with incisors magnified to look like shark's teeth,'[10] as the genteel critic C A Lejeune complained, Dracula bounds over his refectory table and engages in an animalistic struggle with Harker and the vampire woman, the like of which 1950s filmgoers had never seen.

According to *Picturegoer*, Hammer were so keen to preserve Dracula's two-faced secret that studio visitors were instructed only to photograph Lee from behind – a far cry from his dramatic entrance in full make-up at the Frankenstein press reception. The Count's appearances would be similarly rationed in the film itself, reducing him, as per Stoker's novel, to a malignant off-screen presence for much of the action. Dracula pervades the whole picture but is only visible for about six of its 82 minutes. His handful of lines are all over after the introductory scenes with Harker, yet Lee resists the temptation to play them up, instead rapping them out with a throwaway aristocratic insouciance.

Having established Dracula's human credentials, the inhuman ones are emphasised in the remainder of the film. There had been a few feral moments in earlier horror pictures, generally from female performers like Carroll Borland in *Mark of the Vampire* and Elsa Lanchester in *Bride of Frankenstein*. But the sheer concentration of them in Lee's Dracula, coupled with an astonishing athleticism and colossal physical presence, made the performance a truly groundbreaking one. The stunning close-up referred to above, together with the eye-popping ferocity of the battle that ensues, are supplemented by an equally hair-raising encounter in Dracula's crypt, when Harker makes the fatal error of staking the bride (Valerie Gaunt) first. Supine in his sarcophagus, Dracula's face has now acquired a greenish tinge; his eyes flash open in response to Harker's hammer blows and a nostril-flaring look of fury changes to a monstrous grin of triumph as day turns to night.

Dracula is then framed, statue-like, in a French window for his bedroom assault on Lucy (Carol Marsh) and at the bottom of a flight of stairs for the corresponding scene with Mina (Melissa Stribling). Presenting the Count as an unstoppable force to be simultaneously feared and desired, both scenes carry an erotic charge every bit as startling to contemporary audiences as the charnel house details of *The Curse of Frankenstein* had been; indeed, the Mina scene only got past the censor thanks to Tony Hinds' extremely artful, and prolonged, negotiations with the British Board of Film Censors.

The third act chase and grisly climax of *Dracula* are as exciting a ten-minute stretch as is to be found in any Gothic horror picture before or since. The mask of evil perfected by Lee comes to the fore yet again, looking authentically insane as Dracula attempts to bury the abducted Mina alive and like some unidentified man/animal hybrid as he stalks Van Helsing round the library of his castle. The effect is genuinely horrifying, and much enhanced by the strange, discordant brass blaring out from James Bernard's hell-for-leather score. This time it is Van Helsing who makes an athletic spring from the refectory table, flooding the room with morning sun and reducing the Count to a scattering of dust. Brilliantly lit, choreographed, and performed, this triumph of light over darkness was shot, appropriately enough, on Christmas Eve, after which the actors went home and special effects photography continued until 3 January 1958.

Lee's contract for *Dracula* had specified a payment of £60 per day, setting the total at a minimum of £720. Lee recalled receiving £750 and buying himself a grey, second-hand Mercedes on the proceeds. He also came away with some amusing memories to counterbalance the Gothic gravity of the film itself. 'There was one instance,' he recalled, 'where I had to pick up this girl [stuntwoman Daphne Baker] and charge across the graveyard, where I've conveniently dug a grave, and throw her into it ... So I rushed over and picked her up, and then rushed across with her and flung her into the grave, and went straight in on top of her!'[11]

When Baker made way for Melissa Stribling herself, Lee's next plunge was a good-natured gag. 'When it came to my turn,' Stribling maintained, 'I was lying in the bottom of the grave and Chris Lee was nothing if not keen ... He jumped in and made a funny remark to the director about, "You can leave us alone for a while: I'm not going to waste this opportunity."'[12] The film's decadent aroma of graveyard sex, and the hideous allure of Dracula himself, would soon make Stribling an object of envy to female audiences around the world. 'I'm frankly puzzled,' Lee told one reporter. 'An odd sex manifestation. Maybe it's because I tried to make Dracula a romantic and tragic figure. Someone you could feel sorry for.'[13]

SCREAM BOY? NO – DREAM BOY

In between film assignments, Lee continued to appear in various popular TV series of the day. *OSS* was a vehicle for Lee's *Beyond Mombasa* chum, Ron Randell, and in the penultimate instalment, *Operation Firefly*, Lee played Dessinger, a fiendish SS officer involved in a microfilm intrigue in Brussels. The director was C M Pennington Richards and Lee modelled Dessinger on the notorious Reinhard Heydrich. In Peter Maxwell's *Manhunt,* an episode of ITC's popular *William Tell*, heroic Conrad Phillips and mountainous Willoughby Goddard came up against Lee's dastardly Prince Erik, whose habit of hunting humans was reminiscent of Count Zaroff in *The Most Dangerous Game*. (Further Zaroff echoes

Microfilm intrigue in Brussels: with Ron Randell in the Operation Firefly *episode of* OSS *(1957)*

Lurking watchfully in shadow as the saturnine Resurrection Joe, with Boris Karloff, Adrienne Corri and Francis de Wolff in Corridors of Blood *(1958)*

would crop up in Lee's film work.) And in Joseph Sterling's *This Hungry Hell* – a segment of the *White Hunter* series starring Rhodes Reason – Lee was Mark Caldwell, another unscrupulous huntsman, this time hand-in-glove with the slave trade. Having had a life-or-death struggle with a stuffed lion, Lee was amused when the real animal escaped its confinement and caused panic at Twickenham Studios.

Lee's next picture followed in May 1958. A gory account of the discovery of anaesthesia, *The Doctor from Seven Dials* started production at MGM Borehamwood on the 12th, with Boris Karloff in the lead and Robert Day in the director's chair. Producers Associates – namely the young impresario Richard Gordon and Lee's old Highbury boss, John Croydon – had been advised by James Carreras that having Karloff and Lee in the same picture would be a profitable idea. The 70-year-old Karloff was accordingly cast as Dr Thomas Bolton, whose quest to prove that 'pain and the knife can be separated' delivers him into the clutches of the Seven Dials underworld, while a juicy cameo was reserved for Lee as a particularly repellent low-life. ('I play a body-snatcher called Resurrection Joe,' Lee noted soon after production. 'He's a grotesque, pock-marked chap. The girls won't like me at all.'[14]) Despite this winning combination, the film's fortunes were placed in jeopardy when its US sponsors, MGM, changed management during production. As a result, it languished unreleased until 1962, when it emerged under the more exploitable title *Corridors of Blood*.

Beautifully photographed by Geoffrey Faithfull, the film's grimy underworld scenes are rendered in a Dickensian chiaroscuro that owes much to David Lean's classic film of *Oliver Twist*, made ten years previously. And Lee cuts a truly frightening figure closely akin to Dickens' Bill Sikes. Again, the threat is all the more potent for being delivered deadpan. Unencumbered by any significant theatrical experience, Lee was developing instead a pared-down quality of stillness that would guarantee an audience's full attention even if his fellow actors were performing cartwheels. The stillness also ensured that his villains always had an inner life, a life outside the confines of the film in which they're contained. The details, however, are cleverly kept hidden. Lurking watchfully in shadow for most of his screen time, Resurrection Joe comes across as a man who has secrets, probably

With Peter Cushing at an 'autograph party' promoting the New York première of Dracula

completely ghastly ones. This man knows something, but we're never told precisely what. It's the old theory urging filmmakers to suggest the monster, rather than show it, applied to performance.

In tight-fitting, battered frock coat and dog-eared topper – and speaking in soft, caressing East End tones – the lean and hungry Joe has a partner in crime in the burly form of Black Ben (Francis de Wolff), with whom he delivers a corpse to the elderly Dr Blount (Frank Pettingell) while the huge shadow of a child's skeleton hovers over the transaction. The corpses are acquired in the unorthodox fashion perfected by Burke and Hare up in Edinburgh. 'You'll be all right, Tim – nice and comfortable,' Joe tells one bedridden victim (Stratford Johns) as he applies a pillow to his face. The camera then swerves up to Joe's own heavy-lidded face, grinning broadly as he listens to Tim's suffocated screams. Later on, the corpse is revealed to Karloff's Dr Bolton with the pillow still in place. 'He died peaceful, Guvnor,' Joe explains, certain of Bolton's compliance in providing a false death certificate because a notebook, containing vital details of all 53 of Bolton's experiments, has fallen into the hands of Black Ben.

From this point on, the philanthropic but naïve Dr Bolton begins a downward spiral familiar from several of Karloff's earlier roles (and later reproduced by Lee's own Dr Newhartt in *The Oblong Box*). Joe attempts to rape the fulsome Rosa (Yvonne Romain) but is otherwise kept busy by the conniving Black Ben, who sends him on a midnight raid of the hospital dispensary, during which, to Bolton's horror, Joe efficiently kills the night porter. Ben finally decides that Bolton has outlived his usefulness – 'Don't worry, Guvnor,' Joe breathes, 'it'll all be taken care of, nice and tidy' – but Nigel Green's Inspector Donovan suddenly bursts into the tavern with a large number of Peelers in tow. 'It's best I finish him,' Joe mutters as Ben ascends to the roof, and there's a brief echo of *Dracula* as he stalks his prey around the attic room in which Bolton has been imprisoned. As Joe stabs him, Bolton gropes for a vitriol bottle – the same one Joe helped to steal from the dispensary – and splashes it in Joe's face.

Day indulges in a discreet spot of slow-motion here, as Joe recoils in shrieking agony, his head flung back, his black-gloved hands covering his face and a sizzle of bacon applied to the soundtrack. One of the most horribly graphic scenes yet featured in a British horror picture, Lee stumbled blindly into a stove while performing it and badly damaged his knee. Working with Karloff was in other respects less painful. 'During the filming,' Lee recalled, 'he always used to say, "I'm just a poor old man who happens to have strayed in from the street. What am I but somebody who used to sweep up the floors of the studio?" That was his great joke: this poor old man who's so helpless and so useless and only good for sweeping up the studio. So at the wrap party he was solemnly presented with a broom, which he loved. He had a wonderful sense of humour and fun.'[15]

Nine days into the *Seven Dials* schedule, the knee injury already sustained, Lee joined Peter Cushing on Wednesday 21 May for a *Dracula* press reception at the Hungaria restaurant on Lower Regent Street. Also present were Carol Marsh, Melissa Stribling, James and Michael Carreras, and Tony Hinds, together with artfully lit coffins, skulls and other mementos mori. The film's West End première took place at the Gaumont the following evening, where Lee's name appeared in lights alongside Cushing's and the neon legend 'Don't Dare See It Alone!' pulsed enticingly over the Haymarket. A colossal likeness of Lee's Count dominated the frontage, swarming over a blonde victim from whose throat neon blood dripped steadily beside a further legend, 'Who Will Be His Bride Tonight?'

The film was represented at the première by the same group that had attended the Hungaria, plus Terence Fisher and a host of unrelated celebrities like Vera Day, Michael Medwin, Luciana Paluzzi, Jill Ireland, Hardy Kruger, Delphi Lawrence and Lee's *River Plate* companion, April Olrich. ('I walked in in an absolute paroxysm of embarrassment,' Lee noted.[16]) This glitzy opening was followed by the film's record-breaking run over the Bank Holiday weekend, with queues stretching around the block to see what the *Daily Cinema* dubbed 'the horror-sex blockbuster at the Gaumont Haymarket.' And on Sunday the 25th Lee left for New York – his first visit to the US – accompanied by Peter Cushing, Tony Hinds and James Carreras. The following day, Cushing's 45th birthday was celebrated at the top of the Empire State Building, giving Lee a touch of vertigo. Lee's own 36th birthday was marked on Tuesday by a press luncheon at which Universal chief Al Daff presented him with a birthday cake, stabbed by its recipient with suitably bloodthirsty enthusiasm; later, Daff would inform the astonished Hammer representatives that their film had rescued Universal from the brink of bankruptcy.

The New York première followed on Thursday the 29th at the Mayfair Theatre. 'It was midnight – special showing,' Lee recalled, 'and most of the audience were showbusiness. Peter and I sat right under the projection booth at the back and the crowd came in; they were shouting, they all knew each other, they were really in high spirits. Somebody fired a gun – a blank cartridge – and that got a few people's attention. Finally, the lights went down. Along came the credits and there's the tomb with the name 'Dracula', blood smattering on it – and they *roared*! At that point, I said to Peter, "I'm leaving; I can't take any more of this. This is awful." And Peter said, "No – just stay." And this kept going until the famous scene in which Jonathan Harker meets me for the first time ... He feels the presence and he turns around and there, at the top of the stairs, is this silhouette. I tell you, the place erupted. The roof nearly came off ... Perhaps they expected to hear a macabre foreign voice, or see a strange-looking person with a green face or whatever. I just walked down the staircase and said "Mr Harker, I'm glad that you have arrived safely." And the silence was quite remarkable. From then on, we had 'em. For the rest of the film there wasn't a sound.'[17]

Lee spent a fortnight in the US – among other things, he dropped in on Richard Burton at the Morosco Theatre, where Burton was starring with Susan Strasberg in *Time Remembered* – and then returned to England to finish off *The Doctor of Seven Dials*. He also moved from his one-room apartment at 35 Eaton Terrace to a three-bedroom flat in Stack House on nearby Cundy Street, the rent setting him back £8 a week. *Dracula*, meanwhile, was proving a phenomenal summer smash across Rank's entire Gaumont circuit. Amid the expected chorus of revulsion from the critics – more virulent even that that accorded *The Curse of Frankenstein* – there were several plaudits for his own performance; he was described as 'monstrously chilling' in *Picturegoer*, 'thoroughly gruesome' in *Variety* and 'a real fright' in the *Monthly Film Bulletin*. Dudley Carew maintained in the *Times* that 'Mr Christopher Lee makes a saturnine and malignant Count, whose silhouette fits most effectively into a background of shadows, and the part is played straight, as melodramatic parts should be played.' And England's wittiest critic, Paul Dehn of the *News Chronicle*, pointed to the film's high seriousness and equally high sex content when he pointed out that 'Christopher Lee, as Dracula, never seems to have his tongue in his cheek, though he may frequently have it in somebody else's.'

Lee's impact as Dracula led to his first major splash in the fan magazines. At the beginning of August, Gordon Campbell of *Picturegoer*'s Reader Service Department titled his column 'Scream Boy? No – Dream Boy'. Rapidly dispensing with queries regarding Danny Kaye, James Garner, Joan Greenwood and Eric Barker, Campbell devoted the majority of his word count to Britain's newest screen sensation on the principle that 'A bumper female postbag can't be wrong.' 'Christopher Lee is currently boosted as Britain's bloodthirsty monster in *Dracula*,' he wrote. 'But instead of screaming you're dreaming over the man Hammer Films picked to chill you. He's become filmdom's most fantastic heart-throb. He is giving Reader Service girl writers goose pimples. Not wholly for the reason intended. "He's handsome..." "dynamic..." "thrilling," say hundreds of letters. "Tell us more..."'[18]

Hammer had scandalised Britain's critics and thrilled audiences worldwide with a blood-bolted alternative to the bland diet of Britain's mainstream filmmakers. In the same way, Lee had become a kind of necrophile substitute for Rank's clean-limbed teen favourite, Dirk Bogarde. In short, he had become a star.

TERENCE-COLOURED

Picturegoer kept tabs on Lee as the horror boom tightened its grip on the box-office, putting out a 'Horror Special' in November with a Lee interview as its centrepiece. In it, he rehearsed several opinions that he would stick to for decades to come. 'To find out what makes a screen monster tick,' wrote Sarah Stoddart, 'I tracked Lee down to his well-furnished lair in a lush London flat ... Shaking a few skeletons in the cupboards of British studios, he says: "Hammer Films hasn't any particular magic. It's just hit on the idea of making films that picturegoers *want*. Too many producers make films just to please themselves. They imagine the rest of the world cares passionately about the British way of life when the fact is it doesn't."'

As well as disdaining the parochial thinking of British filmmakers – a disdain that would soon propel him towards making films on the Continent in order to consolidate his international reputation – Lee also had no time 'for the critics whose blood is boiling about the spine-chilling moneymakers. "Corrupting influence? They're talking utter rot. A couple of realistic films such as *On the Waterfront* and *Blackboard Jungle* can do more to incite hooliganism than a dozen horror films ... Horror is pure escapism and rattling good entertainment if directed with the skill and polish of *Dracula*."' Lee went further, calling the horror boom 'the best thing that's hit British films for years' and asserting that 'I'd be crazy to turn my back on it now.'[19]

Hammer weren't about to let him, in any case. Though still derided by British critics as mere tuppence-coloured sensationalism, their lurid shockers had converted the company into a major player and the next character lined up for a Hammer make-over was Sherlock Holmes. *The Hound of the Baskervilles* was announced in May, with Cushing and Lee signing up on 1 August. In the wake of *Dracula* and its threat of typecasting, Lee 'felt that this was the time of possible danger for me' and was therefore delighted to be offered a change of image with the imperilled Sir Henry Baskerville, though well aware that the character 'was not the most exciting individual.' On 3 September, Lee joined Cushing and the film's newly appointed Dr Watson, André Morell, at a press reception held at the Sherlock Holmes Pub on Northumberland Avenue, and production began at Bray ten days later.

The Hound of the Baskervilles was by no means the box-office smash Hammer had been anticipating, but it remains perhaps the most engaging, and beautifully rendered, entry in their initial series of costume Gothics. Cushing and Morell are ideally matched as Holmes and Watson, while Lee is perfectly at home playing just the kind of glamorous romantic lead British producers had been denying him for ten years. After Lee's elevation to sex symbol status via *Dracula*, Hammer were unconcerned by the usual objections, though one of them – his height – could have been more tactfully handled by Terence Fisher, whose set-ups often place Lee and the equally lofty Francis de Wolff in towering contrast to Cushing. Cushing was himself six feet tall, a sufficiently dominant height for Holmes in normal circumstances but not here.

Though considerably taller than Conan Doyle's Sir Henry, Lee corresponds exactly to Doyle's other specifications ('thick brows ... sensitive nostrils ... large hazel eyes ... dark and expressive face') and gives Sir Henry intriguing touches of playfulness and vulnerability. Recently arrived from South Africa, he's first seen at his toilette in a London hotel, bristling with affronted hauteur when two representatives of the management respond to his summons over 20 minutes late. The representatives are actually Holmes and Watson, and, when he realises his mistake, Sir Henry at once relaxes, exposing the lordly impatience as a mere front. Back in darkest Devon, he's sufficiently out of touch to exclaim 'Jumble sale? What on earth's that?' when asked to make a contribution by the fluttery Bishop Frankland. Miles Malleson, the inimitable actor/playwright/CND activist playing the Bishop, facilitates some of Lee's most relaxed moments in the picture. Malleson's wittering style raises good-natured smiles from Morell, Lee and John Le Mesurier that look charmingly close to involuntary 'corpsing'. Lee also didn't have to act too hard in a scene involving a marauding tarantula, which among other off-screen accomplishments succeeded in shedding its skin on the studio floor. 'What a filthy thing: horrible,' Sir

MALIGNANT HEROES 1956-1959

Sir Henry Baskerville and the vengeful Cecile (Marla Landi) in The Hound of the Baskervilles *(1958)*

Henry stammers after his skin-crawling encounter with it, echoing Lee's own sentiments exactly.

Later, looking dapper in tweed jacket, jodhpurs and riding boots, Sir Henry initiates a romance with the Hispanic daughter of one of his tenants, and does so with a surprisingly forceful display of noblesse oblige, unaware that Cecile has her own reasons for submitting to his attentions. 'Will you meet me tonight, at the Hall?' he breathes as they embrace. 'We can walk back across the moor...' Outwardly smooth but inwardly rather gauche, he's sufficiently inflamed to suggest an assignation that runs counter to all Holmes' warnings regarding the legendary

Hound of Hell. Sure enough, Cecile rounds on Sir Henry in spitfire fashion after luring him to a mist-wreathed, derelict abbey. 'Swine! You thought it was going to be easy, didn't you?' she hisses, and Sir Henry looks on in blank astonishment and gathering terror as she airs a centuries-old class grievance. Known internationally as a model under her real name of Maria Scarafia, Marla Landi makes a splendidly vindictive femme fatale, generally reckoned more effective than the Hound she unleashes, a performing Great Dane of placid disposition called Colonel. Among several schemes to make the dog seem more ferocious, an attempt to use a midget in Lee's place proved abortive.

The Hound of the Baskervilles wrapped on 31 October; *The Man in the Rue Noire* followed it into Bray less than three weeks later and Lee (who had seen Barré Lyndon's original play, *The Man in Half Moon Street*, at the New Theatre nearly 20 years before) went with it. Cushing, however, did not, rejecting the leading role for reasons unknown and devoting his time, instead, to an exhibition of his watercolours in New Bond Street. The part was passed on to the glacial German actor Anton Diffring. It doesn't seem to have occurred to Hammer to promote Lee into prime position, even though the part – of a glamorous Parisian sculptor who looks 35 but is actually 104 – would have suited him quite nicely.

Hammer's attitude to Lee at this time was a curious one; as one critic has put it, 'Peter Cushing was Hammer's *star* – Christopher Lee was only its monster.'[20] Cushing had come to Hammer prepackaged as a star, albeit a purely domestic one. Lee, however, was a 'monster' of their own creation and, in typically British style, Hammer appear to have been blind to the value of something they had fashioned themselves. The story would be very different by the early 1970s, when the struggling Hammer had come to perceive Lee as their last remaining meal ticket and routinely billed him above Cushing just as he was routinely billed below him in the late 1950s. But, in the meantime, Hammer's attitude meant that Lee had to stand by and watch Anton Diffring and, later, Paul Massie give uninspiring performances in roles better suited to him. He was even deemed dispensible when Hammer got around to making a luscious sequel to *Dracula* in 1960, the story of *The Brides of Dracula* focusing on the easily resurrected Van Helsing rather than the reduced-to-dust Dracula.

As indicated by *The Hound of the Baskervilles*, however, Hammer were willing to entrust Lee with slightly stodgy second leads as well as out-and-out monsters. In *The Man Who Could Cheat Death*, as Terence Fisher's new film was ultimately retitled, he was cast as Dr Pierre Gerrard, a high-minded but somewhat unimaginative surgeon in turn-of-the-century Paris who vies with Diffring's Georges Bonnet for the affections of Janine Dubois (Hazel Court). Faced with a venerable, world-renowned researcher – and properly awestruck – Gerrard nevertheless demurs when Professor Weiss (Arnold Marle) proposes that he perform a slightly outré operation. 'Being a surgeon is a practical business, Professor,' he explains. 'It's necessary to make a living; that doesn't leave very much time for pioneering.'

Though realised with Hammer's customary Technicolor lustre, the film suffers from Diffring's stagey and unsympathetic central performance and from less cleverly disguised corner-cutting than usual. It's also extraordinarily talky by Jimmy Sangster standards. In a typically yellow-saturated drawing room, Gerrard and Inspector Legris (Francis de Wolff) chatter away for what seems like ages, Lee trying to alleviate the static stodge by toying with a pen knife while de Wolff does a ponderous circuit of the room for no good reason other than to liven up his windy slabs of police procedural. The scene does establish, however, that Bonnet has been murdering people at ten-yearly intervals for some seven decades, placing Gerrard in the invidious position of having to tell the besotted Janine to steer clear. Something of a stuffed shirt, all Gerrard can manage to tell her is that 'The man's abnormal.'

Gerrard finally agrees to performing the vital operation that will prolong Bonnet's existence, but Bonnet abducts Janine anyway. Lee gives a fine urgency to a scene in which Gerrard and the Inspector ransack Bonnet's office for a clue to her whereabouts, explaining to Legris that 'I made the incision, but I did *not* perform the operation.' Getting ready to hurry outdoors, Lee underlines the word 'incision' by fastening a cuff-link with unusual savagery. It's then off to Bonnet's lock-up at the Gare du Nord and a fiery climax in which Bonnet crumbles into decrepitude while Janine rushes into Gerrard's arms. Short on visceral excitement, *The Man Who Could Cheat Death* made a comfortable profit but, like the Holmes picture, was not the kind of money spinner Hammer's distibutors had come to expect.

As the film approached the end of its schedule, Lee had one of his first direct encounters with a breed

Pierre Gerrard and Inspector Legris (Francis de Wolff) on the trail of The Man Who Could Cheat Death *(1958)*

'A figure of imperishable sadness,' said the Times: *Kharis in* The Mummy *(1959)*

he was to become very familiar with – the encyclopaedically well-informed horror fan. In its Horror Special, *Picturegoer* had posed a dozen quiz questions relating to horror history, 'Dinner with Dracula' the promised reward. Young RAF recruit Malcolm Downey received his prize shortly before Christmas. 'Two minutes after they shook hands,' reported Sarah Stoddart, 'Lee said: "It's frightening. This boy is a walking encyclopaedia on horror. He knows more than I do. And I'm getting to be quite an expert." For Yorkshire-born Downey, who went along with another airman, Eddie Marr, from Angus, Scotland, the thrills were just beginning. First a toast with Lee in his lush, plush flat in London's Belgravia ... Then into Lee's slinky, jet-black car [actually a car laid on by *Picturegoer*, Lee points out] to The Caprice – London's nightspot rendezvous for the biggest stage and screen stars ... It was a date two picturegoers haven't a ghost of a chance to forget.' [21]

After a brief assignment in Hamburg (discussed below), Lee returned to Bray in 1959 to complete his triumvirate of classic monsters. *The Mummy* went on the floor on 25 February, its script a slightly clumsy Sangster amalgam of elements from Universal's Mummy B-features of the 1940s. Hammer gave it deluxe A-picture treatment, however, even transplanting the unit to Shepperton for the all-important swamp scenes and happily acceding to Universal's insistence that the casting of Cushing and Lee was 'a must'. As Peter Burnup, venerable critic of the *News of the World*, would put it when the film began its blockbusting release in September, 'the now renowned firm of Peter Cushing and Christopher Lee – acknowledged specialists in this line of business – have been brought in to keep the grisly pot continually on the boil.'

The Mummy remains a highly impressive successor to Hammer's previous horror hits. With the usual Hammer personnel excelling themselves in all departments, Terence Fisher gives the film's violent set-pieces stunning impact, as well as investing the film with a memorable, melancholic undertow. Lee's extraordinary performance as the mummified Kharis is central to both effects. Encased in a brilliant but highly uncomfortable make-up by Hammer's new make-up maestro, Roy Ashton, Lee communicates a 4000-year-old sense of love and loss entirely through his expressive eyes and body language. He also lends the Mummy's bludgeoning assaults on the late-Victorian desecrators a truly awesome physical power.

Kharis first appears in answer to the prayers of Mehemet Bey (George Pastell), wrenching himself with almost Bambi-like awkwardness from the blood-red depths of a Home Counties bog. His slime-encrusted head lolls upwards in close-up and the eyes flicker open, after which his resistant legs yank themselves free and he joins Bey on the bank. Issued with his instructions, Kharis' face remains blank but his eyes spark into vindictive life, belying his robotic movements as he lurches off on his first mission. The quality of Lee's mime even earned the praise of highbrow art critic Lawrence Alloway. 'The men in the make-up department and Christopher Lee have done the Mummy very well,' he enthused. 'Its walk, stiff after millennia of entombment, experimentally flexing its limbs as it goes, is a brilliant extension of the original lumbering walk that Karloff created; the dried hollowness of the bandaged body, a powerful crust, is creepily conveyed, too.' [22]

Lee takes every opportunity to emphasise the humanity still extant within Kharis' bandaged crust. Shimmering with slime, Kharis smashes his way through a window grille in the Engerfield Asylum and slithers down the inside wall in pursuit of Felix Aylmer's deranged elder archaeologist. Having throttled him to death, he pauses to direct a measured look of 'Serves you right' at the corpse before striding out. His assaults on the home of Cushing's John Banning are dazzlingly choreographed too, with Kharis pounding through the French windows of Bray's ballroom stage and belabouring Banning as if he were a mere insect. In their first encounter, Banning leaps up to his bookshelf to grasp an ornamental spear and impale the unheeding Kharis on it; in the second, Kharis wrests a rifle from him and flings it out of shot with breathtaking fluidity. On both occasions, the intervention of Banning's wife Isobel (Yvonne Furneaux) brings the violence to a sudden halt. She is, of course, a dead ringer for Kharis' Ancient Egyptian love, Ananka, and Kharis' response on first seeing her is one of the most sensitive things Lee has ever done. Head working almost coyly as he reaches for her, it then lolls down in spaniel-eyed desolation when the perplexed Isobel fails to return his affection.

Sangster's faulty structure introduces two flashbacks mid-film, but both have rewarding moments. One reaches back to 2000 BC and presents Lee's youthful Kharis in splendid ceremonial robes, uttering a funeral oration over Ananka, extolling her 'created form more perfect than those of the Gods' and really meaning it. The other shows the first discovery of the Mummy, trapped in its 'comatose state of living death' – still upright, head bowed, and looking like a giant grey fossil. 'To me the dead are the dead: clay,' says Mehemet Bey later, and that's exactly what Lee looks like in this scene. All ends with Kharis shot to pieces in the swamp, his head blown apart in a nasty sequence that was apparently even nastier before the BBFC got their hands on it. The final submersion, incidentally, was performed by Eddie Powell, his first substitution for Lee in a long career as his stunt double.

Despite Powell's presence, Lee sustained several injuries while working on *The Mummy*, smashing his way through non-breakaway doors and wrenching his neck muscles while carrying Yvonne Furneaux through the swamp, with numerous unprintable oaths issuing from behind the inflexible make-up. Nevertheless, he was sufficiently relaxed about the finished film to offer a sardonic quip at the expense of critics still fulminating over the unacceptable levels of violence in Hammer's films. 'In *The Mummy*,' he countered, 'I only kill three people, and not in a ghastly way. I just break their necks.' [23]

VAMPIRE ON TOUR

On Wednesday 21 January 1959, the ever-circulating C H B Williamson attended the opening of a new Jermyn Street nightclub, Danny's Green Room. The Danny in question was the popular character actor Danny Green, and among the guests were Val Guest and Yolande Donlan, Hy Hazell, Donald Houston, Sid James, Joseph Janni, David Kossoff, Sydney Tafler and Christopher Lee, 'who goes from one film to another and whose only regret is that with current demands he cannot be in two or three places at the same time,' Williamson reported in the Friday edition of *To-Day's Cinema*. 'He told me his fan mail has become worldwide since *Dracula*, but many who write are intelligent and send interesting letters.'

Though in demand and in receipt of interesting fan letters – indeed, in July a fully fledged fan club would be inaugurated in the US by Jessica Wallace – Lee was aware that the impact of *Dracula* had been so great it had left casting directors in just as much of a quandary about how best to 'play' him as they had been when he was unknown. How do you follow a 500-year-old vampire Count? As Lee himself put it, the answer seemed to be, for the time being at least: with 'a raft of sleazy characters.'

'The thriller *The Treasure of San Teresa* sees Christopher Lee back in sinister circulation as the villainous Jaeger, head of a gang of crooks operating in post-war Hamburg.' The pressbook for Alvin Rakoff's film did its best to boost its fourth-billed star but his role amounted to little more than the kind of negligible cameo he'd been used to pre-*Dracula*. The film began production in Hamburg at the end of

MALIGNANT HEROES 1956-1959

The Treasure of San Teresa, Hamburg, February 1959: director Alvin Rakoff tows Lee, Walter Gotell, Nadine Tallier, Marius Goring, Dawn Addams and Eddie Constantine. The leather raincoat would resurface 23 years later in Massarati and the Brain

January 1959 as *Long Distance* (a title retained for its US release); Lee filmed his brief scenes in February just ahead of *The Mummy*. The film was an unofficial companion piece to a previous Sydney Box production that had been shot partly in Berlin. *Subway in the Sky*, directed by Box's wife Muriel, shared most of the same technical personnel and was just going on release as *Teresa* started shooting.

Despite Wilkie Cooper's atmospheric monochrome photography of various wintery German locations, Rakoff's film is an uninvolving thriller in which an American secret service man, Larry Brennan, revisits Hamburg 15 years after a Nazi general instructed him to hide a cache of invaluable jewels in a Czechoslovakian convent. The granite-faced Eddie Constantine is the OSS agent, Dawn Addams is Hedi, the glamorous daughter of the dead general, and together they embark on an Iron Curtain-flouting treasure hunt. There's much to-ing and fro-ing in long distance lorries and stealthy dodging of border guards, together with a bar-room brawl in which the tiny Tsai Chin, later to co-star with Lee in several Fu Manchu pictures, lolls at a bar stool as a Chinese call girl. There's even a daring glimpse of bathtub nudity from Nadine Tallier as Hedi's flatmate, Zizi.

Lee turns up at the 50-minute mark as Inspector Jaeger of the Hamburg police, who, despite insisting that 'I don't like violence,' takes Larry to a garage and has him roughed up by his beefy henchman, Max. He's easily outsmarted by Larry, however, and only reappears for the railroad climax, still clad in a leather raincoat, trilby and muffler. He is in reality a gangster in cahoots with the duplicitous Zizi, and ends up being throttled on the track by Larry. (The stuntmen employed here are easily identifiable as such, particularly the fair-haired one substituting for Lee.) The treasure itself ends up in the river below. As for the leather raincoat, it was bought in Hamburg by Lee himself and hangs in his wardrobe to this day. Thanks to its resemblance to the kind of thing formerly worn by the Gestapo, it earned him many odd looks among the locals while working on *San Teresa* – shades of his effect on Hove during *Battle of the V.1*.

One answer to the question 'How to follow a vampire Count?' was, of course, 'With another vampire Count.' Lee resisted reprising Dracula himself until 1965, but when offered an Italian comedy in the spring of 1959 called *Tempi duri per i vampiri* (Hard Times for Vampires) he saw no harm in accepting, provided that his character was clearly signposted as Baron Roderigo de Braumfürten.

CHRISTOPHER LEE – PART THREE

Always keen to imitate trends from abroad, Italian producers had taken note of the staggering success achieved in Italy by Hammer's first two horrors (retitled *La maschera di Frankenstein* and *Dracula il vampiro*) and a boom in homegrown Gothic would accordingly begin in 1960 with *La maschera del demonio*. *Tempi duri per i vampiri* formed a jocular prelude to this efflorescence.

Known in English-speaking territories as *Uncle Was a Vampire*, the film was directed by comedy specialist Stefano Vanzina, popularly known as Steno, and starred the pint-sized singer-comedian Renato Rascel. Setting a precedent for any number of Italian horrors to follow, it was filmed at a rambling castello overlooking Lake Bracciano near Rome and Lee got to know its owner, the lofty Prince Livio Odescalchi, very well. The film is graced with wall-to-wall bathing beauties and lusciously coloured UltraScope photography by Marco Scarpelli, but the humour fails to translate. Even Italian critics were unamused when the film opened in Rome in October. 'The director attempts to disguise the weakness of the comedy with a parade of beautiful women,' carped one. 'But even the participation of specialist Christopher Lee doesn't produce the desired result.'[24]

The joke of the film, such as it is, is that Lee only gets to bite the unappetising Rascel, leaving Rascel free to nuzzle all the film's resplendent lovelies (Sylva Koscina, Kai Fischer, Lia Zopelli, Susanne Loret) in a single night. Rascel is the impecunious Baron Oswaldo di Lamberteghi, reduced to being a waiter to monied tourists at what was once his own castle. He takes delivery of his Bavarian uncle's casket, from which emerges, some 20 minutes in, not merely the expected groping hand but also a foot shod in a stylish winkle-picker shoe. Lee looks magnificent as a vampire subtly different from Dracula: much more gaunt, sporting significantly bigger fangs, ashen-faced, jet-black hair plastered to his head and with the red flanges of his cloak swept dramatically over each shoulder. Lee's Dracula wouldn't surrender to a red-lined cloak until *Dracula Prince of Darkness*, and there are many pre-echoes of that film and its sequels in Lee's performance, too.

Experimenting with demonic facial expressions absent from his first attempt at Dracula, Lee plays the Baron completely straight, whatever the indignities inflicted on him. When Oswaldo commends his uncle's youthful appearance and snobbishly suggests that 'It's a question of blood,' the Baron rounds on him in a big, grimacing close-up – eyes blazing – that wouldn't have been out of place in *Dracula* itself. Lee is also very alarming as he gazes down from a balcony at the assembled beauties in their evening dresses and when prowling the hotel's battlements at dusk. Hovering, fangs bared, at the window of the delectable Carlotta (Koscina), he sizes up her carotid as she lounges on her bed, listening to a pop ballad on a portable Dansette. Her elderly father enters, absent-mindedly flourishing a cross-shaped coat hanger, and the Baron topples from the balcony into a hedge below. Coming to at cock-crow, he runs wildly past gaily coloured beach umbrellas in search of sanctuary.

'I'm tired, I'm weary of moving from castle to castle, from tomb to tomb,' he explains to Oswaldo later, giving a long account of how he became a vampire, proudly displaying his impressive canines and then sinking them into Oswaldo's throat. Having passed on the curse (and his cloak), the Baron is able to rest in peace for half an hour or so of solid Renato Rascel antics, but returns enraged when one of Oswaldo's victims, the lovely Lilina (Loret), responds to his advances with true love. 'You shouldn't have bothered that girl,' he complains. 'My thirst has become incurable again.' Despite his irritation, he rescues Oswaldo from a deputation of inflamed locals (smoothly debunking vampirism as 'something absurd, ridiculous, incredible') and then goes after Lilina with a horrible fanged smile as Oswaldo makes desperate efforts to cause the cock to crow ahead of time. En route for Bavaria again, the Baron links arms with two other lovelies at the railway station, explaining that 'For 400 years I've been getting in and out of these coffins ... [Now] another destiny awaits me.' As the credits roll and Bruno Martino trills a ritzy Rascel/Martino composition called 'Dracula Cha-Cha-Cha', the girls are seen driving off in a horsedrawn hearse with the Baron comfortably coffined in the back.

Tempi duri per i vampiri is significant as a forerunner of Lee's prolific Continental engagements during the 1960s, and also as an indication that his vampire persona could retain its demonic power even in a lighthearted context. Less happily, the Italian predilection for not bothering to use live sound means that the viewer has to watch Lee while listening to someone else entirely. The sonorous American voice dubbed onto Lee's performance is literally sonorous on this occasion: it's been filtered, rather hokily, through an echo chamber.

SOHO SEX BARONS

Back in England, Lee started work early in August on what Renown Pictures' publicity department would subsequently ballyhoo as 'The Dynamic Drama of Youth MAD about BEAT, Living for KICKS.' The film

The baleful Baron Roderigo at Odescalchi Castle in Stefano Vanzina's Tempi duri per i vampiri *(1959)*

Christopher Lee – Part Three

Kenny and Greta (Delphi Lawrence) observe Simon (Nigel Green) and Jennifer (Gillian Hills) through a two-way mirror in Edmond T Gréville's Beat Girl (1959)

was Edmond T Gréville's *Beat Girl* and the studio was MGM Borehamwood. Later in August the same studio played host to a film focusing on what the posters called 'The neon-lit jungle of the club underworld!' This was Terence Young's *Too Hot to Handle*, and Lee found himself dashing between sets, affixing a pencil moustache for *Too Hot* and removing it for *Beat Girl*. Both films were set in the twilight world of Soho striptease, a hot topic at the time thanks to impresario Paul Raymond having already established his dominion over the district while soft porn magazines like *Kamera* and *Solo* proliferated at an unprecedented rate. In *Beat Girl*, Lee was cast as Kenny, 'smooth and evil' proprietor of the Les Girls strip club, with Nigel Green as his lieutenant Simon. In *Too Hot to Handle*, Lee was the lieutenant, Paul Novak, and Leo Genn the well-heeled boss of the Pink Flamingo club, Johnny Solo.

Beat Girl has since become a minor cult favourite, chiefly for its hilariously clunky snapshot of late 1950s youth culture and for John Barry's stunning jazz-pop score, his first ever film commission. The film's producer George Willoughby had cast the struggling young pop singer Adam Faith on the strength of his appearances on the BBC programme *Drumbeat*; a prescient decision, for by the time *Beat Girl* made its delayed appearance at the London Pavilion on 28 October 1960, Faith had become a teen sensation with several Top Ten hits to his name. *Beat Girl* accordingly sired the first ever soundtrack album for a British film, which climbed rapidly to number 12.

As well as Adam Faith, the assembled teens in *Beat Girl* include Faith's girlfriend of the time, Shirley Ann Field (dubbed with a regal voice quite unsuited to lines like 'Daddy-o, I'm over and out'), Oliver Reed (twitching to the film's driving theme as if in the final stages of epilepsy) and Peter McEnery, a future lion of the RSC who here utters the immortal line, 'Great, Dad, great: straight from the fridge.' The title character, Jennifer, is played by 15-year-old Bardot lookalike Gillian Hills, her glamorous stepmother, Nichole, is French import Noelle Adam and her perplexed father, a modernist architect called Paul Linden, is played by David Farrar. A hook-nosed veteran of classics from the Powell and Pressburger stable, Farrar is completely out of his depth in these surroundings. 'Go on, get out of it, you jiving, drivelling scum,' he splutters impotently as he breaks up one of Jennifer's beatnik gatherings.

The teens frequent a Soho café called the Off-Beat; just across the road is Kenny's sinful establishment Les Girls, where Claire Gordon's Honey stumbles through a fledgling striptease as the oily proprietor watches from his office via a two-way mirror. 'It's the only way I can tell whether the girls are earning their money or not,' Kenny explains. Supremely urbane, he greets the curious Jennifer with a well-rehearsed spiel. 'There's a thrill in this work – all the girls say so – a real thrill,' he coos. 'Besides, it's a shame to waste a nice figure.'

Kenny is clearly attracted to what his henchman Simon calls 'gaol bait' and is delighted when Jennifer reappears. 'The gang gave me the heebies,' she tells him. 'I felt flat.' 'Well, naturally,' he replies, caressing her shoulders and hair. 'What can those children possibly do for you? You need a little help, don't you? One way or another, I think I can offer you quite a future...' Proposing a trip to Paris, he claims that 'You might even have your name up in lights on the Champs Elysée – and that really means something.' Kenny is suddenly stabbed with his own paper knife, however, and when Simon breaks in, we find that the desk lamp has been up-ended beside Kenny's body, giving a nightmare quality to the scene. Jennifer cringes terrified in a corner as Kenny's hardbitten mistress, Greta, emerges from the shadows and says simply, 'I reckon I did us all a favour.'

Faced with the 1950s teen explosion, filmmakers were at a loss and never more so than in *Beat Girl*. The film advertised its identity crisis even on the posters, which drew attention to its 'Exciting BEAT Tunes' while simultaneously running a picture of Gillian Hills in her scanties under a banner that screamed 'This could be your TEENAGE daughter!' The director, Edmond T Gréville, had been straddling the British and French film industries since 1929, taking advantage of his dual nationality to make minor classics like *Noose* and *Marchand d'amour*. According to Lee, 'He was a delightful man. I liked him very much. He was the only Frenchman I've ever met in my life who spoke English without the slightest accent.'

Beat Girl was hack work by Gréville's standards, but it's still spiced with a certain demented charm that helps the viewer through several sluggish passages. It acquired the distinction of being banned in France and only got through in the UK – with an 'X' certificate – after Pascaline's exotic striptease had been all but deleted. (Eye-poppingly rude, this sequence resurfaced on TV and video prints in the 1990s.) Billed third, Lee trots through his villainous paces with practised ease, particularly in his edgy scenes with Delphi Lawrence's disaffected Greta. Formerly a victim of *The Man Who Could Cheat Death*, Lawrence goes mysteriously uncredited in *Beat*

As the duplicitous Novak with Johnny Solo (Leo Genn), Midnight Franklin (Jayne Mansfield) and 'Diamonds' Dinelli (Sheldon Lawrence) in Terence Young's Too Hot to Handle *(1959)*

Girl, despite playing a substantial role with characteristic aplomb.

Too Hot to Handle was Lee's seventh and last assignment for the faithful Terence Young. Filmed by Otto Heller in sumptuous Eastmancolor, its Soho flavour is even less convincing than *Beat Girl*'s, with saucy set-pieces smacking more of an MGM musical than the Raymond Revuebar. Like Heller, the German actor Karlheinz Boehm was about to make *Peeping Tom*, another film focusing, at least in part, on 1950s pornography. Here, Boehm plays journalist Robert Jouvel, who comes to Johnny Solo's Pink Flamingo in search of a scoop. 'Oh, sure,' drawls Lee's spiv-like Novak in an American accent. 'Read all about it. Sexy, sordid Soho, England's greatest shame – send for the missionaries before it's too late.' 'Oh, don't mind him,' Solo apologises. 'He's useful. Besides, I like unpleasant people.' What Solo doesn't realise is that Novak is a double agent, plotting his downfall with rival sex baron 'Diamonds' Dinelli (Sheldon Lawrence), proprietor of the adjacent Diamond Horseshoe club.

The film was a vehicle for the prodigious curves of US import Jayne Mansfield. Den mother to Solo's gaggle of glamour queens, Mansfield's Midnight Franklin advises him against hiring Pony Tail, 'the little blonde with the rock 'n' roll hairdo [who's] hardly out of the Girl Scouts.' (Barbara Windsor, in her first substantial film role, is dubbed here just as clumsily as Shirley Ann Field was in *Beat Girl*, while the film's numerous Americanisms were the work of screenwriter Herbert Kretzmer.) Solo's downfall is eventually brought about, not by Novak and Dinelli, but by a nasty date-rape scenario in which Pony Tail is wined, dined and murdered by the loathsome Mr Arpels (Martin Boddey). About to be led away by the police, Solo is informed of Novak's treachery and the pair exchange reproachful glances across the Pink Flamingo's deserted dancefloor.

Long, lean and sinister, Novak has been a silent presence in the film's most exciting sequence, lurking outside Lambeth Palace with a copy of the *Evening Standard* for camouflage as Midnight waits apprehensively to hand over money to a bunch of blackmailers. A deputation of vicars gets in the way, but one of them is bogus, snatches the money and hurtles down Lambeth Pier with Novak in hot pursuit, his white mackintosh flying in the breeze. Lee's best moments, however, are reserved for Novak's razzmatazz role as MC of 'Gentleman' Johnny Solo's nudie cabaret. 'And now, ladies and gentlemen,' he beams, 'to start the evening for you, we give you London's – now, why stop at London? – we give you the world's most glamorous number, the one and only Midnight Franklin. And you can see for yourselves why all men describe her as – ' Whereupon a bunch of limp male vocalists chime in with 'Hot, hot, much too hot to handle' and the capacious Mansfield sashays into the spotlight.

Another act is introduced with a stream of exotic gobbledegook. 'And now, friends, the Orient beckons,' Novak explains ominously. 'The mysterious East, land of strange barbaric rites, land of the monsoon. For months there has been a drought. The parched earth calls for rain. But the Rain God waits, angry...' The ensuing dance sequence ends with a fully fledged rain storm on stage, a greater extravagance than anything in *Beat Girl*. The film's exploitation ingredients also include the inevitable cat fight in the Pink Flamingo's dressing rooms, while the roster of glamour queens is rounded out by Kai Fischer, last seen in a Mediterranean setting in *Tempi duri per i vampiri*.

The film acquired notoriety even during production, when the producers failed to meet their Borehamwood bills and the unit was accordingly locked out of the studio while the fully paid-up *Gorgo* continued production within. The dispute was rapidly resolved, but not before being splashed all over the newspapers. Undaunted, Jayne Mansfield asserted that '*Too Hot to Handle* is the best film I have made' [25] and immediately moved over to Twickenham to star in *The Challenge* for John Gilling. For his part, Lee claimed to have based Novak on a notorious upper class spiv-cum-socialite of his acquaintance and that the film 'was made with an alternative version for those who preferred Jayne Mansfield with her nipples painted out.' The UK and US versions are conspicuously nipple-free, so there must be a less discreet Continental version out there somewhere, a fact confirmed by Barbara Windsor. She also pointed out that, Continental version or not, 'Jayne Mansfield's bristols had to dominate every scene of *Too Hot to Handle*, even if it meant putting us behind schedule.' [26]

JANUS-FACED

By 1959, Lee's film commitments were leaving little time for television. An exception was made for an episode of *Tales of the Vikings*, a TV spin-off from the 1958 Kirk Douglas vehicle *The Vikings*. Made in Munich for Douglas' own Bryna Productions and syndicated through United Artists Television, the series starred Jerome Courtland, Walter Barnes and the towering Buddy Baer as the titular Vikings, with rewarding roles for British actors like Edmund Purdom, Peter Bull, George Coulouris and June Thorburn. *The Bull* cast Lee as a despotic Norman lord and the legendary, alcohol-addled character star, Wilfrid Lawson, as his Saxon antagonist, with the young Ryan O'Neal as Lawson's son. Lawson's

Professor Driscoll encourages the witchcraft researches of Nan Barlow (Venetia Stevenson) for reasons of his own in The City of the Dead *(1959)*

uniquely cavalier approach to saying his lines reduced director Elmo Williams to despair and provided Lee with one of the funniest anecdotes in his autobiography.

Hammer's meteoric success had inspired many other British producers to leap onto the horror bandwagon, and, after *Corridors of Blood*, Lee's second appearance in a non-Hammer horror film followed in John Moxey's *The City of the Dead*, which began at Shepperton on 12 October. The film's executive producer, New Yorker Milton Subotsky, would later set up a Hammer rival called Amicus and employ Lee on five further occasions. For the time being, *The City of the Dead* was made under the aegis of Vulcan Productions and produced by Donald Taylor, a major figure in the 1930s documentary movement and also a veteran of *Douglas Fairbanks Presents*.

Set in New England, the film is structured around the witchcraft researches in Whitewood Massachusetts of pretty student Nan Barlow (Venetia Stevenson) – but only until the halfway point, when she is shockingly killed off in a satanic ceremony. After that, her brother and boyfriend come looking for her and a second young woman nearly gets the sacrificial treatment too. (Several ill-informed critics have suggested that the film's structure was lifted from Alfred Hitchcock's *Psycho*, failing to notice that *The City of the Dead* began shooting some seven weeks before the Hitchcock picture.) One of the most atmospheric of all British shockers, the picture is smothered in as much ground fog as Shepperton could muster and boasts an extraordinarily baleful femme fatale in Mrs Newless, landlady of Whitewood's conspicuously uninviting Raven's Inn. Effortlessly malevolent, Patricia Jessel was acting with Peter Cushing in *The Sound of Murder* at the Aldwych Theatre during the evenings while playing Mrs Newless during the day.

Lee is Professor Alan Driscoll, the suave but faintly sinister tutor to Nan's group of anthropology students. Lee's East Coast accent is pitch-perfect and he gives Driscoll just the right conceited body language to go with it. Driscoll concludes his account of the Salem witch trials with the mantra 'Burn, witch, burn!', to which Nan's lamebrained boyfriend Bill (Tom Naylor) facetiously replies, 'Dig that crazy beat!' Faced with a gang of teens just as unconvincing as those in *Beat Girl*, Driscoll asserts with unwonted intensity that 'Witchcraft is *not* nonsense' and happily endorses Nan's scheme to do on-the-spot research in distant Whitewood. He also argues hotly with Nan's brother Richard (Dennis Lotis) on the same subject, and his passionate response is finally explained when Nan reaches the end of her researches. Trapped in a cavern underneath the Raven's Inn, she is pinned to a sacrificial altar but our attention is somehow drawn to a hooded figure half-hidden behind Mrs Newless. We get a clearer view of him a few moments later, but Mrs Newless' sacrificial knife is cleverly positioned to conceal his eyes. The knife soon flashes down, however, and there is Driscoll in full view, lips twitching with excitement.

Driscoll is next seen back in his college study, filmed through the bars of a birdcage as he plucks a dove from it and mutters, 'Oh Lord of Light, accept this sacrifice.' He's interrupted by two unexpected callers, handling Patricia Russell (Betta St John) with a laconic but gently obstructive charm that turns ever so slightly threatening when he's faced once more with the persistent Richard Barlow. Things meanwhile gather to a head in Whitewood and Driscoll re-emerges for the attempted sacrifice of Patricia in a mist-wreathed graveyard. We have gathered by this stage that Driscoll, like Mrs Newless and all their cowled confederates, is not merely a Satanist but the reincarnation of a 17th century original. At the stroke of midnight, the dying Bill directs the shadow of a cross onto the assembled worshippers, whereupon Driscoll's arm bursts into flames and his companions rapidly follow suit.

The film is a memorable one – and, as a pastiche American Gothic, remains a firm favourite of American fans under its US title *Horror Hotel* – but Lee's role seems strangely dislocated from the rest of the action. Though a centuries-old associate of Mrs Newless and her spooky friend Jethro Keane (Valentine Dyall), he barely interacts with them in the satanic ceremonies, his major opportunities being confined to his apartment on campus. Milton Subotsky would later make a habit of writing underlength scripts for Amicus; on this occasion, he claimed to have done the opposite, boosting George Baxt's screenplay to feature length by adding a new character. Maybe it was Driscoll. Whether or not he was an afterthought, Lee's cowled face still loomed large on the posters.

From the Janus-faced Professor Driscoll, Lee proceeded to Hammer's MegaScope study in dual personality, *The Two Faces of Dr Jekyll*, which started at Bray on 23 November. Producer Michael Carreras, son of James, was already impatient with Hammer's Gothic formula and felt the urge to 'upgrade' Hammer's image. To this end, he engaged the West End playwright Wolf Mankowitz to write the script at twice Hammer's usual fee and, when Laurence Harvey proved unavailable, assigned the lead (or leads) to the then-hot Canadian actor Paul Massie.

Unfortunately, the no-nonsense Terence Fisher was out of sympathy with Mankowitz's screenplay. And Michael Carreras may have felt that Massie was a 'proper' actor but failed to notice that he was temperamentally unsuited, and unequal, to the gaslit Lyceum mode that Jekyll and Hyde demanded.

The actor who was so suited was third-billed below Massie and 'one of the sweetest actresses I've ever worked with', Dawn Addams. But maybe Lee was better off playing Jekyll's feckless friend, Paul Allen. The very model of a late-Victorian bounder, Allen gets plenty of juicy, epigrammatic one-liners to speak rather than the ponderous musings given to Jekyll and Hyde, and Lee steals the movie without any apparent effort whatsoever. A compulsive gambler, Paul is forever cadging money while simultaneously speaking of the paramount importance of honour, and illustrates Mankowitz's theme – the two-facedness of high society – far more effectively than the literally divided Jekyll/Hyde. Lee's make-up is subtly different from that of the clean-limbed Sir Henry Baskerville: darker around the eyes, more dissipated, and with impressively pronged sideburns to add a touch of the 1870s spiv. Lee himself gives Paul a louche, lazy smile and a certain world-weary glamour, both of which make his essential spinelessness and hypocrisy perfectly clear.

'Paul Allen is here again,' says Jekyll's wife Kitty on his first appearance. 'Don't give in to him, Henry – he's such a useless waster.' Enjoying an extra-marital affair with Paul, Kitty's words are designed to put Jekyll off the scent. The boorish and bearded Jekyll soon turns into the youthful, smooth-chopped Hyde, however, and discovers his wife and best friend waltzing at the 'very nearly halfway respectable' Sphinx Club. 'Mr Paul Allen, is it not?' Hyde asks chirpily. Amiably drunk and clutching a cigar, Paul slurs in reply, 'Not if you're one of my ruddy creditors!' Taking the novice Hyde under his wing, he dubs the icily sexy Kitty 'my frozen honey-pot' but also concedes that 'She's the most perfect parcel of ladyhood you ever set eyes on.' As for Maria, the Sphinx's resident snake-dancer, he advises his new friend to 'Forget it, dear boy. She's not in the prep school class ... Only princes, pashas, millionaires or distinguished actor-managers need apply.'

The crash course in metropolitan vice which follows ('London is your oyster, dear boy, and I'm the one who can open it for you') takes in a low pub, an opium den and a boxing ring, where the pugilist brothers Douglas and 'Tiger' Joe Robinson are seen knocking seven bells out of each other. (The Robinsons, incidentally, ran a gym in Orange Street, off Leicester Square, where Lee was a regular visitor.) Though in his element in these low-life surroundings,

Relaxing at Elstree with producer Michael Carreras, writer Wolf Mankowitz and co-star Dawn Addams during the filming of The Two Faces of Dr Jekyll *(1959)*

Paul is less sure of himself in his chosen milieu of upper class gambling clubs. 'Have you ever known me to welsh on a debt of honour?' he bristles at the end of one typically disastrous game, immediately running to Jekyll for yet another top-up loan. Paul's acceptance of help from Hyde is equally craven, but he finally snaps when Hyde suggests that he should 'procure' Kitty for him as collateral. 'How very amusing,' Hyde gloats. 'Paul Allen, breaker of every law in the moral code, is shocked into morality.'

Himself a snake, Paul ends up being throttled to death by Maria's python, and Lee was no more enamoured of this exotic creature than he had been of *Hound*'s tarantula. *The Two Faces of Dr Jekyll* gave him the chance to round off the 1950s with one of his most stylish characterisations yet, but it didn't provide Hammer with a particularly encouraging start to the 1960s. Running wildly over-budget, it moved to Elstree for a final, unscheduled fortnight and would prove a box-office clinker everywhere it played, its disastrous failure only offset by the terrific business generated by *The Brides of Dracula*. To make matters worse, for US release the scandalised Columbia shredded the film's salacious details in a welter of ugly jump-cuts and insisted on the deletion of Mankowitz's many mild profanities. Lee and the other principals were therefore recalled for further looping (substituting 'darn' for 'damn', 'witch' for 'bitch' etc), whereupon Columbia added insult to injury by offloading the film onto an independent distributor.

Cast as a short-fused pimp in *Jekyll*'s nightclub scenes was the young Oliver Reed, who would eventually clock up nine Hammer credits before moving on to fully fledged stardom with directors like Michael Winner and Ken Russell. 'Christopher used to pick up [character actor] Denis Shaw and myself at Earls Court,' Reed recalled, 'and we'd have to listen to him sing opera all the way down [to Bray]. German opera – all the time!' [27] Like everyone involved with Hammer during the company's halcyon period, Reed recalled the camaraderie at Bray Studios with affection. Lee himself maintained that 'Everyone was extremely friendly. The food was the best in England and the atmosphere in the studio was better than any other I've worked in. There were never any disagreements on the set, never any rows or temperamental outbursts. We all got on together very well. It was a very happy time; probably the happiest time of my career.' [28]

PART FOUR

EURO-ACTOR
1960–1964

In April 1960, the last ever issue of *Picturegoer* was published, making way for an ill-fated teen magazine called *Date*. In that last issue, the magazine which had acclaimed Lee as a 'dream boy' rather than a 'scream boy' published a brief piece called 'How a Bachelor Lives', bracketing him with vocalist Glen Mason as 'two of the most eligible men about town'.

'Both live alone,' explained columnist Pat Gledhill, 'in comfortable, orderly domains kept that way by domestic help daily. Both eat out more often than not. Both throw their socks away at the first sign of a hole ... For Christopher Lee ... bachelorhood presents no problems. "The woman who looks after my flat will cook for me if I want to have friends to dinner. Otherwise I take them out. I give two parties a year, when I return hospitality, but I hold them on a large scale so it means getting someone in to handle the refreshments." ... But don't lose heart, girls,' added Gledhill. 'Christopher Lee intends to change his bachelor status. "I enjoy my life now, but I have no wish to look after myself permanently. I believe that running a home is a woman's job." He merely adds this proviso: "She would have to be someone I could admire – as well as someone who could put up with me!"'[1]

Within a year Lee would make good on this hint and the article would be out of date. He had previously been poised to marry the 19-year-old Swedish beauty Henriette von Rosen – cousin of the ballerina who had appeared with him in *The Nightingale* – but had been reluctant to involve her in the precarious life of an actor and had broken the engagement off. His Hammer celebrity, meanwhile, had brought with it a legion of female fans who would happily have taken Henriette's place. 'Why do girls like me?' he mused on the Elstree set of *The Two Faces of Dr Jekyll*. 'I honestly believe it's because I represent a tragic figure on the screen. My fans aren't horror-struck morons. They're sensitive to romantic loneliness and it's this quality I try to get across in even my most melodramatic roles.'[2]

Having completed *Jekyll* in January, Lee moved back to Bray on 13 April 1960 for an on-camera make-up test for his next Hammer role, that of Tong leader Chung King in *The Terror of the Tongs*. Filming began on the 19th and Lee's scenes were completed by the 29th. Director Anthony Bushell was an actor who had been Olivier's right-hand man during the shooting of *Hamlet* 13 years before, though whether he recalled Lee's unauthorised contribution to that film is not known. An 'X'-rated *Boy's Own* melodrama set in Hong Kong in 1910, *Tongs* was known in production as *The Hatchet-Men* and gave Lee the opportunity to provide a preliminary sketch of one of his most famous roles, Dr Fu Manchu. It also provided him with top billing for the first time in a feature film.

These two points of historical interest are about all that the film has going for it. It's a crude full-colour retread of *The Stranglers of Bombay*, a Hammer subject filmed in monochrome the previous summer, and is hobbled by one of Jimmy Sangster's least inspirational screenplays. 'The old adage that you can't make a good picture from a bad script is admirably demonstrated here,' Sangster wrote in his autobiography. 'Mind you, I don't think the assembled company would have made a good picture even if the script had been good. Apart from the line producer, Ken Hyman, I don't think they were too sure what they were doing.'[3] This is hardly surprising, given that the film only came into being as a means of making the most of an expensive Chinese dockside set built by Bernard Robinson for *Visa to Canton*.

Leader of a kind of Cantonese Mafia, Lee is seen at an early stage conferring 'the ceremonial gauntlet and the sacred hatchet of the Red Dragon' on a dozy, doped-up assassin. He brings an easy, Oxbridge-educated insouciance to lines like 'The police have been entirely ineffectual for the last 100 years and will doubtlyss continue to be so for the next,' and shares

The whip-wielding Kurt Menliff at Anzio for Mario Bava's La frusta e il corpo *(1963)*

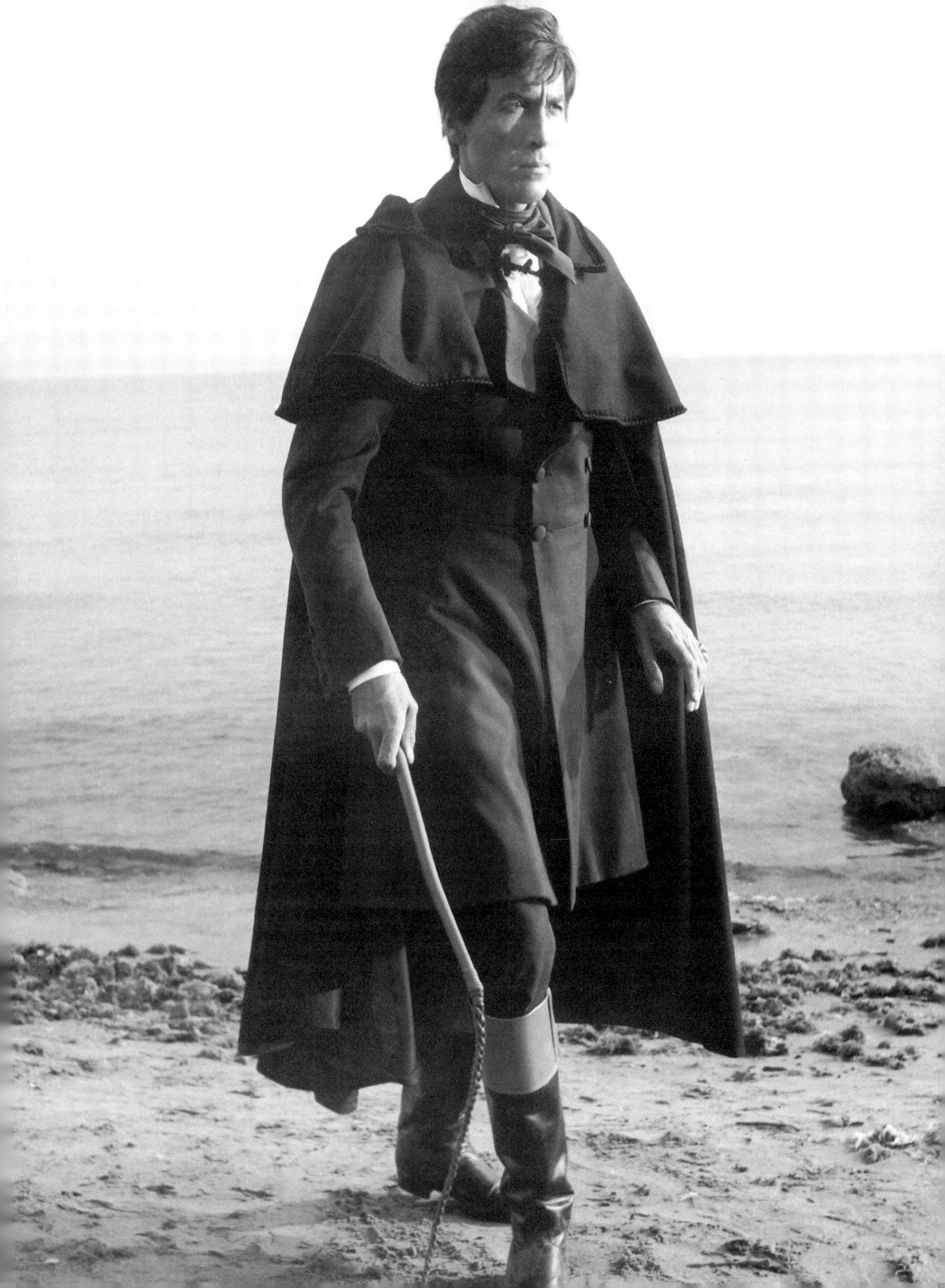

an edgy scene with Brian Worth as a treacherous East India Company official, ending it with an icily underplayed aside: 'He that loves pleasure shall by pleasure fall.' With Geoffrey Toone's bovine hero at his mercy, he claims blandly that 'Of necessity our means of persuasion must be invisible ones.' He then leans forward to utter the immortal line, 'Have you ever had your bones scraped, Captain?' And Bushell cuts in for a tight close-up on Chung King's unmoving face, which betrays no sign of sadistic anticipation as he adds, 'It is painful in the extreme, I can assure you.' Elsewhere, Lee gives the Tong leader an intellectual, almost pedantic air, facing death with Oriental sang froid – 'Like all Occidentals, Mr Harcourt,' he tells the cringing East India Company man, 'you find it impossible to accept the inevitable' – and only betraying a touch of anxiety when the enraged mob breaks into his Tong HQ.

Understandably, Hammer were unsure about pushing the film until it showed a good return in the US and Europe, whereupon it finally opened at the London Pavilion on 30 September 1961 in tandem with William Castle's *Psycho* variant, *Homicidal*. 'The Horror Kings of Britain and America Combine to Thrill You!' screamed the Pavilion's frontage under a colossal reproduction of Lee's face, glowering slant-eyed over Piccadilly Circus. The double-feature did terrific business during its month-long tenure of the Pavilion and then cleaned up in similarly spectacular fashion when released to the ABC circuit in November.

FRENCH LEAVE

After *The Terror of the Tongs*, Lee appeared in the first of several of his pictures that would be made in two languages. Produced by Steven Pallos and *The City of the Dead*'s Donald Taylor, *The Hands of Orlac* – or, to French audiences, *Les Mains d'Orlac* – was entrusted to a director equally at home in British and French studios, Edmond T Gréville. Production started on the French Riviera on 16 May 1960, and, though Lee wasn't required immediately, his commitment put paid to a trade announcement listing him alongside Peter Cushing, John Fraser and June Thorburn as stars of John Gilling's *The Wreckers*, starting on 20 June and eventually retitled *Fury at Smugglers' Bay*.

Filming of *Orlac* extended to 17 July, divided between Shepperton and the Studios de la Victorine in Nice (familiar to Lee from *Bitter Victory*), together with location work in Marseilles. Though much slicker, *Orlac* is cut from much the same cloth as Gréville's *Beat Girl*, sharing a similarly glacial monochrome 'look', a similar sleazy environment and Lee as the chief sleazemonger. Maurice Renard's 1920 novel had already formed the basis of two classic horror films – Robert Wiene's *Orlacs Hände* in 1924 and Karl Freund's *Mad Love* in 1935. Gréville's version retained Renard's basic idea of a famous concert pianist losing his two greatest assets in a train crash (here changed to a plane crash) and then coming close to losing his mind when he suspects that the hands of an executed murderer have been grafted on in their place.

The result is somewhat bland, landed with a mere 'A' certificate in the UK and lacking the wild, hallucinatory edge common to the Wiene and Freund versions. But it looks gorgeous, thanks to the combined efforts of cinematographers Jacques Lemare and Desmond Dickinson, and has an interesting (though not always appropriate) score from the famous jazz pianist Claude Bolling. At first it comes as a surprise that Lee's role is a rough approximation of the part played by Peter Lorre in *Mad Love* rather than the title role essayed by Conrad Veidt in *Orlacs Hände*. The Veidt echo comes instead from a 1929 thriller called *The Last Performance*, in which Veidt's Erik the Great commits murder by means of his trick sword cabinet, just as Lee's Nero

'He that loves pleasure shall by pleasure fall': with minions Roger Delgado and Brian Worth in The Terror of the Tongs *(1960)*

Certifiably insane: nightclub magician Nero doffs his Vasseur disguise in Edmond T Gréville's The Hands of Orlac / Les Mains d'Orlac *(1960)*

does here. A spiv-like burlesque illusionist dubbed 'le Roi du mystère', Nero is partnered by Dany Carrel's petite Li-Lang ('la Reine du charme') and resorts to blackmail when he stumbles upon the unfortunate Steven Orlac's secret. 'If he's got something to hide,' he tells Li-Lang in one of the English version's more extraordinary lines of dialogue, 'he'll pay through the nose 'til his eyes drop out.'

Assembled at Shepperton, various distinguished British thespians – Donald Wolfit, Felix Aylmer, Basil Sidney, Donald Pleasence – dutifully mouthed their lines in French for the 'version Française' but were dubbed in post-production. Not so Lee and the film's stolid American leading man, Mel Ferrer, who filmed at Nice as well as Shepperton and whose French dialogue is preserved in *Les Mains d'Orlac*. 'I think my performance in French,' Lee observed, 'was probably far better than the one in English because I could do more with the language.'[4] Lee's French performance does indeed have a touch more brio, gestural as well as vocal, but in either version he cuts a splendidly hateful figure. The pixie-like Dany Carrel also performed in both languages, as well as contributing a spot of off-hand toplessness to the French version (artfully obscured by Lee's head in the English one) and singing a delightful nightclub number called 'C'est parti'. For his own nightclub performance, Lee was coached by the magician Billy McComb, though, with most of Nero's tricks being achieved by elementary optical effects, McComb's participation was little more than a formality.

Nero first appears over half an hour into the film, poring over a newspaper in the cramped lobby of Marseilles' Hôtel du Midi and immediately smelling an opportunity when Orlac books in. Intrigued, he tells Li-Lang that he thinks he's seen Orlac somewhere before. 'Maybe in gaol,' she mutters, adding reproachfully, 'You hate people. You made me a slut.' 'Made?' he counters smoothly. 'My dear, I couldn't stop you. You were born a slut and you'll always be one. It is I who have lowered myself.' The note of vainglorious self-aggrandisement here is developed later in the picture, with the threadbare Nero referring to himself and the monied Orlac as 'we men of the world' and 'we artists'. In the meantime, however, he learns of Orlac's hand-fixation and visits him in his room, pretending to have been an acquaintance of the executed strangler. Extending a commiserating hand, he says, 'In memory of my poor friend Louis Vasseur, would you permit me to shake his hand?' – and his maniacal laughter rings tauntingly down the corridor as Orlac rushes distraught from the room.

Nero's blackmail campaign even extends to the bedroom of Orlac's Riviera villa, where he issues like a shadow from behind a mirror in which the supine Orlac is reflected. Wearing a grotesque mask, steel pincers for hands and a livid prosthetic scar on his neck, he soon abandons his Vasseur disguise and sits down chummily on the bed. 'It was a very convincing performance, wasn't it?' he twinkles. 'I should have been famous too, you know: as famous as you are.' (Though the lines about being famous are missing from the French cut, the hectic gaiety with which Lee plays the scene makes it clear in both versions that Nero isn't merely opportunistic but certifiably insane.) He then follows Orlac to London and restages his magic act for nightclub manager Felix (Peter Reynolds). Lee's posturings at rehearsal are very funny indeed, but afterwards Nero learns that Felix intends to ditch him and, in response to public demand, build up the glamorous Li-Lang instead. 'If they want your body,' he slyly informs her, 'then they must have it' – and after submitting her to a deliberately botched sword trick, he has a last struggle with Orlac before being apprehended by the police. The climactic fight was a tough one, with Lee banging his forehead on an iron pipe and Ferrer accidentally bloodying his co-star's nose.

Sadly, several of Gréville's visual affectations were dropped in the UK version, while his fanciful French dialogue (written under his usual Max Montagut pseudonym) was brought crashingly down to earth by Donald Taylor's Anglicised equivalent. As for Lee, his French scenes are spiced with amusing extra details, notably when he slaps a passing chorine's bottom rather than merely looking back at it appreciatively as he does in the English version. The oddest variation comes when Nero is hustled away by the police at the end. In English, he is granted a final, trademark burst of insane laughter off-camera, whereas in French he is bundled off in ignominious silence.

Lee's stint in Nice, playing a role entirely in French, must have made his next Hammer engagement, in which he was required merely to affect a French accent, seem like a piece of cake. *Taste of Fear* had been fashioned by screenwriter Jimmy Sangster in the corkscrew mould of Henri-Georges Clouzot's *Les Diaboliques* and involved a Hammer crew spending some two weeks on the French Riviera, picking up glamorous location shots at Cap d'Antibes, Villefranche, Nice and elsewhere. Lee only joined up when the unit returned to Elstree in November and was purposely cast in red herring mode as Dr Pierre Gerrard, coincidentally the same name as his character in a previous Sangster script, *The Man Who Could Cheat Death*. 'My only tip to you is not to be thrown by the presence of Hammer's Tame Fiend, Christopher Lee,' noted critic Felix Barker. 'He plays a French doctor with a very creditable accent and I kept a wary eye on him. I am happy to report that he did not revert to his old Dracula trick of blood-sucking ... There should be an Oscar for such good behaviour.'[5]

Sangster had first offered *Taste of Fear*, then called *See No Evil*, to the veteran producer Sydney Box but the script eventually found its way, by a route almost as circuitous as Sangster's plot, to his old friends at Hammer, who gave Sangster the opportunity to produce the film as well as write it. In doing so, they inaugurated a profitable sideline in chilly black-and-white suspense thrillers that carried them through a sticky patch in the early 1960s when the British censor was taking a much harder line with their colourful Gothic horrors. Directed by former Ealing editor Seth Holt, *Taste of Fear* is a taut little thriller in which wheelchair-bound Penny Appleby comes to her

Dr Pierre Gerrard in Seth Holt's serpentine thriller Taste of Fear *(1960)*

father's Côte d'Azur villa only to find Daddy mysteriously absent. On several occasions, his corpse pops up in 'now you see him, now you don't' style and Penny becomes convinced that her stepmother Jane is conspiring with the family doctor to have her certified insane.

As the last of several clever revelations, we discover at the end that Jane and her chauffeur Bob are the duplicitous conspirators while Penny and Dr Gerrard are involved in a conspiracy of their own, to expose the killers of Penny's father. We also discover that Penny isn't Penny but her former companion Maggie. It's the kind of serpentine plot that Sangster began to specialise in having abandoned the Hammer Gothics, and, like most of its successors, it doesn't stand up to close scrutiny. It's realised, however, with great style by Holt, luminously shot by Douglas Slocombe and held together by a persuasive performance from Susan Strasberg, daughter of Method guru Lee Strasberg.

The other headliners are Ann Todd and Ronald Lewis, with Lee relaxed and quietly authoritative in a smaller role. Penny's first encounter with her father's corpse ends with her plunging into the villa's swimming pool, wheelchair and all, and Dr Gerrard's face emerges from her splashy ordeal in a forbidding medium close-up. Taking her pulse, he remarks glibly that 'Imagination is a very funny thing, you know' and provides her with a sedative. He reappears later on for an edgy lunchtime sequence in which he pronounces that 'Shocks ... can deal the mind a very serious blow, a blow which could affect it permanently,' an observation naturally taken by Penny as an indication that she's likely to go insane. At dinner he broaches the subject of 'hysterical paralysis'. Given that Penny is confined to a wheelchair, in doing so he puts his foot in it again, bringing another meal to an uncomfortable, silent conclusion.

All these tight-lipped exchanges are seen in a new light, of course, when we realise at the end that Gerrard and Penny, or rather Maggie, have been 'acting' all along in order to hoodwink Jane and Bob. Gerrard makes a last appearance on a Riviera clifftop, looking down at Jane's body floating near the rocks below – for reasons too complex to go into, Bob has kicked her over the edge – and then brings the curtain down with the hackneyed line, 'Come away, Maggie: there's nothing more for you here.'

Lee's French accent is impeccable and he still rates *Taste of Fear* as the best Hammer film he ever appeared in, reserving particularly high praise for Seth Holt, whose career was derailed by alcoholism prior to his untimely death in 1971. During shooting, Susan Strasberg was sometimes put off her stroke by the watchful presence on the sidelines of her mother Paula, former mentor to Marilyn Monroe. Lee, meanwhile, was momentarily fazed by a visit from Gary Cooper, who was making *The Naked Edge* on an adjacent stage with Peter Cushing among the supporting cast. 'Can you imagine,' Lee remarked, 'seeing one of the great stars in the history of cinema looking at you from behind a camera? I was literally bereft of speech.'[6] He could add this encounter to his chat at Shepperton earlier in the year with Cary Grant, who was at work on *The Grass is Greener* while Lee was occupied with *Orlac*.

After *Taste of Fear*, Lee was pencilled in for a reunion with Edmond T Gréville. A Cannes-based company, Méditerranée Cinéma, proposed to start shooting their adaptation of the Frédéric Dard bestseller, *Cette mort dont tu parlais*, on 2 January 1961, with Lee cast opposite Dawn Addams. The film materialised as *Les Menteurs*, with Addams on board but with Jean Servais substituting for Lee. *Taste of Fear*, meanwhile, was released on 5 June 1961, not long after the broadcast of one of Lee's increasingly rare forays into television.

One Step Beyond was a series of 25-minute dramas which, like *The Twilight Zone*, explored what director/presenter John Newland called 'man's adventure in the world of the unknown, that mysterious psychic world beyond our five senses.' For its final 13 instalments it moved from the MGM lot in Hollywood to the MGM British Studios at Borehamwood, with Lee's old Fairbanks chum, Peter Marriott, in overall charge. *The Sorcerer* was shown on 23 May 1961 and starred Lee as Oberleutnant Wilhelm Reitlinger, the head of the 23rd Signals Unit in the First World War who suspects that his sweetheart Elsa is entertaining most of the 71st Grenadiers back in Berlin. With the telekinetic help of a weird old farmer (Martin Benson), he's transported 800 kilometres in the blink of an eye and shoots her dead. Gabriella Licudi is a wooden Elsa but, one brief drunk scene excepted, Lee paints a convincing mini-portrait of an unhappy loser, described by his superior officer (Joseph Furst) as 'difficult, troublesome and temperamentally unstable.'

Exploring the Underworld

'He lives in Belgravia,' claimed the publicity material for *The Hands of Orlac*, 'and, though much pursued, is still unmarried.' Shortly before making *Orlac*, however, Lee had been informed by Danish friends of a beautiful painter and Dior model, Birgit Kroencke, whom, they felt sure, would be an ideal match for him. A meeting in Copenhagen on Boxing Day 1960 was followed, on Friday 17 March 1961, by a quiet wedding at St Michael's Chester Square. Without the luxury of a conventional honeymoon – Lee had to start work on an Edgar Wallace picture the following Monday – the newly weds decided to string out their honeymoon across the year, snatching whatever opportunities were available between pictures and starting with a weekend in Brighton. A night at the Royal Albion Hotel was followed by two at the Roedean home of Hammer chief James Carreras.

Interviewed soon afterwards by *Sunday Express* showbiz columnist Jack Bentley, Birgit – or Gitte as her friends called her – claimed that 'I hadn't seen Chris in horror films before I met him. Horror films are banned in Denmark. But I've seen them since and I want him to go on being a screen monster. You see, monsters never get the girl in the end.' Speaking of Gitte in February 1995, Lee pointed out that 'We shall have been married 34 years next month and I still love her as much as I ever did. She's an incredibly patient woman, cheerful and full of fun, which I am not always.'[7]

The Edgar Wallace picture was an Anglo-German co-production called *The Devil's Daffodil* in the UK and *Das Geheimnis der gelben Narzissen* in Germany. Starting with Harald Reinl's *Der Frosch mit der Maske* in 1959, jazzy Edgar Wallace adaptations were wildly popular with German audiences throughout the 1960s, generally with the clean-limbed Joachim Fuchsberger as the hero and the rubber-faced Eddi Arent as the comic relief. Taking their cue from the bestselling taschenkrimis to be found on every German bookstall, the films were known as krimis and united the doom-laden world of Dr Mabuse with a tongue-in-cheek 1960s sensibility.

With Gitte at St Michael's Chester Square, Friday 17 March 1961

Shot at Shepperton and on location in London and Hamburg, *The Devil's Daffodil* saw Steven Pallos and Donald Taylor, producers of *The Hands of Orlac*, cashing in on the trend with a picture shot, like *Orlac*, in two versions. This time, however, some of the film's British actors were replaced by German ones to give the film greater appeal for German audiences. Lee, Marius Goring, Albert Lieven, Ingrid van Bergen and Peter Illing were common to both versions, but *Das Geheimnis* substituted Joachim Fuchsberger for hero William Lucas, Sabina Sesselmann for heroine Penelope Horner and Klaus Kinski for 'daffodil killer' Colin Jeavons. And, again like *Orlac*, Pallos and Taylor chose a director familiar with working in both countries; the Hungarian Akos von Rathony had previously made a breezy farce, *Don't Blame the Stork*, in British studios in 1953.

Lee is Hong Kong detective Ling Chu, necessitating another use of his least favourite prosthetic enhancement, the epicanthic fold around the eyes. Ling Chu teams up with security expert Jack Tarling (Lucas/Fuchsberger) and Scotland Yard's Superintendent Whiteside (Walter Gotell) to solve a series of murders linked to a narcotics racket masterminded by wealthy merchant Raymond Lyne (Lieven). 'Each time the daffodil killer strikes,' panted the pressbook, 'the mystery intensifies. Suspense is as taut as a cheese-cutter when Tarling's chief suspect is found dead – his body covered in daffodils. And then there is the nerve-shaking climax when the killer's identity is revealed and the hunt for the most dangerous man in Britain is on.'

The climax is well-staged but somewhat less than nerve-shaking; it takes place in a cemetery, with the drug-addled killer dragging Lyne's secretary, Anne Rider (Horner/Sesselmann), into a mausoleum where Ling Chu is lying in wait for him. As the father of one of the daffodil-strewn victims, the vengeful Ling Chu is quick to knife the madman, after which Tarling leads Anne to safety and the credits roll. Neatly turned out in a variety of bow ties and straw hats, Ling Chu is a dapper figure much given to oracular pronouncements like 'There is no flotsam without jetsam.' Lee's three Oriental appearances thus far – in *The Nightingale*, *The Terror of the Tongs* and now *The Devil's Daffodil* – make his eventual casting as Fu Manchu seem, in retrospect, inevitable. In the meantime, Ling Chu gave a faintly bookish tone to his honeymoon. 'I had my lines to learn, in English and German,' he reported. 'Contriving a Chinese accent when I spoke the German lines was a new problem. Being fluent in German, Gitte was able to hearken to me, though naturally the Chinese aspect was new to her as well.'

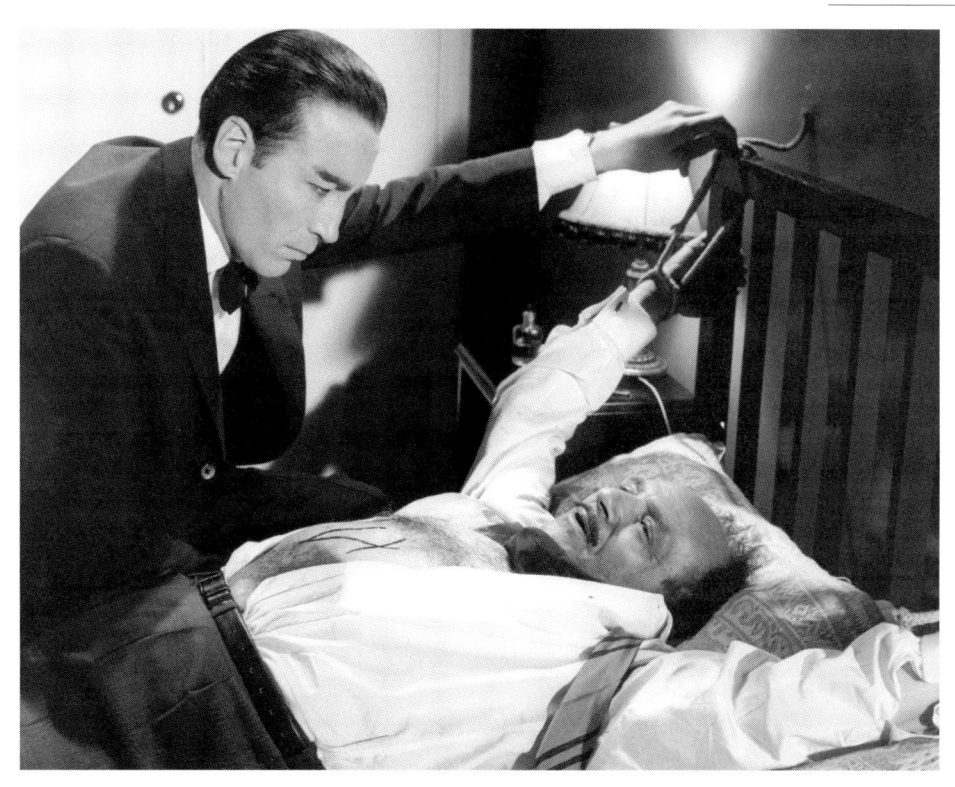

Hong Kong detective Ling Chu interrogates nightclub owner Jan Putek (Peter Illing) in The Devil's Daffodil / Das Geheimnis der gelben Narzissen *(1961)*

Having contributed to one Continental trend, Lee moved on to another, plunging into the gaudy and irrational world of Italian horror pictures. After the jocular tone of *Tempi duri per i vampiri*, Italian horror had assumed a straight face with Mario Bava's highly atmospheric *La maschera del demonio*, which conferred stardom on the sepulchral British beauty Barbara Steele and made a killing in the US when released there as *Black Sunday*. With *Ercole al centro della terra*, which began filming on 29 May 1961, Bava ventured into the extremely lucrative 'peplum' genre (otherwise known as 'sword and sandal' pictures) but chose to turn the film, as one critic has put it, into 'a sort of horror-vampire movie in which only by chance is the hero named Hercules.'[8]

As well as being the godfather of Italian horror pictures, Bava was a master cinematographer and special effects wizard, and had proved his mettle by directing, uncredited, large chunks of Pietro Francisci's *Le fatiche di Ercole* and *Ercole e la regina di Lidia*. As *Hercules* and *Hercules Unchained*, these had been two of the biggest international moneyspinners in the history of the Italian film industry, and the third picture was entrusted to Bava alone. In *Ercole al centro della terra* he set aside the queasy monochrome of *La maschera del demonio* and began experimenting with the abstract use of vividly coloured gel lighting.

He also set himself an unusual challenge. 'I had made a bet,' he explained, 'to shoot a film using only a wall one could take apart, a door and a window and four movable columns; nothing else. I did it by continuing to move those elements around in a series of backgrounds and foregrounds.'[9]

Utilising the bare bones of a temple set familiar from countless Italian epics, Bava smothered it in smoke and bold splotches of colour with results that are often strikingly handsome. Lee is Lico, demonic ruler of the Earth's core, whose palace resides in a strange landscape stained crimson and blue, its apparently lavish throne room open to a blood-red sky. As with *Tempi duri per i vampiri*, the film's English version (*Hercules in the Centre of the Earth*) doesn't retain Lee's original dialogue track, substituting for it a rather weedy voice that fails to match up to his imposing appearance, decked out in a black leather tunic and cloak plus a prototype Beatle wig. In the pre-credits sequence, Lico hovers over a prostrate beauty and the anonymous dubber intones, 'Evil shall triumph, even over the Gods, to dominate the Earth.' Whereupon Bava inserts some memorably creepy shots of groping zombie hands and grating sarcophagus lids.

Lico has Hercules' lover Daianara in his thrall – at one point she responds to his summons by rising

Lico, prince of the Underworld, in Mario Bava's stylish Ercole al centro della terra *(1961)*

from a slab in the plank-like fashion patented by *Nosferatu* – and, to restore her soul, Hercules and Theseus have to journey to the Underworld and recover the Golden Apple. (Just the one – this is a low-budget film.) While Hercules appropriates their prize, his sleeping friends are visited by a charming stone robot that drones 'You must be longer' as it places Theseus on a rack. Seeing that Hercules has evaded this and other hazards, the disconcerted Lico consults a Sibylline oracle. 'You must take into your veins the blood of Daianara,' it tells him. 'With her death, you shall gain eternal life.' Lico limbers up by killing the beautiful Helena, his face reflected in a pool of her blood as he says simply, 'Yes, it was I.' He then carries the white-robed Daianara through cobwebbed catacombs and makes ready to sacrifice her by the light of the moon.

The demented resurrection sequence that follows reintroduces the shrouded zombies glimpsed at the beginning and hurls them in vast numbers at the camera as well as at Hercules. Though the flying ghouls are fitted with visible wires, their battle with Hercules is one of the most remarkable scenes in Bava's portfolio, simultaneously ridiculous and disturbing. Lico himself is immobilised under a polystyrene menhir and, after Hercules has thrown several more at the pursuing zombies, bursts into flames at the rising of the sun.

For all its comic-book accoutrements, *Ercole al centro della terra* is a dark and doom-laden picture, and the actors, including Lee, move through it with a kind of deathly serenity. The blank-faced beauties are Leonora Ruffo (Daianara) and Rosalba Neri (Helena), while the South African muscleman Reg Park gives Hercules himself a suitably bovine impassivity. Giorgio Ardisson, as Theseus, would reappear with Lee in *Katarsis* while Gaïa Germani, hidden behind the mask of the Sybilline oracle, resurfaced as the heroine of *Il castello dei morti vivi*. Though poker-faced in the film, Lee and the amiable Park had severe 'corpsing' problems during the shooting, regularly dissolving into uncontrollable gales of laughter. 'Bava was sitting there, absolutely glaring at us,' Lee remembers, 'and he didn't glare very often. It was my fault.'

After this spell at Cinecittà Studios, Lee returned to Bray for a punishing project called *The Pirates of Blood River*, which started on 3 July. Hammer head James Carreras had noticed a gap in the market around the school holiday period and the company's schedules accordingly began to fill up with highly coloured matinée swashbucklers. Even so, *The Pirates of Blood River* contrives to kick off with big-breasted glamour model Marie Devereux being consumed by piranha fish, confirming that the best of the Hammer swashbucklers would look and feel exactly like the horrors, only with the Gothic edges knocked off. To bolster this impression, Lee would star in two of them while Oliver Reed, Hammer's youthful werewolf, turned up in no fewer than four.

Explaining Hammer's apparent change of direction, producer Anthony Nelson Keys suggested that 'It's a good idea to have a different film. It's like going to the seaside. Everyone has a wonderful time – then comes back refreshed.'[1] '*Pirates* was a fearsome film to work on,' Lee countered in his autobiography. 'Gitte could well have been widowed.' Likened by Lee to the noxious tarn surrounding Poe's House of Usher, a stagnant lake in the middle of Black Park provided the chief dangers, with Lee and his scurvy crew wading waist-deep through the evil-smelling slime and Oliver Reed being hospitalised with an eye infection. Despite these privations, Lee was no doubt pleased to be returning as a star to the buccaneering genre in which he'd made some minor appearances in the 1950s, and his performance as the black-hearted LaRoche is accordingly one of his best to date.

'He's a great man, the Captain,' says the diminutive Mac, played by Hammer regular Michael Ripper. 'As strong as a lion, as cunning as a mongoose, and as vicious as a snake ... He's not like other men: he don't even sweat!' Recycling his French accent from *Taste of Fear*, Lee brings a new mellifluousness to it in a delightfully laconic introductory scene. Setting out his two-faced stall for the benefit of escaped convict Jonathan Standing, he promises to return him to the Caribbean Huguenot settlement lorded over by Jonathan's despotic father, Jason, in return for a cache of gold stored there. When the take-over of the settlement turns predictably violent and Jonathan protests, LaRoche dismisses the homicidal behaviour of his aptly named henchman, Hench, with the coolly philosophical observation that 'Unfortunately, human nature is apt to determine where peace ends and strife begins.'

Complete with a black eyepatch and a paralysed left hand clutched to his side, LaRoche provides a foretaste of Lee's one-eyed Rochefort in *The Three Musketeers* and his disabled ex-Nazi in *Massarati and the Brain*. A quietly dangerous figure, LaRoche seems to exercise complete dominion over his men and presides over a terrifically intense scene in which he outlines his plans to the assembled Huguenots in their Judgment House. 'We do not yield to the Devil!' insists Jonathan's deposed father (played by another Hammer regular, Andrew Keir). 'A very noble and praiseworthy sentiment,' smiles LaRoche in reply, 'but you may change your mind when you find how persuasive the Devil can be.' Unlike Chung King in *The Terror of the Tongs*, whose 'means of persuasion' were exacted in private, LaRoche publicly proposes to execute a Huguenot per day until the location of the treasure is revealed.

Lee delivers lines like 'Mr Hench, you will see to it that no one remains alive' with a suitably cold-eyed imperturbability, but also shows that LaRoche is capable of being hurt when the inebriated Mac amuses his mates with a clutched-hand impersonation of him. Discovering that the gold is stored in a colossal statue of the colony's founder, the pirates set off on a woodland trek back to their ship, towing the statue behind them and taking Jonathan and his father as hostages. Several Black Park trees are chopped down in a gripping ambush sequence and LaRoche finally faces a mutiny led by the disillusioned Mac. An exciting duel with Kerwin Mathews' vengeful Jonathan ends with LaRoche impaled to a tree when Jonathan resorts, rather unsportingly, to throwing his sword at him.

The Pirates of Blood River is one of Hammer's most accomplished entertainments, directed with no-nonsense precision by swashbuckling specialist John Gilling and beautifully photographed by Arthur Grant. The casting, too, is spot on, with the notable exception of Glenn Corbett, a Columbia choice, as Jonathan's friend Henry. The film was double-billed at the Pavilion with Columbia's *Mysterious Island*, the combination of Ray Harryhausen monsters with Hammer's landlocked pirate thrills subsequently smashing box-office records across the ABC circuit and becoming the most successful double-feature of 1962. With no trace of pantomime straining-after-effect, Lee's

Impaled to a Black Park tree as LaRoche in The Pirates of Blood River *(1961)*

smoothly malevolent performance in *The Pirates of Blood River* proved, to attentive viewers, that he was now a screen villain of the master class.

FISHER OUT OF WATER

After diversions in Italy and Berkshire, German assignments assumed centre stage through the remainder of 1961 and into 1962. The first of these was a British co-production, filmed in separate versions, that took Lee to Ireland rather than Germany. In the first week of November 1961, the *Daily Cinema*'s C H B Williamson dropped the following tidbit into his 'Studio wise' column. 'Making the break from comedy ... Paddy Carstairs sends me a note from Dublin telling me his drama is going fine in its fifth week at Ardmore [Studios]. *The Devil's Agent*, he says, has a great cast: Peter Van Eyck, Marianne Koch, Christopher Lee, MacDonald Carey, Helen Cherry, Billie Whitelaw, David Knight, Colin Gordon, Niall MacGuinness [sic] and others. Says JPC, "It's lovely to be back on drama!"' [11]

Elder brother of Hammer's Anthony Nelson Keys, John Paddy Carstairs was the director responsible for Norman Wisdom's early successes and *The Devil's Agent*, a deviation from his comic path, proved to be his last picture. Indeed, his reference to the film 'going fine' may have been wishful thinking. Lee acknowledged that the actors were accommodated 'in a delightful hotel [Conna Hall] whose suites were all named after Irish writers' but also pointed out that the production 'staggered from crisis to crisis as it was never certain whether the money would be coming for the next reel.'

Known in its German version as *Im Namen des Teufels*, the picture cropped up in Williamson's column again four days later. 'Paddy Carstairs tells me Peter Cushing, Peter Vaughan and Mike Brennan are latest additions to the cast of *The Devil's Agent* ... [The film] will complete in the studio on 17 November and then go to Vienna for exteriors.' [12] The reference to Cushing's participation is a further indication of the picture's troubled history. Lee never met his Hammer co-star while working on the film and, when it was released in December 1962, Cushing's scenes had, for reasons unknown, been cut from it.

It's easy to see how this was done, however, because the film is hopelessly episodic and clocks in at a rather undernourished 77 minutes. The humdrum story revolves around wine merchant George Droste (Van Eyck), who is inveigled into becoming a double agent by Lee's monied industrialist, Baron von Staub, when the old friends meet at von Staub's estate in Germany's Soviet sector. Droste soon finds himself delivering packages to Vienna on behalf of the Baron's sister, Countess Cosimano (Cherry), running errands for an American agent (Carey) in Budapest, and smuggling Nazi archives back into West Berlin at the behest of the two-faced General Greenhahn (Marius Goring). The film actually consists of three humdrum stories, clumsily cobbled together, proceeding in disorienting fits and starts, and coming to an inconclusive end in which Droste settles down with Hungarian refugee Nora Gulden (Koch). *The Devil's Agent* betrays signs of its chop-and-change production throughout, though Lee and Helen Cherry are smoothly duplicitous as the German aristocrats-cum-Soviet agents.

From Dublin the Lees decamped to Hamburg for another krimi, based this time on Edgar Wallace's 1932 novel *When the Gangs Came to London*. Despite its multi-national working title – *Gangster in London* – the film became known in Germany as *Das Rätsel der roten Orchidee* and was shown to English-speaking audiences as *The Secret of the Red Orchid*. Shooting stretched from 12 December 1961 to 15 January 1962 at Hamburg's REAL-Film Studio, where Lee was driven to break one of his cardinal rules. The autocratic behaviour of Helmut Ashley made the filming a nightmarish experience and, setting aside his vow never to fall out openly with a director, Lee was moved at one point to retaliate. 'Now I can understand how it was that Hitler was an Austrian!' he exclaimed. Acting in German, Lee was required to play an FBI agent investigating a Chicago mobster who has moved to London. Amongst other effronteries, Ashley presumed to criticise Lee's German-American accent, but it's seamlessly done and certainly preferable to the comically inappropriate

Soviet agent Baron von Staub and unsuspecting vintner George Droste (Peter Van Eyck) in The Devil's Agent / Im Namen des Teufels *(1961)*

American voice dubbed over Lee's dialogue in the English version.

Lee's Captain Allerman glides through most of the action in a trilby and mackintosh, enjoying edgy banter with Eric Pohlmann's elephantine Kirky Minelli and a brief interview with the diminutive Klaus Kinski, playing a rival gang boss oddly described in the opening credits as 'the beautiful Steve.' ('Polente!' – 'Pigs!' – squawks Steve's pet parrot at sight of the Captain.) Lee changes to a beret and commando gear for an abortive security operation, and then appears in pyjamas for some fisticuffs in a sleeping car. 'You're not Norris!' gasps the would-be assassin whom Allerman has disarmed and handcuffed. 'No, Babyface,' Allerman grins as he removes his stick-on moustache and goatee. 'I'm from Chicago, just like you!'

Lee's best scene is a nocturnal one in which he's stalked by another would-be assassin, whips two revolvers from his mackintosh, shoots his pursuer and then twirls the revolvers round his fingers with Wild West aplomb. Blowing down both barrels, he quips 'Doppelt hält besser!' ('Two is better than one!') and strides contentedly into the night. Prefiguring the glib one-liners that would soon become James Bond's stock-in-trade, this delightful moment is somewhat diluted in the English version, where the mystery US voice merely drawls 'Too slow, buddy.' Allerman finally joins his Scotland Yard opposite number (Adrian Hoven) for a subterranean chase and shoot-out, the villain expiring on the pavement above while clutching a parking meter. Eddi Arent is on hand as an exaggeratedly posh 'comedy' butler, the heroine is the lovely Marisa Mell and Minelli's free-spending wife is played by Christiane Nielsen, badgering her husband into a life of organised crime and at one point leafing through an Edgar Wallace paperback. The tone is lighthearted throughout, with full-blown slapstick intruding as the gang warfare escalates and uncredited composer Pete Thomas chucking in bits of 'Mary Had a Little Lamb' and 'Auld Lang Syne' to add to the film's mock-British flavour.

While Lee was occupied with these German pictures, Hammer were at work on a film that he had expressed a wish to appear in as long ago as December 1958. 'Do you know my biggest ambition in horror?' he confided to journalist Sarah Stoddart. 'To star in a remake of The Phantom of the Opera. This film would give me a chance to prove that I can sing.' [13] Still wanting to make 'prestige' subjects, Hammer passed over Lee in favour of Herbert Lom, who gave them a memorably forlorn Phantom but wasn't required to sing in any case. Lee's disappointment may have been tempered somewhat when Terence

Captain Allerman on the track of Chicago gangsters in the Edgar Wallace thriller Das Rätsel der roten Orchidee (1961)

Fisher's film performed poorly at the UK box-office, but for the time being he and Gitte were fully occupied with a move to Switzerland, setting up home there in March 1962. A Swiss residence entailed a less punitive tax bill than a Belgravia one, and made sense, too, given the proliferation of Continental pictures Lee was being offered. Villa Kefissia was a modest bungalow on the northern shore of Lake Geneva, commanding a view of the Rhone Valley and within striking distance of Vevey. In the depths of winter, however, it revealed cracks in its pleasing façade that echoed Lee's growing disenchantment with his Swiss exile, a disenchantment which ensured that it would ultimately last little more than three years. Outwardly bracing, the atmosphere of Switzerland soon proved enervating.

Adjusting to Lake Geneva, Lee took things rather more easily in 1962 than he had in 1961, though this restfulness was not of his choosing. He was required to establish his residency by spending six months in the country out of his first 12, and remembers that

CHRISTOPHER LEE – PART FOUR

'1962 was a bad year, probably the worst year of my career apart from the time when I worked in Simpson's. I wasn't making any money – though, admittedly, the franc was 12 to the pound and the tax that I was paying as a foreign resident was minute.' Soon after his 40th birthday, however, Lee took on his first engagement as a fully fledged 'Euro-actor'. Shot in East Germany and the Republic of Ireland during July and August, *Sherlock Holmes und das Halsband des Todes* was made by Artur Brauner's CCC (Central Cinema Company) at his extremely busy Haselhorst Atelier in Spandau. The film was touted as the 'gruselig-spannenden Leichenrevue' ('the chiller-thriller corpse cabaret') and, presumably because of his success with *The Hound of the Baskervilles*, Terence Fisher was coaxed away from his Twickenham home to direct, bringing with him one of his favourite character actors, Thorley Walters, to play Dr Watson.

'They were doing something that really was impossible to do,' Walters recalled. 'They would have a Frenchman playing with you in one scene speaking French, and the Germans speaking in German in the same scene ... It was impossible to tell, if you were addressing lines to somebody in English and they replied in German and somebody else replied in French, where you were ... We all had trouble with the management,' he added darkly. 'I can't give you more details – libel and that!'[14] Lee is also not to be drawn regarding the film's off-camera controversies, except to say that the tension between Brauner and his associate Heinrich von Leipziger (aka Henry E Lester) caused Terence Fisher to lose his temper for the first and only time in Lee's experience. And, though Lee was becoming used to the kind of Babel described by Walters, Fisher was not and the film was eventually co-directed by his first assistant, Frank Winterstein. The film's production problems also put paid to a proposed follow-up in which Lee's Holmes was to tangle with Jack the Ripper. Deserting Brauner, Leipziger/Lester teamed up with Michael Klinger and Tony Tenser in London and the Holmes/Ripper idea emerged as *A Study in Terror*, starring John Neville.

Ruinously dubbed in its English version (*Sherlock Holmes and the Deadly Necklace*), Fisher's film has acquired a misplaced reputation as a total disaster. In fact, there's nothing much wrong with it that the restoration of Lee and Walters' original dialogue tracks wouldn't put right; that and the removal of a hideously inappropriate jazz score. The reconstruction of 221b Baker Street is meticulously done, as is the period recreation of an Edwardian capital thronged with motor cars rather than horse-drawn cabs. (As was customary during the 1960s, Dublin was used as a stand-in for turn-of-the-century London.) Though bearing virtually no relation to *The Valley of Fear* as initial trade announcements suggested it would, the screenplay is a neat enough puzzle from Curt Siodmak, brother of Robert and writer of Hollywood classics like *The Wolf Man* and *The Beast with Five Fingers*. As for the actors, Hans Söhnker is an agreeably baleful Moriarty (or 'Moriarity' as the American dubbers insist on calling him), while Lee and Walters are ideally cast as Holmes and Watson.

Lee's Holmes is introduced in the guise of a lanky old sea-dog, a rather skimpy get-up that Watson and Mrs Hudson inexplicably fail to see through. Revealing his true self, we find that Lee has been fitted by make-up man Heinz Stamm with an unusually severe widow's peak and a prosthetically enlarged nose, the better to approximate Sidney Paget's original *Strand* magazine illustrations; indeed, as Holmes consults his newspaper, we're treated to several lengthy profile shots to make sure the enhanced hooter doesn't go unnoticed. Lee has pointed out that his Holmes was an attempt 'to play him really as he was written, as a very intolerant, argumentative, difficult man,'[15] and yet his performance is a relaxed and occasionally playful one, providing a blueprint for the almost skittish Holmes he would play in 1990. He indulges in a bizarre fencing match with Watson – a bread knife and a rolled-up copy of the *Times* their chosen weapons – and is all smiles as he elucidates the dying gesture of a Baker Street visitor. He also conducts a couple of interrogations with his knuckles parked nonchalantly on one cheek.

The plot has something to do with the theft of an invaluable necklace that once belonged to Cleopatra. Holmes recovers it from an Egyptian sarcophagus concealed in Moriarty's apartment and then resumes his sea-dog disguise – donkey jacket, eyepatch, walrus moustache, etc – in order to infiltrate Moriarty's docklands gang. In the Hare and Eagle, he disables one of the thugs by throwing a dart at him, after which the anonymous dubber unleashes his pièce de resistance, giving Holmes' sea-dog a ridiculously fey East End accent. A police van robbery is then conducted from the sewers – Lee was disconcerted to learn that the evil-smelling location for this sequence had been a poison gas factory during the war – and Moriarty evades capture on a technicality, though Holmes has the satisfaction of restoring the deadly necklace to the auction rooms right under his nose.

Thanks to the disastrous soundtrack applied to the film's English version, Lee's first stab at Holmes has to remain a tantalising 'might-have-been', but at least the Dublin scenes provided him with an unlooked-for insight into his lineage. Relaxing between takes in a

A Sidney Paget illustration come to life: Holmes and Watson (Thorley Walters) with dying informer Jenkins (Franco Giacobini) in Sherlock Holmes und das Halsband des Todes *(1962)*

local pub (still dressed, somewhat ostentatiously, in the full rig of deerstalker and Inverness cape), he was approached by a group of Romany drinkers. Their probing enquiries into his parentage suggested to him that he might be the inheritor of gypsy blood on his father's side.

SUMMER 1963: OVERWHELMINGLY ITALIAN

From focusing on German productions, Lee headed south for further Gothic adventures in Italy, completing no fewer than four such films in less than three months.

On 7 May 1963, he arrived in Rome to begin filming *La frusta e il corpo* (The Whip and the Body), which marked a reunion with the inspirational Mario Bava. Going into release on 29 August, the film found itself charged with obscenity by a single scandalised cinemagoer (an action that was subsequently dropped). A fabulously over-ripe Gothic melodrama, the film cast Lee as sadistic aristocrat Kurt Menliff, whose own father tells him that 'You're not my son; you're a serpent.' Kurt's whip-wielding romance with his masochistic sister-in-law Nevenka is so strong it survives his death, and it was this taboo-busting S & M relationship that caused the threatened legal

The whip (Kurt Menliff) and the body (Nevenka): with Daliah Lavi in Mario Bava's luscious La frusta e il corpo *(1963)*

action. It also provides an echo of James Mason's behaviour in the old Gainsborough bodice-rippers, as well as laying bare the darker undercurrents of Gothic classics like *Wuthering Heights* and *Jane Eyre*.

Though stamped through and through with Bava's trademark visual magic, *La frusta* also betrays a more contemporary influence. The sea dappled pink by the sunset, Kurt thunders on horseback through the surf as the film begins, an opening that no doubt reminded alert 1960s filmgoers of the many barren shorelines in Roger Corman's popular Poe pictures for AIP. And the echo wasn't accidental. Very much an Italian equivalent to Hammer's Jimmy Sangster, the film's ubiquitous writer, Ernesto Gastaldi, admitted that 'The producers, Ugo Guerra and Elio Scardamaglia, showed me an Italian print of [Corman's] *Pit and the Pendulum* before I started writing it. "Give us something like this," they said … Christopher Lee wasn't free when the project started,' he added. 'Afterwards he became free and his name helped the producers to secure a good minimo garantito from the distributors.'[16]

As Kurt, Lee has never looked more Byronic. Yet again, we have to listen to someone else droning through his dialogue – particularly frustrating, given that the film was shot entirely in English – but there's not a lot of it on this occasion because Kurt is reduced to a ghostly presence for most of his screen time. Kurt gets a frosty reception when reappearing, prodigal son-style, at his ancestral mansion and then corners Nevenka (Daliah Lavi) on the beach. Filmed at Anzio, 20 miles outside Rome, this first encounter is a scintillatingly erotic one. It starts with a passionate kiss and then, as Nevenka subsides onto a rock, Kurt lays into her with his horsewhip. 'You haven't changed, I see,' he sneers. 'You always loved violence.' Once Kurt has laid open the back of her white blouse under a hail of rapid blows, the scene ends with the supine pair enfolding each other on the rocks as Kurt's horse nuzzles the pink-hued surf in the distance. A large part of the film's power derives from the disturbing way in which Bava renders eye-popping displays of sexual violence in the most achingly romantic images.

A storm rising, Kurt retires to his bedroom and is stabbed behind the arras by an unseen assailant – the unhinged Nevenka as it subsequently turns out. Expiring in death-rattling disbelief even as he pulls the dagger from his throat, Kurt is rapidly consigned to the family vault, where his father (Gustavo de Nardo) views the corpse with the grudging observation, 'I had to stand the sight of him alive; it can't be any worse now.' Soon, however, Kurt and his horsewhip appear silhouetted in the purple gloom of Nevenka's bedroom, offering a threat of violence that is extinguished when her handsome but dreary husband (Luciano Stella) intervenes. Kurt's glowering face also appears at a rain-streaked French window, receding into the darkness again in a spooky shot modelled, perhaps, on one of Peter Wyngarde's visitations in Jack Clayton's *The Innocents*.

It soon becomes clear that, like the repressed heroine of Clayton's film, Nevenka is being 'haunted' by her own desires and is quite literally creating a rod for her own back. That Kurt is a phantom reflection of Nevenka's sexual fantasies becomes obvious when she caresses herself longingly in front of a mirror only for Kurt's grinning face to appear in it alongside her. There's a faint echo here of the mirrors Lee held up to Mel Ferrer in *The Hands of Orlac* and Philip Saville in *The Mirror and Markheim*, but the scene proceeds very differently in *La frusta*. Beaten unmercifully, Nevenka cries out 'I hate you!' moments before gnawing passionately on Kurt's knuckles. She's later found slumped in orgasmic abandon over his tomb and, when she tries to 'kill' him at the end, she succeeds only in killing herself. Kurt's remains are then set alight and, as Carlo Rustichelli's beautiful score rises to a rhapsodic crescendo, Bava closes the proceedings on a cheeky close-up of Kurt's still-tumescent whip twitching amid the flames.

Its heavy-duty eroticism butchered into incomprehensibility by the British censor, the film appeared in the UK as *Night is the Phantom*, while in the US it sneaked out under the truly ridiculous title *What*. Lee's role is relatively small but, like *Dracula*, his presence, alternately feared and desired, permeates the entire picture. And the scenes in which he lashes the beautiful Daliah Lavi in a blaze of teeth-clenched ferocity are certainly among the most astonishing in Lee's repertoire. He happily went along with Bava's more outré demands – even kissing the camera lens at one point – but confesses that 'I didn't really understand it. The whole film was meant to be a hallucination, and, of course, that's very difficult to get across.'

'Very weird some of these Italian projects were,' Lee mused in his autobiography, and the weirdest of the lot was Giuseppe Veggezzi's *Katarsis*, which was shot between 14 May and 7 June. This returned Lee to the location used in 1959 for *Tempi duri per i vampiri*; indeed, the Odescalchi Castle overlooking Lake Bracciano seems to have been Italy's equivalent of Oakley Court, the Gothic pile next to Bray Studios that turned up in so many British horror films. First unveiled on 9 September, Veggezzi's film was barely seen and a second attempt at releasing it was made in August 1965, retitled *Sfida al diavolo* (Challenge to the Devil) and supplemented at either end with newly shot material involving gangsters and nightclub performers. Even in this padded form it runs a mere 79 minutes and is heavy-going for at least half of them. The sparsely populated nightclub scenes are seemingly interminable and feature a tubby young monk explaining to an even tubbier chanteuse why he turned his back on a life of petty delinquency.

The lengthy flashback that follows forms the substance of the original *Katarsis* and introduces us to a group of beatniks, three men (one of whom is the future monk) and three women. Having beaten up an innocent man at the roadside, they find their way into a forbidding castle. 'It seemed deserted,' the monk's voice-over informs us, 'and was eerily silent, like an unreal world.' Finding food and drink laid out for them on a cobwebbed table – a very Dracula-like touch – they go wild, presumably thanks to some hallucinogenic contained in the drink, and dance insanely to a tom-tom beat for what seems like hours. 'When the orgy was reaching its height,' we're told, 'a strange person appeared ... an ageless person, a person outside time.' This is Lee, dressed in vaguely Elizabethan garb, supported by a cane and wearing a white wig. 'Time is my enemy,' he philosophises (dubbed into Italian, incidentally; no English rendering of this obscure film seems to exist). 'We are all doomed to die, just as we are to live. I rebel at the injustice of such a fate.' He claims to have sold his soul in order to preserve his lover's beauty and the teenagers, having laughed in his face, agree to search the castle for her body.

Once they've gone, he warms his hands by the fire and, as the clock strikes midnight, turns into a much younger man, beetle-browed, bearded and staring balefully into camera. After this genuinely chilling moment, the endless peregrinations of the juveniles take over, their search leading them into every Freudian nook and cranny of the castle, going up and down spiral staircases, along lengthy corridors, and losing their heads completely in a glass-partitioned upper room. Returning downstairs, their host is white-haired again and it's revealed that his lover was concealed in the fireside clock all along. As the beatniks bury the woman outside, he is seen pondering the clock pendulum as flames encroach. The gang then rediscover their roadside victim and guiltily help him into a car; it's Lee, of course, and the film's half-baked metaphysical pretensions are complete. Though it often looks and feels like a student film, *Katarsis* has loads of atmosphere, shadowy black-and-white photography by Angelo Baistrocchi and Mario Parapetti and a hypnotic score by Berto Pisano. According to Lee, director Veggezzi (or Joseph Veg as he was billed in publicity materials) committed suicide soon after the filming.

Another Italian project, *La vergine di Norimberga* completed filming at De Paolis Studios on 13 July and was released, with remarkable speed, on 15 August. Its 32-year-old director, Antonio Margheriti, had just directed the highly regarded Barbara Steele vehicle *Danza macabra*, and with *La vergine* he retained that film's producer Marco Vicario and leading man Georges Rivière. The film was based on a short story by Frank Bogart that had been published in the pulp series *KKK – i classici dell'orrore*; Vicario was the publisher of the *KKK* series and the role of tormented newlywed Mary Hunter was assigned to his wife, Rossana Podestà. As for the script, it was concocted by Ernesto Gastaldi in collaboration with none other than Edmond T Gréville, director of *Beat Girl* and *The Hands of Orlac*.

With its modern-day setting and string of elaborately conceived murders, the film provides a foretaste of the hugely popular 'giallo' thrillers that would follow it, though the template for them was really set by Mario Bava's *Sei donne per l'assassino* the following year. Except for some stodgy bits of exposition, the first two-thirds of *La vergine di Norimberga* are a sustained nightmare for damsel in distress Mary; indeed, Rossana Podestà doesn't appear in anything other than a nightie until an hour has elapsed. Spending her honeymoon at a Rhineland

Christopher Lee – Part Four

castle that belonged to her husband's presumed dead father, she's plagued by visions of mutilated women that turn out to be all too real. For father-in-law is still on the premises, having been turned into 'a living skull' by Nazi surgeons as a punishment for his involvement in the plot to assassinate Hitler. Taking on the role of a sadistic mediaeval ancestor called the Punisher, he plants one victim in the Iron Maiden of the title and then muzzles another with a cage full of rats. 'The mind of Man is ever at the service of evil,' he explains. 'Nowadays great progress has been made with the aid of science, of course. But the old ways are still the best, believe me!'

The film's images of a beautiful victim with poached eyes and another with half her nose chewed off by rats were extraordinarily strong stuff for the time, as was its black-and-white flashback to the General's agonies at the hands of the Nazi surgeons, a sequence that carries a nasty whiff of Georges Franju's *Les Yeux sans visage*. For all its gloatingly gruesome details, however, Margheriti succeeds in making the film strangely moving. Lee plays Erich, custodian of the castle's torture museum and the mad General's former batman, whose devotion to his old master is such that he sacrifices his life on his behalf. As the castle goes up in flames around them, Erich cradles the expiring General in his arms, a pietà reminiscent of Ygor and the Monster in the old Universal horror series. In a final speech that does nothing to explain his habit of torturing and killing people, the General stammers out his belief that 'The war is over and lost but we go on, sending thousands of men to their deaths. We must stop this slaughter. We will have peace again, Erich.' Whereupon the ceiling collapses, the lovers run into each other's arms outdoors, and the credits roll.

The saturnine Erich is a red herring deluxe and has precious little dialogue; what there is, unfortunately, is dubbed by another actor in the English-speaking release, *Horror Castle*. Lee indulges in some typically eloquent mime, however, as when he is introduced to Mary and responds with a mixed display of self-disgust and simple bashfulness. He also cuts a very frightening, watchful figure while patrolling the castle's crypt, in which the harrassed Mary is hiding. Margheriti was impressed by his British guest star. 'Christopher Lee is a fascinating actor,' he observed. 'He speaks Italian correctly, his origins being Italian, and is a very sweet person, very different from the characters he normally interpreted in horror movies.'[17] Though fitted with a nasty scar disfiguring his left eye and cheek, Lee himself reported that 'It was quite relaxing, for once, to be able to look at somebody else getting the sticky end of the wedge,' referring to the extremely hideous make-up worn by the Yugoslavian actor Mirko Valentin as the skull-faced Punisher.

Barely pausing for breath, Lee was back in Rome on 17 July for a film based on Sheridan Le Fanu's 1871 novella *Carmilla*. *La cripta e l'incubo* (The Crypt and the Nightmare) – produced under the title *La maledizione dei Karnstein* – was directed by Camillo Mastrocinque on location at the Castello di Balsorano in Avezzano. Shot in atmospheric black-and-white, it's an interesting forerunner of the accomplished Barbara Steele vehicle Mastrocinque made three years later, *Un angelo per Satana*. But, according to the film's co-writer Ernesto Gastaldi, 'Mastrocinque was a director of meagre talent. He directed a lot of comic films in which the leading actor [Totò] was also the leading man on the set. When he directed *La cripta e l'incubo*, he was embarrassed. The producers asked [Antonio] Margheriti to help him, but I don't know that he did.'[18]

Dressed and made-up much as he would be in 1970 for *I, Monster*, Lee is Count Ludwig von Karnstein, concerned father of the lovely Laura (Adriana Ambesi, previously seen in *Katarsis*). He dismisses his arcane researches as 'idle curiosity' but is haunted by a family curse that suggests one of his descendants will be a reincarnation of the witch Seera. The narrative cleverly misdirects the audience, and Karnstein himself, into thinking that Laura is the resident vampire and her friend Lyuba (Pier Anna Quaglia) the victim. Torch held aloft, Karnstein finally leads an expedition into his ancestral crypt and the reverse proves to be the case. 'It's across this threshold,' he tells his young librarian, 'that the curse of my family begins. You don't have to come if you don't want to...'

Lee gives these lines no trace of ominous import, delivering them instead with simplicity and genuine concern. (And, thankfully, his own voice is preserved in the English language version, *Crypt of Horror*.) It was perhaps a relief to Lee to play a sensitive and anguished character for a change, though the investigative bibliophile played by Spanish actor José Campos is the more rewarding role. That Karnstein begins the film by engaging a librarian may seem like a conscious echo of *Dracula*, but as the story unfolds Lee has nothing more sinister to do than ruminate reflectively at his fireside and recoil from the tell-tale wounds he finds on Lyuba's throat, dressed on both occasions in a nightgown with 'a great fancy K' embossed on it. Lee's only off-beat moment is provided by Karnstein's relationship with his coquettish parlourmaid Annette (Véra Valmont). 'Why don't we get married?' she asks. 'You could be my daughter,' he

Red herring de luxe: as Erich in Antonio Margheriti's La vergine di Norimberga *(1963)*

'It's across this threshold that the curse of my family begins...' Entering the Karnstein family vault with Jose Campos in the Carmilla adaptation, La cripta e l'incubo *(1963)*

scoffs. 'All right then,' she replies. 'Adopt me.'

For the most part, however, Lee and his fellow actors are upstaged by the crepuscular atmosphere cooked up by Mastrocinque and his cinematographers, Julio Ortas Plaza and Giuseppe Aquari. Laura's nightmare is erotically rendered, with Lyuba turning into a grinning skull when Laura languorously kisses her hand. And, given that Laura and Lyuba look like sexually awakening adolescents, Laura's subsequent shock at discovering a large splotch of blood on her bedsheets carries a surprisingly frank Freudian charge. Elsewhere, a pedlar is found hanged in the belltower with one of his hands missing. It is later pressed into service by the ill-fated Karnstein housekeeper as a flaming Hand of Glory (an exactly similar five-fingered prop would recur in *The Wicker Man*), and the film reaches an agreeably demented crescendo when the dead housekeeper sits up in her coffin and points accusingly at Karnstein's daughter.

FROM HAMMER TO HITCHCOCK

Though domiciled in Switzerland, Lee was still called upon by Hammer from time to time and would take up residence at the Guards Polo Club near Maidenhead in answer to their summons. The financial success of *The Pirates of Blood River* ensured a loose follow-up of sorts, and Lee accordingly took a break from his Gothic exploits in Italy to make *The Devil-Ship Pirates* at Bray. The result was one of the top-earning British films of 1964 and it's not hard to see why. Shot in lustrous 'Hammerscope' by Michael Reed and nimbly directed by Don Sharp, it maintains Hammer's knack for making a modest budget look like a major one and packs in enough swashbuckling action to satisfy bloodthirsty boys of all ages.

Stretching from mid-August to early October 1963, shooting involved danger not merely to the assembled buccaneers, as had been the case on *The Pirates of Blood River*, but to the film crew as well. The Diablo – the devil-ship of the title – had been designed by Bernard Robinson at a cost of £17,000 and set afloat in a flooded gravel pit near Bray. Weighing 40 tons and measuring 120 feet in length, it was an impressive structure but had not been designed to withstand a famished unit surging to one side when the tea-boat came into view. The ship capsized and chaos ensued. Clinging to the aft deck, Lee took the precaution of salvaging continuity girl Pauline Harlow's typewriter.

Don Sharp had been an actor in his native Australia, as well as on BBC Radio, and was initially apprehensive about working with Lee. 'I had seen several of Chris' pictures and I was worried about a range I saw as playing down one line,' he explained. 'But right from our first meeting we got on and, when we talked, it was two actors talking! We'd explore his character and I found myself suggesting depths to Captain Robeles that I hadn't expected I'd be able to do. Chris is tremendously professional and can essay roles that are charming and threatening at the same time – he has a lovely stillness about him. He's a very commanding presence.'[19]

In a Jimmy Sangster scenario faintly reminiscent of Alberto Cavalcanti's wartime classic *Went the Day Well?*, Robeles is the captain of a pirate ship requisitioned by the Spanish Armada, and when it's run aground on the Cornish coast he persuades the credulous inhabitants of the nearest village that England is under the dominion of Spain. 'Bosun,' he barks, 'you will warn the crew that, if any one of them lets slip what really happened to the Armada, I will personally cut out his tongue.' But the villagers gradually come to realise that they've been deceived and find an ally in Robeles' high-minded lieutenant, Manuel. Lee shares a memorably tense scene with Barry Warren, going about his toilet and simultaneously revealing the chip on Robeles' shoulder. 'Your type: you sicken me with your pious attitudes,' he spits. 'I'm going to strip you of your fancy ideas one by one until you're no better than the rest of us.'

In stark contrast to the laconic and underplayed LaRoche in *The Pirates of Blood River*, Lee goes into sneering melodrama mode for Robeles and the result, as David Rider put it in *Films and Filming*, 'is genuinely awe-inspiring'. The eyes are manic, the teeth more often than not clenched, the dialogue hissed out in phrases that drip with contempt. That Robeles is a villain of the darkest hue is made clear to us in the film's opening sea battle, when he summarily executes his Armada liaison Don José (Joseph O'Conor) by shooting him in the back. He wrings information from Cornish teenager Jane (Natasha Pyne) with practised ease and creates a horrible effect when dining with the local Squire, chomping mechanically on his food

Captain Robeles off-duty during the Bray filming of The Devil-Ship Pirates *(1963)*

while staring with dead-eyed lust at the Squire's daughter Angela. Two years later, Lee would size up Suzan Farmer with equally foul, unspoken intentions in another Don Sharp film, *Rasputin the Mad Monk*.

Elsewhere, the manipulative Robeles callously destroys an 11-year-old messenger's faith in his father and efficiently skewers the Squire (Ernest Clark) when he objects to his proposal to take Angela as a hostage. He also hangs the local blacksmith, played by an actor last seen being consumed by piranha fish in *The Pirates of Blood River*, Andrew Keir. Trying to escape in his renovated ship, Robeles is halted by the blacksmith's vengeful son and finally sent sprawling onto the Diablo's flame-wreathed deck by a bullet fired by the dying Manuel. Tanned, trim-bearded and glossy-haired, Lee looks splendid in Robeles' plumes and red velvet but was not exempt from Hammer's usual roster of physical perils. 'I was cut about quite a lot in this film in the fights,' he informed his fan club. 'At the end of the climactic battle with John Cairney, I pitched straight back into the flames rather nearer than I intended. Besides catching my elbows an imperial crack on the deck, I also started to set fire to my wig.'

On their return to the Continent, Lee and the pregnant Gitte were faced next with a painful personal drama. 'I was in bed with flu and my wife Gitte was overdue,' he explained 30 years later. 'Suddenly she turned to me and said, "This is it." I got out of bed and drove her to the clinic in Lausanne. It was the day after President Kennedy was assassinated [23 November 1963] and all the staff in the clinic were glued to the television, watching the footage of his assassination ... I was sent down to the waiting room, where I sat in a state of panic. After what seemed like forever, one of the nurses came down and shouted at me, "You have a daughter." I just said, "My wife, how is my wife?" to which she replied, "She's all right," and then added "for the moment." ... I thought, "Oh my God, she's dying." And then the gynaecologist appeared with this bundle, unwrapped it, and there was my daughter with her two legs in plaster. I nearly went into orbit. Our daughter had been born with both her feet turned inwards ... What should have been the most joyful day of my life turned out to be the worst. I think I had some kind of mental breakdown without realising it.'[20]

A week later, while Gitte was recuperating, Lee took their daughter, Christina, to a London specialist, who wrenched her feet back into position and prescribed the use of splints. These remained in place for some three years and, when Christina was eight, she underwent an operation which successfully aligned her heels. In the meantime, as Lee put it, 'my feelings rotated like a whirlpool, of happiness at the birth of our daughter, and anxiety about Gitte and the unexpected complications with which she had to cope.'

Disorientated, Lee fulfilled his next Hammer commitment at Bray as 1963 edged into 1964. *The Gorgon* is a grey and forbidding film that marked the first and last Hammer reunion of the Cushing-Lee-Fisher team that had done such startling work in the late 1950s. A strange gloss on the Greek myth of the Medusa, it's set in 1910 and locates the last of the Gorgons, Megaera, in Castle Borski, a desolate pile frowning down upon the fearful mid-European community of Vandorf. Young Paul Heitz, investigating the mysterious deaths of his brother and father, comes up against the intransigent Dr Namaroff and enlists the aid of his tutor from Leipzig University, Professor Carl Meister.

In an interesting attempt at ringing the changes on the standard Lee-Cushing casting, the reptilian Namaroff was given to Cushing and the brusquely heroic Meister to Lee. The results are not entirely successful. John Gilling, director of *The Pirates of Blood River*, had fashioned a script that he considered one of his best and was enraged when Tony Hinds made several changes. Whoever was responsible, Namaroff is full of murky motivations that even Cushing can't satisfactorily clarify, while the 41-year-old Lee simply appears too young for the avuncular Meister and his rasping delivery is not always convincing.

Cast in Van Helsing mould, Meister could easily have been played, like Cushing's Van Helsing, as a youngish man of action as well as intellect, but instead he labours under a lengthy grey wig and moustache. Intrusive make-up aside, Lee provides Meister with several foretastes of the suaver hero he would play in *The Devil Rides Out* some four years later. Like the Duc de Richleau, Meister has a lordly way with underlings, informing Patrick Troughton's police chief that the Foreign Secretary is 'a very valued friend of my dear brother' as well as fixing him with a withering glare and barking 'Don't use long words, Inspector: they don't suit you.' First seen toying with a fossil at his Leipzig desk, he doesn't reappear until the 50-minute mark, silhouetted in Paul's Vandorf doorway amid a swirl of autumn leaves – a familiar poetic device of Fisher's. The sinister spell is immediately punctured when Meister says bluffly, 'Well, do you propose to keep me standing out here all night?'

Meister's unravelling of the mystery involves a brief tussle with Namaroff's knife-throwing henchman Ratoff (Jack Watson) and then a face-to-face confrontation with Namaroff himself, Meister brandishing the confiscated knife under the doctor's nose. As a detective, Meister is more bulldozing juggernaut than analytical Sherlock Holmes, but Lee tempers his brusqueness with a fatherly concern for

Professor Meister and Paul Heitz (Richard Pasco) puzzling over the identity of The Gorgon *(1963)*

the wayward Paul. As Paul rhapsodises about Namaroff's beautiful assistant Carla, Meister summarises his problem in no-nonsense style ('I see: you're in love with her') and then, beginning to suspect that Carla is the human face of the dreaded Megaera, he responds to Paul's objections with the crucial line, 'Why shouldn't I? I'm not in love with her.' Among the tortured souls of Vandorf, Meister is the only one without any emotional ties and is therefore free to lop off Megaera's head in the storm-laden climax. This spirited conclusion is unfortunately spoiled by a laughably unconvincing severed head devised by effects man Syd Pearson; as Lee himself put it, 'The only thing wrong with *The Gorgon* is the Gorgon.'[21]

Though miscast, Lee is characteristically watchable, as is Cushing, but the film is really carried by the doomed romance movingly played out by Richard Pasco's Paul and Barbara Shelley's Carla. Though a coldly cerebral exercise, the film proved a commercial winner when paired with Hammer's humdrum *The Curse of the Mummy's Tomb* – 'She had a face only a mummy could love!' shrilled the US posters – but for Lee *The Gorgon* was perhaps most memorable for introducing him to Shelley, who would become his favourite Hammer leading lady. Working with both Cushing and Lee for the first time, she was immediately made aware of the camaraderie between them and enjoyed running through Gilbert and Sullivan patter songs with Cushing and studio-rattling operatic arias with Lee.

On 11 January 1964, a few days before completion of *The Gorgon*, Christina was christened at St Michael's Chester Square, the same church in which the Lees had been married nearly three years earlier. But, not long after their return to Switzerland, Lee was required in March to make his first trip to Hollywood. Lee's misgivings about leaving Gitte and their small daughter behind led to panic attacks on the journey to LA, creating in the former RAF officer a fear of flying that would never leave him. As Lee explains, 'Having to leave a young wife, who'd just had a major operation, and a child who had been born with a serious problem – I was in such a state, thinking I'd never see either of them again. I don't know how I got through the movie.' But, in consultation with Gitte, he had decided that the Hollywood offer couldn't be passed up, especially as it had the name Alfred Hitchcock attached to it.

In the event, Lee's stint at Universal Studios yielded only a brief glimpse of Hitchcock sailing past in a black Cadillac. An instalment of the prestigious TV anthology *The Alfred Hitchcock Hour*, *The Sign of Satan* was shot in six days from Wednesday 11 March and was directed by one of Hitchcock's staff directors,

Burying Harlequin: with Donald Sutherland, Luigi Bonos, Antonio de Martino, Gaïa Germani and Philippe Leroy in Warren Kiefer's splendid Il castello dei morti vivi (1964)

the former film star Robert Douglas. Having met his co-star, Gia Scala, at Douglas' Beverly Hills home, Lee settled into a colossal dressing room and had his make-up needs attended to by Bud Westmore, the man who had designed *The Creature from the Black Lagoon*. The script was adapted from an extremely disturbing Robert Bloch short story called *Return to the Sabbath*; dating from 1945, it had lately been resurrected in Bloch's paperback anthology *Horror-7*. 'In Hollywood to make a horror film,' explained *TV Guide*, 'a European actor insists that he wants no publicity because he fears that a cult of Devil-worshippers may try to kill him.' Or, as Hitchcock puts it in a characteristically droll introduction to the story, 'The scene of tonight's drama [is] Hollywood California ... [and] concerns some doings which would be considered rather peculiar even in that bizarre town.'

'There was a Chinese box effect about my position vis-à-vis this tale,' Lee admitted. Indeed, Barré Lyndon's script provides him with one particularly apposite line when Karl Jorla tells his Hollywood benefactors that 'It was a great opportunity for me to come from Europe and I'm extremely grateful to you for giving me the chance.' Though *The Sign of Satan* isn't quite 'the best horror film ever', as *Films in Review* called it, it's still memorably creepy. Jorla is first seen rising from a mist-wreathed tomb in an Austrian film clip that captures the interest of US producer Max Rubini (Gilbert Green). Cast as Baron Ulmo in Rubini's latest Hollywood horror, Jorla reveals that the sponsors of the Austrian picture were Satanists, that the Black Mass featured in it was the genuine article and that the film was only intended for private circulation. He subsequently goes missing before fulfilling his promise to 'be here early, ready to work' – despite the fact that he's been murdered in the meantime. Fitted by Westmore with a sky-high black wig, Lee gives Jorla a sad-eyed fatalism that lingers long in the memory – as does a fleeting, slow-motion shot of his posthumous return to the studio.

While filming *The Sign of Satan*, Lee was interviewed by the legendary director William Wyler regarding a cameo role in Wyler's film *The Collector*. As it turned out, Wyler and Lee's old friend Mike Frankovich (Columbia's man in the UK) had got their wires crossed: the role had already gone to Kenneth More, who later suffered the ignominy of being cut from the finished film altogether. Lee also played golf at Bel-Air with Ray Milland, dropped in on director Roger Corman, shared numerous Chinese meals with the craggy character star Neville Brand and met the writer Ray Bradbury, who expressed a wish to cast Lee as Mr Dark in a film version of his novel *Something Wicked This Way Comes*. 'To Christopher Lee, who *is* Mr Dark,' he wrote in the flyleaf of Lee's copy, 'with the admiration of his fan Ray Bradbury.' The role would eventually go to Jonathan Pryce when the film finally appeared some 20 years later.

Lee had no opportunity, however, to meet the writer of *Return to the Sabbath* itself, who was also the author of *Psycho*. 'I was working elsewhere,' Robert Bloch recalled, 'and hadn't even been informed of his casting. When not before the camera Christopher spent a miserable stay across the street [from the studio] in a motel infested by termites and supporting actors.' [22] The omission was remedied in August 1965, when Bloch came over to London to write a British picture called *The Psychopath* and got together with Lee, Boris Karloff and Forrest J Ackerman, guru of the US fan magazine *Famous Monsters of Filmland*. Also in 1965, Lee recalled his Hitchcock stint during the course of a telephone interview with the legendary Hollywood gossip columnist Louella Parsons. 'Everyone was very kind, very courteous to me,' he told her. 'I would love to come back, but I can only do that if the right film comes up and they ask for me.' 'If the gentlemen is as charming as he sounded,' Parsons concluded, 'I hope it happens soon.'

Art and Artists

In the meantime, the ubiquitous Odescalchi Castle was pressed into service for Lee's final Italian engagement during this period. *Il castello dei morti vivi* was shot over 24 days, starting on 27 April 1964, and cost a mere $116,000. The identity of the film's director has since given rise to some confusion. The credits on the Italian print call it 'A film by Warren Kiefer' (the film's American screenwriter) but, to satisfy quota requirements, wind up with the legend 'Directed by Herbert Wise' (pseudonym of Luciano Ricci). Furthermore, a 20-year-old Englishman called Michael Reeves (later to direct the remarkable *Witchfinder General*) is billed alongside Fritz Muller as assistant director.

As Lee puts it, 'Reeves did everybody's job: he was producer, director and all three assistants, or so it seemed. Full of enthusiasm, bright as a button and obviously totally dedicated to film – I liked him very much.' 'Just for the record,' Kiefer explained back in 1989, 'there *was* no co-director. Michael Reeves hung around as an unpaid gofer during the production and had nothing whatever to do with the direction or anything else.' The film was one of the first for the young Canadian actor Donald Sutherland, who subsequently named his son after its director, Kiefer.

Despite the confusion surrounding it, *Il castello dei morti vivi* is one of the most engaging and imaginative of all Italian horror pictures, beautifully rendered in icy monochrome by Fellini's sometime cinematographer, Aldo Tonti. Set in the aftermath of the Napoleonic Wars, it begins with a spot of bludgeoning violence in a sylvan setting, in which the malefactor (as we later discover) is the oafish Sandro, collecting human specimens for his ghoulish master, the mad taxidermist Count Drago. Stripped of the death's head make-up he wore as the Punisher, the lantern-jawed Mirko Valentin plays Sandro and Lee, with a neat goatee, dark-rimmed eyes and glossy black hair pasted to his skull, is the necrophile aesthete Drago – reversing the master/servant relationship the two actors played out in *La vergine di Norimberga*.

'Many men waste their lives searching for the secret of life,' Drago pronounces. 'It is the secrets of death that interest me.' The journey to Drago's castle, like Dracula's, is unmarked by the singing of birds. 'It's strange,' someone mutters, 'like another world.' We later discover that Drago has muzzled the birds personally. His hallway is festooned with them – the taxidermy sub-plot of Hitchcock's *Psycho* was presumably an influence here – with dead ravens, eagles, even pelicans artfully arranged on specially installed indoor trees. Drago has summoned an itinerant Commedia dell'Arte troupe to perform at his castle – the influence here appears to have been Bergman's *The Seventh Seal* – and his opening gambit on their arrival is a funereal 'Welcome to my home.' This further echo of *Dracula* is supplemented by a more interesting echo. When Drago refers to 'a new series of experiments,' troupe leader Bruno (Jacques Stanislawsky) asks 'What kind of animal is it?' 'The most interesting and most dangerous animal of all,' Drago replies, making it clear that he is close kin to Count Zaroff of *The Most Dangerous Game*, who made a habit of hunting humans and displaying their heads on his walls.

Drago has perfected a new 'embalming chemical ... an aqueous secretion of a tropical plant,' with which he spikes his guests' cognac. When asked why he doesn't drink too, he explains that 'My health forbids it,' a hypochondriac touch reminiscent of Poe's Roderick Usher. Poe-like, too, is the perfectly preserved corpse of his wife, laid out in a cobwebbed four-poster upstairs and frozen into immobility while regarding herself in a hand-mirror. Drago eventually unveils a forbidden room worthy of Bluebeard himself, peopled with humans who have been calcified rather than merely stuffed. Dipping a scalpel into his lethal embalming fluid, he tells cavalry officer-turned-actor Eric (Philippe Leroy) and the beautiful ingenue Laura (Gaïa Germani) that 'I wish the two of you to play the leading parts in my eternal theatre. You, my friends, will never lose your youth; you will be for ever on the stage...'

If the film sounds like a ragbag of borrowings, it has plenty of artful flourishes of its own, notably some extremely atmospheric scenes set in the sunlit park at Bomarzo, complete with its strikingly weird giant sculptures. A stately funeral procession, led by the top-hatted Drago, takes place here, as well as some compelling sequences in which Sandro pursues the troupe's resident dwarf, Neep (Antonio de Martino). Adding to the film's virtues, there's a lyrical score by Angelo Francesco Lavagnino and an unusually diverting selection of supporting actors. Last seen in *La frusta e il corpo* and often referred to as Italy's Peter Lorre, Luciano Pigozzi is on hand as the troupe's treacherous Harlequin and Donald Sutherland plays not only a gurning police officer but also, bizarrely, a gurning witch, whose beauty was destroyed by Drago's chemical experiments. Given to gnomic utterances like 'Some will live and some will die, before tomorrow's sun is high,' 'she' closes with Drago at the end and stabs him with his own poisoned scalpel. Bent double, hair flopping forward, face frozen into a disbelieving scream, this statue-like demise is among the most memorable of Lee's many screen deaths.

Lee has rarely appeared more sepulchral (make-up artist: Guglielmo Bonotti) and, when the strolling players perform a mock-hanging for him, his delighted laughter and applause is truly manic; nicely balanced, too, by the moronic merriment of Sandro. He delivers Drago's dialogue in his familiar stentorian tones but in unusually light and rapid-fire fashion. That Lee speaks his own dialogue in the English version of the film (*The Castle of the Living Dead*) is particularly miraculous, given that the film's young American producer, Paul Maslansky, succeeded in losing the entire soundtrack and even the continuity reports, making the business of post-synching the film even more tedious than usual. After this brief hiccough, Lee and Maslansky became firm friends, an association that was still bearing fruit in the 1990s.

While filming *Il castello dei morti vivi*, Lee told journalist (and later director) Dario Argento that he expected his next project to be another Italian one, this time co-starring Boris Karloff. This was an AIP project based on H P Lovecraft's *The Dunwich Horror* and to be directed by Mario Bava; it was eventually made in California five years later by Daniel Haller. When the Karloff reunion failed to materialise, Lee opted for *Dr Terror's House of Horrors*, which got underway at Shepperton on 25 May. Inspired by his spell in 1959 as executive producer of *The City of the Dead*, New Yorker Milton Subotsky had relocated permanently and set up a new company called Amicus. *Dr Terror* cost a mere £105,000 and, though denied a West End opening, made a killing when released to the ABC circuit in February 1965.

Subotsky cannily enlisted Hammer mainstays Lee and Cushing for his first foray into Hammer territory; Lee would reappear under the Subotsky aegis on four further occasions, while Cushing finally clocked up an impressive 14. *Dr Terror* locates them on a train bound for Bradley. Lee is one of five passengers – the others are Neil McCallum, Roy Castle, pop DJ Alan Freeman and Donald Sutherland again – who are disconcerted by Cushing's fleabitten Dr Schreck in a life-or-death rendition of the 'nutter on the bus' syndrome. Each of them is given a glimpse of his true self through the medium of Schreck's Tarot deck and each of them turns out at the end to be dead. Subotsky's clunky script gives each story a suitably idiot-proof title – 'Werewolf', 'Creeping Vine', 'Voodoo', 'Disembodied Hand' and 'Vampire' – and the general standard is pretty low. Happily, the ensemble playing in the linking scenes is impressively edgy while Lee is made the centrepiece of the strongest episode, 'Disembodied Hand'.

Lee's Franklyn Marsh is a comic characterisation of some subtlety, a brilliant portrait in miniature that builds up from a series of mere hints a complete picture of the man's anally retentive lifestyle. A tight-lipped art critic, Marsh is trying to board the train when Castle's breezy jazz musician Biff Bailey accidentally closes the door on Marsh's case. Ceremoniously taking his seat, donning his spectacles and unfolding his newspaper, the affronted Marsh directs a withering look at the quailing Biff that no character comedian could have bettered. Having settled in, Marsh rapidly singles himself out as the resident sceptic when faced with Schreck's Tarot cards. 'Really!' he snorts. 'Do we have to suffer all this nonsense? Astrologers, spiritualists, table-rappers –

the entire lunatic fringe – they've been exposed for the charlatans they are over and over again.'

Even at this early stage, Lee is careful to introduce an intriguingly strident note into Marsh's scepticism, whetting our appetite for the inevitable moment when Schreck pricks the bubble of his pomposity. Until then, he remains frozen behind his paper while the others listen agog to Schreck's patter. Asked to identify himself, he maintains conceitedly that 'Most informed people have heard of Franklyn Marsh, art critic,' to which Biff unaffectedly replies, 'Well, I've never heard of you.' Marsh dismisses this slight with a querulous twitch of his newspaper before finally agreeing 'to participate in [Schreck's] ridiculous parlour game' – doing so, however, in a slightly keening voice that betrays the suppressed hysteria underlying his surface smugness.

'Disembodied Hand' is a diverting anecdote in which Marsh grandly informs Michael Gough's fey 'action' painter that 'I live by my vision.' He then demolishes the artist's latest work with ill-concealed relish ('A work of noticeable incompetence, even for Mr Eric Landor') and offers up an ill-advised panegyric over the work of an unknown painter ('Clearly the work of a creative artist of considerable promise'). To his consternation, the promising artist is then introduced to him by a pretty gallery employee (Isla Blair). It's a chimpanzee in stripey top and denim jeans and, having literally been made a monkey of, Lee wipes the smirk of humourless self-satisfaction from Marsh's face in a deeply satisfying display of social humiliation.

Landor's orchestrated campaign of further taunts eventually compels Marsh to run him down in his car. His hand crushed beyond repair, Landor shoots himself. The hand survives, however, and the prim-and-proper art critic is appalled by this loathsome reminder of his crime, crawling relentlessly into every corner of his ordered life and eventually forcing him into crashing his car and losing his sight. Lee's shuddering displays of fear and revulsion when lobbing the hand out of his car window, tonging it into the fireplace or frenziedly attacking it with a paper-knife are an accurate index to the twitchy paranoia Marsh is normally at pains to conceal. In a particularly clever touch, Lee has the guilty Marsh recover from one encounter by sinking into his desk chair and briefly studying his own hands in some perplexity.

Though something of a curate's egg, the film is distinguished by a notably creepy score from the avant-garde composer Elisabeth Lutyens, muted cinematography by Alan Hume and several discreetly effective directorial touches from Freddie Francis. An Oscar-winning lighting cameraman, Francis would become increasingly identified as the director of low-budget horror pictures and was well aware that the first of his seven Amicus assignments was chiefly salvaged by the practised interplay of Cushing and Lee. 'If you want to make horror films,' he commented, 'you can't do better than Peter Cushing and Christopher Lee. They have a wonderful chemistry on screen.'[23]

Franklyn Marsh delivers an ill-considered critical judgment to painter Eric Landor (Michael Gough) in Dr Terror's House of Horrors (1964)

PART FIVE

HOMECOMING
1964–1968

Lee's Swiss exile was taking its toll. A diet of Italian horror pictures coupled with return visits to the UK on Hammer's behalf wasn't quite, as Lee put it, 'the pan-European spread for which we had hoped. It appeared to me that what little I had gained was being thrown away by the restrictions on my freedom to work. I was going through a form of nervous breakdown.'

Traces of Lee's anxious mood cropped up during his next picture, a large-scale Hammer adventure based on Rider Haggard's 1887 novel *She*. Directed by Robert Day, with whom Lee had last worked on *Corridors of Blood*, it began filming in Israel (without Lee) on 24 August 1964 prior to moving into Elstree in September. During the shooting of a scene in which Lee's High Priest Billali oversees the execution of a number of black slaves – who at Ayesha's imperious command are tossed in copious quantities into a sort of indoor volcano – Lee succumbed to a sudden attack of claustrophobia. Having dashed outdoors without explanation, he paced around feverishly, still fully costumed, in the midst of a torrential downpour, only to reappear on the set about 15 minutes later, sheepish and sodden.

She was in line with Hammer's short-lived belief that they should 'think big' in future, a belief fostered by the ever-quixotic Michael Carreras. Despite being Hammer's most expensive film to date (budgeted at close to £325,000), *She* is the first instance of the company's reach visibly exceeding its grasp. It was nevertheless a big hit on release (its chances buoyed considerably by the luscious presence of Ursula Andress, whom the posters touted as 'The World's Most Beautiful Woman!'), and made a further killing when double-billed in 1969 with Hammer's dinosaur extravaganza, *One Million Years B.C.*

Lee looks splendidly saturnine throughout, particularly in an Egyptian-styled headdress –

Hammer's research consultant on the film was Andrew Low, who had fulfilled the same function on *The Mummy* – and offers a tight-lipped portrait in submerged resentment, coupled with much dark-eyed watchfulness and a sad desperation to share in the immortality enjoyed by his Queen. 'High Priests die as easily as other mortals,' Ayesha reminds him as he trembles at her feet, and the theme resurfaces when Billali meets the plucky Cambridge explorer Major Holly in a set of catacombs lined with dessicated, upright mummies. 'High Priests, like myself, to Ayesha,' Billali explains. 'But with one difference: they are dead.' The scene doesn't advance the plot in any way, seeming to have been put in purely for the fans to relish a brief tête-à-tête between Lee and his old antagonist, Peter Cushing. And the film benefits from it. Trying to break through the robotic dignity with which Billali asserts his allegiance to Ayesha, Holly insists that 'Your body does her bidding, but your spirit cries out to be free.' To which Billali solemnly replies, 'Each one of us has his own destiny to fulfil.'

Billali isn't being entirely honest here, for he fully intends to engineer his destiny to his own ends. Aware that Ayesha's flame of eternal youth is due to make one of its rare appearances, he intrudes into the sacred chamber and tells her that 'I have but to enter the flame to become as you are.' With absurd but dramatically expedient contrariness, he fails to do this straight away and instead has a violent set-to with Ayesha's mortal lover Leo (John Richardson). He receives a torch in the face ('causing me to look like Al Jolson,' Lee noted) and is making a desperate lunge for the palpitating blue flames when Ayesha stabs him in the back. Groping pathetically for the flame, Lee gives Billali a final moment of staring-eyed pathos as his body gives up the ghost before he can reach it.

DEVIL DOCTOR

Still shuttling between Vevey and London, Lee began 1965 with a return visit to Shepperton for a second Amicus picture. This began on 18 January and was

In rehearsal with Barbara Shelley for Rasputin the Mad Monk *(1965)*

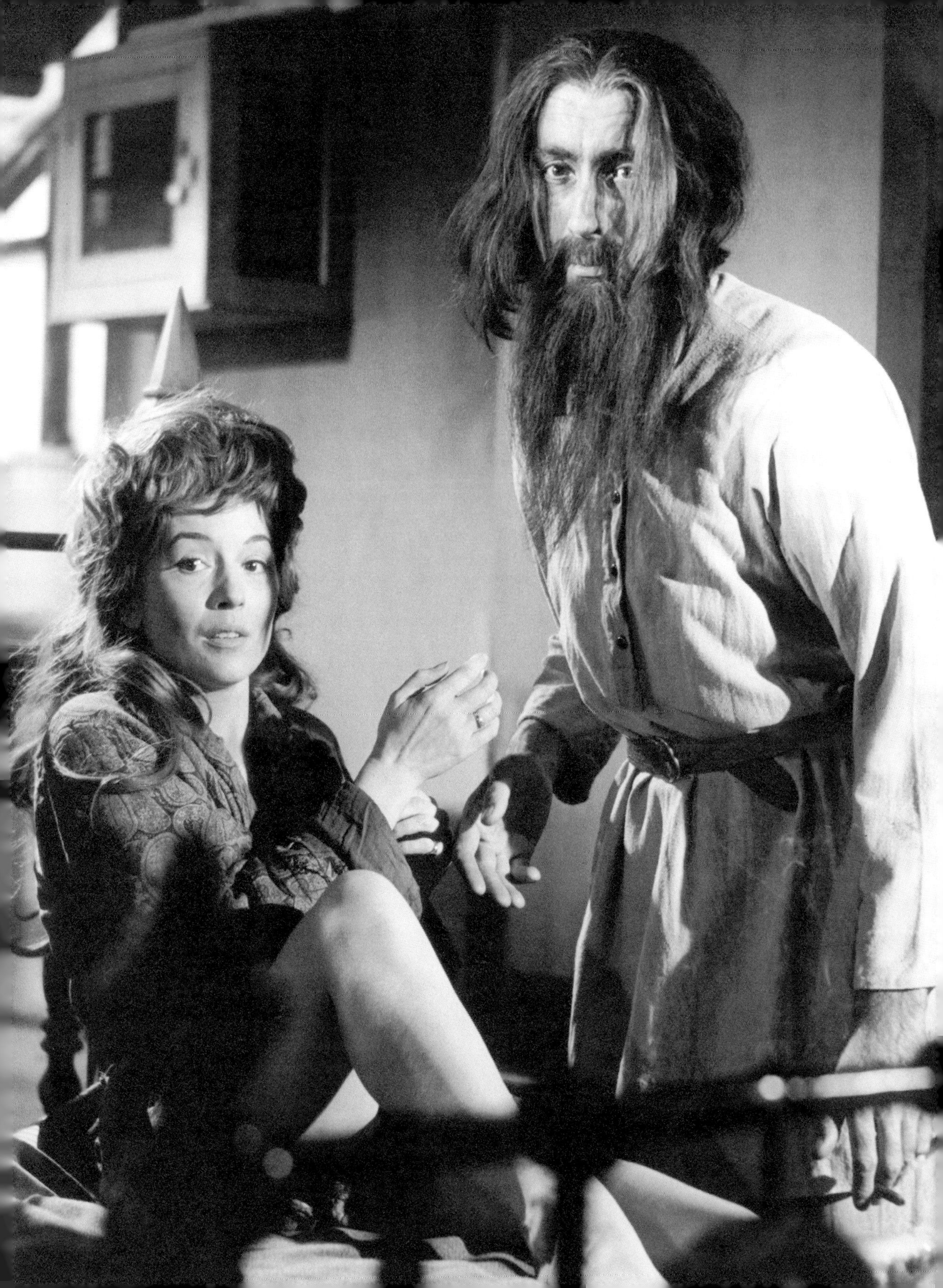

Off-duty at Elstree with Ursula Andress: She *(1964)*

called *The Skull*. Based on a Robert Bloch story, it's a mood piece from start to finish. Though little more than a padded version of one of the horror anecdotes Amicus would normally have featured four or five abreast in a portmanteau picture, *The Skull* is a minor triumph and probably the best picture the company produced. As 'Guest Star', Lee has four brief scenes as Sir Matthew Phillips, a collector of antique curiosa who is much relieved when his prize exhibit, a skull reputed to be that of the Marquis de Sade, is stolen. During the course of the film, fellow collector Christopher Maitland (played by Peter Cushing at his edgiest) finds out why, the hard way.

Cushing and Lee are introduced in an auction room, where auctioneer Michael Gough advertises 'four stone figures, mid 17th century ... [representing] the hierarchies of Hell.' For reasons he doesn't understand, Sir Matthew steadily hikes up the bidding for the grotesque quartet and finally, in a virtually trance-like state, offers £1500 for them. Later, he and Maitland play billiards and Lee gives a nicely haunted quality to his talk of 'invisible beings, spirits from a strange, evil world' that battened on him under the influence of the stolen skull. Lee's jaunty handling of a cigar fails to disguise his disquiet as he explains that 'Sometimes I used to hear them calling me to join them in their ceremonies,' and the disquiet is doomily underscored here by Elisabeth Lutyens' creepy music. The skull-maddened Maitland finally puts Sir Matthew out of his misery by clubbing him to death with Balbarith (one of the nasty little statuettes seen at the beginning), his victim crashing to the green baize amid a picturesque scatter of billiard balls.

From being clobbered by Peter Cushing over a billiard table in *The Skull*, Lee moved on to a highly accomplished *Boy's Own* thriller called *The Face of Fu Manchu*, which began in Ireland on 15 February. Sax Rohmer's 'Yellow Peril', together with his dogged adversaries Nayland Smith and Dr Petrie, had first appeared in print in 1913. By the time Lee got to grips with him, the 'devil doctor' had already been essayed on film several times, most famously in *The Mask of Fu Manchu*, an extremely kinky Karloff vehicle produced by MGM in 1932. But Lee's take on the character would be very different to Karloff's drooling bisexual gargoyle. Indeed, the marble inscrutability of Lee's Fu brings to mind those chilling words from *Macbeth*, 'There's no art/To find the mind's construction in the face.'

'Imagine a person, tall, lean and feline, high-shouldered, with a brow like Shakespeare and a face like Satan, a close-shaven skull and long, magnetic eyes of true cat-green,' wrote Rohmer in his first Fu Manchu novel. 'Invest him with all the cruel cunning of an entire Eastern race, accumulated in one giant intellect ... and you have a mental picture of Dr Fu Manchu, the yellow peril incarnate in one man.' Described like that, there seems very little likelihood of the Chinese ever taking the negative Fu Manchu image to their hearts. But, as critic Helen Lawrenson put it, 'Today's children are far too blasé to fall for this kind of nonsense, and I have a feeling that the new Fu series is more likely to become a campy cult than an incitement to Sinophobia.'[1]

Nevertheless, Lee conceded that 'There were objections [to the film] in San Francisco and other cities with large Chinese populations ... I can only say that I never played Fu Manchu in any way that the Chinese could find offensive ... However, I can understand that the Chinese object to the character being referred to as the Yellow Peril.'[2] The dignity conferred on an otherwise invidious character by Lee was pointed up in *Newsweek*'s review of *Face*, which observed that 'Fu is played by Christopher Lee – tall, ascetic, not particularly Oriental but subtly tragic around the twitching roots of his false mustaches.'

Lee would repeat this characterisation four times over the next three years, but the drop in quality from film to film was more marked even than in his eight outings as Count Dracula over a 15-year period. The films were the brainchild of maverick producer Harry Alan Towers, who also wrote them under the pseudonym Peter Welbeck. The word 'maverick' seems inadequate for this legendary fly-by-night showman, a former child actor, radio producer and ATV executive who, according to one critic, 'has rarely been interviewed over the years, except perhaps by the authorities ... [and who] uses the same press agent as Lord Lucan.'[3] Towers had been arrested in the US in 1961, allegedly for his involvement with a call girl racket, but reportedly jumped bail and only gave himself up 20 years later, paying a paltry fine of $4,200. Astonishingly then, the numerous films he produced in the interim were all made while he was officially 'on the run'.

A highly successful series of early 1960s paperback reprints of Rohmer's original novels provided Towers with one good reason for reviving Fu Manchu, but the colossal success of the James Bond films no doubt provided an even better one. Indeed, *The Face of Fu Manchu* is a delightful evocation of that between-the-wars limbo of imperialist spy fiction which threw up Sexton Blake and Bulldog Drummond, eventually giving birth to the post-war icon that was Bond. 'The producers are so confident of Fu's success that they are preparing screenplays for three more films,' observed Mary Knoblauch in the run-up to the film's release. 'After that it should be time for a showdown between Fu and 007.'[4]

Fu's resemblance to several of Bond's deadly adversaries, notably the Chinese-German mastermind, Dr No, is too obvious to require further elaboration. Indeed, by Lee's own account, his Fu Manchu warm-up in Hammer's *The Terror of the Tongs* had prompted his cousin, Ian Fleming, to ruminate on the possibility of Lee playing Dr No. Fleming's Jamaican neighbour, Noël Coward, was a still stronger possibility but the role eventually went to the American stage actor Joseph Wiseman, whose metal-clawed super-villain in the final third of Terence Young's *Dr No* has much of the flesh-crawling impassivity that Lee would bring to Fu Manchu.

Lee's first Fu vehicle begins with a bogus decapitation for Fu Manchu that was staged at Kilmainham Gaol in County Wicklow. A virtually sacred site in Ireland's troubled 20th century history, the controversy surrounding the filmmakers' use of this location was given an extra kick by the coincidence of Sir Roger Casement's funeral procession passing by while the scene was being shot. The sequence is a memorably eerie one, with rain lashing down after the execution has been accomplished, the white robes of the beheaded Fu fluttering in long shot and Nayland Smith lingering, at attention, long after everyone else has gone. It's later revealed that the executed man was not Fu Manchu at all but a famous Chinese actor going to his death in a hypnotised state – a pleasing nod to the complete absence of theatricality in Lee's hypnotic portrayal.

Sir Matthew Phillips and fellow collector Christopher Maitland (Peter Cushing) in Freddie Francis' The Skull (1965)

The disguised Carl Janssen (Joachim Fuchsberger) and Nayland Smith (Nigel Green) infiltrate their adversary's Tibetan stronghold in The Face of Fu Manchu *(1965)*

Stillness is the key here. Lee himself put it down to purely practical considerations, noting that the 'extremely complicated' make-up for Fu Manchu ensured that 'my features were rendered immobile.' But it goes deeper than that. This Fu can watch a truly horrible scene – in which a hapless Chinese girl struggles silently in a glass chamber as it steadily fills with filthy Thames water – and respond to it with the deadpan observation, 'Another suicide...' There is no lip-smacking exultation in his own villainy anywhere to be seen. It's as if Fu's murderous drive towards world domination were a purely cerebral pursuit, with human beings as expendable pawns in a fiendish intellectual sport.

This sociopathic impassivity would reach chilling heights in Lee's third performance as Fu, but here it contributes to a strikingly weird composition in which the face of Fu's deadly daughter, Lin Tang, looms in the left foreground while Fu himself sits nonchalantly in the right background. Both remain as unmoving, and unmoved, as statues when the rinky-dink dance music on Fu's wireless is suddenly interrupted by news of his latest atrocity: the killing of some 3000 residents of Fleetwick, Essex. As Nayland Smith and his colleagues take a tour of this depopulated backwater, the film carries a brief echo of Wolf Rilla's *Village of the Damned*. Coincidentally, Rilla's father Walter was cast in *Face* as a German professor under threat from Fu Manchu, though he was under threat in reality – almost dy[ing], to Lee – from the flu which afflicted th[e shoot]. Lee himself succumbed to an ear infe[ction].

If, as Lee put it, 'the conditions were [awful]', the results, crisply directed by Don Sh[arp], are genuinely striking. The Dublin locatio[ns, with] grimy industrial bits, are splendidly u[sed, and] looking, as in *Sherlock Holmes und das [Halsband des] Todes*, more like turn-of-the-century London than London itself – and the film abounds in gripping set-pieces, like a car chase in which the pilot of a bi-plane off-handedly drops bombs in the path of Nayland Smith's car. Nigel Green's grimly unflappable Nayland Smith and Karin Dor's fetching Teutonic ingenue are very good value, too.

Lee recalled how Sax Rohmer's widow visited the shoot and told him 'that she thought I looked very much as her husband had intended, and recounted an experience he had had in Limehouse ... On one foggy night he had seen a huge, expensive car draw up before a seedy-looking building and from it step an immensely tall and dignified Chinese followed by a beautiful half-caste girl. They became the models for Fu Manchu and his daughter.'[5] Something of the chill of this anecdote is preserved in the film's location of Fu's nocturnal hideaway beneath a Gothic graveyard, but even more of it is preserved in broad daylight when Fu's tiny daughter, disguised as an old lady, is hurrying towards an imposing car and Fu unexpectedly lurches out of it to hiss 'Run!' The impression of an unknowable evil located in workaday London is powerfully conveyed and strongly reminiscent of Stoker's *Dracula*. Stoker is also recalled in Smith's climactic pursuit of Fu back to his Tibetan stronghold and in a scene where Fu – like Dracula, only rather more talkative – hypnotises an English professor in his study.

Three More Mesmerists

Three other hypnotic characters would come Lee's way in 1965. In April he finally agreed to Hammer's request to play Dracula again, signing a single contract encompassing both *Dracula Prince of Darkness* and *Rasputin the Mad Monk*, two components of a four-picture package that Anthony Nelson Keys proposed to make back-to-back. Rasputin was the lure that persuaded him to don Dracula's mantle once more, now supplemented by the blood-red lining he had successfully resisted back in 1957. And, as Lee prepared to return to his most famous role, he and Gitte also elected to return to London, swopping Lake Geneva for Belgravia, with Boris and Evie Karloff as next door neighbours.

Dracula Prince of Darkness was given the lustre of widescreen Techniscope and, after some 45 minutes of atmospheric scene-setting, furnishes an ingenious means of reviving what the opening narration has called 'the most evil and terrible creature who ever set his seal on civilisation.' In a scene that called down on Hammer howls of critical execration such as they hadn't heard since the late 1950s, an English tourist is suspended like a steer above Dracula's sarcophagus and his blood, of which there's an awful lot, is used to lubricate the Count's dessicated remains. Foreshadowing the kind of thing that would later appear in *The Texas Chain Saw Massacre*, the sequence is thrillingly staged in quasi-religious style by Terence Fisher and provides Dracula with a suitably magical rejuvenation. So magical, unfortunately, that Lee decreed that any human characteristics in the Count would seem incongruous thereafter and should be deleted, including his dialogue. 'As Dracula I never say a word,' he warned his fans. 'As I am already a vampire from the word go, there is nothing I can say – not even a courteous "Well, here we are again," etc.'

As a result, the mask of evil that proved so uniquely frightening in the first film is still present and correct, but this time around the mask is almost all there is. It remains frightening in itself, but the deeper horror of its use in *Dracula* – as a ghastly contrast with the Count's more human moments – is absent. A certain dynamism, from Fisher as well as Lee, is also missing. Several scenes are more or less direct replays of highlights from the first film but don't quite cut it. Dracula's hissing appearance at the

Stepping out on the truncated castle set for Dracula Prince of Darkness *(1965). 'Christopher Lee is as intensely absorbed in his vampire roles as ever [Edmund] Kean was in Overreach,' commented the* Times *film critic David Robinson*

top of the main staircase, framed by marble pillars and backed by a blood-tinted tapestry, is stunning stuff but is supplemented by a strangely listless tussle in which Charles Kent (Francis Matthews) obediently crashes into the Count's fireside footstool just as Jonathan Harker did eight years before. There are many splendid moments, however, as when Dracula corners Kent's wife Diana (Suzan Farmer) and Michael Reed's hellish underlighting causes his eyebrows to spider alarmingly across his forehead.

But Lee's best moments remain those in which he allows a vestige of humanity to creep in. The revived vampire's first appearance, his white face hovering in darkness above the cowering Helen Kent (Barbara Shelley), is a classic. The red light in Lee's eyes seems briefly forlorn – as if to say, 'Well, here we are again, condemned to an eternity of blood-drinking' – before his lips peel back with appalling deliberation to reveal the trademark fangs. And at the end, when Dracula is consigned to an imaginative but clumsily executed end in his own moat, Lee's desperate attempts to avoid sliding into the water are topped by a weirdly heart-rending shriek when he finally does so. The physical hazards seemingly inseparable from a Hammer shoot this time echoed his injury on *The Curse of Frankenstein*. One of Lee's red contact lenses fell out onto the salt-covered plasterboard 'ice' at the climax and was reinserted while a few grains of salt still clung to it, with agonising effect. Lee's stunt double, Eddie Powell, fared much worse, however, nearly drowning during the same sequence.

Dracula's frozen moat, together with several other sets and some of the film's cast, would resurface in Don Sharp's *Rasputin the Mad Monk*, which started filming on 7 June, only three days after *Prince of Darkness* wrapped. Hammer's thoughts had first turned to preparing a tuppence-coloured biopic of Rasputin in 1961, but even four years later the notoriously litigious Prince Yousoupoff was still alive (just). Lee told his fan club that 'As a small boy, my mother tells me I was introduced to Prince Felix Yousoupoff and the Grand Duke Dimitri, two of the assassins of Rasputin. Rather strange. The former still lives in Paris and will not consent to the real story being shown on the screen, which rather ties our hands.'

Indeed it did. Hammer's need to tread carefully for fear of a Yousoupoff lawsuit combined with the film's position in Tony Keys' penny-pinching back-to-back production programme to make *Rasputin the Mad Monk* a rather fragile vessel in which to contain Lee's colossal performance. He threw everything into it, including a mass of historical research but not the Russian accent that he was still considering while shooting the Dracula picture. By 30 June, he was informing his fans that 'I am enmeshed in the making of *Rasputin*, not only figuratively but also literally, as I am festooned in hair from morning to night. This is without doubt the most demanding role I have ever undertaken ... [requiring] more of me as an actor than any part I have ever had. The range is enormous, and the difficulties of presenting this enigmatic character with any degree of reality are nearly insuperable.'

Lee's impatience with the hirsute Rasputin 'look' continued unabated ('All this hair is most irritating,' he grumbled, adding that 'as far as I am concerned the Rolling Stones can have it all!'), but the results are extremely striking. Thirty years later, Lee would self-deprecatingly claim that 'The only character I played over the top, because there was no alternative, was Rasputin.'[6] In fact, his performance is invested with a certain historical plausibility not shared by the film itself while remaining a monumental piece of melodramatic acting done in the grand manner. And, though conceived on an epic scale, Lee's performance is still garnished with telling details. Approaching a woman's sickbed and making ready for a healing sequence of frightening intensity, he nevertheless finds time for a rapid appraisal of the woman's doe-eyed daughter Tania (Fiona Hartford). His subsequent liaison with Tania is surprisingly erotic, as is his seduction of the Tsarina's lady-in-waiting Sonia later on, but his fascination for both is clearly the snake-like fascination of a man who is equal parts megalomaniac, misogynist, manipulator and murderer.

This is made clear in his conversation with a cheery carter who escorts him to St Petersburg (played by the pint-sized Bartlett Mullins but unmistakeably voiced by Hammer veteran Michael Ripper). 'What do we have senses for if not to use them?' rumbles Rasputin. 'To feel, taste, touch, stroke – crush.' His inability to distinguish between stroking and crushing is confirmed when Sonia finally rebels against his mercenary treatment of her (Barbara Shelley, so good in the Dracula picture, is equally incandescent here), and a hair-raisingly violent confrontation culminates in him callously hypnotising her into committing suicide. This scene – with Lee cackling insanely, Shelley shrieking vengefully, both with all stops way, way out – is certainly one of the most astonishing in the Hammer repertoire.

For such a patrician actor, Lee manages a convincing impression of low-life bluster in his scenes of boozy hellraising in the Café Tzigane; his dark-eyed, wordless toast to the aristocratic Vanessa (Suzan Farmer) from across the room seems like a ghastly act of violation in itself. As Rasputin's influence at court deepens, Lee shares powerful

'I'm going to show you what it means to act, not from the surface, but from the soul': Philippe Darvas with protégée Nicole (Jenny Till) in Theatre of Death *(1965)*

scenes with Renée Asherson's impressionable Tsarina and John Bailey's tight-lipped Dr Siglov and eventually splashes a young would-be assassin with vitriol. Played entirely in the dark, with only teasing lines like 'Careful, Peter: there are acids in here' to punctuate it, this scene is something of a tour de force, but it's nothing compared to the extraordinary climax in which two other assassins (Francis Matthews and Richard Pasco) finally succeed in their mission.

Lured into what he supposes will be a hot date with Vanessa, Rasputin is unaware that his narcissistic private self is being spied upon by Pasco's excellent Dr Zargo (and us). Here Lee is clever enough to introduce some charming comic touches as he prepares for his big night with Vanessa, comic touches which artfully increase our apprehension. He vainly smooths his hair and beard, greedily guzzles Zargo's poisoned wine, tosses a chocolate box lid over the back of the sofa prior to impatiently seating himself, even does a discreet double-take on spying the chocolates themselves. He demolishes one, not knowing they're all spiked with cyanide, and then opts to shove three into his mouth at once.

Rasputin's subsequent agonies – retching, screaming and bent almost double – were reportedly the result of consultations with medical men about the effects of cyanide poisoning. Whether accurate or not, they constitute an amazing display of truly baroque acting, culminating in Rasputin, still resplendent in his red silk tunic, crawling slug-like across the floor towards the petrified Zargo and receiving a hypodermic in the neck for his pains. 'He won't die,' Zargo whimpers. 'He *is* the Devil!' Rasputin's reluctance to expire is clearly the prototype of all those 'monster sits up again just when you thought he was dead' scenes that became so familiar in 1980s slasher flicks. But at the end it isn't Rasputin but a weedy rag doll which is defenestrated and hurtles to the ice below, reminding one that, for all Don Sharp's clever efforts at damage limitation, *Rasputin the Mad Monk* is an unworthy vehicle for its star. As Barbara Shelley put it, 'I thought he was brilliant. If it hadn't been a Hammer film, he would have had incredible reviews for that … Really, it's very difficult to work with a great mate and be impressed. Yet he could almost hypnotise me in *Rasputin*. This tremendous inner strength came through.'[7]

A rather less formidable hypnotist fell to Lee's lot in *Theatre of Death*, directed at Elstree by Samuel Gallu, a portly veteran of some 450 TV shows, in October and November. Though cast as little more than a top-billed red herring, Lee conceded that 'I think it may well be quite entertaining' and accurately singled out Gil Taylor's cinematography as 'superb.' Made in Scope for the independent Pennea Productions, the film benefits from a luridly coloured reprise of the kind of Grand

Guignol setting last properly exploited in *Mad Love* back in 1935. The theatre in question is the Paris 'Théatre de Mort' (actually London's old Lyric Hammersmith) and is the setting for some nicely sado-erotic routines while a 'medical' vampire stalks the foggy Paris streets outside.

Lee is Philippe Darvas, the martinet director who inherited the theatre from his father and whose directorial techniques are sadistic in the extreme. When Dilys Watling's Heidi turns in an under-powered performance at rehearsal, her pouting justification that 'I'm hungry; I missed lunch' doesn't go down at all well. Dazzling in a V-necked scarlet sweater, Darvas shows disquieting relish in demonstrating the correct method of committing the various stage atrocities he has devised. 'Lesson number one, my friends,' he intones. 'Always catch your audience. Involvement: the number one priority in all good theatre.' To make us even more worried about him, he has a tendency to hole up in a cobweb-strewn torture chamber beneath the stage, at one point treating himself to a slide show featuring images from *Der Golem*, the 1931 version of *Dr Jekyll and Mr Hyde* and, very cheekily, Valerie Gaunt baring her fangs in *Dracula*.

A portrait of Darvas (complete with removable eyes for undercover surveillance of his employees) seems to be modelled on Lee's Byronic turn in *La frusta e il corpo*, though the flouncy wig he wears in the film points forward to his appearance in *El proceso de las brujas*. A scene in which he hypnotises his pasty-faced protégée Nicole (Jenny Till) with a blue-tinted signet ring provides an echo of *Rasputin* ('Maybe he's doing a Svengali on her,' speculates Ivor Dean's dogged police inspector), as does a sadistic stand-off with Lelia Goldoni's snub-nosed Dani Gireaux. Demolishing Dani verbally in the same way Rasputin did Sonia, Lee has a memorably mad moment as he drags her before a mirror and spits, 'Take a look at yourself! Look at that make-up! It's ridiculous!'

Darvas disappears a scant 45 minutes in (reversing the example of *Dracula Prince of Darkness* and many of Lee's other films), having been around merely to mislead the audience into thinking that he must be the vampire. Before his disappearance, Darvas shares an uncomfortable car journey with Julian Glover's doctor hero, and it's hard not to detect a certain extra-textual impatience in Lee's voice when he asks Glover, 'Does the subject of vampires interest you?'

YELLOW PERIL 2 & 3

Advertised with the creaky tag-line, 'The Sinister Minister of Fear is Here!', *The Face of Fu Manchu* had been a big hit in the US, with an especially impudent publicity campaign reserved for New York. The film's release coincided with the mayoral elections of autumn 1965, and some 500 subways were festooned with placards depicting Fu's face and characteristic fingernail alongside the slogan, FU MANCHU FOR MAYOR. A sequel was inevitable and Harry Alan Towers decided to shoot it back-to-back at Bray Studios with a humdrum crime melodrama directed by John Moxey, who had last worked with Lee in *The City of the Dead*. 'It looks as if I'm going to be asked to do a film next month called *The Man Without a Face*,' Lee told his fans. 'In fact, I have agreed to do it, provided that I am given a final shooting script that is satisfactory. If I do this film it will start on 22 November.'

The film appears to have been delayed until 6 December and became known as *Circus of Fear*. Like most Towers productions, it featured a fair smattering of German actors to give it added Euro-appeal – also to appease Towers' German backers, who called it *Das Rätsel des silbernen Dreieck*. *The Face of Fu Manchu* had showcased not only the elderly Walter Rilla but also krimi favourite Joachim Fuchsberger and Karin Dor, frequently a lovely half-breed in Germany's then-popular Yugoslavian-shot Westerns. *Circus of Fear* located Eddi Arent and Klaus Kinski (last seen with Lee in *Das Rätsel der roten Orchidee*), together with Heinz Drache, in the unlikely environs of Winkfield in Berkshire.

The action begins with a moderately exciting heist staged on Tower Bridge, involves lion-taming scenes that look like stock footage culled from Sidney Hayers' far superior 1959 shocker *Circus of Horrors*, and features a very obvious, thunder-thighed double for Margaret Lee during a knife-throwing act. The dull result is further disfigured by Johnny Douglas' hideously over-emphatic jazz score and is only enlivened by the august presence of Cecil Parker and some nice exterior views of Bray Studios. All in all, it's a sorry waste of some promising source material; German prints reveal it as another Edgar Wallace picture, derived from his 1929 stories *Again the Three Just Men* and *The Law of the Three Just Men*.

In British prints, Lee shared top billing with Leo Genn but his face is obscured by a black hood until well over an hour into the film's running time. Lee justified this absurdly self-effacing role by saying that 'the audience will get a rest from gazing at these mournful features,' though one critic grumbled that 'the girls are going to be disappointed to see so little of Christopher Lee without his mask.'[8] Complete with tweed jacket, jodhpurs and riding boots, Lee is a shady lion tamer called Gregor. 'Years ago he was involved in a serious accident and very badly scarred,' the owner of Barberini's Circus informs us, but

With daughter Christina at Bray Studios while filming The Brides of Fu Manchu *(1966)*

Gregor's face is climactically revealed to be perfectly presentable after all. He is also revealed to be Suzy Kendall's missing father, rather than the uncle we'd been led to believe, and finally takes a tumble over a cliff by way of some very poor back-projection.

The Fu Manchu sequel followed at Bray on 12 January 1966, again under the guiding hand of Don Sharp, and was called *The Brides of Fu Manchu*. 'I am expecting to pop off with Gitte and the producer,' Lee explained, 'to Scandinavia, Holland and possibly France to choose 12 young ladies of impeccable beauty and unimpeachable morals to play the 12 hostages or 'brides' of Fu Manchu ... all of whom represent different countries in Europe. Sounds like quite a good idea.' This old-fashioned publicity wheeze may have helped sell the picture – in the Continental version of the film, the 12 lucky starlets were obliged to go topless – but the infusion of cheesecake does no real favours to an inexplicably dreary follow-up to the splendid *Face*.

After an indigestible replay of the previous film's conclusion, *Brides* proceeds to an authentically sadistic scene in which Fu forces Carole Gray (raven-haired star of Sharp's *Curse of the Fly*) to kill another girl hostage under hypnosis. There's also a nasty sequence in which Marie Versini (Dirk Bogarde's tumbril companion at the conclusion of *A Tale of Two Cities*) is held over a snakepit by the blank-faced brides. There are a great many more genuine Chinese among Fu's henchmen than *Face* could boast, but there are also far too many unappetising German actors clogging up the cast list, together with disturbing indications that Fu is going the way of Lee's Dracula into what Shakespearean critics, speaking of Iago, have called 'motiveless malignity.' For all the bone-freezing spin Lee puts on lines like 'When those men die, I shall rule – and the world will be mine,' one longs for Fu to have some genuinely interesting motive for his power mania.

This failing was pinpointed by several disappointed critics on the film's release in December. 'Fu Manchu, you should have quit while you were ahead,' observed Robert Salmaggi. 'But no, you got lucky with the camp success of *The Face of Fu Manchu* and so you had to make *The Brides of Fu Manchu*. Fooey on you, Fu. You dropped the ball this time out. You stand there like a nudnik with your Rosalind Russell shoulder-pads, your droopy mustache and your outsized fingernails and you shout all sorts of challenges about "The world will soon be mine, all mine!" What would you do with it if you got it? With the sloppy, amateurish way you handle things ... you wouldn't last a single day.'[9] Already worried by Towers' scripts, Lee found himself in agreement with criticisms such as these.

Five Golden Dragons at Hong Kong's Shaw Studios, September 1966: relaxing with George Raft, Dan Duryea, Brian Donlevy, Margaret Lee and (standing) director Jeremy Summers, producer Norman Williams and Rupert Davies

As it is, the script manages at least one reasonably good gag. Fu having threatened to destroy Windsor Castle, his opponents' efforts to protect that national monument are made to look ridiculous when Fu vaporises the 123 people aboard a ship called the Windsor Castle. The picture also has a sufficient grasp of period detail to sneak in a fleeting reference to Nigel Playfair's long-running 1920s revival of *The Beggar's Opera* at the Lyric Hammersmith. But *Brides* is only a shadow of its spirited forerunner, and is further weakened by a Nayland Smith from Douglas Wilmer (then very popular as the BBC's Sherlock Holmes) which is considerably less engaging than Nigel Green's in the previous picture.

Wilmer would show a good deal more spirit in the third entry in the series; so, for that matter, would the film itself. But before proceeding to the next startling developments in the Fu Manchu saga, Towers and his German sponsors entered into an arrangement with Hong Kong's Shaw Brothers. Lee accordingly flew to Hong Kong on 15 September for a brief cameo in an exotic crime caper called *Five Golden Dragons*. The director was Jeremy Summers, whose father Walter had been responsible for *The Dark Eyes of London*, the Bela Lugosi vehicle that had so alarmed Lee in 1939. The result is no more absorbing than *Circus of Fear*, but at least it benefits from some eye-catching backdrops and a very droll (and extraordinarily fey) lead performance from Robert Cummings, here making his last film and styling himself Bob Cummings. The film is also distinguished by Rupert Davies as a Shakespeare-spouting police superintendent and by a trio of extremely attractive leading ladies – Maria Perschy, Margaret Lee and Maria Röhm. But it also has its fair share of floppy-limbed dummies plummeting from high-rise buildings and 'comedy' musical effects during a manic chase round a pagoda.

The five golden dragons of the title are a group of all-powerful crime lords who only turn up near the end. Lee is Golden Dragon No 3, arriving from Beirut in a private yacht and then convening with his fellows under cover of silken robes and some ridiculous Toy Town dragon masks. Doffing their headgear, they are revealed as Dan Duryea (in turquoise), George Raft (in white) and Brian Donlevy (in blue), with Lee in mauve and the final twist reserved for the black-robed No 5. As well as relishing the golf available in Hong Kong, Lee's chief memory of this lumpen comedy-thriller was that Raft spent some six hours talking to him about his youthful misadventures and that 'a film of that would have been better value.' 'And you can imagine what I talked with Lillian Donlevy about,' Lee added. 'At one time her name was Lillian Lugosi.'[10]

Lee spent the first week of October on a promotional visit to Manila with Towers starlets Margaret Lee and Maria Röhm, then returned to Hong Kong for his third dose of the Yellow Peril. *The Vengeance of Fu Manchu* has a genuinely swashbuckling quality and, true to its title, could reasonably have been advertised with the tag-line 'This time it's personal', giving real bite to the proceedings. 'What do you hope to gain from this?' Nayland Smith asks Fu Manchu at one point. 'A certain personal satisfaction, Commissioner,' hisses Fu in reply. Having been routed by the French Foreign Legion at the end of the previous picture, Fu Manchu really means to get even with Nayland Smith this time around. Lee accordingly shows a lot more relish in expounding his vengeful schemes than he did in *Brides*, and benefits, too, from a noticeably more reptilian make-up job. He's also draped in considerably more splendid robes, his headgear even sprouting some fetching peacock feathers. The Hong Kong and Kowloon locations give added authenticity to the proceedings, with Fu and Lin Tang entering a grand palace in stately procession and a flunkey intoning, 'My lord, we welcome you to the home of your ancestors.'

Of the filmmakers' stint at the Shaw Studios, Lee observed some 15 years later that 'We were the first Europeans to make films there; now, everybody's doing it.' He also recalled that 'The Chinese are *not* inscrutable. One member of the Chinese crowd was always pushing himself forward to get into every

The devil doctor back on home ground in The Vengeance of Fu Manchu *(1966)*

shot. His colleagues got so angry they killed him. They chased him down the road towards Hong Kong and actually killed him.'[11] As if taking its cue from this gruesome incident, the sadism of the previous Fu Manchu films is stepped up considerably. There's a slew of ritual killings in the first reel, including a brisk beheading, and the kittenish heroine (Maria Röhm) is subsequently forced, between mimed nightclub numbers, to strangle one of Fu's skulking henchmen.

The central conceit of the film, borrowed from Rohmer's penultimate novel, *Re-Enter Fu Manchu*, is pleasingly sadistic too. After killing off numerous insubordinates, Fu and Lin Tang are seen on horseback on the brow of a hill. 'Now my work can begin,' Fu announces, 'a work of infinite pleasure, a work of vengeance: vengeance against one man.' Douglas Wilmer's Nayland Smith is significantly greyer than in *Brides* and is involved in the setting-up of Interpol. ('Sounds like a patent medicine,' chortles Howard Marion Crawford's Petrie.) His work is complicated, however, by the fact that Fu Manchu has perfected an exact replica of him via plastic surgery. This sub-plot is totally absurd but furnishes a nasty moment when the bandages are removed from a horribly bruised and scarred Wilmer. 'The face of Nayland Smith: the mind of a murderer,' Fu exults in a neat reversal of the first film's title. Later, the chalk-faced Smith substitute murders Smith's Oriental maid, Jasmine, and when the fake Nayland Smith is finally hanged for this transgression, Fu Manchu actually gets to say 'Vengeance is mine.'

On his way back from Hong Kong, Lee stayed for ten days in December at the LA home of Robert Bloch. During this second Hollywood visit, Bloch reported, 'He proved to be an interesting guest, full of amusing anecdotes about British film people and surprisingly well informed about us colonials. His favourite American performer was W C Fields, whom he imitated better than [Ray] Bradbury did, and he was well versed in the artistry of Laurel and Hardy ... A multilinguist with a fine singing voice, Christopher could have enjoyed a career in music as well as films; every morning he sang Wagner in the shower. As a versatile professional,' Bloch added, 'Christopher chafed at the bit identifying him as a star of horror films ... [and] rightly considered himself capable of "straight" performances. It was his hope that he'd find wider opportunity to demonstrate this in American films, and declared his intention to return.'[12]

THE SNAKEPIT AND THE ANGEL OF DEATH

1967 began for Lee with whispers of numerous projects that failed to come to fruition. His stay in Hollywood had yielded an offer to appear in the *Batman* TV series, and other items mentioned in the trades included a stint with Julie Christie in a Grecian epic called *Leonidas*, Brigitte Bardot in a Christopher

Sweating it out with Patrick Allen in Terence Fisher's Night of the Big Heat *(1967)*

Isherwood TV play called *Colonel Hooker and the Lady* and Vincent Price in a Harry Alan Towers item called *The Sleeper Awakes*. Most intriguing of all, Lee was hotly tipped to play Don Quixote in the West End version of the hit Broadway musical *Man of La Mancha*, but one song – 'Impossible Dream' – proved too high for his voice. When it finally opened at the Piccadilly Theatre in April 1968, the role was taken by Keith Michell.

Amid all these exciting possibilities came a reunion with Peter Cushing and Terence Fisher that did nothing to stir echoes of their past glories. Filmed at Pinewood from 20 February to 31 March, *Night of the Big Heat* was shot, ironically, in peculiarly cold weather and was based on a John Lymington novel that had already served as a TV play. Fisher's film of it, produced under the tin-pot auspices of Tom Blakeley's Planet Productions, rarely breaks free of its cramped TV-style dimensions, despite attractive colour photography by Reginald Wyer. The plot has various offshore Little Englanders sweating copiously in an alien-induced heatwave while Lee's mysterious scientist, Godfrey Hanson, lurks about their island collecting evidence to the quivering strains of Malcolm Lockyer's dreadful score.

Hanson is the focus of a 'what the hell's he doing up there?' intrigue reminiscent of James Whale's *The Invisible Man*. Patrick Allen's square-jawed publican finally bursts into Lee's rented room claiming hotly that 'This is my hotel, not your bloody laboratory!' Hanson's lengthy explanation, that 'For the past week this island has become ... the central landing-point for beings from another planet,' is ruinously staged in a phosphorescent red glare – Hanson having turned his quarters into a makeshift dark-room – and is typical of the film's preference for talky dialogue over action. Hanson is an impossibly po-faced part (not helped by a pair of forbidding, black-rimmed NHS spectacles), and Lee can do little with it. As in a few other boring roles that he was saddled with around this time, his frustration is almost visible from time to time, a frustration that would happily ebb away when his roles took a turn for the better in 1969.

Hanson comes up, nevertheless, with a bland statement that, unknown to him, sums up the domestic and sexual tensions afflicting all the characters but himself. 'This heat's bound to lead to irrational behaviour,' he points out, immediately after which Kenneth Cope tries to rape Jane Merrow, who is a pouting, sweat-gilded sex-pot throughout and one of the picture's few redeeming features. Cushing's role is even more thankless than Lee's, and both of them are obliged to tell us over a walkie-talkie about all the things that we can see them doing quite clearly.

Professor Stone meets Emma Peel (Diana Rigg) and John Steed (Patrick Macnee) in The Avengers: Never, Never Say Die *(1967)*

Fisher had demonstrated his lack of sympathy with science fiction as long ago as early 1950s efforts like *Four Sided Triangle* and *Spaceways*, and it contributes to making *Night of the Big Heat* a bona-fide disaster. The final revelation of the invaders – 'looking,' as Lee put it, 'like fried eggs' – contributes even more.

The wintery start to 1967 had been more faithfully recorded in Lee's first stint in the cult TV series *The Avengers*, six years old but now a full-colour marvel of well-oiled elegance shot at Elstree. The story *Never, Never Say Die* was directed by Robert Day in the week ending on 14 February and transmitted on 17 March. As the saucily named Professor Frank N Stone, Lee is a chilly boffin in a silver 'en brosse' wig who spends the first 20 minutes rampaging the countryside in clodhopping boots. His automaton-like behaviour involves threatening telly regulars like Arnold Ridley and John Junkin and seems strangely influenced by any transistor radios in the vicinity. Stone, it is revealed, has created a plastic-coated duplicate of himself and a take-over by similar duplicates is only averted when Diana Rigg's Emma Peel engages in hand-to-hand combat with the robot Stone. The show looked back to Lee's prep school days in his scenes with former schoolboy co-star Patrick Macnee and forward to his role as a bureaucratic 'composite' in *Scream and Scream Again*.

'I am leaving on Monday 19 June for Munich,' Lee subsequently told his fan club, 'where I shall be playing a rather revolting aristocrat in a rather weird semi-surrealistic German film entitled at the moment *The Pendulum*. I really have no idea whether this film will ever be shown outside Europe and it is just possible that this might be an advantage.' Lee's obviously jaded approach to this assignment was unaffected by its promising credentials. *Die*

Schlangengrube und das Pendel (The Snakepit and the Pendulum) was shot between 16 May and 7 July and was touted, rightly, as Germany's first Gothic horror movie since the war. It was directed by Harald Reinl, veteran of numerous German Westerns and krimis, and starred his wife – and Lee's co-star from *The Face of Fu Manchu* – Karin Dor. The American Lex Barker, who had supplanted Johnny Weissmuller as Tarzan in the late 1940s and subsequently became Germany's biggest postwar star in his cowboy role of Old Shatterhand, was also brought in to add a further stiffening of star-power.

But Lee was still not convinced. 'The only thing that I can remember from a brief glance at the so-called script is that I start the film by being placed in an iron mask and am then torn in pieces by four horses. Whatever happens after that could conceivably be something of an anti-climax – but if you were to murmur the magic words "The blood is the life" you would not be far wrong.' And, while shooting his scenes at the Bavaria-Atelier, Lee insisted to German journalist Horst Königstein that 'You could, if you wanted to, call the character a living dead but he is *not* a vampire.'[13] But Lee need not have worried. Redolent of a highly coloured Grimm fairy tale, *Die Schlangengrube und das Pendel* is a strangely charming film, though somewhat short on incident and owing more to Mario Bava's *La maschera del demonio* than its accredited source in Edgar Allan Poe.

Lee plays the absurdly named Count Regula (which sounds like a constipation cure even in German) and is first seen in the condemned cell as he faces execution for the murder of 12 virgins and calls down a curse on his spaniel-wigged accuser. 'Reinholdt von Marienberg,' he intones, 'I shall destroy you, and all your family.' He then has a spiked mask shoved onto his face and is torn apart by horses in full view of the acquiescent townsfolk. These scenes in dungeon and town square are similar to scenes filmed later in the year by Michael Reeves for *Witchfinder General*, though the quartering itself is tactfully represented only by a cartoon drawn by a tale-spinning old man some 35 years later.

Von Marienberg's descendant, Roger Montelis (Barker), then undertakes an engagingly eerie, mist-wreathed coach journey to Regula's castle on Good Friday; the limbs on the trees are human ones, hanged bodies depend from the branches and corpses are scattered underfoot. And in the castle itself, art directors Gabriel Pellon and Werner Maria Achmann have a field day. Regula's decorative scheme includes Bosch-flavoured frescoes, walls studded with skulls, skeletons dressed in suits of armour and vultures picking at bloody morsels on the floor, not to mention a torture chamber with his 12 virgin victims arranged in various artistic postures and Regula himself preserved in a shimmering glass sarcophagus. The sumptuous Lilian von Brandt (Dor) is later assailed by tarantulas, scorpions and lizards, while the snakepit itself features human arms and skulls as well as snakes. The concentration of Gothic images reaches almost ridiculous extremes, but nevertheless creates a genuinely nightmarish setting for Regula's resurrection.

When his manservant Anatol (Carl Lange) cuts his wrist and bleeds green blood onto the lid of Regula's sarcophagus, the Count's limbs are magically reattached and the revived Regula turns out to be a rather forlorn, grey-faced combination of vampire and mad scientist. He's given to sonorous quotations from the Dracula phrasebook ('Welcome to my house' as well as 'The blood is the life'), but seems unutterably desolate and weary as he warns Lilian from his throne that 'I have the blood of 12 virgins; you shall be the thirteenth.' Thankfully, Lee's own voice is preserved in the dubbed version (released in the UK and US as *Blood Demon*) and does much to dispel the effect of an unusually crude, greasepaint-heavy make-up job.

Regula and Anatol are a memorably creepy pair and are finally routed when Montelis, having escaped from the metronomic onslaught of the knife-edged pendulum, tells Regula that 'I too have a pendulum; the pendulum that will destroy you.' Shrinking from Montelis' swinging crucifix, Regula runs at him with an axe but is finally reduced, like Anatol, to dust while the assembled virgins turn to skeletons. *Die Schlangengrube und das Pendel* may not have restored to German horror films the lustre they bore in the pioneering days of silent film, but it has a uniquely hypnotic atmosphere and deserves to be better known.

Pausing only for a brief assignment in Madrid (discussed below) and an appearance on *The Dave Allen Show*, Lee returned to Elstree in August for one of Hammer's most celebrated latterday pictures. He had first recommended Dennis Wheatley's novel *The Devil Rides Out* to James Carreras as long ago as 1963, and when the project finally received Carreras' go-ahead in 1967, the grateful Wheatley urged Hammer to cast Lee against type as the steely Duc de Richleau. This they did, and with Terence Fisher enlisted to direct and the epicene West End star Charles Gray cast as Lee's satanic antagonist Mocata, the conditions were right for a picture in which, as Lee put it, 'The terrible vibrations of evil were clearly felt.'

'I have high hopes for this film,' said Lee shortly after production ended, 'and it will prove, once and for all, that I can be accepted in a completely normal role.' This depends on one's definition of 'normal', for, rather like Van Helsing and Dracula, there are several indications that de Richleau and Mocata are opposite sides of the same coin. And just as his idol Conrad Veidt played a Christ figure in *The Passing of the Third Floor Back* in much the same way that he generally played demonic ones, Lee brings to de Richleau the same frightening intensity he normally applied to his villainous roles. The film delivers its warning against occult dabbling with such extraordinary force because of the absolute seriousness with which it was made. Lee's de Richleau is central to this effect, giving ominous weight to almost every line. This approach would appear heavy-handed in a more 'realistic' context, but here it convinces us right from the beginning that we're watching a life-and-death struggle of cosmic significance.

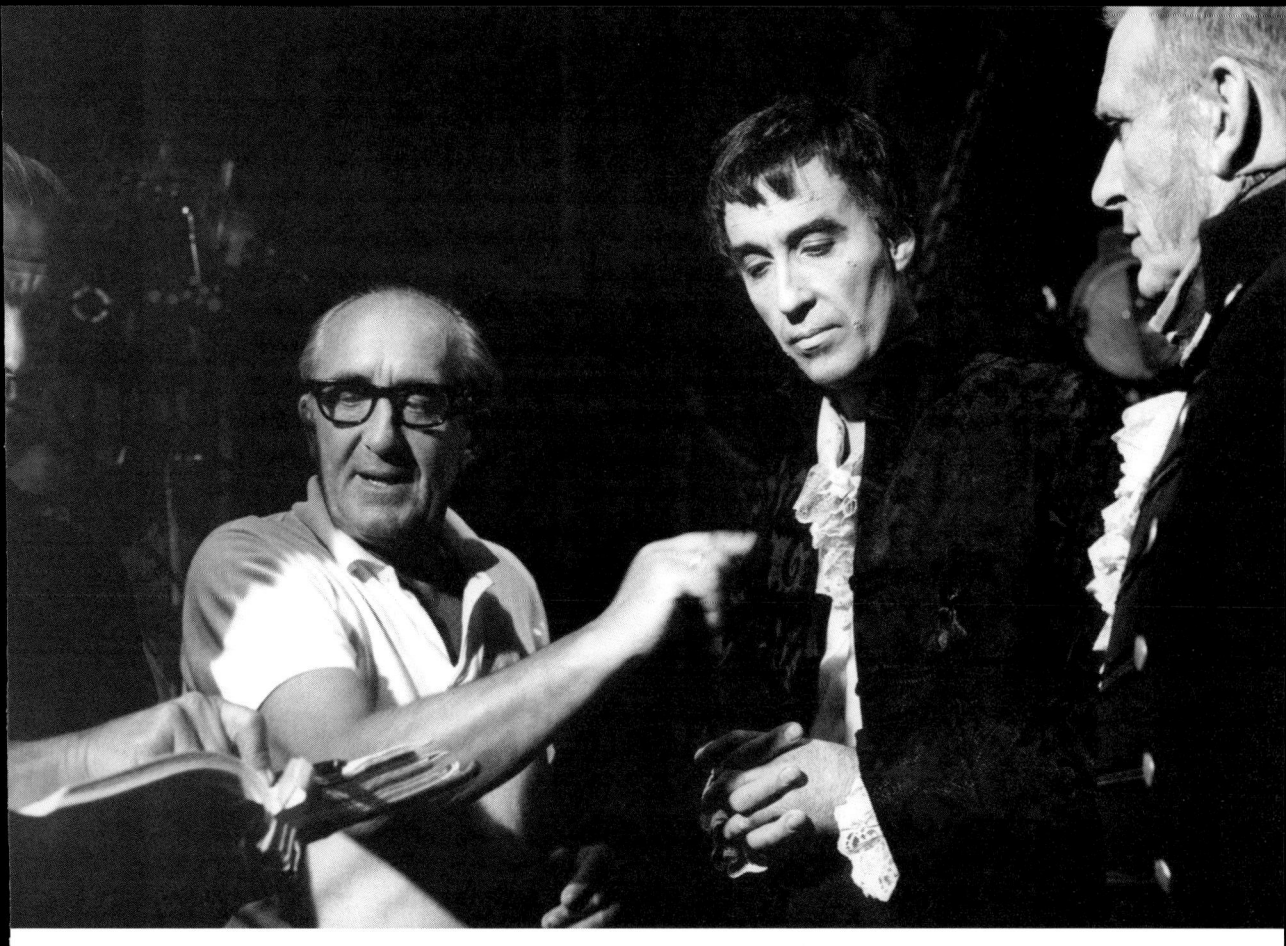

The film is set in the same Sexton Blake-flavoured world exploited by *The Face of Fu Manchu*, but it also has a genuine aroma of that 1920s demi-monde presided over by Aleister Crowley. At Simon Aron's opening cocktail party, laced with numerous disquieting portents of what is to come, Lee expertly layers de Richleau's gathering apprehension with slightly frosty good manners. Packed with incident as well as

Lee and Carl Lange (far right) with director Harald Reinl on the Munich set of Die Schlangengrube und das Pendel *(1967)*

portent, the first 20-odd minutes culminate in a gripping scene in which de Richleau and his slow-witted friend Rex are visited in Simon's observatory by the first of several Mocata-fuelled manifestations.

To relieve nervous tension after this petrifying event – de Richleau's own as well as the audience's – Lee is careful to bring a light, almost comic, touch to de Richleau's lordly nonchalance when planning his next move. Asked by Rex if he can borrow his car, he replies airily, 'Yes; take any of them,' and brings the same breezy sense of noblesse oblige to his determination to consult various forbidden volumes at the British Museum. 'Fortunately, the curator is a friend of mine,' he off-handedly points out. Lee himself followed de Richleau's example in this, spending long hours in the British Museum and coming up with the genuine prayer of exorcism that vanquishes Mocata at the climax.

The first phase of the film ends with a satanic ceremony on Salisbury Plain – James Bernard's music here is stunning, and Lee's cry of 'The Goat of

With Terence Fisher on the observatory set of The Devil Rides Out (1967)

Mendes! The Devil himself!' electrifying – and then the battle lines are finally drawn when de Richleau delivers Simon and fellow sufferer Tanith to the country home of Richard and Marie Eaton. (In the family orientation of these battle lines, the story bears a further resemblance to Stoker's *Dracula*.) The long night spent by the protagonists in a protective pentacle as Mocata hurls various satanic monstrosities at them is one of the greatest set-pieces in horror cinema, brilliantly directed and edited and its effect enhanced even in the quieter moments. When the sceptical Richard complains that 'Frankly, I think we're behaving like a pack of idiots,' de Richleau's measured reply – 'It begins' – is sufficient in itself to induce a fluttering of the stomach. Most frightening of all is the moment when, hearing approaching hoofbeats and otherworldly whinnying from beyond the door, de Richleau quietly informs us that 'He has given up trying to get Simon; he has sent the Angel of Death himself to claim him...'

The explosive arrival of this apparition astride a golden-hoofed, bat-winged steed is so shattering as to render the remainder of the film a slight anti-climax. But when Simon finally thanks God for his deliverance, de Richleau's solemn words of agreement ('Yes, Simon: He is the one we must thank') combine with the Messianic swelling of the music to create a genuinely moving coda. Over 30 years on, Lee claims that '*The Devil Rides Out* remains in my head as an ongoing project,' with hopes of a remake resurfacing at Hammer's every attempt to resuscitate itself. The special effects could be a great deal better in a 21st century rendition, but would the film's naïve, fairy-tale power, notably in the closing shot described above, be reproducible at this late date? Probably not.

YELLOW PERIL 4 & 5

Harry Alan Towers was still calling upon Lee's services on a regular basis. He had even turned up, in a roundabout way, in Towers' Swiss-set rendition of *Ten Little Indians* in 1965, where a taped message of his voice puts the wind up assembled murder suspects like Shirley Eaton, Hugh O'Brian and Mario Adorf. And on 21 July 1967 he flew to Spain for yet another Towers extravaganza, sandwiched between his trip to Munich for *Die Schlangengrube und das Pendel* and the Elstree filming of *The Devil Rides Out*. 'I am proposing to go directly to Madrid,' he informed his fans, 'for a guest appearance in an Anglo-Spanish-American production for Harry Alan Towers, which is vaguely about some sort of female jungle maiden, what you might call a forest bird ... I shall play the part of a famous explorer who is paralysed and confined to a wheelchair. He is also a grandfather, so I shall have to age five years or so.'

Jeremy Summers' *The Face of Eve* was known simply as *Eve* during production (and also on its US release) and features Celeste Yarnall as a female Tarzan abroad in the Amazonian jungle, modelling a fur bikini presumably inspired by Hammer's smash hit *One Million Years B.C.* Yarnall's performance is so weirdly mannered that she appears throughout to be performing in an underwater ballet, and the film in general is ripe for rediscovery by connoisseurs of high camp. Eve is stumbled upon by explorers Mike (Robert Walker Jr) and Gonzalez (Ricardo Diaz), who report her existence to Burke, a small-time showman played, delightfully, by the inimitable, bald-domed American character star Fred Clark. They also appeal to the disabled Colonel Jeffrey Stewart (Lee) to reveal the whereabouts of the fabled Orejano's Treasure. 'I look upon explorers, prospectors and treasure hunters as the most engaging of God's idiots,' he says affably.

Lee's silver-haired character was loosely modelled on the famous 'vanished' Amazon explorer, Colonel Fawcett, and the sub-plot involving the Colonel and his treacherous associate Diego (Herbert Lom) offers a brief glimpse of genuine drama. The Colonel sits forlornly in his wheelchair at his own alfresco birthday party while the locals whoop it up all around him, consoled only by the presence of his long-lost granddaughter Eve (Rosenda Monteros, last seen in *She*). She isn't Eve at all, of course, but has been insinuated into the household by the conniving Diego in the hope of appropriating the Colonel's money. When he reveals that he hasn't any, the bogus Eve removes her blonde wig and tosses it into the Colonel's lap with a spiteful cry of 'Hang this on the wall with the rest of the trophies.' Distraught, the Colonel pursues her and takes a tumble in his wheelchair down a flight of steps. Confusingly, both Eves seem to have been dubbed by the same artist, the ubiquitous Hammer 'voice' Olive Gregg.

Bedridden, the Colonel likens himself to King Lear (a man who 'ignored his friends and trusted his enemies') and finally has the real Eve delivered to him by Mike and Gonzalez. 'Eve, you never knew her but you're your mother all over again,' he rasps moments before expiring. Eve is then mobbed by insensitive reporters, sets about them with her shoe and defiantly rips aside the patterned frock Mike has squeezed her into. Incredibly, the fur bikini is still in place underneath and the credits roll as Eve strides back into the jungle. As in *The Gorgon*, Lee looks conspicuously too young to play a sexagenarian, but this is far and away the least of the film's absurdities.

For his final Fu Manchu instalments, Towers turned to a 30-something Spanish filmmaker called Jesús Franco. Franco, who regularly styled himself Jess among a slew of more fanciful pseudonyms, had made the derivative but extremely effective *Gritos en la noche* (*The Awful Dr Orlof*) in 1961, a film that stands as Spain's first, and possibly best, horror picture. The highbrow horror fanciers at *Midi-Minuit Fantastique* magazine were moved to utter Franco's name in the same breath as Buñuel when faced with it. Franco's subsequent output of well over 150 wildly eclectic but instantly recognisable films has not borne out this lofty comparison but stamps him, nevertheless, as a true auteur, if film theorists permit such high-flown sobriquets in the low-rent surroundings in which Franco generally operates.

Towers himself was not convinced. 'Franco was a terribly nice man but he shouldn't have been allowed to direct traffic,' he observed in 1990. 'He was a jazz musician who played the trombone until he discovered the zoom lens.'[14] The Franco/Towers collaboration nevertheless yielded nine pictures and kept both men fully occupied until the end of the 1960s. But even Franco's most fervent apologists admit that the Towers pictures – despite, or perhaps because of, their relatively healthy budgets and the presence in them of established stars – are among Franco's drearier productions. Lee would appear in five of them, and the whole sequence kicked off with Towers' penultimate Fu Manchu picture.

The Blood of Fu Manchu took Lee to Rio de Janeiro on 30 November. 'I was not very impressed with Rio,'

Colonel Stewart realises the truth about his presumed granddaughter in The Face of Eve *(1967)*

he opined to his fan club. 'I found it a rather tasteless and certainly unglamorous city, terribly crowded and noisy and frighteningly expensive. However, I think *The Blood of Fu Manchu* could turn out quite well and the director, Jesús Franco, is an extremely talented young man.' After an arresting title sequence with Fu and Lin Tang suspended in smoke-wreathed darkness, the film gives early warning of Franco's fondness for wobbly camera movements and precipitate zooms as Fu, holed up in a South American cave, tells a bevy of fettered beauties that 'Each of you has her appointed task with the ten men who are my greatest enemies. You will take them the gift you bear upon your lips: death.'

The plot that unfolds, though forgotten about for long stretches of the picture, sees Nayland Smith numbered among the international dignitaries who fall prey to Fu's 'kiss and kill' concept. As a result, Smith is debilitated by blindness for much of the film – a condition alleviated at the end by a blood-exchange with Frances Kahn's beauteous Carmen – and the role is therefore a pretty thankless one for Nayland Smith mark three, Richard Greene. Some 30 years earlier, incidentally, Greene had played Lee's Sir Henry role in the Twentieth Century-Fox version of *The Hound of the Baskervilles*.

Apart from a brief view of a vintage car early on, the period of the film is ignored altogether, with Lin Tang looking more 'with it' than ever. And towards the end of the film, an incomprehensible montage sequence not only mixes Fu's victims with glimpses of the leather-clad Shirley Eaton (who was simultaneously playing Rohmer's female Fu, Sumuru, in a fetishistic Franco/Towers extravaganza called *The Girl From Rio*), but also blithely includes views of postwar tower blocks and modern sports cars. We are clearly in that parallel universe unique to Franco's filmography, an impression compounded by the antics of a roly-poly, Pancho Villa-styled outlaw (Ricardo Palacios), whose behaviour suggests that we're watching a Spaghetti Western, or possibly a ritzily scored jungle travelogue, rather than a Fu Manchu film. The ramshackle proceedings also include some bare breasts at a gypsy encampment, Maria Röhm in an unbecoming blonde wig, several shady characters dubbed by the same ubiquitous voice-over artiste (Robert Rietty), and – a spark of interest here – the first confrontation between Fu Manchu and Howard Marion Crawford's Dr Petrie.

Lee himself appears unruffled by his bizarre surroundings, indulging in a delivery much more nasal and rapid-fire than in previous outings and skating lightly over some of Towers' most studiedly oracular dialogue. (Example: 'Let him wait like an ant upon an anvil, never knowing when the hammer blow will strike.') At the end, Nayland Smith says 'There: the end of the Lost City,' while Petrie sighs, 'And, thank God, the end of Fu Manchu.' But, true to Franco's only passing acquaintance with narrative coherence, we've seen almost nothing to justify these self-satisfied pronouncements.

Lee's Fu Manchu had made its mark on popular culture – indeed, the *Observer* lightheartedly speculated, first in July 1967 and again in September 1968, on whether Lee's drooping moustaches in the role had influenced the Eastern-flavoured male fashions of Flower Power – but as a commercial property it was fast approaching its sell-by date. As an indication of waning interest in Towers' franchise, *Blood* was retitled *Kiss and Kill* in the US while its predecessor, *The Vengeance of Fu Manchu*, had been available in large parts of America only in black-and-white. A further indication was provided by the last film in the series, *The Castle of Fu Manchu*, which went into production on 10 September 1968 but failed to turn up on British screens until January 1972. The filming of this one was divided between Barcelona and Istanbul (hence the film's strangely anonymous shooting title, *Assignment Istanbul*), though Lee's self-contained scenes were confined to the former.

Again, much of the film is lathered in the kind of eye-straining pop-art filters characteristic of Franco's late 1960s output, while most of the characters have again been revoiced by Robert Rietty. Even one of Lee's lines – 'Bring forth the two prisoners' – has been revoiced by *someone*. Franco himself puts in an appearance, looking shifty in a red fez. The tiny Tsai Chin, a veteran of all five films as Fu's daughter, seems to vary in weight from scene to scene while most other members of the cast play modish 1960s gangsters trying desperately to look 1930s. Richard Greene's Nayland Smith is, again, given almost nothing worthwhile to do, though his Scottish fishing holiday with Petrie is pleasingly reminiscent of a similar vacation for Holmes and Watson in Universal's *The Spider Woman*. Worst of all, the film begins with five minutes of total incoherence as Franco intercuts Burt Kwouk's demise from *The Brides of Fu Manchu* with blue-tinted stock footage of 1950s cruise liner passengers and a truly hopeless model of the iceberg that Fu Manchu has in store for them.

Castle never really recovers from this inept opening, though Lee himself is still able to bring some new touches to his characterisation. He's not only conspicuously leaner and greyer, he's also more reptilian than ever and has taken to smiling a lot

At Grim's Dyke Hall with Barbara Steele and Boris Karloff for Curse of the Crimson Altar *(1968)*

when tormenting his victims. Brought to its highest pitch seven years later in *To the Devil a Daughter*, Lee's concept of the smiling villain lends *Castle* a wintery breath of the sinister which it otherwise lacks. In fact, it comes dangerously close to being unwatchable. As Marjorie Bilbow put it on the film's long-delayed UK appearance, 'Only in the majestic malignancy of Christopher Lee's periodic appearances could this film be said to stop chasing its tail long enough to justify its title.' [15]

After an extremely promising start, the Fu Manchu series had played itself out in record time. 'I did the Fu Manchu pictures because I thought they were a potentially marvellous subject,' Lee explained in 1970. 'I've read all the Rohmer books, and if we had filmed *them* Fu Manchu would have been as successful as James Bond ... [But] the scripts were not what you would call the best in the world.' [16] And, despite his belief in Franco's talents (a belief undimmed to this day), he pointed out that the last two entries were guilty of 'going to magnificent locations and not using them enough' and were 'rushed through so much that instead of cross-cutting, the zoom lens was used in and out all the time from close-up to long shot back to close-up.' [17] Even so, Lee's association with Towers and Franco was by no means over.

BACK TO BRITISH HORRORS

'On our return flight from Rio to London,' Lee informed his fans in the wake of *The Blood of Fu Manchu*, 'I bent over to talk to some people during a stop at Las Palmas in the Canary Islands – and when I straightened up, my back had gone. The pain was appalling.' Back at home, Lee 'spent two very glamorous weeks flat on my back' over the Christmas and New Year holiday, and reported that for a further 'three weeks I have to wear a form of corset and it will be some time before I am completely back to normal and able to forget about this problem. I also got flu on top of everything else and altogether was at a very low ebb.'

Going back to work at the beginning of February in *Curse of the Crimson Altar* (which had started without him on 22 January), Lee still betrayed signs of his recently corseted anxieties. 'Frankly this was one of the very few occasions in my career,' he confided to his fan club, 'when I can honestly say I did not enjoy my work ... because I was in a state of constant apprehension about my wretched back.' As a result, *Crimson Altar* is one of the very few occasions in Lee's career when he fails to redeem a boring role in an even more boring film.

The picture was produced by Tigon British, a new Hammer rival that had recently been responsible for the stupendous *Witchfinder General*, and was shot by

Christopher Lee – Part Five

that film's brilliant cinematographer, Johnny Coquillon, at W S Gilbert's former home, Grim's Dyke Hall near Harrow. Nominally based on H P Lovecraft's story *Dreams in the Witch House*, the film is atmosphere-free and notable mainly for its pathetic middle-aged attempts at portraying the hip new 'swinging' scene in the wilds of Berkshire. Also for entirely wasting its three iconic stars – Lee, Boris Karloff and, returning from a string of influential Italian horrors, the British-born beauty Barbara Steele. The director responsible was Vernon Sewell, who had last worked with Lee on *Battle of the V.1* in 1957.

Lee's role as Squire Morley is interminably talky and most of his dialogue consists of deeply tedious exposition. In tweed jacket and horn-rimmed spectacles, he swops seemingly endless brandies with the wheelchair-bound Karloff and only begins to show signs of his true nature when searching for a ceremonial dagger in the cobwebbed attic. It turns out that Morley is the descendant of the 17th century witch Lavinia (played by Steele in green-hued face and horned headdress). To avenge himself on the bovine hero (who is the descendant of Lavinia's chief accuser), he tethers his own niece, Eve, to an altar and utters a great deal of mumbo jumbo over her before being shot in the hand by Karloff. The place goes up in flames and, ascending to the roof, Morley turns, rather unexpectedly, into Lavinia. 'He was mad,' Karloff sighs. 'For years I've suspected he had a sick mind. Thought he was a warlock!' If only the script had allowed us a few more glimpses of Morley's 'sick mind'; apart from exposing his niece's purple lingerie, he remains in an affable Home Counties straitjacket throughout and the picture follows suit.

The film was featured in a March 1968 instalment of the BBC's *Film Review* programme, in which presenter Philip Jenkinson visited Grim's Dyke Hall and encountered its three resident icons, while back in January – bad back notwithstanding – Lee had been seen with Barbara Steele, Milton Subotsky and others in a *Whicker's World* discussion called 'A Handful of Horrors'. And shortly after completing *Crimson Altar*, Lee's neighbour Karloff presented him with a signed photo inscribed 'Dear Christopher. Many, many more together, I hope.' This possibility was ruled out when Karloff died, aged 81, at Midhurst on 2 February 1969.

The Lee family followed *Crimson Altar* with a recuperative holiday in Barbados, but Lee's continuing back problems ensured that his stunt double Eddie Powell was extensively employed in *Dracula Has Risen From the Grave*, which started shooting at Pinewood – only the second Hammer film to be shot there – on 22 April 1968. Shots of Lee jumping over parapets or carrying Veronica Carlson's Maria are actually shots of Powell. Remarkably, however, Lee managed to perform Dracula's energetic demise, in which he is spectacularly impaled on an enormous gold crucifix, unassisted save for one brief side-long shot in which Powell is seen bent almost double over the cross.

Lee's astonishing death agonies during this scene, beautifully poised on that fine line between the ghastly and the ridiculous, are a return to the glory days of his mime work in *The Curse of Frankenstein* and *The Mummy*. Struggling 'like a fly on a pin,' as Lee put it, and staring in disbelief at the hands that have proved unable to remove the crucifix, Lee finally allows his head to loll despairingly upwards (not downwards, as in the earlier films) to reveal stigmatic tears of blood. His cloak finally drops from the blood-dripping cross as it previously slid under the ice in *Dracula Prince of Darkness* and flapped forlornly on the floor of his library in *Dracula*.

One of Hammer's most arresting climaxes, the shooting of this blood-drenched scene on Wednesday 29 May was watched by Sir Henry Floyd, Lord Lieutenant of the County of Buckinghamshire, visiting Pinewood in order to confer upon Hammer Film Productions a coveted Queen's Award to Industry. 'After the Lord Lieutenant and his wife, who I'm sure had never been in a studio in their lives, had been watching all this without any expression at all on their faces,' Lee recalled, 'there was a long, long silence and then, very clearly and very penetratingly, he turned to his wife and said, "You know, my dear, that man is a member of my club."'[18]

Two days earlier, Lee had celebrated his 46th birthday performing another exacting scene, in which the atheist hero's attempt to destroy the Count fails to work. 'It was all wrong that Dracula should have been able to remove the stake,' Lee protested. 'I objected at the time, but it was overruled. It is an extremely gruesome sequence: the blood comes pouring out.'[19] The scene is barnstorming stuff nevertheless, and Lee manages to supplement it with a nice detail of his own when, having torn the stake from his heart, the Count appears briefly disorientated, not knowing quite where to look for his aggressor before lobbing the bloody stake at his retreating back.

The scene is typical of the film, a gaudily coloured package of show-stopping moments that ensured its colossal Stateside success when released there in March 1969 with the support of an especially facetious Warner Bros/Seven Arts ad campaign. Freddie Francis, who was enlisted to direct when Terence Fisher broke his leg in a road accident, gives the film a bewitching

Wednesday 29 May 1968: while filming Dracula Has Risen From the Grave, *Sir Henry Floyd, Lord Lieutenant of the County of Buckinghamshire, came to Pinewood to present Hammer Film Productions with a Queen's Award to Industry*

fairy-tale look together with a stronger dose of eroticism than ever. Still relatively youthful-looking in *Prince of Darkness*, Lee is now a perceptibly middle-aged vampire but with no reduction in his sexual allure. Barbara Ewing's lusty Zena becomes positively addicted to his attentions but, as in the previous film, Dracula only enslaves redheads in order to get at blondes. Having tired of Zena, the Count reposes in his coffin and, like some loathsome ill-natured invalid, instructs his dog-collared disciple to 'Destroy her.'

His subsequent bedroom scenes with the radiant Maria, much enhanced by James Bernard's scintillating score and Francis' curious use of amber filters, are as precise a distillation of the Gothic 'Demon Lover' archetype as can be imagined. (In France, the film was retitled *Dracula et les femmes* and advertised with the slogan 'un Don Juan aux dents très longues.') Francis comes up with numerous felicitous touches; at one point Dracula becomes a mere feature of the décor when he steps from the shadow of his upended coffin lid into the miasmic light of his basement hideaway, at others he is a red-eyed demon, lashing his horses onward with maniacal zeal. The film is by no means the best of Hammer's Dracula follow-ups – a conspicuously drippy romance between the young leads makes sure of that – but it does feature some of Lee's most indelibly frightening moments in the Dracula role.

Lee's exertions in this film are particularly remarkable given his increased misgivings about Hammer's approach to the character. 'That was the one,' he asserted, 'that established the pattern of writing a screenplay which really had nothing whatever to do with Dracula then saying, "Now, how can we fit Count Dracula into this?"'[20] Furthermore, he was becoming exasperated by 'the same monotonous dirge from Hammer about not having enough money for my salary.' Having turned the film down initially, he found himself badgered over the telephone by James Carreras himself, 'saying "You must do this film, on my knees I beg you, I'm 62 years old and I cannot take the stress and strain. Do you know how many people you will keep from working at Hammer if you don't agree to do this film?" It really was a form of emotional blackmail. Plus, by then he'd made a deal with a major distributor, and there'd have been hell to pay if he didn't deliver the Dracula film he'd promised.'[21]

During production of *Dracula Has Risen From the Grave*, Lee was heard on BBC Radio 3 as the captain of spaceship Cetus-7, the Ahab figure in a 75-minute adaptation of Ray Bradbury's *Moby Dick* variant *Leviathan '99*, which was broadcast on 3 May. Bradbury had given the script to Lee with the request that he use his influence to get it made. Herman Melville's white whale was replaced by a white comet that has cost the Captain his sight, and Donald McWhinnie in the *Listener* referred to Bradbury's story as 'the poetry of science fiction,' adding that 'I shall remember particularly the voice of ... Christopher Lee, drifting awesomely through the caverns of the air.' Several years later, Bradbury himself recalled in *Vertex* magazine that Lee 'played the Captain and played it beautifully.'

Just after his stint in Barcelona for *The Castle of Fu Manchu*, Lee returned to Elstree in October for another guest appearance in *The Avengers*. In *The Interrogators* (directed by Ealing veteran Charles Crichton and broadcast on New Year's Day 1969), he plays Colonel Mannering, boss of a veritable torture chamber in which the endurance of British agents is severely tested. One of the victims is Steed's new associate, Tara King (Linda Thorson). 'I modelled my military moustache on my father,' Lee told the *Sunday Mirror*, 'and selected my medal ribbons with some care. I have made this Colonel a mixture of many phoney officers I've met ... a blend of megalomania, power lust and sadism.'[22]

In November Lee moved to Shepperton for an American International production, nominally based on Edgar Allan Poe, that should have reunited him with Michael Reeves, the young director who had been an assistant on *Il castello dei morti vivi* four years before and had since given British horror a strident wake-up call with the brutal and brilliant *Witchfinder General*. Reeves' dissatisfaction with the script, and worsening depression, saw him withdraw from the project before filming began, and on 11 February 1969 he was mysteriously found dead at his flat in Cadogan Place.

The Oblong Box had pressed on without him under the direction of Gordon Hessler, former associate producer of *The Alfred Hitchcock Hour*, and Lee's 'special guest star' status as Dr Newhartt proved more rewarding than Vincent Price's passive central role as Julian Markham. Julian's disfigured brother Sir Edward (Alister Williamson) seeks to escape his confinement by feigning death and is delivered by unwitting bodysnatchers to the doctor's surgery. 'The penalty for graverobbing is the noose, isn't it?' Sir Edward crows. 'And, happily or not, my body is alive enough to tell the tale.' Newhartt submits to this spot of post-prandial blackmail, worrying about how he will explain Sir Edward's presence as a house guest ('One has to observe the conventions') and clearly not believing a word of Sir Edward's claim that he has been 'turned inside out by sorcery.' After his pretty housemaid (Sally Geeson) has spent a night of passion with the masked Sir Edward, Newhartt pettily gives her her marching orders ('I'm sure that with

Dr Newhartt submits to the blackmail threats of the masked Sir Edward Markham (Alister Williamson) in The Oblong Box *(1968)*

your abilities you will find suitable lodgings and an appropriate position,' he sniffs) and, when she too tries blackmail, issues a chilling warning to the effect that 'I might find myself buying *your* pretty little body one day: for a guinea or two.' Elsewhere, Lee has little to do other than flourish a quill pen and peer through microscopes while a skull perches ominously on his filing cabinet. But when Ivor Dean's police superintendent quizzes him about a cloak of his that has been found splashed with 'the blood of a tart in London who got her throat cut,' Newhartt sees him off with sardonic aplomb and a barely disguised curl of contempt. But he finally has his own throat cut by Sir Edward's serrated knife, though the squib that draws blood here is not entirely convincing. Nor is the film, crippled as it is by a final revelation of Sir Edward's disfigurement that must count as one of the biggest anti-climaxes in horror history.

But it did bring Lee together with Vincent Price for the first time. 'It was not until I was dying, with my throat cut, that my story intersected with Vincent's,' Lee recalled. 'He was swathed in a cloak like a tent, and by mistake rolled me onto it so that the camera could relish my death agony to the full, and kept hissing "You're lying on my train!" as I gurgled.' Price himself observed that he had been apprehensive about meeting Lee, having been led to expect a chilly and unapproachable individual, but that, on first meeting, 'We took one look at each other and started laughing ... We find each other hysterically funny. I'm really devoted to him. I think he's one of my very few good friends in the business.'[23]

PART SIX

BEYOND THE GRAVEYARD
1969–1971

As the 1960s wore on, Lee must have found some of the scripts being submitted to him indistinguishable as well as undistinguished. 'Now my vengeance is complete,' grins Fu Manchu on successfully blackening the name of Nayland Smith in *The Vengeance of Fu Manchu*. In *Die Schlangengrube und das Pendel*, Count Regula looks over his bubbling retorts and calculates that 'A few more seconds and my vengeance is complete.' While Dracula himself, having disposed of an irritating young pastry cook on the rooftops of Keinenberg in *Dracula Has Risen From the Grave*, tells his latest handmaiden that 'Now my revenge is complete.' Lee said all these lines in the space of little more than 18 months, but the only thing that could reasonably be called complete at this period was his own disenchantment.

He was mollified to some extent by the press hubbub surrounding Hammer's acquisition of the Queen's Award to Industry, much of which focused in appreciative terms on his own contribution. 'It is really Mr Lee, [Hammer's] monster king, who should collect,' observed Alix Palmer in the *Daily Express* on the very morning (22 April 1968) that *Dracula Has Risen From the Grave* went into production, while in the *Times* on the same day, Henry Blyth asked the rhetorical question, 'Why ... has such success come to Hammer's monster-in-chief, Mr Christopher Lee, who can justifiably be described as a typical Englishman? A product of Wellington, a prominent cricketer in his school days, a scratch golfer, and a man of Edwardian demeanour – tall of figure, austere, and immaculately dressed ... [But] there is nothing really incongruous about an actor who spends much of his time in the Gothic gloom of a medieval dungeon ... and the rest of it thinking difficult putts at Sunningdale, for to each task must

be brought a careful and refined technique; a staid and even an austere approach.'

In *Photoplay*, Lee appeared equally sanguine about his identification with horror, though shying away from the word itself. 'It would be silly to be upset about success,' he pontificated. 'No, I consider myself very fortunate to be a specialist in a small field. That's very important for an actor who wants to keep busy.' But, in the same interview, there was perhaps a touch of defensiveness in his assertion that he'd only made one true horror picture. '*The Curse of Frankenstein* was a real horror film because it was gruesome, gory, revolting and beastly. The others are pure escapist entertainment, acting as an emotional safety valve by playing on people's love of being frightened.'[1] And his true feelings were captured by Alix Palmer, to whom he admitted, 'Of course I would like to do big things other than fantasies, because I know I am capable. It's not a case of the clown who wants to play Hamlet, but it's pretty close to it.'

1969 was to prove an extraordinarily prolific year for Lee, and among the familiar diet of Hammer and Harry Alan Towers there were signs that 'big things other than fantasies' might be within his grasp after all. First, however, tribute was paid to Lee's pre-eminence among screen vampires by two showbusiness legends, Peter Sellers and Sammy Davis Jr.

At Sellers' invitation, Lee popped up as one of seven credited guest stars in Joe McGrath's *The Magic Christian*. An adaptation of Terry Southern's 1959 novella of the same name, the film is a genuine cinematic folly, a satire of conspicuous consumption that is itself a monstrously overblown example of it. It's also an example of the British film industry splashing out recklessly with the American dollars soon to be withdrawn from it, as well as embarrassing evidence of Sellers' increasing detachment from reality. His self-indulgent antics as Sir Guy Grand aren't funny in the slightest, and one critic has numbered *The Magic Christian* among no fewer than seven late 1960s Sellers vehicles that are

Tuesday 27 May 1969: Uta Levka joins Lee (47) and Vincent Price (58) as they celebrate their shared birthday at Mme Tussaud's during the filming of Scream and Scream Again

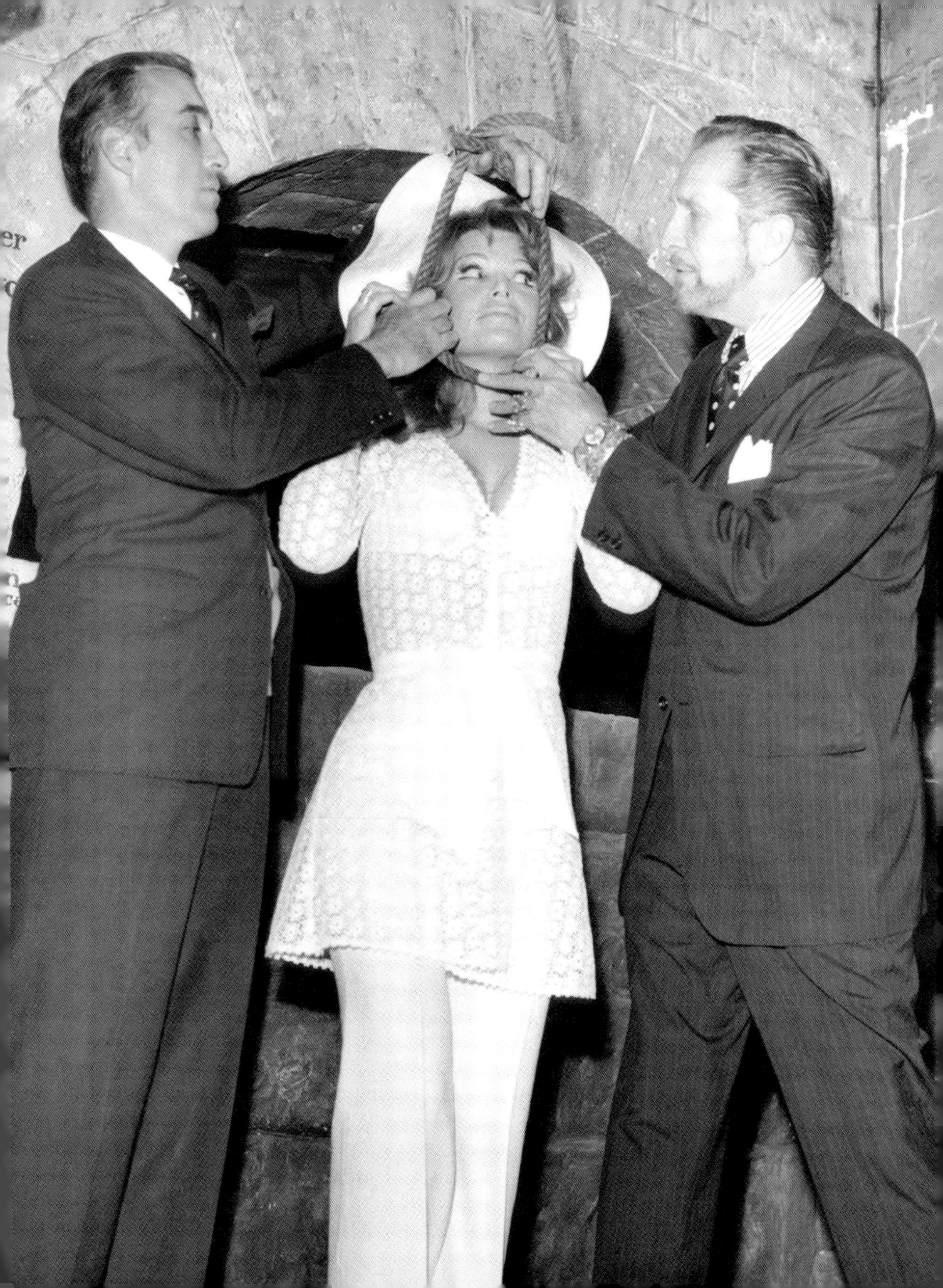

the kind of 'films which ought to be shipped to a desert island and screened continuously to those responsible for them.'[2]

The shooting of the picture at Twickenham sprawled from 3 February to 2 May, during which time Sellers' co-star, Ringo Starr, was at work on the Beatles' last album, *Abbey Road*. As well as describing the film as 'an adventure in a new field for me,' Lee told his fans that 'During my three days at the studio I met the Beatles for the first time, and they appear to be very pleasant young men. It would seem that they are going through a very anxious time at the moment.' This last observation was all too accurate; indeed, *The Magic Christian* remains a mesmerising monument to that hysterical period in which the sun set on the euphoric optimism of the 1960s and rose again on the jaded cynicism of the 1970s.

The film's roster of familiar British faces – TV personalities as well as character actors – is astonishing, and most of them go uncredited. Uttering only four words, Lee turns up towards the end as 'Ship's Vampire' aboard what TV newsreader Michael Aspel calls a 'fantastic new dream ship, the Magic Christian.' First seen in waiter's livery and reflected in a mirror, he looms into white-faced close-up as he bares his fangs at the snooty lady passenger to whom he has just served tea. He's then seen in full vampire rig striding in slow-motion down the ship's futuristic corridors as the camera tracks precipitately backwards (very impressive, this), and finally invades the bridge to enfold ship's captain Wilfrid Hyde-White, which acts as a cue for the film to go climactically berserk.

Later in the year, Lee and Peter Cushing spent a morning at Shepperton Studios at the invitation of Sammy Davis Jr, a devoted fan of their Hammer work. Directed by Jerry Lewis, *One More Time* began on 30 June and was a sequel to the previous year's Davis Jr/Peter Lawford vehicle *Salt and Pepper*.

Ready to enfold Wilfrid Hyde-White, unflappable captain of The Magic Christian *(1969)*

Laboured, self-admiring stuff, it's laden with in-jokes – Davis Jr and Lawford were both members of Hollywood's so-called Rat Pack – but on a less epic scale than *The Magic Christian*. Exploring the bowels of Pepperworth Castle, Davis Jr stumbles upon a hidden laboratory, complete with a daft-looking monster, a girl tethered to a table and two familiar faces. 'Aha!' cries Cushing's Baron. 'We have a visitor!' Then Lee's Count says 'Won't you join our little party?' and toasts the intruder with a glass of blood. The gag lasts a mere five seconds or so, but is proof, if any were needed, that by 1969 Cushing and Lee had become part of the fabric of popular culture.

LOCH NESS MONSTER, MONMOUTH ASSIZES

One director who paid no heed whatsoever to Lee's Dracula image was the legendary Billy Wilder, and in so doing he provided Lee's career with one of its periodic turning points. At Pinewood to make *The Private Life of Sherlock Holmes* in May 1969, Wilder needed a suitably imposing actor to play Holmes' mysterious brother Mycroft after George Sanders had vacated the role.

'I owe a great debt to Billy Wilder because I was trying to break the shackles of typecasting at the time,' Lee recalled. 'I remember him saying, bless him, "I'm not concerned with what you've done or what you're best known for. I'm only concerned with whether you're the right actor to play this part in my picture."'[3] Wilder's lack of interest in Lee's public image was dropped only once. 'We made the film around and about the south shore of Loch Ness,' Lee wrote, 'and as we stepped out to do our first shot in Castle Urquhart, by that spooky stretch of dark water, bats came wheeling out. Billy said, "You must feel quite at home here." It was the only reference he ever made to my past, and I was profoundly grateful.'

A lavish production for the Mirisch Corporation, *The Private Life of Sherlock Holmes* took some six months to make, including two and a half weeks in Scotland, and seemed a strange departure for the Austrian-born director of such classics as *The Lost Weekend, Sunset Boulevard, Some Like It Hot* and *The Apartment*. A witty deconstruction of the Sherlock Holmes myth, it abounds in exhilarating gags – Wilder's latterday collaborator, I A L Diamond, was co-writer of a script which the actors were encouraged to treat like Holy Writ – but is chiefly memorable for the elegiac spell of romantic fatalism it weaves around Holmes himself. Robert Stephens, who had a nervous breakdown during production, plays Holmes as a whey-faced, slightly fey malcontent much given to theatrical flourishes but afflicted by some unspecified

Cushing and Lee with Sammy Davis Jr on the Shepperton set of One More Time *(1969)*

melancholia. This, together with the film's gorgeous production values and stellar supporting cast, makes *The Private Life of Sherlock Holmes* an uncommonly charming and affecting picture.

This was all lost on Wilder's sponsors at United Artists, who, having watched in alarm as the film exceeded both its schedule and budget, eventually demanded the excision of two of its segments, 'The Case of the Upside-Down Room' and 'The Dreadful Business of the Naked Honeymooners'. Mysteriously, Wilder acceded to this adulteration despite having the right to final cut in his contract. 'This is the story of our lives in the cinema,' Lee lamented. 'Someone somewhere makes a decision that the film is too short or too long or whatever. If it's too long, some 22-year-old genius proceeds to cut it without the slightest knowledge of what he's doing or why.' [4] The film proved a commercial failure on its belated release at the end of 1970, with audiences unmoved by critical endorsements like that of the *Observer*'s Tom Milne, who announced that '*The Private Life of Sherlock Holmes* goes straight into my Ten Best of 1970 list.'

Though the film failed, there's little doubt that Lee's severe but sardonic Mycroft caused blinkered casting directors to readjust their spectacles. A shadowy Establishment figure, bald-domed and military of bearing, Mycroft is first encountered indulging in an unusually scientific method of wine decanting at the Diogenes Club (a 'stodgy and seemingly calcified establishment,' according to Holmes). 'A treat for you,' he tells Holmes and Watson, 'a very old Madeira: 1814,' adding, in a delightful tidbit for Holmes aficionados, that 'I see you so rarely. How long has it been? Not since the case of the Greek interpreter.'

Receiving a letter touching on 'the national security', Lee does some excellent monocle-popping business reminiscent of his youthful efforts in *Trottie True* and gives a deliciously condescending comic edge to his subsequent reappearance at Urquhart Castle. Expertly disguising the fact that Mycroft's role here is as a mouthpiece for some rather belated exposition, he sneeringly informs Sherlock that 'You, my dear brother, have been working for the Wilhelmstraße,' and then reveals that Sherlock's wilting client, Gabrielle Valladon, is actually a German agent called Ilse von Hoffmansthal. 'Am I going too fast for the best brain in England?' he asks with withering mock-solicitude.

Showing Mollie Maureen's dwarfish Queen Victoria the revolutionary submersible 'Jonah' (tricked out with a Loch Ness Monster headpiece to deter the inquisitive), Mycroft is crushed when she declares it 'unsportsmanlike, un-English and in very poor taste.' Thinking quickly, he determines to dispose of the German spies who have been dogging Sherlock's

With Mollie Maureen and director Billy Wilder at work on The Private Life of Sherlock Holmes *(1969)*

footsteps, proposing with fine-tuned relish to 'invite them aboard for the final journey: 700 feet, straight down.' He then bears Ilsa away in an open carriage and finally informs Sherlock by mail that she has been executed by the Japanese. Lee gratefully described the picture as 'streets ahead of any I've ever done ... [with] a wonderful director, superb script, fine part and a magnificent production; well, you can't ask for more, can you? But it took me 23 years and over a hundred pictures before I got it!'[5]

While limbering up for Mycroft, Lee had contributed an undemanding cameo to an American International/Amicus co-production called *Scream and Scream Again*, which started at Shepperton on the same day, 5 May, that the Wilder film began at Pinewood. Based on Peter Saxon's novel *The Disorientated Man*, this was directed by Gordon Hessler in a hard-edged, up-to-the-minute fashion quite different from *The Oblong Box*, owing more to the gritty style of the American director Don Siegel. A strange but extremely powerful mixture of science fiction, vampire picture, police procedural and conspiracy thriller, the film is also notable for being the first teaming of Vincent Price, Peter Cushing and Christopher Lee and for botching the opportunity completely.

Cushing comes and goes in the blink of an eye, Price makes the most substantial contribution but is mainly confined to the film's final third, while Lee's role remains frustratingly shadowy. As Fremont of British Intelligence, he gives his minions an unfussy debriefing about half an hour in (in an office oddly decorated with African carvings) and then, looking swish in trilby and furled umbrella, liaises with a hook-nosed continental Fascist (Marshall Jones) in a teeming Trafalgar Square. He finally turns up in a Rolls-Royce at the end to put paid to Price's Dr Browning in a vat of yellow acid and then to mutter 'It's only just beginning' as the credits roll. We've just about gathered by this stage that Fremont is one of a master race of synthetic composites created by Browning but, thanks to Christopher Wicking's garbled script, audiences are likely to be as mystified by the narrative as Lee and Price professed to be. The action, however, is consistently gripping, notably a breathless police pursuit of Michael Gothard's bionic young serial killer, and contributed to the film's robust box-office performance in 1970.

While *Scream and Scream Again* unfolded at Shepperton, Commonwealth United, the company responsible for *The Magic Christian*, were devoting the summer of 1969 to something much more sober: a new screen version of Shakespeare's *Julius Caesar*. It was by all accounts the film 'everyone' wanted to be in that year; this, and Lee's growing concern to prove himself in mainstream pictures, may account for his willingness to play the very small role of Artemidorus. Despite his minimal involvement, Lee received 'also starring' credit alongside Jill Bennett immediately after the film's seven headliners: Charlton Heston, Jason Robards, John Gielgud, Richard Johnson, Robert Vaughn, Richard Chamberlain and Diana Rigg.

A lavish but strangely bloodless adaptation, the film is totally destroyed by Robards' paralysingly robotic Brutus; rarely has a normally exceptional actor looked less happy. Lee's scene was filmed on Friday 27 June and involved him pushing his way to the front of a horde of extras and pleading with Gielgud's Caesar to 'Read this schedule.' Caesar doesn't, of course, and proceeds to the Senate where he's hacked to pieces by the conspirators. According to Lee, director Stuart Burge addressed only one sentence to him by way of guidance: 'Of course, you do realise, don't you, that Artemidorus is quite, quite mad?' But Burge was canny enough, nevertheless, to throw in a nod to Lee's horror celebrity by including Artemidorus in a nightmarish montage representing Calphurnia's premonitory dream.

After his brush with Sir John Gielgud, and during a break in his work on *The Private Life of Sherlock Holmes*, Lee took the opportunity to pop across to Portugal – Leria, to be precise – for a return engagement with Jesús Franco. *El proceso de las brujas* (Trial of the Witches) acquired the catchy title *The Bloody Judge* in its English-speaking manifestations and was another of Franco's collaborations with Harry Alan Towers. Thanks to films like *La marca del hombre lobo* and *La residencia*, Spain was on the brink of an extraordinarily productive horror boom of which slavish 'adaptations' of foreign hits would form a notable part. The impact of Michael Reeves' *Witchfinder General* had reverberated well beyond the UK and *El proceso* reproduces all its salient features with painstaking attention to detail but almost zero inspiration.

Writing, as usual, as Peter Welbeck, Towers shifts the action of *Witchfinder* forward a few decades in order to give a loose account of the fearsome Judge Jeffreys and the Monmouth rebellion. Bruno Nicolai's score reproduces the romantic sweep of Paul Ferris' for *Witchfinder*, while Franco regularly treats us to shots of sunlight piercing through tree branches, the image with which Reeves' film begins. And Towers clearly lavished some money on the picture, because Franco manages to stage the kind of reasonably credible battle sequence that the budget-conscious Reeves

'Hail, Caesar! Read this schedule!' With Derek Godfrey, Charlton Heston and John Gielgud in Julius Caesar (1969)

was careful to avoid. Towers also gives us a few insights into Jeffreys' motivation; several more, in fact, than Vincent Price was given in delineating Matthew Hopkins. Jeffreys is seen penning earnest self-justifications in his journal, and at one point quaveringly informs an underling (José María Prada) that 'Justice is a terrible thing, Palafox, but' – and here Lee suddenly turns coldly manic – 'Justice must be *done*!' But somehow these touches don't add up to much and Jeffreys remains a strangely boring character. With most of his scenes given over to exposition he doesn't stand a chance of becoming the inscrutable force of evil represented by Hopkins.

Though mainly functional, Jeffreys is still given some juicy lines of pastiche Jacobean to speak and Lee puts them over in a metallic voice suggestive of the strange forces that impel Jeffreys' hysterical belief in the letter of the law. At the beginning, he sits in spaniel-wigged splendour in a very Hispanic-looking Old Bailey and oozes gimlet-eyed malice as he pronounces sentence: 'The accused, Alicia Gray, will be examined – *thoroughly* – for abnormality of mind and body.' In the meantime, he takes the lascivious opportunity to size up the other so-called 'witch', who turns out, surprise surprise, to be the future Mrs Harry Alan Towers, Maria Röhm.

Later, he affirms his belief that these witches should be 'stamped out like rats in a granary, else we shall never cleanse England of this pestilence.' Lee also relishes fruity lines like 'I have a title, rogue: use it, or I'll have your tongue by the roots,' and gives conviction to Jeffreys' horror of the blood-spattered dreams that afflict him. 'Would that but once you had seen one of your own sentences carried out,' says the similarly spaniel-wigged Leo Genn in explanation of these dreams, and the film then dwindles to a curiously low-key ending in which the condemned Jeffreys, having finally seen an execution from his prison window, expires of a heart attack.

Despite the presence in the lower depths of Franco's ubiquitous Swiss collaborator, Howard Vernon (as a leotarded torturer obviously modelled on Boris Karloff in *Tower of London*), *El proceso* is hard to follow and, with Franco's jazz-fuelled exuberance thoroughly dampened by the conventional subject matter, rather dull to boot. For the German version, *Der Hexentöter von Blackmoor* (The Witch Killer of Blackmoor), Franco spiced things up with some ten minutes of saucier footage, including the nude Maria Röhm being fondled by an exploratory hand that purports to be, but isn't, Lee's. 'One must shrug,' Lee reflected later. 'There's no scope for hiring private eyes to vet what is happening in every film when one's back is turned.'

Lee didn't know it yet, but Towers and Franco had pulled a similar stunt on him earlier that year, when George Sanders was contracted as the aristocratic narrator of their *De Sade 70* project but had to withdraw through illness. When Wolfgang Preiss also dropped out – his wife had been in a road accident – Towers got on the phone to Lee and pleaded with him to forsake his planned weekend of golf and come to Barcelona instead. Lee did so, rapidly polished off his scenes as Dolmance (wearing the same smoking jacket he'd worn in *Sherlock Holmes und das Halsband des Todes*) and was home again, none the wiser, by Monday.

The torrid result, in which Swedish starlet Marie Liljedahl becomes the doped-up plaything for Franco regulars Jack Taylor and Maria Röhm, was released in the US as *Eugénie ... the Story of Her Journey Into Perversion* and as *Marquis de Sade's Philosophy in the Boudoir* in the UK, where it came to Lee's attention that his name was being prominently displayed on an Old Compton Street sex cinema. For the record, *De Sade 70* is one of Franco's most imaginative and lustrous-to-look-at productions, with Lee on especially good form as the oracular master of ceremonies. And he bore no grudges in any case. 'Jess is a much better director than he's given credit for,' he opined. 'He's

Capital punishment: Judge Jeffreys finally catches a glimpse of his own handiwork in The Bloody Judge, *aka* El proceso de las brujas *(1969)*

As Dolmance, smooth narrator of Jesús Franco's *De Sade 70* (1969), released in the UK as *Marquis de Sade's philosophy in the Boudoir*

very limited by what he is allowed to do financially, and by the actors and schedules at his disposal. I don't consider him to be a hack director; after all, he was Orson Welles' assistant on *Chimes at Midnight*.'[6] Further torrid movie offers would come from the novelist Edna O'Brien – her script was bluntly entitled *Stud* – and from director Just Jaeckin, whose notorious skin-flick *Story of O* eventually featured Anthony Steel rather than Lee.

Variations on a Theme

'Imagine my surprise when I discovered on my return from Portugal,' Lee wrote to his fan club president, Gloria Lillibridge, on 27 August 1969, 'that my agent, with the very best of intentions, has virtually committed me to playing Dracula for the fourth time in yet another Hammer production ... My agent's excuse ... is that I am receiving three times the money I have ever received for a Hammer film.' And that wasn't all. 'At a mass meeting of my agents yesterday,'

Lee continued, 'I was told that the situation in the film industry at the moment is extremely precarious, that the major American companies are in dire straits and that production is being cut down enormously in the next few months. I have discovered that all this is in fact true and ... in view of this I must, as a family man, take all precautions necessary to safeguard our financial position.'

It was indeed true. Many of the American majors were facing financial disaster (Hammer's sponsors, Warner Bros/Seven Arts, lost some $52 million in 1969) and several of them were being taken over by faceless conglomerates unconnected with filmmaking. The concerns of their London-based offshoots mattered little in this new climate, and so the long process began that would see the British film industry more or less extinguished by the turn of the 1980s.

As for Lee, his reluctance to play Dracula again was further complicated by the fact that he had already committed himself to a non-Hammer Dracula

Partially rejuvenated, Count Dracula encounters Lucy (Soledad Miranda) in El Conde Drácula *(1969)*

film. He informed Lillibridge that 'On 3 November I start what I hope will be positively my last film for Hammer. The tasteful title is *Taste the Blood of Dracula*. As usual, words fail me, as indeed they will also do in the film. Frankly, rather than deliver some of the lines in the script, I would prefer to say nothing at all ... However, here comes one amusing aspect of the whole mess. I have long wanted, as you know, to do Bram Stoker's *Dracula* as he wrote it. I have now agreed to do this, for three weeks on location starting on 13 October. So I will be playing the role twice in the space of two months.'

Lee's participation in this 'authentic' Dracula was slightly delayed; on 13 October he was only just completing his work on *The Private Life of Sherlock Holmes*. He then went straight to Barcelona for *El Conde Drácula*. Another Franco/Towers collaboration, this was originally announced as a multi-million dollar project with Vincent Price as Van Helsing and Terence Fisher at the helm. The end product was a rather more humble affair, with Herbert Lom as Van Helsing (made-up like a blue-rinsed version of Lee's Duc de Richleau in *The Devil Rides Out*) and Franco stalwarts Paul Muller, Jack Taylor and Maria Röhm further down the cast list. Franco's then-muse, Soledad Miranda, was cast as Lucy – she was tragically killed in a car crash two years later, aged 27 – and Klaus Kinski weighed in as Renfield. Perhaps because he had once spent three months in a madhouse himself, he remains one of the very best Renfields on record, though granted only one word of dialogue and not even told by the devious Towers that he was appearing in a Dracula picture.

Lee himself was rightly sceptical of the whole Towers/Franco set-up by this stage, telling his fans that 'Knowing what the producer can in fact produce, you won't be surprised if it is not good, and I shall be delightfully surprised if it is.' The film has come in for a lot of criticism – for its bizarre deviations from what was advertised as the first faithful rendition of Stoker's story, for its Victorian England that looks more like an episode of *The High Chaparral*, for a disintegration scene at the end unparalleled in its uselessness – but the first half hour comes close to realising the hopes that Lee initially cherished for the entire picture.

Franco gives these scenes a genuinely dreamlike atmosphere, with Harker's journey to Castle Dracula undertaken in an unearthly blue haze of scudding fogs and attended on the soundtrack, in a typically wild Franco touch, by jungle sound effects seemingly culled from an old Tarzan picture. Having doubled as his own muffled coachman, Lee's Count then emerges from the shadows in answer to Harker's knock and remains the only accurate representation of Stoker's Dracula ever committed to film. (Gary Oldman's bizarrely pompadoured Widow Twanky lookalike in Francis Coppola's 1991 version hardly qualifies in this respect.) Lee's snow-white hair and handlebar moustache are supplemented by a sallow complexion, apricot-coloured lips and a quite riveting vein of maniacal self-absorption. Sad as well as mad, this Dracula utters a string of oracular non-sequiturs in a forlorn, gravelly voice that seems genuinely to issue from the grave. Particularly resonant is a phrase penned by Towers rather than Stoker: 'I am not young, and yet I am restless.'

The highly atmospheric setting for Harker's interview with the Count was a castellated room in Barcelona's Barrio Gótico; it had reportedly been the scene, some four centuries earlier, of King Ferdinand and Queen Isabella receiving Columbus on his return from discovering America. Retiring to the 16th century fireside for Dracula's martial reminiscences, Lee turns in his chair to utter the immortal Stoker line, 'Listen to them – the children of the night. What music they make!' Franco pans down to Dracula's fangs glimmering under his moustache at this point, and Lee's delivery, controlled yet quietly fanatical, is at least the equal of Lugosi's baroque phrasing in 1930. 'I think Christopher Lee is brilliant – great,' Franco recalled. 'He did this [monologue] and made the scene in such a brilliant way.'[7]

Even in this section, however, Franco muffs several golden opportunities, notably the primal scene in which Dracula interrupts his vampire brides as they swarm over the supine Harker, which carries none of the explosive impact the corresponding scene was given in the Hammer *Dracula*. And after that, with Dracula correctly reduced to a shadowy, mainly off-screen presence, the curiously wooden supporting cast (of which Franco himself forms a part) fails miserably to sustain audience interest. It is also after this opening section that the film abandons all pretence at fidelity to the novel; indeed, the dubbing for the German version (*Nachts wenn Dracula erwacht*) even abandons the Count's transfer to London, limiting his globetrotting to Budapest, a sensible move given the preponderance of palm trees on show.

Having grown young on Lucy's blood and therefore looking as darkly Hispanic as everybody else in the picture, Lee himself provides the film's only remaining highpoints. Standing on his balcony and hissing out malign instructions, he is the very image of Stoker's rejuvenated vampire, and in two brief scenes towards the end – one with a passing prostitute, the other with a Russian sea captain – Lee ensures that the film captures the chilly essence of the novel better than any other adaptation. But set against these moments are inane ones like a scene in which, rather than unleash a plague of rats on his pursuers as per Stoker, Dracula animates a bunch of moth-eaten stuffed animals. Fox, warthog, badger, owl, deer, ostrich, raven, even a swordfish – all are quite obviously being joggled towards the camera by an unseen hand, and the result is almost blissfully absurd.

Despite this, the film made over 40 million pesetas in Spain, a truly phenomenal sum that may have compensated Towers for its virtual non-appearance in English-speaking territories. In the US, its release under the title *Count Dracula* was delayed by a lawsuit arising from its projected distributor going out of business, while in the UK (where it became *Bram Stoker's Count Dracula*) it had to wait until 1973 for a very limited run, though *Films Illustrated* caught up with it and observed that 'It is rare that a name actor is so ill-served by a production.'

Back in London, Lee arrived at Elstree in the second week of November for the long-threatened *Taste the Blood of Dracula*, which had started under Peter Sasdy's direction on 27 October. Fan club member Jill Basten visited Lee at the studio, first encountering him 'sinisterly garbed as the arch fiend Dracula … [and] behaving in a decidedly unfiendish manner, endeavouring to fulfil the wishes of a group of small boys who wanted him to frighten them! They remained resolutely unperturbed in spite of all his efforts … "Fans of the future," said Christopher with a mischievous glint in his eye.'

Children may have been present at the studio, but Peter Sasdy's *Taste the Blood of Dracula* turned out to be the least childish of Hammer's Dracula pictures since the first, and also the most accomplished. Anthony Hinds' script had originated as a Dracula subject without Dracula, Hammer's reluctance to pay Lee's salary having prompted Hinds to create a decadent English disciple of the Count's called Lord Courtley. Warner Bros/Seven Arts took one look at this, however, and, mindful of the tremendous success enjoyed by *Dracula Has Risen From the Grave*, insisted on Lee's participation.

The screenplay having been rewritten to accommodate him, Lee eliminated much of his dialogue – his shooting script is peppered with exasperated marginalia like 'Dracula's lines are half-witted' and 'Suggest-suggest-suggest!' – and in the process helped to underline the film's most interesting theme, which presents Dracula as an inscrutable Anti-Father urging Edwardian youngsters to rebel against their hypocritical elders. By 1969, this generation-gap theme was nothing if not topical, and Hammer's ingenues were rapidly decreasing in age in accordance with it; Barbara Shelley, a beauteous victim as recently as *Prince of Darkness*, would surely have been pencilled in for the heroine's anguished mother had she been considered for *Taste the Blood*.

Lee himself is given a splendid crashing chord on being resurrected. 'They have destroyed my servant,' he says of the three Edwardian patriarchs responsible for Courtley's death. 'They will *be* destroyed.' (Lee changed this from the script's much less impressive 'You destroy my servant, you will be destroyed.') Elsewhere, he swirls impressively around Scott MacGregor's gorgeous church interior and sees off Isla Blair's Lucy Paxton with a truly frightening fixed glare and razor-toothed lunge. But, though playing a vital role in the action, Dracula is a more shadowy presence than ever in this picture. 'It's a clever premise, there's no denying that,' Lee said of the film. 'And it has the best cast of the Dracula sequels … But again, where is Dracula?'[8] Lee was also unhappy with Sasdy's decision to dwell on the Count's throat-piercing repasts (previously shielded by his cloak or some such), nor did he enjoy the brief use of contact lenses that were not only blood-shot but entirely crimson and pupil-free.

Martin Jarvis was cast as one of the film's rebellious young people and 30 years later provided an intriguing account of it in his memoirs. The star 'was hardly ever on the set. We filmed day after day without meeting him. One morning, I sensed a different atmosphere. The crew moved about with anxious faces. The make-up people seemed nervous … An hour later everything went quiet. Suddenly a tall cloaked figure manifested itself on the set, ready for work. Not a moment was wasted. By the end of the day it seemed as if his entire part was in the can.'

In one scene, Jarvis and the fanged Isla Blair succumbed to a severe case of 'corpsing', their incessant giggles ruining several takes. 'Count Dracula himself, played by the impeccable Christopher Lee, was not amused as he lurked behind Isla, waiting for the camera to whip-pan to his final reaction. He suggested darkly that we leave the set until we had control of ourselves. He was right, of course.' And Lee's poker-faced attitude to the material provided Jarvis with an acting lesson that 'Peter Barkworth hadn't covered at RADA.' Unable to muster a sufficient 'shock-horror reaction' in one scene, he was reminded of Alan Badel's dictum, 'It doesn't matter how big it is as long as it's filled from inside,' and marvelled at how actors like Lee, Cushing and Price 'can play this kind of thing on a monumental scale yet never appear to be going over the top. They are always true to the situation, however extraordinary it may be. Their screen behaviour is always filled from inside.'[9]

FROM AVANT-GARDE TO AMICUS

At the turn of the 1970s, Lee was greatly enthused by a project called *Salem Come to Supper*, in which a Swedish farmer is unjustly incarcerated in a lunatic asylum and goes to extraordinarily intricate lengths to avenge himself. The producer was his old *Orlac* co-star, Mel Ferrer, but, having acquired the property and even paid for rewrites, Lee was disagreeably surprised when Max von Sydow was cast as Salem instead. The result was Laslo Benedek's *The Night Visitor*, with von Sydow backed up by Liv Ullman, Per Oscarsson and Trevor Howard. 'The failure of *The Night Visitor* with its high echelon cast,' asserted *Cinefantastique* with unwitting appositeness, 'suggests an interesting idea: how would the same script have looked with a totally different set of actors, say, Christopher Lee as the revenge-crazed Salem, Barbara Steele doing her specialty as the witchy wife who prods others to do evil acts, Klaus Kinski as the wild-eyed doctor and Peter Cushing as the determined investigator? It almost sounds like a horror masterpiece.'

Mourning his loss of the *Salem* project, Lee started 1970 instead with one of the most unusual assignments of his career. Pedro Portabella was a young Catalonian filmmaker who, along with Gonzalo Suárez, Vicente Aranda, Jorge Grau and others, had formed part of the so-called 'Barcelona School' during the 1960s. The heir to a fortune founded on Danone yoghurt, Portabella had co-produced Luis Bunuel's *Viridiana*, had his passport revoked by the Franco regime and directed an impressionistic, semi-documentary barrage against Spain's decadent upper classes called *Nocturne 29*. In 1969 he made *Cuadecuc Vampír*, an extraordinary phantasmagoria nominally focused on the making of *El Conde Drácula* and shot in 16mm black-and-white, while the following year he

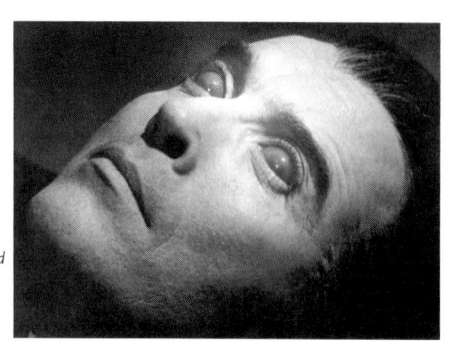

The Hammer Dracula resurrected a third time in Taste the Blood of Dracula *(1969)*

invited Lee back to Barcelona for another monochrome meditation on government oppression called *Umbracle*. 'I can't begin to explain it!' Lee announced. 'It's a most extraordinary and way-out script. It's not a commercial proposition; it's not a commercial picture.' According to Portabella, Lee agreed to appear in *Umbracle* 'on condition that he had time off to sample the local golf courses.'[10]

'How do you classify these films?' asked Jonathan Rosenbaum of the *Village Voice*. 'Are they horror movies, political statements, formal studies of sound affecting image, homages to the silent cinema, private reveries, or laconic portraits of contemporary Spain?' Rosenbaum concluded that they are 'like stray pages from ancient books, drifting through an alien environment where they figure like half-remembered dreams belonging to another time and place.'[11]

Cuadecuc Vampír is certainly a mesmerising experience. 'Cua de cuc' means 'worm's tail', presumably a reference to the film's position as a poetic addendum to Franco's Dracula picture. Indeed, the opening credits make the bizarre claim, in Catalan, that 'This film was made during the filming of *Dracula* by Jesús Franco, produced for Hammer Films [sic] from an idea by Joan Brossa and Pere Portabella.'

The opening of the film is rendered virtually in negative, an extraordinary effect achieved by Portabella buying up a load of ancient film stock and removing most of the emulsion. A crew member is seen spraying fake fog in preparation for Harker's coach journey; Dracula's fireside expostulations are shown with a full complement of exposed arc lights; Lee is seen climbing into his coffin, making himself comfortable and being attended by a man with a cobweb-making machine. Long passages are silent, though sometimes punctuated by insistent knocking sounds or the hammering of pneumatic drills.

We're subsequently shown close-ups of the clapperboard and the continuity stopwatch, not to mention an obviously string-propelled bat. Soledad Miranda is seen smoking a cigarette in bed while a shot is set up; later we see her neck wounds being attached. Maria Röhm rehearses with a trendy leopardskin coat draped over her crinoline; Herbert Lom has his goatee trimmed. When the vampire brides are staked, a technician is seen lobbing blood into Jack Taylor's face. Lee strides onto the woodland location in a pair of sunglasses and salutes at sight of the camera; later he ceremoniously removes his red contact lenses and fake fangs.

Finally, Portabella ventures into Lee's dressing room. Reflected in multiple mirrors, Lee addresses Portabella's crew in French and then, in English, reads the death of Dracula from Stoker's book, with learned

Thursday 1 January 1970: returning from a break in Barbados with Gitte

asides about Bowie and Kukri knives. He finally looks directly into camera and the film ends. Lee's is the only voice in the entire picture. With Franco's crew members as much a part of Portabella's action as the actors, *Cuadecuc Vampir* achieves a memorably eerie blurring of fantasy and reality; in demystifying the filmmaking process, it's somehow a thousand times more mysterious than the picture it springs from. As Rosenbaum put it, 'A check-up on Franco's film reveals a sow's ear; Portabella took the same actors, sets, part of the action and plot, and turned it into a poem.'[12]

Again concocted by Portabella in association with the artist-poet Joan Brossa, *Umbracle* is less digestible. Its title is taken from a sheltered Barcelona park known as 'the shady place', perhaps likening the Spanish people under General Franco to plants denied sunlight. 'He [Portabella] told me he had seen much of my work and wanted to film a symbolic interpretation of me,' Lee explained. 'How could I resist? I feel an actor should tackle as many kinds of cinema as possible, and *The Shady Place* was certainly breaking new ground for me.'[13]

Of course, the film is more a symbolic interpretation of General Franco, its disconnected images ranging from Lee peering at pickled exhibits in Barcelona's Museo de Zoologia to his striding the streets in shades and a black suit like an East End gangster. The images flickering like early film, Lee buys a cigar and then sees a man bundled into custody in the street outside. A Catalan and a Spaniard issue matter-of-fact diatribes against state censorship, there's a lengthy clip from an old Pedro Lazaga film and a couple of clowns spar with each other on a stage. Lee shares an elevator with Jeannine Mestre, one of the vampire brides from *El Conde Drácula*, and, having been encouraged by Portabella to improvise, suddenly says 'I'm going to sing.' Sure enough, he's next seen on a stage, the camera whirling around him as he belts out excerpts from *The Damnation of Faust* and *The Flying Dutchman*. He then removes his tie prior to a spirited recitation of Poe's *The Raven*, and has just got to the last line when the cameraman drops the camera. Order is restored, Lee utters Poe's final doom-laden word ('Nevermore') and then stares stonily into the lens for a seeming eternity before the scene is cut. 'People supposed it to be a still,' he lamented later.

He is then seen talking animatedly to Jeannine Mestre on an ornate sofa – the scene is played silent – after which she reclines nude in bed as he decorates her with jewellery. Chickens are seen going to their doom on a conveyor belt as the Carpenters croon '(They Long To Be) Close To You' and footage of silent movie comedians is intercut with Lee emerging from the Metro. Lee later ascends a mountain on a funicular railway and finally swots a fly. The creature waggles helplessly on a white blotter and the film ends. 'For all its critical nosegays,' Lee concluded, 'it's possible that only Portabella and perhaps his mentor Buñuel fully understood it.' Both the Portabella pictures were showcased at New York's Museum of Modern Art and London's National Film Theatre, while for Lee they provided an opportunity to meet the celebrated Spanish artists Joan Miró and Antoni Tàpies.

After these fascinating flirtations with 'art' cinema, Lee returned to Elstree in May 1970 for Hammer's tackiest production yet. *Scars of Dracula*, mounted with indecent haste after Hammer's previous Dracula subject, was funded by EMI, American finance having largely been withdrawn from Hammer as from most other sectors of the British film industry. The film's only connection with the handsomely mounted *Taste the Blood* lies in its title typography. Dracula's ashes have somehow returned to Transylvania, a laughably phoney vampire bat throws up on them, and the Count is back in business even before the credits roll. The result is a simple-minded penny dreadful with conspicuously cheapskate sets, and its only interest lies in its increased level of sadism, director Roy Ward Baker having determined that if he was going to make a horror film he was going to make sure it was really horrid.

Much of the plot revolves around a callow student/philanderer called Paul Carlson. (Christopher Matthews, passable as a fumbling scientist in *Scream and Scream Again*, is pretty obnoxious here.) Dracula himself, however, is granted an unprecedented amount of screen time. Somewhat unflatteringly photographed in *Taste the Blood*, Lee here looks more ghoulish and pasty-faced than ever. 'In the later films,' Lee reflected, 'they would have difficulty matching my appearance to the way I looked in the earlier Dracula films. I remember that we never had the same wig from one film to the next … [and] as I got older, and my face lost some of its natural elasticity … the make-up artists would try to cover that with facial make-up … Oddly enough, by the time Hammer shot the two modern-day Dracula sequels in the early 1970s, the make-up technology and photography had advanced to the stage where I actually look better in those two films – and my appearance is uniform from one to the next, although they were shot a year apart – than I do in the earlier sequels.' [14]

Scars contains numerous unwelcome surprises (female vampires have sex with mere mortals, vampires can stab one another to death, vampires can even stoop to poisoning people's breakfasts), together with a reasonable ration of dialogue for Dracula. But in his old role of frosty yet hospitable host, Lee is required to do little more than proffer red wine to his guests on three separate occasions. (He gets it from a tacky little mini-bar contraption in his reception area, the castle's reduction to the level of Woolworths Baroque being explained by the fact that Michael Ripper and other angry villagers torched the place in the first reel.) But even in these dubious surroundings, Lee conjures some extraordinarily powerful moments. He bites fellow vampire Anouska Hempel with a horribly mad, red-eyed compulsion, and there's a startling scene in which, with demonic glee, he brands Patrick Troughton's Klove with a red-hot sword, conferring upon him the titular scars of Dracula.

Lee finally creates an electrifying effect when he turns his attentions to Wendy Hamilton's Julie. Sinking his fangs into her throat, he looks up from his repast with fathomless eyes directed squarely at us, the audience; Lee's oft-quoted theory regarding 'the loneliness of evil' is served up unadulterated in this single shot. In the end, Dracula's predilection for throwing things (an upright brazier in *Dracula*, a stake in *Has Risen*, organ pipes in *Taste the Blood*) finally proves his undoing when, poised to hurl a metal spike at the young lovers, it's struck by lightning and he plunges in flames from the battlements with a very satisfying bellow of rage and disbelief.

In July, Lee was at Shepperton for six days to play the lead in the third segment of a four-decker Amicus anthology far more genteel than its gruesome title, *The House that Dripped Blood*, would suggest. Like all four episodes, 'Sweets to the Sweet' was based on a short story by Lee's friend Robert Bloch and personally adapted by him, and like Franklyn Marsh in *Dr Terror's House of Horrors*, Lee's character in it is a man frozen into harsh and unyielding behaviour by fright. 'John Reed,' we're told by the estate agent narrator, is 'a quiet man and a dangerous one – to himself.' Arriving at his new home accompanied by his tiny daughter (Chloë Franks), Reed's affirmative answer to the estate agent's observation that Jane is 'a lovely child' is reluctant, stiff, token. Further hints are dropped, as when Reed agrees, with barely concealed distaste, that Jane is 'the living image' of her mother. The denouement is a chilling one (Jane, it transpires, is a dab hand at voodoo, just like the late Mrs Reed) and the story shows Lee in his best tight-lipped mode, though at one point he has Reed relax sufficiently to discard his *Financial Times* and take up a paperback copy of one of Lee's own favourite books, *The Lord of the Rings*.

The fourth and final story in Peter Duffell's film is also worth mentioning for its casting of Jon Pertwee as a grandiloquent horror star who, at work on a new potboiler called *Curse of the Bloodsuckers*, stabs his cane through the film's cardboard castle for all the world as if he were on the set of *Scars of Dracula*. Though the part more properly belongs to Vincent Price (who was in fact approached by Amicus), several commentators have mourned the fact that Lee wasn't cast in it. 'Self reflexivity' would certainly have been taken to unprecedented extremes had Lee been required to extol the horror movies of the past and, mentioning *Dracula*, point out that he was referring to 'the one with Bela Lugosi, of course – not this new fellow.'

IN SEARCH OF VARIETY

Another Amicus assignment beckoned, but before starting work on it Lee became involved in an entirely different project. 'Christopher Lee, high priest of horror films, has stepped from the grave to the groove to become a pop singer,' remarked the *Sunday Mirror* in September. 'Due out next month is the single 'I Am Yours', with Mr Lee, minus fangs and batwings, emerging as a stylish ballad singer.'[15] Sadly, Lee decided that the song (together with its B-side, 'The Seasons') was unsuitable and it was never

Pins and needles: feeling the effects of voodoo in the 'Sweets to the Sweet' episode of The House that Dripped Blood *(1970), with Hugh Manning*

issued, leaving his next quixotic tilt at the pop charts until the end of the century.

In the meantime, work began at Shepperton on Lee's next picture, another Amicus item, on 10 October. Lee had told his fans that he considered the title of his last Amicus picture 'diabolical'; now he was faced with something called *I, Monster*. 'I can assure you that that title will be changed one way or the other,' he claimed prior to shooting. It wasn't, but its hokey title proved to be the least of the film's problems. Milton Subotsky had concocted a new version of the Jekyll and Hyde story, adding a Freudian spin (he'd recently married a psychologist) but changing the principal's names to Marlowe and Blake. Worse, a cursory reading of *New Scientist* magazine had convinced him that it was possible to make a 3-D film on the cheap.

Christopher Lee – Part Six

The thoroughly degraded Mr Blake – ie, Mr Hyde – in I, Monster *(1970)*

The director, 22-year-old Stephen Weeks, was engaged by Subotsky a matter of days before the film was due to start shooting. Having directed a powerful Tigon featurette called *1917*, Weeks had shown Lee six minutes of test footage shot in an old church and accordingly found himself in the middle of a nightmare on *I, Monster*. Subotsky's cock-eyed 3-D scheme required that the camera should travel from left to right, but, as Weeks observed later, 'it was all absolute fantasy. There was this Super-8 test of Subotsky's new baby crawling across a lawn, but no one could see the effect ... Then Tony Curtis, the art director, decided it'd work if the travel was right to left. So I ended up making a film filled with static speeches where everything had to move left to right on sets built the other way round.'[16]

Lee, his co-star Peter Cushing and everyone else involved with the project were thoroughly mystified by Subotsky's intransigence. 'To me, it doesn't look like 3-D even with the glasses on,' Lee complained. 'I don't think anyone else thinks it looks like 3-D, except possibly for Milton Subotsky and [his business partner] Max Rosenberg, who have literally had to force themselves into believing that it is 3-D.' With the eleventh hour abandonment of the process, the result was a film running a scant 80 minutes – nearly half an hour of scripted tracking shots had gone by the board – and a quiet burial in a double-bill with Peter Collinson's Susan George vehicle, *Fright*. This is a shame, because *I, Monster* contains one, or rather two, of Lee's most striking performances.

The film's duality theme is stated straight away, as Weeks' camera pans from a monkey in a cage to the frock-coated Marlowe and finally comes to rest on a two-headed baby preserved in a jar. The unsmiling Marlowe's visible distress when forced to kill a cat doesn't prepare us for his first drug-induced transformation, which, apart from dark-rimmed eyes and subtly enlarged teeth, is achieved entirely by acting. Blake grins mischievously, lights a bunsen burner with playful relish, makes a face at the monkey, admires himself in a mirror and then takes up a laboratory mouse. He has just selected a scalpel when arrested by clock chimes. Carl Davis' otherwise dreary score goes all Kurt Weill at this point, emphasising the jaunty, almost childlike nature of the early Blake. For his second transformation, he ventures outdoors, putting on his cloak with fey precision and almost mincing down the street as he twirls a stolen walking stick. He hisses suddenly at a passing urchin and laughs at his own jest, becoming even more ingratiatingly sinister when seen in mad-eyed close-up as he charms a backstreet landlady.

According to Marlowe's notebook, the third change we see is actually the ninth, revealing a thoroughly degraded Blake, hair dropping out, nose flattened, teeth rotted, warts appearing. Marlowe's liberated 'id' is still boyish, struggling to shake off his 'superego' but not really knowing what to do with himself when he does, even retiring to his squalid rented room and weeping in frustration after being snubbed by an acid-tongued prostitute (Marjie Lawrence). But when he determines on revenge, the childlike Blake becomes a nightmarish reincarnation of Marlowe's dreaded father. 'Like all fashionable doctors,' Marlowe has told us, 'my father carried a gold-headed cane. He used it for other things besides walking.' Now, in the film's most memorable sequence, Blake pursues Annie through the streets and beats her to death with just such a cane.

Lee's contrast between the stiff-backed Marlowe and the increasingly crook-backed Blake is an extraordinary achievement, reminiscent of Jean-Louis Barrault's Jekyll and Hyde in Renoir's 1959 TV film, *Le testament du Docteur Cordelier*, and at least as impressive. Eventually, Blake asserts himself without recourse to Marlowe's liberating drug and the protesting remnants of Marlowe are still visible as he flees wildly through a swirl of autumn leaves, coming to rest at an outdoor aviary. When a little girl glimpses him through the revolving bars of this contraption, Weeks' visual reference to the windmill climax of James Whale's *Frankenstein* is supplemented by Lee's ineffably pathetic gesture of defeat, lolling his head in shame just as he did in *The Curse of Frankenstein* and *The Mummy*.

Despite the obvious presence of a stuntman when Blake trashes his laboratory and then plunges in flames down a staircase, the final scenes are distinguished by several startlingly grotesque Lee close-ups as he struggles to push Cushing's Utterson out of a window, a set-up very similar to the end of *Rasputin the Mad Monk*. The film is decorated with many artful touches introduced by Weeks in an effort to overcome the obstacles placed in his path by Subotsky – there are any number of strange angles, fish-eye lenses, overhead shots etc – and has an unusually authentic atmosphere of Edwardian London. But the compromised result, again like *Rasputin the Mad Monk*, remains an unworthy vehicle for Lee's bravura performance.

Kicking off 1971, Lee's old association with Tony Tenser's Tigon British, for whom he had made *Curse of the Crimson Altar* three years earlier, was rekindled when he joined the cast of *Hannie Caulder*. While making *Scars of Dracula* he had claimed that 'To do a Western is the dream of my life.'[17] Six months later the dream was realised. The film's eight-week schedule began on 18 January in Almería, long the favoured location for so-called Spaghetti Westerns. Sixty per cent of the film's $1,400,000 budget came from Tigon and the remainder from Curtwel, a company run by Raquel Welch and her husband Patrick Curtis. Curtis was confident that the sight of his beauteous wife attired in nothing but a poncho and a gun belt would acquire the same iconic status she had enjoyed in a fur bikini in Hammer's *One Million Years B.C.* Indeed, on location in Spain Curtis expressed his admiration for 'the way Jimmy Carreras works,'[18] unaware that, back in Wardour Street, Carreras was preparing to abandon the rapidly sinking Hammer ship.

Given Hammer's dwindling fortunes, it was perhaps just as well that a quite new Christopher Lee was on show in *Hannie Caulder*. A brutal rape/revenge melodrama, the film is compromised by director Burt Kennedy's apparent uncertainty as to how seriously it should be treated. (Though a horse opera specialist and protégé of the cult director Budd Boetticher, Kennedy was best known for his spoof James Garner vehicles, *Support Your Local Sheriff!* and *Support Your Local Gunfighter*.) The picture begins with a blood-spattered bank raid straight out of *The Wild Bunch*, but the three nasty brothers responsible for it – and, later, for repeatedly raping the heroine – are played rather disconcertingly for laughs by Ernest Borgnine, Strother Martin and the splendidly wall-eyed Jack Elam. Ken Thorne's soaring score also verges on the parodic. But there are moments of serenity along the rough-and-tumble route, and several of these are provided by Lee.

In order to have her revenge, Raquel Welch's Hannie falls in with a jaded bounty hunter, Thomas Luther Price (Robert Culp), who offers to teach her to shoot and takes her across the Mexican border to meet ace gunsmith Bailey. Lee's character is given a great deal of expository build-up by Price; we learn that Bailey 'first set up shop in New Orleans [and] when the war come, he switched over to making guns for the Confederate Army.' Also that, having fled in 1863, he now lives by the seashore with 'a Mexican wife and more young 'uns than you can count on your fingers.' But, amid all this exposition, it's never explained why Bailey speaks with an English accent. 'Reason I take such pains with the outside of a gun,' he points out, 'is because I've always thought death

Expat gunsmith Bailey demonstrates his wares in Hannie Caulder *(1971)*

very unattractive. Mean, rotten thing: no getting back at it. Least I can do is add a bit of style.' Rhythmically, Lee's lines were clearly intended for an American, but his performance is so relaxed, and his appearance so splendid, that we never question the presence of a patrician Englishman in the Mexican wilderness. With his black beard fetchingly streaked with grey and a beat-up sombrero on his head, Lee creates a charmingly laconic character quite unlike anything he had previously been called upon to play.

The tranquillity of Bailey's existence, with the ocean at his front door and hordes of little niños under his benevolent care, is rudely disrupted when a bunch of swarthy Mexican bandits thunder through the surf towards his secluded homestead. The exciting gun battle that ensues is chiefly intended to convey that Hannie still hasn't quite got the stomach for killing, but also shows us that Bailey's skill with rifles is by no means confined to crafting them. Lee's is just the sort of appealing character whom we expect to be expediently sacrificed at a moment like this, but, gratifyingly, he survives to see off Culp and Welch with a wave of his sombrero before a touching final shot in which he casts a loving look at one of his little sons. Lee certainly fares a lot better than the film's other guest star, his former Charm School associate Diana Dors, whose spell as 'Madame' is of the 'blink and you'll miss it' variety.

Lee may have been cast against type in *Hannie Caulder*, but while working on it he was given a vivid reminder of how powerful his identification with demonic roles still was. 'I was walking down a centre street of a local village in Spain,' he recalled. 'A very small village; only one street. All the women, mothers and grandmothers – all completely dressed in black – rushed into the street and grabbed all of their children and put them indoors. They also gave me the sign against the Evil Eye.'[19]

Lee's next major project followed in September and gave him the opportunity to examine such superstitious behaviour in more detail. *In Search of Dracula* (aka *Pa jakt efter Dracula*) was the brainchild of the Stockholm-based American director Calvin Floyd and was a TV documentary based on the as yet unpublished book of the same name by Raymond T McNally and Radu Florescu. The book's hopelessly flimsy theory regarding Vlad Tepes, bloodthirsty Voivode of Walachia in the 15th century – namely that he was the direct model for Stoker's Dracula – has since been very thoroughly demolished, but its stranglehold on the popular conception (or misconception) of Dracula is by now immovable. Floyd's documentary (which was made available in several versions, the longest clocking in at over 70 minutes) marked the beginning of this stranglehold, not to mention a noticeable upswing in the fortunes of the Romanian tourist board.

It opens with a highly impressive credits sequence, utilising Vlad-based graphics and some stirring music by Floyd himself, and then lapses into the first of several clips from *Scars of Dracula*. That out of the way, Floyd's beautiful location shots give one an idea of what a proper film of the novel might look like, one

Recreating Vlad Tepes at Bran Castle for the Calvin Floyd documentary Pa jakt efter Dracula *(1971), otherwise known as* In Search of Dracula

that, unlike Stoker himself, took the trouble to go to Transylvania. Lee is on hand as narrator – the script is a clunky one, unfortunately, even featuring misquotations from the novel – and at two points he appears in talking-head mode, sporting a bushy moustache (the remains of his *Hannie Caulder* beard) and a vaguely windswept look despite being comfortably ensconced in a studio. In voice-over, Lee refers to his first Dracula film by its American title and makes mention of its six sequels, an indication that he was called back to add further narration in 1974, when the decision was made to pad the film to feature length for a hoped-for theatrical release. Sadly, the stock footage in the long version, most it from various silent movies, becomes maddeningly irrelevant, as does a laborious digression into the genesis of *Frankenstein* at the Villa Diodati.

Lee is also on hand to impersonate Vlad Tepes and Stoker's Dracula. Regarding his uncannily accurate appearance as the former, Lee observed that 'I was togged up in moustache, fur hat and flowing robes to wander about [Vlad's] forests and castle of Bran,' recalling also that 'When we alighted at Pojana, above Brasov, it suddenly became seven degrees colder, the moon hoisted itself over the crags ... and a bat brushed past my face. "They know," said Calvin.' Lee's scenes as Dracula are just as impressive. In a white wig, conspicuously lacking the traditional widow's peak and offset by jet-black brows and moustache, he descends some steps to enfold an uncredited victim in a scene based compositionally on his encounter with Barbara Shelley in *Dracula Prince of Darkness*. And at the end, he is finally about to bite the girl when he looks up and genially addresses the audience in an adapted version of the curtain speech from the 1920s *Dracula* play. 'Just remember,' he concludes with a doom-laden change of tone, 'there *are* such things!' – and the film ends with a gratifyingly melodramatic crash of music.

Hip Teens, Bluff Brits

1971 was a testing time for Lee, resulting in his embracing a superstition of his own. Sifting through no fewer than 16 proposals, he selected four and dutifully signed the contracts. All four fell through. (One of them was a particularly appetising notion: another Western, *Tomorrow's Dawn* was due to start on 22 March with director Peter Collinson and prospective co-stars Eli Wallach and Telly Savalas, plus two other Lees – Lee Van Cleef and Lee J Cobb.) 'The mistake I had made,' he recalled nearly 20 years later, 'was telling everyone that I was going to be in these films, [so] I had nothing to fall back on. That experience made me very superstitious about telling people what I'm going to do. Now, I only tell them what I *have* done.'[20]

In the unusual position of having time on his hands, Lee spent two days in Columbia's Wardour Street basement at the behest of director Ben Kadish and producer Peter Marriott, the latter familiar from the long-ago *Douglas Fairbanks Presents*. *Theatre Macabre* was a plush series of half-hour dramas for Polish television in which Lee topped and tailed each story, all of them derived from classic horror writers. No mere talking head, he was costumed in a fashion appropriate to each episode and was also provided with suitable props. In one, for instance, he played an organ grinder, complete with monkey; in another he used the very chair in which Oliver Reed's Father Grandier had recently been burned to death in *The Devils*. It was also in this limbo period that he was made the subject of one of the National Film Theatre's prestigious John Player discussions, events which had recently focused on such luminaries as Dirk Bogarde, David Niven, Terence Rattigan, Shirley MacLaine and Rex Harrison. He was interviewed at the NFT on Sunday 1 August by the film critic Philip Strick, subsequently repeating the experience, interviewed this time by David Castell, at the Newport Film Theatre in Monmouthshire on Sunday 24 October.

Reviewing *The Private Life of Sherlock Holmes* in the *Sunday Telegraph* the previous December, Margaret Hinxman had observed that 'Christopher Lee ... is so commandingly good that this must surely be the end of shabby Draculas for him.' But, some ten months later, Lee's string of broken contracts forced him to bow to the inevitable and agree to James Carreras' pleas that he appear in *Dracula Today*, directed at Elstree by Alan Gibson. Despite being reunited with Peter Cushing's Van Helsing after a lapse of 14 years, Lee was horrified by the film's inane script, which resurrected the Count in a contemporary Chelsea so ill-observed that its 'hip' teenagers seem no more up-to-date than those in *Beat Girl*. As was customary by now, Lee chopped out most of the Count's dialogue, which, coming this time from the pen of Don Houghton, was noticeably more florid than the stuff Tony Hinds used to concoct but every bit as banal. Out went such drivel as 'I am Dracula, Lord of Darkness, Master of the Walking Dead! I am the Curse, the Apollyon, Angel of the Destroying Furies! I am the Apocalypse!' 'I think he should have something to say in these films,' Lee had tartly observed back in 1968, 'though when he does speak it has to be something worth saying.'[21]

Dracula A.D. 1972, as it became known, begins with a moderately exciting Victorian prologue in which Dracula and the 'original' Van Helsing –

Cushing subsequently plays his grandson in the main body of the film – fight to the death atop a runaway coach. Puzzlingly, this sequence is set in 1872, 13 years before the events chronicled in Hammer's first *Dracula*, but narrative continuity was the least of Hammer's concerns at this late stage. Effective though it is, it's hard not to think that this scene of two ageing icons locked in mortal combat was merely a source of amusement to 'switched-on' youth audiences of 1972. If so, they would have found much more to tickle them as the film progressed, particularly in the utterly cardboard younger characters intended to 'reflect' them.

Lee is required merely to die, be resurrected, bite three people (one of whom is a man) and then die again, and all his scenes bar the opening one are set in a musty old church. A Renfield substitute, preposterously named Johnny Alucard, supplies him with Caroline Munro and Marsha Hunt (his first black victim) and, to his credit, Lee's disillusionment with Hammer's procedures is never visible at any point. Indeed, though pushing 50 he looks splendidly imposing in the part and gives it some frighteningly feral moments that are close to his best. His clinch with Caroline Munro is especially nasty, with Dracula looking skyward after the first bite, blood leaking down over his chin, then resuming his attack with a horrid, mock-coital jerk.

Later, he remonstrates with the ridiculous Alucard by pointing an extremely threatening finger at the camera and snarling '*You*, and your line, have been chosen!' And in his final confrontation with Van Helsing, he recaptures some of the red-eyed animality he displayed in the corresponding scene in *Dracula*, even slinging an upright brazier at him just as he did in 1957. He tosses in a line from the book ('You would play your brains against mine? Against me who has commanded nations?') and then, also as per Stoker, is climactically stabbed with a knife. Reasoning that this wouldn't be sufficient for 1970s gorehounds, Houghton then sends him out into the graveyard, where he ends up stumbling ignominiously into a hole in the ground and, with much glopping of bright-red Kensington Gore, is impaled through the back with a shovel.

Lee's disdain for Hammer's Dracula productions was at its height by this time and becoming increasingly vocal. 'All I get to do is to stand around on unhallowed ground, sweep down corridors and make the odd pounce or two,' he vociferated. 'Nobody can write dialogue for Dracula ... In the new film I have one original Stoker line, but that's yelled out at a distance of a hundred years. I've told Hammer that, unless certain conditions are met, I shall not play the role again.'[22] For his part, James Carreras cynically observed in *Bizarre* magazine that 'He has been saying this for years about Dracula, but he keeps on playing Dracula. If he said every time the press interviewed him, "I love Dracula, I'm going to play Dracula forever," the press would stop interviewing him.'

A much happier Cushing/Lee vehicle followed a month or so after *Dracula A.D. 1972* finished shooting. On 6 December Lee started work on an Anglo-Spanish co-production called *Pánico en el Transiberiano* at Estudios Madrid 70 in Daganzo; Cushing flew over to join him a week later. Directed by Eugenio Martín, the film cost some $350,000 and on its Spanish release the following year netted in excess of 26 million pesetas. And when belatedly issued in the UK as *Horror Express* in June 1974, the film received a much more enthusiastic critical reception than was normally accorded Cushing and Lee's purely British horrors.

Spain's short-lived but amazingly productive horror boom was in full swing when *Horror Express* was made, but it never acquired an iconic star other than the stocky ex-weightlifter Jacinto Molina, who styled himself Paul Naschy for his many fur-faced incarnations as 'el hombre lobo'. It was an extraordinary coup, then, for Scotia International to engage the services of the men whom Dilys Powell later dubbed 'the twin pillars of [England's] native horror cinema,'[23] and their presence no doubt did much to ensure the film's impressive takings. The film scored a yet greater coup in providing them with arguably the most delightful and even-handed showcase of all their co-starring vehicles. The chemistry and warmth between Cushing and Lee is perhaps so marked in this film because they needed every bit of it off-camera as well as on. Not only were they working in what Lee remembers as 'a thoroughly horrible little studio in the middle of nowhere,' but Cushing's wife Helen had died on 14 January and he was afflicted by the profound grief that would remain with him until the end of his life.

As recorded by Mark A Miller in his 1995 book devoted to the Cushing/Lee canon, the prospect of being on foreign soil for his first Christmas without Helen led Cushing to announce his withdrawal from *Horror Express* even as producer Bernard Gordon picked him up at the airport. Gordon left it to Lee to talk Cushing round, which Lee did by studiously avoiding the topic and subjecting his old friend instead to a concentrated blast of the anecdote-driven camaraderie they had enjoyed since 1956. Cushing received further emotional support when he joined Lee, Gitte and eight-year-old Christina in their hotel suite on Christmas Day. A few days earlier, the Lees had had an emotional

'Monster? We're British, you know!' With Peter Cushing and Julio Pena in Pánico en el Transiberiano, aka Horror Express *(1971)*

moment of their own at a festive cast-and-crew gathering, when Christina began dancing and leaping about with a facility she had never shown before.

Horror Express is a handsomely appointed and wittily scripted gem, with Lee and Cushing as rival anthropologists, Professor Saxton and Dr Wells, getting together to do battle with a shape-shifting alien creature on board the Trans-Siberian Express. Holmes and Watson are recalled here but also the bluff Britishers, Charters and Caldicott, from Hitchcock's trainbound classic, *The Lady Vanishes*. 'Oh yes: England,' smiles Silvia Tortosa's doe-eyed Countess on hearing their accents. 'Queen Victoria, crumpets, Shakespeare.' And when Julio Peña's police inspector, himself the alien's host by this stage, tries to put them off the scent by suggesting that *they* might be infected, Cushing is granted the immortal line, 'Monster? We're British, you know!'

The script elsewhere is wildly eclectic, featuring a wild-eyed Rasputin lookalike (Alberto de Mendoza) who is actually referred to as a 'mad monk' at one point, a silky Mata Hari-style spy (played by Helga Liné, a long-serving queen of Euro-horror) and a bunch of third act Cossacks led by Telly Savalas. And at the end it suddenly turns into a zombie picture, with Lee shooting and slicing his way through hordes of reacti-vated Cossacks before joining Cushing for a thrilling finale which is a cliffhanger in the most literal sense.

Cushing is on thoroughly mischievous, birdlike form as Dr Wells, with a twinkle in his eye that entirely belies his real-life bereavement, while Lee's haughty persona is seen at its most relaxed and effective as Saxton, all the more so for his willingness to have it punctured from time to time by a little gentle humour. And with his bristling moustache, grey-flecked hair and no-nonsense worsted suit, he looks every inch the intellectual adventurer of Edwardian fiction. Convinced that his 'box of bones' recovered from a Manchurian cave will ensure that 'the very origin of Man is determined,' he gets a shock when he discovers that his cherished Missing Link has gone missing for real and that the box contains only the blood-stained corpse of a railway employee. 'My God,' he gasps, 'it's the baggage man!' – bearing out Margaret Hinxman's observation that 'Both Lee and Cushing have developed a dapper way of saying an idiotic line straight, while still communicating the joke of it to the audience.'[24] Howard Hawks' *The Thing* remade in the dazzling colours of a Euro-Western, *Horror Express* held out great hopes for further Cushing/Lee collaborations, which would continue to proliferate in 1972.

PART SEVEN

FROM SCAREMONGER TO SCARAMANGA

1972–1975

In February 1971, the *Motion Picture Herald* published a poll of 1,600 cinema managers called 'Britain's Best for 1970'. The list of the 25 most popular film stars saw Lee coming in seventeenth, with people like Julie Andrews, Oliver Reed, Charlton Heston, Peter O'Toole and Burt Lancaster lagging behind him. 'I am the fourth most popular British actor on that list,' Lee noted. 'But nothing appeared about it in the British press. Nothing.'[1]

Still waiting for casting directors to get the 'message' provided by *The Private Life of Sherlock Holmes*, Lee was increasingly bothered in the early 1970s by the spectre of typecasting, and was determined to exorcise it. He also had some pretty withering views about the film business in general, notably the 'complete hypocrisy' surrounding various taboo-busting, headline-hogging blockbusters of the period. 'There is less violence in ten or twelve Hammer films than in five minutes of one of these art films,' he stormed, 'and in these [art] films, the violence is real, not fantasy.'[2] This disgruntled mood was salved somewhat by the continued adoration of his fans, whose centre of operations had recently shifted from the USA to the Worthing home of his new fan club president, Dorene Hazell. And his mailbag yielded some unusual tributes, notably one from a Romanian correspondent claiming that 'We have formed a club for you because you are, without doubt, the most terrible actor in the world.' Tickled by this confusion of 'terrifying' with 'terrible', Lee considered the letter one of the funniest he had ever received.

Back in the UK after their exertions in *Horror Express*, Cushing and Lee were whisked straight into *The Creeping Flesh*, a World Film Services/Tigon co-production which started at Shepperton on 31 January 1972 with Freddie Francis at the helm. This time it's Cushing who harbours wild evolutionary theories, unearthing a colossal humanoid skeleton and inadvertently unleashing the so-called Evil One upon the world at the outset of the 20th century. The family tragedy outlined in the film is just as bleak, with Cushing's Emmanuel Hildern haunted by the dementia into which his late wife descended and conferring it upon their daughter Penelope in the grimmest of self-fulfilling prophecies. Lee plays Emmanuel's embittered half-brother James, who, as superintendent of the Hildern Institute for Mental Disorders, is responsible first for Emmanuel's wife, then for his daughter and finally for poor Emmanuel himself.

The film's overtones of Shakespearean tragedy are confirmed by its structure, with the main plot centred on Emmanuel's astonishing anthropological find and the sub-plot devoted to James' experiments in the asylum, the two strands eventually intertwining with disastrous results. Toying off-handedly with his half-brother's fragile feelings, Lee invests the hateful James with sub-zero emotional coldness. His feigned concern when discussing the death of Emmanuel's wife gives place to the merest suspicion of a smirk as their conversation proceeds and finally to the steeliest of stares as he expresses his determination to win the Richter Prize that Emmanuel also has his eye on. 'I want to make it quite clear, Emmanuel,' he says, 'that I do not propose to continue to subsidise your ridiculous expeditions to the ends of the Earth to prove your lunatic theories about the origin of Man.'

James' habitual curtness is visible even in his two encounters with Duncan Lamont's dour police chief, who has been charged with apprehending escaped lunatic Lenny. (Lenny's misadventures with the crazed Penelope not only form yet another plot strand but also utilise the grimy *Oliver!* street sets last seen in *I, Monster*.) As well as calmly emptying three bullets into the back of another escapee, James is subsequently seen testing his 'electrical wave theory' on a severed arm in a tank. 'Unfortunately,' he observes conceitedly, 'in the state of society as it exists today, we are not permitted to experiment on human

With Maud Adams in the ninth instalment of Eon's long-running 007 series, The Man with the Golden Gun (1974)

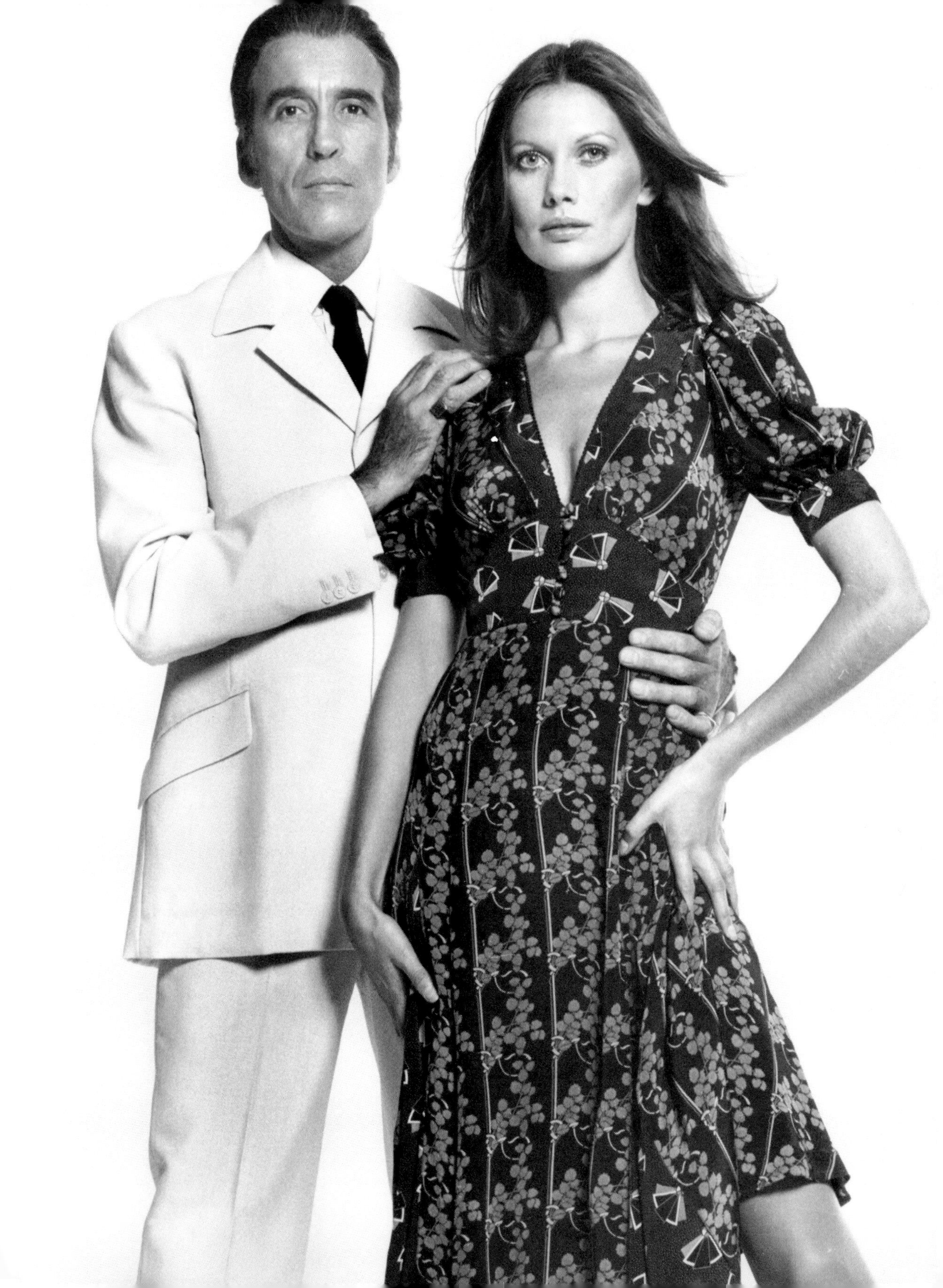

Relaxing at Shepperton with Lorna Heilbron and Jenny Runacre while filming The Creeping Flesh *(1972)*

beings: *normal* human beings.' But when Penelope is delivered to his door, her mutated blood cells convince him that Emmanuel has been doing just that and he determines to take a close look at Emmanuel's laboratory. Well aware of his half-brother's pathological fear of hereditary insanity, he informs Emmanuel of Penelope's incarceration with unconcealed relish and then abducts the monstrous skeleton, unaware that it has a habit of taking on flesh when exposed to water. In a triumph of dramatic irony, the oblivious James hoists himself out of his overturned and rain-soaked carriage only moments before the creature's fleshy hand puts in an appearance.

A doom-laden coda finds Penelope and her father confined to James' asylum as he airily dismisses the suggestion that they are his niece and brother. 'I'm a sort of authority figure for them,' he explains, 'so naturally I appear in their fantasies.' Insouciant smugness oozing from every pore, he also points out that they have been inmates of his ever since 'the year I won the Richter Prize,' bringing the film to a truly painful conclusion. Thanks to an unusually clever script, it's quite possible that the entire story really *is* one of Emmanuel's 'fantasies' and that James isn't any relation to him after all. Either way, Lee plays the character with frosty aplomb and his scenes with Cushing positively crackle.

CHARLEMAGNE

While *The Creeping Flesh* continued its tenure of Shepperton during March, Lee spent a single Saturday morning with Donald Pleasence and Norman Rossington on another British horror, *Death Line*. Unusually gruesome for its day, the film was produced by Lee's old associate from *Il castello dei morti vivi*, Paul Maslansky, and directed by a young American known for his Coca-Cola commercials, Gary Sherman. Made for only £80,000, the film went on to become a smash hit and remains one of the most powerful of all British horror films, particularly for the elegiac spell of sadness it weaves around its scrofulous, troglodyte protagonist, referred to merely as 'The Man'.

The only living descendant of a group of tube workers buried alive in an 1890s tunnel cave-in, his cannibalistic forays onto the platform at Russell Square station arouse the interest of Holborn's mean-spirited Inspector Calhoun. Though clearly included mainly for marquee value, Lee's two-minute cameo as Stratton-Villiers MI5 is thematically important and icily effective to boot. A 1970s manifestation of the Establishment callousness that sealed the fate of the tunnel workers some 80 years before, Stratton-Villiers appears as if from nowhere while Calhoun and Det Sgt Rogers are nosing around the home of a missing civil servant. Complete with bowler hat, furled umbrella and Old Etonian tie, Stratton-Villiers coolly warns them that their investigations are liable to ring Establishment alarm bells. Class animosity pulsing between them, the shabby Calhoun objects that 'This is my manor, and the villains in it are mine.' 'Well, you're welcome to them, old thing,' Stratton-Villiers twinkles threateningly in reply, 'so why don't you just run along and arrest a few?'

Though Lee's blackly comic scene is only frightening on a cerebral level, the film as a whole is gut-wrenchingly good and testimony to the fact was provided by one of Lee's fans. 'My husband, knowing I'm a great fan of Mr Lee, took me to see *Death Line*,' wrote Christine Pugh of Gosport to her fellow members in a 1974 fan club bulletin. 'I was two weeks away from having my first child, and by the time the film ended, I was so frightened to death I thought I was going to give birth.' The baby, incidentally, finally appeared on 27 May, Lee's birthday, and was duly called Christopher.

One project mooted in 1972 but never filmed was a Hammer picture called *Victim of His Imagination*. Scripted by Don Houghton and to be produced by Howard Brandy, this was to have starred Lee alongside Hammer's current darling, Shane Briant, in a potentially fascinating story outlining the genesis of *Dracula*. Ignoring the Vlad the Impaler nonsense espoused by *In Search of Dracula*, Houghton had hit upon a much more plausible model for the Count in Bram Stoker's autocratic thespian employer, Henry Irving. Though the ethereal Briant was an odd choice to play man's man Stoker, Lee's Irving is surely one of the great missed opportunities of British horror. Tellingly, Peter Cushing had been approached to play Irving – unsuccessfully, as it turned out – by the BBC back in the 1950s.

While Henry Irving hovered in limbo, Lee turned producer in April 1972 for a film called *Nothing But the Night*. Reports of Lee's interest in setting his own film company date back as far as 1967, and by 1970 he had teamed up with the former Hammer producer Anthony Nelson Keys to form Charlemagne Productions, so named because of the Carandini family's ancestral links to the Frankish king. 'I had made many films for other companies which grossed big profits,' Lee explained. 'So we decided it was time we had a fair share of what was due us. What we did for other companies we could do for ourselves. Moreover, we wanted to choose our own properties and play the kind of parts I wanted to play.'[3]

Armed with the screen rights to three Dennis Wheatley novels (*The Satanist*, *The Haunting of Toby Jugg* and *To the Devil a Daughter*) and two more by John Blackburn (*Bury Him Darkly* and *Nothing But the Night*) – together with an original screenplay by Robin Squires called *Portrait of Barbara* – Lee and Keys approached the Rank Organisation and saw the Wheatley projects turned down flat. *Nothing But the Night*, however, was given the go-ahead and started shooting at Pinewood on 17 April. 'You have to try and sell a picture on a package deal,' Keys explained a week into shooting. 'The package on this one was Christopher Lee, Peter Cushing, Tony Keys, possibly Diana Dors and director Peter Sasdy. That was the conception I gave to the Rank Organisation to start with ... They said yes, and away we go. And we'll just have to keep our fingers crossed.'[4]

The deal Keys offered to Rank may have been an attractive one, but the deal offered by Rank in return was anything but. The film was rushed onto the floor with a frugal budget that didn't run to a second unit or even special effects, while the schedule was an unrealistic 30 days. Thanks to these constraints, and a script by Brian Hayles that could have done with several rewrites to infuse some logic into it, *Nothing But the Night* was an unfortunate start for Charlemagne. Indeed, with Rank's stinginess applying to publicity as well as production, it proved an unfortunate end, too. Despite Lee and Cushing

Stratton-Villers MI5 pulls rank on the humble Inspector Calhoun (Donald Pleasence) in Gary Sherman's remarkable Death Line *(1972)*

Christopher Lee – Part Seven

joining forces for a cinema-hopping promotional tour, the film's box-office failure in 1973 proved a mortal blow to the company.

The story revolves around an offshore Scottish orphanage where the elderly trustees have been transplanting their personalities into the children as a means of cheating death. Lee plays Colonel Charles Bingham, a severe CID man who joins with pathologist Sir Mark Ashley (Cushing) to work out what's going on. On location near Dartmoor, Lee sampled the golf course at Thurlsdon with Cushing as caddy, but the pair had less fun in the film itself, both of them visibly floored by their wafer-thin characters. Lee's opening exposition of the case in Cushing's office is smoothly done, and the climactic scene in which the children tether him like a steer and almost propel him into a bonfire is also effective, with Lee appealing to the children and the surviving trustees in appropriately strangulated tones. But inbetween he seems ill at ease, unable to invest the fearsome Bingham with any leavening shafts of humour. It's almost as if Lee the actor had to take a back seat to Lee the producer, labouring under all the headaches imposed by Charlemagne's Rank paymasters.

To make matters worse, there are two gruesomely uncharismatic second leads (Keith Barron and Georgia Brown), who share a saxophone-laden romantic interlude for no properly motivated reason, and numerous scenes of red-wigged fugitive Diana Dors charging about in highly conspicuous fashion while helicopters and police dogs fail completely to spot her. Peter Sasdy, whose recent work for Hammer had contained many artful flourishes, brings none to this picture, seeming as stymied by the screenplay as everyone else. Even the film's composer, Malcolm Williamson, was disgruntled. 'I love Tony Keys as much as Lee,' he conceded, '[but] it was director Peter Sasdy that provided the temperament for that production ... You respond to the visual atmosphere when you write new music. *Nothing But the Night* had virtually nothing for me to work with visually.'[5]

'When I make my first personal film,' Lee had promised himself in 1971, 'everything has got to be right – script, director, cast.'[6] It's clear that Rank's sudden offer of backing caused these luxuries to be set aside, though the main question arising from *Nothing But the Night* is why Lee should have given himself such a boring part: until one realises that there aren't any interesting ones. The dullness of Lee's role and his enervated account of it was picked up even by some of his fans. In a surprisingly hard-hitting observation for a fan club bulletin, Juliette Bentley of Gloucester claimed that 'Colonel Bingham was yet another in the line of uptight,

With Peter Cushing, Michael Gambon and Fulton Mackay on location in the West Country for Nothing But the Night *(1972)*

From Scaremonger To Scaramanga 1972-1975

The not-so-sinister teaser: as the affable Lord Summerisle in The Wicker Man *(1972), displaying a hothouse exhibit subsequently consigned to the cutting room floor*

bad-tempered, humourless characters (Franklyn Marsh in Scotland Yard this time), which to put it bluntly is all Christopher seems to do when he plays ordinary people. At villains and anything out of the ordinary he is unsurpassed: sensitive, subtle and various: but give him the role of a reasonably ordinary, everyday person and they all come out the same.' Happily, waiting in the wings was another film set on an offshore Scottish island, and in it Lee would exorcise the grim shade of Colonel Bingham by giving one of his most relaxed and engaging performances yet.

Another Offshore Island

With the eventual fate of *Nothing But the Night* as yet unclear, Lee spent much of the remainder of 1972 'in the middle of very protracted financial negotiations towards getting the kind of deal that we will accept.' Interviewed at Elstree on 22 December, Lee confirmed that a number of prospective sponsors had offered 'to put money into Charlemagne ... [but] we have not been able to progress very far with the actual setting up of a financial structure to a point where we can say we've got all the money in the bank and we will make our next picture. If it works out ... we will be able to make two pictures a year for at least five or six years.'[7]

Amidst these negotiations, Lee was offered a role specially written for him in a British Lion project called *The Wicker Man*. The script – detailing a fiendish, yet deadly serious, practical joke devised by a pagan community on an offshore Scottish island – was by Anthony Shaffer, who had recently come to prominence with *Sleuth* (play and film) and the screenplay for Hitchcock's *Frenzy*. The film's schedule began on 16 October, its 25 Scottish locations ranging across some 190 miles and creating an entirely believable ambience for the island fiefdom presided over by Lee's Lord Summerisle. Convinced that *The Wicker Man* would be 'the best-scripted film I ever took part in,' Lee had agreed to contribute his services – like Shaffer and its director Robin Hardy – for no fee.

Despite, or more probably because of, its checkered career on release and the continuing mystery surrounding a considerable amount of footage excised by panicked distributors, *The Wicker Man* has assumed a position of giddy eminence in the pantheon of so-called 'cult' movies. And it's certainly one of the most beguiling and strikingly intelligent of all British horror pictures, utilising a whole range of tried-and-tested genre conventions and turning them ingeniously on their heads. Among these conventions is Lee himself, whose mere presence gives audiences the coded message that Summerisle must be a villain before triumphantly wrongfooting them with a heavy dose of beaming benevolence on his first meeting with Edward Woodward's tight-lipped Sergeant Howie.

Tweedy, sometimes kilted – with a leonine shock of hair reminiscent of 'Nuada, our most sacred god of the sun' – Lee's Summerisle is disconcerting not for any calculated villainy but purely because of his unnervingly steady gaze and half-amused smile, neither of which gives the viewer a clear idea of where he's coming from. This ambivalence is maintained throughout, and even at the very end of the film, when it's become clear that Summerisle has orchestrated a devious plot to burn Howie to death as a human sacrifice, it remains impossible to hate him. His schemes may be appalling but they're perfectly permissible according to the religion followed by his island subjects. As he observes when accused by Howie of being a pagan, he is 'A heathen, conceivably, but not, I hope, an unenlightened one.'

Typical of the script's uniquely flavoursome dialogue, this line is favoured with a big yet unreadable close-up of Summerisle, underlining his inscrutability. Does he espouse the beliefs which the upright Howie finds so repugnant out of the 'expediency' practised by his grandfather, who was first to assume control of the island, or out of the 'love' subsequently felt by his father? Whether assuring Howie that 'We don't commit murder up here; we're a deeply religious people,' or responding with a bland show of mystification as Howie hurls a dead hare at his feet, Lee maintains a light touch throughout and is careful to preserve Summerisle's secret. 'It's a complex role,' he pointed out several years later. 'While being genuine, the character had to carry the sense that something was not quite right in that village, and you can't quite put your finger on it ... It's the abnormal that lurks behind the normal which makes a film like this work so successfully. It's what you don't see rather than what you do, what is suggested rather than shown in detail.'[8]

In the longer versions of the film, Summerisle is first seen at night as he offers up a kilted teenage boy as 'another sacrifice for Aphrodite' – ie, for sexual initiation at the hands of Britt Ekland's Willow MacGregor. Pausing among the Summerisle foliage, he recites a few lines of modified Walt Whitman to a pair of copulating snails, the sombre lyricism of Lee's delivery making it immediately clear that Summerisle is a man of culture and refinement. When we see him again, his ideological clash with Howie represents the centrepiece of the film. On a tour of his estate – a composite, incidentally, of the Logan Botanical Gardens with two castles, Culzean and Lochinch – Summerisle explains to the affronted Howie why he considers that the Christian God 'had his chance and, in modern parlance, blew it.' And Howie's explosive objections are met with just the kind of unruffled insouciance calculated to irritate a good 'Christian copper' even further.

As the May Day festivities get under way, Summerisle is seen at his most genial, practising a Highland reel while dressed in a suitably sunny yellow polo neck and a charmingly incongruous pair of sneakers. The ensuing procession qualifies as perhaps the strangest spectacle in British cinema, and at its head is perhaps its strangest component, Summerisle in his traditional role of the 'man-woman, the sinister teaser, played by the community leader or priest.' It's surely Lee's most outré incarnation: white-faced, dressed in a lilac frock and squaw-like black wig, the sneakers still firmly in place as he flourishes a sickle and a sprig of mistletoe. Summerisle pirouettes with a kind of stiff solemnity in advance of a traditional dance-drama that includes the Salmon of Knowledge, the Hobbyhorse, Old Brazenface and the rest – all en route to Howie's fiery 'appointment with the Wicker Man.'

The clifftop climax, filmed at the Machars peninsula, is stunningly staged and finds Lee back in his leather-patched tweeds for a deft unravelling of the mystery, much of it relayed in close-up as his golden aureole of hair flutters in the breeze. As sacrificial victims, he informs Howie, 'Animals are fine, but their acceptability is limited. A little child is even better – but not nearly as effective as the right kind of adult...' In that final phrase the scales fall from the audience's eyes as much as Howie's, and few actors could have laced it with the ominous import Lee does. He switches immediately to a tone of beatific compassion as Summerisle assures Howie that 'Believing what you do, we confer upon you a rare gift these days: a martyr's death.' He betrays the slightest flicker of anxiety when Howie defiantly nominates him as next year's sacrifice, then holds his hands aloft before the setting sun. 'Reverence the sacrifice,' he intones, and, with a rousing chorus of 'Summer is icumen in,' the film hastens to its astonishing end.

Ever since seeing the 'finished' film in British Lion's Soho basement in 1973, Lee has been vocal in his dismay at the studio butchery inflicted upon it. And with good reason; his Lord Summerisle is a delightfully ambiguous creation deserving of the best possible showcase. 'I don't know that Lee's done anything better than that,' Anthony Shaffer observed some 20 years later. 'He's absolutely formidable in that mauve frock and that fright wig. It's a sensationally good performance. Lee is absolutely amazing in the picture.'[9]

NEVER MORE

At the mercy of a peculiarly hectic schedule, Lee returned from Scotland on 14 November and left for

Hollywood the very next day. He was due to take part in his first TV movie, a droll Sammy Davis Jr vehicle for Paramount called *Poor Devil*. 'Naturally I play the Devil,'[10] he pointed out crisply – in the silk-jacketed entrepreneurial style, he might have added, of *Playboy* boss Hugh Hefner. 'I had three wonderful weeks,' Lee remarked. 'Never have I received such appreciation, such courtesy, such kindness and good humour as I did on the set at Paramount. I was applauded when I walked onto the set, and that's never happened to me in a British studio in all my life.'[11]

When the film was transmitted on ABC the following year, however, audiences failed to warm to the antics of Davis Jr as an incompetent minor demon lorded over by Lee's Lucifer and a projected spin-off series was scrapped. The fate of *Poor Devil* is hardly surprising given that it is strangely unfunny. The production and costume design, plus Morton Stevens' funky score, are the sort of thing lovingly recreated in the 1998 hit, *Austin Powers: International Man of Mystery*. But Robert Scheerer's leaden direction misses comic opportunities at every turn and TV stalwarts like Jack Klugman and Adam West are left flailing. Lee has some diverting moments, whether reflecting on future recruits ('Hell hath no better prospect than a good man scorned') or past successes ('That Adam: he was a tough proposition'), but even he resorts, presumably in desperation, to yelling several of his lines by the end.

Though parodic, Lee's role gained him an unusual fan in Anton La Vey, High Priest of San Francisco's Church of Satan, who sent him two of his books, inscribing them 'To Christopher Lee – a fine actor and a perfect devil!' Lee also took the opportunity, on 24 November, to address the Count Dracula Society at LA's Ambassador Hotel, his audience including such luminaries as Forrest J Ackerman, Reginald LeBorg, A E Van Vogt and Lee's old friend Robert Bloch.

On his return, Lee had a breather lasting little more than 24 hours before starting work on a small Glenbeigh production called *Dark Places*. Directed by his old associate Don Sharp, this has Robert Hardy as a former mental patient, Edward Foster, who inherits an old house and becomes possessed by the shade of its former inmate. Hardy is no film star, however – the numerous scenes in which he mopes around the house, going steadily crazy, seem interminable – and the four actors billed above him (Lee, Joan Collins, Herbert Lom and Jane Birkin) play totally peripheral roles. The sub-plot in which Lee and Collins are involved is especially tedious. As the local GP, Ian Mandeville, and his oversexed sister Sarah, they want to get their hands on a cache of money concealed in the house before Foster does and only the faint whiff of

Lucifer in the style of Hugh Hefner: Poor Devil *(1972)*

incest between them enlivens their handful of scenes. Realising that Sarah has slept with Foster, Mandeville rounds on her with 'You dirty, filthy little slut!' Whereupon she caresses his cheek and pouts, 'Poor Ian, don't you sometimes wish that I wasn't your sister?'

Lee recalls that '*Dark Places* was shot in a condemned house near Pinewood and was an extremely uncomfortable film to make.' The result is stodgy and unmemorable, though its scenes of Mandeville dressing Foster's wounded knee and subsequently treating him for hypertension provide a faint foretaste of the rapport between Lee and Hardy in *A Feast at Midnight* over 20 years later. Lee also gets to utter the kind of warning normally reserved for Transylvanian innkeepers. 'The villagers won't go near the place,' he observes. 'They swear it's haunted by the children.' His only moment of distinction comes when Mandeville, having discovered that his sister has been strangled to death by the out-of-control Edward, finds himself at the wrong end of a pick-axe and comes out with a panicked shriek of 'Edward!' just before the blow is struck.

1972 concluded with Lee's last appearance as Dracula; indeed, director Alan Gibson wrapped *Dracula is Dead and Well and Living in London* at Elstree on 3 January 1973, 15 years to the day since the original *Dracula* wrapped at Bray. Audience tastes had

Smiling through The Satanic Rites of Dracula with Peter Cushing (1972)

changed radically in the intervening period and there is virtually nothing in *The Satanic Rites of Dracula*, as it came to be entitled, that recalls the robust, fairy-tale simplicity of its distinguished progenitor other than the continued presence of Lee and Cushing. A gaudy stew of full-frontal nudity and brutal set-pieces, the film is nevertheless a vast improvement over *Dracula A.D. 1972*, to which it is a direct sequel, while its two stars perform, as ever, as if nothing is amiss.

Though the usual palaver of resurrecting the Count is happily passed over this time round, it still takes over half an hour before Dracula puts in an appearance. When he does, it's in a highly erotic scene in which he swarms vaporously under a vibrating door and enfolds the kidnapped Valerie Van Ost on a crude camp-bed. The modern-day Van Helsing, meanwhile, is unravelling a convoluted plot involving a newly perfected strain of bubonic plague and four highly placed grandees indulging in satanic ceremonies. He winds up at a mysterious tower block built on the site of the deconsecrated church in which he killed Dracula two years before. There, in the only scene in the Hammer series in which Lee is divested of his cloak, the Count masquerades in silhouette as property developer D D Denham, a disguise that pitches him somewhere between Fu Manchu and Howard Hughes. But in the cheerful manifesto that he presents to Van Helsing he sounds more like a representative of the then-topical Festival of Light.

'There is a group of us,' Lee explains in a vaguely Lugosi-like accent, 'who are determined that the decadence of the present day can and will be halted. A new political regime is planned. To lend weight to one's arguments, amid the rush and whirl of humanity, it is sometimes necessary to be persuasive...'

Don Houghton's script is charmingly satirical in a comic-strip kind of way, while Lee stitched into it several lines adapted from Stoker. As well as 'the rush and whirl of humanity' line quoted above, at the climax Dracula bellows boastfully that 'My revenge has spread over centuries, and has just begun!' – although, with his schemes literally going up in flames by that stage, the line could have been better positioned. But the tense countdown-to-midnight scene preceding the inferno is suspensefully done and Lee, with a surprisingly large amount of dialogue, is magnificent in it. The Lugosi-like tones set aside, he introduces 'the instrument of my final conquest: swifter, more awesome than the Black Death: the plague,' and refers to his panicky acolytes as 'the four horsemen of my created Apocalypse.' He alludes almost wistfully to the 'release' of death and then points an extremely threatening finger at the camera just as he did in *A.D. 1972*, hissing '*You*, Van Helsing, are now one of the four.' Narrowing his eyes at the stroke of midnight, he wills one of his flunkeys to smash the vial of plague-carrying germs and all hell breaks loose.

Dracula finally comes to an appropriately Messianic, though somewhat undignified, end, plunging his way through a hawthorn bush and being impaled by Van Helsing on the other side. The cosmic death wish expressed by the Count in this picture may have been a subtextual nod from Houghton to Lee's own, by now overwhelming, desire to put an end to Dracula once and for all. *Satanic Rites* was ignominiously double-billed in the UK with an American hybrid called *Blacula* and failed to appear in Stateside cinemas until 1978. It also proved to be the final straw for Lee, bringing him, as he put it, to 'my irrevocable full stop.' Soon afterwards he announced that 'I've done enough. That chapter of my life is closed. For several reasons. I felt the films were getting further and further away from the original Stoker conception. When you lose interest in a character you should not continue to play it. I felt it was becoming too easy. The challenge had gone. I lost belief. I lost faith. I said goodbye.'[12]

MONSIEUR CYCLOPS

After the intense activity that rounded out 1972, Lee took things a little more easily at the beginning of 1973. From 9 to 11 February he was ensconced in the Alpine ski resort of Avoriaz for the first Festival International d'Avoriaz du Film Fantastique, where he saw such pictures as Steven Spielberg's *Duel* and Mario Bava's *Antefatto* (*Twitch of the Death Nerve*). As President of the jury, he insisted, in the teeth of French opposition, that *Duel* be given the Grand Prix, a move that ensured its cult acceptance and which Spielberg would bear in mind when casting *1941* some five years later.

Also while there, he was reportedly offered four pictures: *Tendre Dracula* by director Alain Robbe-Grillet (a film with the same title, starring Peter Cushing, was made 12 months later by Pierre Grunstein), *La confession* for Claude Chabrol, *Mort profonde* (a story set at the Avoriaz Festival itself and to co-star Fernando Rey, Stephane Audran and Maurice Ronet), and *Eulalie quitte les champs* for Jérôme Savary. In an echo of 1971, only one of these – the last – was eventually made. The US broadcast of *Poor Devil* followed on the 14th – it had to wait a further 12 months before reaching the UK – and Lee was no doubt gratified to find himself singled out in the *Los Angeles Times* as 'a splendidly sinister Lucifer.'

This restful period was a prelude to one of the most encouraging phases in Lee's career, with prominent roles in blockbusters produced by Ilya Salkind and Albert R Broccoli just around the corner. As a result, the non-appearance of the projected *Poor Devil* spin-off series was only a passing disappointment. 'Because I didn't do *Poor Devil*,' Lee explained to his fans, 'I did *The Three Musketeers* and from the Musketeers undoubtedly came *The Man With the Golden Gun*. Mr Broccoli had seen it and he'd seen *The Wicker Man*, so if I'd done that TV series I might still have been doing it ... It was a blessing in disguise that I didn't do it, although I was looking forward to it at the time.'

On 10 May, Salkind's $5 million Alexandre Dumas adaptation, *The Three Musketeers*, began filming in Madrid's Cerralbo Museum, though the bulk of the four-month schedule would utilise Toledo as a substitute for 17th century Paris. The notion of remaking *The Three Musketeers* had occurred to the 26-year-old Salkind back in September 1972. The idea then was to film in Budapest and cast the Beatles, no less. Famous for directing them in *A Hard Day's Night* and *Help!*, Richard Lester was brought on board and determined to portray the period as it really was. ('You should be aware,' he pointed out, 'that, even though it's a romantic piece, everyone was pretty filthy, that they never washed and they urinated on all those tapestries that are now in the museums.'[13]) The Beatles idea having been set aside (presumably because the group had broken up over two years before), 55 locations were chosen (104 according to some reports), 110 sets erected and the proverbial cast of thousands enlisted to decorate them. The film's numerous headliners, ranging from Charlton Heston as Cardinal Richelieu to Faye Dunaway as Milady de Winter and Jean-Pierre Cassel as Louis XIII, were a stellar lot and Lee, cast as 'the Cardinal's living blade' Rochefort, was billed sixth.

The Three Musketeers (The Queen's Diamonds) opened in Paris on 13 December – Lee remembered 'the entire cast crossing the Champs Elysée at 8.15 at night in a drizzle in their evening clothes on foot, which I think startled the crowds slightly' – and rapidly became a worldwide hit. By that time, however, 'the entire cast' had got wind of an unusual development. 'Soon *The Four Musketeers (The Revenge of Milady)*' trumpeted the film's closing credit titles, together with an enticing montage of scenes that hadn't made it into *The Three Musketeers*. As Lee put it, the film had 'somehow bifurcated into two films, such was the quantity of celluloid in the can.' The trade papers buzzed briefly with threats of legal action from some of the actors' representatives, but these efforts were stymied when it was discovered that Salkind had cannily used the ambiguous term 'project' in their contracts. Lee himself was unconcerned, pointing out mildly that 'It was reasonable to do this rather than waste the richness of the material.'

'I fear you, Eminence. I also hate you.' The Comte de Rochefort with Cardinal Richelieu (Charlton Heston) in Dick Lester's all-star 'project' based on Alexandre Dumas' The Three Musketeers (1973)

Faced with this rich material, Lester emphasises as much grime and grit as he can but also brings to the film a vein of Goonish humour harking back to his first picture, *The Running, Jumping and Standing Still Film*, which he had made in tandem with the Goons in 1959. Spike Milligan himself turns up in the first Musketeers instalment, improbably cast as Raquel Welch's husband, but the rest of the film's abundant humour is less engaging. 'Lester's Gaggadocio,' as the *Evening Standard* dubbed it, consists mainly of Spanish actors bumbling about in long shot as accident-prone low-life types while patently dubbed and not very amusing one-liners are pasted over their slapstick routines.

Much better are the ravishing visuals, courtesy of art director Brian Eatwell and cinematographer David Watkin, together with some convincingly brutal sword fights orchestrated by fencing wizard Bill Hobbs. The filming, as Lee put it, was 'a physically exhausting stream of battles with men 20 or 30 years my junior: Oliver Reed, Michael York, Richard Chamberlain. Nothing was faked; we were all quite badly knocked about.' Reed sustained an impaled hand, York nearly lost an eye, Frank Finlay was slammed in the face with a 2 by 4; even Raquel Welch sprained her wrist and elbow in a climactic wrestling match with Faye Dunaway. As for Lee, he wrenched a shoulder in a night fight with York and tore a ligament in his left knee while duelling with Reed. And all these injuries were sustained in Iberian temperatures approaching 120°.

The one-eyed Rochefort – 'surely Peter Pan's Captain Hook in live-action form,'[14] as critic Annie Stonian aptly described him – is one of Lee's most relaxed performances, darkly witty, broodingly resentful of his clerical master and every bit as deadly as Reed's Athos gives him out. 'If you see him walking on the other side of the road one day,' he warns York's wet-behind-the-ears d'Artagnan, 'don't bother to cross over.' But d'Artagnan has already encountered 'that villain without an eye'; in the film's second scene Rochefort nonchalantly plays bowls while offering a dazzling stream of deadpan insults directed at d'Artagnan's broken-down steed. 'It was certainly a change to have an audience laughing at his remarks instead of screaming,' wrote Australian admirer Nikki White to her fellow fan club members. 'His acid comments on d'Artagnan's horse and general appearance had the [Sydney] audience in fits. He was so delightfully arrogant and sardonic. He looked good, too, in his red velvet and black eye-patch.'

Lee also has effective moments when breaking into Welch and Milligan's bedroom – splaying his fingers and admiring the gloves adorning them as

Milligan makes absurd attempts to load a gun – and in a frankly farcical sequence where he holds a wardrobe door closed, oblivious to the fact that York's fingers are caught in the gap. In a tense two-handed scene with Heston's monolithic Cardinal Richelieu, he airily passes off the unhappy outcome of his latest mission ('I failed; one does, occasionally'), proceeds to accuse the Cardinal, very politely, of 'vaulting ambition' and finally admits through gritted teeth that 'I fear you, Eminence. I also hate you.' After a delightfully nostalgic scene with his old Hammer co-star Francis de Wolff (playing an obstructive sea captain who demands a countersigned passport from Rochefort), Lee indulges in a set-piece encounter with York in a darkened wood. Lit by lanterns and flashing rapiers, the fight concludes when Rochefort is felled by an uprooted tree ineptly wielded by d'Artagnan's manservant Planchet (Roy Kinnear).

The film was set before the Queen Mother on 25 March 1974 (the third of Lee's films to be accorded the 'Royal Film Performance' accolade) and *The Four Musketeers (The Revenge of Milady)* reached the nation's cinemas a year later. *Newsweek* hailed this second picture as 'icy and artfully executed, without the pretence to lightheartedness that falsified its predecessor ... Villainy, rather than banter, wit and horseplay, reigns in this second part.' Indeed, Lester's promise that the Dumas project had given him 'a chance to look coldly at the heroes and warmly at the villains'[15] is finally borne out in this instalment, though the heroes are still allowed to direct some choice insults at their antagonists, with Porthos calling Rochefort and his lover Milady 'two birds of prey in fine feathers' and Rochefort himself 'the Cardinal's jackal.'

The film begins with a replay of d'Artagnan's ceremonial acquisition of the musketeers' tabard from the first picture and then proceeds to a charming scene in which Rochefort is at the mercy of a notably inept firing squad. 'Reload!' squawks their leader (Bob Todd), whereupon Rochefort, in a sally joyfully repeated by several reviewers, harrumphs 'Why bother? I may die of old age.' Rescued by the musketeers, he pauses to retrieve and dust off his plumed hat before mounting his getaway horse and abducting Raquel Welch's Mme Bonancieux in a rumbustious marketplace scuffle. In Milady de Winter's boudoir at bathtime, a conspiratorial exchange is given a kinky undertow as Rochefort, having apparently filled her bathtub with blood, lovingly trails his fingers in it. 'I remember the scene I played with Faye Dunaway,' Lee recalled in 1975. 'Right away she put her finger on it – the sexual undertones, the light touch – just like that.

Marvellous. I was enormously impressed; she had never met me before that.'[16]

During a protracted, prat-falling fight on a frozen lake with d'Artagnan, both participants fall splashily through the ice in a scene typical of Lester's method of staging battles with maximum verisimilitude prior to debunking them with slapstick. (For Lee, the scene was also reminiscent, perhaps, of the closing moments of *Dracula Prince of Darkness*.) As events gather to a head at the convent of St Cecilia in Armentières, Rochefort determines that 'I'll take care of the knight errants' and, after a major set-to with Athos, finds himself face to face with d'Artagnan in the church itself. Lester makes much use here of artful long shots, framing the balletic movements of the duellists under an imposing arch as white-robed nuns scatter like panicked doves, and Rochefort is finally skewered in Christ-like pose to a lectern, complete with leather-bound Bible.

Before his lengthy stint as Rochefort, Lee had begun his involvement with a peculiar project in Paris called *Eulalie quitte les champs*, a 'Films d'aventure et d'amour' production originally mooted, as noted above, at the Avoriaz Festival. Lee had first encountered 'Le Grand Magic Circus' when their iconoclastic stage show came to London's Roundhouse; at Jérôme Savary's invitation he then found himself making a film with them. The result, also known as *Le Boucher, le star et l'orpheline*, ran into problems at an early stage. The money disappeared and production only resumed on 8 September. Memorably off-beat, the film involved Lee in an improvisational free-for-all on the streets of Paris and, as such, represented his closest brush with art cinema since his collaborations with Pedro Portabella.

Caught up in the improvisational mayhem of Eulalie quitte les champs, *released as* Le Boucher, le star et l'orpheline *(1973)*

For some of the picture he was required to play a bungling secret agent – not only dressed in white but *painted* white – and journeyed to the snow-covered Massif Central near Grenoble to light explosive fuses. Elsewhere, he explained, 'I play me. As I come riding up the street in Paris, I'm greeted by the entire cast of the real Magic Circus and they chase me into a funeral parlour ... while performers from the film, dressed as Mao, Che and Nero, look in through the windows.' Apparently nobody knew that the building Lee had been instructed to dash into was a funeral home, and he was quite horrified when he found there 'an unhappy bereaved couple ... discussing the death of a relative with an understanding undertaker. What they must have thought when I burst in, followed by this incredible motley gang, fairly boggles the imagination. The nearest comparison I can make with the players in the Magic Circus is with the original players in *Saturday Night Live*.'[17] Of whom, more later.

After *Eulalie* Lee was looking forward to appearing with Mark Lester, Nathalie Delon and Jon Finch in a 'dawn of man' adventure called *The Dreamtime*. A French/Italian/Bulgarian co-production, André Farwagi's film was set to start shooting on 1 October, then was put back to November and finally disappeared altogether from the forward schedules of France's trade press. There was also talk of something called *Jack the Ripper Goes West* for producer Euan Lloyd, to be filmed in Madrid in October. ('There is a great deal of historical evidence,' Lee opined, 'that Jack the Ripper could have emigrated to the United States.'[18]) Both projects would resurface, with no more concrete results, in 1974.

Rounding off 1973, there were distinct echoes of *Douglas Fairbanks Presents* and *The Errol Flynn Theatre* when Lee appeared in an episode of Anglia TV's *Orson Welles Great Mysteries*, a show that would itself pave the way for *Roald Dahl's Tales of the Unexpected*. A rather somnolent exercise, Alan Gibson's *The Leather Funnel* starred Lee, hollow-eyed and grey-faced, as 'an ageing bachelor brother' to Jane Seymour in a convoluted story adapted from a Conan Doyle original. After that, Lee sailed into 1974 with an offer from the National Theatre, then still domiciled at the Old Vic. On 19 February he was a guest on the first edition of *Just a* [Derek] *Nimmo* and at the end of March he went to Pinewood for a heavily made-up appearance as Zandor in ATV's lumbering epic *Space: 1999*. In Charles Crichton's *Earthbound*, Zandor shares a tender psychic bond with Barbara Bain's Dr Helena Russell; though benevolent, he also arranges an extremely nasty end for a duplicitous earthling played by Roy Dotrice. Neither commitment seems preferable to a stint at the Old Vic, but the magnitude of Lee's next film makes it clear that turning down the NT's offer was a shrewd move after all.

ONE LIGHT, ONE DARK
The week after the Royal première of *The Three Musketeers*, Thames TV broadcast Christopher Lee's *This Is Your Life* on Wednesday 3 April. Enticed into performing a sword fight with Bill Hobbs for the children's magazine programme *Magpie*, Lee found himself presented with the familiar red book by the equally familiar Eamonn Andrews. Among the guests were Trevor Howard, Oliver Reed, Peter Cushing, Vincent Price and 'the most attractive blood group in pictures,' as Lee dubbed them – Veronica Carlson, Valerie Van Ost and Joanna Lumley. Filmed tributes were sent in by Charlton Heston, Patrick Macnee and Sammy Davis Jr, while 10-year-old Christina claimed that, despite having seen her father on TV as Count Dracula, her dreams of Donny Osmond remained undisturbed.

The next day, Lee journeyed to Madrid to tape introductions for a seven-week, seven-film tribute to him on Spanish TV and then went straight to Paris for

As Zandor in the Earthbound *episode of Gerry Anderson's* Space: 1999 *(1974). The wig was adapted for use by Peter Cushing, Margaret Leighton and Leo McKern in later instalments*

From Scaremonger To Scaramanga 1972-1975

On This is Your Life, *Oliver Reed told Eamonn Andrews and the viewers at home that Lee used to charge for use of his Mercedes back in their Hammer days. Lee didn't bother to contradict him (1974)*

Alain Schlockoff's third Convention Française du Cinéma Fantastique, where he was presented with a gold medal for services to the cinema and introduced *The Wicker Man*. For his next trip Lee went further afield, departing on Saturday 13 April for 'the middle of nowhere for a week – the south of Thailand.' This was just the beginning of perhaps his most high-profile assignment yet, an assignment which would move on to Hong Kong and Bangkok before settling at Pinewood in June and finally wrapping at the end of July.

The whole thing had begun over lunch at the White Elephant in Curzon Street, when director Guy Hamilton had offered Lee the title role in the next James Bond picture, *The Man With the Golden Gun*. The worst characterised villain in Ian Fleming's novels, Francisco Scaramanga turned out to be by far the best characterised villain in Eon's blockbusting Bond franchise, courtesy of a witty script by Tom Mankiewicz (first draft) and Richard Maibaum (second draft), together with some fine-tuning by Lee and Hamilton themselves. 'When I first read the script,' Lee told the *Times*, 'I visualised Scaramanga as a straight-down-the-middle heavy. The villains are always the centre of curiosity in Ian's books: Bond doesn't change but they do. But I must agree that Scaramanga is not one of his most impressive murderers ... So Guy and I, after a lot of talk, decided to make Scaramanga a little like Bond himself, a counter-Bond if you like, instead of the murderous, unappetising thug of the novel ... When we were out filming in Thailand down on the Andaman Sea, Guy kept on saying to Roger Moore and myself, "Enjoy it, enjoy it! Lightly! Lightly!" And enjoy it we did.'[19]

Filming near Phuket, off the Malay peninsula, was centred on the tiny island of Khow-Ping-Khan, which doubled as Scaramanga's tropical hideaway. The budget may have been in the $7,000,000 area – 'More was spent in one day than on the whole of *Nothing But the Night*,' Lee ruefully informed his fans – but working conditions were still subject to the vagaries of the local weather. 'We were there at the beginning of the monsoon period,' Lee continued, 'both in Hong Kong and Thailand, so the suffocating, stifling heat was like being in a Turkish bath all the time – draining and exhausting and tiring – making everybody irritable.'

Despite this sense of monsoon oppressiveness, Lee began perfecting a stylish and truly dangerous character whom he airily described to Eon's publicists as 'just a misdirected individual with a lot of hang-ups.' The contest between Bond and Scaramanga is made all the more potent by the film's 'opposite sides of the same coin' motif. Modelled by Mankiewicz on the clash between Alan Ladd and Jack Palance in *Shane*, it actually plays much more like an old RKO thriller from 1932, *The Most Dangerous Game*, in which Leslie Banks' Count Zaroff is a trigger-happy island dweller convinced that Joel McCrea's great White Hunter is his alter ego. Though Scaramanga is given no more screen time than the average Bond villain, he carries far more symbolic weight. 'If, as we are invited to speculate, he really is Bond's shadow,' one critic has hazarded, 'what does that tell us about Bond?'[20]

Taking aim as the sociopathic Francisco Scaramanga in The Man With the Golden Gun *(1974)*

Presumably in acknowledgment of this, the screenwriters devoted their familiar 'teaser' pre-credits sequence to the villain rather than the hero, a move faintly reminiscent of the opening of *From Russia With Love* but otherwise unprecedented in the Eon series. The film begins with a view of Scaramanga's island paradise as the man himself strides out of the sea, though Lee in white swimming shorts doesn't have quite the same impact as Ursula Andress' similar emergence in *Dr No*. He towels himself dry, revealing one of Lee's more peculiar prosthetic enhancements – what Bond later calls 'a superfluous papilla,' or third nipple – and then dons a tracksuit for a deadly game with hatchet-faced Hollywood heavy Marc Lawrence in Scaramanga's customised Honky Tonk shooting gallery. Production designer Peter Murton here rejects Ken Adam's Dr Mabuse-style designs familiar from other Bond pictures, going instead for an abundance of skewed angles and mirrored surfaces more suggestive of Dr Caligari. The prized golden gun is clutched in the beak of a stuffed raven, Scaramanga dispatches his opponent with ease and then turns to a wax effigy of Roger Moore's Bond, blasting the fingers off it with castrating relish.

Weird and compelling though it is, this teaser sequence has the unfortunate effect of neutralising the film's climax, which, substituting Moore for Lawrence, more or less replays it shot for shot. Both scenes were filmed at Pinewood in the last week of July and, though Lee gives Scaramanga a memorable moment of confusion and disbelief as he succumbs to Bond's bullet, the second go-around can't help but come across as something of a damp squib. Even so, Lee sustained a severe burn on his chest while filming it. 'It looked as though I'd been hit by a shell!' he told his fans. 'I won't tell you what I said; you can use your imagination. Even Roger's sense of humour deserted him.' Indeed, Moore's final one-liner as he looks down at the stricken Scaramanga – 'Flat on his coup de grâce' – is delivered without a hint of the twinkling facetiousness that overcame his 007 in subsequent films.

True to his claim that 'We have so much in common, Mr Bond', Scaramanga is elsewhere given several bon mots of his own. He disposes of Richard Loo's Hai Fat with cold-blooded nonchalance and informs a panicked flunkey that 'Mr Fat has just resigned; I'm the new chairman of the board.' Then, striding poker-faced outdoors: 'He always did like that mausoleum. Put him in it.' Resplendent in a white suit and an interesting tan make-up, Lee is at his sardonically humorous best in several scenes with Roger Moore; indeed, the fact that both actors, one light, one dark, were graduates of Pinewood's cloying 1940s entertainment *Trottie True* adds an extra frisson to the film's duality theme. Sliding serenely into the seat next to Bond's at a boxing match – with Andrea Anders (Maud Adams), the woman both have slept with, propped up glassy-eyed and dead beside them – Scaramanga smoothly explains something of his circus upbringing and his childhood trauma on encountering a mortally wounded elephant. 'You see, Mr Bond, I always thought I liked animals,' he grins. 'Then I discovered that I liked killing people even more.'

At Scaramanga's island retreat, he greets Bond with huge bonhomie and then, in a foolish sub-plot grafted on by Maibaum in the second draft, shows off the massive solar power installation his Chinese sponsors have thoughtfully constructed for him. Though Lee manages a gratifyingly mad gleam as he demonstrates his solar-powered bazooka (immolating Bond's seaplane with a cheery 'This is the part I *really* like'), he's required in this scene to tell Bond that 'Science was never my strong point,' an amazingly dopey admission from Maibaum that the science fiction sub-plot really has no place in the picture whatsoever. Back to the real business of the film, Lee presides over a scintillating lunchtime sequence in which he and Moore are joined by Britt Ekland's featherbrained Mary Goodnight. ('I like a girl in a bikini: no concealed weapons,' quips Scaramanga.) Though fantastically urbane, Lee keeps Scaramanga's sociopathic streak visible at all times. 'You see, Mr Bond,' he explains, 'like every great artist I want to create an indisputable masterpiece once in my lifetime: the death of 007, mano a mano, face to face.' The scene crackles with flavoursome dialogue, and Lee is careful to introduce a brief twinge of insecurity into the steady mania of Scaramanga's eyes when Bond refuses to play along.

The Man With the Golden Gun is routinely taken to be one of the least accomplished Bond films and it was certainly one of the least commercially successful, though, with a worldwide gross of over $97 million, Eon can't have been unduly concerned. It's disfigured by laborious car chases, a horribly unfunny redneck character left over from *Live and Let Die*, and by the topical but irrelevant solar power angle. But the local colour is as ravishing as ever and in Lee's fetishistic Scaramanga it has arguably the strongest villain in the entire series, an accomplishment which Lee graciously attributed to his director. 'Guy Hamilton got something out of me on this picture which I've never been able to show on the screen,' he said. 'In his own words, he got the spook out of me. He got the Dracula out of me ... He's getting me to do this picture in such a light way that you can hardly believe this man is as lethal as he is. He's getting me to smile. He's getting me to laugh, which, I must admit, I don't find very easy to do as an actor. He's getting the lightness of performance out of me, the contrasts...' [21]

In fact, Hamilton was merely consolidating a process already well advanced in Lee's recent performances as Rochefort and Lord Summerisle, returning him to the light touch he had been capable of in the 1950s but which had been partly extinguished by a run of depressingly monolithic parts in the mid-1960s. And his triumph as Scaramanga carried with it a more specific satisfaction. Only five years before, the film's co-producer, Harry Saltzman, had reportedly pooh-poohed the notion of casting Lee in *Battle of Britain* on the grounds that audiences would never accept Dracula in a Spitfire.

ACTOR ON TOUR

Though prospective employers had been contacting his agent on the strength of Scaramanga even before *The Man With the Golden Gun* went into production, Lee informed his fans on his return to London that 'I've no idea what my next picture's going to be. I've still got this contract to do *Dreamtime* in Turkey the last two weeks of August.' Though Jean-Louis Trintignant's name was now attached to the project, *The Dreamtime* had no more luck getting made in 1974 than it had in 1973, and the same applied to the long-gestating *Jack the Ripper Goes West*. As for the second Charlemagne film, *To the Devil a Daughter* was now mooted as a co-production with Hammer, who, by June 1974, were joint owners with Charlemagne of seven Dennis Wheatley properties acquired by Lee and Tony Nelson Keys. With a skeleton staff of only 11, Hammer embarked on what turned out to be the Herculean task of bringing *To the Devil a Daughter* to the screen and the first thing to go by the board was an optimistic start date of 4 August.

As screen assignments foundered, Lee filled in his time by venturing into different fields. Back in 1966, he had recorded Stoker's *Dracula* for producer Russ Jones as a limited edition, two-record set (doing all the voices, including the women). Later the same year, he provided the introduction to a Jones publication called *Christopher Lee's Treasury of Terror*, in which stories by Stoker, Rudyard Kipling, August Derleth and others were rendered in comic-strip form by artists from the *Creepy* and *Eerie* stables. Now, eight years on, both extra-curricular concepts were resurrected. First, he

With Jon Finch shortly before a near-death experience on Shearwater Lake for Diagnosis: Murder *(1974)*

contributed a magnificently textured voice-over to a Don Houghton-scripted Dracula story for Hammer City Records, one of many desperate attempts by Michael Carreras to replenish the Hammer coffers. Next, he entered the field of horror anthologies previously occupied by Alfred Hitchcock and Boris Karloff. Cooked up in tandem with the prolific anthologist Peter Haining, the perplexingly titled *Christopher Lee's New Chamber of Horrors* – Lee had favoured *The Graveside Companion* – was published by Souvenir Press on 31 October. 'Waiting to emerge are 16 stories of sheer terror,' screamed the ads, 'each one introduced by the acknowledged Crown Prince of Terror, Christopher Lee.'

Lee was unhappy with the result. 'Look at it,' he urged journalist Suzanne Lowry. 'I asked them not to use the word 'horror' in the title; I asked them not to use a picture of me as Dracula on the cover. But they've done both.'[22] (He was even more unhappy when Lowry wrote up her interview and erroneously claimed that he had played the Count 15 times.) Decamping to W H Allen, and replacing Haining with Michel Parry, Lee signed up for four further anthologies which were taken up by Warner Paperback Library in the US. W H Allen further suggested that he write an autobiography, a notion first put to him by the novelist James Hadley Chase back in the 1960s. Lee would plunge into the task in earnest in 1975.

His recording career, meanwhile, was evolving in unexpected directions. At the invitation of Paul McCartney, he appeared on the cover of the top-selling Wings album *Band on the Run*, his fellow 'band members' including James Coburn, Clement Freud, Kenny Lynch, John Conteh and Michael Parkinson. A mooted duet with David Bowie failed to materialise, however, and the same went for a 'rock oratorio' by Simon Heath called *Mephistopheles*, planned as both an LP record and a TV special. Lee remained committed to this project over several years, claiming that it could be 'even bigger than *Tommy*.' One 'concept' album that did get off the ground was *The King of Elfland's Daughter*, based by Bob Johnson and Peter Knight of folk-rock favourites Steeleye Span on a story by one of Lee's favourite authors, Lord Dunsany. Lee journeyed to Brussels in 1976 to record his narration, sharing the bill with Mary Hopkin, P P Arnold and others.

Rounding off 1974, Lee opted for a trip to Bristol for a TV movie, later released theatrically, called *Diagnosis: Murder*. 'I sincerely hope they change the title,' Lee grumbled as he left for the HTV West studios on 19 October. Going back and forth on the picture for five weeks, Lee's suggestion that the film should be retitled *The Practitioner* was finally ignored. Both director Sidney Hayers and writer Philip Levene were veterans of *The Avengers* and the film was the second collaboration between HTV and Silhouette Films; the first, *Deadly Strangers*, had starred Hayley Mills and Sterling Hayden and was also a Hayers/Levene concoction.

The rather dour proceedings revolve around Lee's playboy psychiatrist, Dr Stephen Hayward, who hides his nefarious schemes behind an affable, tweedy exterior. He also hides his doped-up wife Julia (Dilys Hamlett) in a remote farmhouse in order to facilitate his affair with his doting secretary Helen (Judy Geeson). 'Let me tell you something, Helen,' he says.

'Each year there are at least half a dozen unsolved murders. Tea?' Though chiefly motivated by greed, there's a cold-hearted intellectual purpose involved in Hayward's plot, too. 'I was also rather curious about myself,' he explains. 'I wanted to see how I would react when the police arrived.' He performs splendidly under interrogation but, when he's climactically hoodwinked into drowning Helen in a weighted sack rather than Julia, suspicious coppers Jon Finch and Tony Beckley are on hand to arrest him. 'Like most psychiatrists he's a bit of a nutter,' Finch concludes.

Lee and Finch have some effective cat-and-mouse encounters but, though a pleasant enough picture, *Diagnosis: Murder* is hardly a memorable one – except, perhaps, for the participants. It was shot at Sopworth House near Malmesbury and on Shearwater Lake near Warminster. There, early in November, Lee was required to manoeuvre a motor-boat in ever-tightening circles at 40 to 50 mph and, when the boat containing Hayers and the camera crew came in too close, he reported that 'Jon Finch and I and five other people were as near to being killed as it is possible to be.'

Finishing the film on 22 November, Lee left a week later for Los Angeles and a promotional tour of *The Man With the Golden Gun* alongside Maud Adams and the diminutive Hervé Villechaize. Lee acknowledged ruefully that the process 'was bound to be more about the Gun than about the Man,' but on the *Tonight* show on 2 December, he was unable to produce the gold-plated prop thanks to a misunderstanding with US Customs. Cajoled by Johnny Carson stand-in (and former Rat Pack member) Joey Bishop into doing an impromptu spot of singing instead, Lee chose Iago from *Otello*. Via Patrick Curtis, he next found himself at the Playboy Mansion, where a sneak preview of *The Four Musketeers* was laid on specially, and then visited Universal, watched an episode of *Kojak* being filmed and was courted as a possible guest star. The tour subsequently embraced San Francisco, Denver, Dallas (by which stage the impounded Golden Gun had been returned), Fort Worth, Atlanta, Chicago and finally New York, where Lee spent three days trapped in a hotel suite by over-zealous reporters. He was safely back in London, nevertheless, for the world première of *The Man With the Golden Gun* on 19 December.

Into 1975, and Lee was off to Leeds on 24 February for a singing appearance on the religious programme *Stars on Sunday*, sharing the bill with his old mentor Douglas Fairbanks Jr. 'No Scars This Sunday' quipped the *TV Times*. Between the programme's recording and eventual transmission on 20 April, Lee found himself embroiled in another US promotional tour. As well as participating around this time in a number of televised 'Pro-Celebrity' golf tournaments, he committed himself to an 18-day American stint on behalf of *The Four Musketeers*, starting on 10 March – and this time he was on his own.

From snow-covered Boston Lee moved on to Philadelphia and then Washington. There he was looked after by Dave Polland, a PR guru normally occupied with Presidential inaugurations, and 'briefly said "How do you do?" to Robert Redford and Dustin Hoffman, preparing for the picture they're going to do about Watergate.' Further stopovers in Charlotte, Tampa, Cleveland, Minneapolis, St Paul and Seattle were interleaved with restful visits to Disneyworld and Arnold Palmer's Golf and Country Club in Orlando before the tour ended with *The Four Musketeers*' Beverly Hills première. In Hollywood, the lofty Lee was reportedly vetoed as a potential guest murderer on *Columbo* by the show's pint-sized star, Peter Falk, but Lee was mollified by the fact that Falk seemed to be the only person in America who didn't want him. 'Everywhere I went everybody seemed to know me,' Lee reflected. 'I was really overcome by enthusiasm literally everywhere.' Astonished by this warm reception, Lee's thoughts began turning in a direction that would have career-changing consequences some 12 months later.

For the time being, however, the most conspicuous result of Lee's American tour was a heartfelt endorsement from Muhammad Ali. Lee heard that, when interviewed on the Jarvis Astaire

Tuesday 18 March 1975: meeting up with the Champion in Cleveland. 'Now stand opposite me and give me that look,' said Ali. 'What look?' 'You know, that look you give people on the screen and it chills the very marrow in their bones...'

show, Ali had numbered him among the six most interesting people in the world. Their paths finally crossed in Cleveland on 18 March, where Ali pledged that 'When I beat Chuck Wepner ... I'm going to tell the whole wide world that I won this fight for you, for Christopher Lee.' Lee subsequently watched the championship fight on closed circuit TV at Hugh Hefner's home as part of a stellar gathering that included Robert Evans, James Caan, Ryan O'Neal, Stuart Whitman, Hugh O'Brian, Jim Brown, the currently notorious Linda Lovelace and the subsequently notorious O J Simpson. According to Lee, 'the whole room erupted' when the victorious Ali made good on his pledge. 'One could tour a thousand whistlestops promoting a film,' Lee observed later, 'and never get together as much promotion as Ali bestowed in five seconds.'

Two of Lee's companions that evening turned up in his next picture. Based at the tiny Killarney Studios, *The Diamond Mercenaries* began its eight-week schedule in South West Africa at the end of March. As well as O J Simpson and Hugh O'Brian (who was deputising for Jack Palance), the cast included Telly Savalas and Peter Fonda, with the beauteous Maud Adams — Lee's ill-fated mistress in *The Man With the Golden Gun* — thrown in for token 'femme' interest. Fresh from a brief stint with Adrienne Corri and producer George Brown at Warsaw's British Film Week, Lee joined up in early May, by which time, he recalled, 'Telly Savalas had already gone back to America for his nightclub act and the next *Kojak*.'

Director Val Guest had once been responsible for such classics as *The Quatermass Xperiment*, *80,000 Suspects* and *The Day the Earth Caught Fire*, but he had lately dwindled to the level of *The Au Pair Girls* and the smash hit *Confessions of a Window Cleaner*. In *The Diamond Mercenaries* he seems to have been striving to reproduce the glamour of recent pictures like *Gold* and *Diamonds Are Forever* but the result often looks and sounds like a rough cut, disfigured in particular by the screaming horror of Georges Garvarentz's score. As the poetry-reading Major Chilton, Lee is one of five mercenaries who mount a bloody assault on a closely guarded diamond stockade, and in several scenes the film comes across like a criminalised version of Lee's last desert escapade, *Bitter Victory*. 'My part is not the biggest in the world,' Lee reported, 'largely due to my own wishes. The original part was of a Frenchman: "Mon ami," "Mon brave," and all that kind of thing, which I thought was unnecessary and dangerously like caricature.' Lee reconceived the character as a shady, sociopathic, knife-wielding ex-Guards officer, explaining that 'I knew people like this in the war.'

Lee's Chilton has the best scene in the picture, for what it's worth, when he visits a lanky, lingerie-clad prostitute (Marina Christelis) and produces a flick knife instead of the requested 20 rand. When Danielle's next customer intrudes, Chilton explains sweetly that 'The world has just lost a very average whore, Mr Nelson ... Let's just say I'm a rather dissatisfied customer' — and then nonchalantly disposes of him too. For the raid itself, Chilton kills several guards with a machine gun and then is killed himself when his jeep overturns in a spectacular chase sequence. The powdered windscreen scattered under his dead face like diamonds, Chilton is held aloft by his companion 'Bopper' Alexander (Simpson) and his limp body is peppered with machine-gun fire as Alexander makes his escape. This is the second best scene in the picture.

Working on the film, Lee was amazed by the devil-may-care South African stuntmen and charmed by his co-stars Fonda and Simpson; he was also grateful for the opportunity to see something of his

As the vicious Major Chilton in Val Guest's The Diamond Mercenaries *(1975)*

half-brother Nicolas and family. 'I adored those two weeks,' Lee reported later. 'It brought back memories of the war in North Africa, when I felt so well and life was so exciting and adventurous. Even when I got sand in my hair, eyes, nose, mouth, ears – even my food – I revelled in it and didn't mind a bit.'

Better Than Sitting About

High hopes followed by bad pictures are a fact of every film star's life; as Lee himself has put it, 'I have been in some very indifferent films, but I don't know any actor who hasn't.'[23] *The Evil Force* is another matter, however. 'Why would he lend his name to this trash?' asked the reviewer in *Cinefantastique*. The truth is, he didn't. Copyright 1975, it's a crude US potboiler about a Manson-style mass murder and the paranormal revenge wreaked upon the perpetrators. It's known by at least two other titles, *Revenge of the Dead* and – the one that really gets Lee's goat – *Meatcleaver Massacre*. 'I certainly never did a picture with that title!'[24] he exclaimed in 1984.

Looking dapper in black blazer and red tartan trousers, Lee turns up at either end of the picture to utter some entirely irrelevant ruminations about the supernatural. Having described the depredations of 'coal-black, dog-headed hags with bat's wings, blood-shot eyes and snakes for hair' at one end of the film, he returns at the other to recite an epic poem about a battle between an Egyptian and an Alaskan shaman. The footage, about eight minutes in all, was shot for the purposes of an abandoned documentary, probably during Lee's Hollywood stint for *Poor Devil* in late 1972. Sold on to 'Group 1 Productions' without Lee's knowledge, it formed an opportunistic wraparound for a picture he knew nothing about until many years later, when that dreaded alternative title began turning up in filmographies. 'Today there is a need for a new kind of horror film,' he had cannily observed back in 1974. '*Rosemary's Baby* was excellent and so is *The Exorcist*.'[25] *Meatcleaver Massacre* was not the new kind of horror film he had in mind.

Back in Wardour Street, Hammer, too, were keenly aware of 'the need for a new kind of horror film.' The phenomenal success of *The Exorcist* had made it clear, if it hadn't been clear already, that Hammer's medium-budget Gothics were no longer viable. Of the many projects on the company's schedule in 1974, *To the Devil a Daughter* had accordingly been pushed to the front but it was to endure an extraordinarily tortuous gestation. By the end of the year it was no longer a Hammer/Charlemagne co-production, despite Tony Nelson Keys' continued involvement in the fraught matters of script and casting, and by June 1975 a German co-producer was finally found in Terra Filmkunst. Though budgeted at $1,000,000 (an unprecedentedly high sum for a Hammer film), Keys' services as producer were deemed too expensive and he retired to Richmond as secretary of the Stage Golfing Society. When the film finally began production on 1 September, therefore, Lee was the only link to its origins as a Charlemagne project.

Lee had been pencilled in for the role of defrocked priest Father Michael Rayner since Day One. The search for his antagonist, however, had caused numerous headaches, and the actor eventually assigned the role, Richard Widmark, was so dismayed by what he saw as the amateurism of the film that he took to calling Hammer 'Mickey Mouse Productions'. For his part, the film's director Peter Sykes let slip that 'We are known as the Pink Page Production Company at the moment because we're changing the script so rapidly.'[26] Christopher Wicking's characteristically garbled screenplay remains a conspicuous flaw in the finished film but in other respects *To the Devil a Daughter* retains 'the terrible vibrations of evil' that Lee felt in *The Devil Rides Out* while pushing Hammer with some style into post-*Exorcist* explicitness.

The plot, which is actually far more straightforward than Wicking allows it to be, involves Rayner's efforts to create an avatar, or human incarnation, of his demonic deity Astaroth. The chosen vessel is novitiate nun Catherine Beddows, whose panicky father entrusts her to the care of occult novelist John Verney. Sweetly reasonable yet implacably malevolent, Rayner is one of Lee's most alarming characterisations. He presides coolly over the delivery of the demonic baby, tethering the mother's knees and ankles and explaining to his followers, with a saintly smile, that 'Margaret knows the only way it must be born. It won't be easy. It won't be pleasant.' When the baby emerges (out of frame, thank goodness), the camera sails past the revolted reactions of Rayner's helpers before settling on Rayner himself, beaming down at the new arrival with Cheshire Cat satisfaction and then crooning to the expiring Margaret in tones of almost Messianic sympathy.

Rayner is so blandly frightening in this sequence that Sykes allows a tight close-up of his quietly mad face to fade for a seeming eternity while the film moves on to its next phase. Decamping from Germany to England, Rayner officiates at an orgiastic ceremony, with kinky cut-aways a thousand times filthier than anything that had been permitted in *The Devil Rides Out*. (Lee's brief flash of rearview nudity, however, was provided by the faithful Eddie Powell.) He also takes to the telephone, affable and unruffled as he torments the nervy Beddows with visions of his telephone cord turning into a snake, then tightly controlled as he threatens the defiant Verney with 'On your head be it...'

And in his final muted showdown with Verney (a queasy sequence shot at West Wycombe's Mausoleum monument), he briefly tempts him with a vision of Catherine frontally nude. This shot – rather a startling one, given that Nastassja Kinski, daughter of Lee's old co-star Klaus, was only 16 when the film was made – is followed by further beatific smiling as Rayner promises that 'When this ceremony has been performed, I shall destroy you, John Verney.' He then allows Rayner a twinge of Lord Summerisle-style unease when Verney reveals that he knows more about the Book of Astaroth than Rayner suspected and, in a famously anti-climactic ending, is finally routed when Verney chucks a stone at him. Lee's own voice has been joined to the chorus of disapproval regarding this conclusion but the film's atmosphere is so disquieting and its tone so oddly cerebral that a more slam-bang climax would seem out of place. Cerebral disquiet, however, was hardly the recipe for Hammer's commercial salvation. Though the film would perform robustly at the UK box-office, it was barely visible in America and accordingly became the last Hammer Horror to date.

While filming it, Lee left on 6 October for a fortnight in Vancouver, undertaking the journey, he said, 'as a labour of love and a love of labour.' Tom Drake's *The Keeper* was a small picture shot on 16mm by Lionsgate Productions; the picture was so small, in fact, that, on his return to London, Lee found a belated letter from Canadian Equity urging him not to participate in it because it was a non-union affair. 'It's really got enormous possibilities,' Lee had enthused back in August, 'a mixture almost of *Batman* and *Arsenic and Old Lace* and a lot of other things.' But a bout of flu and the almost incessant rain that poured down during his stay in British Columbia dampened Lee's spirits somewhat, and the completed film sank without trace until picked up by obscure video labels in the 1980s. This is just as well, for *The Keeper* is a childish and amateurish effort best left buried.

Set (very shakily) in 1947, it has Lee as boss of the Underwood Asylum, subjecting his patients to Pavlovian torments while scheming to 'become the richest and most powerful man in the world.' Looking exactly as he does in *To the Devil a Daughter*, Lee limps along on a cane fitted with a hypnotic glass eye and croons a soothing mantra to the inmates while unleashing cheesy psychedelic opticals via an organ-like console. 'Love the Keeper: obey the Keeper:

With Nastassja Kinski and the blood of Astaroth at West Wycombe's Mausoleum Monument in To the Devil a Daughter *(1975)*

the Keeper will keep you alive,' he purrs, only to be climactically trapped in his own aversion chamber prior to losing his head and being led away by the cops. The young leads – Sally Gray (aka Mrs Tom Drake) and Tell Schreiber – are a grisly pair, there's an even grislier little boy involved and the only worthwhile thing about the film, which purports to be a crazy comedy incidentally, is the ambiguous look Lee turns to the camera for the final freeze-frame.

After a stint in Bavaria to complete his work on *To the Devil a Daughter*, Lee's last assignment in 1975 took him, in November, to what was then called Rhodesia for a German-backed film directed by Jürgen Goslar and known under a multiplicity of titles: *Der flüsternde Tod*, *Whispering Death*, *Albino*, *Night of the Askari* and, for its brief theatrical run in the UK, *Death in the Sun*. 'Death Wish in the Sun' would have been nearer the mark, as the film's rape-revenge scenario – based on a true story – transfers *Death Wish* to the veldt with numerous sadistic details outstripping anything in Lee's horror pictures.

Though top-billed, Lee's role as a firm but fair military policeman is fairly peripheral, conceding centre stage to James Faulkner's grief-crazed Terrick, who becomes an outlaw in seeking to avenge the rape and murder of his beautiful fiancée Sally (Sybil Danning). The terrorist perpetrator, played by the German actor Horst Frank, is perhaps the most repulsive villain ever committed to film, an albino negro who rapes the heroine in a scene of eye-popping unpleasantness. 'She began to scream and scream and scream,' he drools later. 'You should've heard her. It was quite wonderful – and *very* stimulating.' He finally expires with mud all over his face, looking like a Black and White Minstrel and observing that 'Killing me won't change anything.'

The film was criticised for placing South Africa's political problems in an exploitative context, though Lee himself did what he could by adding 'lines to the effect that justice should relate equally to black and white' and insisting on the casting of black actor Sam Williams. 'I can't think of a better way to help integration, myself,' he pointed out. 'An integrated film crew and cast.'[27] As the so-called 'big mambo', Lee's Bill is seen carousing in a crowded military bar rocking to the sing-song strains of 'Parlez-vous' and performs mock surgery on an inebriated colleague. 'Before an operation,' he announces, 'it is customary to administer an anaesthetic. Snakebite serum has proved to be extremely effective ... The injection will be administered from the rear. Prepare the patient!'

Acting as an uproarious counterpoint to the film's many scenes of genuine torture, the fun is brought to a sudden halt by the ringing of alarm bells and the

As 'the Member in Charge' – with real-life Rhodesian policeman – in Der flüsternde Tod (1975), briefly glimpsed in the UK as Death in the Sun

moving discovery of Sally's corpse. Bill reappears in shorts, mobilising his men with the rousing observation that 'One false move and you will destroy everything that we have taken years to achieve: the rule of law and order, and justice, and the support of the Africans.' Though urbane and relaxed – and presumably drawing upon his own wartime experience with Rhodesia's police force – Lee is overshadowed by the film's parade of atrocities, which makes it a rip-roaring success when considered purely as exploitation. It's also beautifully photographed by Wolfgang Treu.

'How actors such as Lee and Trevor Howard (as the dead girl's rheumy-eyed father) can find themselves in films like this is a puzzle,' commented David Castell in *Films Illustrated*. 'They should have stern words with their agents.' It was, of course, no puzzle at all. With the British film industry entering its ignominious death throes, Lee considered his recent engagements to be 'better than sitting about, but there still remained more sitting about than I liked.' He had been assured that his performance as Scaramanga would waft him 'to the fleece-lined clouds of guaranteed and well-paid work.' But now, some 12 months after *The Man With the Golden Gun* had opened, it was becoming clear that those clouds existed only in America; angry storm clouds were all that could be seen gathering over British studios. 'Reviewing the situation, it occurred to me that an actor must go where the work is and not merely where the taxes are,' Lee concluded. His stint at Paramount for *Poor Devil* and the success of his recent US promotional tours – together with the urgings of Billy Wilder, Richard Widmark and Universal executive Taft Schreiber – had convinced him, in close consultation with Gitte, to move to Hollywood.

PART EIGHT

FROM BELGRAVIA TO BEL-AIR 1976–1982

'It's as simple as this,' Lee claimed two years into his Hollywood residency. 'In America, they say "Welcome, welcome. We like your work." Not "We like you as *Dracula*, we like you in *horror* films," but "We like your *work*." There they accept success; they are happy for you. In Britain, any degree of success is met with envy and resentment.'[1] Lee saw this culture of envy and resentment as not necessarily endemic to the British but as emanating from the current government and its punishing levels of taxation. Typecasting, however, was a greater spur even than taxes in motivating his removal to LA. 'I went to America because I knew perfectly well that if I had stayed in this country I would have made a very adequate living, but I would have gone on making the same sort of film ... [becoming] progressively disenchanted and disinterested. And if the actor becomes bored, so does the audience – it's very contagious.'[2]

Preparing to leave the UK, Lee could look with some satisfaction at the number of actors who had followed him into the Dracula role and interpret it as a healthy sign of his having left the character behind. His retirement from the field dated back to January 1973 and, consciously or not, had unleashed a sudden flood of alternative Draculas. Within six months, Jack Palance, Udo Kier and David Niven had all assumed Dracula's mantle and there were plenty more to follow, notably Louis Jourdan in a splendidly detailed BBC version directed by Lee's co-star from *The Mirror and Markheim*, Philip Saville. Indeed, Lee himself was approached in Washington by a theatrical entrepreneur anxious to revive Hamilton Deane's old *Dracula* adaptation on Broadway. Deciding that the play could only expect derisive laughter from 1970s audiences – and unaware that the intention was to camp it up anyway – Lee turned the offer down. Frank Langella was a big hit when the production finally emerged in 1977, but the following year made the fatal error of repeating his affected performance in a seriously intended, big-budget film version that bombed spectacularly.

Lee may have left Dracula behind, but he was happy, nevertheless, to play a vampire in France as a prelude to his Hollywood move and an ironic farewell to the typecasting problem. En route to Los Angeles, the Lees paused in Paris 'to mop up some available work' in a droll Edouard Molinaro comedy called *Dracula Père et Fils*, which began its eight-week schedule at the Studios de Billancourt on 16 March 1976. Though announced in the French trade press under that title, Lee asserted that he was under the impression the film was called merely *Père et Fils*, and the resulting confusion gave rise to a spiteful broadside in *Cinefantastique*: 'Copping his plea about doing the picture, Lee maintained that he fought against the titling of the film ... saying "It is totally misleading. I do not play the part of Dracula in the picture ... The reason I did it was not to parody myself, which I do not do, but because by doing this I can close the door very firmly on the vampire. Let's put it that way. And I feel this is my last word on the subject, if I may say so." Yes, Chris, but is it your last picture on the subject?'[3]

As a matter of fact it was, and an uncommonly charming one too. Based on Claude Klotz's novel *Paris-Vampire*, it benefits from sumptuous production values, a spooky score by Vladimir Cosma and flavoursome dialogue by Jean-Marie Poiré ('fils' of Gaumont chief Alain Poiré). The credits are relayed through the vellum leaves of an ancient, candlelit book and inform us that we are in 'Transylvanie 1784'. The opening minutes – panicked passengers on board a benighted coach, damsel delivered to the door of the nearby castle – are played entirely straight. In a neat reversal of expectations, only when Lee appears does the comedy begin.

The character is at no point called Dracula; imposingly outfitted in brocaded frock coat, lacy jabot and

Saturday 25 March 1978: with John Belushi at New York's Rockefeller Center in Saturday Night Live

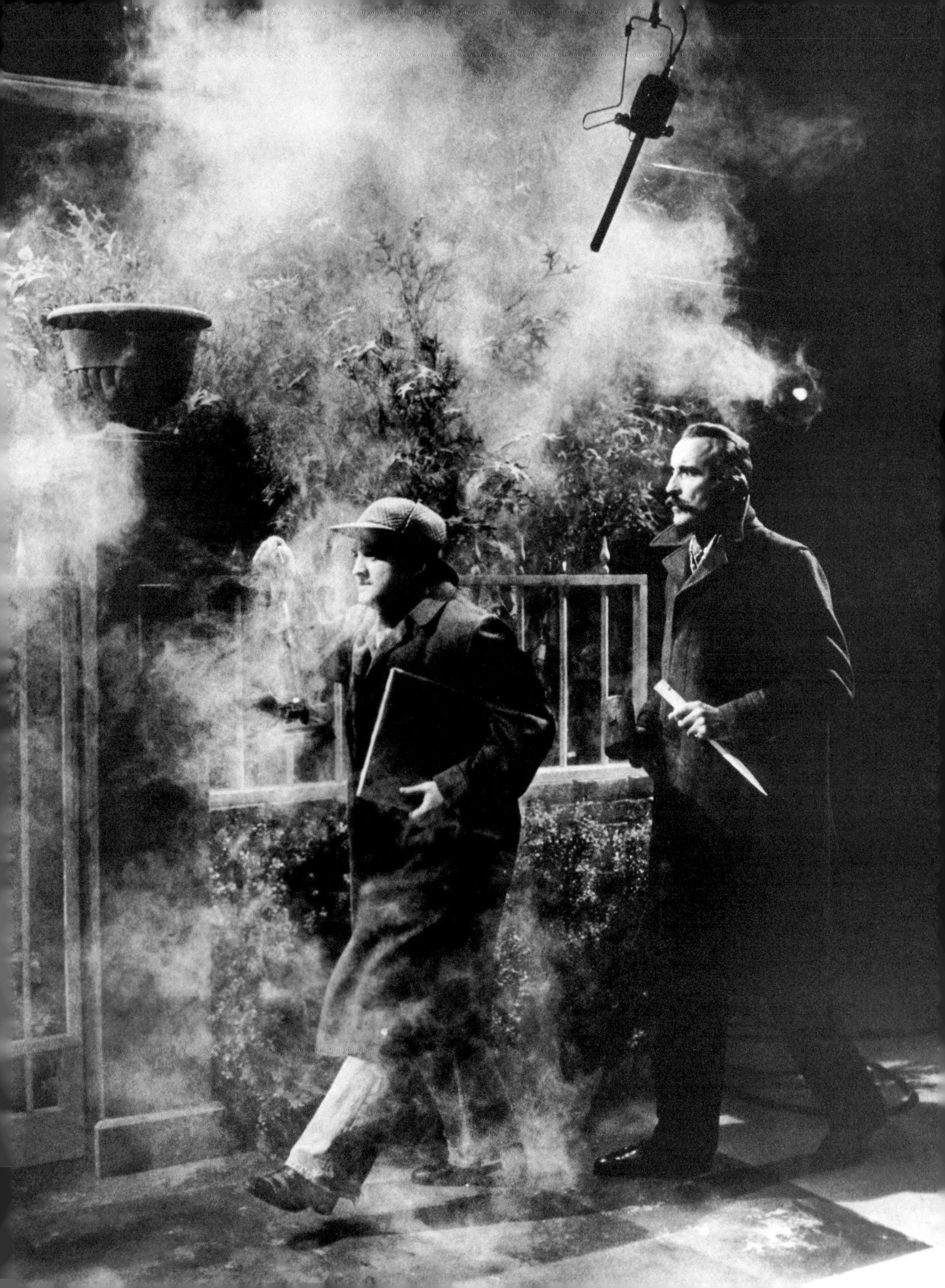

With director Edouard Molinaro and Catherine Breillat (herself a future film director) at the Studios de Billancourt, at work on the delightful Dracula Père et Fils *(1976)*

lengthy grey wig, he doesn't conform to the standard image of Dracula either. He emerges from behind a bronze effigy of himself and, at his first courtly utterance of 'Welcome my dear,' his comely visitor (Catherine Breillat) faints on the spot. After some discreetly handled congress in his coffin, she bears the Count a son and is then accidentally destroyed by the dawn. Molinaro floods the screen in searing yellow here as a prelude to a very funny scene – 'cinq ans plus tard' as the vellum pages tell us – in which the Count barks at his insubordinate son, 'Ferdinand, drink your blood and go to bed, do you hear?'

A vellum title then announces '116 ans plus tard' and the Count is seen sucking on a cigar as he supervises his gawky son's first attempt at full-blown vampirism. 'I refuse to feed you out of a bottle for the rest of your life,' he hisses. 'You're 116 years old and without your first victim!' Finally we reach 'de nos jours' and a Communist takeover sees the Count complaining to Ferdinand that 'This regime doesn't hold anything sacred.' Fleeing, father and son are accidentally buried at sea in their separate coffins. Ferdinand ends up in France, the Count – netted by a trawler along with numerous fish – in England.

So far the film is an engaging and gently amusing delight, preferable by far to other horror-comedies like *Dance of the Vampires* and *Love at First Bite*. And the momentum continues for a while as the Count hits London and becomes a big horror star not unlike Christopher Lee. Filming 'The Man from Transylvania', he vampirises his co-star (Anna Gael) for real but then callously sends her out into the sunlight when she becomes troublesome. And, travelling to France to make 'Les amours du vampire', he is unexpectedly reunited with Ferdinand at the airport. Here, at the last hurdle, the film stumbles slightly. Though played by the skilled comic actor Bernard Menez, Ferdinand is sufficiently pasty-faced and geeky to make his furtive visits to blood banks and morgues more genuinely sinister than Molinaro perhaps intended. And the film is also unsure of its effects when father and son start to vie for the favours of the beautiful Nicole, who has tried to interest the Count in an ad campaign for Permadent toothpaste.

Nicole is played by Molinaro's then-wife, Marie-Hélène Breillat; also Catherine Breillat's sister, she causes the Count to see in her a reincarnation of his lost love, a hoary old plot device used with a straight face in some other Dracula films. There are a few diverting moments of French farce here – much opening and closing of bedroom doors – but the film's swollen Gallic running time nudges two hours and finally defeats Molinaro's invention. Lee, however, scores a grey-faced triumph as the autumnal Count, whether conveying perplexity when he sinks his teeth into a blonde-wigged inflatable doll or maiden-auntish modesty as he plucks a sheet up to his neck when disturbed in his coffin. And, despite these gently comic touches, we still know exactly what Nicole means when she says that 'It gives you the chills, the way he looks at you. He can read all the woes of the world in his face. It's as if he'd been alive for centuries.'

Molinaro subsequently made the smash hit *La cage aux folles*, while Lee decamped to the USA. What happened when *Dracula Père et Fils* went to America, however, counts as one of the most atrocious bastardisations of an accomplished picture in recent memory. Calling the film *Dracula and Son*, Quartet Films Inc tacked on a juvenile cartoon prologue extolling it as 'the Dracula movie to end all Dracula movies' and lopped it down to around 80 minutes, complete with horribly dubbed, and horribly unfunny, wisecracks totally alien to the elegance of the French original. A proper version of the film, complete with Lee's fruity English dialogue track, wasn't seen by English-speaking audiences until 22 years later.

High and Low

Renting out their Belgravia flat and jettisoning their Rolls-Royce altogether, the Lees settled into LA and acquired a Buick and a Chevrolet instead. 'We live between Wilshire and Bel-Air on one side and Beverly Hills and Westwood on the other,' Lee explained on a brief return trip to England, 'and we have a marvellous view for miles and miles of the whole of the Hollywood Hills and way down to the sea at Santa Monica. I don't want to live in a house. I much prefer to live in a flat – or, as they say over there, an apartment.'[4]

Staunch Europeans adjusting to a mild case of culture shock, the Lees' feelings about their new circumstances were rather more ambivalent than that quote suggests. 'Actually we were on the eighth floor,' Lee pointed out in his autobiography, 'with a deep draught of smog directly we opened a window.' The Bel-Air Country Club was a mere five minutes away, however, so Lee soon found himself playing golf with Howard Keel, George C Scott, Ray Bolger, Vic Damone, Jack Lemmon, even Fred Astaire. He also got to meet such legendary veterans of the silent screen as Hal Roach, Clarence Brown and Adolph Zukor.

Lee's arrival in Hollywood didn't go unnoticed by indigenous casting directors. 'The number of British exiles living in Hollywood is growing larger all the time,' observed *Photoplay* columnist Barbra Paskin, 'and the latest addition to the colony is Christopher Lee. His arrival here was hardly inconspicuous. Instead of spending a few months quietly settling into his new home, he immediately went to work in one of the year's biggest films.'[5]

Twenty years after making *The Curse of Frankenstein*, Lee kicked off his Hollywood phase with seventh billing in the deluxe cast of Jerry Jameson's *Airport '77*. Alongside him were such Tinsel Town luminaries as Jack Lemmon, Lee Grant, Joseph Cotten, James Stewart and *That Lady* herself, Olivia de Havilland. A contrived sequel to *Airport* and *Airport 1975*, filming began on 9 August, comprised location work in Florida followed by interiors back on the West coast at both Universal and CBS, and concluded on 4 November. The plot for this one has Robert Foxworth's duplicitous co-pilot deliberately 'losing' his 747 in the Bermuda Triangle but accidentally crashing it into an oil rig. The plane sinks to the ocean floor like a sealed tomb and the scene is set for sundry soap opera melodramatics.

As repressed English oceanographer Martin Wallace, Lee was required to die in a heroic effort to rescue his fellow passengers and, because Martin is described as 'an experienced scuba diver' and several tons of water would be involved in the sequence, he spent a week in the Universal pool being coached by the legendary aquatic stuntman, Manfred Zendar. Lee's subsequent efforts resulted in his being presented with a Stunt Men's Association belt buckle. 'I valued it more than I would an Oscar,' he wrote. 'I showed it to Jack [Lemmon] as we sat together, soaking wet, in a small caravan. I remarked that I couldn't help wondering why we were doing this. "Because we're fucking crazy," said Jack.' Just how crazy Lee revealed on his return trip to England two years later. 'I went down in that tank time and time again for three solid days,' he explained. 'I had to remain perfectly still for a full minute, holding my breath, with my eyes and mouth open. What I didn't realise was that, if I hadn't exhaled properly on the way up, if I'd got one bubble of air, it would have gone straight to my brain and killed me.'[6]

The completed scene is a tense one, with Martin accompanying the pilot (Lemmon) to the 747's hold and attempting to unlock the bulkhead. The Englishman is expendable, of course, and the disastrous result of his efforts is a memorably spooky shot in which his corpse floats upward – limp, glassy-eyed, hair pluming in the current – past a window through which his vindictive wife happens to be looking. She says nothing at first but rapidly loses her head and later, when an attempt is made to raise the plane and all hell breaks loose, she is heard to scream 'Martin! Martin! Help me!'

This is a poignant moment, given the spiky nature of their relationship as portrayed earlier in the film. Splendidly played by Lee Grant, Karen is an alcoholic shrew who can't stop herself from mocking her tight-lipped husband's sexual prowess and even his accent. Explaining his passion for diving to the sympathetic Julie (Kathleen Quinlan), Martin maintains that 'It's wonderful down there; in fact, it's about the only time I ever really feel free.' Later, he's conspicuously absent from the scenes of the plane crashing into the sea (was Lee not available that week?), but reappears, hair mussed, to reassure the crumbling Karen and then to make his heroic gesture. 'Can't you forget about people for once and think about yourself?' Karen pleads. 'It's other people thinking about themselves,' Martin stoically replies, 'that got us down here in the first place, Karen.'

The Wallaces' relationship is a totally clichéd one, but at least it has a bit of grit; indeed, it constitutes the only grit in a distressingly gritless, and witless, film. The kind of computerised product of mid-1970s Hollywood which, for all its mega-budget credentials, looks and feels like a TV movie, *Airport '77* has 'corporate concept' stamped all over it. The particular concept here is that 1970s staple, the disaster movie, and the film's deadening parade of soap opera stereotypes – blind pianist, cute kids, old codgers finding love, even a doctor who turns out to be a vet – would be reproduced with deadly satirical accuracy in *Airplane!*. Early in 1979, Lee would be offered a role in the latter but turned it down. Lee's decision marked the beginning of a new career for bland leading man Leslie Nielsen, who henceforward became a white-haired, deadpan comedian of engaging brilliance.

For all its vacuity, *Airport '77* was, commercially, the cream of the Hollywood crop, but Lee followed it with two zero-budget science fiction pictures which he still points to as the only films he regrets having made. 'I've never, ever gone into a picture thinking that it was going to be a disaster,' he insisted in 1985, adding, however, that on some occasions 'I may have found out within 24 hours that it was going to be a disaster.'[7] *Starship Invasions* was presumably one of these. Filmed at Toronto's Hal Roach Studios from 18 October to 5 December 1976, the film was known in production as *The Winged Serpent* (a nod to the exotic insignia worn by Lee and his malevolent cohorts) and was due to be released as *Alien Encounter* before Columbia, distributor of Steven Spielberg's upcoming *Close Encounters of the Third Kind*, threatened legal action.

The final release title was intended to echo *Star Wars* instead, which sadly was not upcoming but had been released in May 1977, four months ahead of *Starship Invasions*. An embarrassing farrago featuring what *Cinefantastique* charitably described as 'a Saturday morning cartoon level of sophistication,' *Starship Invasions* seemed, if possible, doubly pathetic in the wake of *Star Wars*. 'When I read the script,' Lee recalled, 'I thought it was a very interesting idea that people would communicate telepathically on the screen … I didn't realise that I would be given a funny hat to wear and a rather ridiculous outfit. But the director [Ed Hunt] certainly was keen and hard-working. He was not sufficiently experienced, let's put it that way.'[8] The notion that the film's two alien races, engaged in a tin-pot struggle for control of the Earth, should communicate telepathically was in fact no more than a budget-cutting dodge to avoid using live sound, and results in numerous shots of Lee's Captain Rameses, stony-faced and ill at ease, staring into the camera as his remarks issue in voice-over from the ether.

At least he wasn't required to learn any of the script's outstandingly vacuous dialogue, unlike his co-star Robert Vaughn, whose Canadian UFO expert at least wasn't required to wear any of the film's utterly laughable Outer Space costumes. Lee's 'agent of barbarism and chaos' looks absurd in a black jumpsuit and attached headpiece, but no more so than the tin-foil androids and curvy alien glamour girls squeezed into unflattering white leotards. Despite a reported budget of over $2 million, the sets are cardboard and the special effects papier maché, while the overall feel of the film is that of a high school parody that, unfortunately, expects to be taken seriously. '*Starship Invasions* appears to have been made on a budget that might better have been used to supply hot dogs for a small picnic,' commented Janet Maslin in the *New York Times*. 'The flying saucers look like hubcaps, the spacelings' bodysuits are baggy

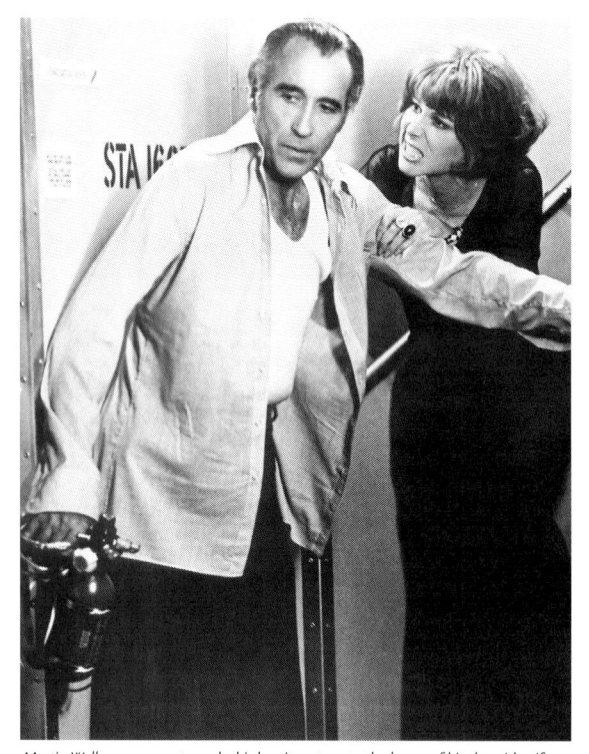

Martin Wallace prepares to make his heroic gesture, to the horror of his shrewish wife Karen (Lee Grant), in Airport '77 (1976)

and the Christopher Lee part isn't even properly played by Christopher Lee.'

End of the World followed in April 1977 and, like *Starship Invasions*, was in US theatres by September. 'I've never minced matters about that film,' Lee maintains. 'I was categorically told by the producers, and so was my agent, that Arthur Kennedy, John Carradine, José Ferrer and many others had signed to do certain parts in that picture.'[9] When he turned up, however, they weren't there – though three performers of more or less comparable stature (Lew Ayres, Dean Jagger and MacDonald Carey) were, not to mention one-time *Lolita* Sue Lyon as a fetching ingenue. Directed by John Hayes, the film was one of the fledgling productions of 22-year-old Charles Band, later the entrepreneur behind the extraordinarily prolific video labels Empire and Full Moon. It was regularly triple-billed at drive-ins with two of Band's previous efforts, an 'X'-rated version of *Cinderella* and a tale of automotive possession called *Crash*, in which Sue Lyon co-starred with none other than José Ferrer and John Carradine, which perhaps explains the confusion about their projected involvement in *End of the World*.

Blessed with an authentically barmy screenplay by Frank Ray Perilli, *End of the World* is by no means the embarrassment that *Starship Invasions* is. It gets off to an especially arresting start as Lee's Father Pergado, looking much as he did in *To the Devil a Daughter*, ventures into a diner and asks distractedly 'to call the police before it's too late.' Before he can do so, however, the payphone blows off the wall, the coffee machine explodes and the proprietor, doused in scalding coffee, plunges blindly into his own neon sign. Wandering back to the Convent of St Catherine, Pergado is greeted at the door by himself. Identical to a famous scene in Henrik Galeen's 1926 doppelgänger classic *Der Student von Prag*, this is yet another of those odd echoes of Conrad Veidt's career that crop up persistently in Lee's. The bogus Pergado is in reality an alien called Zindar – not to be confused with Zandor from *Space: 1999* or, for that matter, the Zendar who had coached Lee in *Airport '77* – and observes that 'You humans are just beginning to understand cloning. We mastered it many years ago. We took on the appearance of Father Pergado and the six nuns in this mission because we were forced to for our experiments.'

While the mind is still boggling over the exploitational masterstroke of alien-possessed nuns, we gather that Earth has been sentenced to death for its ecological crimes. We've already heard about an earthquake in China and a volcanic eruption in Africa (though we've seen neither of them: this is a low-budget picture); now Zindar unleashes a stock-footage tidal wave. He can destroy cars and other obstructions telekinetically – this is achieved by superimposing Lee's eyes over the object in question – and, having briefly manifested himself as the bug-eyed humanoid he really is, he crosses over to the 'other side' accompanied by plucky protagonists Sue Lyon and Kirk Scott (star of Band's *Cinderella*). Whereupon the world really does end, and with a suitably apocalyptic bang.

Lee acquits himself honourably, all things considered – few actors could say 'We want that variance crystal and we want it now!' with such conviction – and the film has a certain makeshift charm exemplified by the presence in a party sequence of virtually the entire Band clan, including Charles' first wife Meda and film director father, Albert, not forgetting screenwriter Perilli. Nevertheless, Lee must have been stung when the film was described in *Cinefantastique* as 'Another step down for Christopher Lee, who had better start watching his step.'

MIND OVER MARTIAL ARTS

End of the World began production in Los Angeles on 16 April 1977, though Lee's involvement wasn't announced until three days later. By that time he was already involved with *Return from Witch Mountain*, which had started shooting in Burbank on the 11th. Yet another science fiction subject, the telekinesis and telepathy in this one were left to a pair of sickly-sweet extraterrestrial children, Tia and Tony Malone. The film had the distinguished Disney badge on it and – still more attractive to Lee – gave him the opportunity to act opposite the legendary Hollywood grande dame, Bette Davis. 'I was thrilled to work with her,' he enthused. 'The fact that it was a comedy about children was beside the point.'[10]

The film was a sequel to Disney's 1973 hit *Escape to Witch Mountain* and was again directed by the young Englishman John Hough, whose credits included a spirited latterday Hammer Horror called *Twins of Evil*. There's nothing very spirited about *Return from Witch Mountain*, however. Like *Starship Invasions* and *End of the World*, it came out in the wake of *Star Wars* and must have been found wanting by pre-teenage connoisseurs even then. This newly sophisticated audience could well have been put off, too, by the film's conspicuously nauseating gaggle of street kids, one of whom asks at the end, 'If we wuz to go back to school, could we get as smart as Tia and Tony?' 'Maybe even smarter!' chirrups the ever-radiant Tia. With powers that make the picture seem like a Children's Film Foundation version of Brian De Palma's recent horror hit *Carrie*, Tia and Tony are indifferently played

Letha Wedge (Bette Davis) and Professor Victor Gannon up to no good in the Disney adventure Return from Witch Mountain *(1977)*

by Kim Richards and Ike Eisenmann and the real fun is left, as usual, to the scheming villains.

Lee is Professor Victor Gannon, a trilby-hatted charlatan in league with Davis' purse-lipped Letha Wedge ('looking Pasadena fashionable,' as the *Hollywood Reporter* put it) and attended by a hatchet-faced henchman called Sickle (Anthony James). 'There are no miracles, Letha,' Victor complacently claims as they roll into view in a sleek black Citroën, 'only scientific explanations for everything.' He soon admits, however, that Tony wields 'a force capable of counter-manding the basic physical law of gravity' and, as the villains drink a toast to what Victor calls 'molecular mobilisation' and Letha dubs 'molecular capitalisation,' we seem to be in a 'good villain/bad villain' situation. But Victor shows his true colours when he determines to 'scratch' Tia because of the telepathic threat she poses to his hypnotic dominance over Tony. And Lee may have felt the shade of Sax Rohmer at his shoulder when Victor, sizing up a sprawling plutonium plant, claims that 'This is the first step towards my becoming the most powerful man in the world.'

The villains are climactically levitated onto a precarious workmen's pallet – Lee is seen twirling in mid-air as he makes the ascent – and the film reaches a predictably saccharine conclusion. Like *Airport '77*, *Witch Mountain* has the flavourless texture of a TV movie and presents no challenge to its grown-up co-stars. Bette Davis was clearly aware of this when she presented Lee with a signed photo inscribed 'Chris: Hope one day we really act in a film,' underlining the words 'really', 'act' and 'film'. 'Both seem to have fun with their roles,' claimed one critic, 'obviously realising it's no talent stretch nor even a credit either will linger over when writing future memoirs. But both deliver like pros, as expected, and give the film a stature and identity it wouldn't otherwise enjoy.'[11]

By that time, however, Lee's memoirs had already hit the bookshops. Memorably entitled *Tall, Dark and Gruesome*, they were published by W H Allen in July 1977 and featured a striking, mock-sinister cover portrait of Lee staring balefully at prospective buyers. Nobody was too put off, however, as the book sold out in no time at all, despite Lee being unavailable for promotional purposes. The book had been a major undertaking – 'So far, I've recorded eight hours on tape and I've got as far as the end of Day Two: 28 or 29 May 1922,' he had told his fans back in 1975 – but the result was well worth it. As one critic observed, 'Mr Lee's keen sense of humour (and great gift of mimicry) do not come across in either his television appearances or the sombre film roles he has made his speciality ... In a witty and intensely readable book, we learn of aspects of his life outside showbusiness and come away with a picture of a man, of good birth and background, who is perhaps faintly embarrassed by the way he earns his living.'[12]

Lee's lack of an opportunity to display his comic talents was soon to be put right in spectacular style, but in the meantime he moved on to MGM's massive TV mini-series, *How the West Was Won*, directed by Bernard McEveety. The English gunsmith of *Hannie Caulder* was now a Czarist aristocrat, the Grand Duke Dmitri, encountering Sioux Indians in the Wild West alongside Horst Bucholz's Count Sergei in season two, episodes one to three. 'I think one reason it had an extraordinarily successful impact on the American public – very high ratings – was because nobody had ever seen a Western with Cossacks in it,'[13] Lee suggested.

Conversely, Wild West thrills transplanted to an Eastern setting were a feature of Lee's next film assignment, *Caravans*, a $12 million adaptation of James A Michener's bestseller that began its 16-week schedule on 29 August and was the first film to be made entirely on location in Iran. A longtime associate of Clint Eastwood, director James Fargo had a stellar cast at his disposal – including headliners Anthony Quinn, Jennifer O'Neill, Michael Sarrazin and Iran's premier film star, Behruz Vosoughi – but the result is an elephantine saga that quickly loses its grip on the viewer. The story of a beautiful Senator's daughter who escapes her marriage by taking up with a band of nomads on the Afghanistan border, it purports to be set in 1948 but kicks off with a Missing Persons photo of O'Neill that's clearly from her 1970s modelling portfolio. Nor do things get any better after that.

Lee's part as Machiavellian politician Sardar Khan was described in advance reports as 'the plum role' but there's little sign of it in the finished film. He appears in two brief scenes, both shot at Isfahan's Shah Abbas Hotel, and doesn't look especially exotic – close-cropped beard, shirt and tie, dark sash, red-striped robe. He makes the most, however, of cultivated observations like 'We keep our women in seclusion, covered and lacking the rights of a camel, and yet we dedicate most of our poetry to them.' Later, while discussing the worsening nomad crisis with his CIA liaison (Barry Sullivan) and his nephew Colonel Vazrula (Vosoughi), Khan callously observes that 'I do not propose to be embarrassed by it.' And that's about all. Lee's scenes were reportedly shortened in post-production, but it was perhaps just as well that his contribution was relatively small, given the resounding chorus of critical raspberries that greeted the film on release the following year. According to the *New York Times*, 'Films like *Caravans*

make one wonder if the Radio City Music Hall deserves to be saved. It opened there November 2, all grisly two hours of this fake epic.'

It was becoming clear that, though Lee's move to Hollywood saw him mixing in more exalted company and in higher-profile projects, it did nothing to safeguard him from the potential for disaster that accompanies any film. His next picture, however, not only reunited him with producer Paul Maslansky but also remains a charmingly off-beat favourite of Martial Arts enthusiasts. Richard Moore's *The Silent Flute* cost $4 million and was renamed *Circle of Iron* in the US, though retaining its production title in the UK. Starting in Israel on 30 October, it was based on an ageing treatment by James Coburn and the recently deceased Bruce Lee, both of whom were at one point poised to star in it. Jeff Cooper filled in as Cord, the musclebound centrepiece of this picaresque adventure, while David Carradine, famous for his role in the *Kung Fu* TV series, played the four roles earmarked for Bruce Lee.

For viewers immune to the lure of Martial Arts action, it's a very long haul indeed before Lee makes his entrance, the preceding footage enlivened by a tribe of troglodyte monkeymen and an engaging cameo from Eli Wallach as a man who's been half-immersed in a cask of oil for ten years in an attempt to dissolve his troublesome lower half, specifically 'that terrible thing between my legs.' Lee turns up in the final ten minutes as Zetan, guardian of the mirrored book that has been the object of Cord's quest all along and a saintly figure rather than the fearsome one we've been led to expect. His first gesture is to present Cord with a peach-coloured rose, after which he takes him on a tour of his Oriental flower gardens (largely made up of some beautiful

Cord (Jeff Cooper) encounters the saintly Zetan in Circle of Iron *(1977)*

matte paintings) and observes that harmony 'permeates everything here.' Faintly reminiscent of Lord Summerisle's tour of his orchards in *The Wicker Man*, this restful scene precedes Cord's encounter with the longed-for book. A piercingly mournful expression crossing his face, Zetan then utters the film's final philosophical message: 'There is no book, Cord: no enlightenment outside yourself.' It's a brief but extraordinarily dignified performance, providing a genuinely tranquil end to a hectic picture.

PYRENEES TO PINEWOOD

Hollywood in the 1970s had been triumphantly infiltrated by the so-called 'Movie Brat' generation of anarchic young directors, among them Martin Scorsese, Steven Spielberg, George Lucas, Francis Coppola and Brian De Palma. Most of them were conspicuously bearded and most of them paid tribute to Lee when meeting him in person; some even offered him jobs. John Landis tempted him with his ragbag of sophomore skits, *Kentucky Fried Movie*, but was turned down when Lee realised he was required to do a Fu Manchu in it – 'and I had no wish to be sucked back into that.'

Also in the spring of 1978, John Carpenter was at work on a small horror picture called *Halloween* that went on to earn $55 million. He offered Lee the Dr Loomis role eventually assigned to Donald Pleasence. 'I don't regret that,' Lee insisted in 1995. 'I said there was nothing in this character, all he does is say "This man is dangerous and mad." And then I was offered *The Fog* by John Carpenter – the part of the priest. I said I'd play him if you make him into a strong man, not a weak man.'[14] Carpenter was clearly unwilling to do this, giving the part to Hal Holbrook instead, but later told Lee that he had been right: had Father Malone been stronger, the film itself would have been stronger.

The esteem in which Lee was held by a younger generation had a happier outcome when he agreed, reluctantly at first, to act as 'Guest Host' in a 1978 edition of the cult TV sketch show, *Saturday Night Live*. At New York's Rockefeller Center on 25 March, Lee found himself reliving the horrors of live television in the company of wildly inventive soon-to-be-stars like Dan Aykroyd, John Belushi and Bill Murray. 'By the time we did it,' he remembered, 'I was on the biggest high I've ever had in my life! So were they, but in a slightly different way. I really shouldn't say that, because of the terrible tragedy that happened to John Belushi. I've never understood how these things happen. He had genius.'[15]

As well as hosting the show, Lee appeared in various sketches as Sherlock Holmes (shoving a ten-dollar bill up one nostril), Van Helsing (staking a copy of Richard Nixon's memoirs), Professor Higgins (trying to improve the mangled diction of Gilda Radner) and as Death himself, appropriating a puppy dog but meeting his match in its girlish owner, Laraine Newman. ('I'm sorry about Tippy ... Every day I'm given a list of lives that have to end. It's not the greatest job in the world but it's a living.') In doing so, Lee showed America, and its casting directors, that he could be funny. On NBC's *Tomorrow Show* on 30 May, he not only shared the bill with Brooke Shields on the eve of her 13th birthday but also told interviewer Tom Snyder that the *Saturday Night Live* crew were possessed of 'a kind of divine madness' and that they were 'the most dedicated group of professional people I think I've ever worked with.'

After that, Lee's next film could only be an anti-climax. '*The Passage* is so awful you must suspect it was designed to be someone's tax write-off,' sneered Vincent Canby in the *New York Times*. 'As such, it should be a smashing success.' The film's ten-week schedule began in the Pyrenees on 27 March and then transferred to Nice's Victorine Studios, though Lee's scenes were filmed entirely on location. Based by screenwriter Bruce Nicolaysen on his novel *Perilous Passage*, the film has American academic James Mason and family being smuggled out of wartime France by Basque shepherd Anthony Quinn while doggedly pursued by Nazi nutter Malcolm McDowell. Lee is a gypsy patriarch who risks his life to help them.

The director was J Lee Thompson, journeyman veteran of titles as diverse as *No Trees in the Street* and *Conquest of the Planet of the Apes*. The film is a by-the-numbers WWII melodrama disfigured by a level of sadism undreamed of in Lee's old Hammer Horrors. Michel Lonsdale has his fingers chopped off in a very nasty scene indeed, while Kay Lenz is raped in similarly gloating fashion. For the first atrocity, McDowell's bug-eyed SS madman is skittishly outfit-ted in a chef's hat; for the second, he reveals, believe it or not, a swastika-embossed jockstrap. Both these ludicrous embellishments were reportedly dreamt up by McDowell himself. Von Becker could have been a genuinely frightening figure; instead, McDowell plays him, grotesquely, for laughs as a posturing SS ninny, thereby sinking the film completely.

Lee, by contrast, is a solemnly dignified Romany, dusting off the French accent last heard in *The Pirates of Blood River* and looking splendid in a bushy moustache, battered trilby, dusty donkey jacket and frayed mittens. His scenes were filmed near Lourdes and its famous grotto, and for his spectacular demise – in which he's bound to a chair beside a babbling

With Malcolm McDowell, Robert Rhys, Anthony Quinn, Patricia Neal, Kay Lenz, James Mason and Paul Clemens while filming The Passage *near Lourdes (1978)*

stream, doused in petrol and turned into a human torch – he was required to be 'soaked to the skin for two days in a row. I had only myself to blame, however, because I'd seen exactly the same thing done by the SS to Yugoslavian partisans in 1944 and had therefore suggested it to J Lee Thompson.'

The role is a brief but affecting one, and perhaps served Lee as a means of paying tribute to his own gypsy ancestry. Convinced that 'the only safe place to be is in the country,' the gypsy ignores his own advice and is soon at the reins of his covered wagon, passing through a town square decorated with hanged corpses. Dark-eyed and rueful, he observes that 'It's not just the Jews that are killed by the Germans. Those are my people. We also are of inferior blood.' Once the refugee family has moved off over the snow-covered mountains, Von Becker catches up with the gypsy encampment and its leader stoically mutters 'We must all die sometime' as his tormentor toys sadistically with a lit cigarette holder. Lee's mixture of sad-eyed fear and dogged defiance is stirring stuff, but unfortunately he has to share the scene with the ridiculous McDowell.

Budgeted at $4.5 million, Ernest Pintoff's *Jaguar Lives!* began in Madrid on 24 June and is similarly ridiculous. Another Martial Arts opus, it shared executive producer Sandy Howard with *The Silent Flute* but jettisoned that film's air of Zen spirituality in favour of garbled James Bond-style intrigue. To bolster the impression, no fewer than five Bond veterans were pressed into service: Donald Pleasence, Joseph Wiseman, Barbara Bach, John Huston and, of course, Lee. The star, however, was the 33-year-old, undefeated world heavyweight karate champion Joe Lewis, playing the high-kicking Jonathan Cross, codename Jaguar. As well as boasting of his globetrotting production that 'There won't be a single studio shot in it,' producer Derek Gibson explained that 'We want to create a new American movie hero in Joe. He's got what it takes to be a new screen Flynn or Eastwood, or a Raquel Welch with balls ... This film is the first in a series of four we have planned with Joe playing Jonathan Cross.'[16]

In what turned out to be the one-and-only Jonathan Cross caper, Lee crops up in the Tokyo section – filmed in Madrid – playing English drugs baron Adam Cain, an old friend of the hero's from 'that unpleasantness in Cambodia.' It's a brief appearance, as was becoming customary at this time, but a pleasantly urbane one. 'Poor Adam Cain,' he sighs mock-ruefully, 'doomed to a life of international finance...' He also gets to talk on the telephone with Capucine and stand by appreciatively as Cross makes short work of a gaggle of Oriental thugs. Some of the other guest stars are in and out even quicker: Barbara Bach barely features and, apart from a word or two during each credits sequence, Woody Strode appears to have been cut out altogether.

Careful to select what he called short roles, as distinct from merely small ones, Lee had nevertheless

With Mickey Rooney on a return trip to Pinewood for Arabian Adventure *(1978)*

been suffering from a run of rather weedy cameos for some 12 months, and it took a return visit to England to restore him to full strength. *Arabian Adventure* began on 24 July, looking a little weedy itself by comparison to its Pinewood stablemate, Richard Donner's *Superman*. But it provided Lee, who started work on it on 8 August, with the welcome opportunity to pay tribute to his idol Conrad Veidt.

Kevin Connor's film is an amiable variant on *The Thief of Bagdad* with Lee in the equivalent of the old Veidt role (here called Alquazar), bosomy 18-year-old newcomer Emma Samms as his stepdaughter Princess Zuleira and Oliver Tobias as a Prince Hassan hailing, it seems, from Dagenham rather than Arabia. A bona-fide remake of *The Thief of Bagdad* had coincidentally just vacated Shepperton. There, the Veidt substitute had been Terence Stamp, who, by the end of the year, would be playing the title role in a disastrous West End production of *Dracula*. A further Stamp coincidence involved his role as General Zod in *Superman*, which Lee had been offered at the inception of the project two years before; unable to return to England at that early stage of his Hollywood residency, Lee had been forced to decline.

Arabian Adventure is yet another of Lee's pictures from this period that suffered by comparison to the all-conquering *Star Wars*. It's OK as Saturday matinée fodder but its quaint notions of what young cinema-goers were after would have gone down better in 1964 than 1978. And Brian Hayles' flavourless script is recognisably the work of the man who made such a mess of *Nothing But the Night*. Saddled by Hayles with a thoroughly one-dimensional character, Lee nevertheless has several agreeable moments as the wicked Alquazar. His introduction is particularly impressive. As a lithe belly dancer (Suzanne Danielle) bows low in front of him, the camera pans up from his feet to his hands, splayed like spiders on his knees, then passes a livid red sash at his midriff and finally catches his face as it leans into the light and an ominous three-note motif reverberates on the soundtrack. Elsewhere, he utters several lines that could have come straight out of the Fu Manchu phrasebook, claiming, for instance, that 'I will possess all the riches of the world, its kings will grovel before me, and I will be denied nothing!'

Alquazar, it is revealed, has sold his soul as a 'sacrifice to the Evil Ones'. His white-robed conscience is imprisoned in the so-called Mirror of the Moon, a kind of ectoplasmic TV set, and Lee plays both roles. With Lee as a soulless sorcerer striding through subterranean caverns ablaze with hellish flames – and Tobias as a young adventurer traversing a zombie-filled lake in quest of the magical Rose of Elil – the film carries several echoes of the much more imaginative *Ercole al centro della terra*. Alquazar has a more florid brand of invective than the impassive Lico, however; he denounces Milo O'Shea's rascally Khasim as 'You scum! You streak of spittle in the dust! You entrails of a diseased worm!' and then turns him into a very large toad. He finally goes completely mad while threatening the winsome Majeed ('Give me the Rose or I will feed your flesh to the dogs of Jadur!') and is rather hurriedly dispatched, via some not very persuasive special effects, into a cleft in his own caverns.

The film's performances are distinctly variable – Samms is obviously dubbed, Tobias totally disengaged, Mickey Rooney quite indescribable, poor Peter Cushing virtually invisible. As Majeed, 11-year-old Puneet Sira was the film's Sabu substitute and was also a devotee of the comic strips in *House of Hammer* magazine. 'I was totally in awe of this man,' he recalled in 1993. 'But what really surprised me the most was that he was totally opposite to the characters that he played. I found Christopher Lee very humble. On the set, he kept to himself. He was content reading the paper, just getting up for the rehearsals and doing his shots and then going back to his paper.'[17]

Though happiest while reading the news and puffing on his pipe (a habit reacquired while filming *The Diamond Mercenaries*), Lee was besieged by press interviewers during his brief stay and also had plenty of 'catching up' to do. 'During the course of our roast beef Pinewood lunch,' reported one journalist, 'we had cause to pause to greet at least 20 old buddies of Mr Lee's who had previously worked with him on Israeli, Swiss or American locations, as well as greeting a string of unconnected celebrities such as Jim Dale, Kenneth More and Nicolas Roeg.'[18] While in the UK, Lee also oversaw the publication of his third W H Allen anthology, *The Great Villains* – declining an offer to do a US one-man show based around it – and was involved in less harmonious negotiations with Mayflower Books. Their paperback reprint of *Tall, Dark and Gruesome* was scheduled for November and on its front cover, to Lee's disgust, was a red-eyed still from *The Satanic Rites of Dracula*.

U-BOATS AND MOTORBIKES

Lee's first TV movie during his Hollywood phase was *The Pirate*. Based on a torrid Harold Robbins bestseller, he had made it in a brief pause between *The Passage* and *Jaguar Lives!* and was cast as Arab doctor Samir al-Fayd, Franco Nero's presumed dad. Their fellow players were a lustrous lot, including Anne

With Franco Nero and Jeff Corey in Ken Annakin's epic TV movie, The Pirate *(1978)*

As Polish meteorologist Professor Lechinski in the Alistair Maclean adaptation Bear Island *(1978)*

Archer, Olivia Hussey and Stuart Whitman, and the director was British veteran Ken Annakin. Clocking in at a staggering four hours, it was considerately transmitted in two parts. 'Whatever your subjective feelings about the Harold Robbins potboiler that spawned this miniseries, forget them,' urged the *Hollywood Reporter*, 'because the current effort has style, skill and ... a surprising amount of conviction to its credit ... [with] a bevy of mature performances that anchor the film, from Eli Wallach, Christopher Lee, Michael Constantine, James Franciscus and Jeff Corey.'

As *The Pirate*'s blockbuster histrionics unspooled on TV at the end of November, Lee's next theatrical feature began on the 27th. *Bear Island* revived his association with both Peter Snell, producer of *Julius Caesar* and *The Wicker Man*, and Don Sharp, director of five of his earlier pictures. The film was an Anglo-Canadian co-production and divided its time between British Columbia, Alaska's Glacier Bay and Pinewood. Loosely based on an Alistair Maclean novel, it replaced Maclean's snowbound film crew with a snowbound scientific expedition at work on Bear Island, a benighted spot in the Arctic Ocean north of Norway, home of a NATO Early Warning System and one-time home of a German U-boat base. With a homicidal saboteur on the team, the film rapidly gets into a *Ten Little Indians* situation, with bits of *The Thing* thrown in, and Lee's Polish meteorologist, Professor Lechinski, is one of the chief red herrings.

As part of the 1970s vogue for all-star big-budget jamborees, *Bear Island* is notable for its profligate array of fake accents. The American Barbara Parkins plays an Englishwoman; the English Vanessa Redgrave a Norwegian; the American Richard Widmark a German; even the Canadian Donald Sutherland has to make the minimal adjustment to play an American. Lee's well-tried facility for accents stands him in good stead in this variable company. His soulful Pole is certainly a lot easier on the ear than Redgrave's Norse psychologist, whose horribly mangled line readings have to be heard to be believed. This menagerie of weird accents was contained on the Ljubov Orlova, a Soviet liner that doubled as the film's Morning Rose and as floating hotel for the cast and crew. Lee had already learnt to walk on snowshoes in the icy environs of Stewart, British Columbia's most northerly sea port; now, in Alaska, he found the extreme cold 'was at times intense enough to garble our speech.' Perhaps that was Redgrave's problem.

The film itself is a leaden exercise, carrying little of the charge Don Sharp brought to his previous brush with Alistair Maclean, *Puppet On a Chain*, for which he had directed some dazzling second unit action sequences. It doesn't even carry the charge contained in David MacDonald's *Snowbound*, a remarkably similar British spy thriller from 1947. When Barbara Parkins' vindictive minerologist takes an early bath, courtesy of a conspicuously unexciting avalanche, Lee's Lechinski is soon suspected of having fired the avalanche-inducing shot. He also has a disconcerting habit of making lone journeys away from the camp each night. Outfitted in goggles and face mask, he mournfully explains that 'Much of my life I have spent in detention camps of both sides. After an hour or two in that complex I have to get out.'

Lechinski calls the nearby U-boat graveyard 'the home of the grey sharks' but is not involved in the film's spookiest sequence, in which Sutherland's troubled marine biologist explores the abandoned U-boats and finds several skeletons, including that of his own father. Lechinski is finally felled by a sabotaged radio mast and Sharp works in a bit of very obvious Dracula imagery – Lee lying supine with blood trickling from the corner of his mouth and slowly flickering his eyes open in response to a shot of adrenalin. Despite this cheeky touch, Sharp was full of admiration for his old colleague. 'There are visual moments that still stay with me,' he recalled. 'One is of Chris alone in the freezing snow outside the weather station ... simply standing – very still, of course – but you feel the loneliness of the man, the solitude which he wrapped around himself as a protection. You feel it because Chris has this ability to communicate with an audience even when he is apparently doing nothing.' [19]

Lee wasn't done with U-boats quite yet. While filming *Arabian Adventure* in London, he'd been telephoned by Steven Spielberg, the meteorically successful young director responsible for *Jaws* and

Close Encounters of the Third Kind. The latter, in particular, had made a big impact on Lee. 'It had everything I like in a film,' he claimed. 'Style, beauty, fantasy bordering on reality, visual imagination and, above all, the sense of a thinking, creative mind behind it all.'[20] Lee lost no time, therefore, in accepting the role of Nazi U-boat captain Von Kleinschmidt in Spielberg's next project, *1941*, which started shooting on 20 November. Shuttling between *Bear Island* in Alaska and the Spielberg project at Culver City, Lee was obliged to juggle his facial hair, appearing moustachioed for Lechinski and clean-shaven for Von Kleinschmidt. (The same problem had come up on *Beat Girl* and *Too Hot to Handle* 19 years before.) He was also required to speak entirely in German while his Japanese opposite number, Toshiro Mifune, railed at him entirely in Japanese.

Reminiscent of the brain-reeling procedures employed in some of Lee's Euro-productions of the early 1960s, the babel was this time retained in the final cut, the joke being that, though speaking in different languages, the rival submarine commanders can understand each other perfectly. Cinemagoers, meanwhile, were provided with subtitles. 'The Führer was right,' Lee screams. 'There is no place in the Reich for you yellow swine!' To which Mifune replies, 'You can take your Third Reich and shove it up your ass!' Amazingly, this running gag between Lee and Mifune counts as one of the more sophisticated conceits in a bloated slapstick enterprise described in the *New York Times* as being 'as much fun as a 40-pound wristwatch.' Spielberg had had such golden progress up to this point that the press deemed him ready for a fall, and with *1941* he played straight into their hands.

The film begins with Susan Backlinie reprising her legendary nocturnal swim from the opening of *Jaws*, being goosed from below not by a Great White shark but by the surfacing submarine. Self-mockery, self-indulgence or self-aggrandisement? The question reverberates through the entire ramshackle two hours of *1941* (boosted by a further 30 minutes for TV and video), with the gags occasionally hitting but for the most part missing. Chronicling the panic let loose on America's west coast in the immediate aftermath of the attack on Pearl Harbor, the film's bizarre set-pieces steer surprisingly close to historical fact but are laid on so thickly they pall in record time. The film's closest relative is Stanley Kramer's 1963 folly *It's a Mad, Mad, Mad, Mad World* and, in Lee's filmography, the undisciplined mess that is *The Magic Christian*.

As for Lee's participation, it provides an echo of some of his 1950s roles and yet another reminder of Conrad Veidt, several of whose latterday pictures cast him as Nazi officers. It also sees him returning to the world of *Saturday Night Live*, with young guns John Belushi and Dan Aykroyd prominent among the cast. And it gives him a few diverting moments of slapstick. Von Kleinschmidt finally announces that 'I'm not about to lose my life because of some crazy Jap ideals' and attempts to take over the sub, whereupon Mifune unceremoniously tosses him overboard. Curiously, he doesn't reappear, though several other characters hit the drink and bob up again quite happily. In fact, a scene in which he was washed ashore – the only Nazi ever to set foot on American soil – before being apprehended by Slim Pickens was one of several sequences removed by Spielberg after a catastrophic preview at his 'lucky theatre' in Dallas.

Shooting Von Kleinschmidt's waterlogged arrival on American soil – a scene dropped from the film's release print – with director Steven Spielberg and co-star Slim Pickens: 1941 *(1979)*

Harvey Holroyd (Martin Mull), daughter Joanie (Jennifer McAllister) and Skull, charismatic leader of 'a faggot motorcycle gang', in Bill Persky's sardonic Serial *(1979)*

Another featured Lee threatening Pickens with a coathanger, a scenario painstakingly restaged by Spielberg two years later in *Raiders of the Lost Ark*.

The Spielberg assignment had borne Lee deep into 1979 but his next picture was a great deal funnier and remains perhaps the most intriguing of his whole Hollywood period. *Serial* started shooting on 29 May under the direction of Bill Persky, a veteran of TV sitcoms, and was based on a 1976 'novel with drawings' by Cyra McFadden. Set in Marin County, the film's satire of middle-class 'me generation' obsessives couldn't help but seem a bit belated by the time the film came out in March 1980, but it's still bracingly funny and witheringly well observed. Something of its jaded flavour is contained in an alfresco hippy wedding sequence, in which the lanky Sally Kellerman invokes 'You-ness, me-ness, us-ness, we-ness, your-ness, my-ness, our-ness: happiness.' 'Sameness,' mutters spectator Martin Mull under his breath.

Lee's role is a small but distinctly memorable one, amply justifying his being billed fourth after Mull, Tuesday Weld and Kellerman. He was cast as Luckman, a glamorous, silver-suited businessman who doubles as Skull, the leader of 'a faggot motorcycle gang.' As a passing psychiatrist explains, 'During the week they're completely normal but on weekends they dress up like Hell's Angels and listen to a lot of Judy Garland records.'

Twenty years after *Too Hot to Handle* and *The City of the Dead*, Lee gave Luckman/Skull the same refined American cadences as Novak and Professor Driscoll, and considered his acceptance as an American in an American picture one of *Serial*'s chief satisfactions. He was also reunited with motorcycles for the first time since a wartime stint in Malta 36 years before, roaring into view at a funeral and insisting gravely that 'My men are not pansies. We have terrorised entire communities. We are tough dudes, Holroyd.' Elsewhere, he complains that some of his 'clients have certain Victorian prejudices about what guys do with their weekends,' and delivers the line with just the tiniest glimmer of a petulant moue.

A triumph of off-beat casting, the role confirmed Lee's talent for deadpan humour. 'This is an American comedy,' he explained in Paramount's production notes. 'It is essentially and totally a part of the American scene ... a wonderful mixture of slapstick, farce, wit and satire, and, of course, it all has to be played totally seriously. You don't play it funny; you play it straight within the comedic situation.' Lee's reference to the film being thoroughly American proved prophetic; it went unseen in the UK until surfacing on video in 1984. Nevertheless, he had a ball making it and observed that 'In *Serial* I used language the like of which I never thought I would ever use in a movie ... and it does not bother me a bit. One just has to look at it as being part of what one might call 'contemporary conversation'. As long as it is not done in an offensive way or a tasteless way, I see nothing wrong.'[21]

Lee's stint with San Francisco's Hell's Angels – they were, as he put it, 'the genuine fireball' – included thundering across the Golden Gate bridge to the tune of Steppenwolf's 'Born To Be Wild' and mounting a climactic motorcycle raid on the posh premises of a mauve-robed religious cult. Resplendent in his leathers, Skull is handed a red rose by a young male initiate who reverently intones 'We love you.' Skull's response reportedly brought the house down at the press preview. Dandling the rose reflectively and unleashing a twinkling smile, he says simply, 'Well, that's very easy to say, but are you willing to prove it?'

INTO THE '80S

On 28 August 1979, Lee attended the LA première of Takeo Nakamura's *Nutcracker Fantasy*, a Japanese puppet animation feature derived from Tchaikovsky and E T A Hoffmann. Along with *Laugh-In* veteran Jo Anne Worley, Lee had provided the English language version with an impressive range of voices, not forgetting a couple of operatic songs. The following year Lee joined Angela Lansbury, Alan Arkin, Mia Farrow and others in voicing Arthur Rankin's *The Last Unicorn*, an appealing cartoon feature that made it to cinemas two years later. Lee provided the sepulchral tones of the fearsome King Haggard, a mad monarch whose throneroom resembles a tomb.

Lee was meanwhile maintaining a strong TV presence, first as Miguel in *Captain America II*, broadcast on 23 November 1979, and then as Marcus Valorium, playing opposite the young Ted Danson, in *Once Upon a Spy*, which followed on 19 September 1980. Both these vacuous pilot films were directed by Ivan Nagy, subsequently notorious for his 1990s involvement with Heidi Fleiss and already, according to Lee, 'a real slave driver'. In both, Lee is cast in standard 'rent-a-villain' mode, though he does what he can to ring the changes by voicing Miguel with a rumbling baritone and skating much more lightly over the inanities in Valorium's dialogue.

In *Captain America II*, he is described as 'the man behind the airport slaughter at Copenhagen, the massacre at the World Cup track meet and most of the kidnappings and executions of diplomats all over Europe.' He develops a gas that accelerates the ageing process a thousandfold and, when hoist by his own petard at the end, succumbs to instant decrepitude in unintentionally comical fashion. *Once Upon a Spy* is *You Only Live Twice* remade in the style of *Starsky and Hutch* – the magpie screenwriter was none other than Jimmy Sangster, long since decamped to America – and has Lee's super-villain aiming a 'molecular condenser beam' at the Hoover Dam. A restful role, Valorium is confined to a motorised wheelchair throughout and comes out with familiar megalo-maniac pronouncements like 'Gentlemen, we are now embarking on our first step towards the creation of an orderly new world.' Shamelessly plundering the James Bond recipe book, Sangster steals a march on the Bond series in only one respect – the use of a female 'M' figure in the person of glamorous Oscar nominee Eleanor Parker. Having long admired her from afar, Lee was sorry not to meet her during the filming.

After making *Once Upon a Spy*, Lee spent two days in San Francisco on an Italian production called *Save the Last Dance For Me*. Of its range of alternate titles – *Steigler, Stiegler*; *Desperate Moves*; *Rollerboy* – the latter

You Only Live Twice remade in the style of Starsky and Hutch: Marcus Valorium plots world domination from his motorised wheelchair in Once Upon a Spy (1980)

Christopher Lee – Part Eight

is the name under which it was finally reviewed some six years later. 28-year-old *Little House on the Prairie* veteran Steve Tracy, whom Lee referred to as 'a sort of pocket Gene Wilder', plays nerdish 17-year-old roller-skater Andy Steigler, whose picaresque adventures in San Francisco eventually lead him, about 60 minutes in, to Boxer's School of Assertiveness Training.

Though an Englishman, Lee's Dr Carl Boxer is a satirical figure straight out of *Serial* rather than the clumsy comedy of *Rollerboy*. A charlatan psychiatrist who has written the self-help bestsellers 'Punch Your Way to Success' and 'I'm OK You're Inferior', he greets Andy with a smartly delivered kick in the pants. 'See: your first lesson,' he announces. 'Never trust anybody.' He points proudly to a newspaper headline – 'Dr Boxer Uses Sadism to Build Lives' – then demands $1500 in cash. Relenting, he tells Andy disdainfully that 'We do have a once-a-year special for twerps and old ladies; it will cost you 65 dollars.' Attended, bizarrely, by a tiny tuxedoed henchman called Anthony (Selwyn Emerson Miller III), he is then seen holding imperious court over his other students, whom he privately refers to as 'fat, grubbing worms who will never amount to anything.' The way Lee elides his lines in throwaway fashion during this sequence is beautifully done and maximises their comic effect. He finally imparts to Andy a secret assertiveness technique – 'With the Move of Moves you will always have the upper hand' – and is slightly disconcerted when it turns the boy, temporarily, into a gum-chewing thug.

Rollerboy is a pretty gauche entertainment, and Lee's delightfully fruity cameo is its highspot by a very long distance. But it has a strangely bewitching charm of its own, together with an unusually engaging heroine (Dana Handler) and a roster of pop songs co-written by its director, Ovidio G Assonitis. Some of these, notably 'Disco Man', are truly gruesome, but one, 'The Road to California', is an extraordinarily affecting, harmonica-saturated ballad that plays over Andy's journey from Oregon to San Francisco and is then cannily used again over the end credits. Sadly, the film disappeared more or less without trace.

Lee's temporary Americanisation continued apace; at the end of June 1980, he played nasty fashion mogul Dale Woodman in the two-part *Charlie's Angels* story, *Angel in Hiding*, a new-season opener that introduced Tanya Roberts into the Angels fold. Lee made a point of accepting one-off TV roles while turning down series commitments. He explained why in 1986. 'At one time or another,' he maintained, 'I was approached by every one of them – *Dynasty*, *Dallas*, *The Colbys*, *Remington Steele*, all those episodic shows ... I've always said no because you tend to find yourself with 15 other guest stars and the word goes round that you're on the skids ... Chuck Heston doesn't think that way, I realise that. But although I've known him for years and years and made *The Three* and *The Four Musketeers* with him, I have no idea why he does *The Colbys*. You'll have to ask him. I made a thriller with Joan Collins, too, called *Dark Places*, but I'm not tempted to pop up in *Dynasty* either.' [22]

Rather than appear in soap operas, Lee opted for further globetrotting. He fretted over the fact that Gitte couldn't always come with him, left instead 'to suffocate in the cultural vacuum of Los Angeles,' but she took to making solo trips to exotic climes normally shunned by film crews. She was able to accompany him, however, on his two chief excursions of 1980; indeed, the evidence is up there on the screen.

First up was another Paul Maslansky assignment, *The Salamander*, which started on 18 June and required Lee to go to Rome the day after finishing his *Charlie's Angels* role. Gitte turns up at either end of the picture as the wife of Prince Baldassare, director of Italy's Counter Intelligence agency. Lee, of course, is Baldassare, a thinly veiled portrait of the right-wing war hero Prince Borghese. Though adapted by Rod Serling from a Morris West novel, the film's fact-based

Dr Carl Boxer, author of the self-help bestseller 'I'm OK You're Inferior', with his sidekick Anthony (Selwyn Emerson Miller III) in Rollerboy (1980)

'This is Italy. We are all salamanders.' Prince Baldassare is led away by the police in The Salamander (1980); Claudia Cardinale is seated at right, Gitte at extreme left

account of an attempted Fascist coup ensured that it was never shown in Italy. The one-and-only directorial effort of Peter Zinner, who had edited pictures like *The Godfather* and *The Deer Hunter*, it has Franco Nero as Dante Matucci, a colonel in the Carabinieri who uncovers a sinister plot in tandem with Anthony Quinn's powerful industrialist Bruno Manzini, the so-called Salamander. Lee is Matucci's boss, Baldassare, an urbane figure who preaches political pragmatism before turning out to be the chief culprit, aided and abetted by Eli Wallach's rat-faced General Leporello.

After a nasty scene in which an old man is dentally tortured and then defenestrated, Baldassare urges Matucci to hole up in Zurich for the sake of his own skin. 'Think of how you will enjoy your burial, Matucci, while you wait for the resurrection,' he says enigmatically. Even more enigmatic is his glib observation when arrested at the end: 'This is Italy. We are all salamanders.' The scene preceding his arrest, in which Manzini gathers together Italy's great and good for an accusatory film show, is much the best in the picture. As Matucci points the finger, both Baldassare and Leporello look gratifyingly thunderstruck and Matucci ultimately takes over Baldassare's job. But the film is in other respects a lumbering intrigue and had to wait three years before being granted a patchy release.

Still outside Hollywood, Lee then joined David Carradine and Stockard Channing in the politically volatile Zimbabwe for a crazy car race comedy called *Rally*, which was finally released as *Safari 3000* after an intermediate title change to *Two in the Bush*. Directed by Harry Hurwitz, the film began its 12-week schedule in October. Lee plays the impressively moustachioed Count Lorenzo Borgia – 'It's ironic that I should be cast as a descendant of a family that once intermarried with my own' – and he comes across as a live action version of the indefatigable saboteur, Dick Dastardly, from the children's cartoon series *The Wacky Races*. Unfortunately, his 'Muttley' is not a snickering dog but a ludicrous character called Theodor, played with grotesque overstatement by the diminutive Hamilton Camp.

Much of the comedy is clearly improvised and Lee plays it smoothly and lightly; for an actor who once admitted that he found it difficult to laugh on screen, it's charming to see him beaming unaffectedly all over the place in this picture. Camp, by contrast, mugs furiously from beginning to end and is never in the least bit funny. When he croons an absurd ditty called 'Baboons on the Road', Lee puts his head in his hands in despair, a gesture that could easily be mistaken for a judgment on Camp rather than Theodor.

The improvisational nature of their scenes is detectable when the Borgia name is confused with both Victor Borge and Ernest Borgnine ('Yes: fine actor,' Lee booms), and also in various jokey nods to the real Christopher Lee, notably his facility with languages and frustrated aspirations to be an opera singer. 'What a voice: opera's loss,' wheezes Camp as Lee warbles operatically from the driver's seat. 'Thank you,' Lee replies. 'I had thought of it seriously at one time, as you know.' Some of the improvisations were curtailed, however; an intriguing scene of Borgia and Theodor smoking pot in the former's private jet was consigned to the cutting-room floor. 'I had to ask for professional advice, *of course*, as I did not know how to act stoned,' Lee reassured his fans.

With Stockard Channing, and 'Caligula', in car-race caper Safari 3000 *(1980)*

After a promising opening, the film devolves into a ramshackle mess distinguished only by some diverting splashes of local colour. The teams involved in the car race are crude national stereotypes and occasionally sexual ones, too; for the 'gay' team, the film's hairdresser and wardrobe supervisor were pushed in front of the camera. Lee has great fun yodelling his delight in the open road and also when showing off his tame cheetah, Caligula, in a failed seduction scene with Stockard Channing. He gives an agreeable twinkle, too, to the line 'Americans: a graceless people,' an amusingly mild response to Carradine's suggestion that he should 'take [his] car and shove it up [his] aristocratic ass.' As in *The Salamander*, Gitte appears briefly, this time sitting at a bar and giving Channing's baby baboon a drink, while Lee rounds off the whole thing, having been trounced by Carradine in the race, with a defeated cry of 'La commedia é finita.' Viewers unimpressed by Hamilton Camp's gurning attempts at humour will be unaware that the 'comedy' ever began.

NAME YOUR POISON

Set, like *Rollerboy*, in San Francisco, Steve Carver's *An Eye for an Eye* began production on 7 January 1981 and by August was making pots of money at the US box-office. 'Chuck Norris doesn't need a weapon ... He *is* a weapon!' screamed the ads for this one, Lee's third Martial Arts picture. Budgeted at $3.8 million, the film was the fifth starring vehicle for the charisma-free Norris, who had been undefeated world middleweight karate champion from 1968 to 1974 and was now determined to provide a John Wayne-style role model for directionless American kids. To this end, he was cast in *An Eye for an Eye* as the crusading Sean Kane, who describes himself as 'just another out-of-work ex-cop with a score to settle.'

As Morgan Canfield, revered head of TV news station Channel 6, Lee is required to reiterate his bland villain routine for the umpteenth time and does so with his usual élan. An avuncular, pipe-smoking figure, Canfield runs a TV exposé on a drug-smuggling racket while secretly masterminding it. This duplicity is revealed in a surprisingly desultory fashion but Lee subsequently gets to toy with Maggie Cooper's enterprising Heather ('Such a persistent child,' he purrs) and announces, as the relaxed host of a drug smugglers' convention, that 'Nothing could possibly penetrate our security.' This turns out to be a vain boast, as Canfield ends up on the floor being throttled by the vengeful Kane in a scene given rather more realism by Norris than Lee found comfortable.

What else is there to say about *An Eye for an Eye*? Virtually nothing. It's the kind of American

'Happy days are here again.' John McKenzie goes down with his ship in Goliath Awaits *(1981)*

production-line pap that Lee's British and Continental films had never been, whatever their imperfections. 'You know the stuff if you know any Californian Kung Fu at all,' observed critic Al Clark. 'People keep going to see it, though: mock-Easterns have replaced pretend-Westerns as the favoured undemanding night out.' And Clark perceptively added that 'Christopher Lee ... wears his best "Is this what I went to Hollywood for?" expression throughout.'[23]

Was this, in fact, what Lee went to Hollywood for? Perhaps not, but there was no doubt that he had done what he set out to do – to prove that he could get along quite nicely without recourse to red contact lenses and extended canine teeth. He was still largely identified as a villain, but that in itself didn't worry him; as he has accurately pointed out on numerous occasions, villains are almost invariably more interesting than heroes. And, most importantly, he had unearthed a hitherto unsuspected gift for comedy. The pictures coming his way, however, were another matter. After a number of high-profile projects when he was still relatively new to Hollywood – *Airport '77*, *Caravans*, *1941* – the feature films being offered him had lately dwindled to the level of *An Eye for an Eye* (popular rubbish) and *Safari 3000* (unpopular rubbish). Indeed, his most accomplished project around this time was another TV movie, *Goliath Awaits*, filmed in May 1981 and transmitted on 17 and 23 November.

After *Arabian Adventure*, director Kevin Connor had himself decamped to America and made a delightfully gruesome horror-comedy called *Motel Hell*. In *Goliath Awaits*, he reunited Lee with his *Arabian Adventure* co-star Emma Samms, who again played Lee's daughter. Budgeted at $4 million and shot on the Queen Mary at Long Beach and at Columbia's Burbank studio, the film co-starred Mark Harmon, John Carradine, Robert Forster, Jean Marsh and, as Lee's sinister right-hand man, Frank Gorshin.

Its agreeably wild narrative had apparently been waiting to be filmed for some 14 years. Sunk in the North Atlantic in 1939, the Goliath turns out to be playing host to an entire undersea community. Former third engineer John McKenzie has become in the meantime a kind of God-like Nemo figure, his well-intentioned despotism deftly sketched in by Lee.

'I have to age 40 years,' Lee remarked. 'But the character's personality also changes, and that's what attracted me to the part. He has a remarkable mind, and he devises all sorts of ways for the passengers and crew to survive. He's a technician, an inventor, a father figure and a sort of Santa Claus character to the children; eventually he becomes a benevolent dictator. But like all dictators, when things stop going his way, he lashes out.' [24] The film ends on an elegiac note as McKenzie, deserted by his subjects, stands forlornly in his hydroponic garden, waiting for the Goliath to go up in smoke and listening to a scratchy 78 of his favourite song, 'Happy Days Are Here Again'.

A less momentous television project had taken Lee to Toronto for a single day at the beginning of 1981. *Tales of the Haunted* was directed by Gordon Hessler and written by the former AIP executive Louis M Heyward, both of whom had been behind *The Oblong Box* and *Scream and Scream Again*. A five-part pilot with guest stars of the calibre of Jack Palance, the show was advertised as 'The unique late night alternative' with 'Your host, Christopher Lee' and its component parts were later refashioned into a TV movie called *Evil Stalks This House*. 'I wrote the pilot myself, which was basically a rip-off of H P Lovecraft,' Heyward recalled. 'I knew Christopher Lee from the AIP days ... He agreed to host the pilot and, if it went, the series. He just loved working, pure and simple. We sold the pilot and it played in syndication, but it never went any further than that. I wasn't sorry.' [25]

Perhaps it was this brief stint as a 'horror host' that inspired another offer from the new brood of Hollywood horror-mongers. John Carpenter had tried to engage Lee's services twice; now it was the turn of Wes Craven. Foundering somewhat in the lean period between *The Hills Have Eyes* and *A Nightmare on Elm Street*, Craven tried, and failed, to add the lustre of Lee's name to his 1981 project, *Swamp Thing*. According to Lee, 'I simply said, "Look, if you can come up with something I haven't done before, let's talk about it." But it was really, in a sense, the mixture as before, and I wasn't all that interested.' [26] Craven plumped instead for Louis Jourdan, who had already followed Lee's lead in playing Dracula and would subsequently turn up as a Bond villain in *Octopussy*.

Lee chose instead to get right away from Hollywood. Budgeted at $7 million, Philippe Mora's *The Return of Captain Invincible* was touted as Australia's most expensive film ever and occupied Sydney's Seven Keys Studio from 23 November 1981 to 15 March 1982. An ambitious parody of the superhero sub-genre, the result is a wildly undisciplined slapstick comedy that isn't nearly as funny as it thinks it is but is nevertheless a difficult film to dislike. And Lee's role as the nefarious Mr Midnight, though it seems at first sight exactly 'the mixture as before', has a few outré features that were an obvious lure to Lee and make it one of the most delightful of all his screen appearances.

Alan Arkin – 'the most diversely talented performer I've ever shared a frame with' – is Captain Invincible, an alcoholic, washed-up superhero whose day is long past. Rehabilitated by the US government for one final mission, he describes Mr Midnight as 'my arch enemy; hell, everybody's arch enemy as far back as I can remember.' The notion of Invincible and Midnight, Good and Evil, as timeless antagonists is amusingly set up in an imaginative black-and-white pre-credits sequence. In a series of mock-newsreels chronicling Invincible's past exploits, Midnight is visible in 1920s Chicago as a cigar-chewing 'mystery big-shot racketeer'; in Nazi Germany, he's at Hitler's right hand as the Führer's 'industrialist crony', and he's even an interested observer at the McCarthy hearings, where Invincible is castigated for wearing a red cloak. And, hearing from an underling about 'that slob that's been getting all the VIP treatment,' the contemporary Midnight murmurs reflectively, 'An old fighter? I wonder...' Whereupon Lee's eyes glisten and his jaw muscles tighten in his signature style and the battle is on.

Much of the action is devoted to Invincible's blundering attempts at regaining his invincibility, interspersed with the obligatory ration of cut-aways to the omniscient villain in his bizarre HQ. For some reason, Midnight is attended by Julius, a bearded little gremlin like something out of *Star Wars*. Midnight also has a tendency to burst into snatches of Wagner. He gleefully demonstrates his dog-eat-dog attitude by feeding tidbits to a pet frog ('Teatime for Jeremy...'), feeding the frog to a python, then feeding the python to a vulture and finally tucking into roast vulture himself. He refers to the meal as 'A veritable feast of thanksgiving on this, the eve of a glorious New Order,' and proceeds to expound his atrocious masterplan, 'Operation Ivory'. 'When the pure genetic Americans discover what I have done to clean up that rotting cesspool that they call New York,' he gloats, 'they will carry me into the White House on their shoulders.'

Done with Lee's usual gimlet-eyed panache, this is all pretty familiar Fu Manchu stuff, though the Nazi eugenics angle is a faintly distasteful innovation. The

Scaling the heights of high camp: Mr Midnight and assorted dancing girls in The Return of Captain Invincible *(1981)*

real fun begins when the film forsakes slapstick comedy for musical comedy. Bursting into song on the subway, Invincible's trilling of 'Evil Midnight' is intercut with sleazy interjections from Midnight himself. 'Long before the crack of doom there was Evil in the air,' he rumbles. 'Long before we left the womb there was Evil everywhere!' – and he cracks a colossal whip as a bunch of *Flashdance*-style chorus girls sashay into view in fetish underwear.

Even better, in his final confrontation with Invincible, Midnight gets a number to himself, also penned by Richard Hartley and Richard O'Brien of *Rocky Horror Show* fame. Sneeringly referring to Invincible as 'a nonentity whose ticket to oblivion is about to be punched,' Midnight reveals a rainbow-coloured indoor bar and namechecks, in song, the dizzying variety of drinks with which he proposes to break Invincible's spirit. 'Have a short or a port or a snort of any sort,' he booms – and the dancing girls slink back in, suggestively vibrating their cocktail shakers. Scaling the heights of high camp, Lee then waggles his knees and flutters his hands as he launches into the sax-driven chorus: 'If you don't name your poison/I'll have to get the boys in/And you'll never see another Tequila sunrise.' And in doing so, he steals the picture.

Sadly, the film then dwindles to an incoherent ending in which Midnight wades around his indoor mock-up of the New York State coastline before Invincible topples him with, appropriately enough, a giant globe. The scene is as much of a damp squib as many James Bond denouements, notably that of *The Man With the Golden Gun*. And the film itself is decidedly hit-or-miss and frequently juvenile. But in it Lee consolidated the great achievement of his Hollywood period. Less hidebound than their UK counterparts, US casting directors had been a crucial factor in bringing before the public a newly relaxed Christopher Lee. Shakespeare, in Malvolio, and Buster Keaton, in his entire career, had shown that the unsmiling, outwardly dignified comedian is often the funniest of all. On the same principle, Lee proved in *The Return of Captain Invincible* that he could retain his dignity while simultaneously laughing at himself. For that reason, 'Name Your Poison' remains one of his finest hours.

PART NINE

ANOTHER HOMECOMING
1982–1989

In May 1982, Lee turned 60 and could reflect on the fact that 'The move to the States was a good one and gave me the opportunity to play an incredible variety of parts.'[1] But there was a less congenial side to his time in Los Angeles, springing not merely from the sharp practices endemic in the film industry but also from the deadening Beverly Hills lifestyle. These misgivings combined with several other factors, notably a major health scare, to ensure that the Lees were back in London for good by the time he was 63.

Lee's TV presence was maintained, meanwhile, with a one-off appearance in *Evening at the Improv*, a popular comedy show produced by Patrick Macnee's son Rupert. Lee treated viewers to the Sylvester the Cat and Yosemite Sam impersonations normally confined to his phone conversations with Peter Cushing and sang selections from *Man of La Mancha*. Harvey Hart's *Massarati and the Brain* was a more conventional project, an exotic crime caper for Aaron Spelling Productions transmitted on 26 August. In it, Lee's Victor Leopold is a bespectacled ex-Nazi 'linked with terrorist groups so vicious even the PLO disowns them.' He crosses swords with monied soldier of fortune Massarati, played by Daniel Pilon (last seen in the execrable *Starship Invasions*), and with Massarati's revoltingly precocious 10-year-old nephew, the 'Brain' (Peter Billingsley).

Saddled with another boring 'rent-a-villain' role, Lee based his characterisation, right down to a gloved and paralysed hand, on Artur Axmann, head of the Hitler Youth. Spending most of his screen time wearing the same SS leather raincoat he wore in *The Treasure of San Teresa* in 1959, he has one gratifying moment when Leopold's henchmen gag the ghastly child prodigy. 'D'you know something, mein junge?' he hisses. 'You talk too much...' Ann Turkel and Camilla Sparv are also involved in an adventure dismissed in the *Hollywood Reporter* as possessing 'glamour and class, vapid though they ultimately are' – which could easily be a thumbnail sketch of life in 1980s LA.

Another TV movie followed on 17 September, this time for the powerful producer Ed Feldman. A cloyingly saccharine confection, *Charles & Diana A Royal Love Story* took Lee back to England briefly and hit TV screens in record time; it had only begun shooting at Shepperton on 5 July. The 1981 Royal Wedding had struck an international chord and, while director James Goldstone got to grips with his version of the tale, a rival version – *The Royal Romance of Charles and Diana* – was already underway in New York for CBS. Goldstone's young leads were David Robb and Caroline Bliss; the remainder of the Royal Family were played by Margaret Tyzack, Mona Washbourne and Lee as the Duke of Edinburgh. Another veteran of *The Devil Rides Out*, Charles Gray, weighed in as Diana's father, Earl Spencer.

'Arriving on the set,' claimed a reporter for *Screen International*, 'one was immediately struck by entirely how physically unlike their real-life counterparts the actors were, but as director Goldstone is at pains to explain, lookalikes were never the intention.'[2] Maybe so, but, according to Lee, his old schoolfriend Patrick Macnee was sent home when his resemblance to Earl Mountbatten was considered insufficient; David Langton of *Upstairs Downstairs* fame was drafted in to replace him. As for Lee, he was duly fitted with blond eyebrows and thinning blond hair, but the producers demurred when he suggested they go the whole hog and give him blue contact lenses. Though dubious about the queasy business of impersonating a real-life Royal, Lee made up for his paucity of dialogue by addressing numerous unheard comments to Tyzack's Queen and pointing things out to her in characteristic Prince Philip style. By an ironic quirk, the CBS Duke was played by Stewart Granger, the actor for whom Lee had served as stand-in back in the late 1940s.

Heart trouble: the wicked Kato in Mio, min Mio! *(1986), also known as* The Land of Faraway

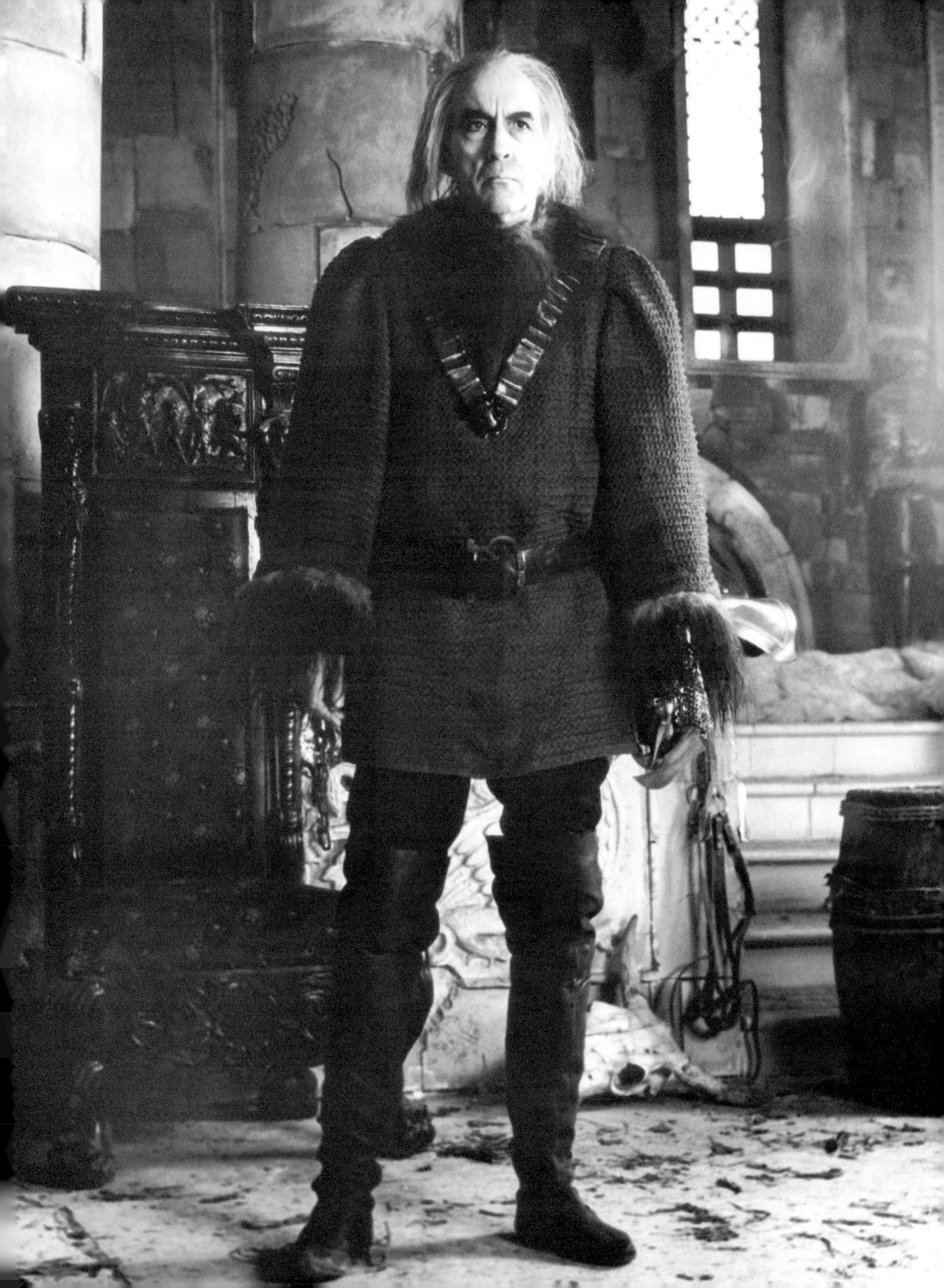

The longest shadow of them all: Roderick Grisbane avenges a 40-year-old family grievance in House of the Long Shadows *(1982)*

Long Shadows, Ten Times the Light

Remaining in the UK after his stint as Prince Philip, Lee opted to appear in a horror film for the first time since 1975. Most such offers had come in recent years from Hollywood sources – and all had been turned down – but at least one had been made by an old associate from Lee's days in British horror. Back in 1980, as Lee recounted it, 'I got a message from my agent asking me if I would like to do a picture with Milton Subotsky and I said, "Yes. After all these years, what does he have planned?" So he told me he's going to do a picture called *The Monster Club*. I said, "That's enough. We need go no further!"' [3]

House of the Long Shadows, however, was another matter. The umpteenth film version of the Earl Derr Biggers warhorse *Seven Keys to Baldpate*, the project had been dreamt up by Menahem Golan of London Cannon Productions in February 1982 and started shooting at East Tisted's Rotherfield Park on 9 August. The lure for Lee was the opportunity to share the bill with Peter Cushing, Vincent Price and John Carradine. (The last two, incidentally, *had* agreed to appear in *The Monster Club*.) With a combined age of 276, these four horror icons were the 'long shadows' of the title and their participation in the film was a press agent's dream.

'I suppose I was expecting some bitchiness and prima donna behaviour,' mused director Pete Walker, 'but that hasn't happened. They are consummate professionals; they never blow a line or miss a mark. You learn in this business that you get what you pay for, and they are giving real value for money.' [4] Walker had started out in the twilight world of British sex-ploitation but in the mid-1970s had produced a clutch of hard-edged and unusually brutal horror pictures. He seemed an odd choice, then, to preside over a nostalgic thriller like *House of the Long Shadows*, but cosy 'old dark house' subjects were apparently what he'd been yearning to make all along. The film is rather dawdlingly paced and is handicapped by some distinctly underwhelming juveniles – not to mention a remarkably lame pay-off – but as a vehicle for Lee, Cushing and Price it's much more satisfying than their bitty contributions to *Scream and Scream Again*. Blessed with equally juicy roles, all three are at the very top of their form and with the added bonus of John Carradine and Walker veteran Sheila Keith – whom Lee remembered with affection from his early days at the Connaught Theatre – the picture is exactly as Walker described it: value for money.

Cushing and Price are Grisbane brothers Sebastian and Lionel, one lisping and fearful, the other supercilious and flamboyant. The gnarled

Carradine is their oracular father Lord Grisbane – not really very plausible, since he was only five years Price's senior – and Keith is their alternately vindictive and lachrymose sister, Victoria. After suitably grand entrances for Cushing and Price, Lee gets the same treatment some 45 minutes in, looming beetle-browed out of the darkness and announcing himself as monied property developer Corrigan.

The scattered Grisbanes have reconvened at Baldpate Manor in order to free their youngest sibling Roderick, whom they imprisoned in an attic room over 40 years before. But when Lionel asserts the Grisbanes' ancestral claim to the house, the tight-lipped Corrigan drops a bombshell. 'History holds no sway with the present, Mr Grisbane,' he says firmly. 'Particularly in view of the fact that I intend to tear this house down and sell off the land for industrial development.' Appropriately, Victoria then launches into an ear-splitting rendition of 'The Force of Destiny' at the pianoforte. Positioned on the same sofa as the enraptured Sebastian, Corrigan's tiny flinch of distaste at Victoria's efforts is a priceless Lee touch, immediately followed by a stark look of gob-smacked amazement when she rushes tearfully from the room. The queasy sense of social embarrassment continues at the dinner table and, as people start dying, Corrigan is persuasively presented as the voice of reason, advising the juveniles to 'Leave this place at once: with a lunatic brother roaming around, God knows what will happen.'

With Sebastian, Victoria, Lord Grisbane and several others all dead, the scene is set for the film's climactic twist – not, perhaps, an unexpected one but handled by Lee with thrilling melodramatic relish. Alone with Lionel, Corrigan reflects on the fact that 'Destiny and retribution are often inter-related, aren't they?' Lee introduces a tiny pause here, the subtle play of his features a wonder to behold as he drops in one final word: 'brother...' Jaw muscles tightening and eyes changing in an instant to a look of adamantine malice, he then explains that 'For 40 years I have waited for this one final moment of revenge ... I, your *dear* brother Roderick, have come here to pass sentence as judge – and executioner.'

In a barnstorming climax, Corrigan sees off Lionel with a double-bladed axe and then removes his bow tie in order to throttle the hopeless hero. The slow turn of Corrigan's head as he hears the heroine bleating in fear is a classic moment, and his subsequent plunge down the stairs, writhing contortedly with the axe planted in his own midriff, is charmingly reminiscent of *Dracula Has Risen From the Grave*. Moments later, however, the film springs a further revelation – that the Grisbanes have all been actors engaged by the hero's venal publisher (Richard Todd) to add fuel to his latest horror novel. Screenwriter Michael Armstrong may have hoped that this ending would give the proceedings a certain Pirandellian spin, but it strikes most viewers as an unforgivable cheat. Even here, however, Lee and Price have some spiteful fun pretending to be what would later become known as 'luvvies'.

Only briefly visible on its cinema release the following year, *House of the Long Shadows* came in for some predictable sniping from the press. *Time Out*, for example, claimed that 'Christopher Lee [is] so wooden that it's hard to tell if he's in a coffin or not.' As conceited critical gags go, this is more conceited than most but impossible to substantiate from a viewing of the film itself, in which Lee's performance is fluid, relaxed, at ease. With Price on hand to give the proceedings an agreeable flourish of high camp, and Cushing to provide a beautifully etched study in stammering fear, Lee's function in the film was to infuse it with some old-style terror mixed with pathos, and this he did in grand style, proving that he was still master of a genre he had formally forsaken.

Thanks to new companies like Palace, Goldcrest and Virgin, British cinema in the early 1980s was showing some misleading signs of vitality, and it was for Goldcrest that Lee gave his next performance. The illusory nature of the British 'revival' is perhaps indicated by the reliance on dreamy evocations of Britain's colonial past like *Heat and Dust* and *A Passage to India*. Goldcrest's *The Far Pavilions*, a large-scale mini-series released theatrically in some territories, is in similar vein. Budgeted at around $14 million, it was based on M M Kaye's weighty bestseller of the same name and started its 15-week schedule in Jaipur on 10 January 1983, finally reaching British TV screens in January of the following year.

Directed by Peter Duffell, whom Lee had last encountered on *The House that Dripped Blood*, the film featured Ben Cross and Amy Irving as star-crossed lovers in the halcyon days of the British Raj. Cross was flavour of the month thanks to *Chariots of Fire* while Irving was soon to marry Steven Spielberg; indeed, Spielberg visited the unit while scouting locations for his upcoming film *Indiana Jones and the Temple of Doom*. Among the picture's peculiarities, the leathery Rana of Bhithor was played by the Italian actor Rossano Brazzi and then dubbed in post-production by David de Keyser – with an Italian accent. Stranger still, the theatrical cut took the extraordinary liberty of removing Sir John Gielgud's performance as Cavagnari in its entirety. Along with Gitte, Gielgud had been one of the few participants not to succumb to what Lee called 'gut-rot' at the team's HQ in the sometime palace of the Maharajah of Jaipur. 'If only visitors to India could leave their stomachs behind,' Lee noted sardonically, 'they would be better fixed to face the hazards and enjoy the charm of filming with Indians.'

Cast as Irving's philosophical uncle Kaka-ji Rao, Lee looks splendidly imposing in his Indian robes and manages to avoid the 'Goodness gracious me' taint that would engulf Alec Guinness' Professor Godbole in *A Passage to India*. He has some amusingly laconic moments – muttering 'Children, children: most unseemly' as some tiny royals mimic Western-style dancing, for example – and a touching one when out riding with the moonstruck hero. 'It is thus that young men look and speak and sigh when they think of their belovéd,' he cannily observes, adding that 'I too was young once, although to look at me now you might not believe that.' He goes on to explain that, after his wife succumbed to cholera, he fell in love with another woman but 'She was not of my caste and she was of mixed blood, and afterwards – afterwards I could not find another woman to take her place.'

Providing a mournful index in this speech to the racial divide separating the hero and heroine, Lee is required elsewhere to lead an elaborate wedding procession, flanked by Omar Sharif and Ben Cross and backed up by innumerable extras and a fleet of ceremonial pachyderms. The horses were unused to the elephants, the elephants were unprepared for the ritualistic clash of cymbals, and the result was a high-speed bolt on the part of the horses with Lee and his companions still in the saddle. The clouds of dust that were stirred up during this stampede caused Lee to add asthma to the horrors of 'gut-rot'. The wedding itself is a sumptuous affair, beautifully captured by the celebrated cinematographer Jack Cardiff and presided over by a genuine pandit, who earned Lee's admiration for his 'remarkable breath control'.

Back in the USA, Lee next participated in realising the dreams of Shelley Duvall, the saucer-eyed actress who had caused a stir in Stanley Kubrick's *The Shining* and as Olive Oyl in Robert Altman's *Popeye*. In order to make *Faerie Tale Theatre*, Duvall formed her own Platypus Productions, lavished $500,000 on each episode and staffed them with actors and technicians drawn mainly from the Altman stable. 'Not since the long ago *Shirley Temple Storybook*,' observed one critic, 'have TV audiences been rewarded with such sugar-plum family entertainment.'[5] And not since *Tales of Hans Andersen* in 1953 had Lee been involved in a straightforward fairy tale, rather than the 'X'-rated variety in which he'd made his name.

Among the series' casting coups were Scaramanga's former henchman, Hervé Villechaize, as *Rumpelstiltskin*, Mick Jagger and Barbara Hershey in *The Nightingale* and Susan Sarandon and Klaus Kinski in Roger Vadim's take on *Beauty and the Beast*. For Graeme Clifford's *The Boy who Left Home to Find Out About the Shivers*, Peter MacNicol was the boy and Christopher Lee – who better? – provided the shivers as the Sorcerer, doubling as the charmingly muddle-headed King Vladimir. Also in the cast assembled at the ABC Television Center were David Warner and, as Lee's hunchback assistant, Frank Zappa. MacNicol later claimed that 'Christopher has a very surprising and, I believe, completely unknown adeptness at witty, urbane comedy. It's a pity that we will never see what he would have done with the part of Elliot in Noël Coward's *Private Lives*, or any number of Coward vehicles, or Maugham plays. He is wonderful, and dry, and sardonic.'[6]

A different kind of sorcery was showcased in a 22-minute featurette, released in February 1984, called *New Magic*. In this, special effects guru

As the philosophical Kaka-ji Rao in Peter Duffell's lavish Goldcrest mini-series, *The Far Pavilions* (1983)

As the muddle-headed King Vladimir – with Peter MacNicol and Frank Zappa – in The Boy Who Left Home to Find Out About the Shivers, *a 1983 instalment of* Faerie Tale Theatre

Douglas Trumbull blazed a trail for his revolutionary Showscan system, which projected 70mm footage at 60 frames per second, two and a half times faster than normal film. Wall-to-wall screens were required, with projectors specially designed to provide ten times more light than usual, in order to give the showstopping effect of '3-D without the glasses'. Trumbull's system would eventually be superseded by the similarly panoramic IMAX technology.

'I play a Mr Kellar,' Lee pointed out, 'who was a famous conjuror-magician who really existed ... It really is, in a way, the story of *The Sorcerer's Apprentice* told in a modern idiom. The sorcerer's apprentice is a projectionist [Gerrit Graham] who proceeds to foul up everything in the projection room and then decides to explain to the audience how I perform my magic ... Then at the end I come back and catch him at it, and of course I banish him from my sight. I then deliver the final two or three minutes of dialogue straight at the camera ... explaining to the public how Showscan works, without becoming too technical.'[7] Lee went on to describe Trumbull's visual and sonic effects as 'quite unique, unlike anything I've ever seen,' but some reviewers were more blasé. 'It's surprising that such a ballyhooed process doesn't deliver more,' opined Randy Palmer in *Cinefantastique*. 'But when an extreme close-up of Christopher Lee's face fills the screen, we become starkly aware of the detailed Showscan image; the picture is *so* sharp and clear that every line and blemish etched into an actor's face comes into focus. Showscan may even require new make-up techniques as well as new projection systems.'

PUNKS IN PRAGUE, AND ELSEWHERE

After *The Far Pavilions*, Lee was happy to return to India the following year for a promising picture called *The Bengal Lancers*. The script, about a vanished regiment on the Northwest frontier, was intriguing, the director was Stephen (*I, Monster*) Weeks and Lee's co-stars included Michael York, Trevor Howard, Weeks' regular collaborator Ronald Lacey and Howard's wife Helen Cherry. Weeks had been working on the project since 1977 and had finally been offered financial backing, to the tune of $6 million, by the Pakistani shipping magnate Mahmud Sipra.

With the cast put up at another converted Maharajah's palace, this time in Jodhpur, the film began shooting on 13 February 1984 and closed down two weeks later. Lee had been given an early indication of impending trouble when a deputation of crew members asked him to intervene on their behalf regarding non-payment of their wages. Meanwhile, cries of 'Hair in the gate!' were going up after almost every take and the baffled cinematographer Walter Lassally found himself unjustly accused of producing out-of-focus footage. Weeks has subsequently expounded an elaborate theory regarding suspect rushes reports and questionable insurance claims.

Lee's response was more temperate. 'It should not ever happen,' he wrote. 'But it happens quite often.' Another Weeks project from around this time – an Arthurian fantasy called *The Avalon Awakening*, in which Lee was pencilled in for the Dean of Glastonbury Cathedral – failed to get beyond the script stage.

Unhappily, Lee's final spate of Hollywood assignments didn't have the plug pulled on them. Cheap and witless 1980s trash, *The Rosebud Beach Hotel* began in March and reunited him with Harry Hurwitz, the affable director of *Safari 3000*. With the inexorable rise of home video, it was now possible to aim films directly at viewers' sitting rooms, bypassing cinemas altogether and going instead for a newly defined youth audience sometimes characterised as the 'pizza and a six-pack' crowd. Lee's final Hollywood pictures would have 'straight-to-video' stamped all over them and their bottom-of-the-barrel quality would perhaps form part of his motivation for returning to England the following year.

Known in production as *The Big Lobby*, *The Rosebud Beach Hotel* divided its time between the Hollywood Roosevelt Hotel for interiors and Santa Monica's Shangri-La Hotel for the beach-fringed location shots. As hotel magnate Clifford King, Lee has an amusing opening scene in which he fences insanely with a snivelling accountant. Then, pondering the question of appointing a new manager, he announces that 'It's just what the Rosebud Beach Hotel needs: new blood,' giving a certain self-mocking emphasis, of course, to the final phrase. He subsequently engages Matches Monahan of 'Fire for Hire' to destroy the hotel, unaware that his daughter (Colleen Camp) has appointed herself as assistant to the young manager (Peter Scolari), whom he can't stand. An old softy really, he finally rescues Scolari from the about-to-blow building and offers the young couple the insurance money as a wedding present. The film has plenty of inanely juvenile gags and numerous topless girly bell-hops to tickle the American teenagers who formed its target audience.

Having been reunited with Harry Hurwitz, Lee was next reunited with Philippe Mora, the Paris-born, Melbourne-raised director responsible for *The Return of Captain Invincible*. In 1978, Lee had missed the opportunity to appear in John Carpenter's epoch-making *Halloween*. Joe Dante's *The Howling* caused a similar stir among horror fans two years later and, with a sequel mooted, Lee felt that it would do no harm, after *House of the Long Shadows*, to dip a second toe into the waters of Gothic horror. He cannot have known that the several sequels to *The Howling* would be cynically conceived as a money-spinning straight-to-video franchise and that the first of them would be arguably the worst. Nor that it would acquire the risible subtitle *Your Sister is a Werewolf* in the US and, incredibly, *Stirba – Werewolf Bitch* in the UK.

Apart from some Van Helsing-style exposition shot in a Hollywood house designed by Frank Lloyd Wright, *Howling II* took Lee to Czechoslovakia's Filmove Studio at Barandow. Starting work on the film on 13 August 1984, Mora maintained that 'We are not going to dwell on the gore aspect. Christopher Lee doesn't like it and neither do I, as I think there is a very fine line between horror and disgust.' [8] The even finer line between horror and hilarity, however, is recklessly transgressed by the film's shockingly bad prosthetics, which make Transylvania's gathering of flat-faced werewolves look like rejects from *Planet of the Apes*. Tirelessly badgering Mora and others, Lee reminded them of the basic anatomical truth that wolves have snouts, but his complaints went unheeded. In a triumph of understatement, he noted later that the upright werewolves gave the film 'a children's theatre aspect.'

The film opens quite promisingly, with a moderately exciting rock instrumental over the credit titles together with scraps of modified Goya imagery and some fetching glimpses of East European local colour. It proceeds to a funeral staged at the Jewish Cemetery outside Prague, where Lee's 'occult investigator' Stefan is seen loitering by Kafka's grave. He then turns up at a raucous punk club, donning a trendy pair of wraparound shades in order to observe a werewolf 'pick-up'. The lupine temptress is Marsha Hunt, Lee's black victim from *Dracula A.D. 1972*, and the punk milieu is also reminiscent of that film in being nearly ten years out of date. The juveniles, Annie McEnroe and Reb (*Captain America*) Brown, are a notably weedy pair but Lee still manages to chill the blood when asked by McEnroe, 'Where do we have to go to find Stirba?' 'To the dark country,' Lee intones in reply. 'To Transylvania...'

The remainder of the film contains scene after scene of an ineptitude and fatuity that has to be seen to be believed, all of them cut to the staccato rhythm of a rock video. Stirba's rejuvenation ceremony is studded with topless wolf-girls and the ridiculous bursts of hirsute wolf-sex are only slightly grislier than the obligatory hero/heroine love scene. At the end, the vengeful Stefan turns out to be Stirba's ageless brother and her incestuous advances to him involve sending out cheapskate laser beams from her fingertips. Stirba herself is vividly portrayed by the spectacularly bosomed Sybil Danning, an actress familiar from three previous Lee projects (*The Three Musketeers*, *Der flüsternde Tod* and *The Salamander*) and by 1984 the undisputed Queen of Exploitation.

As for Lee, his gravitas while impaling Ferdy Mayne on a titanium stake, or solemnly asserting that

'At midnight on that day all werewolves will reveal themselves,' is, as usual, impeccable. But, in this bargain-basement context, his total seriousness can't help but look more than a little ridiculous. And, physically, he looks unusually grey and ill in the picture, the reason for which would become clear the following year. In the meantime, Lee's Stefan had brought forth a warm endorsement from director Mora. 'Not only is Lee the total professional,' Mora claimed, 'I also call him the self-focusing actor. If out of the corner of his eye he can see that the focus-puller isn't really doing his job, he'll move back three inches and get into focus himself. He's wonderful and I have a lot of time for him ... He really sells the audience on the fantasy without ever going over the top.' [9]

Lee's final picture while domiciled in Hollywood, *Jocks*, started on 26 November in Las Vegas under the title *Road Trip*, marking yet another reunion, this time with Steve Carver, director of *An Eye for an Eye*. Though room is found for veterans like Lee, R G Armstrong and Richard Roundtree, the film is chiefly given over to the ghastly misadventures of a group of repulsive, basketball-playing teens and the whole thing is swamped in unlistenable American power-pop of the period. (The main offender is an ear-bleeding monstrosity called 'Powerplay', performed by Jimmy Osmond.) What is the patrician Christopher Lee doing in this horrific, *Porky's*-flavoured milieu? Playing White, the eccentric president of Los Angeles College, flourishing a sword at Beetlebaum, his beleaguered head of sports (Armstrong), and telling him in no uncertain terms that 'I want to win: I want that championship.' With Lee turning up in the opening scene and indulging in crazed swordplay, the film immediately recalls *The Rosebud Beach Hotel* and, also like that film, he is given one or two self-referential gags. Once Armstrong has gone, he takes up the en garde position and, clearly mad as a hatter, hisses to himself, 'And now, musketeers, we meet again...'

At the opposite end of the film, he reappears in a Las Vegas hotel, grimaces in horror when kissed by the euphoric Armstrong during the climactic championship and is last seen making eyes at a lanky blonde whom we know to be a man in drag. 'The pièce de resistance of my portion,' Lee remembered, 'was a scene in which I realise that the girl I madly love, who has invited me to her room, is a man' – but this pay-off appears to have been cut. In the handful of scenes that remain, Lee abandons the light comic touch of *Serial* and *Rollerboy* in favour of a stentorian delivery that isn't nearly as funny.

Lee was disorientated by the film's nocturnal schedule – filming in Las Vegas' Barbary Coast Casino necessitated working from 1.00 am until midday –

On the look-out for lycanthropes in a Prague punk club in Philippe Mora's dreadful Howling II *(1984)*

but simultaneously he had more serious grounds for disquiet. 'At that time I often felt mysteriously tired,' he recollected. 'Walking along the road, even on the level, was a drag. The slopes on the golf course seemed like a ploughed field to climb. My beloved doctor, Maxine Ostrum, said I had the blood pressure of a man of 30. But the heartbeat was irregular.'

Home via Harley Street

While working on *Jocks*, Lee was contacted by William C Faure of the South African Broadcasting Corporation. Would he play Lord Bathurst in Faure's TV mini-series devoted to the so-called 'Black Napoleon', *Shaka Zulu*? Lee had long been fascinated by the subject and had recommended it on several occasions to the executives at Hammer; indeed, the title cropped up as part of their ill-fated 1974 production programme. Faure's version had expanded from a purely local enterprise, possibly to be performed entirely in Zulu, to a colossal venture costing close to 30 million rand and sponsored by the US distributor, Harmony Gold.

Faure began work in September 1984 and his British guest stars arrived in South Africa early the following year. With apartheid still in place, the series aroused much controversy, but, as with *Der flüsternde Tod* some ten years earlier, Lee was of the opinion that integration between blacks and whites could only be assisted by co-operative ventures of this kind. Among the white actors who presumably agreed with him were Edward Fox, Robert Powell, Fiona Fullerton, Trevor Howard and Kenneth Griffith. (The latter even contributed to the script.) Lee's brief scenes were filmed at Groote Schuur, the State President's mansion in Cape Town, and amount to little more than an uneasy interview with Roy Dotrice's George IV. Clad only in a nightshirt and with a simpering doxy on one knee, the King warns the scandalised Bathurst to sort out the Zulu problem or else. According to Lee, a great deal of Dotrice's outré business with a large sausage hit the cutting-room floor. Fittingly, most of the white characters are pretty peripheral, with centre stage conceded to local actor Henry Cele, who bestrides the many hours of *Shaka Zulu* like a colossus.

After a flying visit to the UK, where *The Return of Captain Invincible* had finally achieved a short run at the Knightsbridge Minema, Lee's next film was an Anglo-Swedish co-production shot at the Swedish Film Institute's Film House Studios from 28 January 1985. *The Face* eventually made it to video as *Mask of Murder* and was directed by the prolific Swedish director Arne Mattsson. The film's snow-covered Swedish locations doubled for a small Canadian community, Nelson, which is being terrorised by a serial killer. The culprit turns out to be the granite-jawed Bob McClay (Rod Taylor), who, outfitted in a featureless mask, could easily come out of one of the Italian 'giallo' pictures that had been so popular in the 1970s.

Though dubbed the Swedish Hitchcock, Mattsson was no Mario Bava or Dario Argento and the film has none of the imaginative flair lavished on the better gialli. Lee, Taylor and co-star Valerie Perrine are surrounded by numerous Swedish actors who have been grotesquely dubbed into English; even the sepulchral English actor Terrence Hardiman suffers the indignity of being dubbed into American. Totally miscast, Lee is the local police chief, Jonathan Rich, whom we first encounter on his birthday mouthing unlovely lines like 'The psychiatrists … can't make up their minds whether [the killer's] problem is in his head or in his balls.' He's subsequently hospitalised and, having listened to Hardiman's lip-smacking account of how marriage alone can turn men into psychopaths, replies mildly that 'I knew there was a reason I remained single.' The film has a moderately intriguing conclusion in which the Inspector finds in McClay's desk a copy of *Playboy* with the centrefold's throat neatly sliced across, meaning that, though McClay has been exonerated, Rich secretly knows the truth. But in other respects the film is a listless and faintly distasteful thriller, rapidly consigned to a deserved oblivion in the video bargain bins.

Lee's last few films had been a pretty depressing bunch and were symptomatic of the problems he faced in a Hollywood quite different from the one he'd arrived in nine years earlier. In the 1980s, the kind of all-star jamborees popular in the previous decade, with plenty of opportunities in them for seasoned character actors, had given place to the vogue for effects-laden 'event' movies. 'I've accomplished what I intended to do by coming here,' he reflected during the filming of *Jocks*, 'although I have not starred in a major American movie as a first or second name. It's very unlikely that I would because … today films seem to fall between two extremes. There are special effects movies, costing huge sums of money – for which people get *paid* huge sums of money – in which you forget the acting, because there is no necessity for it. And there are teenage movies.'[10]

Whether or not Lee was aware of the fish-out-of-water nature of his two appearances in what he called 'kid pictures', he had more pressing reasons to leave Hollywood behind in the spring of 1985. One of them, perhaps, was the subconscious desire to die at home if he had to die at all. A Santa Monica specialist had confirmed that his heart fluttered, specifically the mitral valve of the left ventricle, and the message was clear. 'I had to have open-heart surgery to repair a leaking

Jonathan Rich grasps the real identity of Nelson's serial killer in Arne Mattsson's Mask of Murder *(1985)*

valve,' he recalled. 'My heart was beginning to enlarge and wasn't pumping properly. I got terribly tired just walking – ordinary walking, not climbing. I got scared to death ... That was hell, believe me. I'm not talking about the pain; I'm talking about the fear.'[11]

The Lees returned to Belgravia permanently in April 1985 and, soon after Lee's 63rd birthday, the operation took place at the Harley Street Clinic in June. Lee left letters for both Gitte and Christina in case it should prove unsuccessful and was clinically dead for part of the procedure while his heart was frozen and the valve repaired. The cardiac surgery was supplemented by a punishing regime of physiotherapy, but after only six weeks of recuperation Lee felt the need to return to work.

This he did in a prestigious Channel 4 drama called *The Disputation*. Set in Barcelona in 1263, it cast Lee as King James I of Aragon, a liberal ruler who organises a disputation between representatives of the Jewish and Catholic faiths. Appropriately, the role was physically an undemanding one – indeed, the entire play could just as easily have been presented on radio as TV – but Lee was required to paint, with the lightest of brushstrokes, a portrait of a man harrowed by his conscience. The result is a performance of extraordinary delicacy, combining the shattered magnificence of a mediaeval monarch with many subtle touches of everyday humanity as he wrestles with a textbook case of Catholic guilt. Given to smiling wanly as the debate rages around him, Lee's James is a man who'd rather be remembered as 'a great Catholic King' than 'a Jew-loving whoremonger.'

Directed by Geoffrey Sax for Electric Rainbow Productions, the play is scored by Michael Nyman, economically staged on minimalist sets left over from the Welsh National Opera's *Ernani*, has lavish costumes by Maria Björnson and matches Lee with four distinguished stage actors. Alan Dobie, Bernard Hepton, Helen Lindsay and Bob Peck are s upplemented by a refugee from the 1970s punk explosion, Toyah Willcox, who plays the King's lisping, unaffected mistress. 'I can face an army of Moors but I can't face Hell,' he tells her, while his Father Confessor tells *him* that 'Your desire for fair play could lead you to within measurable distance of Hellfire.' Lee has two riveting conversations with Dobie's Rabbi Moses ben Nachman, serene and sorrowful encounters quite different to the melodramatic plane occupied by Peck and Lindsay's Jew-baiting characters. It's possible that the world-weary grace with which Lee negotiates the play's religious probings was intensified by his recent brush with death.

Corporate queasiness over its subject matter ensured that *The Disputation* went out over a year

Shattered magnificence: as James I of Aragon in the Channel 4 drama, The Disputation *(1985)*

after it was made, on 21 December 1986. Lee was singled out in the *Independent* for 'a cameo of attractive naturalness' and in *Time Out* for 'a performance of considerable sensitivity and power.' Rightly convinced of the play's quality, Lee did all he could to support it, maintaining that 'Any story like this which is so accurate historically is interesting, particularly about a religious conflict which is still going on ... Anti-Semitism somehow refuses to go away. Synagogues were bombed only this year. I have seen the swastikas daubed on the Simon Wiesenthal Centre in Los Angeles and across gravestones in France and Germany. *The Disputation* is a plea for more tolerance and understanding.'[12]

From Channel 4 Lee moved on to a stint in Moscow. Vladimir Grammatikov's *Mio, min Mio!* – known in English-speaking territories as *The Land of Faraway* – started on 11 March 1986 and was a co-production of Gorky Film, Nordisk Tonefilm and the Swedish Film Institute. Based on Astrid Lindgren's children's stories, graced with miniatures by Bond alumnus Derek Meddings and fitted with a lilting theme – 'Mio, My Mio' – by Abba stalwarts Benny Andersson and Björn Ulvaeus, the result is an engaging fairy tale with a memorably baleful appearance from Lee in its third act. The principals, however, are a highly accomplished pair of small boys: Nicholas Pickard as Mio and, shortly before landing the lead role in Spielberg's *Empire of the Sun*, Christian Bale as his friend Jum-Jum.

Afflicted by what he called 'the standard frustrations of Russian filmmaking at that time' – notably a disinclination on the part of the crew to do anything before lunch – Lee also found his accommodation off-putting, despite the fact that his room in the National Hotel commanded a splendid view of Red Square and was dominated by a huge refectory table reputed to have been used by Lenin. Supplied with a large consignment of complimentary caviar, the Lees celebrated their silver wedding anniversary around this historic table on 17 March. And, having so recently undergone open-heart surgery, it was perhaps piquant for Lee to find himself cast as a man who literally has a heart of stone.

As an indication of the film's pleasingly naïve scheme, the credits of *Mio, min Mio!* are laid out over a mock-mediaeval painting of a white castle topped by fluttering doves, while across a forbidding causeway looms a black castle attended by ravens. 'There is something called the Land Outside,' little Mio is warned by his father, the King (Joseph Bottoms). 'It lies beyond the Forest of Mysteries.' Whether or not screenwriter William Aldridge was aware that Transylvania translates as the Land Beyond the Forest, Lee is ideally cast as the despotic ruler of this shadowy domain, at the mere mention of whose name – Kato – the skies rumble and autumn leaves swirl in alarm.

But Mio and Jum-Jum are determined to confront the dreaded Kato, an ancient knight fitted with a mechanical hand and reputed to have turned all the local children into birds. Progressing through subterranean caverns studded with skeletons, the two become separated. Mio loses his footing but is saved from a precipitous fall by a metallic pincer that providentially grasps his wrist and hoists him upwards. After a build-up of well over 60 minutes, this is a grand entrance for Lee, rapidly followed by Kato's mystified examination of Mio's magic sword. 'This is the most dangerous sword I have ever seen in my castle,' he breathes. 'It cannot be used to kill the good and the innocent...' Lee gives Kato an affecting twinge of perplexity as he asks himself 'What shall I do with it?', deciding finally that 'I will throw it into the dead lake.'

Having imprisoned Mio and Jum-Jum, Kato is next seen sitting alone in his cavernous throne room, joylessly using a feather to tickle an unperturbed toad that sits on a metal plate in front of him. Divested of his chain-mail hood, we see that Kato resembles a colossal bird of prey – black eyebrows shaped into quills, a balding dome with matted grey hair straggling down at either side, filthy fur fringes edging his chain-mail tunic. Having recovered his sword and escaped his confinement, Mio gains entrance and a blistering duel ensues. Kato stalks his tiny antagonist with insane deliberation, cleaving a marble table in two with one blow and then unleashing a leaf-strewn whirlwind. He also calls up a blazing fireball, orchestrating its movements with his mailed fist but admitting defeat when Mio absorbs it into his sword.

And here Lee introduces the humanising twist, giving Kato's words a graceful edge of noble resignation. 'I have known for a long time that this moment would come,' he says forlornly. 'But remember, Prince Mio: even if you kill me, you cannot destroy Evil. Another Kato will come, and another, and another – and what can you do about it? Nothing.' Impaled by Mio, he slumps onto his throne and murmurs, 'At last I am free of this heart of stone. It has crushed and smothered me so long.' Giving a tiny sigh, his head lolls in Lee's familiar fashion and he falls to rubble, his heart a glimmering red stone among the fragments. Mio takes it to a window and it flutters away as a tiny bird. The castle collapses, House of Usher style, and the curse is lifted from the local children just as it was from Mina in *Dracula* – a film Lee had insisted all along was no more than an adult fairy tale. It's one of Lee's more low-key death scenes but an extremely powerful one. Kato is a brief role but provides proof of what *The Boy who Left Home to Find Out About the Shivers* had suggested: that Lee was the perfect choice to provide small cinemagoers with a healthy dose of terror.

OLD FRIENDS

The remainder of 1986 and much of 1987 were chiefly given over to reunions with old associates Arne Mattsson, Franco Nero, Edouard Molinaro and – returning after an absence of some 18 years – none other than Jesús Franco.

Mattsson's *The Girl* started without Lee on 17 March and is a picture that harks back not only to *Lolita* but also to the kind of arthouse erotica with which Mattsson had made his name in the 1950s. Franco Nero is a successful lawyer, Peter Berg, who becomes embroiled with a scheming teenage minx called Pat and a convoluted money-laundering plot, with much of the action devoted to scenes of the 40-something Berg, and others, getting to grips with a consistently nude, under-age partner. For Vincent Canby in the *New York Times*, it was a 'truly awful English-language Swedish melodrama.' Canby also noted that 'the 14-year-old Swedish girl' around whom the plot revolves 'is played by Clare Powney, who is English, clearly not 14 and appears to have studied acting with Pia Zadora.'

Lee turns up in the film's final minutes as Peter Storm, a bespectacled police inspector who discovers Berg's corpse after Pat has calculatedly left the gas on. 'There's something here that doesn't quite fit,' he muses, subsequently grilling the unfortunate Hans (Mark Robinson) and coming to the mistaken conclusion that he was the culprit. A British picture shot in Stockholm, *The Girl* provides a faint echo of *Valley of Eagles*, with Lee now promoted to full Jack Warner status, but the film's only other interesting feature is its foreshadowing of torrid Hollywood thrillers like *Basic Instinct*.

By June Lee was in France making a three-hour television drama for TF1 called *Un métier de Seigneur*. Ten years after their collaboration on *Dracula Père et Fils*, director Edouard Molinaro cast Lee as 'Fog', chief of British Intelligence during the fall of France in 1940. The rights to Pierre Boulle's novel had formerly rested with Warner Bros, but no American star could be persuaded to play the highly ambiguous figure of Lieutenant Cousin. Pierre Arditi was up to the challenge, however, and the other headliners were Evelyne Bouix, Alessandro Vantini, Annie Girardot and Jay Benedict. Lee met Boulle himself during the shoot and the result went out in two 86-minute instalments, starting on 6 December. According to French columnist Bernard Ales, the film was full of 'résistance, collaboration, torture, trahison.'[13]

Another television project ended less happily. An American/Italian/German co-production, Simon Langton's highly engaging *Casanova* was filmed in October and November in Spain and Italy; 'associate producer' credit went to the former James Bond beauty, Luciana Paluzzi. Lee's duties as a cuckolded Polish Count, Branicki, involved little more than fighting a pistol duel with Richard Chamberlain over Hanna Schygulla (improbably cast as Chamberlain's mother) in the film's closing minutes. The project's other stars included Sylvia Kristel, Ornella Muti and Sophie Ward, with a healthy crop of *Musketeers* veterans alongside Lee and Chamberlain: Faye Dunaway, Frank Finlay, Roy Kinnear. Also like the *Musketeers* films, it was written by the novelist George MacDonald Fraser. Though well received when first transmitted on 1 March 1987, some versions contrived to drop Lee's brief scenes in an attempt at reducing the film to a more manageable length. Lee assuaged his disappointment by making public appearances in support of a new CD release of Stravinsky's *The Soldier's Tale*, issued in February and featuring Lee playing all the speaking parts: the narrator, the soldier, the Devil, even the ingenue.

Celebrating his fortieth anniversary as an actor, Lee moved smoothly from Stravinsky to a return engagement in Alicante with Jesús Franco. *Operación cocaína*, also known as *Dark Mission Flowers of Evil*, began its four-week schedule in March 1987 with a budget of $800,000. A cheapskate drug-smuggling thriller, it was sponsored by France's indefatigable exploitation merchants Eurociné, who had been behind Franco's first hit, *Gritos en la noche*, and had since collaborated with him on such mind-boggling curios as *The Bare-Breasted Countess*. Lee plays Luis Montana, in reality the fugitive Luis Morel, a former associate of Fidel Castro. With an unlikely backstory – born in Sheffield in 1933, he spent 20 years in Cuba as a left-wing activist – Montana is reunited with his Hispanic daughter Linda, who soon stumbles upon his secret.

Lee's naturalistic playing of their reunion dinner is complicated by Franco's insistence on overlaying the scene with perpetually barking dogs – also by his young co-star Cristina Higueras, who was apparently a delight to work with but whose English dialogue is frequently incomprehensible. Thereafter, Lee really earns his money during an explosive telephone call – 'Words, words, words!' he rails at his unseen interlocutor – which is overheard by the perplexed Linda. Swathed in a capacious robe at his poolside, Montana's neck scar confirms his true identity and the film ends in a welter of helicopter attacks and

With Christopher Mitchum and Cristina Higueras in the threadbare Eurociné thriller Operación cocaína *(1987)*

random explosions. French porn diva Brigitte Lahaie dies a heroic death in these gun battles and Lee is given an effective speech as Montana tries to explain himself to Linda. 'Your mother was murdered by American imperialists,' he rasps. 'They killed all the leaders of the revolution, all of them – Che Guevara, everybody – everybody except *me*.' Moments later, however, a grenade is thrown into his car and he's machine-gunned for good measure.

The film is lathered in rinky-dink Hispanic muzak (guilty composer: Louis Albarado) and features Chris Mitchum, son of the sleepy Robert, shambling through the action in a virtually catatonic state. While making *Operación cocaína*, Franco was approached by the French video mogul René Chateau to make a relatively big-budget horror picture called *Les prédateurs de la nuit*, and in so doing proved that he could still make a film with his old off-the-wall fervour. But *Operación cocaína* and Lee's next picture with him, *La Chute des aigles*, display none of it.

Things would improve in 1988, but not immediately. *Operación cocaína* is, perhaps mercifully, extremely hard to find; Lee's next film, *Olympus Force*, was sneaked out as a Japanese laserdisc. Directed by James Fortune and Robert Garofalo, the film's $4 million budget was provided by a young Greek shipping tycoon called John Draikis, who also played one of the leading roles. Production began in Athens on 25 January with Linda Thorson, Joss Ackland, Ronald Lacey and Richard Todd in the cast. In March, Lee and Page Three 'stunner' Linda Lusardi were added when further star-power was deemed necessary. Garofalo had been in touch with Lee before, regarding a project called *Waterloo 2* in which Lee was to have played Wellington alongside Ronnie Barker as an inept field surgeon.

A glimpse of the rough assembly of *Olympus Force*, which carries the subtitle *The Key*, is a truly excruciating experience. The moronic story involves Athene (Thorson) and Hermes (Draikis) descending from Olympus to avenge the desecration of Delphi by a gang of international terrorists. These crime-busting immortals get mixed up, as the film's lavish promotional brochure puts it, in 'outlandish adventures in hotel rooms, jacuzzis, music shops, Japanese restaurants and the ancient Olympic stadium' before hijacking 'a small gin palace of a boat owned by war veteran Filly (Christopher Lee) accompanied by his latest bathing beauty (Linda Lusardi).' Tracking the villains to a giant ocean liner, they summon Poseidon who obligingly blows the liner out of the water. End of picture. Lee is on blimpish form, complete with Panama hat, MCC tie and the swimsuited Lusardi stretched across his lap as he regales her with non-stop wartime reminiscences. 'Great comfort to me, my stories,' he sighs. 'All I have left these days.' Somebody obviously realised that the film was unreleasable (even in a 1980s straight-to-video market where almost anything went) and sensibly buried it. Everywhere except Japan, at any rate.

With bathing beauty Linda Lusardi in the unreleased – in fact, unreleasable – Olympus Force The Key *(1988)*

A more low-key Euro-production – Anglo-Dutch this time – was *Murder Story*, which began its five-week schedule in Amsterdam on 21 April 1988. Written and directed by Eddie Arno and Markus Innocenti, this tale of American teenagers tangling in Holland with a fiendish right-wing plot is an innocuous, even artless piece but has a great deal more going for it than similar projects like *Mask of Murder*. 'Bigger casting for the youngsters,' opined *Variety*, 'plus a more topical central mystery could have elevated this acceptable picture to must-see status.' Alexis Denisof, as Tony, and Stacia Burton, as Marty, may not qualify as big names but they're an engaging pair and carry the picture with some conviction. Even so, the film's opening 15 minutes are marked by total incoherence until Lee's stabilising influence is introduced.

Playing novelist Willard Hope (Amsterdam resident, so-called Master of the Macabre and author of 'Bloodbath'), he's first seen sitting glumly behind a pile of books at an almost deserted book-signing. Tracked down by Tony to a nearby diner, he responds with droll, elder statesman calm to Tony's youthful enthusiasm, claiming airily that 'It's a freer country than most' and offering desultory recommendations regarding the menu. ('The soup's good.') Lee is on wonderfully relaxed form here, so much so that he has neglected to remove the bangle from his wrist that he wears in 'real life'.

The boy is struggling to put together the plot of a Willard Hope-style bestseller from a random jigsaw of newspaper clippings, one of which sets the spring-and-autumn pair onto the trail that will result in Hope's death. 'He's taking me to a porn cinema,' Hope tells Marty in some astonishment, and, despite the fact that Amsterdam is bristling with demonstrators brandishing 'Weg met Porno' placards, the investigators proceed undaunted. Referring to 'a scene where I was filmed coming out of a porno shop,' Lee grumbled later that 'a photograph of my doing so appeared in the press without any acknowledgment that it was an exercise in fiction.'

Puffing nonchalantly on his pipe, Hope is then grilled by an American detective (Jeff Harding) and is sufficiently intrigued by the deepening mystery to visit the nearest Bibliotheek and get to grips with a microfiche. He's then cornered at home by the villains, however, and Tony later discovers his white-faced corpse slumped in a below-stairs cupboard. At this point, the film still has nearly 40 minutes to run and it's a shame that the casting director's imagination (and possibly the film's financial resources) ran out sufficiently to cast the uncharismatic American actor Bruce Boa as the main villain. And Arno and Innocenti make matters worse by zooming crudely

Novelist Willard Hope outside an Amsterdam porn shop in Arno and Innocenti's Murder Story *(1988)*

into a vast close-up of Boa's mouth during his didactic speeches regarding 'the New American way'. But the scenes of Lee as a heroic oldster trying to keep pace with Tony and Marty have an undeniable charm.

OLD FRANCE

In July 1988, Lee took the opportunity to extend his relationship with Harmony Gold, sponsors of *Shaka Zulu*, with another brief cameo in a marathon mini-series epic. Buzz Kulik's *Around the World in 80 Days* starred Pierce Brosnan as a prissy Phileas Fogg and Eric Idle as his Gallic manservant Passepartout, with Lee, Patrick Macnee and Simon Ward on hand to play whist with Fogg at the Reform Club. The location was actually the Travellers' Club in Pall Mall – of which, Lee noted, his maternal grandfather had once been the secretary – and Lee was required to place the crucial bet on which the globetrotting plot revolves. Lee responds to Fogg's conceited claims with a withering show of incredulity almost as intimidating as his luxuriant muttonchop whiskers. 'This engagement also gave me the opportunity to share a scene with an actress I have always considered superb,' Lee adds, 'the late and much lamented Lee Remick, who appeared as Sarah Bernhardt.'

After this, Lee made a belated return to his old role as the musketeers' one-eyed antagonist Rochefort. Dividing its time between Pinewood and Madrid's Estudios Roma and budgeted at $17 million, *The Return of the Musketeers* was an Anglo-French-Spanish co-production that took its cue from Dumas' novel *Twenty Years After*. 'It would have been unwise to make a sequel very soon after the original films,'

The withered Rochefort with his long-lost daughter Justine (Kim Cattrall) in The Return of the Musketeers *(1988)*

claimed director Dick Lester, 'but the thought of us all rendezvousing to examine our operation scars and to discuss our arthritis was too good to miss.'[14] There must be better reasons for making a film than this and, as it turned out, the picture was to have a tragic outcome. Like the earlier instalments, *Return* was shot around Toledo in the punishing heat of a Castillian summer, beginning on 22 August and wrapping on 15 October. Halfway through, however – on Wednesday 21 September – the tubby comic actor Roy Kinnear fell off his horse while traversing a Toledo bridge with the musketeers. The completed film was subsequently dedicated to his memory. 'Roy's death spread such a pall of misery,' Lee wrote, 'that it was surprising the film was ever finished and, in truth, the world would have lost nothing much if it hadn't been.'

Though a reasonably engaging entertainment, the film is hard to watch for scenes like the one in which Michael York's ageing d'Artagnan literally stumbles over his old manservant, Planchet, in the marketplace. Their entire exchange is played out with no view of Kinnear at all and with somebody else's voice on the soundtrack. There are also ill-advised lines like 'Planchet, get on your horse if you can.' Elsewhere, the picture features several interesting innovations, notably a trip to England with Alan Howard as a warty Cromwell, Bill Paterson as golf enthusiast Charles I and Billy Connolly as the royal caddy. Even Cyrano de Bergerac noses his way into the action at one point in the person of Jean-Pierre Cassel, who played Louis XIII in the earlier films. The creaky veterans are supplemented by upcoming talents like C Thomas Howell (Athos' son) and Kim Cattrall ('Rochefort's bastard' Justine), and the whole thing is ravishingly photographed by Bernard Lutic, cinematographer for the gossamer 'comédies et proverbes' of Eric Rohmer.

As for Rochefort, the former Captain Hook lookalike is now a straggle-haired shadow, emerging from 17 years of 'rotting in the Bastille' and trying to cope with his daughter's determination to avenge the death of her mother, Milady de Winter. 'What could I do?' he pleads. 'I was bleeding my life out in the church at Armentières when they took her.' When pressed about the identity of the kidnappers, he says gravely, 'Better you should never know. Believe me, my child' – and here Lee reverently touches his pierced heart – 'they are fatal men.'

A highly equivocal heroine, Justine is introduced to us in the process of committing an axe murder, and Rochefort is visibly shaken – indeed, shaking – when she cajoles him into executing the English King. Sailing back to France, Rochefort is conspicuously absent from a major shipboard skirmish (which made a welcome change for Lee after his exertions of 1973) but succeeds in stamping out a saboteur's fuse, unaware that the musketeers have artfully lit a separate one. 'It's all right, Justine,' he cries, 'I've put it out!' – whereupon the ship blows to smithereens. Though the elderly Rochefort is a much less forbidding figure than before – indeed, almost a pathetic one – the film's publicity manual nevertheless referred to Lee as 'the Poet Laureate of motion picture menace'.

While filming *The Return of the Musketeers*, Lee popped across to Madrid as a favour to Paul Maslansky. There he performed a brief cameo in Gene Quintano's romantic comedy-thriller, *Honeymoon Academy*, later released to video as *For Better or For Worse*. Robert Hays (from *Airplane!*) and Kim Cattrall (from *The Return of the Musketeers*) are an American couple honeymooning in Spain; one of them, unknown to the other, is a spy. Lee crops up 35 minutes in and is dead four minutes later. As a crumpled old counterfeiter who in gaol has had 'ample time to perfect my masterpiece,' he capers into view in a side street, decked out in beret, spectacles and a generous sprinkling of snow-white stubble. He shakes Cattrall's hand with a joke-shop buzzer in his palm and giggles inanely at his own jest. Moments later, he's shot down in the marketplace and dies in Hays' arms, the buzzer still buzzing even as he expires. Lee's skittish turn enlivens a leaden entertainment which in most other respects is nearly unwatchable.

After these Iberian adventures, Lee moved to France for a lavish bicentennial celebration of that country's establishment as a republic. Budgeted at $50 million, *La Révolution Française* was a French-Italian TV co-production, its first three-hour instalment, *Les années lumière*, directed by Robert Enrico and the second, *Les années terribles*, by US import Richard T Heffron. Work on the latter began on 16 January 1989 with a starry cast including Sam Neill, Claudia Cardinale, Peter Ustinov, Dominique Pinon and Massimo Girotti, plus Klaus-Maria Brandauer as Danton and Andrzej Seweryn as Robespierre. The casting of mini-series monarch Jane Seymour as Marie Antoinette caused patriotic outrage among indigenous stars like Isabelle Adjani, Catherine Deneuve and Isabelle Huppert; Seymour subsequently added insult to injury by persuading the producers to cast her two small children as well.

Having been one of the few aristocrats in *A Tale of Two Cities* who wasn't required to mount the scaffold, Lee now presided over it in his role as state 'exécuteur' Charles Henri Sanson, the so-called Monsieur de Paris, consultant to Dr Guillotin on the construction of his infernal machine and, oddly enough, a fervent monarchist. Unsurprisingly, Lee's services were required only for *Les années terribles* and he spent a fortnight in a disused airfield outside Paris, up to his elbows in mud and gore as he methodically decapitated virtually the entire dramatis personae. 'Nobody, Sarnya, can accuse you of

Danton's death: Monsieur de Paris appeases the mob in La Révolution Française: les années terribles *(1989), a mammoth TV movie also released to cinemas*

nepotism,' Lee told the series' octogenarian producer Alexandre Mnouchkine, a cousin by marriage whom Lee had known since before the war. 'After 42 years you offer me my first job with you.'

Whether Mnouchkine was aware of Lee's previous brushes with state executioners is unclear, however. Not only had Lee played Sanson before in a 1955 episode of *The Adventures of the Scarlet Pimpernel* – on both occasions, Lee determined to make him 'more aristo than the aristos ... by no means a butchering slob' – but he had also known England's long-serving hangman, Albert Pierrepoint. And before that, he had been dragged unwillingly, aged 17, to see the execution at Versailles of serial killer Eugen Weidmann, which turned out to be France's last public use of the guillotine. As for his own mock-decapitation of Jane Seymour 50 years later, he murmured an unscripted 'Courage, madame' to her as she ascended the scaffold – 'and Peter Ustinov (otherwise Mirabeau) said this added "a grace note to the whole scene."'

There are no grace notes to be found in Jesús Franco's *La Chute des aigles*, assuming one can find this extremely obscure film at all. Divided between Spain and France, its five-week schedule began on 2 May and provided Lee with a handy substitute for an aborted Italian project he had been expecting to make – Annalisa de Simone's *Il monastero*. *La Chute (Fall of the Eagles)* is a dreary WWII drama that offers no scope for Franco's improvisational stock-in-trade. Listless hack work, it's clogged with musical interludes that range from a saccharine score by Franco's regular collaborator, Daniel J White, to interminable production numbers lifted directly from *Cabaret*. The period flavour, such as it is, collapses completely where the female characters are concerned, all of whom sport spangly evening dresses and backcombed hair redolent of the 1980s rather than the 1940s. And the action set-pieces, notably a snowbound train ambush, are ineptly staged.

As in his previous Franco picture, Lee plays a troubled father, Walter Strauss, whose daughter Lilian (Alexandra Erlich) announces her intention to marry pianist Karl Holbach (Ramon Sheen). 'You've been in love 24 times,' Walter scoffs, whereupon she claims that they're more or less married anyway, having already made love. 'You have the effrontery to say that to me?' he bristles. She signs on for service on the Eastern Front and there's a vaguely touching moment as Walter turns up silently at the station to watch her train receding into the distance. 'I think she left to get away from me,' he confesses over a glass of schnapps to a friendly Jewish landlady, who is later carted off by the SS as Walter looks on helplessly. Lee appears suitably remote in his wire-rimmed spectacles and ever-present bow tie, but that's about as much as can be said in the film's favour.

BLACK SPOT

Lee plunged further into 1989 with one of the most astonishing characterisations of his career. Starting on 12 May with two weeks at Pinewood followed by another four in Jamaica, Fraser C Heston's *Treasure Island* remains arguably the definitive version of R L Stevenson's buccaneering yarn. Aimed at cable TV in the US but given a well-deserved theatrical release elsewhere, the film was made by the Turner Network in association with British Lion, which meant that Lee's old friend Peter Snell was in place as executive producer. And from their first collaboration, *Julius Caesar*, came Charlton Heston (Fraser's dad) as a hook-nosed Long John Silver. Heston was making a habit at this time of playing parts wildly unsuited to him in lavish TV movies – Thomas More, Sherlock Holmes – but, happily, the rascally Silver is not one of them.

'*Treasure Island* starts off with an intensity which sets the pace for the entire story,' asserted TNT's publicists, and that intensity was largely the responsibility of Oliver Reed as the ill-fated Billy Bones and Lee as his dread nemesis Blind Pew, who will stop at nothing to get hold of a coveted map in Bones' possession. Lee's scenes at the Admiral Benbow Inn marked a reunion not only with Reed but also with Christian Bale from *Mio, min Mio!*, here cast as the teenage hero Jim Hawkins, and, as Jim's mother, Isla Blair from *Dr Terror's House of Horrors* and *Taste the Blood of Dracula*.

Pew, we're told, lost his sight in the same shipboard skirmish that cost Silver his leg, and on his first nocturnal appearance he greets young Jim with a deceptively sweet-natured façade and a wheedling East End accent. 'Would some kind friend,' he wheezes, 'tell a poor blind man what's lost the sight of his eyes in the service of King George – Gawd bless 'im – in what part of the country he might now be?' This opening gambit is as long as Pew's dissimulation lasts, however. Draped in a filthy, hooded gaberdine and supported by a stick, he soon reveals himself as nothing less than a human embodiment of the Grim Reaper. 'He looked like Death,' Silver says of him later in the picture, and it comes as no surprise when Bones, having been handed the so-called Black Spot by Pew, very quickly drops dead. And Lee gives a truly awful deliberation to Pew's words as he effects the fateful hand-over. 'Yes,' he breathes contentedly. 'Now that's done. Oh ye-e-e-es...'

The role is entirely redefined by Lee's mere presence, and to bolster this transformation some delightful horror motifs are introduced. Pew is

ANOTHER HOMECOMING 1982-1989

Treasure Island (1989): scurvy old shipmates Billy Bones (Oliver Reed), Long John Silver (Charlton Heston) and the terrifying Blind Pew

heralded on both his appearances by the ominous tapping of his cane and is subject to a dramatic unmasking straight out of *The Phantom of the Opera*. When the grimy binding is whipped away from his face, we see a filmy right eye that could be the same appliance Lee wore in *The Curse of Frankenstein*. The rotted teeth are familiar from *I, Monster*. The livid mark of a fire brand running diagonally across his left eye could be an intermediate stage of his 'human torch' demise in *Scars of Dracula*. These reminiscences of Lee's horror roles were surely not accidental. Consciously invoked by Fraser Heston and his make-up team, they help to make the meeting of Bones and Pew something much more resonant than a reckoning between two avaricious old sea-dogs.

Lee's blind gropings when unmasked carry a further echo of *The Curse of Frankenstein*, specifically the Creature's pathetic flailing when shot in the eye. A rumbustious battle ensues as Pew's scurvy crew erupt into the inn, and Pew's shrieking face when he wrestles with mother and son in a window frame is the equal of anything in Lee's bona-fide horror pictures. (It's also reminiscent of similar attempts at defenestration in *Rasputin the Mad Monk* and *I, Monster*.) Nor does Lee neglect to add a final note of pathos, making it clear that this figure of Fate is himself pathetically vulnerable. 'How I wish I'd put his eyes out!' he screams as he emerges from the melée and Jim escapes his clutches. Then, as Dr Livesey's horsemen thunder inexorably towards him and his shipmates scatter in alarm, Pew surrenders briefly to babbling bewilderment – 'You won't leave old Pew, mates: not old Pew!' – before issuing a final ironic cry of 'Damn your eyes!' and disappearing in spectacular fashion under the pounding hooves of the oncoming horses.

Though Lee's presence is felt for less than ten of the film's 132 minutes, his performance was singled out by several reviewers. 'Christopher Lee,' commented the *Daily Mail*, 'surprisingly manages to out-act even Olly and, with noisy snarl, rotting teeth and missing eyes, provides a handy lesson for any would-be scene stealer.' And, according to *What's On in London*, Lee's 'all-too-brief performance ... alone makes the film worth seeing.' The best accolade of all came from the *Chicago Tribune*, which claimed that Lee's Blind Pew 'makes Freddy Krueger look like Santa Claus.' The comparison with the pizza-faced, razor-fingered protagonist of *A Nightmare on Elm Street* and its sequels was an apt one. Though only a dabbler in macabre roles by this time, Lee could still, in the space of a fleeting cameo, overshadow the most inescapable anti-hero of 1980s horror.

While the *Treasure Island* crew decamped to Jamaica, Lee spent the run-up to his 67th birthday at Leominster Priory, where on 25 and 26 May he provided the narration for a new recording of Prokofiev's *Peter and the Wolf* alongside the English String Orchestra and its conductor Sir Yehudi Menuhin. He was then off to South East Africa to make a horror picture for Blue Rock Films. Starting on 4 June and shot under the title *Panga*, the project was retitled *Witchcraft* for UK video and, absurdly, *Curse III: Blood Sacrifice* for the US, despite its having no connection whatever to any previous *Curse*. Once again, a perfectly respectable film had suffered, as Lee puts it, from the attentions of 'some genius dreaming up an idiotic alternative title.'

It was a particularly sad fate given the high hopes held for *Panga* by the local industry and the imported talents both before and behind the cameras. British director Sean Barton was a former editor who had cut pictures like *Return of the Jedi* and *Jagged Edge*, while female lead Jenilee Harrison had spent some three years playing Jamie Ewing in *Dallas*. Based on a story by Richard Haddon Haines, the film is fetchingly set in 1950, when Elizabeth Armstrong, the American wife of a wealthy cane farmer, inadvertently incurs the wrath of a local witchdoctor. An efficient and handsomely photographed shocker, it's only let down by the lumbering sea spirit cobbled together by Hollywood effects house Chris Walas Inc. At the end we're allowed far too close a look at it and it resembles the Creature from the Black Lagoon's overweight brother.

Claiming that 'I've seen things that can't possibly be explained by modern science,' Lee's bearded Dr Pearson is a Van Helsing figure outfitted in a floppy white suit and a tatty Panama hat. He has a bad case of asthma – 'If I overdo it,' he explains, 'I begin to sound like a rusty drainpipe' – and so, apparently, does the monster, whose homicidal forays are given to us in POV shots overlaid with the sound of laboured breathing. Pearson's red herring status is built up of further hints: he displays an unhealthy interest in a ceremonial witchdoctor's stick and is glimpsed visiting the witchdoctor himself at his hut. More sinister still, during the heroine's nocturnal travails in the cane fields we see him in a clearing making incantations with the aid of the ceremonial stick – a scene which, according to Lee, made the crew members uneasy for fear that something might genuinely be conjured up.

As the film enters its final phase, Elizabeth has been through a lot – she's found her husband hung up among the carcases in the cold store and their estate manager's head has fallen off before her very eyes. (This character is played by the imposing Henry Cele, *Shaka Zulu* himself.) She takes refuge at the home of her elderly friend Anthea Steel (Zoë Randall) and babbles on about how Pearson must be the killer. 'I've known Dr Pearson for 20 years,' Anthea scoffs. 'He's a compassionate man; anyone from these parts will tell you.' Pearson then turns up in person and is given an impressive monologue in which to exonerate himself.

With Elizabeth's rifle trained on him – and punctuated by spasms of darkness as a storm comes up and interferes with the electricity – Pearson explains that his interest in local superstition began when his own father fell foul of it. 'My mother found his severed head on the lawn,' he stammers. 'It was – moving. The cane rats had got it, you see. They were fighting for it – *inside* the skull.' Precisely controlled, Lee makes this speech an object lesson in his long-standing theory that leaving the horror to an audience's imagination is always more effective than showing it to them in detail, and the ridiculous sea spirit then comes along to prove it once and for all. We learn later that Pearson's incantations were performed over a sacrificial goat in an effort to allay the sea spirit's anger. Only once the film is over do we realise that, apart from this brief spot of goat sacrifice, Pearson doesn't really *do* anything. Even when a scream is heard from an upstairs bedroom and he utters the generic line 'It's in the house,' Pearson leaves it to the plucky Anthea to go up and blast the creature out of a second storey window. It's a nice role, however, and very nicely put over.

BACK TO HOLLYWOOD

The snowy stubble sported by Blind Pew had developed into a trimly tailored beard for Dr Pearson, and Lee retained the facial hair when arriving in Hollywood in July to start work on *Gremlins 2 The New Batch*. Production had begun on 26 May and, judging from the script, Lee had assumed that his role as mad scientist Dr Catheter would necessitate an unkempt Einstein look. Joe Dante, the 42-year-old director of such 1980s hits as *The Howling*, *Innerspace* and the original *Gremlins*, politely suggested Lee take a look at the streamlined laboratory set that had been built on Warners' Stage 16. Having done so, Lee realised that his usual smooth self was required and the beard was accordingly shaved off.

With Steven Spielberg among its executive producers, *Gremlins 2* is, like Spielberg's own *1941*, a latterday *Hellzapoppin'* stuffed with as many movie in-jokes per square inch as movie buff Dante could squeeze in. In this self-referential context, Lee has clearly been included as a living movie reference and plays up to his iconic status with relish. The action takes place in the colossal New York headquarters of media giant Daniel Clamp (an obvious dig at the real-life Donald Trump), which contains in its upper reaches a genetics lab called the Splice o' Life Inc. The lab-coated Catheter is lord of this domain, aided and abetted by a Tweedledum and Tweedledee pair called Martin and Lewis (itself a movie reference), played by tubby, carrot-topped twins Don and Dan Stanton.

Lee's Catheter is an effortlessly droll creation, offering a wicked parody of the generic mad scientist while simultaneously playing the character totally straight. 'Oh, Dr Catheter, this just came for you,' says a flunkey, whereupon Catheter's eyes light up in unholy glee – 'Oh, splendid! This must be my malaria!' – only for his smile to fade as he grumbles, 'Just rabies. I've *got* rabies...' Encountering Gizmo, one of the winsome Mogwai creatures featured in the first *Gremlins*, he recoils in distaste ('Cute, isn't it?') and is granted some very funny reaction shots as he watches it dancing to a pop record ('He *likes* this music?'). He then reflects on the possibility of investigating its 'body structure' and is filmed through the bars of its cage as he leers, 'And for that, my little friend, we'll just have to *cut* you...'

Some 30 minutes elapse before Catheter reappears, with Dante's manic set-pieces proliferating in the interim along with cameos from several other veterans of post-war horror and science fiction: Dick Miller, Kenneth Tobey, Al Lewis, John Astin. On his return, Catheter is seen toting an enormous pod familiar from *Invasion of the Body Snatchers* and tries

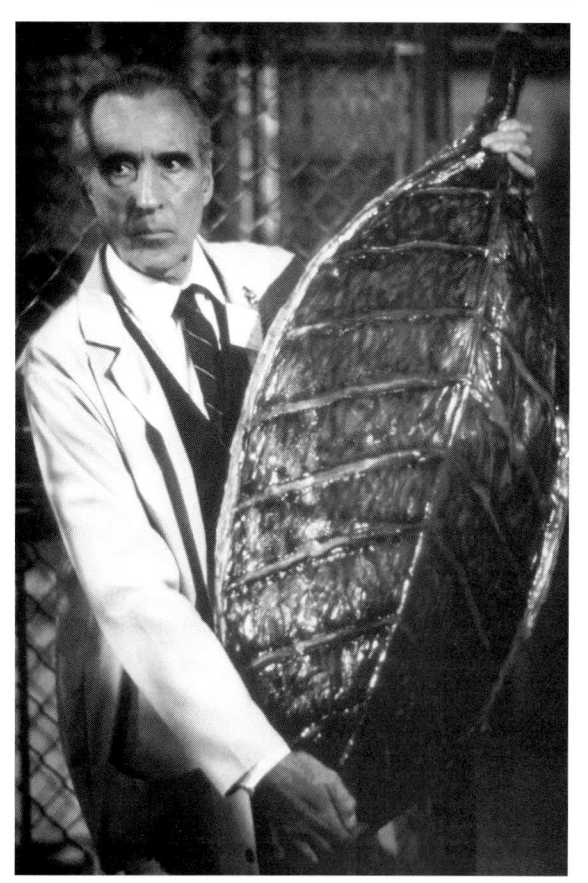

Dr Catheter with in-joke pod in Joe Dante's money-spinning Gremlins 2 The New Batch *(1989)*

to negotiate with one of Gizmo's less sweet-natured Mogwai brothers. Spookily underlit, he leans towards it and grins coaxingly, 'There's a good creature. Now, let's talk this over. I can get you diseases. You'd like that, wouldn't you?'

Spurning Catheter's advances, the furry creature metamorphoses into a hideous, scaly gargoyle with the velvet voice of Tony Randall. Like the prehistoric skeleton in *The Creeping Flesh*, the Mogwai are Jekyll and Hyde creatures that respond in disagreeable fashion to being doused in water, and soon Clamp Plaza is overrun by them. 'We can't let them get away,' Catheter bellows. 'All they have to do is to eat three or four children and there'd be the most appalling publicity!' As the chaos escalates, he's seen roaming the corridors, muttering 'The horror! The horror!', and he finally admits that 'There are some things that man was not meant to splice.' Here, the gremlins live up to their name by causing the film stock to corrode (for cinemagoers) and the TV to flip into alternative channels (for video viewers), and

In Austria with Ian Hogg, Yolanda Vasquez and Michael Brandon in the functional TV movie The Care of Time *(1989), broadcast over a year late thanks to Anglia's sensitivity regarding the impending Gulf War*

Catheter finally determines to break out the elephant guns. A gremlin is lurking inside the locker, however, and attaches itself to his hand; another, charged up with electricity, cooks Catheter in an electrical vortex and he pitches forward, presumably in death.

Though rather summarily written out of the film, Lee's stint in *Gremlins 2* gave him the chance to appear in the kind of high-profile Hollywood hit he'd been starved of throughout the 1980s. '*Gremlins 2* is a really funny film,' Lee enthused, 'but frightening too, and the special effects are marvellous – it becomes remarkably real. There were 75 animators working on the creatures alone.'[15] Elsewhere, he observed tersely that 'After some of the *people* I've worked with, acting with lumps of inanimate fur was quite a refreshing change.'[16]

As a pleasing side-effect to the success of *Gremlins 2*, Joe Dante became a faithful friend. 'I like actors anyway, and here's a guy I grew up watching,' he observed. Anticipating a po-faced Brit, he found instead that Lee 'was a riot. He was very funny. He's got hundreds of stories, which he will tell you at the drop of a hat. Sometimes they're too long to hear the end of before you have to do a take, so I went back into the mode I used on *The Howling* when John Carradine would tell me stories that were too long just before a take. I started doing the slates so I could hear half the story, then we'd do a take, and while I was waiting for the camera to get ready, I would hear the rest of the story before I did the slate.'[17] For his part, Lee was astonished to find that 'He knew all my films and was quoting stuff from 25 or 30 years back. "Do you remember this line from so-and-so?" And he was right every time.'[18]

Lee's remaining 1980s commitments took him to Austria and Italy. Directed by John Davies, *The Care of Time* was shot between July and September and budgeted at $3 million. A slick but run-of-the-mill Anglia TV movie, it was adapted by Alan Seymour from one of Lee's favourite authors, Eric Ambler, and wasn't broadcast until 26 August 1991. As Karlis Zander, a shady former Foreign Legionnaire turned international 'fixer', Lee was partnered by Michael Brandon, former star of *Dempsey and Makepeace*, and donated a number of snaps of himself as a boy and an Intelligence officer for a scene in which Zander's past is pieced together. The most memorable thing about this engagement for Lee was the fact that it was shot in Klagenfurt, where he had worked in Intelligence at the end of the war. 'I took the same route that I took all those years ago,' Lee says. 'It was uncanny. It made me feel very uneasy. I remembered what had happened around there and everything I'd seen. Thousands of men, women and children behind a high wire fence, dressed in the most bizarre way, in a kind of tattered uniform. I was told they were White Russians who'd fought with the Germans and Serbians who were anti-Tito. And the world knows what happened to them.'

For his final engagement in 1989, Lee went to Rome in November to co-star alongside Alberto Sordi, Laura Antonelli and Lucia Bosé in *L'avaro*, an extremely loose adaptation of Molière's 17th century comedy *L'Avare* (*The Miser*). The veteran comic Sordi had already appeared with Antonelli in an adaptation of *Le Malade imaginaire* (retitled *Il malato immaginario*), and *L'avaro* was intended as a follow-up. Lee was cast as a mercenary Cardinal, not included in Molière's original, who earmarks his literally poisonous sister for marriage to Sordi's paranoid penny-pincher, Arpagon. Once Lee had done his bit, the film's 14-week schedule dragged on until February 1990, taking in Madrid as well as Rome.

The engagement was not one of Lee's happiest, for he quickly discovered that the film's director, Tonino Cervi, was a puppet of the star, Sordi. At the Palazzo Farnese, Lee was driven to distraction by Cervi's typically noisy Italian crew – also by Sordi's habit of murmuring all his fellow actors' lines under his breath – and succumbed to an uncharacteristic loss of temper. These distractions also caused him to forget his lines during a particularly convoluted monologue, an experience unique to an actor who claims 'to have a mind in which lines stick, so that sometimes if I wake in the night I hear them again from long-ago, half-forgotten films.' Nevertheless, the finished picture is a ravishing entertainment, offering a richly coloured snapshot of 17th century Europe through its gorgeous cinematography, costumes and set design, while Lee is very funny indeed in a scene in which the Cardinal dons a blond spaniel wig and pays an incognito visit to Antonelli's bordello.

Lee's far-sighted decision to establish himself as a 'Euro-actor' back in the 1960s was standing him in good stead some three decades on. This was just as well given the pitiful pass to which British films had sunk by 1990, with production reaching a rock-bottom level unmatched since 1924. 'One of the great tragedies of the British film industry,' Lee claimed while preparing to make *L'avaro*, 'is that for so many years they have concentrated exclusively on the domestic picture for the domestic market. That is one of the major reasons why our industry barely exists. There is nothing wrong with making a picture that represents the British way of life, but it has got to be commercial ... Even now I am absolutely stunned by some of the films we are still making in this country. The moment you know who is in them, the story and who is directing, you know it's not going to work. It's absolutely fatal.'[19] Lee had been issuing dire warnings of this kind for over 20 years and, as a result, was able to face the 1990s with a great deal more confidence than Britain's navel-gazing film producers.

As Cardinal Spinosi in Tonino Cervi's Molière adaptation/ Alberto Sordi vehicle, L'avaro *(1989)*

PART TEN

NEW HORIZONS
1990–1999

At the turn of the 1990s, Lee was well past retirement age but his workaholic tendencies made the notion of resting on his laurels a non-starter. 'Oh no, what for?' he exclaimed. 'I can't spend the rest of my life – I don't know if that's five minutes or five years – playing golf or travelling. Very nice, but after a while I'd get bored. I wonder what people do when they retire at 65 or less; what do they do with their lives?'[1]

Lee's first role in the new decade was in a $5 million phantasmagoria called *The Rainbow Thief*, which began at Shepperton on 26 February. The producer was Vincent Winter (who, as a child actor, had received billing, unlike Lee, in *The Dark Avenger*) and the director was Alejandro Jodorowsky, maker of cult classics like *El Topo* and *Santa Sangre*. The script was written by Mexico's Berta Dominguez D (who also appears in the film) and had reportedly been around for over a decade, with Pablo Picasso at one time earmarked to design it and Salvador Dalí to play the lead.

Lee's role as 80-year-old millionaire Rudolf van Tanner was more congenial than the parts played by Peter O'Toole and Omar Sharif. While Lee spent most of his time liberally festooned with bare-bottomed centrefolds, Sharif and O'Toole struggled through 150,000 gallons of sewer water (at least one of which Sharif claimed to have swallowed during rehearsals) before moving to Gdansk in the first week of April. The bizarre result was denied a theatrical release but turned up on video in the US. The film's relative invisibility is a shame, for Lee dominates its opening reel with an engagingly crazed comic performance.

As O'Toole's aristocratic Uncle Rudolf – immaculate in tails, jodhpurs and pince-nez – Lee is seen pouring champagne for his numerous Dalmatians in what is quite obviously the Shepperton conservatory. Mounting a Dalmatian-spotted dodgem car, Rudolf cues up 'The Ride of the Valkyries' on a gaily coloured Wurlitzer juke box and scoots happily around while clashing a pair of cymbals together in time to the music. 'I hope you all like bones!' he says to a swarm of grasping relatives (the sour-faced Sheila Keith among them). 'The caviar, of course, goes to the dogs; spoiled, aren't they?' His guests have barely had time to toy with their beef bones when he drives them out with a clash of cymbals and a demented cry of 'My God, what I want is some real live flesh!' Madame Rainbow's girls are accordingly drafted in, eight lovelies in skimpy, rainbow-coloured lingerie who totter about to a funky Latin number before leading the ecstatic Rudolf to bed. Clad now in nightshirt and bed socks, he croons 'Plaisir d'amour' to them before expiring from their incessant tickling.

Jump-started by Madame Rainbow herself (played by Britain's homegrown porn diva, Linzi Drew), he expires a second time before being jump-started with electricity by a group of paramedics. Having uttered one last operatic phrase he lapses into a coma, leaving Sharif and O'Toole to play out the rest of the picture as a rather wearing amalgamation of *The Elephant Man*, *The Phantom of the Opera* and several others. Lee's performance is brilliantly zany, with an insane gleam that makes the remainder, for all Jodorowsky's directorial flourishes, appear dull. Reporting from the Venice Film Festival on 8 September, *Variety* complained that the film was uncharacteristically whimsical and found both Sharif and O'Toole underwhelming. 'Lee is more successful in his brief appearance as the uncle,' the reviewer added, 'and his character is closer to the usual inhabitant of a Jodorowsky film.'

Another cameo followed, but a considerably less rewarding one. Budgeted at $15 million, Gordon Hessler's *Shogun Mayeda* (US title: *Journey of Honor*) began on 20 April in Japan and moved to Dubrovnik three weeks later. There, Lee joined up to play Philip IV of Spain, receiving a Samurai deputation in quest

As Quaid-e-Azam, Mohammed Ali Jinnah, with cast of thousands in the controversial Jinnah (1997). 'The role of a lifetime,' commented Kevin Thomas in the Los Angeles Times. 'Lee is tremendously moving in his ability to illuminate the inner life of a man of unflinching dignity.'

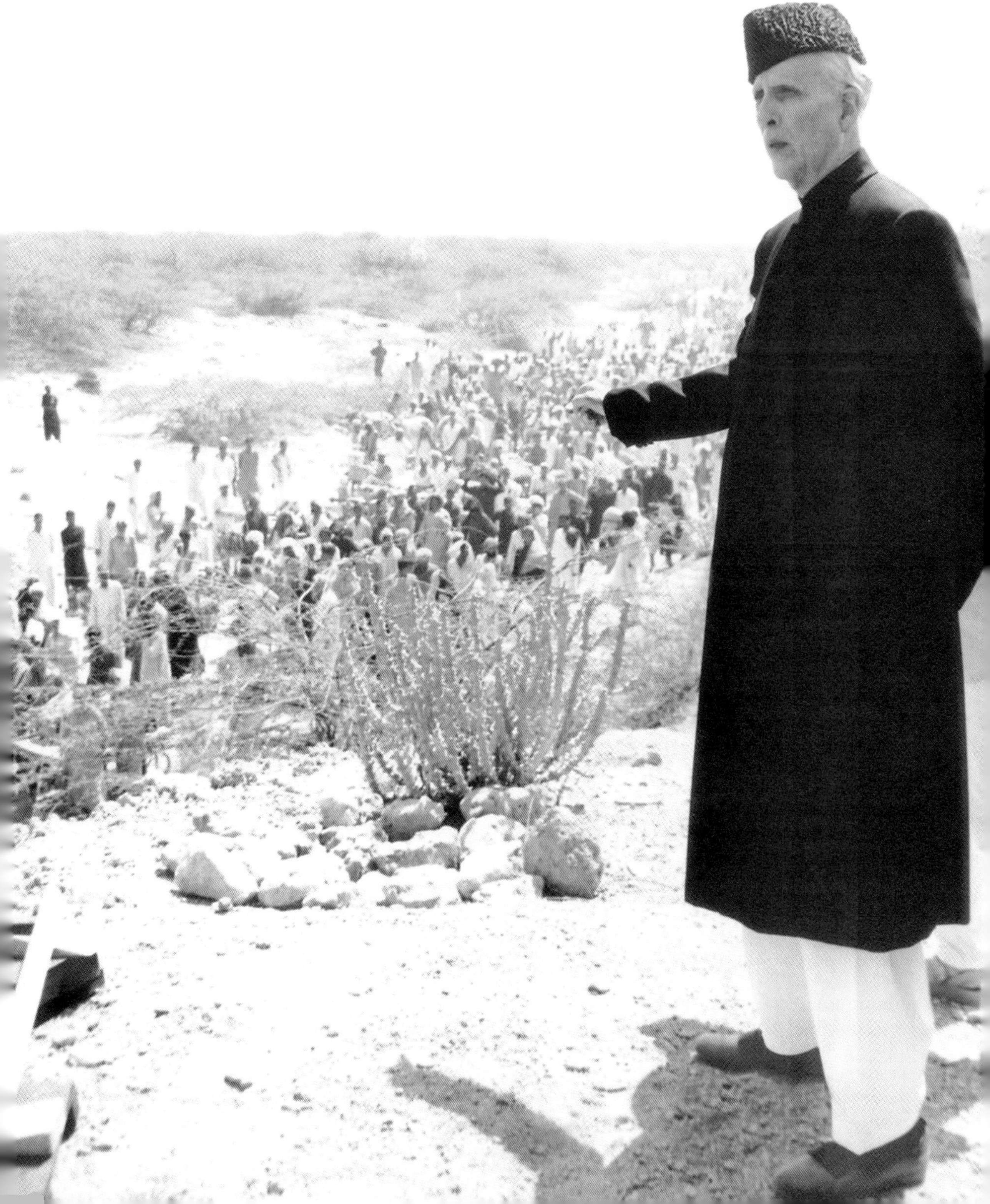

Cueing up 'The Ride of the Valkyries' as the completely crazed Uncle Rudolf in The Rainbow Thief *(1990)*

of flintlocks in the Cadiz of 1602. Saddled with an unbecoming grey bob, Lee's King is saved from death when Mayeda (Sho Kosugi) literally grabs the assassin's arrow in flight, and then watches a lengthy combat between Mayeda and the hot-headed Don Pedro (David Essex). And that's about it. Hessler had previously worked with ninja superstar Kosugi on two 1980s hits, *Pray for Death* and *Rage of Honor*, but was less happy with their third collaboration. For Hessler's non-Japanese guest stars, the film was an unhappy experience all round, particularly for David Essex, who nearly lost an eye during one of the film's more dangerous moments.

RETIREMENT HOLMES

Later in 1990, the mercurial Harry Alan Towers reappeared on Lee's horizon for the first time in 21 years. 'I'm about to start work on a major television project,' he announced, 'a mini-series called *The Golden Years of Sherlock Holmes*. It's going to be eight one-hour adventures set in the days when Holmes is a worldwide celebrity and can't go anywhere without meeting equally famous people who welcome him as a friend. Against wonderfully exotic backgrounds he does the good old Sherlock Holmes stuff and solves mysteries ... Incidentally,' he added, 'Holmes will be Christopher Lee and Watson is Patrick Macnee, both slightly in their dotage I guess. I do believe in having the protean character actors in my movies. There aren't so many around unfortunately. There are no new Christopher Lees or Peter Cushings. Their number is dwindling every day. It's very sad, but time marches on.' [2]

The 'eight one-hour adventures' idea was soon supplanted by two movies for cable TV running an exhausting three hours apiece and sponsored by Harmony Gold. *Sherlock Holmes and the Leading Lady* began in Luxembourg on 27 August – prophetically, Lee remarked to Grand Duke Jean that filmmaking could become big business there – and wound up on 20 October. Lee then had a mere two days back in London to receive the relevant jabs before starting *Incident at Victoria Falls* in Zimbabwe.

Peter Sasdy, the prickly Hungarian director of *Taste the Blood of Dracula* and *Nothing But the Night*, was engaged to take charge of the first while Bill Corcoran directed the second. With a rather sketchy approach to period detail, some dodgy supporting actors and lazy, labyrinthine plots, the films are no more successful than *Sherlock Holmes und das Halsband des Todes* in providing Lee's Holmes with a worthwhile framework. There remains a great deal of charm, however, in the crusty interplay between Holmes and Watson 'in their dotage'. Macnee was cast only after Towers' original choices for Watson, Nigel Stock and Gordon Jackson, had died, but the fact that he and his co-star had been at school together gives an added 'second childhood' zest to their scenes together.

As a result, Lee stumbled across a 'corpsing' problem previously encountered only with Ferdy

Mayne, Reg Park and Hammer veteran Michael Ripper. 'Patrick, who is one of my oldest friends, possesses a quality which convulses me,' he noted. 'It's quite unintentional on his part and I'm afraid I've behaved on occasion quite disgracefully, but he plays it so wonderfully well – this blank disbelief that crosses his face when Holmes comes up with an outrageous suggestion.'[3] Interviewed in the same magazine, Macnee made light of the problem. 'I wouldn't say that at all. We're two highly professional people; he's one of the best actors living and we just did it ... I had four horrifying months on it as it was, and two of them in Africa and rising 70 years old. It's enough for me. But if anyone asks me to do any more, and if Chris wants to do them, of course I would.'[4]

In both pictures Lee presents Holmes as an outwardly frosty but inwardly rather fruity old man, with a discreet wave in his blue-grey hair and an impressive pair of sideburns at odds with the ascetic look favoured by most Holmes interpreters. (What he doesn't have, happily, is the enlarged nose perfected for *Sherlock Holmes und das Halsband des Todes*.) *Sherlock Holmes and the Leading Lady* concerns a hijacked explosive device in the volatile Vienna of 1910 and reacquaints Holmes with his female nemesis Irene Adler (played by the improbably youthful soap opera queen Morgan Fairchild). In some severely misjudged romantic scenes, Lee and Fairchild seem to be acting in separate films – though Holmes' response to Irene's offer of marriage, virtually choking on his champagne in misogynist alarm, remains a delightfully funny moment.

Leadenly directed by Sasdy, *Leading Lady* is grimly amateurish in most departments, but is redeemed by the epic sweep of Corcoran's *Incident at Victoria Falls*, which sets Holmes on the trail of the stolen Star of Africa in Capetown. Despite having roasted in African temperatures of over 100° Fahrenheit during the shoot, Lee appears to be enjoying himself hugely here. Treating the script as if it were a comedy of manners by Pinero, he succeeds in making the master sleuth a gently absurd figure without in any way diminishing his intellectual glamour. In one extraordinary sequence, Holmes and Theodore Roosevelt are seen sitting nonchalantly on the pointed nose of a moving steam locomotive, both Lee and Claude Akins clearly having disdained doubles for the scene. The films are enhanced by other good-value guest stars like John Bennett as Sigmund Freud, Jenny Seagrove as Lillie Langtry, Joss Ackland as Edward VII and Richard Todd as Lord Roberts.

Lee's chief engagements in 1991 took him to Germany, Wales, Italy and finally Czechoslovakia. *Wahre Wunder* was an unusual assignment, a multi-part 'people show' made in a week in Munich for satellite TV. Lee was on hand as the German-speaking host, introducing ordinary German citizens who had experienced 'real-life wonders' but leaving the complex business of interviewing them to TV personality Sabrina Fox. A more conventional project, Robert Knights' *Double Vision* started on 15 September and was one of four Mary Higgins Clark adaptations cooked up by France's Canal Plus and Steve Walsh Productions of Cardiff. It was budgeted at £1.65 million, filmed in London and at the Egerton Grey Hotel near Cardiff Airport, and got no further than US video. Lee's friend from *The Return of the Musketeers*, Kim Cattrall, plays a dual role as twins Caroline and Lisa, one a repressed scientist in Massachusetts, the other a louche wannabe actress in London. Deputising for Jean-Pierre Cassel, Lee is Lisa's sugar daddy Mr Bernard, whose extremely accommodating French wife (Macha Méril) explains that 'My husband has a weakness for young girls; I arranged for him to meet Lisa.'

In his well-spaced scenes, Lee goes through most of the familiar 'old man with young mistress' situations, coping with Lisa's embarrassing eruption

Retirement, Holmes? With Patrick Macnee's Dr Watson in Sherlock Holmes and the Leading Lady *(1990)*

into a christening party and later complaining feebly that 'You're asking me to burn every bridge, and I'm not a young man.' Lisa strips down for his benefit to a fairly astonishing set of PVC underclothes and is subsequently murdered in her benefactor's boathouse. Inexplicably unaware of this, he shares a highly charged final scene with Caroline, whom he takes to be Lisa, and is touchingly shattered when he realises his mistake. As well as being disfigured by some truly horrific soft-rock songs as incidental music, the film is stuffed with imagery relating to twins, premonitions and drowning, all of it garbled and unconvincing, and in this climactic scene Lee's country house decorations include a giant reproduction of Seurat's watery masterpiece 'The Bathers'. Whether the filmmakers were aware that Lee had played Seurat himself some 40 years earlier is unclear.

Jackpot was a much more ambitious undertaking. Touted as Italy's most expensive film (reports of its budget waver between $14 million and $20 million), it started production on 10 October at the Villa Balbianello on Lake Como before transferring to Cinecittà. Reminiscent of an old Hammer picture called *The Damned* and a more recent Disney one called *Tron*, the story concerns a group of isolated pre-teenage geniuses who experiment with virtual reality while perfecting an anti-ageing cream. Filming was complicated by the fact that neither the director, Mario Orfini, nor the leading man, Adriano Celentano, nor the leading child actor, Totò Cascio from *Cinema Paradiso*, could speak English, though the film did give Lee the opportunity to work with former *Baby Doll* Carroll Baker, playing the ageing beauty who sponsors the children's research.

'She's got a wonderful sense of humour,' Lee pointed out, 'and, believe me, she needed it, because we all had to work very hard ... The movie is in English, so Adriano spoke it phonetically as we shot. We had to get it right each time, as much as possible, so that when Adriano got it right, Carroll and I wouldn't have made a mistake at our end.'[5] The result must be the only film in history that includes a slavering camera-crawl up the scantily clad body of an 80-year-old, though the body is that of a beauty queen and only the face is octogenarian. Uncertain in tone throughout, *Jackpot* comes across like a computer-literate product of the Children's Film Foundation, with virtual reality sequences that already seemed dated in 1991 and a similarly old-fashioned Giorgio Moroder score.

Lee is Cedric, faithful butler to the Baker matriarch who introduces the children to Celentano's simple-minded gardener, Furio. In full white-gloved Jeeves mode, Lee has several drily humorous moments, as when Baker recoils from a sudden blast of sunlight, moaning 'It kills! It kills!', and he mutters sardonically, 'So, on occasion, do butlers.' He also goes jogging with Celentano and Bryony Martin's prodigiously gifted Violet, and gives a knitting lesson to Kate Vernon (the rejuvenated version of Baker) in which his bristling black eyebrows seem to take on an independent, caterpillar-like life. Humanised by the home-spun philosophy of the 'holy fool' Furio, the junior boffins join him, Pied Piper-style, in a life-affirming dance as the credits roll. It's a maudlin end to a misconceived movie.

During the *Jackpot* schedule, Lee took a snow-covered ten-day break to film the *Austria March 1917* episode of *The Young Indiana Jones Chronicles* at a mock-up castle outside Prague. The director was the former stuntman Vic Armstrong and Lee was cast as Austria's slippery Foreign Minister, Ottokar, Graf Czernin. Mastermind of the series was *Star Wars* creator George Lucas, establishing a

As Cedric the butler with Totò Cascio, one of numerous child prodigies in Mario Orfini's Jackpot (Classe speciale), *aka* Cybereden *(1991)*

connection that would bear spectacular fruit for Lee some nine years later.

1992 was an unusually restful year. Lee lent his voice to David Thwaytes' animated version of *The Beauty and the Beast*, hosted *Kino '92 Extra* from the Cannes and Berlin Film Festivals for German TV and, having turned 70, went to Zagreb's Jadran Film Studios in August for an Alistair Maclean adaptation called *Death Train*. A co-production between Yorkshire International Films and Jadran Film with further input from British Lion, the picture was written and directed by David S Jackson and produced, like Lee's previous Maclean subject, *Bear Island*, by his old friend Peter Snell. A functional thriller with Pierce Brosnan and Patrick Stewart heading the cast, it appears to have got no further than TV movie status despite bearing the legend 'Dolby Stereo in selected theatres' on its closing credits.

Lee is renegade Russian general Konstantin Benin, who holds the West to nuclear ransom in the belief that 'The Soviet Union's rebirth starts here.' Lee speaks in orotund Russian almost throughout (subtitles thoughtfully provided) and wears medals from his own extensive collection of military insignia. More importantly, he makes Benin a rather sad and fatalistic old soldier rather than the raving maniac he could have been. Benin has good reason for being fatalistic. Referring to the nuclear blunder that set the plot in motion, he explains that 'The accident in [the] lab has irradiated me too,' and urges a subordinate to 'maintain silence and imagine your shining future' with a touching awareness that they won't have one. Leaving his isolated bunker, he's called a 'Commie sack of shit' by Ted Levine and is finally gunned down in an aeroplane by *Baywatch* beauty Alexandra Paul. As he expires, his hand crawls up to activate the bomb anyhow.

THE LAST DINOSAUR

In 1993, Lee was the proud recipient of the Dilys Powell Award for Lifetime Achievement from the London Film Critics' Circle. His films that year were rather less prestigious, however. *Funny Man* was the brainchild of writer/director Simon Sprackling and began on 19 July at a disused mental hospital in Henley-on-Thames, with the film's 71-year-old guest star completing his scenes at the very beginning of the five-week schedule. 'That helped,' Sprackling admitted, 'because at first we thought we were out for a light ale, and when he turned up we realised we were making a movie.'[6] Though worried by the numerous swear words in Sprackling's script, Lee felt that it was highly original and also welcomed the opportunity to support young British filmmakers.

As renegade Russian general, Konstantin Benin, in another Alistair Maclean adaptation, Death Train *(1992)*

'The crew is certainly the youngest I have ever worked with,' he remarked. 'Certainly the most enthusiastic and dedicated.'[7]

In the film's pre-credits poker game, Lee's Callum Chance loses his ancestral home to an odious record producer called Max Taylor (Benny Young) and is described by him as 'the weirdo in a white suit [with] a cute line in theatrics.' 'You're a funny man, Mr Taylor,' Chance replies, 'but I've met funnier. And so will you...' In the remainder of the film, which is awash with lager-lout surrealism and a hit-or-miss stream of vulgar vaudeville routines, Chance is heard reciting bits of Lewis Carroll's *The Walrus and the Carpenter* as well as winking roguishly from behind a house of cards in what appears to be a white-walled lunatic asylum – or is he possibly God in Heaven? Taylor and his retinue are being messily picked off, meanwhile, by a repulsive, wisecracking combination of Harlequin, Freddie Krueger and Mr Punch (Tim James). Finally, Lee contributes to the film's nursery singalong over the closing credits, his rumbling vocal introduced by the Funny Man with the words, 'Come on, Guvnor – lend a hand!'

Though an acquired taste, the uniquely British vulgarity of *Funny Man* is infinitely more inventive than the hackneyed, and uniquely American, inanity of Lee's next picture. Alan Metter's *Police Academy: Mission to Moscow* started on 13 September and was shot in Moscow and St Petersburg. The seventh and,

With George Gaynes in post-Glasnost Russia for the Paul Maslansky production Police Academy: Mission to Moscow *(1993)*

to date, last feature in Paul Maslansky's money-spinning *Police Academy* franchise, it transplants the series' brainless police recruits to post-Glasnost Russia and features Lee as the elderly Commandant Rakov, decorated with a bristling walrus moustache and at least ten times as many medals as *Death Train*'s General Benin. Head of the welcoming committee at the airport, Rakov goes through an absurd routine of ceremonial kissing with his US opposite number (George Gaynes), gets to grips with a computer game ('I have to get to the next level,' he complains) and finally presides over a massed meeting of genuine militia men in Red Square, announcing from the podium that 'Americans and Russians are brothers!' Despite this praiseworthy sentiment, and the radically changed political climate in Russia itself, cast and crew nevertheless had to lie low for four days while hard-line Communists attempted a takeover and Moscow's White House was shelled by tanks.

On 25 October, Vincent Price died in Los Angeles, aged 82. 'The world has lost a great actor and I have lost a wonderful friend,' Lee commented sadly, adding that 'During the years that my wife and I lived in Los Angeles, we were able to see a good deal of Vincent and his wife, Coral Browne, and it was one of the joys of our time there.'[8] As the cinema's roster of Gothic icons began to dwindle, contemporary filmmakers were falling over themselves to produce souped-up versions of the old Gothic classics to titillate the jaded palates of 1990s cinemagoers, and Lee soon grew tired of being asked about them. One journalist even quoted the warning that had been faxed to him by Lee's management prior to their interview: 'Try not to ask him to compare his British horror classics with today's big-budget Hollywood films as this pisses him off,'[9] it read. Lee did formulate a pithy means of evading the subject, however. 'Somebody asked me the other day what the difference was between the first Dracula picture I did and Coppola's. Or between the first Frankenstein film I did and Branagh's. And I said, "Oh, about $40 million."'[10]

The sum spent on Lee's next picture was a very straitened £500,000. The fledgling director/producer team of Justin Hardy and Yoshi Nishio had raced to set up a film project in order to qualify for the government's Business Expansion Scheme (deadline: 31 December 1993) and conceived a story set in a prep school. A direct appeal to young stockbrokers on the floor of the Stock Exchange, together with a large investment from a German yacht builder, produced the desired budget and then, as Nishio put it, 'Justin and I sat down to work out who would be the scariest schoolteacher ever. It had to be Lee.'[11] For his part, Lee was reminded of his experience over 20 years earlier, when he had appeared in *The Wicker Man* for Hardy's father Robin and had taken no fee. For *A Feast at*

Midnight, as the new film was called, Lee generously allowed history to repeat itself. The film's five-week schedule accordingly began at Hawtreys, a public school near Durley in Wiltshire, at the end of March.

Having supported one group of young British filmmakers on a project aimed squarely at the 'pizza and a six-pack' crowd, Lee was now supporting a group working on an altogether more genteel subject. The scenario cooked up by Hardy and Nishio focused on unloved Magnus Gove (Freddie Findlay), who arrives at the forbidding Dryden Park and rebels against the fashionably healthy diet imposed by the avuncular principal. Utilising the sophisticated gourmet techniques instilled in him by his father, he sets up a clandestine feasting society. Lee was cast as Dryden Park's fearsome Latin master, Major Victor E Longfellow, his initials earning him the sobriquet 'Velociraptor' among his pupils. Apprised of his nickname, the Raptor dismisses its source – Steven Spielberg's dinosaur smash *Jurassic Park* – as 'Ghastly Hollywood rot.'

Just as Magnus was introduced with a close-up of his Converse sneakers stepping from a taxi, so the Raptor is first encountered, at night, as a pair of shimmering brown Oxfords alighting from his private car. Lee accompanies this entrance with a pronounced throat-clearing – just the kind of idiosyncratic tic with which teachers habitually identify themselves – and then is given a classic horror build-up as his feet mount the stairs and a huge shadow looms outside the dormitory in which 3A are quaking in their beds. Lee based his characterisation on Geoffrey Bolton, his Classics master at Summer Fields whose erratic temper had been brought on by shellshock in the Great War. 'Schoolmasters all have their acts,' Lee observed. 'They use them to keep discipline ... I think a lot of these men were really very kind underneath: vulnerable, just like my character in the film. Few were real sadists ... I can sympathise with the Raptor,' he added. 'If you're dealing with Classics, you're dealing with the rhythms of meticulous languages. When he goes into a rage it is partly to get results, but partly real hurt, because some wretched boy puts wrong words into the mouth of Cicero.'[12]

Lee makes a delightful show of lordly disdain as he tosses the boys' exercise books back at them ('This is the most appalling Thursday test it has ever been my misfortune to mark') and is very funny indeed when foraging in his washing basket and fishing out a dinky pair of striped briefs. 'Charlotte,' he gasps as his gawky daughter (Lisa Faulkner) cringes in embarrassment, 'what could possibly have possessed you to believe that these are *mine*?' A widower, he flirts with the roly-poly matron, Miss Plunder (Carol Macready), in a stream of unwitting double entendres better suited to one of the smuttier Carry On films. Though it was a shame that Hattie Jacques was no longer around to provide an echo of their flirtatious

The fearsome Major Longfellow quizzes tiny Magnus Gove (Freddie Findlay) in A Feast at Midnight *(1994)*

scenes from *Trottie True*, it was the note of redemption provided by the Raptor's romance with Miss Plunder that clinched Lee's interest in the part.

The Raptor stands on his dignity at all times and is all the funnier for it, especially when Lee abandons his own, appearing in a track suit and cloth cap for a cross-country run in the Savernake Forest or striding up to the crease only for a cricket ball to hit him in the groin. He is also the centrepiece of an elaborate *Jurassic Park* pastiche when he patrols a darkened kitchen in which the Scoffers are hiding – a sequence given an agreeably unearthly quality by Hardy – and, when his speccy daughter lets down her hair and becomes a rebellious beauty in a slinky black dress, Lee makes the Raptor's stammering attempts at establishing a dialogue with her genuinely touching. He also has an intriguing exchange with Robert Hardy's impish Headmaster. 'Empires were not built on rabbit food,' the Raptor harrumphs as he surveys the platefuls of Frusli bars in the staff room, to which the Head gently replies, 'We don't *have* an Empire anymore.' The film is a straightforward, and sometimes cloying, entertainment, but, for those in search of a subtext, maybe this is it. Lee is charmingly portrayed throughout as a dinosaur, an aristocratic relic of a lost world struggling in vain to acclimatise himself to a new one. Perhaps, then, the 'Empire' referred to is the thoroughly extinct British Film Industry.

Unhappily, the film was savaged by critics on its fleeting West End release as an over-priced matinée attraction in May 1995. Hardy was unrepentant, noting the film's cult success in the USA and insisting that 'If you can't sympathise with rich and privileged children, that's your problem.'[13] That Lee could sympathise with privileged children had been made clear when Stuart Hawley, playing the school bully Bathurst, became distressed while shooting a scene in which the other boys pelt him with food. 'What was very sweet was that it was Christopher who took the little boy away when he started to cry,' Hardy recalled, 'and explained to him that for 230-odd films Christopher had had stakes rammed into his heart and had had, basically, people hurling food at him, and how that, ultimately, is the role the baddie has to play.' At the film's wrap party, Lee urged his small co-stars on no account to become actors and, having heard that Hawley wanted to join the SAS, presented him with his own SAS tie from the Second World War. 'And this little boy just burst into tears,' said Hardy, 'and we all burst into tears. It was such an extraordinary gift.'[14]

Shortly after completing *A Feast at Midnight*, Lee went to Canterbury's tiny Talking Shop studio on 17 May 1994 to record the narration for an American documentary entitled *Flesh and Blood The Hammer Heritage of Horror*. Lee's fellow narrator was Peter Cushing, a week away from his 81st birthday just as Lee was a week away from his 72nd. Though extremely frail, Cushing was buoyed by Lee's hale and hearty presence and delighted with his gift of a Sylvester the Cat hand-puppet. The voice-over session lasted some two hours, after which the studio was cleared while Lee screened videos of old Warner Bros and Tom & Jerry cartoons for Cushing. Watching the pair doubled over with laughter, the documentary's director, Ted Newsom, was aware that he had organised 'the one last teaming of the neatest couple of villains the screen has given us.'

'Christopher Lee put on an incredible act that day,' he added, 'one of the most impressive and poignant performances I've ever seen. Like most great performances, there was emotional truth at the core. His fondness and joy at being with a friend wasn't acting. The acting came in what he did *not* reveal to the small audience at Talking Shop, at least while Cushing was around. After Joyce Broughton [Cushing's long-serving secretary] drove the old gentleman off, Lee's sardonic witticisms, laughter and bonhomie transformed into dark impatience. A telephone interview he did with a BBC reporter was abrupt and cool. On the drive back to London, he spoke about his war years, collectors, the weather, anything but the events of earlier in the day. He didn't dare reveal what he was truly feeling while Cushing was there. He had known the man for nearly 40 years. And he knew, as did we all, that they would never see each other again.'[15]

So it proved. The documentary was shown by the BBC in two parts, on 6 and 13 August. Cushing died at the Pilgrim's Hospice in Canterbury on Thursday the 11th. On 12 January 1995, Lee went to St Paul's Church in Covent Garden to read one of the lessons at Cushing's memorial service, and soon afterwards enlarged on his feelings regarding Cushing's death. 'He and I used to keep in touch all the time. We shared certain jokes and characters. He would do Jimmy Durante and I would do Sylvester the Cat ... I am not a person who makes friends easily, casually. Real friendship is rare. You must know that.'[16]

Pharaohs and Knights Templar

Also in 1994, Lee ventured back into television for a hi-tech revival of the 1970s children's favourite *The Tomorrow People*. In a four-parter called *The Rameses Connection*, he played the Pharaoh Rameses reincarnated in the present day as Sam Rees, and at one point was required to dress up in much the same

Tuesday 17 May 1994: Cushing and Lee meet for the last time to record the narration for Flesh and Blood The Hammer Heritage of Horror

Ancient Egyptian robes he'd worn 35 years before in *The Mummy*. He also went to Johannesburg to host a 13-part TV anthology called *Edgar Allan Poe's Tales of Mystery and Imagination*; other actors involved included Moray Watson, Freddie Jones, Catherine Schell, Susan George and Patrick Ryecart. 'Because *The Masque of the Red Death* is one of my personal favourites among Poe's stories,' he explains in the only instalment available for inspection, 'I've chosen this time to become a little more – well – *personally* involved.' He accordingly plays both Prince Prospero and the Red Death in the story that unfolds, the standard of which is so distressingly awful that Dark Films' apparent failure to get the series transmitted comes as no surprise at all.

More restful engagements included Lee's first venture into the fledgling field of CD-ROM. Having already recorded a pilot for an interactive history of comics, he next appeared as Dr Marcus Grimalkin, velvet-jacketed host of Media Design Interactive's

Ghosts, a disc uneasily poised between computer game and paranormal encyclopaedia. He also became involved in the snowballing 'talking book' market. He had recorded two riveting collections of Poe tales in the late 1970s and in the 1990s he would add to his portfolio such horror standards as *Frankenstein*, *The Phantom of the Opera* and *Dr Jekyll and Mr Hyde*, together with two Dennis Wheatley novels (*Strange Conflict* and *The Devil Rides Out*), a selection of Agatha Christie stories, several Sherlock Holmes adventures, even *The Fog* and *The Exorcist*. Rounding off 1994 in style, he was the subject of a Guardian Interview at the National Film Theatre on Sunday 6 November.

In 1995, Lee was a guest castaway on Radio 4's *Desert Island Discs* and indulged in some charming on-camera reminiscences for a clumsily made video project called *The Many Faces of Christopher Lee*. He spent a sunny April afternoon back at Bray Studios, shooting introductory wraparounds for an 18-strong US series called *One Hundred Years of Horror*. The director was Ted Newsom once again and Lee was filmed in front of the ballroom doors he had smashed through in *The Mummy*. 'It was very emotional,' he said when the job was done. 'The day was full of memories. Some very happy memories and some very sad ones, as so many of the people who were a part of Hammer's success have gone ... When I went inside, I said to the woman who runs the studio [Beryl Earl], "Do you see that little corridor, the one that leads out to the garden? That was one of our sets." She couldn't believe it.'[17]

It wasn't all nostalgia, however. In Roger Young's TV epic *Moses* – shot on location in Ouazarzate and Agadir as part of an on-going Italian/American series of 1990s Bible stories called *La Bibbia* – Lee was cast opposite Ben Kingsley, David Suchet and another former Dracula, Frank Langella. Also in the cast was Philippe Leroy, last seen in *Il castello dei morti vivi*. 'I played the Pharaoh Rameses II,' Lee pointed out, 'mostly with my back to the camera, after seeing the material.'[18] After this reminiscence of his role in *The Tomorrow People*, Lee's only movie in 1995 was an inauspicious one, shot in Toronto between June and August and finally bringing him together with John Landis, who had tried to cast him nearly 20 years earlier in *Kentucky Fried Movie*. Unwilling then to reprise his Fu Manchu, Lee was happy in *The Stupids* to deliver an exhilarating piece of self-parody that occupies little more than two or three minutes at the picture's mid-point but remains the only conceivable reason for watching it.

Apparently aimed at children, the brainless antics of Tom Arnold's Stanley Stupid and his equally cretinous family were greeted with open-mouthed amazement when unveiled the following year.

The Evil Sender in his hellish fairy grotto in The Stupids *(1995)*

A touch of Ivan the Terrible: as Azaret the Enchanter in Lamberto Bava's Italian/German TV epic, Sorellina e il principe del sogno (1995)

According to the *New York Times* of 31 August 1996, 'The Stupids opened yesterday to audible yawns among the audience of eight that turned out for the first show at the Criterion in Times Square.' Lee is the Evil Sender, discovered in the hellish fairy grotto in which he hordes all the nation's undelivered mail (as in 'Return to Sender'). 'Poor Jenny Miller: nobody coming to *her* wedding,' Lee sighs, slicing open a letter with his Nosferatu-honed fingernails before tossing it disdainfully into the flames. He then outlines 'a crime so unthinkable that no-one has ever dared to attempt it: to rob an entire nation of its garbage.' Saddled with verbal garbage like this, Lee nevertheless creates a charmingly fruity vignette, rounding on a snivelling postboy with a pointing finger straight out of *Dracula A.D. 1972* and ending his scene with a reverberating boom of maniacal laughter.

Lee was by now turning down more roles than he was taking up. A chance meeting in Wiesbaden with Artur Brauner, the man behind Lee's German films in the 1960s, led to an offer to star in Menahem Golan's *Luise knackt den Jackpot* as lofty butler to lottery winner Marianne Sägebrecht and her feckless husband Oliver Reed; Lee left the job to David Warner. He opted instead for further television, this time at a castle in Slovakia, where his role as the Enchanter in a lavish, two-part Italian-German fairy tale called *Sorellina e il principe del sogno* saw him being directed by Mario Bava's son Lamberto. Lee based his wintery make-up on Nikolai Cherkassov in the title role of Eisenstein's *Ivan the Terrible* but was irritated by constant, contract-flouting suggestions that he should work well into the night, doggedly resisting all blandishments to do so.

The most wicked wizard imaginable – and a gratifyingly substantial role to boot – the Enchanter tells the doe-eyed heroine Alisea (Nicole Grimaudo) that 'People stopped calling me by my name a long time ago, but you may call me Azaret.' Stuffed with lively, computer-generated household implements straight out of Disney's *The Sorcerer's Apprentice*, Azaret's emerald-hued lab is a cobwebbed delight. His three brides, meanwhile, reside on slabs in the dusty catacombs while their souls are embodied on his chest as babbling mouths straight out of the weirder reaches of Surrealist painting. Azaret plans to add the grown-up Alisea (Veronica Logan) to his collection and, when her sweetheart Demian (Raz Degan) tries to thwart him, he animates several unstoppable suits of armour just like Conrad Veidt's Baron von Kempelen in *Le Joueur d'échecs*. A grizzled version of Lico in Bava père's *Ercole al centro della terra*, Azaret reveals his true vampiric colours when he subdues Demian and claims that 'I can only exist by inhabiting your body; I need your youth.' Though turning rather kitsch in its second instalment, *Sorellina* is a wonder to behold and comes complete with some disarmingly simple special effects from another sort of wizard, Sergio Stivaletti.

A similar, though much more benevolent, role followed in September 1996, when Lee journeyed to the Vilnius Studios in Lithuania to shoot four episodes of *The New Adventures of Robin Hood*. As Olwyn, a Gandalf figure possessed of magical powers, Lee stubbornly preserved his English accent despite the fact that the remainder of the show's predominantly English cast had been prevailed upon to speak in American. The following June, Lee would reprise his Olwyn on a return trip to Vilnius, providing a handy stop-gap between *Jinnah* and *Talos the Mummy*.

Olwyn was dwarfed, however, by the part Lee had played just prior to his first spell at Vilnius. With the fearsome Lucas de Beaumanoir, Grand Master of the Knights Templar, Lee was playing his first role for BBCTV in 45 years. Stuart Orme's six-part mediaeval epic *Ivanhoe* was conceived along very different lines to the Roger Moore vehicle in which Lee had appeared in 1957. Stripey tights were out, realistic grime and grit were in; the Northumberland locations were 'colder even than Alaska,' Lee pointed out. As de Beaumanoir, he appears with a monastic tonsure and a mottled, almost charred complexion – strangely appropriate, given his propensity for burning people at the stake. Introduced in episode three with a discreet roll of thunder, he plays the character as an utterly humourless, and utterly insane, religious

As religious maniac Lucas de Beaumanoir, Grand Master of the Knights Templar, in the BBC's Ivanhoe (1996)

zealot, bent on the annihilation of women and Jews alike. In one extremely unpleasant scene, he has Isaac of York (David Horovitch) restrained by a pair of thugs before forcibly baptising him with Holy Water. And, after presiding with impeccably twisted logic over a trumped-up witch trial, he introduces the humanising element in a queasy sequence in which he visits Isaac's imprisoned daughter, Rebecca (Susan Lynch).

'Your shift will burn first, of course, and all men will gaze upon that fleshly shape that Lucifer has given you for their seduction,' he breathes. 'Every part of your body will be stripped of this unholy pelt as your skin, too, begins to blister and burn away. You will be able to watch for some minutes before those lustrous eyes melt...' Lee tactfully underplays the kinky overtones of de Beaumanoir's speech while simultaneously making them as clear as day. 'It is very sexual,' he maintained, 'and I thought the only way to play it was to suggest the terrible repression, not only of this man, but perhaps the monastic orders even up to this day. The Grand Master is probably a virgin. He wants to burn Rebecca but at the same time go to bed with her. I say nothing. It's all in the eyes. I don't know what Sir Walter Scott would think. Go for it, probably.'[19] Paying further tribute to Scott, Lee subsequently recorded *Ivanhoe* as a BBC talking book to coincide with the series' transmission.

1996 wound up with an epic TV adaptation of Homer's *The Odyssey*, filmed from 14 October in Turkey and Malta with interiors at Shepperton. In charge was the distinguished Russian director Andrei Konchalovsky, and the stellar cast included Armand Assante (Odysseus), Greta Scacchi (Penelope), Geraldine Chaplin (Eurycleia), Jeroen Krabbe (King Alcino), Irene Papas (Anticlea) and Isabella Rossellini (Athena). Lee's powerful cameo as Tiresias was filmed at Shepperton in a single day. There were no takers, however, for a proposed remake of the old Tod Slaughter barnstormer, *Sweeney Todd, the Demon Barber of Fleet Street*, even with Joe Dante attached as director, Peter Snell as producer, Michel Parry as writer and, possibly, Angela Lansbury as co-star. This, and other disappointments like it, made Lee despair of a new breed of cine-illiterate studio executives whom he memorably described as '15-year-olds with their caps on backwards.' They were hardly the kind of people likely to give him the opportunity to play his other septuagenarian dream parts – Ivan the Terrible and Don Quixote.

Pakistan Zindabad

1997 marked the 50th anniversary of Lee's first film appearance and was also the 50th anniversary of the founding of Pakistan. Though seemingly unrelated, these facts made Lee's next project an unusually appropriate one. It was also his most challenging and, by a long distance, the most controversial. *Jinnah* was the brainchild of Professor Akbar Ahmed, a Cambridge academic and leading authority on Islam who wished to right a wrong perpetrated by Richard Attenborough's *Gandhi*. In that film, Ahmed argued, Mohammed Ali Jinnah, founder of Pakistan, was grievously misrepresented as a cynical manipulator, pressurising Britain into dividing India purely to satisfy his personal ambition. 'It was a great film,' Ahmed conceded, 'but Jinnah's role was a travesty, a distortion of history ... Why would millions of Muslims have seen him as a Moses figure if he was so cold? They would have walked into the sea if he had asked them to.'[20]

The role of Quaid-e-Azam (the Great Leader) was assigned to Lee after Jeremy Irons had turned it down amid growing unrest about a white actor playing an Asian. 'Once I had signed to play the role,' Lee recollected, 'I did all the research I possibly could. I read every book, saw old newsreels, listened to tapes of his speeches. Because of his time in England he had no accent, which made it considerably easier for me. When I put on his distinctive clothes – the long white Sherwani coat and the baggy Shalwar trousers – people actually called me "Mr Jinnah." I bleached my eyebrows white, and had a white streak in my hair three inches wide, just as he did. In the end [the likeness] was quite uncanny ... Someone objected, "But you're taller than he was." My answer was simple: the man was a giant, whether you agree with him or not.'[21]

Director Jamil Dehlavi began the film's three-month schedule in Karachi on 3 March, backed by a partly British crew and the proverbial cast of thousands. Lee immediately became aware, however, of a virulent campaign against the project, a campaign orchestrated by local newspaper editor Imran Aslam, who got up a petition demanding that Lee be arrested and deported. 'I tried to defuse the situation,' Lee maintained. 'I told them, "If you can find a Pakistani actor to do it, I'll go home!" They couldn't, so the cameras started rolling.' But Aslam and his supporters were not to be put off. 'They ranted, "This man has portrayed a lot of bad people!" I was accused of playing 'lethal characters' in horror and sex films. The sex bit was news to me, I have to say ... I had an armed bodyguard with me day and night in case someone tried to kidnap me,' Lee continued, 'and 12 armed guards surrounding me every day when I drove to the set. They were in a convoy of open army trucks clutching Kalashnikovs.'[22]

The negative publicity eventually took its toll; the government withdrew its promised investment three weeks into the film's schedule and the production

Mohammed Ali Jinnah with sister Fatima (Shireen Shah) and Liaquat Ali Khan (Shakeel, in spectacles at left) in Jinnah *(1997)*

company, Quaid Project Ltd, was only able to raise two thirds of the deficit, making do with a final budget of £6 million and adjusting the shooting schedule accordingly. And the controversy didn't end there. Many of the film's details were denounced as indecent or 'un-Pakistani'; despite the fact that Jinnah succumbed to lung cancer a year after Partition, scenes showing him coughing were objected to along with much else. The actresses were called prostitutes and Ahmed was still receiving death threats as general release approached. Calling the film a Hindu and Zionist plot, activists swore to raze to the ground any cinemas playing it and to attack all those involved; 'Either they will die or I will die,' [23] claimed industrialist Mia Azhar Umin. The continuing turmoil ensured that, though seen at the Montreal, Cairo and London Film Festivals in 1998, the film's Pakistan release was delayed until summer 2000, when it also began to crop up in Western cable TV schedules.

The film is a strange concoction, often deeply moving but also, thanks to a wavering narrative line that chops back and forth between various flashbacks, somewhat daunting to those unversed in the bloody history of Partition. The central conceit is a naïve one, with Jinnah being rushed to hospital in 1948 and looking back over his life with the help of a cherubic guide whose celestial computers are malfunctioning.

(The distinguished Indian actor Shashi Kapoor also got into hot water over his role in the film, with hostile observers misinterpreting it as the Archangel Gabriel and demanding that he be repatriated.) This vein of 'magic realism' becomes truly bizarre when the old Jinnah is seen sitting on a park bench and conversing with his younger self (Richard Lintern), or offering him his enthusiastic support at a public meeting, much to the young Jinnah's understandable perplexity. And it finally becomes silly when Nehru and Gandhi, no less, are discovered sharing Kapoor's computer consoles.

The acting is somewhat mixed, too, with Robert Ashby (Nehru) and Maria Aitken (Edwina Mountbatten) smoothly professional while James Fox's extraordinarily wooden last Viceroy can most charitably be looked upon as a tongue-in-cheek caricature of stuffed-shirt Englishness. But the film looks beautiful – cinematographer Nick Knowland's soft, suffused lighting is remarkable and Lee acknowledges him as the film's main creative force – while Lee himself gives a performance compact of sadness. He's first seen on a stretcher, virtually luminous with lung cancer and ready for Kapoor's muddled, post-mortem preparation of his 'case'. He watches himself locking horns with Mountbatten (who offers Jinnah the premiership of India on the principle of making 'the biggest bounder the head prefect') and, when shown the decline and death of his young wife Rutti, makes the elegiac admission that 'I loved her ... but I never taught myself to *show* that love.'

Ahmed described Jinnah as a Victorian at heart, and Jinnah's inability to learn from his emotional mistakes is underlined in an exceptional scene set in his Lahore residence in 1946. Tightly buttoned up behind his mandarin collar, he is asked by his jodhpured daughter (Vaneeza Ahmed) if she may marry a Parsee, as he did. He forbids it, however, closing the subject by grimly reinserting his monocle, putting a cigarette back between his teeth and ostentatiously returning to his copy of the London *Times*. Later, he announces the creation of Pakistan with a grandly Presidential flourish – 'I am nobody's Emperor; I am a soldier in the service of the birthright of Pakistan' – and deals with the ensuing outbreak of violence with unruffled ease. As a riot is broken up by tear gas, a bearded insurgent comes at Jinnah with a shovel, but Jinnah turns on him with a withering scorn handled by Lee in truly electrifying style. 'Islam doesn't need fanatics like you,' he barks. 'Islam needs men of vision who will build the country. *Now grow up!* – and serve Pakistan.'

The film pauses for a bizarre fantasy trial sequence, in which Jinnah resumes his advocate's wig and gown to grill Mountbatten and a blimpish British general (John Nettleton), concluding his interrogation with a sardonic reference to 'Honour among thieves.' But the film reaches its true climax in the deserts of Pakistan as hordes of Jinnah's followers turn out to watch his triumphal progress. The violence has deepened in the meantime and millions have lost their lives on the sub-continent, but his followers' veneration is undiminished. A refugee father (Talat Hussain) apologises to Jinnah for his little daughter's forgetfulness – 'I am sorry, sir, we beg your forgiveness for her not recognising you, but she is only a child' – and Jinnah gulps back tears as he mournfully replies, 'It is I who should ask *you* for forgiveness, for any part I have had in what has happened to you.'

Jinnah's Victorian façade melts away with his tears, just as Lee himself softens into a genuinely moving vulnerability after a long legacy of monolithic characters. Lee modestly gives the credit for this to Hussain – 'He played it so simply, so beautifully that I simply couldn't restrain my tears' – but that is what great acting is all about, after all: reacting as well as merely acting. The camera spirals away from this touching exchange as the vast crowd breaks into an exhilarating chant of 'Pakistan zindabad!' and the credits roll to the uplifting strains of the Pakistan National Anthem.

Even this extraordinarily emotional ending caused consternation among the film's detractors – Jinnah's tears for the victims of Partition apparently marked him as unpatriotic – and it's a great pity that the political trouble surrounding the film succeeded in eclipsing one of Lee's most heartfelt performances. There were whispers of an Oscar nomination, but these hopes were dashed by the film's prolonged invisibility. Instead, Lee had to content himself with the enthusiastic approbation of John Malkovich, president of the jury at the Cairo Film Festival, and some glowing press reports, including an Associated Press review that likened him to John Gielgud and Ralph Richardson. As for Ahmed, he had succeeded in his aim to show that not all Muslim leaders are built along Gaddafi and Saddam lines, and was more than happy with Lee's magisterial account of Jinnah. 'I would like to salute this man,' Ahmed concluded. 'He is not only a world name, he is magnificent in the film. His performance is amazing – and, just as important, he is an officer and a gentleman.'[24]

Millennium Gothic

Lee's next picture was also set in 1948 – his section of it, at any rate – but was a very different proposition, taking him three days rather than three months. *Talos the Mummy* began in Luxembourg on 3 September (one of a slew of films shot there since Lee's prophetic remark back in 1990) and was fitted with a 1940s pre-credits sequence in which Lee was to assume centre stage as patrician archaeologist Sir Richard Turkel.

Unfortunately, the film's all-important special effects appear to have been done back to front; they're for the most part rather good but the stuff featured in the prologue is laughably bad. Sir Richard is sliced in two by the malign force exhaled by Talos' opened tomb, and the computerised offal round his midriff has terrible trouble keeping up with him as he drags himself painfully across the floor. But Lee's performance is a greater embarrassment to the film than its dodgy CGI work. The straight-faced conviction he confers upon its first nine minutes cannot be maintained thereafter, for, with the honourable exception of Louise Lombard as Sir Richard's feisty granddaughter, the younger cast members are far too post-modern to take this *Boy's Own* stuff seriously and clearly don't believe a word of it.

Though theatrically released in some territories, the film was consigned to video in the US and UK, hitting the shelves a mere five days before Universal's block-busting remake of *The Mummy* hit cinemas, with the result that *Talos* was consigned to footnote status at a single stroke. 'With *Talos*,' director Russell Mulcahy claimed during production, 'I've made a Mummy film

With Alun Armstrong in the opening minutes of Tim Burton's millennial smash hit, Sleepy Hollow (1999)

starring my idol Christopher Lee and I've cut him in half in what will be a show-stopping death scene. It doesn't get any better than this.' [25] Happily for Lee, his participation in neo-Hammer Horrors would shortly get a great deal better than this.

In the meantime, he was occupied with a new edition of his autobiography, issued by Gollancz on 23 October and supplemented with some 60 pages of extra material to account for the 20 years that had elapsed since the first. He also contributed the voice of Death to Channel 4's *The Wyrd Sisters*, a six-part animated adaptation of Terry Pratchett's *Discworld*, and then moved decisively into the world of popular music. An album entitled *Christopher Lee Sings Devils, Rogues and Other Villains: from Broadway to Bayreuth and beyond* had been issued in 1996 – it included several operatic arias as well as particularly mind-blowing renditions of 'Mack the Knife' and 'Ghost Riders in the Sky' – and in 1997 he appeared in his first rock video, for the 'boy band' Damage.

The following year he got together with vocalist Gary Curtis to record the single 'Wand'rin' Star'. This was followed in 1999 by a combined version of 'It's Now or Never' and 'O sole mio', Curtis warbling the Elvis Presley section and Lee belting out the Italian operatic bits. Lee could add these to a growing CD collection that included his crack at Chief Sitting Bull in *Annie Get Your Gun*, *The King and I* with Valerie Masterson and even *The Rocky Horror Show*, in which he contributed the saucy incidentals mouthed by Charles Gray in the film version.

Astonishing stuff for a man in his late seventies, but by September 1998 Lee was ready to resume the more conventional business of mere acting with a third stint in *The New Adventures of Robin Hood* at Vilnius. Christmas Day marked the transmission of writer/director Dirk Maggs' *The Gemini Apes*, a pretty ghastly concoction advertised as 'BBC Radio 4's action-packed Christmas audio movie,' in which Lee was cast as a bio-geneticist who sends trained chimpanzees into space. And on 18 March 1999 Lee went to Leavesden Studios to film a brief but juicy cameo in *Sleepy Hollow*. Another neo-Hammer, this was conceived on a much grander and more imaginative scale than the fleabitten *Talos*. Tim Burton, inspirational director of cult favourites like *Ed Wood* and *Mars Attacks!*, had concocted a very loose adaptation of Washington Irving's *The Legend of Sleepy Hollow*, larding it with echoes of Mario Bava and Roger Corman as well as Terence Fisher and commencing production in October 1998 with a budget of $70 million.

The result proved to be Burton's biggest success yet, no mean feat given that his previous pictures included *Batman* and *Batman Returns*. Though sensory overload becomes a danger in the film's closing stages, *Sleepy Hollow* is an exhilarating Gothic fantasia, far more coherent than the harebrained hashes of Gothic served up by Francis Coppola and Kenneth Branagh. Lee's role comes at the very outset and serves a symbolic function, letting the audience know that Burton, who had previously offered wildly imaginative 'deconstructions' of the horror genre in films like

Beetlejuice and *Edward Scissorhands*, was here tackling horror head-on and for real. As the forbidding Burgomaster who sends Johnny Depp's Ichabod Crane to upstate New York to investigate a series of mystery decapitations, Lee was pleased to note that 'I set the ball, or rather the heads, rolling.' Burton frames his baleful close-ups in front of a statue of the American eagle, its wings sprouting from Lee's head as if he were Justice incarnate, and Lee obliges with a repeat performance of his uniquely threatening pointing-at-the-camera routine from *Dracula A.D. 1972*.

Lee's other duties in 1999 were largely at the behest of the BBC, whether narrating a television documentary about Egyptian burial practices (*Empire of Death*) or singing 'Mad Dogs and Englishmen' in a radio gala marking Noël Coward's centenary. Much more momentous, he started work on *Gormenghast* on 24 March and was occupied by it, on and off, until 12 July. Gestating for five years, this four-part adaptation of Mervyn Peake's bizarre post-war masterpieces *Titus Groan* and *Gormenghast* – long considered unfilmable – was brought to the screen by director Andy Wilson at Shepperton Studios. 'I think we've painted ourselves into a corner with adaptations of 19th century classics,' Wilson observed. 'There's another tradition in English storytelling that combines elements of fantasy, the grotesque, comedy, circus sideshow, that's highly visual as well as cerebral. *Gormenghast* is all those things.'[26] A living exemplar of this non-genteel vein of English storytelling, Lee was accordingly cast as Flay, guardian of Gormenghast tradition and cadaverous retainer to Lord Sepulchrave, 76th Earl of Groan. Joining him were distinguished actors like Ian Richardson, Celia Imrie, Richard Griffiths, Zoë Wanamaker, Eric Sykes and Spike Milligan, with the rising star Jonathan Rhys-Meyers as the Machiavellian kitchenboy Steerpike. Indeed, of Britain's theatrical upper crust, Lee's own niece (Xandra's daughter), Harriet Walter, was one of the few performers not involved in *Gormenghast*.

Lee had known Peake himself during the 1950s, rendezvousing with him at the same venue, Harrods Library, where he had first encountered Dennis Wheatley. He brings a ruined grandeur to Flay, speaking in a strangely fractured, monosyllabic utterance and plunging into an epic battle with Griffiths' monstrous Swelter with all the old melodramatic dementia intact. More significantly, the vein of vulnerability he had been developing in *A Feast at Midnight* and *Jinnah* comes to the fore when Flay is banished from Gormenghast by the Countess Gertrude, his crime: flinging a cat at Steerpike. Packing his traps, he trudges into exile with a heart-touching sense of desolation and disbelief. At the end of one episode, he creates a uniquely mournful effect merely by walking through a forest clearing and gazing through a telescope at the distant spires of his beloved Gormenghast. And, for long-term Lee followers, the carpet of autumn leaves he has to traverse here is irresistibly reminiscent of one of the key scenes in *The Curse of Frankenstein*.

With its 120 sets created by the visionary designer Christopher Hobbs, innovative cinematography by Gavin Finney and a constant stream of baroque set-pieces, the end result seems to have perplexed British TV viewers bred on a cosy 1990s diet of simpering Jane Austen adaptations. *Gormenghast* was the BBC's first major offering for the new millennium, nevertheless, just as *Sleepy Hollow* was the first smash hit of the new century in the nation's cinemas. In fact, Lee's role in *Sleepy Hollow* triggered a sudden upsurge of high-profile casting for him, making 'people realise that I'm still around, still above ground, and still working ... You can give the performance of your life in a film which doesn't make money and nobody wants to know. But you can have a smallish part, like I have in *Sleepy Hollow* – and within 48 hours my manager was getting telephone calls from casting directors.'[27] At the turn of the century, Lee accordingly landed major roles in two of the most eagerly awaited fantasy pictures for years.

As mournful manservant Flay in the BBC's phantasmagoric Gormenghast *(1999)*

PART ELEVEN

INDIAN SUMMER
2000 and beyond

'It was while I was making *Gormenghast* that I was first asked to meet Peter Jackson,' Lee recalls. 'I'd heard that a film version of *The Lord of the Rings* was on the cards, and naturally I felt that to be involved in it would be tremendous. I read the books when they first came out and had met Tolkien personally. So I wanted very much to be in it. I met Peter, along with a couple of casting people and a video camera, in a very small back room in a church on the Tottenham Court Road. Having read a brief scene between Gandalf and Frodo – though I knew that I was too old for Gandalf really – I went back to Shepperton to continue with *Gormenghast*. Then a few days later my agent called me to say they were sending the script of the first picture and that they wanted me to play Saruman. Dreams don't come true very often, but in this instance they did.'

Shrouded in an elaborate cloak of secrecy, the three parts of *The Lord of the Rings* were based, like *Gormenghast*, on some of Lee's favourite books and took him to New Zealand on 27 January 2000. Peter Jackson, director of the outrageously gory *Braindead* and the sensitively observed *Heavenly Creatures*, had been engaged by New Line Cinema to bring J R R Tolkien's trilogy to the screen and added Lee to a stellar cast that included Elijah Wood, Ian McKellen, Liv Tyler, Viggo Mortensen, Cate Blanchett and Ian Holm.

Lee had long nursed an ambition to play Gandalf the Grey but was ideally cast, in any case, as Gandalf's mysterious opposite, Saruman the White. His first day of shooting entailed a 3.30 am start – 'That was a new one, even to me' – but he considered that the end result would more than justify the effort. 'I had a marvellous time in Wellington,' he claims. 'Peter Jackson's challenge was to take this fantasy, which is one of the most extraordinary epics ever written – I compare it somewhat with *The Iliad* and *The Odyssey*, quite frankly – and transfer it to the screen and make it believable, which I'm quite convinced he's done. As a director, Peter is extremely precise; knows exactly what he wants. He reminds me in some ways of Billy Wilder.'

Ian McKellen concocted an eloquent internet shooting diary, 'The Grey Book', in which he explained that his first encounter with Lee was in a scene in which 'Gandalf visits his fellow Istar at the Orthanc Tower, where Saruman consults his seeing stone, the Palantir. I don't feel face to face with Dracula, Sherlock Holmes, Fu Manchu all at once because Christopher looks saintly in his robes. And there is work to be done.'

McKellen also observed that 'Christopher Lee proves that a distinctive voice is an asset in the movies ... His 200 (or is it 300?) films have robbed theatre audiences of a resounding Shakespearean. Spread across the black throne under Orthanc's vasty roof, he looked like King Lear in age and authority. He is 78 years old, handsome and powerful. When he speaks, all I see and hear is Saruman, my old associate gone wrong. Except once, when he rounded off a speech, at Peter Jackson's suggestion, with a snarl. To be within four feet of a Lee snarl is unsettling.' And, in a lavish souvenir album concocted for cast and crew, McKellen wrote opposite his portrait as Gandalf the charming message, 'Just when I'd given up hope of being in a Christopher Lee movie...'

Peter Jackson himself offered an extremely perceptive insight into one, or rather two, of Lee's greatest acting tools. 'In front of the camera he has this wonderful ability to do something to his eyes,' he told the *New York Times*' David Edelstein. 'They suddenly glaze over and then gleam in a very chilling way; it's as if he turns on an internal light. When you've got your shot he turns it off and he's back to being his warm self.'[1] Lee, Jackson recalled, 'was one of the first actors we went to see in London. His

The ambiguous Count Dooku, aka Darth Tyranus, was introduced to cinemagoers when Star Wars: Episode II – Attack of the Clones *opened in summer 2002*

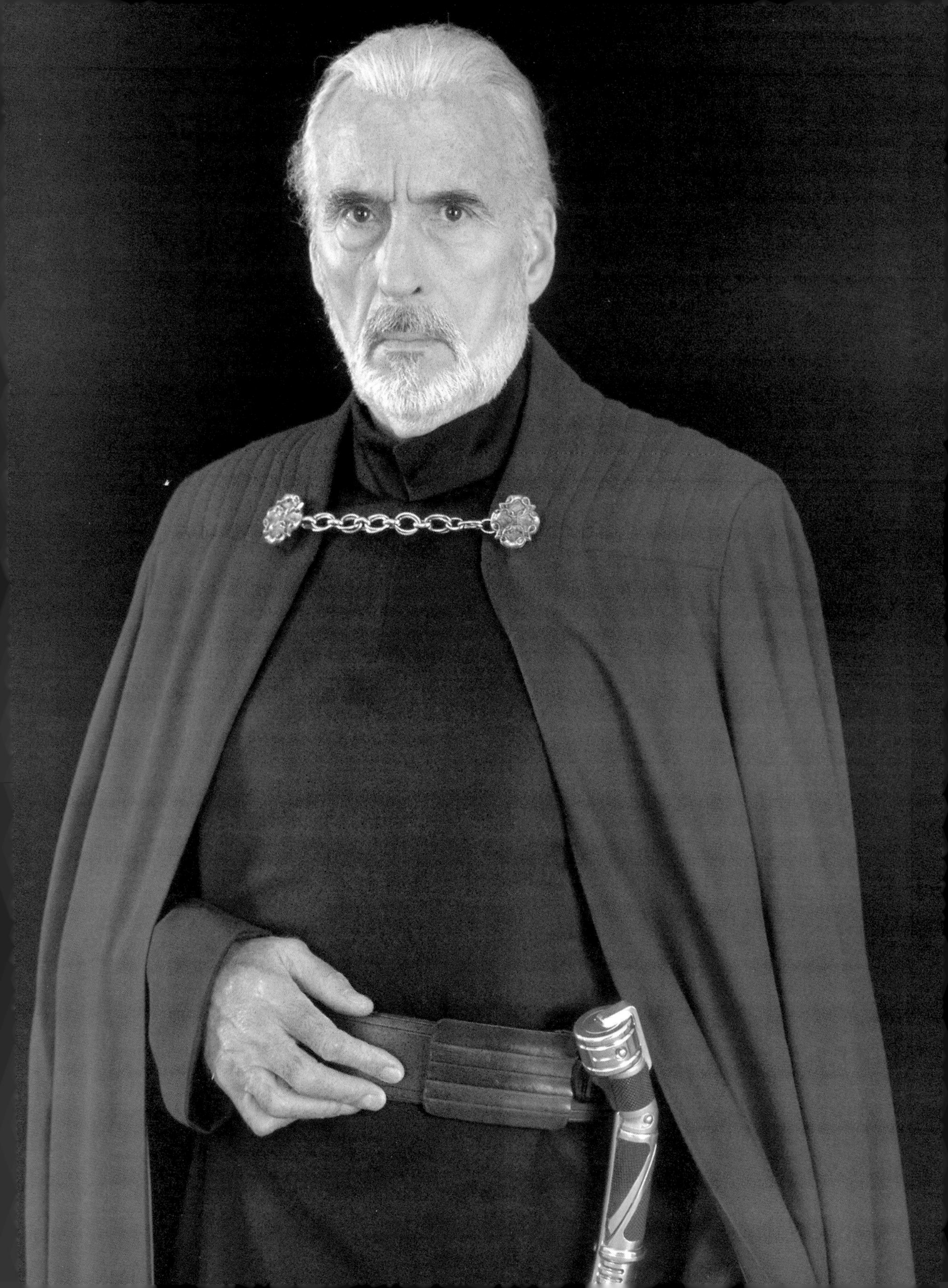

As the smouldering Saruman in The Lord of the Rings: The Fellowship of the Ring, *which was released to worldwide acclaim in December 2001*

enthusiasm and knowledge of Tolkien's work was one of the factors that helped when we decided to cast him, although I had already thought about using him because I had seen a lot of his Hammer films when I was young. And the first James Bond movie I ever saw was *The Man With the Golden Gun* ... Then, on Christopher's last day of shooting, I finally brought my poster for *The Man With the Golden Gun* down with me and had him sign it. It was really great fun to finally be able to work with Christopher Lee.'[2]

Buoyed by these ringing endorsements, Lee returned to Ouazarzate in June, after a five-year absence, for *In the Beginning*, which trod some of the same ground as *Moses*. This time, however, Lee was cast as Rameses I, leaving his old role of Rameses II to a distinctly underwhelming Art Malik. By this time, Lee's fan club, dormant throughout the 1990s, had been revived on the internet. 'Mine is a brief appearance,' he told its members, 'but important to the story. It was directed by an old friend, Kevin Connor. And another good friend, Martin Landau, played Abraham ... It was very enjoyable, apart from the daily sandstorm, usually during our lunch.'

The Old Testament made over as a marathon comic-strip, the show unspooled in two parts on NBC during November. Attended by Steven Berkoff's Potiphar, Lee's Pharaoh is introduced with the golden wings of his eagle-shaped throne sprouting from either side of his head-dress (presumably Connor's nod to Lee's close-ups in *Sleepy Hollow*) and is on very fearsome form as he dismisses his cringing seer.

'Why do I pay you?' he storms. 'I pay you to solve the mystery of my dreams!' He has better luck with the gifted young interpreter Joseph, played by muscle-bound Eddie Cibrian.

Returning from Morocco, Lee recorded another Elvis Presley number, 'Surrender', with Gary Curtis and also turned down a stage offer to play Prospero in *The Tempest*. An enlightened yet vengeful magician in charge of spirits and mis-shapen monsters on an uncharted island, the role would have been perfect for him but – Ian McKellen's comments about 'a resounding Shakespearean' notwithstanding – resuming a theatre career after a lapse of 45 years was not a realistic proposition for a man approaching 80. Yet another momentous job was just around the corner, in any case.

Mind Over 'Method'

After lying dormant for 16 years, the *Star Wars* franchise had returned to cinema screens, and phenomenal box-office returns, in 1999 with *Star Wars: Episode I – The Phantom Menace*. George Lucas accordingly began *Episode II* at Fox's Sydney studios on 26 June 2000 with a budget hovering around the $115 million mark. Lee left for Australia on 31 July, spending three weeks on the set of *Star Wars: Episode II* as part of an impressive star line-up that also included Ewan McGregor, Natalie Portman, Hayden Christensen and Samuel L Jackson.

'I'd heard that George was a brilliant technician,' Lee points out, 'a great creator and innovator, but also that he was very quiet and reserved. Well, I can tell you that George is one of the most articulate people I've ever met; once you get him started, he seems to know something about everything. He's a polymath, he really is. And his reputation for being unapproachable is certainly not correct. In fact, he said on the telephone when offering me the part, "We'll have fun." And I was very glad to hear it. Working with George was indeed fun; he was very helpful and appreciative, and the atmosphere on set was very relaxed.

'I'd never seen anything like the first *Star Wars*; I don't think anybody had,' he adds. 'The thing that really amazed me was that great aerial chase through the canyons. The film created a whole new era of what could be done on the screen. And it all came out of George's mind. As far as I'm concerned, he invented, as Tolkien did, a whole new world; new characters, new images, even, to a certain extent, a new language.'

Lee's old co-star, Peter Cushing, had played Grand Moff Tarkin in the original film back in 1976. ('I found that name very funny, I have to admit,' Lee reveals. 'So I rang Peter up and said, "What is a Grand Moff, and what is a Tarkin?" And he said, "I haven't the faintest idea, dear boy!"') Now Lee was cast as 'a charismatic separatist' and, with the production cloaked in just as much secrecy as *The Lord of the Rings*, he would reveal no more than the fact that 'I have quite a lot to say and a good deal to do.' Indeed, Lee's character name – Count Dooku – and villainous disposition were only confirmed by George Lucas early in 2001, in the foreword to this book. 'Christopher has a certain persona,' Lucas later explained. 'You wouldn't cast him in a remake of *Father Knows Best*. He's formidable.'[3]

Lee's first scene as the renegade Sith Lord – 'in Japanese,' he points out, 'dooku means poison, but I wouldn't necessarily call him evil' – involved the character escaping from the so-called Stalgasin Hive astride a nifty air-speeder. His extensive involvement with the film's blue- and green-screen work began right there, with none other than Lucas' old chum, Francis Coppola, looking on from the sidelines.

With the film's manifold CGI wonders due to be pasted in at a later date, acting opposite nothing presented Lee with no great problem. 'You have to rely on George's descriptions in the script and, of course, on your own imagination,' he explains. 'If you've any instinct and experience as a performer, you can see just about anything. There are technical details one has to attend to, of course – eyelines and so on – but otherwise it's all in the mind's eye. Method actors need more of an external stimulus and would therefore have a lot of problems doing this kind of work. In my view, the Method is only *a* method; it's helped a great many actors but ruined a great many, too.'

Scrupulously avoiding a Method-style request for his 'motivation', Lee nevertheless enquired into Dooku's history – 'What exactly *are* the Sith?' he began – whereupon the diligent Lucas suspended filming for some 15 minutes with a detailed account of the Sith Lords and how Dooku became one of the 'Lost 20' on his defection from the Jedi.

Lee rounded off the year 2000 with two brief engagements during October, the first taking him back 65 years to his scholarship exam at Eton College with M R James. For BBC Scotland, he travelled to Elton Hall near Peterborough to record four James stories for TV broadcast at Christmas: *Number 13*, *The Stalls of Barchester Cathedral*, *The Ash-Tree* and *A Warning to the Curious*. The director was Eleanor Yule and, as billed in *Radio Times*, the collective title – a signal compliment to Lee but, as he is at pains to point out, not entirely fair to M R James – was *Christopher Lee's Ghost Stories for Christmas*. It was

Giving life to the scholarly horrors of Montague Rhodes James: a virtuoso performance in BBC Scotland's quartet of Ghost Stories for Christmas *(2000)*

James' contemporary, Algernon Blackwood, who first blazed a trail for 'talking head' chillers on the small screen back in the late 1940s. The trail had since gone cold but the inspired combination of M R James and Christopher Lee suggested it could yet be rekindled.

Lee's own recommendation for inclusion in the series was a tale called *Count Magnus*, perhaps the most horrific story ever located in Sweden, a country that held a lifelong fascination for James just as it has for Lee. But, even without the face-sucking ghastliness of *Count Magnus*, Lee brings a riveting combination of academic joviality and the genuinely sepulchral to the four chosen stories. With the material cleverly adapted by Ronald Frame (and reportedly trimmed further in post-production), Lee's timing in all four is a model of precision, and his childlike habit of drumming his hands on his knees while warming to his stories suggests very clearly that career academics never grow up. His increasingly desperate iteration of 'I must be firm' in *The Stalls of Barchester* counts as something of a tour de force, while his handling of *Number 13*, complete with characteristically spot-on Danish accents, turns a potentially humorous story into something very disturbing indeed.

The background to these cosy fireside chats consists of a rather limited selection of creepy cutaways and an even more limited selection of reaction shots from Lee's gathered undergraduates, with centre stage being conceded to the narrator himself at all times. That narrator is *not*, however, M R James – as far as Lee is concerned, at any rate. Yet post-production seems to have made it pretty clear that he is; when the first proper close-up of Lee in each segment is accompanied by a disembodied voice intoning 'Montague Rhodes James', there seems to be no other conclusion the viewer can draw.

Which leaves one with a curious philosophical question. If, while playing a role, the actor thinks he isn't playing a specific Cambridge antiquary but just a generalised one, can he legitimately be said to be playing the specific one just because the producers impose that identification at a later date? Suffice to say that, whether playing James himself or merely his mouthpiece, Lee restored life to James' purse-lipped prose in a way that cried out for, but did not receive, a second dose the following Christmas.

Having proved himself the ideal James interpreter, Lee then spent a weekend in Bordeaux narrating (in French) Calliope Productions' *Les Redoutables*, a series of 13 brief TV vignettes concocted by Mathieu Guillermo and directed by such luminaries as Claude Chabrol and Georges Lautner. 'For the tension to reach its height,' Guillermo explained, 'I wanted the stories to be played by the smallest possible cast and feature a minimum of scenery and effects. Each scenario conforms to the following pattern: we begin with a humdrum situation and, little by little, disturbing elements are brought in to disrupt the apparent calm.'[4] To provide the disturbing element in the final instalment, 'Confession', director René Manzor required Lee to appear in person – as Death, no less.

The result is a dazzlingly realised short, with a venal curé (Ticky Holgado) indulging in all sorts of activities while he's ostensibly hearing people's confessions – working on crossword puzzles, filling in his tax return – until receiving a real jolt when 'un mystérieux confesseur drapé de noir' turns up on the other side of the grille. Yes, it's the Grim Reaper himself, who begins apologetically enough ('Je ne sais pas par où commencer, car la liste est trop longue') prior to unleashing a rainstorm within the church and handing over his scythe to the astonished curé.

Lee's cowled harbinger of doom is properly forbidding but also sports a charmingly autumnal twinkle in his eye, a twinkle retained for a 'making of' featurette included on the series' DVD release. Speaking for the most part in French, Lee broke briefly into English for a final, playful admonition: 'Death wishes you all a long and happy future, and I shall not come for you too soon...' Diverting though this engagement was, Lee was undismayed when a second series, shot in English, went ahead in Canada without him.

With Saruman and Count Dooku imminent, Lee was now the recipient of numerous scripts (including *Blade II* and *The She Creature*) in which he had zero interest. Instead, in February 2001 he went to Barcelona at the invitation of Media Park SA for a documentary series called *Érase una vez en Europa* (*Once Upon a Time in Europe*). Lee topped and tailed all 13 instalments, the perfect host for a series which celebrated the explosion of weird and wonderful movies in Europe from the late 1950s to the mid-1970s. Closely modelled on the UK series *Eurotika*, the show's galaxy of polyglot interviewees included numerous people associated with Lee's old movies, including Eugenio Martín, Carlo Rustichelli, Jesús Franco, Helga Liné, Artur Brauner, Antonio Margheriti, even Patrick Mower.

ROYAL ACCOLADE

Also in February 2001, Lee went to Munich to accept a Lifetime Achievement Award from the German video industry – further awards were to come thick and fast in the upcoming months – prior to joining other *Lord of the Rings* alumnae at the Cannes Film Festival in May. With a mouth-watering 20-minute preview shown to the press, this marked the beginning of the feverish anticipation preceding the release of the first film in the trilogy, *The Fellowship of the Ring*. This didn't happen until December, however, so there was time in July for Lee to return to Wellington for some retakes.

During a four-day break in Singapore, however, he trapped his left hand in a hotel door, severely damaging his two middle fingers in an echo of the occasion, 47 years earlier, when Errol Flynn had done something similar to his right hand. The surgeon and anaesthetist charged with repairing the damage were both called Dr Lee, which was the only thing their namesake found amusing in the whole painful scenario. In the finished film, Saruman's Napoleonic habit of concealing his left hand in his flowing white robes is a direct result of this accident.

Before his return trip to Wellington, Lee had been created a Commander of the British Empire in the Queen's Birthday Honours List, the official investiture subsequently taking place on 20 November. His niece, Harriet Walter, had received the same honour before him. 'As far as I'm concerned, Harriet got hers for achievement and I got mine for survival,' he modestly maintains.

A mysterious confessor, robed in black: with Ticky Holgado in Les Redoutables *(2000)*

CHRISTOPHER LEE – PART ELEVEN

Tuesday 20 November 2001: Christopher Lee CBE

Soon afterwards, Lee and Walter 'went public' about their relationship for the first time via a charming double-interview in the *Observer* magazine. 'She has an iron will, and so have I,' Lee observed.

'In that way, we are very much alike. As an actor you need an iron will to have the self-discipline.' The interview also gave Lee an opportunity to conjure memories of his mother, who had died back in 1981.

'Many of [Harriet's] performances have been very much based on my mother's behaviour,' he pointed out. 'In *The Royal Family*, which she acted in recently at the Haymarket with Judi Dench, she *was* my mother. All that rather camp comedy and dramatic gestures.'[5]

'To me as a child,' Walter recollected, 'my uncle was a roving, exotic bachelor figure who swanned in once in a while. The heart-rate went up when he walked in the door. Perhaps it was his wonderful deep voice but he seemed to have an extraordinary power over you ... Sometimes we watched him at work at Bray Studios, where they did the Hammer films,' she added, 'and it all made me think: "Acting – that's what I want to do." ... Because I've done 'serious' plays, perhaps I'm more obsessed with the theatre than my uncle is. But he's got many more interests – he's well read, speaks several languages and he's well known in the profession for being a real gentleman. In recent years, after reading about the idiot pranks of the Russell Crowes of this world, I've come to value him as a role model.'[6]

Limbering up for the release of Peter Jackson's first *Rings* epic, Lee visited Copenhagen for an intriguing project unrelated to the film. With the Tolkien Ensemble, he recorded music from *The Lord of the Rings* (notably Treebeard's song) preparatory to a live concert and CD release. And, after a trip to Athens in October to pick up another Lifetime Achievement award, this time from the Panorama of European Films, 2001 drew to a spectacular close in December with another visit to Copenhagen. Accompanied by Viggo Mortensen, Lee and Gitte attended Denmark's gala premiere of *The Fellowship of the Ring* at the request of that country's Queen. Herself an avid *Rings* enthusiast, she had actually illustrated the Danish edition and took the opportunity of presenting Lee with a copy of it. The film itself, meanwhile, was to create an impact that extended well beyond northern Europe.

'I want people to appreciate what has been achieved,' Lee explained later. 'Before *Lord of the Rings*, some people would have just classed Peter Jackson as a horror director. But there is a mind there. Somebody once asked me how I found Peter Jackson and I said: "Well, I parted his hair and there he was." Look what he has done. He persuaded New Line to invest in making three films at the same time. When I first read *Lord of the Rings* I wanted to see a film of it. But at that time the technology wasn't there, there was no such thing as CGI.'[7]

First seen descending the steps of the Orthanc Tower, Lee's Saruman, immaculate in flowing white, does indeed look like King Lear, as Ian McKellen put it, or else some towering Biblical prophet, or even God himself (the vengeful Old Testament variety, at any rate). The camera pans down eloquently from the cawing rooks encircling Saruman's dark-hued abode to the verdant greenery of its gardens – greenery soon to be wiped out as Saruman's monomania takes over – and all seems sweetness and light as the two wizards confer in the open air. In Saruman's grim, blue-striped study, however, Gandalf gets his first intimations that his old associate has gone over to the dark side, particularly when Saruman describes the dreaded Sauron, with barely concealed relish, as 'a great eye, lidless, wreathed in flame...' Lee is favoured with giant close-ups here, an impressively hooked nose looming into view below luxuriant eyebrows that beetle across the full width of the 70mm screen. Resplendent on his throne, he conveys Saruman's power-mania with the subtlest brushstrokes – yet it pulses unmistakably, unnervingly, from the screen.

When Gandalf realises the full extent of his old friend's madness and tries to escape, Jackson supplements a nod to Brian De Palma's *Carrie* (as Saruman shuts the doors on Gandalf merely by looking sidelong at each of them in turn) with a blisteringly violent fight that plays like a white-bearded version of *The Matrix*. It's hard, too, not to be reminded of the wizards' contest played out by Boris Karloff and Vincent Price in Roger Corman's *The Raven*, with the combatants flinging each other around Orthanc prior to Saruman's climactic cry of 'I gave you the chance of aiding me willingly, but you have elected the way of *pain*!'

Later, Saruman is seen urging his Orc helpers to denude the landscape – with a discreetly retroflexed 'r', he orders his minions to 'R-r-r-rip them all down' as they busy themselves among the trees – prior to patrolling his Satanic mills and grimacing in triumph as a warrior Orc struggles into being in a welter of amniotic fluid. As Saruman chants in Quenya in order to unleash an avalanche on the fellowship, Orlando Bloom's rather fey Legolas aptly observes that 'There's a fell voice on the air...' And the same voice subsequently strikes a genuine chill when instructing his number one Orc to 'Bring them to me alive and unspoiled. *Kill* the others.' In all Saruman's appearances, Lee's self-satisfied half-smile suggests an almost childlike glee in his own awful machinations, a glee delightfully at odds with his saintly, white-robed appearance. Together with the preternatural gleam in his eye that so impressed Peter Jackson, it makes the viewer all too aware that, for Saruman, the access of power equals the irretrievable loss of sanity.

'There's a famous phrase that "Power corrupts, and absolute power corrupts absolutely,"' Lee reflected later. 'Well, that's what happens to Saruman, because he wants to take over Sauron's power and become the Lord of the Rings himself. Saruman sees what's going on through the Palantir and he thinks he can take over, but that's the greatest mistake he's ever made in his entire existence, which is many thousands of years ... When he first came to Middle-earth he was the noblest, finest and most powerful of all the Istari, but of course all that changes as his quest for power leads him towards the dark side.'[8]

No stranger to playing evil geniuses, Lee brought half a century's experience to this one and the result has a uniquely hypnotic power much enhanced by its state-of-the-art surroundings. Lee was disappointed by the excision of Saruman's dialogue expressing his frustration at being trapped within a frail human shell, but his presence still looms large in the film's hectic progress and makes an indelible impression.

He wasn't about to rest on his laurels, however, though yet another came his way in February 2002 in the form of an *Evening Standard* Lifetime Achievement Award. Later that month, he was at Ealing Studios for further work on *Star Wars: Episode II*, now fitted with the subtitle *Attack of the Clones*. And there was a slew of promotional work to deal with, too, taking Lee to Germany, Finland and New York, where he rubbed shoulders with Barry Levinson, Alfonso Cuaron, Norman Mailer, Martin Scorsese and, of course, Peter Jackson.

BUS SHELTERS WORLDWIDE

Star Wars: Episode II – Attack of the Clones finally hit theatres on 16 May, revealing Lee's Darth Tyranus as a much more ambiguous figure than the smouldering Saruman. Strange winged creatures encircle Dooku's tower stronghold on Geonosis just as birds of ill-omen surround Saruman's at Isengard. But Dooku himself is an affable, almost avuncular figure, while his separatist plot frequently seems more reasonable than the arrogant posturings of characters like Obi-Wan Kenobi and Mace Windu.

'Granted,' wrote Mark Caro in the *Chicago Tribune*, 'movies inspired by *Flash Gordon* serials aren't designed for character depth, but ... *Episode II* is at its most provocative as it makes you unsure about who the bad guys really are.'[9] To underline this ambiguity, Lee brings a sad fatalism to his interrogation of the suspended Obi-Wan, heaving a very heavy sigh as he references a character played by Liam Neeson in the previous instalment: 'Qui-Gon always spoke very highly of you. I wish he were still alive. I could use his help right now...' Lee's own take on the character's ambiguity is a straightforward one:

'Dooku is a typical product of a military academy,' he explains. 'He's a soldier. But he's much more than that; he's a politician. He's a very brilliant and clever man; just look at the way he persuades his allies to go along with his scheme, and the way he dupes Obi-Wan Kenobi. He's ambitious, he's ruthless, he's lethal. But he has a sincere grievance against what he considers a corrupt Republic.'

Presiding at a rust-coloured amphitheatre and attended by various green-faced Viceroys, Lee brings a similarly regretful twinkle to his sardonic warning to Samuel L Jackson's Mace Windu that 'You're impossibly outnumbered.' If the Stalgasin Hive's array of spitting CGI beasties and wave upon wave of droid battalions don't knock the viewer for six, there remains a final confrontation in Dooku's Geonosis hangar that won rave reviews from just about every critical quarter. According to Lou Lumenick of the *New York Post*, 'For my money, the rip-roaring light-saber battle that climaxes this blockbuster alone justifies the price of admission. The combatants are Yoda – yes, the sage Jedi master, now a full-fledged special effect rather than a puppet, though still voiced by Frank Oz – and Count Dooku, a scheming former Jedi played by 80-year-old icon Christopher Lee, who here tops even his saturnine villainy in *The Lord of the Rings: The Fellowship of the Ring*.'[10]

In the UK, meanwhile, Chris Hewitt of *Empire* magazine extolled 'Yoda's astonishing, crowd-pleasing battle with Count Dooku' as 'a showdown that is – inarguably – the *Star Wars* saga's greatest single moment.' The following year, Lee would put in an appearance at the Empire Awards to pick up a gong for (somewhat to his bemusement) 'Best Scene', having previously received an award from the same magazine for Lifetime Achievement.

'We tried a lot of things in that fight to discover what worked best,' Lee recalls. 'We started it in Australia and finished it at Ealing – it was a lengthy process.' The result is a truly breathtaking display, with the CGI pyrotechnics nicely balanced by some hokey Lucas dialogue irresistibly reminiscent of classic exchanges between Basil Rathbone and Errol Flynn. 'Brave of you, boy,' grins Dooku. 'But I would have thought you had learned your lesson.' 'I am a slow learner,' replies the beardless Anakin Skywalker implacably.

Having disarmed Obi-Wan, Dooku is faced down by Anakin in a dazzlingly edited lightshow of stroboscopic blues and reds prior to cutting his opponent's arm off and mournfully lolling his head in a gesture familiar from so many of Lee's earlier performances. Finally, the diminutive Yoda makes his entrance and, as in *The Fellowship of the Ring*, there's a nostalgic whiff of *The Raven* as the two combatants unleash their magical powers on one another. 'It is obvious that this contest cannot be decided by our knowledge of the Force,' Dooku finally concedes, 'but by our skills with a light sabre...' The ensuing duel between cinema's tallest leading man and smallest special effect provides a delightful summation of the numerous sword fights Lee has performed on screen

The Star Wars saga's greatest single moment?
As Count Dooku in Star Wars: Episode II – Attack of the Clones

– albeit one assisted (as is only reasonable when one of the duellists is in his late seventies) by CGI wizardry.

Lee finally hit 80 on 27 May, celebrating it with his first-ever visit to his ancestral Buckinghamshire home, Hartwell House. Three days later, he was off to

New Zealand again for further work on the upcoming *The Two Towers*, spending ten days on a trio of extra scenes that, in the end, weren't used. In July, Lee filmed two items for a BBC series called *Essential Poems (To Fall in Love With)*, a melange of romantic poetry devised by the glamorous Daisy Goodwin. For Kahlil Gibran's *On Marriage*, he was filmed against the stained glass of a Putney church and subsequently reproduced as a God-like hologram looming over Piccadilly Circus and other landmarks; for R S Thomas' *A Marriage*, he gave a very simple rendition from an armchair in a local old people's home.

More awards followed. In September, he received a Golden Clapperboard in Monte Carlo as 'the best interpreter of literary works on film', and the following month he picked up a World Award for Lifetime Achievement in Vienna, being handed his bronze miniature of Rodin's *Penseur* by Mikhail Gorbachev. 'It was fascinating, revealing,' Lee recalls. 'You suddenly find yourself talking to somebody who was one of the most powerful men in the world, who in fact changed the 20th century, changed our world.'

The Christmas launch of *The Two Towers* was somewhat coloured for Lee by the death, on 12 December, of his 85-year-old sister Xandra. He was buoyed up, however, by the enthusiastic critical response to the film, which mirrored the plaudits bestowed upon its predecessor. 'Jackson is one of the very few directors able to fluently combine live-action footage and digital animation,' commented Ty Burr in the *Boston Globe*, 'and he has a gift for pop-Wagnerian grandeur that reclaims cinema's primal power. The skirmish midway through between the heroes and Saruman's hyena-riding troops rivals Kurosawa's desperate choreography, and the Helm's Deep wrap-up is as clear as a military diagram and a frightening, panicky chaos.'

Burr also playfully alluded to the film's accidental topicality, pointing out that *The Two Towers* 'is a war film when all is said and done – one that's definitely not for children – and some will take that all the way to the metaphorical bank ... If you want to see Saddam Hussein in that fiery eye of Mordor, be my guest – if you squint, Christopher Lee's Saruman might even pass for Osama bin Laden – but keep in mind that it would be just as easy for someone else to see George W Bush.'[11]

The Two Towers is indeed a war film, a dark and forbidding fable that succeeded in taking even more money at the box-office than its somewhat sunnier predecessor. Lee's Saruman is seen orchestrating his armies, exerting his hypnotic power over Bernard Hill's decrepit King Théoden and conferring with his repulsive sidekick, Wormtongue (Brad Dourif). But his screen time is more limited than before, with Saruman's baleful presence looming over the action at all times but making little direct contribution to it.

Having had some of his footage cut from *The Fellowship of the Ring* and not reinstated for the extended DVD release, Lee is happy to report that 'In *The Two Towers* DVD, they've put back quite a lot of my material. In the theatrical version, there isn't a great deal of me, although Saruman's shadow hangs over the whole film and the other characters talk about him all the time.' The final confrontation at Isengard between Saruman and the fellowship, which forms the climax to Tolkien's second book and which Jackson had shot early in 2000, is cannily being kept back for inclusion in the third instalment of the trilogy, *The Return of the King*.

At the very end of 2002, Lee found himself having to fend off press speculation – mistaken, as it turned out – that he was due to take over the role of Professor Dumbledore in the *Harry Potter* films. With the original Dumbledore, Richard Harris, having died only days before, it was a process he found especially distasteful. In response to his resounding 'No comment,' the *Sunday Telegraph*'s 'Mandrake' column nevertheless pointed out that 'no self-respecting blockbuster can be made these days without Lee in the cast.' And on Boxing Day, the *Times* added to the adulation, nominating him as 'Actor of the Year' and recommending him for an even greater accolade. 'Partly because the Brits love longevity,' explained columnist Andrew Pierce, 'but mainly because he dominates the movie of the year, *The Two Towers*, with his performance as the evil wizard Saruman, knocking drippy Sir Ian McKellen into a cocked helmet. Go on Ma'am, make this fine old English ham a K.'[12] Though Lee would hardly endorse Pierce's description of Ian McKellen as 'drippy' – or, indeed, the description of himself as a 'ham' – it was nevertheless a nice thought.

2002 had been a momentous year, with the forbidding features of Darth Tyranus, light sabre in hand, and Saruman, brooding over the fateful Palantir, staring out from bus shelters across the globe. Lee had even been reproduced in the form of numerous souvenir toys to assist the marketing campaigns of both Lucasfilm and New Line, and shared none of the revulsion expressed by Alec Guinness for such miniaturised exploitation. 'In my view,' he says, 'these toys are very important. They continue to promote the films, they continue to promote my part in them and they continue to put me in front of the public. There are literally dozens of these figures, and I know that the revenue from them is crucial to the companies who produce these

Along with Darth Tyranus, Lee's monomaniac Saruman the White introduced a new generation to his riveting screen presence

extremely expensive pictures. And such marketing is obviously done on the basis of what you've put up there on the screen. I'd say it's just what an actor needs.'

Movie Magician

Into 2003, and on 27 February Lee left for France to start work on Olivier Dahan's *Les Rivières pourpres 2: Les Anges de l'apocalypse*, which had started filming three days earlier. This was a $25 million follow-up to 1999's *Les Rivières pourpres*, which had made a mint in France and acquired a cult reputation overseas, under the title *The Crimson Rivers*, as a sort of Gallic *Seven* or *The Silence of the Lambs*. It was memorably characterised in the *Seattle Times* as 'The most American French movie ever ... like a Hollywood blockbuster that accidentally got made by smart people.'

The new film, scripted by Luc Besson, retained the original's 'odd couple' investigative team of Pierre Niémans and Max Kerkèrian, with Jean Reno reprising the Niémans role and Benoît Magimel supplanting Vincent Cassel as Kerkèrian. Camille Natta was on hand to decipher the religious riddles thrown up by the team's investigation of a series of ghastly murders in Germany and eastern France, while Lee, cast as a mysterious German ancient called Heimerich, described the charismatic Reno as 'the most helpful and generous actor I have ever worked with'. Lee's work on the film encompassed Metz and Clarmont Ferrand as well as Paris, proceeding in fits and starts until early June. The finished film is due for release in France on 28 January 2004.

In May, Lee was voted in at number 31 in Channel 4's poll of the nation's 100 favourite film stars, a late addition to the millennial mania for entirely meaningless lists but still a gratifying accolade. The following month, now aged 81, he proceeded to Wellington once more to complete further pick-up shots for the final instalment of *The Lord of the Rings*.

Christopher Lee – Part Eleven

Prior to setting out on his octogenarian travels, Lee told the *Guardian* that 'I cannot wait for *The Return of the King*. It is the climax and people will get an overall picture of Middle-earth and of Tolkien ... They can't not give awards to *The Return of the King*. When there were no Best Picture or Best Director [Academy] awards for *The Fellowship of the Ring*, I thought it was a disgrace. The other [nominated films] were good movies but they did not even compare. You can't compare anything to these films. You cannot compare it with *Star Wars* or *The Matrix*, which I didn't understand a word of. There will never be anything like it again ... I love to work and to be able to still be working is wonderful; after all, how many roles are there for 81-year-olds? It has been hard work but definitely worth it.'[13]

It certainly was hard work, and continued to be so, as Lee proved by following his Wellington stint with an immediate move to Sydney for his second appearance as Count Dooku, aka Darth Tyranus, in George Lucas' *Star Wars: Episode – III*. He's aware that Dooku is due for some form of terminal retribution in the new film, only admitting to a desire for the character to be 'transformed into Darth Tyranus on a more permanent basis. I think it sounds much grander than Dooku...'

Despite his workaholic tendencies, Lee has expressed jocular misgivings about Peter Jackson's projected remake of *King Kong*. 'I sent a message to Peter the other day,' he reveals. 'I said, "You're not getting *me* into a gorilla suit."' He also hopes that a loose follow-up to *The Wicker Man*, currently titled *Mayday*, may yet go before the cameras, as well as being intrigued by an offer to play Professor Moriarty in a Sherlock Holmes picture called *The Baker Street Irregulars*. And, on top of all that, there's talk of a live-action version of the 1980 animated feature *The Last Unicorn*, in which this time Lee would add more than just his voice to the role of King Haggard.

'Just think of all the appalling people you'll meet!' That dire warning, issued by Lee's mother back in 1946, still seems valid mid-way through her son's sixth decade as a film actor. Whether inveighing against '15-year-olds with their caps on backwards' (ie, studio executives) or the moronic mating dances entered into by casting directors and producers, Lee has some pretty jaded opinions about the film industry. 'It depends who is 'hot',' he explained back in 1997. 'No one thinks about what happens to something hot: it cools or burns out. It's better to be permanently warm ... Casting is done on the basis of what you're paid and even if you make ten duds in a row it doesn't seem to matter... So many 'stars' are

Tuesday 14 May 2002: Lee joins co-star Hayden Christensen and director George Lucas at the Odeon Leicester Square for the UK premiere of Star Wars: Episode II – Attack of the Clones

petrified of having a real actor anywhere near them. I've seen them come and seen them go. They have a shelf life of five years.'[14]

Though quite happy being permanently warm, Lee is getting perilously close to being hot after his work on the *Lord of the Rings* and *Star Wars* sagas. Thanks to the staggering global success of both franchises, Saruman and Darth Tyranus have between them awakened a whole new generation to Lee's riveting screen presence, as well as reminding older cinemagoers of his unrivalled legacy of screen villains. And not just cinemagoers, but casting directors too. 'I'm being offered more work at the moment than at any other time in my whole career,' Lee confirms.

And his jaded views regarding the film business have been tempered somewhat by his recent encounters with Tim Burton, Peter Jackson and George Lucas, all three of them visionary directors in their different ways and all credited by Lee with 'the three I's – inspiration, imagination and instinct. They know what they want, they know how to get it and they care about what they're doing. That's really the characteristic common to all three. They care, they really care.'

The fantastic worlds created by Burton, Jackson and Lucas epitomise, for Lee, the magic that he considers the essence of cinema. He long ago expressed his determination to transport an audience rather than rub its nose in 'slice of life' realities. 'I believe that cinemagoers want to see something quite different from their own lives,' he insisted in 1962. 'Most of them aren't in the slightest bit interested in themes from everyday life. Thrillers, by contrast, are always popular. So I aim to entertain my audiences in as thrilling a style as I can.'[15]

Convinced of the magical properties of film-making, he's well aware that some of his own films have been less than magical. But, good, bad or indifferent, he's dignified them all and, in many cases, brought to them a magic of his own. Small wonder that, in recent years, he has so often been cast as an enchanter or magician – which makes that stage offer to play Prospero all the more tantalising. Unlike Prospero, however, Lee has no intention of 'abjuring' his magic; as noted earlier, retirement is not on his agenda. Fate cast him in the sepulchral mould of his idol, Conrad Veidt, while conferring on him the mantle previously worn by Boris Karloff. But, at the beginning of the 21st century, that mantle has yet to find a worthy successor. Christopher Lee's sinister glamour and monumental presence are unique.

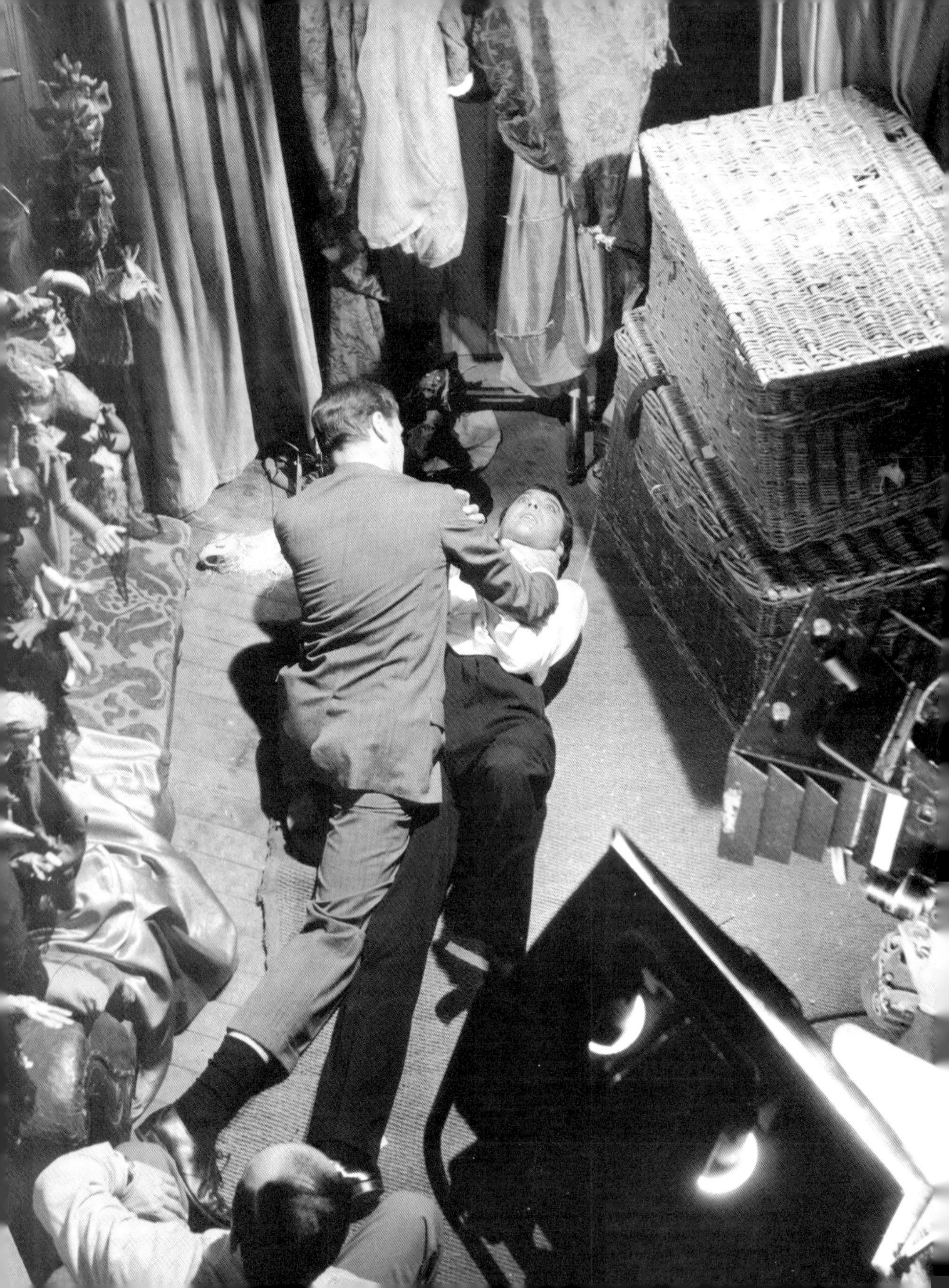

Appendix I: Film and Television Chronology

Listed below are Christopher Lee's appearances as an actor in films and television, arranged, as far as possible, in chronological order of production. All productions, except those marked b/w, are in colour. Titles given are those by which the films are known in their native countries – which, in the case of a co-production, means more than one title. UK and US titles, where different, are noted in parentheses.

Television productions are marked with an asterisk, and TV movies or mini-series are further marked with the acronym 'TVM'. Transmission dates (tx) are given when known; UK dates are those for the London region of the Independent Television network, except where stated otherwise. Tx dates attached to programmes made outside the UK relate to first broadcast in their country of origin. In the case of US broadcasts, the relevant network (CBS, NBC, ABC etc) is given or else an indication that the programme was syndicated, ie, not sold to a major network but broadcast on a channel-by-channel basis. TV productions which gained a theatrical release are identified as such but taken to be films and therefore not marked with an asterisk. Lee's numerous guest appearances on TV chat shows are not included; his documentary work as host/narrator, however, is listed in Appendix II, as are his contributions to animated films.

Many thanks to Julian Grainger for his invaluable work in filling in numerous blanks regarding production companies, alternate titles, countries of origin and other minutiae.

1946

Kaleidoscope # 3 *
BBC TV [GB] b/w tx (live) 20 December
director: Molly Terraine
[participant in 'Word Play' segment]

1947

Kaleidoscope # 5 *
BBC TV [GB] b/w tx (live) 17 January
d Molly Terraine
[participant in 'Word Play' segment]

Corridor of Mirrors
Cartier-Romney Productions/Apollo Films [GB] b/w
d Terence Young
[Charles]

One Night With You
Two Cities Films [GB] b/w
d Terence Young
[Pirelli's assistant]

Hamlet
Two Cities Films [GB] b/w
d Laurence Olivier
[palace guard, unbilled]

Penny and the Pownall Case
Highbury Productions/Production Facilities [GB] b/w
d [H E] 'Slim' Hand
[Jonathan Blair]

My Brother's Keeper
Gainsborough Pictures [GB] b/w
d Alfred Roome
[policeman; scenes deleted]

Saraband for Dead Lovers
[US: *Saraband*]
Ealing Studios [GB]
d Basil Dearden
[Duke Antony von Wolfenbuttel; scenes deleted]

1948

Song for Tomorrow
Highbury Productions [GB] b/w
d Terence Fisher
[Auguste]

Scott of the Antarctic
Ealing Productions [GB]
d Charles Frend
[Bernard Day]

Trottie True
[US: *Gay Lady*]
Two Cities Films [GB]
d Brian Desmond Hurst
[Hon Bongo Icklesham, unbilled]

1949

They Were Not Divided
Two Cities Films [GB] b/w
d Terence Young
[Chris Lewis]

Prelude to Fame
Two Cities Films [GB] b/w
d Fergus McDonell
[journalist, unbilled]

1950

Captain Horatio Hornblower R.N.
[US: *Captain Horatio Hornblower*]
Warner Bros First National Productions [GB]
d Raoul Walsh
[Spanish captain, unbilled]

1951

Valley of Eagles
Independent Sovereign Films [GB] b/w
d Terence Young
[Holt (Swedish detective)]

The Crimson Pirate
Warner Bros First National/Norma Productions [GB/US]
d Robert Siodmak
[Joseph (attaché), unbilled]

Struggling with Mel Ferrer in The Hands of Orlac / Les Mains d'Orlac *(1960)*

I Made News # 3:
The Theft of the Pink Diamond *
BBC TV [GB] b/w tx (live) 2 November
d Leonard Brett
[Commissaire de Police]

Babes in Bagdad
Danziger Brothers [US]
d Edgar G Ulmer
[slave trader, unbilled]

1952

Paul Temple Returns
Nettlefold Productions [GB] b/w
d Maclean Rogers
[Sir Felix Raybourne]

Top Secret
[US: ***Mr Potts Goes to Moscow***]
Associated British [GB] b/w
d Mario Zampi
[Russian spy in hotel foyer, unbilled]

Moulin Rouge
Romulus Films [GB]
d John Huston
[Georges Seurat, unbilled]

Innocents in Paris
Romulus Films [GB] b/w
d Gordon Parry
[Lt Whitlock, unbilled]

Douglas Fairbanks Presents *
Douglas Fairbanks Productions [GB] b/w (production schedule continued into 1953) shown in US on NBC as ***Douglas Fairbanks Jr Presents***
– *Destination Milan*
d Lawrence Huntington
tx US 25 March 1953; also formed part of UK theatrical release of the same title; then tx UK 28 September 1959
[Svenson]
– *American Duel*
d Lance Comfort
tx US 8 April 1953; also formed part of UK theatrical release ***The Triangle***; then tx UK 5 October 1959
[Franz]
– *The Parlour Trick*
d Lawrence Huntington
tx US 22 April 1953; also formed part of UK theatrical release ***Thought to Kill***; then tx UK 16 November 1959
[Junior Counsel]
– *Moment of Truth*
d Lance Comfort
tx US 7 October 1953, UK 25 June 1959
(matador)
– *The Death of Michael Turbin*
d Bernard Knowles

tx US 18 November 1953; also formed part of UK theatrical release of the same title; then tx UK 4 September 1959
[Radenko]
– *International Settlement*
d Lawrence Huntington
tx US 31 March 1954; released theatrically in UK as short film; then tx UK (series title ***Crown Theatre***) 26 June 1956
[Antonio]

1953

Tales of Hans Andersen / H C Andersens Sagor *
Scandinavian American Television Company [US/Sweden/GB] b/w
d Tom Connochie, Åke Ohberg
– *The Nightingale* [no known tx in UK]
[Emperor of China]
– *Wee Willie Winkit* [tx 1 October 1955]
[student]
– *The Cripple Boy* [tx 8 October 1955]
[Olle]
– *The Old House* [no known tx in UK]
[old man]

Colonel March of Scotland Yard:
At Night All Cats Are Grey *
Panda Films [GB] b/w tx US
4 October 1954 (ABC), UK
22 October 1955
d Phil Brown
[Jean-Pierre]

The Mirror and Markheim
Motley Films [GB] b/w TVM released theatrically as short film then tx UK
22 December 1956 (under title ***The Evil Thoughts*** as part of ***The Errol Flynn Theatre***)
d John Lemont
[Visitant]

1954

Douglas Fairbanks Presents *
Douglas Fairbanks Productions [GB] b/w shown in US on NBC as ***Douglas Fairbanks Jr Presents***
– *The Refugee*
tx US 21 April 1954, UK 18 June 1956
d Michael McCarthy
[Carl]
– *Street of Angels*
tx US 2 June 1954, UK 13 June 1956
d Arthur Crabtree
[Maurice]
– *The Awakening*
tx US 14 July 1954, UK 7 March 1956
d Michael McCarthy
[factory boss]

– *A Line in the Snow*
tx US 18 August 1954, UK 16 May 1956
d Michael McCarthy
[Brackett]
– *The Last Knife*
tx US 20 October 1954, UK (series title ***Crown Theatre***) 20 August 1956
d Michael McCarthy
[Tolsen]
– *Border Incident*
tx US 26 January 1955, UK 4 April 1957
d Derek Twist
[official]

Crossroads
Bartlett Productions [GB] b/w (short)
d John Fitchen
[The Ghost]

That Lady
Atalanta Pictures [GB]
d Terence Young
[Captain of the Guard]

The Dark Avenger
[US: ***The Warriors***]
Allied Artists [GB]
d Henry Levin
[French knight in tavern, unbilled]

Police Dog
Douglas Fairbanks Productions [GB] b/w
d Derek Twist
[Johnny]

Final Column
Danziger Productions [GB] b/w
tx US (ABC; series title ***The Vise***)
14 January 1955; released in UK as part of theatrical feature ***Final Column***; then tx UK (series title ***Tension***) 31 August 1962
d David MacDonald (plus co-d, uncredited, Joseph Losey)
[Larry Spence]

The Price of Vanity
Danziger Productions [GB] b/w
tx US (ABC; series title ***The Vise***)
20 May 1955; released in UK as part of theatrical feature ***Man in Demand***; then tx UK (series title ***Tension***) 8 April 1963
d David MacDonald
[Richard Martell]

Strangle Hold
Danziger Productions [GB] b/w
tx US (ABC; series title ***The Vise***)
8 July 1955; released in UK as theatrical short; then tx UK (series title ***Crooked Path***) 8 January 1960
d Ernest Morris
[Brookes]

Douglas Fairbanks Presents *
Douglas Fairbanks Productions [GB] b/w (production schedule continued into 1955) shown in US on NBC as
Douglas Fairbanks Jr Presents
– *The Wedding Dress*
tx US 13 July 1955, UK 23 October 1956
d Roy Rich
[Lt Krainski]
– *The Immigrant*
tx US 12 December 1955, UK 16 May 1957
d Michael McCarthy
[Makarenko]

1955

Alias John Preston
Danziger Photoplays [GB] b/w
d David MacDonald
[David Garrity, alias John Preston]

Storm Over the Nile
London Films Productions [GB]
d Terence Young, Zoltán Korda
[Karaga Pasha]

The Cockleshell Heroes
Warwick Film Productions [GB]
d José Ferrer
[Commander Alan Grieves]

The Adventures of the Scarlet Pimpernel: The Elusive Chauvelin *
Towers of London [GB] b/w
tx 9 November (first scheduled 19 October: not shown); syndicated in US
d Michael McCarthy
[Louis]

Moby Dick Rehearsed * (unfinished)
[GB] b/w (intended for the Ford Foundation Television-Radio Workshop's series *Omnibus* on CBS)
d Orson Welles
[Stage Manager, afterwards Flask]

Private's Progress
Charter Film Productions/Boulting Brothers/British Lion [GB] b/w
d John Boulting
[Major Schultz, unbilled]

The Adventures of Aggie: Cut Glass *
Mid-Ocean Films [GB] b/w
tx 3 December 1956 (Midlands), 27 April 1957 (London)
d John Guillermin
[Inspector Hollis]

Port Afrique
Coronado Productions [GB]
d Rudolph Maté
[Franz Vermes]

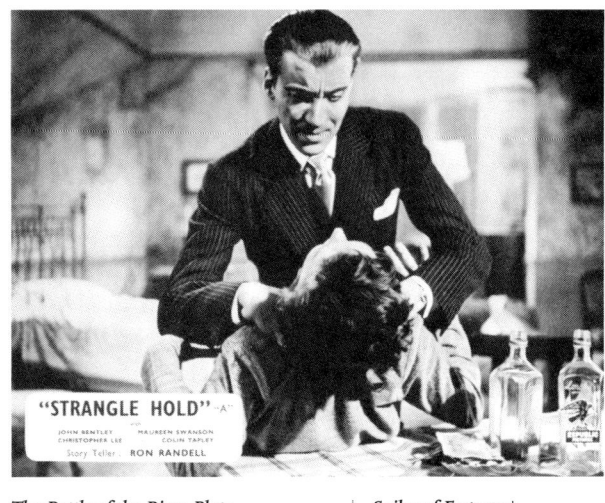

The Battle of the River Plate
[US: *Pursuit of the Graf Spee*]
Arcturus Productions [GB]
d Michael Powell, Emeric Pressburger
[Manolo]

Douglas Fairbanks Presents *
Douglas Fairbanks Productions [GB] b/w (production schedule continued into 1956) shown in US on NBC as
Douglas Fairbanks Jr Presents
– *The Man Who Wouldn't Escape*
tx US 1 October 1956, UK (series title *Saturday Playhouse*) 8 September 1956
d Michael McCarthy
[Luis]
– *Crown of the Andes*
tx US 5 November 1956, UK (series title *Summer Theatre*) 15 June 1957
d Francis Searle
[Felipe Nagy]

1956

Beyond Mombasa
Hemisphere Productions [GB]
d George Marshall
[Gil Rossi]

Assignment Foreign Legion *
Intel Films [GB] b/w
– *The Anaya*
tx UK 7 December 1956, US (CBS) 24 December 1957
d Lance Comfort
[El Abba]
– *As We Forgive*
tx 1 February 1957 (unlisted in *TV Times*); listed repeat 24 April 1958; no known tx in US
d Don Chaffey
[Rodin]

Sailor of Fortune *
Mid-Ocean Films [GB] b/w
(US syndication: 1957)
– *The Desert Hostages*
tx 16 December 1956
d Michael McCarthy
[Yusif]
– *Stranger in Danger*
tx 17 February 1957
d Michael McCarthy
[Carnot]

The Errol Flynn Theatre *
Motley Films [GB] b/w
(see also *The Mirror and Markheim*)
– *The Fortunes of War*
tx UK 22 September 1956, US 5 April 1957 (syndicated)
d John Lemont
[General Hamelin]
– *The Model*
tx 10 November 1956; no known tx in US
d Lawrence Huntington
[Maurice Gabet]
– *Love Token*
tx UK 12 January 1957, US 10 May 1957 (syndicated)
d Peter Maxwell
[Comte de Merret]

The Traitor
[US: *The Accursed*]
Fantur Productions [GB] b/w
d Michael McCarthy
[Dr Neumann]

Ill Met By Moonlight
[US: *Night Ambush*]
Rank Organisation Film Productions [GB] b/w
d Michael Powell, Emeric Pressburger
[German officer at dentist, unbilled; scene deleted in some versions]

As Brookes, a murderous gentleman's gentleman in the Danziger featurette, Strangle Hold

Fortune is a Woman
[US: *She Played With Fire*]
Frank Launder/Sidney Gilliat [GB] b/w
d Sidney Gilliat
[*Charles Highbury*]

The Curse of Frankenstein
Hammer Film Productions [GB]
d Terence Fisher
[*The Creature*]

1957

Gay Cavalier: The Lady's Dilemma *
George King Productions [GB] b/w
tx 25 June; no known tx in US
d Lance Comfort
[*Colonel Jeffries*]

Bitter Victory / Amère victoire
Transcontinental Films/Productions
Robert Laffont [GB/France] b/w
d Nicholas Ray
[*Sgt Barney*]

White Hunter: This Hungry Hell *
Beaconsfield Productions [GB] b/w
tx 3 October 1960 (Midlands);
US syndication from 1957
d Joseph Sterling
[*Mark Caldwell*]

The Truth About Women
Beaconsfield Productions [GB]
d Muriel Box
[*François Thiers*]

OSS: Operation Firefly *
[series title sometimes listed in *TV Times* as *Office of Strategic Services*]
Buckeye Enterprises [GB] b/w
tx 4 January 1958, US (ABC)
13 January 1958
d C M Pennington Richards
[*Dessinger*]

Ivanhoe: German Knight *
Sydney Box Productions/Screen Gems
[GB/US] b/w
tx 16 February 1958 (Midlands),
18 February 1958 (London); syndicated
in US
d Lance Comfort
[*Sir Otto*]

A Tale of Two Cities
Rank Organisation Film Productions/
a Betty E Box production [GB] b/w
d Ralph Thomas
[*Marquis St Evrémonde*]

William Tell: Manhunt *
ITC [GB] b/w tx 24 January 1959;
US syndication from 1957
d Peter Maxwell
[*Prince Erik*]

Battle of the V.1
[US: *Missile from Hell*]
Criterion Productions [GB] b/w
d Vernon Sewell
[*Brunner*]

Dracula
[US: *Horror of Dracula*]
Hammer Film Productions [GB]
d Terence Fisher
[*Count Dracula*]

1958

Corridors of Blood
Anglo Amalgamated/Producers
Associates [GB] b/w
d Robert Day
[*Resurrection Joe*]

The Hound of the Baskervilles
Hammer Film Productions [GB]
d Terence Fisher
[*Sir Henry Baskerville*]

The Man Who Could Cheat Death
Hammer Film Productions [GB]
d Terence Fisher
[*Dr Pierre Gerrard*]

1959

The Treasure of San Teresa
[US: *Long Distance* aka *Hot Money Girl*]
Orbit Productions [GB] b/w
d Alvin Rakoff
[*Inspector Jaeger*]

The Mummy
Hammer Film Productions [GB]
d Terence Fisher
[*The Mummy/Kharis*]

Tales of the Vikings: The Bull *
Bryna Productions [US] syndicated in
US from 1959; no known tx in UK
d Elmo Williams
[*Norman knight*]

Tempi duri per i vampiri
[US: *Uncle Was a Vampire*]
Maxima/CEI Incom/Mountfluor/
Compagnia Cinematografica [Italy]
d Steno (Stefano Vanzina)
(English prints credit Pio Angeletti)
[*Baron Roderigo*]

Beat Girl
[US: *Wild for Kicks*]
Renown Pictures [GB] b/w
d Edmond T Gréville
[*Kenny*]

Too Hot to Handle
[US: *Playgirl After Dark*]
Wigmore Productions/Associated British
[GB]
d Terence Young
[*Novak*]

The City of the Dead
[US: *Horror Hotel*]
Vulcan Productions [GB] b/w
d John Moxey
[*Professor Alan Driscoll*]

The Two Faces of Dr Jekyll
[US: *House of Fright*/*Jekyll's Inferno*]
Hammer Film Productions [GB]
d Terence Fisher
[*Paul Allen*]

1960

The Terror of the Tongs
Hammer Film Productions [GB]
d Anthony Bushell
[*Chung King*]

The Hands of Orlac / Les Mains d'Orlac
Riviera International Films/Société
Cinématographique des Studios de la
Victorine/Pendennis Films
[GB/France] b/w
shot in English and French versions
d Edmond T Gréville
[*Nero/Néron*]

One Step Beyond: The Sorcerer *
Collier Young/Lancer Films [US/GB]
b/w
tx US (ABC) 23 May 1961,
UK 17 January 1962
d John Newland
[*Reitlinger*]

Taste of Fear
[US: *Scream of Fear*]
Hammer Film Productions [GB] b/w
d Seth Holt
[*Dr Pierre Gerrard*]

1961

The Devil's Daffodil / Das Geheimnis der gelben Narzissen
[US alternate title: *The Daffodil Killer*]
Omnia/Rialto Film Preben Philipsen
[GB/West Germany] b/w
shot in English and German versions
d Akos von Rathony
[*Ling Chu*]

Ercole al centro della terra
[US: *Hercules in the Haunted World*,
UK: *Hercules in the Centre of the Earth*]
SPA Cinematografica [Italy]
d Mario Bava
[Lico]

The Pirates of Blood River
Hammer Film Productions [GB]
d John Gilling
[La Roche]

The Devil's Agent / Im Namen des Teufels
Emmet Dalton Productions/CCC Filmkunst [GB/West Germany] b/w
shot in English and German versions
d John Paddy Carstairs
[Baron von Staub]

Das Rätsel der roten Orchidee
[US: *The Secret of the Red Orchid*]
Rialto Film Preben Philipsen [West Germany] b/w
d Helmut Ashley
[Captain Allerman]

1962

Sherlock Holmes und das Halsband des Todes / Sherlock Holmes La Valle del terrore / Sherlock Holmes et le collier de la mort
[UK/US: *Sherlock Holmes and the Deadly Necklace*]
CCC Filmkunst/INCEI Film/Critérion Film [West Germany/Italy/ France] b/w
d Terence Fisher, Frank Winterstein
[Sherlock Holmes]

1963

La frusta e il corpo / Le Corps et le fouet
[UK: *Night is the Phantom*, US: *What*]
Vox Film/Leone Film/Filmsonor [Italy/France]
d John M Old (Mario Bava)
[Kurt Menliff]

Katarsis
[re-release title (1965): *Sfida al diavolo*]
Films della Mangusta [Italy] b/w
d Giuseppe Veggezzi (aka 'Joseph Veg')
[Old Man: Faust/Mephistopheles]

La vergine di Norimberga
[US: *Horror Castle*, UK: *The Castle of Terror*]
Atlantica Cinematografica Produzioni [Italy]
d Anthony M Dawson (Antonio Margheriti)
[Erich]

La cripta e l'incubo / La maldición de los Karnstein
[UK: *Crypt of Horror*]
MEC Cinematografica/Hispamer Film [Italy/Spain] b/w
d Thomas Miller (Camillo Mastrocinque)
[Count Ludwig Karnstein]

The Devil-Ship Pirates
Hammer Film Productions [GB]
d Don Sharp
[Captain Robeles]

The Gorgon
Hammer Film Productions [GB]
d Terence Fisher
[Professor Meister]

1964

The Alfred Hitchcock Hour: The Sign of Satan *
Shamley Productions [US] b/w tx US (CBS) 8 May 1964, UK 16 June 1968
d Robert Douglas
[Karl Jorla]

Il castello dei morti vivi
[UK, US: *The Castle of the Living Dead*]
Serena Film/Filmsonor[Italy/France] b/w
d Warren Kiefer
(also credited on Italian prints: Herbert Wise aka Luciano Ricci)
[Count Drago]

Dr Terror's House of Horrors
Amicus Productions [GB]
d Freddie Francis
[Franklyn Marsh]

She
Hammer Film Productions [GB]
d Robert Day
[Billali]

1965

The Skull
Amicus Productions [GB]
d Freddie Francis
[Sir Matthew Phillips]

The Face of Fu Manchu / Ich, Dr Fu Man Chu
Hallam Productions [/Constantin-Film] [GB/West Germany]
d Don Sharp
[Fu Manchu]

Dracula Prince of Darkness
Hammer Film Productions [GB]
d Terence Fisher
[Dracula]

Rasputin the Mad Monk
Hammer Film Productions [GB]
d Don Sharp
[Rasputin]

Theatre of Death
[US alternate title: *Blood Fiend*]
Pennea Productions [GB]
d Samuel Gallu
[Philippe Darvas]

Circus of Fear / Das Rätsel des silbernen Dreiecks
[US alternate titles: *Psycho-Circus/ Circus of Terror*]
Circus Films/Proudweeks Films/a David Henley film [/Constantin-Film] [GB/West Germany]
d John Moxey (credited on German prints: Werner Jacob)
[Gregor]

1966

The Brides of Fu Manchu / Die 13 Sklavinnen des Dr Fu Man Chu
Fu Manchu Films/a David Henley film [/Constantin-Film] [GB/West Germany]
d Don Sharp
[Fu Manchu]

Five Golden Dragons / Die Pagode zum fünften Schrecken
Blans Film [/Sargon/Constantin-Film] [GB/Liechtenstein/West Germany]
d Jeremy Summers (credited on German prints: Joachim Linden)
[Golden Dragon # 3]

The Vengeance of Fu Manchu / Die Rache des Dr Fu Man Chu
Babasdave Films [/Terra Filmkunst] [GB/West Germany]
d Jeremy Summers
[Fu Manchu]

1967

The Avengers: Never, Never Say Die *
Telemen/ABC Television [GB]
tx UK 17 March, US (ABC) 31 March
d Robert Day
[Professor Stone]

Night of the Big Heat
[US: *Island of the Burning Damned*]
Planet Productions [GB]
d Terence Fisher
[Godfrey Hanson]

Die Schlangengrube und das Pendel
[UK, US: *Blood Demon*]
Constantin-Film [West Germany]

CHRISTOPHER LEE – APPENDIX

Friday 15 September 1967: Dennis Wheatley visits the Elstree set of The Lost Continent, *a Hammer/Wheatley subject made concurrently with* The Devil Rides Out. *Lee had first met Wheatley at a Harrods literary lecture ten years earlier, in the first week of filming* Dracula

d Harald Reinl
[Count Regula]

The Face of Eve / Eva en la selva
[US title: *Eve*]
Udastex Films/Hispamer Film/Sargon/Towers of London/Ada Films [GB/Spain/Liechtenstein]
d Jeremy Summers
[Colonel Stewart]

The Devil Rides Out
[US: *The Devil's Bride*]
Hammer Film Productions [GB]
d Terence Fisher
[Duc de Richleau]

The Blood of Fu Manchu / Der Todeskuß des Dr Fu Man Chu / Fu Manchú y el beso de la muerte
[US alternate titles: *Kiss and Kill/Against All Odds*]
Udastex Films/Terra Filmkunst/Ada Films [GB/West Germany/Spain]
d Jesús Franco
[Fu Manchu]

1968

Curse of the Crimson Altar
[US: *The Crimson Cult*]
Tigon British/American International [GB]
d Vernon Sewell
[Morley]

Dracula Has Risen From the Grave
Hammer Film Productions [GB]
d Freddie Francis
[Dracula]

The Castle of Fu Manchu / Die Folterkammer des Dr Fu Man Chu / Il castello di Fu Manchu / El castillo de Fu Manchú
Towers of London/Terra Filmkunst/Italian International Film/Producciones Cinematográficas Balcázar [GB/West Germany/Italy/Spain]
d Jesús Franco
[Fu Manchu]

The Avengers: The Interrogators *
ABC Television/Thames Television [GB]
tx UK 1 January 1969, US (NBC) 20 January 1969
d Charles Crichton
[Colonel Mannering]

The Oblong Box
American International Productions [GB]
d Gordon Hessler
[Dr Newhartt]

1969

De Sade 70 / Wildkatze / Die Jungfrau und die Peitsche / Marquis de Sade's 'Philosophy in the Boudoir'
[US: *Eugénie ... the Story of Her Journey into Perversion*]
Sargon/Producciones Cinematográficas Balcázar/Hape Film/Video-Tel International [Liechtenstein/Spain/West Germany/GB]
d Jesús Franco
[Dolmance]

The Magic Christian
Grand Films [GB]
d Joe McGrath
[Ship's Vampire]

Scream and Scream Again
American International/Amicus Productions [GB]
d Gordon Hessler
[Fremont]

The Private Life of Sherlock Holmes
Phalanx Productions/Mirisch Productions/Sir Nigel Films [GB/US]
d Billy Wilder
[Mycroft Holmes]

252

Julius Caesar
Commonwealth United Productions/
a Peter Snell production [GB]
d Stuart Burge
[Artemidorus]

El proceso de las brujas / Il trono del fuoco / Der Hexentöter von Blackmoor / The Bloody Judge
[US alternate title: *Night of the Blood Monster*]
Sargon/Fénix Cooperativa Cinematográfica/Prodimex Film/Terra Filmkunst/Towers of London [Liechtenstein/Spain/Italy/West Germany/GB]
d Jesús Franco
[Baron George Jeffreys, Lord Chief Justice]

One More Time
Chrislaw Productions/Trace-Mark Productions [US]
d Jerry Lewis
[unbilled guest appearance with Peter Cushing]

El Conde Drácula / Nachts wenn Dracula erwacht / Il conte Dracula / Bram Stoker's Count Dracula
[US: *Count Dracula*]
Sargon/Fénix/Corona/Filmar/Towers of London [Liechtenstein/Spain/West Germany/Italy/GB]
d Jesús Franco
[Count Dracula]

Cuadecuc Vampir
Films 59/Pere Portabella [Spain] b/w
d Pedro Portabella, Joan Brossa
[himself]

Taste the Blood of Dracula
Hammer Film Productions [GB]
d Peter Sasdy
[Dracula]

1970

Umbracle
Films 59 [Spain]
d Pedro Portabella
[himself]

Scars of Dracula
Hammer Film Productions [GB]
d Roy Ward Baker
[Dracula]

The House that Dripped Blood
Amicus Productions [GB]
d Peter Duffell
[John Reed in segment 'Sweets to the Sweet']

I, Monster
Amicus Productions/British Lion [GB]
d Stephen Weeks
[Marlowe/Blake]

1971

Hannie Caulder
Tigon British/Curtwel Productions [GB]
d Burt Kennedy
[Bailey]

Theatre Macabre *
Film Polski [Poland] 26 x 25 mins
TV anthology for US broadcast
d Ben Kadish
[host]

Pa jakt efter Dracula
Aspekt Film and SFP [Sweden]
TV drama-documentary; expanded version released theatrically in US as *In Search of Dracula The Legend and the Vampire Tradition*
d Calvin Floyd
[himself/Vlad Tepes/Dracula]

Dracula A.D. 1972
Hammer Film Productions [GB]
d Alan Gibson
[Count Dracula]

Pánico en el Transiberiano / Horror Express
Granada Films/Benmar Productions [Spain/GB]
d Gene Martin (Eugenio Martín)
[Professor Alexander Saxton]

1972

The Creeping Flesh
Tigon British/World Film Services [GB]
d Freddie Francis
[James Hildern]

Death Line
[US: *Raw Meat*]
K-L Productions (Jay Kanter/Alan Ladd Jr) [GB]
d Gary Sherman
[Stratton-Villiers MI5]

Nothing But the Night
[US: *The Resurrection Syndicate*]
Charlemagne Productions [GB]
d Peter Sasdy
[Colonel Charles Bingham]

The Wicker Man
British Lion [GB]
d Robin Hardy
[Lord Summerisle]

Poor Devil *
Paramount Pictures [US] TVM
tx (NBC) 14 February 1973,
tx UK (BBC1) 19 February 1974
d Robert Scheerer
[Lucifer]

Dark Places
Sedgled/Glenbeigh [GB]
d Don Sharp
[Dr Ian Mandeville]

The Satanic Rites of Dracula
[US: *Count Dracula and His Vampire Bride*]
Hammer Film Productions [GB]
d Alan Gibson
[Count Dracula]

1973

Le Boucher, le star et l'orpheline
[alternate titles: *Eulalie quitte les champs/Magic Circus*]
Films d'aventure et d'amour [France]
d Jérôme Savary
[Satanus/himself]

The Three Musketeers (The Queen's Diamonds) / Los tres mosqueteros (Los diamantes de la reina)
The Four Musketeers (The Revenge of Milady) / Los cuatro mosqueteros (La venganza de Milady)
Film Trust/Este Films [Panama/Spain] (single 'project' released as two films)
d Richard Lester
[Comte de Rochefort]

Orson Welles Great Mysteries: The Leather Funnel *
Anglia Television [GB] tx 13 July 1974
d Alan Gibson
[Arnaud]

1974

Space: 1999 *
Earthbound
ITC/RAI/Group Three Productions [GB/Italy]
tx UK 4 December 1975,
US 19 January 1976 (syndicated)
d Charles Crichton
[Zandor]

The Man With the Golden Gun
Eon Productions [GB]
d Guy Hamilton
[Francisco Scaramanga]

Diagnosis: Murder
Silhouette Film Productions/HTV

[GB] TVM released theatrically
d Sidney Hayers
[Dr Stephen Hayward]

1975

The Diamond Mercenaries
[US: *Killer Force*]
Michelangelo Productions [Switzerland]
d Val Guest
[Major Chilton]

To the Devil a Daughter / Die Braut des Satans
Hammer Film Productions/Terra Filmkunst [GB/West Germany]
d Peter Sykes
[Father Michael Rayner]

The Keeper
Lionsgate Productions [Canada]
d Tom Drake
[The Keeper]

Der flüsternde Tod
[UK: *Death in the Sun*, US: *Albino/ Night of the Askari*]
Lord Film Produktion [West Germany]
d Jürgen Goslar
[The Member in Charge: Bill]

1976

Dracula Père et Fils
[US: *Dracula and Son*]
Gaumont/Productions 2000 [France]
d Edouard Molinaro
[The Count]

Airport '77
Universal Pictures [US]
d Jerry Jameson
[Martin Wallace]

Starship Invasions / L'Invasion des soucoupes volantes
Hal Roach Studios [Canada]
d Ed Hunt
[Captain Rameses]

1977

Return from Witch Mountain
Walt Disney Productions [US]
d John Hough
[Dr Victor Gannon]

End of the World
Charles Band Ltd/The Irwin Yablans Company [US]
d John Hayes
[Father Pergado/Zindar]

How the West Was Won *
MGM Television [US] tx US (ABC) 12/19/26 February 1978
d Bernard McEveety
[Grand Duke Dmitri]

Caravans / Karevanha
Ibex Films/FIDCI [US/Iran]
d James Fargo
[Sardar Khan]

Circle of Iron
[UK: *The Silent Flute*]
Volare Productions [US]
d Richard Moore
[Zetan, Keeper of the Book]

1978

Saturday Night Live *
NBC Productions [US] tx (live) 25 March
d Dave Wilson
[guest host]

The Passage
Hemdale Holdings/Passage Films/Monday Films [GB]
d J Lee Thompson
[The Gypsy]

The Pirate *
Harold W Koch Productions/Warner Bros Television [US] TVM tx in two parts (CBS) 21/22 November
d Ken Annakin
[Samir al-Fayd]

Jaguar Lives! / El felino
Jaguar Productions/Films Internacionales [US/Spain]
d Ernest Pintoff
[Adam Cain]

Arabian Adventure
EMI/Badger Films [GB]
d Kevin Connor
[Alquazar]

Bear Island / Le Secret de la banquise
Selkirk Films/Bear Island Films/ Columbia Pictures/Canadian Film Development Corporation [GB/ Canada]
d Don Sharp
[Professor Lechinski]

1979

1941
A-Team Productions/Universal Pictures/Columbia Pictures [US]
d Steven Spielberg
[Von Kleinschmidt]

Captain America II *
[on-screen title: *Captain America*; aka *Captain America: Death Too Soon*]
Universal City Studios [US] TVM tx in two parts (CBS) 23/24 November
d Ivan Nagy
[Miguel]

Serial
Paramount Pictures [US]
d Bill Persky
[Luckman/Skull]

1980

Once Upon a Spy *
Columbia Pictures Television/David Gerber Productions [US] TVM tx 19 September
d Ivan Nagy
[Marcus Valorium]

Rollerboy
[US video: *Desperate Moves*, UK video: *Steigler, Stiegler*]
Chesham [Italy]
d Ovidio G Assonitis (aka Oliver Hellman)
[Dr Carl Boxer]

Charlie's Angels: Angel in Hiding *
Spelling-Goldberg Productions [US] TVM tx in two parts (ABC) 16/23 November
d Dennis Donnelly
[Dale Woodman]

The Salamander / La salamandra
Orbi/ITC Films International/Opera Film Produzione [GB/Italy]
d Peter Zinner
[Prince Baldassare]

Safari 3000
Levy-Gardner-Laven Productions/ MGM-UA Entertainment [US]
d Harry Hurwitz
[Count Lorenzo Borgia]

1981

Tales of the Haunted *
Barry & Enright Productions/Global Television Network/Gaylord Productions [US] tx daily 12-16 July (syndicated)
d Gordon Hessler
[host]

An Eye for an Eye
Frank Capra Jr/Avco Embassy [US]
d Steve Carver
[Morgan Canfield]

Goliath Awaits *
A Larry White-Hugh Benson

Productions presentation of a Larry White/Cay-Jay production in association with Columbia Pictures Television [US] TVM tx in two parts (OPT) 17/23 November; in UK 10/11 June 1982
d Kevin Connor
[John McKenzie]

The Return of Captain Invincible
Willara/Seven Keys [Australia]
d Philippe Mora
[Mr Midnight]

1982

Massarati and the Brain *
Aaron Spelling Productions [US] TVM tx (ABC) 26 August
d Harvey Hart
[Victor Leopold]

Charles and Diana A Royal Love Story *
Edward S Feldman Co/St Lorraine Productions [US] TVM
tx (ABC) 17 September
d James Goldstone
[Prince Philip]

House of the Long Shadows
London Cannon Films [GB]
d Pete Walker
[Corrigan/Roderick Grisbane/Bernard]

1983

The Far Pavilions / I paviglioni lontani / Palast der Winde
Goldcrest Films and Television/Home Box Office/Geoffrey Reeve and Associates [GB/US/Italy/West Germany] TVM released theatrically; tx UK (C4) 3/4/5 January 1984, US (HBO) 22/23/24 April 1984
d Peter Duffell
[Kaka-ji Rao]

New Magic
Brock-Trumbull Film [US]
'Showscan' short
d Douglas Trumbull
[Mr Kellar]

Faerie Tale Theatre: The Boy Who Left Home to Find Out About the Shivers *
Platypus Productions/Gaylord Production Company [US]
tx US (SHO) 17 September 1984, UK (C4) 27 December 1990
d Graeme Clifford
[King Vladimir/The Sorcerer]

1984

The Bengal Lancers (unfinished)
Evan Grove Productions [GB]
d Stephen Weeks

The Rosebud Beach Hotel
The Big Lobby Co/Almi Films [US]
d Harry Hurwitz
[Clifford King]

Howling II
[US alternate title: *Howling II ... Your Sister is a Werewolf*, UK video: *Howling II Stirba – Werewolf Bitch*]
Cinema '84/Hemdale Holdings/Granite Productions/Euro Film Fund [US]
d Philippe Mora
[Stefan]

Jocks
Ahmet Yasa/Mount Olympus Productions [US]
d Steve Carver
[President White]

1985

Shaka Zulu *
Harmony Gold/South African Broadcasting Corporation/Tele-München [US/South Africa/ West Germany] TVM tx (US syndication) 24/25/26 November, 2/3 December 1986
d William C Faure
[Lord Bathurst]

Mask of Murder
Master Film Production/an Arne Mattsson production [GB/Sweden]
d Arne Mattsson
[Jonathan Rich]

The Disputation *
Electric Rainbow Productions/Channel 4 [GB]
tx (C4) 21 December 1986
d Geoffrey Sax
[James I of Aragon]

1986

Mio, min Mio! / Mio, moj Mio
[UK, US: *The Land of Faraway*]
Nordisk Tonefilm/Gorky Film Studio/Norway Film Development Corporation/Svenska Filminstitutet/Sovin Film [Norway/Sweden/Soviet Union]
d Alexander Grammatikov
[Kato]

The Girl
Lux Film/an Arne Mattsson production [GB/Sweden]
d Arne Mattsson
[Peter Storm]

Un métier de seigneur / Un mestiere da signori / Der Verräter *
TF1 Films Productions [France/Italy/West Germany] TVM tx 6 December
d Edouard Molinaro
[Fog]

Casanova / Il veneziano Vita e amori di Giacomo Casanova *
Konisberg-Sanitsky Company/Reteitalia/Taurus Film/Hessischer Rundfunk [US/Italy/West Germany] TVM tx (ABC) 1 March 1987
d Simon Langton
[Count Branicki; scenes deleted in some versions]

1987

Operacíon cocaína
[US: *Dark Mission Flowers of Evil*]
Siodmak/Eurociné [Spain/France]
d Jesús Franco
[Luis Morel]

1988

Olympus Force The Key
Atlantis Pictures/General Entertainment Investments [GB]
d James Fortune, Robert Garofalo
[Filly]

Murder Story
Murder Story/Reeve and Partners [Netherlands/GB]
d [Eddie] Arno & [Markus] Innocenti
[Willard Hope]

Around the World in 80 Days / Il giro del mondo in 80 giorni / Put oko sveta *
Harmony Gold/Rete Europa/Valente- Baerwald/Salon/Avala [US/Italy/ West Germany/Hong Kong/Yugoslavia]
TVM tx (NBC) 16/17/18 April 1989
d Buzz Kulik
[Stuart, Reform Club member]

The Return of the Musketeers / Le Retour des mousquetaires / El regreso de los mosqueteros
Timothy Burrill Productions/Fildebroc/Cine 5/Iberoamericana Films [GB/France/Spain]
d Richard Lester
[Rochefort]

Honeymoon Academy
[UK video: *For Better or For Worse*]
Trans World Entertainment/Sarlui-Diamant Productions/Fidelity Films/Paul Maslansky Productions [US]
d Gene Quintano
[*Lazos*]

1989

La Révolution Française 2ème époque: les années terribles / The French Revolution The Terrible Years / La rivoluzione Francese Anni di terrore
Films Ariane/Films A2/Laura Film/Antea/Central TV/Alliance Communications [France/Canada/Italy/West Germany/GB]
TVM released theatrically
d Richard T Heffron
[*Sanson*]

La Chute des aigles
[export title: *Fall of the Eagles*]
Eurociné [France]
d Jesús Franco
[*Walter Strauss*]

Treasure Island
Agamemnon Films/British Lion [US/GB] TVM released theatrically
d Fraser C Heston
[*Blind Pew*]

Panga
[UK video: *Witchcraft*,
US video: *Curse III Blood Sacrifice*]
Blue Rock Films [South Africa]
d Sean Barton
[*Dr Pearson*]

Gremlins 2 The New Batch
Amblin Entertainment/Warner Bros [US]
d Joe Dante
[*Dr Catheter*]

The Care of Time *
Anglia Films [GB] TVM tx 24 August 1991
d John Davies
[*Karlis Zander*]

L'avaro / L'Avare / El avaro
Splendida/Çarthago/Pathé/Velarde/Cinecittà/RAI/TVE [Italy/France/Spain]
d Tonino Cervi
[*Cardinal Spinosi*]

1990

The Rainbow Thief
Timothy Burrill Productions [GB]
d Alejandro Jodorowsky
[*Uncle Rudolf*]

Journey of Honor / Shogun Mayeda
Mayeda Productions/Sanyo Finance/Sho Kosugi Corp/Sho Productions [US/Japan]
d Gordon Hessler
[*Philip IV of Spain*]

Sherlock Holmes and the Leading Lady *
Harmony Gold/Banque et Caisse d'Epargne de l'Etat Luxembourg/Banque Parabis Luxembourg/Silvio Berlusconi Communications [US/Italy/GB] TVM tx (US syndication) 16/23 August 1992
d Peter Sasdy
[*Sherlock Holmes*]

Incident at Victoria Falls *
[on-screen prefix: **Sherlock Holmes The Golden Years**] details as in previous entry TVM tx (US syndication) May 1992
d Bill Corcoran
[*Sherlock Holmes*]

1991

Double Vision *
Caméras Continentales/Telescene Film Group/Canal+/M6/Antenne 2/Gemini Film/a Steve Walsh production [France/Canada/Germany/GB] TVM
d Robert Knights
[*Mr Bernard*]

Jackpot (Classe speciale)
[export title: *Cybereden*]
Eidoscope/Canal+/Stelia Cinematografica [Italy/France]
d Mario Orfini
[*Cedric*]

The Young Indiana Jones Chronicles: Austria March 1917 *
Lucasfilm Television/Amblin Television/Paramount Television [US]
tx (ABC) 21 September 1992
d Vic Armstrong
[*Ottokar, Graf Czernin*]

1992

Death Train
[alternate titles: *Alistair Maclean's Death Train / Detonator*]
Yorkshire International Films/J & M Entertainment/British Lion/Jadran Film/USA Pictures [GB/Yugoslavia/US]
d David S Jackson
[*General Konstantin Benin*]

1993

Funny Man
Nomad Productions/Redman Entertainment [GB]
d Simon Sprackling
[*Callum Chance*]

Police Academy: Mission to Moscow
Warner Bros [US]
d Alan Metter
[*Commandant Rakov*]

1994

A Feast at Midnight
Kwai River Productions [GB]
d Justin Hardy
[*Major V E Longfellow*]

The Tomorrow People: The Rameses Connection *
Tetra Films/Thames TV/Central TV [GB]
tx 4 January to 1 February 1995
d Roger Gartland
[*Sam Rees/Rameses*]

Edgar Allan Poe's Tales of Mystery and Imagination *
Dark Film/JadranFilm [South Africa]
no known tx
d Hugh Whysall, Neil Hetherington, Jakov Sedlar
[host of all 13 episodes plus Prince Prospero/ the Red Death in **The Masque of the Red Death**]

1995

La Bibbia: Mosé / Moses *
LUBE/Lux Vide/Turner Film/Beta Film/RAI/Quinta Communication/France 2 Cinéma/Antena 3/ARD/MTM/Ceská Telerize/NCRV/BSkyB/Taurus Film [Italy/Germany/France/Spain/US/Czechoslovakia]
TVM tx (RaiUno) 18/19 December
d Roger Young
[*Rameses II*]

The Stupids
Savoy Pictures Entertainment/New Line Productions/Imagine Entertainment [US]
d John Landis
[*Evil Sender*]

Sorellina e il principe del sogno / Prinzessin Alisea *
Anfri/Sat 1/Canale 5 [Italy/Germany]
TVM tx (Canale 5) 2/4 January 1996, (Sat 1) 20 December 1996

Film And Television Chronology

Monday 14 March 1966: an astonishing star line-up at the rehearsal for the Royal première of Born Free: from left to right, Catherine Deneuve, CL, Raquel Welch, Woody Allen, Ursula Andress, Dirk Bogarde, Julie Christie, Virginia McKenna, Bill Travers, Deborah Kerr, Rex Harrison, Rachel Roberts, Warren Beatty, Leslie Caron, James Fox and Suzanna Leigh

d Lamberto Bava
[Azaret, the Enchanter]

1996

Ivanhoe *
BBC/Arts & Entertainment Network [GB/US] tx 26 January to 16 February 1997 (CL in episodes 3, 4, 5, 6)
d Stuart Orme
[Lucas de Beaumanoir]

The New Adventures of Robin Hood *
Tarnview/Dune/Metropole Television/Warner Bros International Television/Productions et Editions Cinématographiques Françaises/ Baltic Ventures International/ Weintraub-Kuhn Productions [US/France]
– *Robin and the Golden Arrow* [tx TNT 27 January 1997]
d Joe Coppoletta
– *Legend of Olwyn* [tx 24 February 1997]
d Terry Marcel
– *A Race Against Death* [tx 3 February 1997]
d Terry Marcel
– *Nightmare of the Magic Castle* [tx 7 April 1997]
d Dimitri Logothetis
[Olwyn]

The Odyssey / Die Abenteuer des Odysseus / Odissea *
[alternate title: *Homer's Odyssey*]
Hallmark Entertainment/American Zoetrope/ProSieben Media/Mediaset/ Skai TV/Kirchgruppe [US/Germany/ Italy/Greece]
TVM tx (NBC) 18/19 May 1997, (Canale 5) 28/29 September 1997
d Andrei Konchalovsky
[Tiresias]

1997

Jinnah
Quaid Project/Petra Films/Dehlavi Films [Pakistan/GB]
d Jamil Dehlavi
[Quaid-e-Azam, Mohammed Ali Jinnah]

The New Adventures of Robin Hood: The Sceptre *
details as above; tx TNT 11 October
d Terry Bedford
[Olwyn]

Talos the Mummy
Cine Grande/7th Voyage/KNB EFX Group/Carousel Pictures [US/Luxembourg]
d Russell Mulcahy
[Sir Richard Turkel]

1998

The New Adventures of Robin Hood: The Auction *
details as above; tx TNT 13 December
d Joe Coppoletta
[Olwyn]

1999

Sleepy Hollow
Paramount Pictures/Mandalay Pictures/American Zoetrope/Dieter Geissler Filmproduktion/Karol Film Productions [US/Germany]
d Tim Burton
[Burgomaster]

Gormenghast *
BBC TV/WGBH (Boston)/Chum City [GB/US/Canada]
tx (BBC 2) 17 January to 7 February 2000
d Andy Wilson
[Flay]

2000

The Lord of the Rings: The Fellowship of the Ring, The Two Towers, The Return of the King
New Line Cinema [US]

d Peter Jackson
[Saruman the White]

Am Anfang / In the Beginning *
Babelsberg International/Betriebs/
Hallmark Entertainment/NGP
Holding [DL/US]
TVM; US tx (NBC) 12/13 November,
DL tx (RTL) 4/5/ November 2001
d Kevin Connor
[Rameses II]

Star Wars: Episode II – Attack of the Clones
Lucasfilm [US]
d George Lucas
[Count Dooku/Darth Tyranus]

Ghost Stories for Christmas *
(*The Stalls of Barchester, The Ash Tree, Number 13, A Warning to the Curious*)
BBC Scotland [GB] tx (BBC2) 23, 26, 29, 31 December
d Eleanor Yule
[The Antiquary]

Les Redoutables *
Calliope Production [France]
'Confession' tx (13éme Rue) 21 January 2001
d René Manzor
[narrator of all 13 instalments and Death in *Confession*]

2001

further filming for *The Lord of the Rings: The Fellowship of the Ring*

2002

further filming for *Star Wars: Episode II – Attack of the Clones*

further filming for *The Lord of the Rings: The Two Towers*

2003

Les Rivières pourpres 2: Les Anges de l'apocalypse
[international title: *Crimson Rivers 2: Angels of the Apocalypse*]
Légende Entreprises/EuropaCorp/StudioCanal [France]
d Olivier Dahan
[Heimerich]

further filming for *The Lord of the Rings: The Return of the King*

Star Wars: Episode III
Lucasfilm [US]
d George Lucas
[Count Dooku/Darth Tyranus]

APPENDIX II: OTHER CREDITS

Voice and narration work includes:
Ten Little Indians [voice of Mr U N Owen] d George Pollock 1965 [1]
Victims of Terror: Stories in Stone / Victims of Vesuvius [on-screen narrator] d Harold Baim 1967 [2]
Revenge of the Dead / The Evil Force / Meatcleaver Massacre [on-screen narrator] d Evan Lee 1975 (see page 167) [1]
Muhammad Ali: Truth Victorious [on-screen narrator] d Norman Weissman 1975 [1]
Mysteries from the Unknown: The Occult [on-screen narrator] d Victor Hochberg; tx (US syndication) 7 September 1977 *
Nutcracker Fantasy [voice of Uncle Drosselmeyer and others] d Takeo Nakamura 1979 [1]
The Last Unicorn [voice of King Haggard] d Arthur Rankin Jr, Jules Bass 1980 [1]
Errol Flynn: Portrait of a Swashbuckler [on-screen narrator] d Craig Haffner 1983 (syndicated March 1987) *
Witness the Impossible [host] 52-min 'magic' special 1983 *
The Many Faces of Sherlock Holmes [on-screen narrator] d Michael Muscal 1985 [3]
Walhalla [German version; voices of Thor and Odin] d Peter Madsen, Jeffrey Varab 1986 [1]
Secret World [host] p Alan Sloan 25 x 30 min episodes 1988 *
The Phantom of the Opera [on-screen introduction to video reissue of 1925 film] d Michael Armstrong 1990
Ghost [narrator] d Simon Hicks (video release) 1991
Fear in the Dark [narrator] d Dominic Murphy tx (Channel 4) 31 October 1991 *
The Beauty and the Beast [voice of Monsieur Renard] supervising d Timothy Forder; animation d David Thwaytes 1992 [1]
Flesh and Blood The Hammer Heritage of Horror [co-narrator] d Ted Newsom; tx in two parts (BBC1) 6, 13 August 1994 *

100 Years of Horror [on-screen narrator] d Ted Newsom (18-part series) 1995 *
Strictly Supernatural [narrator of episodes *Séance, Tarot, Astrology*] d Ludo Graham, Justin Hardy (three-part series for Learning Channel) 1996 *
100 Years Count Dracula [host] d Peter Goedel 52-min documentary for Mediakonzept 1997 *
A Century of Science Fiction [narrator] d Ted Newsom 1997 *
The Wyrd Sisters [six-part animated series; voice of Death] d Mark Hall; tx (Channel 4) 18 May to 22 June 1997 * [4]
The Art of Singing [narrator, British version] d Donald Sturrock; two parts (*The Movie Era/The Age of Television*) both tx (BBC2) 2 January 1998 *
Empire of Death [narrator] d Peter Minns tx (BBC2) 31 May 1999 *
Érase una vez en Europa [host] d Carles Prats tx (Vía Digital) in 13 parts from 3 March 2002 *
Stolen [voice] animation d Joanne Simpson, Pat Gavin (promotional film for Save the Children) first shown in cinemas 28 April 2002 [2]
Essential Poems (to Fall in Love with) [poetry readings in 2nd and 5th programmes of five] d Helen Simpson tx (BBC2) 15, 18 February 2003 *

[1]   indicates feature film
[2]   indicates short film
[3]   this material was subsequently cannibalised for use as introductions to video reissues of the Basil Rathbone/Holmes films
[4]   available on US video as *Soul Music*

—   Lee's prolific dubbing work in the 1950s included Guy Hamilton's *Manuela* and Jacques Tati's *Monsieur Hulot's Holiday* (all voices). Seasons 2 and 4 of *Douglas*

Fairbanks Presents were partly filmed in West Germany and part of season 3 in Italy, utilising local actors, many of whom Lee subsequently re-voiced
- Lee is seen playing golf in Michael Seligman's short film *Golf in the Sun*, 1972
- Lee is also credited in John Landis' *Innocent Blood* (1992), which utilises a clip from *Dracula*; other rogue appearances (uncredited) include *Homicide and Old Lace*, a 1969 episode of *The Avengers* which incorporates a clip from *Never, Never Say Die*, and Michael Carreras' 1963 pop musical *What a Crazy World*, in which Joe Brown and Susan Maughan go to see *The Curse of Frankenstein*. James Mason, Shelley Winters and Sue Lyon do the same in Stanley Kubrick's *Lolita* (1962)
- Lee has also been the subject of *Cinema* (tx ITV 4 March 1971, d Roger Tucker), *This is Your Life* (tx ITV 3 April 1974, d Peter Webb), *An Invitation to Remember* (tx ITV 20 August 1989, d Mike Mansfield), an episode of *The World of Hammer* (*Hammer Stars: Christopher Lee*, tx C4 21 October 1994), the video release *The Many Faces of Christopher Lee* (d Colin Webb 1995), one of the many five-minute instalments of *Turning Points* (BBC 1998), and the 2003 documentaries *The Making of a Legend* and *Christopher Lee: A Life in Films*. The latter is a companion piece to the present book.

Appendix III: Apocrypha

A career as long-lived and wide-ranging as Christopher Lee's has inevitably given rise to more than its fair share of misinformation. Several published filmographies greatly exaggerate his number of credits – as can be seen above, there are quite enough of them as it is – by listing the same film numerous times in the belief that its alternate titles (or even its pre-production titles) represent separate films.

In addition, several projects that got no further than being announced in the trade press have been listed as finished films. These include *An Unknown God* (West German, 1985), *The Avalon Awakening* (British, 1988) and *Il monastero/The Monastery* (Italian, 1989), together with a 1995 Kevin Connor project called *The Knot*. Further unmade projects to beware of, other than those mentioned in the main text, are *Diabolica/La diabolika Lady* (Italian, 1965: to have co-starred Barbara Steele), *Dialogue of Death* (Italian-Spanish, 1971: to have been directed by Antonio Margheriti), *The Farm* (Canadian, 1972), *The Spirit of England* (Anglo-Spanish, 1974: to have been directed by Don Chaffey), *Oltre il tempo/Beyond Time* (Italian, 1977), *Moon in Scorpio* (Anglo-Canadian, 1979: to have been directed by Silvio Narizzano), *The Khyber Horse* (British, 1984: proposed follow-up to *The Bengal Lancers*, itself abandoned), *Doom Ship* (British, 1987: to have co-starred Britt Ekland) and *Fire Below* (American, 1987: eventually made, without Lee, as *Bloodstone*).

Completed films which wrongly appear in Lee's filmographies include *The Luck of the Irish* (a British comedy of 1948), *99 mujeres/99 Women* (one of the Harry Alan Towers/ Jesús Franco pictures from the late 1960s) and two 1980 productions, *Blood Beach* and *Sunday Games*. The confusion surrounding the latter has arisen because Lee appeared in a US TV quiz show of the same name in the same year. Lee has also been erroneously credited with a 1983 US mini-series called *Sadat* and the 1997 Harry Alan Towers production *Marco Polo*. Late 1960s filmographies list a Swedish film called *Deserve the Fair* and a similar situation applies to a late 1980s item called *Couleur passion*. It has not been possible to establish what these projects were, but Lee confirms that, whatever they were, he did not appear in them.

The most persistent errors involve *Obsession* and *The Longest Day*. The former is a British thriller from 1948, directed by Edward Dmytryk, in which Lee is said to have played a policeman in the entourage of Naunton Wayne.

A still exists of a PC bearing a passing resemblance to Lee, but Lee is adamant that it is not him. A lengthy US profile published in 1973 (in *Cinefantastique* Volume 3 number 1) made the ludicrous claim that, while making *Ercole al centro della terra* in 1961, 'Lee also found work doing several stunting bits in Darryl Zanuck's all-star production of *The Longest Day*.' This error proceeds from the presence in the film of a French actor vaguely resembling Lee. And, for the record, Lee is not to be confused with either the BBC Radio dramatist Christopher Lee, the Australian screenwriter Christopher Lee or the Cambridge historian Christopher Lee.

Testing for the title role in Harald Reinl's Winnetou, *a German Western in the popular 'Shatterhand' series, 1962*

Draconian discipline at the Hildern Institute for Mental Disorders in The Creeping Flesh *(1972)*

SOURCE NOTES

INTRODUCTION
1. M Ronan, *The Reluctant Villain*, Montage August 1960
2. Raymond Durgnat, *Erotism in Cinema*, Films and Filming January 1962
3. quoted in Ken Ferguson, *The Real Face of Christopher Lee*, Photoplay December 1965
4. quoted in the *Evening News* 4 July 1967
5. quoted in the *Sunday Telegraph* 18 August 1991
6. quoted in Mark A Miller, *Christopher Lee and Peter Cushing and Horror Cinema*, Jefferson NC 1995
7. Theodore Strauss, *The Return of the Somnambulist*, New York Times 12 May 1940
8. quoted in Audrey Williamson, *Frankenstein's Successors on the Screen*, the *Times* 11 January 1960
9. quoted in Betty Harris, *Villain by Accident*, Modern Screen June 1941
10. Richard Raine, *Please Do Not Faint When You See This*, Evening News 2 May 1957
11. review of *The Mummy*, the *Times* 28 September 1959
12. Christopher Lee, *What Horror Means to Me*, Picturegoer Film Annual 1959-60, London 1959

PART ONE: RANK CHARMER
1. quoted in the *Observer* [*Life* magazine] 30 April 1995
2. quoted in *Empire* March 1993
3. *Observer* [*Life* magazine], op cit
4. ibid
5. Diana Dors, *Swingin' Dors*, London 1960
6. *The Cinema* 27 November 1946

7. Norman Hudis, *The Way to the Stars*, undated Rank publicity feature
8. *Worthing Herald* 18 July 1947
9. Hudis, op cit
10. *Worthing Gazette* 19 May 1948
11. *Worthing Gazette* 2 February 1949
12. *Worthing Herald* 11 February 1949
13. *The Cinema Studio* [weekly] 13 July 1949
14. quoted in *The Cinema Studio* [weekly] 1 February 1950
15. *The Cinema Studio* [monthly] October 1951
16. *The Cinema* 8 April 1952

PART TWO:
TV AND OTHER TRIALS

1. quoted in *TV Times* 27 April 1956
2. *To-Day's Cinema* 9 July 1952
3. *To-Day's Cinema* 9 February 1953
4. quoted in Robert W Pohle Jr and Douglas C Hart, *The Films of Christopher Lee*, Metuchen NJ 1983
5. Robert Muller, *The Other Fairbanks*, Picture Post 19 February 1955
6. quoted in the *Daily Sketch* 6 December 1955
7. *The Cinema* 2 February 1955
8. quoted in *The Cinema* 26 May 1955
9. quoted in the *Evening News* 8 February 1956
10. quoted in Brian McFarlane, *An Autobiography of British Cinema*, London 1997
11. quoted in *Little Shoppe of Horrors* # 12, April 1994
12. quoted in *To-Day's Cinema* 31 October 1955
13. Ian Carmichael, *Will the Real Ian Carmichael...*, London 1979
14. quoted in *Essex Weekly News* 24 November 1955
15. Ivor Brown, *All's Welles*, in *Theatre 1954-5*, London 1955
16. Russell Davies (ed), *The Kenneth Williams Diaries*, London 1993
17. Michael Powell, *Million Dollar Movie*, New York 1995
18. Richard Combs in *Film Comment* Vol 31 # 2, March/April 1995
19. *Million Dollar Movie*, op cit
20. quoted in *To-Day's Cinema* 28 November 1955
21. quoted in *TV Times* 7 September 1956
22. Peter Richards in *Film Comment*, op cit
23. *Million Dollar Movie*, op cit
24. quoted in Francis Koval, *Films in 1951*, Sight and Sound 'Festival of Britain' Special, July 1951

PART THREE:
MALIGNANT HEROES

1. *To-Day's Cinema* 13 August 1956
2. quoted in *Hammer Horror* # 1, March 1995
3. letter in *Little Shoppe of Horrors* # 10/11, July 1990
4. reprinted in *Hammer Horror* # 1, op cit
5. Pohle and Hart, op cit
6. *An Autobiography of British Cinema*, op cit
7. ibid
8. Dirk Bogarde, *For the Time Being*, London 1998
9. *Is Jimmy Carreras King of Nausea?*, Daily Express 23 May 1958
10. *Dracula's Macabre Decline*, Observer 31 May 1958
11. quoted in *Fangoria* # 41, January 1985
12. quoted in *Little Shoppe of Horrors* # 4, April 1978
13. quoted in Sarah Stoddart, *Chillers a Menace? Rubbish, says Christopher Lee*, in Picturegoer 1 November 1958
14. ibid
15. quoted in *Scarlet Street* # 8, Fall 1992
16. quoted in *Dracula: The Complete Vampire* [Starlog Movie Magazine # 6], 1992
17. composited from interviews in *Starlog* Movie Magazine # 6 and *Scarlet Street* # 8
18. Gordon Campbell, *Scream boy? No – dream boy*, in Picturegoer 2 August 1958
19. *Chillers a Menace?* op cit
20. Denis Meikle, *A History of Horrors: The Rise and Fall of the House of Hammer*, Lanham MD 1996
21. Sarah Stoddart, *Dracula Keeps That Date*, in Picturegoer 20 December 1958
22. Lawrence Alloway, *Monster Films*, in Encounter Vol 14 # 1, January 1960
23. reprinted in Leslie Halliwell, *The Filmgoer's Book of Quotes*, London 1973
24. *Intermezzo* Vol 14 # 22/23, 15 December 1959
25. quoted in *To-Day's Cinema* 23 October 1959
26. Barbara Windsor and Robin McGibbon, *All Of Me*, London 2000
27. quoted in *A History of Horrors*, op cit
28. ibid

PART FOUR:
EURO-ACTOR

1. Pat Gledhill, *How a bachelor lives*, Picturegoer 23 April 1960
2. quoted in Sarah Stoddart, *Horror Heart-Throb*, Picturegoer 9 January 1960
3. Jimmy Sangster, *Do You Want It Good or Tuesday? From Hammer Films to Hollywood! A Life in the Movies*, Baltimore MD 1997
4. quoted in Pohle and Hart, op cit
5. *Evening News* 30 March 1961
6. quoted in Marcus Hearn and Alan Barnes, *The Hammer Story*, London 1997
7. quoted in the *Daily Mail* 27 February 1995
8. Antonio Bruschini, *Horror all' Italiana 1957-1979*, Firenze 1996
9. quoted in Luigi Cozzi, *Il creatore di mostri: Mario Bava*, in Il giaguaro Vol 1 # 2, May 2000
10. quoted in *Kinematograph Weekly* 3 August 1961
11. C H B Williamson, *Studio wise*, Daily Cinema 6 November 1961
12. ibid, 10 November 1961
13. quoted in *Picturegoer* December 20 1958
14. quoted in *Little Shoppe of Horrors* # 10/11, July 1990
15. quoted in *Cinefantastique* Vol 3 # 1, Fall 1973
16. quoted in Tim Lucas, *What Are Those Strange Drops of Blood in the Scripts of Ernesto Gastaldi?*, Video Watchdog # 39, May/June 1997
17. quoted in Bruschini, op cit
18. Lucas, op cit
19. quoted in *Hammer Horror* # 4, June 1995
20. *Daily Mail*, op cit
21. quoted in Mark A Miller, op cit
22. Robert Bloch, *Once Around the Bloch: An Unauthorised Autobiography*, New York 1993

CHRISTOPHER LEE – SOURCE NOTES

23 quoted in *Monsterland* December 1985

PART FIVE:
HOMECOMING

1 Helen Lawrenson, *Fu Manchu Strikes Again, Holiday* February 1966
2 Pohle and Hart, op cit
3 Allan Bryce, *Harry Alan Towers Interviewed, Shock Xpress 1*, London 1991
4 Mary Knoblauch, *The Return of Fu Manchu, Chicago American* 31 October 1965
5 *Christopher Lee's New Chamber of Horrors*, London 1974
6 quoted in *Interview* # 6, June 1996
7 quoted in *Scarlet Street* # 14, Spring 1994
8 *Daily Cinema* 4 October 1967
9 Robert Salmaggi, *Fu-Get It, World Journal Tribune* 15 December 1966
10 Pohle & Hart, op cit
11 ibid
12 Bloch, op cit
13 quoted in *Aus der Fabrik des Bösen II*, in *Film* vol 5 # 12, December 1967
14 quoted in Bryce, op cit
15 *CinemaTV Today* 15 January 1972
16 quoted in *L'incroyable cinéma* # 5, Autumn 1971
17 ibid
18 quoted in *Little Shoppe of Horrors* # 13, November 1996
19 quoted in *Supernatural Horror Filming* # 1, January 1969
20 quoted in *Starlog* Movie Magazine # 6, op cit
21 ibid
22 quoted in the *Sunday Mirror* 29 December 1968
23 quoted in Victoria Price, *Vincent Price: A Daughter's Biography*, New York 1999

PART SIX:
BEYOND THE GRAVEYARD

1 quoted in *Photoplay* September 1968
2 Robert Murphy, *Sixties British Cinema*, London 1992
3 quoted in *Time Out* 11-18 July 1990
4 quoted in *Movie Collector* # 8, November/December 1994
5 quoted in *L'incroyable cinéma*, op cit
6 quoted in *Starlog* Movie Magazine # 6, op cit
7 quoted in *The Dark Side* # 38, February/March 1994
8 quoted in *Little Shoppe of Horrors* # 13, November 1996
9 Martin Jarvis, *Acting Strangely*, London 1999
10 Pedro Portabella interviewed by Josephine Botting, Barcelona, May 2000
11 Jonathan Rosenbaum, *Portabella at the NFT – A New Vision from Spain, Time Out* 22-28 September 1972
12 ibid
13 quoted in Peter S Haigh, *The Fantastic 'Fang Mail' of Christopher Lee, ABC Film Review* November 1970
14 *Little Shoppe of Horrors* # 13, op cit
15 *Mr Ghoul in the Groove, Sunday Mirror* 20 September 1970
16 quoted in *The Dark Side* # 45, April/May 1995
17 quoted in *L'incroyable cinéma*, op cit
18 quoted in *Today's Cinema* 16 March 1971
19 quoted in Mark A Miller, op cit
20 quoted in Susan de Muth, *Lee Way, What's On in London* 25 July 1990
21 *Supernatural Horror Filming*, op cit
22 quoted in *Films Illustrated* # 17, November 1972
23 review of *The Creeping Flesh, Sunday Times* 4 March 1973
24 review of *Horror Express, Sunday Telegraph* 26 June 1974

PART SEVEN:
FROM SCAREMONGER TO SCARAMANGA

1 quoted in *Many Bloodsuckers, Films Illustrated* # 2, August 1971
2 quoted in Michael White, *A Tall Terrible Tale*, the *Guardian* 11 March 1972
3 quoted in *Variety* 4 July 1973
4 quoted in *Cinefantastique*, Vol 2 # 3, Winter 1973
5 quoted in *Little Shoppe of Horrors* # 10/11, July 1990
6 *Many Bloodsuckers*, op cit
7 quoted in Chris Knight, *London Scene: Cushing and Lee, Cinefantastique* Vol 2 # 4, Summer 1973
8 quoted in *Cinefantastique* Vol 6 # 3, Winter 1977
9 quoted in *Movie Collector*, op cit
10 quoted in *Evening Standard* 15 November 1972
11 as 7
12 quoted in *Photoplay* December 1974
13 quoted in Mark Shivas, *Lester's Back and the Musketeers Have Got Him, New York Times* 5 August 1973
14 in *Film Dope* # 34, March 1986
15 *Daily Mail* 18 October 1973
16 quoted in *Cinema Canada* April 1976
17 quoted in Pohle and Hart, op cit
18 quoted in *Photoplay* January 1974
19 quoted in John Higgins, *From Scaremonger to Scaramanga*, the *Times* 12 December 1974
20 Alan Barnes and Marcus Hearn, *Kiss Kiss Bang Bang! The Unofficial James Bond Film Companion*, London 1997
21 quoted in *Cinefantastique* Vol 4 # 1, Spring 1975
22 quoted in Suzanne Lowry, *Teething Pains, Guardian* 7 November 1974
23 quoted in the *Independent* 24 December 1997
24 quoted in *Fangoria* # 42, February 1985
25 quoted in *Daily Mail* 4 March 1974
26 quoted in *Screen International* # 4, 27 September 1975
27 *Cinema Canada*, op cit

PART EIGHT:
FROM BELGRAVIA TO BEL-AIR

1 quoted in David Castell, *Tall Dark and No Longer Gruesome, Films Illustrated* # 86, October 1978
2 quoted in *The Stage and Television Today* 23 November 1989
3 *Christopher Lee plays Dracula for the last time... again!, Cinefantastique* Vol 5 # 4, Spring 1977
4 Christopher Lee interviewed by Peter Nicholson, Pinewood Studios, August 1978
5 Barbra Paskin, *New Vistas for Chris, Photoplay* May 1977
6 Castell, op cit

7   quoted in David Del Valle, *Tall Dark and Gruesome*, *Films and Filming* # 372, September 1985
8   ibid
9   ibid
10 ibid
11 *Hollywood Reporter* 10 March 1978
12 David Castell in *Films Illustrated* # 72, August 1977
13 Nicholson interview, op cit
14 quoted in *Premiere* August 1995
15 quoted in *Fangoria* # 42, February 1985
16 quoted in *Hollywood Reporter* 23 May 1978
17 quoted in Mark A Miller, op cit
18 James Cameron-Wilson, *The 'Most Terrible Actor'*, *What's On in London*, 29 September 1978
19 Mark A Miller, op cit
20 quoted in *What film gave you the most pleasure during 1978?*, *Films Illustrated* # 90, February 1979
21 Pohle and Hart, op cit
22 quoted in *Today* 15 December 1986
23 in *The Film Yearbook 1983*, London 1982
24 quoted in *Cinefantastique* Vol 11 # 4, December 1981
25 quoted in *Filmfax* # 62, August/September 1997
26 quoted in Bill Warren, *Splendid-Lee*, *Fangoria* # 150, March 1996

Part Nine:
Another Homecoming

1   quoted in De Muth, op cit
2   in *Screen International* 21 August 1982
3   quoted in *Fangoria* # 41, January 1985
4   quoted in *Screen International* 11 September 1982
5   Alvin H Marrill, *The Television Scene*, *Films in Review* August/September 1983
6   quoted in *Fangoria* # 150, March 1996
7   quoted in *Fangoria* # 42, February 1985
8   quoted in *Starburst* # 78, February 1985
9   ibid
10 quoted in Del Valle, op cit
11 quoted in Mark A Miller, op cit
12 quoted in *Today* 15 December 1986
13 *Ciné-Revue* Vol 66 # 24, 12 June 1986
14 quoted in distributor's production notes: *The Return of the Musketeers*
15 De Muth, op cit
16 quoted in *Empire* July 1990
17 quoted in Bill Warren, *Dracula is Not Rising from the Grave Anytime Soon*, *Fangoria* # 94, July 1990
18 *Empire*, op cit
19 quoted in *The Stage and Television Today*, 23 November 1989

Part Ten:
New Horizons

1   quoted in *Shivers* # 13, December 1994
2   quoted in *The Dark Side* # 2, November 1990
3   quoted in Richard Valley, *Interview With the Ex-Vampire*, *Scarlet Street* # 5, Winter 1992
4   quoted in Richard Valley, *Have Bowler Will Travel*, as above
5   quoted in Bill Kelley, *What Dracula Is Up To*, *Imagi-Movies* # 2, Winter 1993/4
6   quoted in the *Guardian* 16 May 1994
7   quoted in *Film Review* Special, Summer 1995
8   quoted in *Scarlet Street* # 13, Winter 1994
9   quoted in the *Observer* [*Life* magazine], op cit
10 quoted in Tristan Davies, *The Last King of Horror*, the *Daily Telegraph* 2 March 1995
11 quoted in the *Daily Telegraph* 20 May 1995
12 quoted in David Robinson, *Hammer head*, the *Times* 25 May 1995
13 quoted in the *Times* 2 June 1995
14 quoted in *Hammer Horror* # 3, May 1995
15 Ted Newsom, *Canterbury Tales*, in *Little Shoppe of Horrors* # 13, November 1996
16 the *Observer* [*Life* magazine], op cit
17 quoted in *Hammer Horror* # 5, July 1995
18 *Splendid-Lee*, op cit
19 quoted in *Radio Times* 1 February 1997
20 quoted in the *Daily Telegraph* 28 June 1997
21 quoted in the *Guardian* 25 September 1998
22 ibid
23 quoted in the *Observer* 12 September 1999
24 *Guardian* 25 September 1998, op cit
25 quoted in *Shivers* # 50, February 1998
26 quoted in *Radio Times* 15 January 2000
27 quoted in Bob Badway, *Prince of Darkness and Light*, *Filmfax* # 80, August/September 2000

Part Eleven:
Indian Summer

1   quoted in David Edelstein, *An Actor So Prolific It's Downright Scary*, in the *New York Times* 12 May 2002
2   quoted in *Starburst Yearbook* [*Starburst Special* # 55], December 2002
3   Edelstein, op cit
4   quoted in Hélène Marzolf, *Treize petits noirs*, in *Télérama* # 2661, 10 January 2001
5   quoted in Ann McFerran, *Relative Values*, *Observer Magazine* 5 May 2002
6   ibid
7   quoted in Victoria Barrett, *The Good, the Bad and the Christopher Lee*, in the *Guardian* 29 May 2003
8   *Starburst Yearbook*, op cit
9   Mark Caro, [review of *Star Wars Episode II*] *Chicago Tribune* 12 May 2002
10 Lou Lumenick, *Forceful return of George Lucas' serial thriller*, *New York Post* 12 May 2002
11 Ty Burr, *An epic of legendary proportions*, *Boston Globe* 18 December 2002
12 Andrew Pierce, *Making a Name in 2002*, in the *Times* 26 December 2002
13 Barrett, op cit
14 quoted in *Radio Times* 1 February 1997
15 quoted in 'Argus', *Christopher Lee: als Liebhaber unmöglich*, in *Bravo* # 2, 13-19 January 1963

Index

All italicised titles relate to film or TV productions except where indicated; page numbers in bold type refer to illustrations

Achmann, Werner Maria 118
Ackerman, Forrest J 101, 155
Ackland, Joss 204, 217
Adam, Noelle 72
Adam and Evelyne 23
Adams, Maud 149, 163, 165, 166
Addams, Dawn 69, **69**, 76, **77**, 83
Addison, John 14, 37
Adorf, Mario 120
Adventures of Aggie, The 43
Adventures of the Scarlet Pimpernel, The 43, 208
After the Ball [musical play] 36-7
Ahmed, Akbar 227, 229
Ahmed, Vaneeza 229
Airplane! 174, 207
Airport '77 173-4, **174**, 175, 176, 189
Aitken, Maria 228
Akins, Claude 217
Albarado, Louis 204
Aldridge, William 202
Alfred Hitchcock Hour, The 99-101, 126

Alias John Preston 40-1, **41**, 48
Ali, Muhammad 165-6, **165**
Allen, Irving 42
Allen, Patrick **116**, 117
Ambesi, Adriana 95
Amère victoire see *Bitter Victory*
American Duel 11, 34-5
Anderson, Gene 53
Andersson, Benny 201
Andress, Ursula 104, **106**, 162, 257
Andreu, Mariano 37
Andrew, Stella 24
Andrews, Eamonn 160, **161**
Angeli, Pier 44
Annakin, Ken 182
Antonelli, Laura 213
Aquari, Giuseppe 96
Arabian Adventure **180**, 180-1, 182, 189
Archer, Anne 182
Ardisson, Giorgio 86
Arditi, Pierre 203
Arent, Eddi 84, 89, 112
Argento, Dario 102, 200
Arkin, Alan 185, 190
Armstrong, Alun **230**
Armstrong, Michael 195
Armstrong, R G 199
Armstrong, Vic 218

Arne, Peter 42, 47
Arness, James 267
Arno, Eddie 205
Arnold, P P 164
Arnold, Tom 224
Around the World in 80 Days 205
Ashby, Robert 228
Asher, Jack **52**, 53, 59
Asherson, Renée 111
Ashley, Helmut 88
Ashton, Roy 67
Aspel, Michael 130
Assante, Armand 227
Assignment Foreign Legion 47
Assonitis, Ovidio G 186
Astin, John 211
As You Like It [play] 22-3, 36
Atienza, Edward **44**, 44
Augustine, Peter 48
Avalon Awakening, The 198
L'avaro 213, **213**
Avengers, The **117**, 117, 126, 164, **264**
Awakening, The 36
Aykroyd, Dan 178, 183
Aylmer, Felix 68, 81
Ayres, Lew 175

Babes in Bagdad **28**, 28-9, 39
Bach, Barbara 179

Backlinie, Susan 183
Baer, Buddy 74
Bailey, John 111
Bailey, Robin 18
Bain, Barbara 160
Baistrocchi, Angelo 93
Baker, Carroll 218
Baker, Daphne **59**, 60
Baker, Roy Ward 140
Baker Street Irregulars, The 245
Bale, Christian 202, 208
Ball, Vincent 39
Band, Charles 175
Band on the Run [album] 164
Bannen, Ian 56, 57
Bardot, Brigitte 116
Barker, Lex 118
Barker, Ronnie 204
Barnes, Walter 74
Barron, Keith 152
Barry, John 72
Bartlett, Sy 37
Bartok, Eva **27**, 28
Barton, Sean 210
Bartrop, Rowland **48**
Bass, Alfie 56
Bates, Michael 18
Batman [TV series] 116
Battle of Britain 163
Battle of the River Plate, The 43-4, **44**, 48
Battle of the V.1 58, 69, 125, **265**
Bava, Lamberto 225
Bava, Mario 85-6, 91-93, 102, 118, 200, 225, 230
Baxt, George 76
Bear Island **182**, 182, 183, 219
Beat Girl 71-4, **72**, 74, 80, 93, 183
Beatles, The 130, 157
Beaton, Cecil 55
Beatty, Robert 36
Beauty and the Beast, The 219
Beckley, Tony 165
Belushi, John 171, 178, 183
Bender, Alexander 15
Benedict, Jay 203
Bengal Lancers, The 197
Bennett, Jill 133
Bennett, John 217
Benny, Jack 16
Benson, Martin **34**, 34, 83
Benthall, Michael 36
Bentley, John 29, **29**, 40
Berglund, Joel 27
Bergman, Ingrid 16
Berkoff, Steven 234
Bernard, James 53, 60, 119, 126
Berridge, Mona 22
Besson, Luc 243
Beyond Mombasa 45-6, **45**, 60
Billingsley, Peter 192
Birkin, Jane 155
Bishop, Joey 165
Bitter Victory 18, 53-5, **54**, 56, 80, 166
Björling, Jussi 27
Björnson, Maria 201
Black, Vivienne 15
Blackman, Honor **269**
Blair, Isla 103, 138, 208
Blakeley, Tom 117
Blanchett, Cate 232
Bliss, Caroline 192

Colonel Mannering and Tara King (Linda Thorson) in The Avengers: The Interrogators *(1968)*

Bloch, Robert 100, 101, 106, 116, 141, 155
Blood of Fu Manchu, The 121-2, 123
Bloody Judge, The 112, 133-4, **134**
Bloom, Orlando 239
Boa, Bruce 205
Boddey, Martin 74
Boehm, Carl 49, 74
Bogarde, Dirk **48**, 48, 49, 56-8, 64, 113, 145, **257**
Boles, John 29
Bolling, Claude 80
Bolton, Geoffrey 221
Bond, Derek 21
Bonos, Luigi **100**
Bonotti, Guglielmo 102
Border Incident 36
Borgnine, Ernest 143, 188
Bosé, Lucia 213
Bottoms, Joseph 202
Boucher, le star et l'orpheline, Le 157, **159**, 159-60
Bouix, Evelyne 203
Boulle, Pierre 203
Boulting, John 26, 43
Bowie, David 164
Box, Betty E 56-7
Box, Muriel 55, 57, 69
Box, Sydney 53, 69, 82
Boy Who Left Home to Find Out About the Shivers, The 196, **197**, 202
Bradbury, Ray 101, 116, 126
Bradley, Leslie 28
Brandauer, Klaus-Maria 207
Brand, Neville 101
Brandon, Michael **212**, 213
Brandy, Howard 151
Brauner, Artur 90, 225, 237
Bray, Robert **47**, 48
Brazzi, Rossano 195
Breillat, Catherine 172, **172**
Breillat, Marie-Hélène 172
Brennan, Mike 88
Bresslaw, Bernard 50
Brett, Leonard 28
Briant, Shane 151
Brides of Fu Manchu, The 113, 113-4, 116, 122
Brittain, RSM 'Tibby' 24
Britton, Tony 22
Broccoli, Albert R 'Cubby' 42, 157
Brosnan, Pierce 205, 219
Brossa, Joan 139
Broughton, Joyce 222
Brown, Reb 198
Brown, Georgia 152
Brown, George 166
Brown, Phil 35
Browne, Coral 21, 220
Bryan, Dora 42
Bucholz, Horst 177
Bunuel, Luis 121, 138, 140
Burge, Stuart 133
Burke, Patricia 22
Burton, Richard **54**, 54-5, 63
Burton, Stacia 205
Burton, Tim 230-1, 245
Bushell, Anthony 18, 78, 80
By Candlelight [play] 18
Byrne, Eddie 47
Byron, Kathleen 25

Cairney, John 98
Callard, Kay 40
Calvert, Eddie 46
Camp, Colleen 198
Camp, Hamilton 187, 188
Campbell, Ian **272**
Campos, José 95, **96**

Captain America II 185, 198
Captain Horatio Hornblower R.N. 25-6, **25**, 27
Carandini, Niccolò 15
Caravans 177, 189
Cardiff, Jack 196
Cardinale, Claudia **187**, 207
Care of Time, The **212**, 213
Carey, MacDonald 88, 175
Carey, Phil 44
Cargill, Patrick 23
Carlson, Veronica 125, 160
Carmichael, Ian 23, **42**, 42, 43
Carpenter, John 178, 190, 194-5
Carradine, David 187, 188
Carradine, John 175, 189, 212
Carrel, Dany 80, 81
Carreras, James 50, 55, 55, 56, 59, 61, 63, 83, 86, 118, 126, 143, 145, 146
Carreras, Michael 63, 76, **77**, 104, 164
Carstairs, John Paddy 88
Cartier, Rudolph 16
Carver, Steve **188**, 199
Casanova 203
Cascio, Totò 218, **218**
Cassel, Jean-Pierre 157, 206, 217
Castello dei morti vivi, Il 86, **100**, 101-2, 126, 150
Castle, Roy 102
Castle of Fu Manchu, The 122-3, 126
Cattrall, Kim **206**, 206, 207, 217
Cele, Henry 200, 210
Celentano, Adriano 218
Cervi, Tonino 213
Chabrol, Claude 157, **237**
Chamberlain, Richard 133, 158, 203
Channing, Stockard 187, **188**, 188
Chaplin, Geraldine 227
Charles and Diana A Royal Love Story 192
Charlie's Angels 186
Chase, James Hadley 164
Cherry, Helen 24, 88, 197

Chin, Tsai 69, 122
Christelis, Marina 166
Christensen, Hayden 235, **244**
Christie, Julie 116, **257**
Chute des aigles, La 204, 208
Cibrian, Eddie 234
Cilento, Diane 55
Circle of Iron 177-8, **177**, 179
Circus of Fear 112-3, 114
City of the Dead, The **75**, 75-6, 80, 102, 112, 184
Clanton, Ralph 24, **24**
Clark, Ernest 98
Clark, Fred 121
Clarke, T E B 'Tibby' 56
Clemens, Paul **179**
Clifford, Graeme 196
Cobb, Lee J 145
Coburn, James 164, 177
Cockleshell Heroes, The 42
Cole, George 21, 30
Collector, The 101
Collins, Joan 155, 186
Collinson, Peter 142, 145
Colonel Hooker and the Lady 117
Colonel March of Scotland Yard **33**, 35
Columbo 165
Comfort, Lance 34, 36, 47, 53
Conde Drácula, El 5, 135-7, **136**, 138-9, 140
Confession, La 157
Confession **237**, **237**
Connaught Theatre 18, 22, 23, 36, 194
Connochie, Tom 35
Connolly, Billy 206
Connor, Kevin 180, 189, 234, 245
Constantine, Eddie **69**, 69
Constantine, Michael 182
Constant Nymph, The [play] 18
Cooper, Gary 83
Cooper, Jeff 177, **177**
Cooper, Maggie 188
Cooper, Wilkie 45, 69

Cope, Kenneth 117
Coppola, Francis 178, 230, 235
Coquillon, Johnny 125
Corbett, Glenn 87
Corcoran, Bill 216, 217
Corey, Jeff **181**, 182
Corman, Roger 92, 101, 230, 239
Corri, Adrienne **61**, 166
Corridor of Mirrors 16-7, 30
Corridors of Blood 61, 61-3, 75, 104
Cosma, Vladimir 170
Cotten, Joseph 173
Court, Hazel 16, 66
Courtland, Jerome 74
Coward, Noël 36, 107, 196, 231
Cowan, Theo 15
Cox, Jack 29
Crabtree, Arthur 36
Cravat, Nick 27
Craven, Wes 190
Crawford, Howard Marion 116, 122
Creeping Flesh, The 148, **150**, 150, 211, **260**
Crehan, Patrick 15
Crichton, Charles 126, 160
Crimson Pirate, The **27**, 27-8
Cripple Boy, The 35
Cripta e l'incubo, La 95-6, **96**
Cross, Ben 195
Cross, Hugh 22
Crossroads 35-6
Crown of the Andes **39**, 39
Croydon, John 19, 61
Crutchley, Rosalie 56, 57
Cuadecuc Vampir 138-40
Cuaron, Alfonso 240
Culp, Robert 143, 144
Culver, Roland 55
Cummings, Bob 115
Curse of Frankenstein, The 11, 50, **52**, 52-3, 55, 56, 58, 60, 63, 110, 125, 128, 173, 209, 231
Curse of the Crimson Altar 123, **123**, 124, 143

CHRISTOPHER LEE – INDEX

Curse III: Blood Sacrifice see *Panga*
Curtis, Gary 230, 235
Curtis, Patrick 143, 165
Curtis, Tony [art director] 142
Cushing, Peter 7, 18, 31, 50, 52, 52-3, 58, **62**, 63, 64, 66, 67, 68, 75, 80, Sybil 169, 198, 102, 103, 104, 106, **107**, 117, 130, **131**, 132, 138, 142, 143, 145-7, **147**, 148, 150, 151-2, 152, 156, **156**, 157, 160, 181, 194-5, 216, 222, **223**, 235
Cybereden see *Jackpot*

Daff, Al 63
Dahl, Arlene 49
Dainton, Patricia 18, 29, **29**, 35
Damage 230
Danielle, Suzanne 180
Daniely, Lisa **46**, 47
Danning, Sybil 169, 198
Danson, Ted 185
Dante, Joe 198, 211-3, 227
Danziger, Harry Lee and Edward J 29, 39-41, 47
Dark Avenger, The **38**, 38, **46**, 214
Dark Mission Flowers of Evil see *Operación cocaína*
Dark Places 155, 186
Dave Allen Show, The 118
Davies, John 213
Davies, Rupert 38, **114**, 115
Davis, Bette 175-6, **176**
Davis, Carl 142
Davis, Sammy, Jr 128, 130, **131**, 155, 160
Dawson, Anthony 37
Day, Robert 61, 62, 104, 117
Dean, Ivor 127
Dearden, Basil 20-1
Death in the Sun see *Der flüsternde Tod*
Death Line 150-1, **151**
Death of Michael Turbin, The **34**, 34
Death Train 219, **219**, 220
Deckers, Eugene 44-5, **270**
Degan, Raz 225
De Havilland, Olivia **37**, 37-8, 173
Dehlavi, Jamil 227
Del Giudice, Filippo 15
Delgado, Roger 25, **80**
De Keyser, David 195
De Martino, Antonio **100**, 102
De Mendoza, Alberto 147
De Nardo, Gustavo 92
Denisof, Alexis 205
Denning, Doreen 35
Depp, Johnny 231
De Sade 70 134, **135**
Desert Island Discs [radio] 224
Design for Living [play] 22
De Simone, Annalisa 208
Destination Milan 34
Devereux, Marie 86
Devil Rides Out, The 98, 118-20, **120**, 136, 167
Devil's Agent, The 88, **88**
Devil's Daffodil, The 84, **85**
Devil-Ship Pirates, The 96-8, **97**
De Wolff, Francis **61**, 62, 64, **66**, 66, 159
Diagnosis: Murder **164**, 164-5
Diamond, I A L 130
Diamond Lil [play] 21
Diamond Mercenaries, The 166, 181
Diaz, Ricardo 121
Dickinson, Desmond 80
Dieterle, William 39
Diffring, Anton 28, 48, 66
Disputation, The 201, **201**

Dobie, Alan 201
Dodds, Olive 15
Dominguez D, Berta 214
Donlevy, Brian **114**, 115
Donlevy, Lillian 115
Dor, Karin 108, **112**, 118
Dorne, Sandra 16, 39, 40, **41**, 41
Dors, Diana 15-6, **144**, 151, 152
Dotrice, Roy 160, 200
Double Vision 217-8
Douglas, Johnny 112
Douglas, Kirk 74
Douglas, Robert 100
Douglas Fairbanks Presents **11**, 32, 34, 34-5, **36**, 36, **39**, 39, 47, 75, 145, 160
Dourif, Brad 242
Drache, Heinz 112
Dracula [double-album] 163
Dracula [play] 145, 170
Dracula 8, **11**, 51, 56, 58-60, **59**, **61**, 62, 63-4, 66, 68, 93, 95, 101, 109, 112, 125, 137, 141, 146, 155, 202
Dracula A.D. 1972 145-6, 156, 198, 225, 231
Dracula Has Risen From the Grave 124, 125-6, 128, 137, 141, 195
Dracula Père et Fils 170, **172**, 172-3, 203
Dracula Prince of Darkness 71, 109-10, **109**, 112, 125, 126, 138, 145, 159
Draikis, John 204
Drake, Tom 168
Dreamtime, The 160, 163
Drew, Linzi 214
Dr No 107, 162
Dr Terror's House of Horrors 40, 102-3, **103**, 141, 208
Duffell, Peter 141, 195
Duggan, Tommy 34
Dunaway, Faye 157, **158**, 159, 203
Dunwich Horror, The 102
Durbridge, Francis 29
Duryea, Dan **114**, 115
Duvall, Shelley 196
Dyall, Valentine 76

Earl, Beryl 224
Easton, Jock 16, 25
Eaton, Shirley 120, 122
Eatwell, Brian 158
Eddington, Paul 22-3
Edgar Allan Poe's Tales of Mystery and Imagination 223
Eisenmann, Ike 176
Ekland, Britt 154, 163, 245
Elam, Jack 143
Elliott, John 22
Empire of Death 231
End of the World 175
Érase una vez en Europa 237
Ercole al centro della terra 85-6, **86**, 181, 225
Erlich, Alexandra 208
Errol Flynn: Portrait of a Swashbuckler 47
Errol Flynn Theatre, The **46**, 46-7, 160
Essential Poems (to Fall in Love With) 242
Essex, David 216
Eugénie ... the Story of Her Journey into Perversion see *De Sade 70*
Eulalie quitte les champs see *Le Boucher, le star et l'orpheline*
Eureka Stockade 20
Evans, E Eynon 23
Evans, Peggy 19

Evening at the Improv 192
Evil Force, The 167
Evil Stalks This House see *Tales of the Haunted*
Evil Thoughts, The see *The Mirror and Markheim*
Ewing, Barbara 126
Eye for an Eye, An 188-9, 199

Fabian, John 28
Face of Eve, The 120-1, **121**
Face of Fu Manchu, The 106-9, **108**, 112, **113**, 119
Faerie Tale Theatre 196, **197**
Fairbanks, Douglas, Jr 31, 32, 34-5, **36**, **39**, 165
Fairchild, Morgan 217
Faith, Adam 72
Faithfull, Geoffrey 61
Falk, Peter 165
Fall of the Eagles see *La Chute des aigles*
Fargo, James 177
Farmer, Suzan 98, 110
Far Pavilions, The 195-6, **196**, 197
Farrar, David 49, 72
Farrow, Mia 185
Farwagi, André 160
Faulkner, James 169
Faulkner, Lisa 221
Faure, William C 199
Feast at Midnight, A 155, 220-2, **221**, 231
Feldman, Ed 192
Ferrer, José 30-1, 42, 53, 175
Ferrer, Mel 81, 92, 138, **274**
Field, Shirley Ann 72, 74
Final Column 40
Finch, Jon 160, **164**, 165
Findlay, Freddie 221, **221**
Finlay, Frank 158, 203
Finney, Gavin 231
Fischer, Kai 71, 74
Fisher, Terence 19, 21, 50, 53, 58, 59, 64, 66, 67, 76, 90, 98, 109, 117, 118, **120**, 125, 136, 230
Fitchen, John 36
Five Golden Dragons **114**, 114-5
Flat Next Door, The [play] 175
Fleming, Ian 12, 107, 161
Flesh and Blood The Hammer Heritage of Horror 222, **223**
Floyd, Calvin 144-5
Floyd, Henry **124**, 125
Flüsternde Tod, Der 169, **169**, 198, 199
Flynn, Errol 38, **46**, 46-7, 237, 240
Fog, The 178
Fonda, Peter 166
Forbes, Bryan 42
For Better or For Worse see *Honeymoon Academy*
Forster, Robert 189
Fortune, James 204
Fortune is a Woman 48-9, **49**
Fortunes of War, The **46**, 46-7
Four Musketeers, The 157, 159, 165, 186
Fox, Edward 200
Fox, James 228, **257**
Fox, Sabrina 217
Foxworth, Robert 173
Frame, Ronald 236
Francis, Freddie 103, 125, 126, 148
Franciscus, James 182
Franco, Jesús 121, 122, 123, 133, 134-5, 136-7, 139, 202, 203-4, 208, 237

Frank, Horst 169
Frankovich, Mike 101
Franks, Chloë 141
Fraser, George MacDonald 203
Freeman, Alan 102
French, Harold 23
Frend, Charles 21-2
Friend, Philip 34
Frusta e il corpo, La **79**, 91-3, **92**, 102, 112
Fuchsberger, Joachim 84, 108, **112**
Fueter, Willy 18
Fullerton, Fiona 200
Funny Man 219
Furneaux, Yvonne 38, 68
Furse, Judith 18
Furst, Joseph 83
Fury at Smugglers' Bay 80

Gabor, Eva 55, **55**
Gael, Anna 172
Gallico, Paul 54
Gallu, Samuel 111
Gambon, Michael 152
Garofalo, Robert 204
Garvarentz, Georges 166
Gastaldi, Ernesto 92, 93, 95
Gaunt, Valerie 60, 112
Gay Cavalier 53
Gaynes, George **220**, 220
Geheimnis der gelben Narzissen, Das see *The Devil's Daffodil*
Geeson, Judy 164
Geeson, Sally 126
Gemini Apes, The [radio play] 230
Genn, Leo 45-6, **45**, 53, 72, **73**, 134
George, Susan 142, 223
Germani, Gaïa 86, **100**, 102
Gerrard, Rupert 24
Ghosts [CD-ROM] 223-4
Ghost Stories for Christmas 235-7, **236**
Giacobini, Franco 91
Gibson, Alan 145, 155, 160
Gibson, Derek 179
Gidding, Nelson 35
Gielgud, John 133, **133**, 195, 229
Gillam, Melville 18
Gilliat, Sidney 15, 49
Gilling, John 74, 80, 87, 98
Girardot, Annie 203
Girl, The 202-3
Girotti, Massimo 207
Glover, Julian 112
Goddard, Alf 31, **31**
Goddard, Pat 16, 17
Goddard, Paulette 29, 47
Goddard, Willoughby 60
Godfrey, Derek **133**
Golan, Menahem 194, 225
Goldner, Charles 18
Goldoni, Lelia 112
Goldstone, James 192
Golf in the Sun 245
Goliath Awaits 189, 189-90
Goodliffe, Michael 49
Goodwin, Daisy 242
Gorbachev, Mikhail 242
Gordon, Bernard 146
Gordon, Claire 73
Gordon, Colin 25, 88
Gordon, Richard 61
Gorgon, The 98-9, **99**, 121
Goring, Marius 35, 43, 49, **69**, 84, 88
Gormenghast 230-1, **231**, 232
Gorshin, Frank 189
Goslar, Jürgen 169
Goss, Helen 15
Gotell, Walter **69**, 84

Gothard, Michael 132
Gough, Michael 103, 103, 106
Graham, Gerrit 197
Grammatikov, Vladimir 201
Granger, Stewart 20-1, 23, 192
Grant, Arthur 87
Grant, Cary 83
Grant, Lee 173, **174**
Grant, Peter 41
Gray, Carole 113
Gray, Charles 118, 192, 230
Gray, Sally 169
Grayson, Kathryn 44
Green, Gilbert 100
Green, Nigel **54**, 54, 62, **72**, 72, 108, 108, 114
Gregg, Everley 28
Gregg, Olga 121
Gregson, John 21
Greene, Lorne 47
Greene, Richard 122, **269**
Greenwood, Joan 21, 63
Gremlins 2 The New Batch **211**, 211-3
Gréville, Edmond T 72, 73, 80, 82, 83, 93
Griffith, Kenneth 200
Griffiths, Richard 231
Grimaudo, Nicole 225
Grose, Lionel 32, 35, 39
Guerra, Ugo 92
Guers, Paul 57
Guest, Val 68, 166
Guillermin, John 43
Guillermo, Matthieu 237
Guinness, Alec 25, 242
Gurney, Rachel 44
Gynt, Greta 49

Hackman, Gene 10
Haining, Peter 164
Halloween 178, 198
Hamilton, Guy 161, 163
Hamilton, Wendy 140
Hamlet 18, 78
Hamlett, Dilys 164
Hammer Presents Dracula [album] 164
Hand, H E 'Slim' 19-20
Handler, Dana 186
Hands of Orlac, The 80-2, **81**, 83, 84, 92, 93, 138, **246**
Hannie Caulder 143-**4**, **143**, 145, 177
Hardiman, Terrence 200
Harding, Jeff 205
Hardy, Gene 54
Hardy, Justin 220, 222
Hardy, Robert 155, 222
Hardy, Robin 153
Harlow, Pauline 96
Harmon, Mark 189
Harris, Julie 55
Harris, Robert 37
Harrison, Jennilee 210
Hart, Harvey 192
Hartford, Fiona 110
Hartley, Richard 191
Harvey, Laurence 42, 55, 76
Hasso, Signe 35
Hawkins, Jack 49, **49**
Hawley, Stuart 222
Hayers, Sidney 112, 164, 165
Hayes, John 175
Hayles, Brian 151, 180
Hays, Robert 207
Haystead, Mercy 36
Hayter, James **20**
Hazell, Dorene 148
Hearne, Richard 18
Heath, Simon 164

Heffron, Richard T 207
Heilbron, Lorna **150**
Heller, Otto 28, 55, 74
Helpmann, Robert 36
Hempel, Anouska 140
Henley, David 15
Henson, Gladys 42
Hepton, Bernard 201
Herbert, Percy 42
Hercules in the Haunted World see *Ercole al centro della terra*
Hessler, Gordon 126, 132, 190, 214, 216
Heston, Charlton 133, **133**, 148, 157, 158, 159, 160, 186, 208, **209**
Heston, Fraser C 208, 209
Heyward, Louis M 190
Higueras, Cristina 203, **203**
Hill, Bernard 242
Hills, Gillian **72**, 72, 73
Hinds, Anthony 50, 58, 60, 63, 98, 137, 140, 145
Hitchcock, Alfred 99, 100, 101
Hobbs, Bill 158, 160
Hobbs, Christopher 231
Hobson, Rodney 16
Hogg, Ian **212**
Holgado, Ticky 237, **237**
Holloway, Stanley 18
Holm, Ian 232
Holt, Patrick 36, 41
Holt, Seth 82, 83
Homolka, Oscar 30
Honeymoon Academy 207
Hopkin, Mary 164
Horner, Penelope 84
Horovitch, David 227
horror anthologies edited by CL 163-4, 181
Horror Express see *Pánico en el Transiberiano*
Hough, John 175
Houghton, Don 145, 151, 156, 164

Hound of the Baskervilles, The 64-5, **65**, 66, 76, 77, 90
House that Dripped Blood, The **141**, 141, 195
House of the Long Shadows **195**, 195-6, 198
Hoven, Adrian 89
Howard, Alan 206
Howard, Sandy 179
Howard, Trevor 42, 138, 160, 169, 197, 200
Howell, C Thomas 206
Howling II 198-**9**, **199**
How the West Was Won 177, **267**
Hume, Alan 103
Hunt, Ed 174
Hunt, Marsha 146, 198
Hunter, Ian 49
Huntington, Lawrence 34
Hurst, Brian Desmond 23
Hurwitz, Harry 187, 198
Hussain, Talat 229
Hussey, Olivia 182
Huston, John 10, **30**, 30-1, 179
Huston, Walter 10
Huth, Harold 32, 38
Hyde-White, Wilfrid 55, **130**, 130
Hylton, Jane 16
Hyman, Eliot 56
Hyman, Ken 78

I Accuse! 53
Idle, Eric 205
Illing, Peter **36**, 36, 84, **85**
Ill Met By Moonlight 10, **48**, 48, 58
I Made News 28
Immigrant, The 39
I, Monster 95, 141-3, **142**, 148, 197, 209
Imrie, Celia 231
In the Beginning 234-5
Incident at Victoria Falls 216-7
'Ingle' (Harcourt George St Croix Rose, CL's stepfather) 12, 14
Im Namen des Teufels see *The Devil's Agent*
Innocenti, Markus 205
Innocents in Paris **31**, 31
In Search of Dracula see *Pa jakt efter Dracula*
International Settlement 34
In the Beginning 232
Irving, Amy 195
Irwin, John 16
Isherwood, Christopher 117
Ivanhoe (1957) 53, 226
Ivanhoe (1996) 226-7, **226**

Jackpot (Classe speciale) **218**, 218
Jackson, Dan **45**
Jackson, David S 219
Jackson, Freda 56
Jackson, Gordon 43, 216
Jackson, Peter 232, 234, 239, 240, 242, 245
Jackson, Samuel L 235, 240
Jack the Ripper Goes West 160, 163
Jacques, Hattie 23, 221
Jaeckin, Just 135
Jagger, Dean 175
Jaguar Lives! 179, 181
James, Anthony 176
James, M R 12, 235-7
James, Tim 219
Jameson, Jerry 173
Jarvis, Martin 138
Jeavons, Colin 84
Jenkinson, Philip 125
Jessel, Patricia 75
Jinnah 215, 226, 227-9, **228**, 231
Jocks 199, 200
Jodorowsky, Alejandro 214
Johns, Stratford 62
Johnson, Bob 164
Johnson, Richard 133
Jones, Freddie 223

With James Arness in the popular MGM mini-series How the West Was Won *(1977)*

With Simon Ward in The Leather Funnel, *a Conan Doyle adaptation included in the Anglia TV anthology* Orson Welles Great Mysteries *(1973)*

Jones, Marshall 132
Jones, Russ 163
Joseph and His Brethren 40
Journey of Honor see *Shogun Mayeda*
Julius Caesar 132-3, **133**, 182, 208
Junge, Alfred 37
Junkin, John 117
Jürgens, Curt 54, 54-5
Just a Nimmo 160
Justice, James Robertson 42

Kadish, Ben 145
Kahn, Frances 122
Kaleidoscope 16
Kapoor, Shashi 228
Karloff, Boris 11, 29, **33**, 35, 50, **61**, 61-3, 68, 101, 102, 106, 109, **123**, 125, 134, 164, 239, 245
Katarsis 9, 86, 93, 95
Keaton, Buster 36
Keen, Geoffrey 49
Keen, Malcolm 49
Keeper, The 168-9
Keir, Andrew 87, 98
Keith, Sheila 18, 22, 194-5, 214
Kelber, Michel 55
Kellerman, Sally 184
Kelly, Maura **17**
Kelly, Sean 54
Kendall, Suzy 113
Kennedy, Burt 143
Kent, Jean 22, 23, 49
Kentucky Fried Movie 178, 224
Keys, Anthony Nelson 86, 88, 109,
   110, 151, 152, 163, 167
Kiefer, Warren 101
King, George 23, 53
King of Elfland's Daughter, The [album] 164
Kingsley, Ben 224
Kinnear, Roy 159, 203, 206
Kino '92 Extra 219
Kinski, Klaus 84, 89, 112, 136, 138, 168, 196
Kinski, Nastassja **168**, 168
Klugman, Jack 155
Knight, David 88, **265**
Knight, Esmond 47
Knight, Peter 164
Knights, Robert 217
Knowland, Nick 228
Knowles, Bernard 34
Knox, Alexander 40-1
Koch, Marianne 88
Kojak 165, 166
Konchalovsky, Andrei 227
Korda, Alexander 41-2
Korda, Zoltán 42
Koscina, Sylva 71
Kosugi, Sho 216
Krabbe, Jeroen 227
Krasker, Robert 37
Kretzmer, Herbert 74
Kristel, Sylvia 203
Kulik, Buzz 205
Kwouk, Burt 122

Labourdette, Elina 55
Lacey, Ronald 197, 204

Lacoste, Raymond 28
Lahaie, Brigitte 204
Lambert, Gavin 54
Lambert, Jack 42
Lamble, Lloyd 40
Lamont, Duncan 40, 56, 148
Lancaster, Burt 27-8, 148
Landau, Martin 234
Land of Faraway, The see *Mio, min Mio!*
Lander, Eric 40
Landi, Marla **65**, 65
Landier, Jean 31
Landis, Harry 54
Landis, John 178, 224
Lange, Carl 118, **119**
Langella, Frank 170, 224
Langton, David 192
Langton, Simon 203
Lansbury, Angela 185, 227
Lassally, Walter 197-8
Last Knife, The 36
Last Unicorn, The 185
Last Unicorn, The [projected live-action version] 245
Latham, Stuart 18
Latimer, Hugh 17
Launder, Frank 15, 49
Lautner, Georges 237
Lavagnino, Angelo Francesco 102
La Vey, Anton 155
Lavi, Daliah 95, **92**, 92, 93
Lawford, Peter 130
Lawrence, Delphi 63, **72**, 73-4
Lawrence, Marc 162
Lawrence, Marjie 142
Lawrence, Sheldon **73**, 74
Lawson, Wilfrid 74-5
Leakey, Phil 50, **52**, 52, 58
Leather Funnel, The 160, **268**
Lee, Christina (CL's daughter) 98, 99, 113, 146-7, 160, 201
Lee, Estelle Marie (CL's mother) 12, 14, 238-9, 245
Lee, Lt Col Geoffrey Trollope (CL's father) 12, 14
Lee, Gitte [Birgit Kroencke] (CL's wife) 83-4, **84**, 87, 98, 99, **139**, 146-7, 169, 186, **187**, 188, 195, 201, 202, 239
Lee, Gypsy Rose 29
Lee, Margaret 112, **114**, 115
Lee, Xandra (CL's sister) 12, 230, 242
Lees, Tamara 23
Le Fort, Robert 31
Lemare, Jacques 80
Le Mesurier, John 64
Lemmon, Jack 173
Lemont, John 35
Lenz, Kay 178, **179**
Leonidas 116
Le Roux, Maurice 54
Leroy, Philippe **100**, 102, 224
Lester, Richard 157-9, 205-6
Levene, Philip 164
Leviathan '99 [radio play] 126
Levin, Henry 38
Levine, Ted 219
Levinson, Barry 240
Levka, Uta **129**
Lewis, Al 211
Lewis, Jerry 130
Lewis, Joe 179
Lewis, Ronald 42, 42, 83
Libel [play] 22
Licudi, Gabriella 83
Lieven, Albert 84
Liljedahl, Marie 134

Lillibridge, Gloria 135, 136
Lindsay, Helen 201
Liné, Helga 147, 237
Line in the Snow, A 36
Lintern, Richard 228
Lister, Moira 20
Lloyd, Euan 160
Lockyer, Malcolm 117
Lodge, David 42
Logan, Veronica 225
Lom, Herbert 47, 89, 121, 136, 139, 155
Lombard, Louise 229
Longden, John 40
Lonsdale, Michel 178
Loo, Richard 162
Looks Familiar 269
Lord of the Rings, The [novel sequence] 141, 232, 239
Lord of the Rings, The [CD release] 239
Lord of the Rings: The Fellowship of the Ring, The 232, **234**, 234, 235, 237, 239-40, 242, 245
Lord of the Rings: The Two Towers, The 242, **243**
Lord of the Rings: The Return of the King, The 242, 243, 245
Loret, Susanne 71
Lorraine, Guido 45
Losey, Joseph 40
Lotis, Dennis 75
Love Token 47
Low, Andrew 104
Lowe, Arthur 35
Lucas, George 7, 178, 218, 235, **244**, 245
Lucas, William 84
Luise knackt den Jackpot 225
Lumley, Joanna 160
Lusardi, Linda 204, **204**
Lutic, Bernard 206
Lutyens, Elisabeth 103, 106
Lynch, Susan 227
Lyndon, Barré 14, 66, 100
Lyon, Sue 175, 259

MacDonald, David 39-40, 182
MacGregor, Scott 138
Mackay, Fulton 152
Macnee, Patrick 12, 117, **117**, 160, 192, 205, 216-7, 217
MacNicol, Peter 196, **197**
Macready, Carol 221
Maddern, Victor 42
Maddox, Jennifer 22
Magic Christian, The 128, 130, **130**, 132, 183
Magimel, Benoît 243
Magpie 160
Maggs, Dirk 230
Maibaum, Richard 161, 163
Mailer, Norman 240
Mains d'Orlac, Les see *The Hands of Orlac*
Maitland, Marne 28
Malik, Art 234
Malkovich, John 229
Malleson, Miles 64
Man in Demand **40**, 40
Mankiewicz, Tom 161
Mankowitz, Wolf 76, **77**, 77
Manning, Hugh 141
Man of La Mancha [musical play] 117, 192
Mansfield, Jayne **73**, 74
Man Who Could Cheat Death, The 66, **66**, 73, 82
Man Who Wouldn't Escape, The 39

Man With the Golden Gun, The **149**, 157, 161-3, **162**, 165, 166, 169, 191, 234
Many Faces of Christopher Lee, The [video documentary] 224
Manzor, René 237
Margheriti, Antonio 93, 95, 237, 259
Marle, Arnold 66
Marquand, Christian 53
Marquis de Sade's 'Philosophy in the Boudoir' see *De Sade* 70
Marriott, Peter 32, 39, 83, 145
Marsh, Carol **17**, 22, 36, 60, 63
Marsh, Jean 189
Marshall, George 45-6
Marshall, Zena 16, **17**
Martin, Bryony 218
Martín, Eugenio (Gene) 146, 237
Martin, Sheila **17**
Martin, Strother 143
Martini, Nino 18
Martino, Bruno 71
Mask of Murder 200, **200**, 205
Maskell, Virginia 23
Maslansky, Paul 102, 150, 186, 207, 220
Mason, Glen 78
Mason, James 8, 92, 178, **179**, 259
Masque of the Red Death, The 223
Massarati and the Brain 69 [caption], 87, 192
Massie, Paul 66, 76
Masterson, Valerie 230
Mastrocinque, Camillo 95, 96
Maté, Rudolph 45
Mathews, Kerwin 87
Mathieson, Muir 25
Matter, Fred **54**
Matthews, Francis 39, 110, 111
Matthews, Christopher 140
Mattsson, Arne 200, 202
Maureen, Mollie 131, **132**
Maxwell, Lois 17
Maxwell, Peter 60
Mayday 245
Mayne, Ferdy 36, 198, 217
Mayo, Virginia **25**, 26
McAllister, Jennifer **184**
McCabe, Evelyn **20**, 21
McCallum, John 27
McCallum, Neil 102
McCarthy, Michael 36, 39, 43, 47
McCartney, Paul 164
McComb, Billy 81
McDonell, Fergus 25
McDowell, Malcolm 178, **179**, 179
McEnery, Peter 72
McEnroe, Annie 198
McEveety, Bernard 177
McGinnis, Niall 88
McGoohan, Patrick 43
McGrath, Joe 128
McGregor, Ewan 235
McKellen, Ian 232, 235, 239, 242
Meddings, Derek 201
Medina, Patricia 58
Medwin, Michael 23, 63
Mell, Marisa 89
Melly, Andrée 47
Melvin, June 16
Menez, Bernard 172
Mengarelli, Julius and Mario 35
Menteurs, Les 83
Menuhin, Yehudi 210
Mephistopheles [rock opera] 164
Méril, Macha 217
Merrow, Jane 117
Mestre, Jeannine 140
Métier de Seigneur, Un 203

Metter, Alan 219
Michael, Ralph 19, **20**, 21
Mifune, Toshiro 183
Miles, Bernard 49
Milland, Ray 101
Miller, Dick 211
Miller, Selwyn Emerson, III 186, **186**
Milligan, Spike 158, 159, 231
Mills, John 21
Mio, min Mio! **193**, 201-2, 208
Miranda, Soledad **136**, 136, 139
Miró, Joan 140
Mirror and Markheim, The 35, 47, 92, 170
Mitchum, Chris **203**, 204
Mnouchkine, Alexandre 208
Moby Dick Rehearsed 42-3
Model, The 47
Molinaro, Edouard 170, **172**, 172, 202, 203
Molinas, Richard 28
Moment of Truth 34
Monastero, Il 208
Monsieur Hulot's Holiday 31
Monster Club, The 194
Monteros, Rosenda 121
Moore, Eileen **33**
Moore, Richard 177
Moore, Roger 22, 23, 53, 161-3, 226
Mora, Philippe 190, 198, 199
More, Kenneth 21, 49, 101, 181
Morell, André 39, 64
Morgan, Charles 18
Moroder, Giorgio 218
Morris, Ernest 39-40
Morris, Lana 34
Morris, Mary 39
Mort profonde 157
Mortensen, Viggo 232, 239
Moseby, Karl 35
Moses 224, 234
Moss, W Stanley 'Billy' 47, 48
Moulin Rouge **30**, 30-1, 42
Mower, Patrick 237
Moxey, John 75, 112
Mulcahy, Russell 229
Mull, Martin **184**, 184
Muller, Fritz 101
Muller, Paul 136
Mullins, Bartlett 34, 110
Mummy, The 5, 11, **67**, 67-8, 69, 125, 223, 224
Munro, Caroline 146
Murder Story **205**, 205
Murray, Bill 178
Murray, Pete 16, **17**
Murray, Stephen 56, 57
Murton, Lionel 43, **44**
Murton, Peter 162
Muti, Ornella 203
My Brother's Keeper 16, 21

Nagy, Ivan 185
Nakamura, Takeo 185
Natta, Camille 243
Naylor, Tom 75
Neal, Patricia **179**
Needs, James 53
Neill, Sam 207
Neri, Rosalba 86
Nero, Franco 181, **181**, 187, 202, 242 [caption]
Nettleton, John 229
New Adventures of Robin Hood, The 226, 230
Newland, John 83
Newley, Anthony 42, 44
New Magic 196-7

Newman, Laraine 178
Newsom, Ted 222, 224
Nicolai, Bruno 133
Nicolaysen, Bruce 178
Nielsen, Christiane 89
Nightingale, The 35, 78, 84
Night of the Big Heat **116**, 117
Night Visitor, The 138
Nimmo, Derek 160
1941 **183**, 183-4, 189
Nishio, Yoshi 220, 221
Noble, Shaun **17**, 21
Noble Spaniard, The [radio play] 25
Norden, Denis **269**
Norris, Chuck 188
Nothing But the Night 151-3, **152**, 161, 180, 216
Nutcracker Fantasy 185
Nyman, Michael 201

Oberon, Merle 47
Oblong Box, The 62, 126-7, **127**, 132, 190
O'Brian, Hugh 120, 166
O'Brien, Edna 135
O'Brien, Richard 191
O'Casey, Ronan **54**
O'Conor, Joseph 97
Odyssey, The 227
Ohberg, Åke 35
Old House, The 35
Olivier, Laurence 18, 35, 50
Olrich, April 43-4, **44**, 63
Olympus Force The Key **204**, 204
Once Upon a Spy 185, **185**
Once Upon a Time in Europe see *Érase una vez en Europa*
O'Neal, Ryan 74, 166
O'Neill, Jennifer 177
One Hundred Years of Horror 224
One More Time 130, **131**
One Night With You 18
One Step Beyond 83

Operación cocaína **203**, 203-4
Orfini, Mario 218
Orme, Stuart 226
Orson Welles Great Mysteries 47, 160, **268**
O'Shea, Milo 181
Osmond, Jimmy 199
OSS **60**, 60
Ostrum, Maxine 199
Othello [play] 27
O'Toole, Peter 148, 214
Owen, Bill 34
Oxley, David 48
Oz, Frank 240

Page, Genevieve **271**
På jakt efter Dracula **144**, 144-5, 151
Palacios, Ricardo 122
Pallos, Steven 80, 84
Paluzzi, Luciana 63, 203
Panga 210
Pánico en el Transiberiano 146-7, **147**, 148
Papas, Irene 227
Paramor, Norrie 46
Parapetti, Mario 93
Park, Reg 86, 217
Parke, Macdonald **28**, 29
Parker, Cecil 56, 57, 112
Parker, Eleanor 185
Parker, Robert 16
Parkins, Barbara 182
Parlour Trick, The 34
Parry, Gordon 31
Parry, Michel 164, 227
Parry, Natasha 23
Parsons, Louella 101
Pascaline 73
Pasco, Richard **99**, 99, 111
Passage, The 178-9, **179**, 181
Pastell, George 67
Paterson, Bill 206
Patterson, George 29

Alquazar off-duty: with Richard Greene, Honor Blackman and chairman Denis Norden in Thames TV's nostalgia quiz, Looks Familiar, broadcast on 9 November 1978

Paul, Alexandra 219
Paul, Raymond 38
Paul Temple Returns **29**, 29-30, 31, 35
Peake, Mervyn 231
Pearson, Syd 99
Peck, Bob 201
Peck, Gregory **25**, 26
Pellegrin, Raymond **54**, 54
Pellon, Gabriel 118
Peña, Julio **147**, 147
Pennington Richards, C M 53, 60
Penny and the Pownall Case **19**, 19-20, 21
Penrose, John 17
Penwarden, Hazel 23
Perilli, Frank Ray 175
Perrine, Valerie 200
Perschy, Maria 115
Persky, Bill 184
Pertwee, Jon 141
Pettingell, Frank 62
Phillips, Conrad 16, 60
Pickard, Nicholas 202
Pickens, Slim **183**, 183-4
Pierrepoint, Albert 208
Pigozzi, Luciano 102
Pilon, Daniel 192
Pinon, Dominique 207
Pintoff, Ernest 179
Pirate, The **181**, 181-2
Pirates of Blood River, The 86-8, **87**, 96, 97, 98, 178
Pisano, Berto 93
Pithey, Wensley 43
Pitoeff, Sacha 57
Plaza, Julio Ortas 96
Pleasence, Donald 56, 57, 81, 150, 151, 178, 179
Plowright, Joan 43
Podestà, Rossana 93
Pohlmann, Erich 89
Poiré, Jean-Marie 170

Police Academy: Mission to Moscow 31, 219-20, **220**
Police Dog 38-9
Polland, Dave 165
Pooley, Olaf 19
Poor Devil **155**, 155, 157, 167, 169
Portabella, Pedro (Pere) 138-40
Port Afrique 44-5, 270
Portman, Eric 17
Portman, Natalie 235
Powell, Eddie 68, 110, 125, 167
Powell, Michael 10, 38, 43-4, 48, 49, 72
Powell, Robert 200
Powney, Clare 203
Prada, José María 134
Preiss, Wolfgang 134
Prelude to Fame 8, 25, 26
Pressburger, Emeric 10, 38, 43-4, 48, 72
Price, Dennis 37, 43, 49
Price, Vincent 117, 126, 127, **129**, 132, 134, 136, 138, 141, 160, 194-5, 220, 239
Price of Vanity, The **40**, 40
Private Life of Sherlock Holmes, The 11, 130-2, **132**, 133, 136, 145, 148, 271
Private's Progress 43, 47
Proceso de las brujas, El see *The Bloody Judge*
Purcell, Noel 28
Pyne, Natasha 97
Quaglia, Pier Anna 95
Quentin Durward 40
Quinlan, Kathleen 173
Quinn, Anthony 177, 178, **179**, 187
Quintano, Gene 207
Quitak, Oscar 48

Radner, Gilda 178
Rafferty, Chips 20

Raft, George 114, 115
Raikes, R P 42
Rainbow Thief, The 214, **216**
Rakoff, Alvin 68-9, **69**
Randall, Tony 211
Randall, Zoë 210
Randell, Ron 35, 40, 45-6, **60**, 60
Rankin, Arthur 185
Rascel, Renato 71
Rasputin the Mad Monk 98, **105**, 109, 110-11, 112, 143, 209
Rätsel der roten Orchidee, Das 88-9, **89**, 112
Ray, Aldo 45
Ray, Nicholas 53-5
Reason, Rhodes 61
Redgrave, Vanessa 182
records/CDs featuring CL 141, 163-4, 203, 210, 230, 235
redoutables, Les 237, **237**
Redway, John 50
Reed, Donna 45-6, **45**
Reed, Michael 96, 110
Reed, Oliver 72, 77, 86, 87, 145, 148, 158, 160, **161**, 208, **209**, 210, 225
Reeves, Michael 101, 118, 126, 133
Refugee, The 36
Reinl, Harald 84, 118, **119**, 238 [caption]
Remick, Lee 205
Rennie, Michael 58, **265**
Reno, Jean 243
Return from Witch Mountain 175-6, **176**
Return of Captain Invincible, The 190-1, **191**, 198, 200
Return of the Musketeers, The 205-7, **206**, 217
Révolution Française: les années terribles, La **207**, 207-8
Reynolds, Peter 82
Rhodes, Christopher 34, **39**, 39
Rhys, Robert **179**
Rhys-Meyers, Jonathan 231
Ricci, Luciano 101
Rice, Joan 38
Rich, Roy 39
Richards, Kim 176
Richardson, Ian 231
Richardson, John 104
Richfield, Edwin 25
Rickman, Rex 'Ricky' 15, **17**, 21
Ridley, Arnold 117
Rietty, Robert 122
Rigg, Diana 117, **117**, 133
Rilla, Walter 108, 112
Ripper, Michael 87, 110, 140, 217
Rivière, Georges 93
Rivières pourpres 2: Les anges de l'apocalypse, Les 243
Robards, Jason 133
Robb, David 192
Robbe-Grillet, Alain 157
Roberts, Tanya 186
Robinson, Bernard 53, 59 [caption], 78, 96
Robinson, Douglas and 'Tiger' Joe 76-7
Robinson, Mark 203
Robson, Flora 21
Roc, Patricia 18, 47
Rogers, Maclean 29-30
Röhm, Maria 115, 116, 122, 134, 136, 139
Roland, Gilbert 37-8
Rollerboy 185-6, **186**, 188, 199
Romain, Yvonne 62
Roman, Ruth 54

Romney, Edana 16-17
Roome, Alfred 21
Rooney, Mickey **180**, 181
Rory, Rosanna 47
Rosay, Françoise **37**, 37
Rosebud Beach Hotel, The **198**, 199
Rosenberg, Max J 142
Rossellini, Isabella 227
Rossington, Norman 150
Roundtree, Richard 199
Rowe, Frances 33
Ruffo, Leonora 86
Runacre, Jenny 150
Rustichelli, Carlo 92, 237
Ryecart, Patrick 223

Safari 3000 187-8, **188**, 189, 198
Sägebrecht, Marianne 225
Sailor of Fortune 47
Salamander, The 186-7, **187**, 188, 198
Salkind, Ilya 157
Sallis, Peter 43
Saltzman, Harry 163
Samms, Emma **180**, 181, 189
Sanders, George 10, 130, 134
Sangster, Jimmy 52, 58, 66, 67, 68, 78, 82, 92, 97, 185
Saraband for Dead Lovers 20-1
Sarrazin, Michael 177
Sasdy, Peter 137, 138, 151, 152, 216, 217
Satanic Rites of Dracula, The 155-7, **156**, 181
Saturday Night Live 11, 160, **171**, 178, 183
Savalas, Telly 145, 147, 166
Savary, Jérôme 157, 159
Saville, Philip 16, 35, 92, 170
Sax, Geoffrey 201
Scacchi, Greta 227
Scala, Gia 100
Scardamaglia, Elio 92
Scarpelli, Marco
Scars of Dracula 140-1, 143, 144, 209
Scheerer, Robert 155
Schell, Catherine 223
Schlangengrube und das Pendel, Die 117-8, **119**, 120, 128
Schlockoff, Alain 161
Schreiber, Taft 169
Schreiber, Tell 19
Schuster, Hugo 25
Schygulla, Hanna 203
Scofield, Paul 37
Scolari, Peter 198
Scorsese, Martin **178**, 240
Scott, George C 10, 173
Scott, Kirk 175
Scott of the Antarctic 21-22, **21**, 27
Scream and Scream Again 117, **129**, 132, 150, 194
Seagrove, Jenny 217
Searle, Francis 39
See Naples and Die [play] 23
Sellars, Elizabeth 34
Sellers, Peter 128
Serial **184**, 184-5, 186, 199
Serling, Rod 186
Sesselmann, Sabina 84
Sewell, Vernon 58, 125
Seweryn, Andrzej 207
Seyler, Athene 56
Seymour, Alan 213
Seymour, Jane 160, 207, 208
Sfida al diavolo see *Katarsis*
Shaffer, Anthony 153, 154
Shah, Shireen **228**
Shaka Zulu 199-200, 205, 210

A Moroccan mystery for Franz Vermes and Colonel Moussac (Eugene Deckers) in Rudolph Maté's Port Afrique (1955)

270

Shakeel 228
Sharif, Omar 196, 214
Sharp, Don 96, 98, 108, 110, 111, 113, 155, 182
Shaw Brothers 114
Shaw, Denis 77
Shawlee, Joan 43
She 104, **106**
Sheen, Ramon 208
Shelley, Barbara 99, **105**, 110, 111, 138, 145
Sherlock Holmes and the Leading Lady 216-7, **217**
Sherlock Holmes und das Halsband des Todes 90-1, **91**, 108, 134, 216, 217
Sherman, Gary 150
Shields, Brooke 178
Shiner, Ronald **31**, 31
Shogun Mayeda 214, 216
Shop at Sly Corner, The [play] 23
Sidney, Basil 18, 81
Sign of Satan, The 99-101
Silent Flute, The see *Circle of Iron*
Sim, Alastair 31
Simons, William 35
Simpson, Norma 16
Simpson, O J 166
Siodmak, Curt 90
Siodmak, Robert 27, 90
Sipra, Mahmud 197
Sira, Puneet 181
Skull, The 106, **107**
Sleeper Awakes, The 117
Sleepy Hollow 230-1, **230**, 234
Slocombe, Douglas 83
Smith, Constance 16, 23
Snell, Peter 182, 208, 219, 227
Snyder, Tom 178
Söhnker, Hans 90
Solon, Ewen 27
Something Wicked This Way Comes 100
Somlo, Josef 15
Song for Tomorrow **20**, 21, 50
Sorcerer, The 83
Sordi, Alberto 213
Sorellina e il principe del sogno **225**, 225
Soul Music see *The Wyrd Sisters*
Space: 1999 160, **160**, 175
Sparv, Camilla 192
Spector, Maude 37
Spenser, Jeremy 25
Spielberg, Steven 157, 174, 178, 182-4, **183**, 195, 202, 211, 221
Sprackling, Simon 219
Stainton, Philip 31
Stamm, Heinz 90
Stanislawsky, Jacques 101
Stanton, Don and Dan 211
Starr, Ringo 101
Starship Invasions 174-5, 192
Stars on Sunday 165
Star Wars: Episode II – Attack of the Clones 7, 8, **233**, 235, 240-1, **241**
Star Wars: Episode III 245
Steel, Anthony 16, 23, **42**, 42, 49, 135
Steele, Barbara 85, 93, 95, **123**, 125, 138, 245
Steeleye Span 164
Steigler, Stiegler see *Rollerboy*
Stella, Luciano 92
Stephens, Robert 130, 132
Sterke, Jeanette 40
Sterling, Joseph 61
Stevens, Morton 155
Stevenson, Venetia **75**, 75

Stewart, James 173
Stewart, Patrick 219
Stivaletti, Sergio 225
St John, Betta 40, 76
Stolen 258
Stone, John 16
Storm Over the Nile **42**, 42
Story of O 135
Strange Hold 40, 249
Strasberg, Susan 63, 83
Streeter, Sydney 43
Street of Angels **36**, 36
Streuli, Peter 22
Stribling, Melissa 60, 63
Strick, Philip 145
Strode, Woody 179
Stud 135
Stupids, The **224**, 224-5
Subotsky, Milton 75, 76, 102, 125, 141-2, 194
Suchet, David 224
Sullivan, Barry 177
Summers, Jeremy **114**, 114, 121
Superman 180
Sutherland, Donald **100**, 101, 102, 182
Swamp Thing 190
Sweeney Todd, the Demon Barber of Fleet Street 227
Sykes, Eric 231
Sykes, Peter 167
Sylvester, William 36

Tabori, Paul 40-1
Tafler, Sydney **42**, 42, 68
Tale of Two Cities, A 5, **56**, 56-8, 113
Tales of Hans Andersen 35, 196
Tales of the Haunted 190
Tales of the Vikings 74-5
talking books narrated by CL 224, 226
Tall, Dark and Gruesome [autobiography] 176-7, 181, 229
Tallier, Nadine **69**, 69
Talos the Mummy 229-30
Tapies, Antoní 140
Taste of Fear **82**, 82-3, 87
Taste of the Blood of Dracula 135-6, 137-8, **138**, 140, 141, 208, 216

Tati, Jacques 31
Taylor, Donald 75, 80, 82, 84
Taylor, Gil 111
Taylor, Jack 134, 136, 139
Taylor, Rod 200
Tempest, The [play] 235, 245
Tempi duri per i vampiri 69, **70**, 71, 74, 85, 95
Tendre Dracula 157
Ten Little Indians 120
Tenser, Tony 90, 143
Terraine, Molly 15, 16, 17-8
Terror of the Tongs, The 18, **78**, 79, 79, 84, 107
Terry-Thomas 43
That Lady **37**, 37-8, 173
Theatre Macabre 145
Theatre of Death 111, 111-2
Theft of the Pink Diamond, The 28
Thesiger, Ernest 55
They Were Not Divided 23-4, **24**, 27
This Is Your Life 160, **161**
Thomas, Pete 89
Thomas, Ralph 56
Thompson, J Lee 178, 179
Thorburn, June 35, 74, 80
Thorne, Ken 143
Thorpe, Richard 40
Thorson, Linda 126, **204**, 264
Thought to Kill 34
Three Musketeers, The 87, 157-9, **158**, 160, 186, 198
Thwaytes, David 219
Till, Jenny 111, 112
Tobey, Kenneth 211
Tobias, Oliver 180, 181
Todd, Ann 83
Todd, Bob 159
Todd, Richard 195, 204, 217
Tomorrow People, The 222-3, 224
Tomorrow's Dawn 145
Tonti, Aldo 101
Toone, Geoffrey 80
Too Hot to Handle 72, **73**, 74, 183, 184
Tortosa, Silvia 147
To the Devil a Daughter 122, 151, 163, 167-8, **168**, 169, 175

Towers, Harry Alan 35, 43, 107, 112, 114, 117, 120, 121, 123, 128, 133, 134, 136, 137, 216, 245
Tracy, Steve 186
Traitor, The 47-8, **47**
Treasure Island 208-10, **209**
Treasure of San Teresa, The 68-9, **69**, 192
Treu, Wolfgang 169
Triangle, The 34
Trottie True 22, 23, 55, 131, 163, 222
Troughton, Patrick 98, 140
Trubshawe, Michael **24**, 24
Trumbull, Douglas 197
Truth About Women, The 55-6, **55**
Turkel, Ann 192
Turner, George 52
Turner, Tim 38
Tutin, Dorothy **56**, 57
Twist, Derek 36, 38
Two Faces of Dr Jekyll, The 11, 76-7, **77**, 78
Tyler, Liv 232
Tyzack, Margaret 192

Ulmer, Edgar G 28
Ulvaeus, Björn 201
Umbracle 138-40
Underdown, Edward 24
Urquhart, Robert 52, 53
Ustinov, Peter 207, 208

Valentin, Mirko 95, 101
Valk, Frederick 30
Valley of Eagles **26**, 26-7, 203
Valmont, Véra 95
Van Bergen, Ingrid 84
Van Cleef, Lee 145
Van Eyck, Peter **88**, 88
Van Eyssen, John 42, 47, 48
Van Ost, Valerie 156, 160
Vantini, Allesandro 203
Vanzina, Stefano 71
Vasquez, Yolanda 212
Vaughan, Peter 88
Vaughan Williams, Ralph 22
Vaughn, Robert 133, 174
Veggezzi, Giuseppe 93

Veidt, Conrad 10, **10**, 11, 14, 35, 41, 49, 80, 119, 175, 180, 225, 245
Vengeance of Fu Manchu, The 115-6, **115**, 122, 128
Vergine di Norimberga, La 93, **94**, 95, 101
Verney, Guy 18
Vernon, Howard 134
Vernon, Kate 218
Versini, Marie 56, **56**, 113
Vicario, Marco 93
Victim of His Imagination 151
Victims of Terror: Stories in Stone 258
Villechaize, Hervé 165, 196
Villiers, Mavis 17
Vitale, Milly 58
Von Leipziger, Heinrich 90
Von Rathony, Akos 84
Von Rosen, Elsa-Marianne 35, 78
Von Rosen, Henriette 78
Von Sydow, Max 138
Vosoughi, Behruz 177

Wahre Wunder 217
Walhalla 258
Walker, Pete 194
Walker, Robert, Jr 121
Wallace, Jessica 68
Wallach, Eli 145, 177, 182, 187
Walter, Harriet (CL's niece) 231, 237-9
Walters, Thorley 55, 90, **91**

Walsh, Raoul 25-6
Wanamaker, Zoë 231
Ward, Simon **268**, 205
Ward, Sophie 203
Warner, David 196, 225
Warner, Jack 21, **26**, 26-7, 203
Warren, Barry 97
Washbourne, Mona 192
Watkin, David 158
Watling, Dilys 112
Watson, Jack 98
Watson, Moray 223
Watt, Harry 20
Waxman, Harry 27
Wedding Dress, The 39
Weeks, Stephen 142-3, 197
Wee Willie Winkit 35
Welch, Leslie 16
Welch, Raquel 143, **144**, 158, 159, **257**
Weld, Tuesday 184
Welles, Orson 42-3, 47, 135
Wells, Ingeborg 36
West, Adam 155
West, Mae 21
Westmore, Bud 100, 101
Wheatley, Dennis 118, 151, 163, 231, **252**
Whicker's World 125
White, Daniel J 208
White Hunter 61
Whitelaw, Billie 88

Whitman, Stuart 166, 182
Wicker Man, The 96, **153**, 153-4, 157, 161, 178, 182, 220, **272**
Wicking, Christopher 132, 167
Widmark, Richard 167, 169, 182
Willcox, Toyah 201
Wilde, Cornel 45
Wilder, Billy 130-2, **132**, 169, 232
Williams, Elmo 75
Williams, Gwen 23
Williams, Kenneth 43
Williams, Norman 35, **114**
Williams, Sam 169
Williams, Sumner **54**
Williamson, Alister 126, **127**
Williamson, C H B 'Willy' 23, 32, 50, 68, 88
Williamson, Malcolm 152
William Tell 16, 60
Willoughby, George 72
Wilmer, Douglas 114, 116
Wilson, Andy 231
Wind and the Rain, The [play] 23
Windsor, Barbara 74
Wings 164
Winnetou 259
Winter, Vincent 214
Winterstein, Frank 90
Wiseman, Joseph 107, 179
Wishing Well, The [play] 23
Witchcraft see Panga
Witty, John 25

Wolfit, Donald 47-8, 58, 81
Wood, Elijah 232
Woodbridge, George 27
Woods, Gaynor 23
Woodward, Edward 153, **272**
Woolf, John and Jimmy 30, 31
Worley, Jo Anne 185
Worth, Brian 18, 80, **80**
Wyer, Reginald 117
Wyler, William 101
Wymore, Patrice 47
Wyrd Sisters, The 230

Yarnall, Celeste 121
York, Michael 158, 159, 197, 206
Young, Benny 219
Young, Freddie 46
Young, Muriel 40
Young, Roger 224
Young, Terence 16-7, 18, 23, 37, 42, 44, 72, 74, 107
Young Indiana Jones Chronicles, The 5, 218
Yousoupoff, Felix 110
Yule, Eleanor 235

Zampi, Mario 30
Zappa, Frank 196, **197**
Zendar, Manfred 173, 175
Zetterling, Mai 47, 55
Zinner, Peter 187
Zopelli, Lia 71

Traditional dance-drama in idyllic Summerisle surroundings: as 'the sinister teaser' with Ian Campbell (bearded) and Edward Woodward (masked) in The Wicker Man *(1972)*

APPENDIX II • STAGE, SCREEN AND RADIO

FILM

1939
Edward Small Productions-UA (USA): *The Man in the Iron Mask*
Hal Roach Studios (USA): *A Chump at Oxford*
RKO Radio (USA): *Vigil in the Night*
RKO Radio (USA): *Laddie*

1940
Republic (USA): *Women in War*
Columbia (USA): *The Howards of Virginia*
MGM (USA): *John Nesbitt's Passing Parade – The Hidden Master* [short]
MGM (USA): *John Nesbitt's Passing Parade – Dreams* [short]
MGM (USA): *John Nesbitt's Passing Parade – The Woman in the House* [short] *
MGM (USA): *John Nesbitt's Passing Parade – Return from Nowhere* [short] *
[* PC's scenes recycled from *Dreams*]

1941
Columbia (USA): *They Dare Not Love*

1942
Canadian Ministry Films (Canada): *We All Help* [short]

1946
Crown Film Unit (GB): *It Might Be You* [short]
Crown Film Unit (GB): *The New Teacher* short]

1947
Two Cities (GB): *Hamlet*

1952
Romulus (GB): *Moulin Rouge*

1953
Warwick (GB-USA): *The Black Knight*

1954
Coronado (GB): *The End of the Affair*
Republic (USA): *Magic Fire*

1955
Rossen Films-UA (USA): *Alexander the Great*

1956
Harlequin (GB): *Time Without Pity*
Hammer (GB): *The Curse of Frankenstein*

'Mine's a MINOR'
says PETER CUSHING
APPEARING IN THE FILM 'MAGIC FIRE'

2/9 for 20
PLAIN OR CORK TIPPED
ALSO IN SMALLER PACK

"De Reszke" Product

ISSUED BY GODFREY PHILLIPS LIMITED

—317—

1957
Hammer (GB): *The Abominable Snowman*
Rank (GB): *Violent Playground*
Hammer (GB): *Dracula*

1958
Hammer (GB): *The Revenge of Frankenstein*
Warner Bros (USA): *John Paul Jones*
Hammer (GB): *The Hound of the Baskervilles*

1959
Hammer (GB): *The Mummy*
Triad (GB): *The Flesh and the Fiends*
Charter (GB): *Suspect*

1960
Hammer (GB): *The Brides of Dracula*
Aubrey Baring Productions (GB): *Cone of Silence*
Hammer (GB): *Sword of Sherwood Forest*
Mijo (GB): *Fury at Smugglers' Bay*
New World (GB): *The Hellfire Club*
Pennebaker-Baroda (GB): *The Naked Edge*

1961
Hammer (GB): *Cash On Demand*
Hammer (GB): *Captain Clegg*
Constantin-Criterion (Germany-Ireland): *Im Namen des Teufels* [*The Devil's Agent*] *
[* PC's scenes deleted]

1962
White Cross (GB): *The Man Who Finally Died*

1963
Hammer (GB): *The Evil of Frankenstein*
Hammer (GB): *The Gorgon*

1964
Amicus (GB): *Dr Terror's House of Horrors*
Hammer (GB): *She*

1965
Amicus (GB): *The Skull*
Aaru [Amicus] (GB): *Dr Who and the Daleks*
Planet (GB): *Island of Terror*

1966
Aaru [Amicus] (GB): *Daleks' Invasion Earth 2150 A.D.*
Hammer (GB): *Frankenstein Created Woman*
Amicus (GB): *Torture Garden*

1967
Foundation (GB): *Some May Live*
Planet (GB): *Night of the Big Heat*
Titan (GB): *Corruption*
Tigon (GB): *The Blood Beast Terror*

1969
Hammer (GB): *Frankenstein Must Be Destroyed*
Titan-Lucinda (GB): *Incense for the Damned*
AIP-Amicus (GB): *Scream and Scream Again*
Chrislaw-Trace Mark (GB): *One More Time*

1970
Hammer-AIP (GB): *The Vampire Lovers*
Amicus (GB): *The House That Dripped Blood*
Amicus-British Lion (GB): *I, Monster*

1971
Hammer (GB): *Twins of Evil*

APPENDIX II • STAGE, SCREEN AND RADIO

Amicus-Metromedia (GB): *Tales from the Crypt*
Hammer (GB): *Dracula A.D. 1972*
Hammer (GB): *Fear in the Night*
AIP (GB): *Dr Phibes Rises Again*
Granada-Benmar (Spain-GB): *Pánico en el Transiberiano* [Horror Express]

1972

World Film Services-LMG (GB): *The Creeping Flesh*
Amicus-Harbor (GB): *Asylum*
Charlemagne (GB): *Nothing But the Night*
Amicus-Harbor (GB): *~ ~ And Now the Screaming Starts!*
Hammer (GB): *Frankenstein and the Monster from Hell*
Hammer (GB): *The Satanic Rites of Dracula*

1973

AIP-Amicus (GB): *Madhouse*
Amicus (GB): *From Beyond the Grave*
Amicus (GB): *The Beast Must Die*
Hammer-Shaw Brothers (GB-Hong Kong): *The Legend of the 7 Golden Vampires*

1974

Hammer-Shaw Brothers (GB-Hong Kong): *Shatter*
Films Christian Fechner (France): *La grande trouille* [Tender Dracula]
Tyburn (GB): *The Ghoul*
Tyburn (GB): *Legend of the Werewolf*

1975

Lawrence Friedricks Enterprises (USA): *Shock Waves* [Death Corps]
Combat (GB): *Trial by Combat*
Poseidon-Getty (GB-USA): *The Devil's Men*

1976

Amicus (GB): *At the Earth's Core*
Lucasfilm-Twentieth Century-Fox (USA): *Star Wars*
Ottokar Runze-Orfeo (Germany-Spain): *Die Standarte* [Battleflag]
Cinévidéo-Tor (Canada-GB): *The Uncanny*

1977

Naxos-Film (Germany-USA): *Hitlers Sohn* [Hitler's Son]

1978

Barkarow-Melsom (GB): *The Detour* [short; PC as narrator]
Elsinore (GB-Zambia): *A Touch of the Sun*
Badger (GB): *Arabian Adventure*

1980

Almena-Fort (Spain-USA): *Misterio en la isla de los monstruos* [Mystery on Monster Island]

1981

MB Diffusion (Spain-USA): *Asalto al casino* [Black Jack]

1982

Paramount-Kingsmere (USA-GB): *Top Secret!*
London Cannon (GB): *House of the Long Shadows*
London Cannon (GB): *Sword of the Valiant – The Legend of Gawain and the Green Knight*

1985

Compact Yellowbill-Tambarle (GB): *Biggles*

RADIO

1941
NBC (USA): *Outward Bound, The Grandpa Family, Bitter Sweet*

1943
BBC: *Mendelssohn, Destination Unknown*
BBC: *The Lay of Horatius*

1946
BBC: *Wednesday Matinée – A Fourth for Bridge*
BBC: *Orley Farm* [serial]

1947
BBC: *Saturday Matinée – The Face of Teresa, Radio Theatre – It Speaks for Itself*

1948
ABC (Australia): *Beau Brummell*

1949
BBC: *Saturday-Night Theatre – Alien Corn*

1951
BBC: *PC 49 – The Case of the Tenth Green*

1954
BBC: *A Book at Bedtime – Natural Causes*

BBC: *Morning Story – The Bride in the Bath*
BBC: *The Gay Lord Quex*

1955
BBC: *Wife for Sale*

1964
BBC: *Loyal Servant*

1966
Stanmark: *Doctor Who* [not broadcast]
BBC: *The Strong Are Lonely*

1967
BBC: *The Burnt Flowerbed*

1973
BBC: *The Price of Fear – The Man Who Hated Scenes*

1977
BBC: *Aliens in the Mind* [six-part serial]

1990
BBC: *Human Conflict*

TELEVISION

1951
BBC: *Eden End*
BBC: *When We Are Married*

1952
BBC: *Pride and Prejudice* [six-part serial]
BBC: *Bird in Hand*

BBC: *If This Be Error*
BBC: *Asmodée*
BBC: *For the Children – The Silver Swan*

1953
BBC: *Number Three*
BBC: *Asmodée* [repeat performance of

1952 production]
BBC: *Epitaph for a Spy* [six-part serial]
BBC: *Wednesday Theatre Presents – A Social Success*
BBC: *Rookery Nook*
BBC: *The Road*
BBC: *Anastasia*
BBC: *The Noble Spaniard*
BBC: *Portrait by Peko*

1954
BBC: *Tovarich*
BBC: *Beau Brummell*
BBC: *The Face of Love*
BBC: *Nineteen Eighty-Four*

1955
BBC: *The Creature*
BBC: *The Moment of Truth*
BBC: *The Browning Version*
BBC: *Richard of Bordeaux*

1956
BBC: *Home at Seven*

1957
BBC: *Sunday-Night Theatre – Gaslight*

1958
BBC: *The Winslow Boy*
BBC: *Uncle Harry*

1962
ABC: *Drama 62 – Peace with Terror*

1963
BBC: *The Spread of the Eagle* [episodes four to six – *Julius Caesar*]
BBC: *Comedy Playhouse – The Plan*

1964
BBC: *Star Story – The Yellow Cat* [not transmitted]

BBC: *Story Parade – The Caves of Steel*

1965
BBC: *Cribbins*
BBC: *Thirty-Minute Theatre – Monica*

1967
ABC: *The Avengers – Return of the Cybernauts*

1968
BBC: *Sir Arthur Conan Doyle's Sherlock Holmes* [16-part series]

1969
BBC: *The Morecambe and Wise Show* [two episodes]

1970
BBC: *The Morecambe and Wise Christmas Show*

1973
BBC: *The Morecambe and Wise Show*
ITC: *The Zoo Gang – The Counterfeit Trap*
Anglia: *Orson Welles Great Mysteries – La Grande Bretèche*

1974
ITC-Rai: *Space: 1999 – The Missing Link*

1976
Avengers Film & TV: *The New Avengers – The Eagle's Nest*
ABC Circle (USA): *The Great Houdini* [TV movie]

1978
Thames: *The Morecambe and Wise Show*

1980
ITC-Cinema Arts: *Hammer House of Horror – The Silent Scream*
Hallmark (USA): *A Tale of Two Cities* [TV movie]
Thames: *The Morecambe and Wise Christmas Show*

1983
Anglia: *Tales of the Unexpected – The Vorpal Blade*
20th Century Fox (USA): *Helen Keller The Miracle Continues* [TV movie]

1984
Tyburn: *The Masks of Death* [TV movie]

AWARDS

1953-54
National Television Award – *Daily Mail* – for Outstanding Actor of the Year

1955
Guild of Television Producers and Directors Best Performance Award (Winston Smith in *Nineteen Eighty-Four*)

1956
Television Top Ten Award – *News Chronicle* – for Best Actor (Viewers' Gallup Polls)

1973
Licorne d'Or Award – Convention Française du Cinéma Fantastique, Paris – for Best Actor (Mr Grimsdyke in *Tales from the Crypt*)

1976
Best Actor Award – Festival Internacional de Cinema Fantàstic i de Terror, Sitges (Dr Lawrence in *The Ghoul*)

1983
Best Actor Award – Festival Internacional de Cinema Fantàstic i de Terror, Sitges (Sebastian Grisbane in *House of the Long Shadows*) – shared with Vincent Price, Christopher Lee and John Carradine for the same film